I0819645

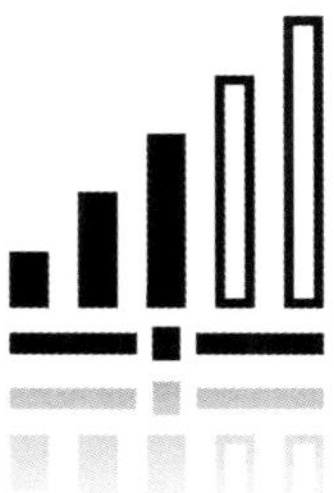

ON RECORD 1988 G. BROWN

CONTENTS

ON RECORD ENTRIES ARE NOT ORDERED ALPHABETICALLY, BUT ORGANIZED INTUITIVELY—A MIXTURE OF SEGUES BY MUSICAL GENRE OR STYLE.

007 INTRODUCTION

008 TRACY CHAPMAN
010 MELISSA ETHERIDGE
012 EDIE BRICKELL & NEW BOHEMIANS
014 TANITA TIKARAM
016 TONI CHILDS
018 MICHELLE SHOCKED
020 JOAN JETT & THE BLACKHEARTS
022 COWBOY JUNKIES
024 ANITA BAKER
026 BRENDA RUSSELL
028 BILLY OCEAN
030 FOUR TOPS
032 THE TRAVELING WILBURYS
034 KEITH RICHARDS
036 THE KINKS
038 CROSBY, STILLS, NASH & YOUNG
040 BRIAN WILSON
042 ROBERT PLANT
044 BAD COMPANY
046 THE MOODY BLUES
048 MIKE + THE MECHANICS
050 3
052 ROBIN TROWER
054 CHEAP TRICK
056 STEVE MILLER
058 CHICAGO
060 DARYL HALL & JOHN OATES
062 LITTLE FEAT
064 38 SPECIAL
066 LYNYRD SKYNYRD
068 JIMMY BUFFETT
070 BRUCE HORNSBY & THE RANGE
072 HUEY LEWIS & THE NEWS
074 GRAHAM PARKER
076 RICHARD THOMPSON
078 LEO KOTTKE
080 RANDY NEWMAN
082 TONIO K.
084 PAT McLAUGHLIN
086 KENNY LOGGINS
088 BILL MEDLEY
090 ELTON JOHN
092 JANE'S ADDICTION
094 THE SUGARCUBES
096 WAS (NOT WAS)
098 THE CHURCH
100 BIG PIG
102 PAUL KELLY & THE MESSENGERS
104 JOHN MAYALL
106 GEORGE THOROGOOD & THE DESTROYERS
108 ELVIN BISHOP
110 JOE LOUIS WALKER
112 THE ROBERT CRAY BAND
114 THE JEFF HEALEY BAND
116 TOMMY CONWELL & THE YOUNG RUMBLERS
118 HENRY LEE SUMMER
120 THE GEORGIA SATELLITES
122 THE SMITHEREENS
124 TREAT HER RIGHT
126 CAMPER VAN BEETHOVEN
128 LET'S ACTIVE
130 THE FEELIES
132 THE BEARS
134 INFORMATION SOCIETY
136 TACKHEAD
138 UNDERWORLD
140 ERASURE
142 THE PRIMITIVES
144 THE PROCLAIMERS
146 VAN MORRISON & THE CHIEFTAINS
148 HOTHOUSE FLOWERS
150 THE BIBLE
152 TIM & MOLLIE O'BRIEN
154 SAM PHILLIPS
156 SANDI PATTI
158 STRYPER
160 DANZIG
163 SAM KINISON

164 BON JOVI
166 AC/DC
168 OZZY OSBOURNE
170 SCORPIONS
172 JUDAS PRIEST
174 IRON MAIDEN
176 METALLICA
178 MEGADETH
180 QUEENSRŸCHE
182 YNGWIE MALMSTEEN
184 POISON
186 L.A. GUNS
188 RATT
190 WINGER
192 DAVID LEE ROTH
194 BULLETBOYS
196 KINGDOM COME
198 LIVING COLOUR
200 FISHBONE
202 BOBBY BROWN
204 TIFFANY
206 NEW KIDS ON THE BLOCK
208 KENNY G
210 AL JARREAU
212 LIZ STORY
214 TUCK & PATTI
216 ACOUSTIC ALCHEMY
218 ROB WASSERMAN
220 SHADOWFAX
222 STANLEY JORDAN
224 NAJEE
226 ZIGGY MARLEY & THE MELODY MAKERS
228 TOOTS
230 VAN HALEN
230 U2
230 R.E.M.
234 PAULA ABDUL
234 TAYLOR DAYNE
234 SHEENA EASTON
238 ROD STEWART
238 SADE
238 ENYA
242 STEVE WINWOOD
242 ROBERT PALMER
242 NEIL YOUNG & THE BLUENOTES
246 PETER CETERA
246 BETTE MIDLER
246 BARBRA STREISAND
250 MARTIKA
250 KYLIE MINOGUE
250 SAMANTHA FOX
254 PUBLIC ENEMY
254 RUN-D.M.C.
254 PRINCE
258 M.C. HAMMER
258 MORRIS DAY
258 JOHNNY KEMP
262 GUY
262 J.J. FAD
262 AL B. SURE!
266 D.J. JAZZY JEFF & THE FRESH PRINCE
266 ROB BASE & D.J. E-Z ROCK
266 FAT BOYS
270 PET SHOP BOYS
270 CLIMIE FISHER
270 JOHNNY HATES JAZZ
274 A-HA
274 SIOUXSIE & THE BANSHEES
274 COCTEAU TWINS
278 JOHN HIATT
278 MORRISSEY
278 JULIAN COPE
282 MAXI PRIEST
282 THE WATERBOYS
282 THE POGUES
286 THE BANGLES
286 JANE WIEDLIN
286 PAT BENATAR
290 BOY MEETS GIRL
290 WILL TO POWER
290 JON ASTLEY
294 NEW EDITION
294 THE BOYS
294 BOYS CLUB
298 JIMMY PAGE
298 LITA FORD
298 VIXEN
302 BLUE ÖYSTER CULT
302 ANTHRAX
302 SLAYER
306 CINDERELLA
306 EUROPE
306 KIX
310 EDDIE MONEY
310 GLENN FREY
310 GRAYSON HUGH
314 KARYN WHITE
314 CHERRELLE
314 SAM BROWN
318 TEDDY PENDERGRASS
318 IVAN NEVILLE
318 DEON ESTUS
322 CAMEO
322 LEVERT
322 SURFACE
326 CROWDED HOUSE
326 THE PURSUIT OF HAPPINESS
326 RHYTHM CORPS
330 TALKING HEADS
330 OINGO BOINGO
330 BOOK OF LOVE
334 DURAN DURAN
334 THE ESCAPE CLUB
334 THE GODFATHERS
338 STEVE EARLE
338 LYLE LOVETT
338 K.D. LANG
342 DWIGHT YOAKAM
342 RODNEY CROWELL
342 KEITH WHITLEY
346 REBA MCENTIRE
346 PATTY LOVELESS
346 K.T. OSLIN
350 THE DESERT ROSE BAND
350 RESTLESS HEART
350 SOUTHERN PACIFIC
354 BOBBY MCFERRIN
354 TAKE 6
354 GEORGE HOWARD
358 KATIE WEBSTER
358 JAMES BROWN
358 WILLIE DIXON
362 SLICK RICK
362 ICE-T
362 WYNTON MARSALIS
363 RANDY TRAVIS
363 GEORGE STRAIT
363 HIGHWAY 101
364 LUCINDA WILLIAMS
364 SHONA LAING
364 THE DEIGHTON FAMILY
365 RICK ASTLEY
365 THE GREGG ALLMAN BAND
365 CELLARFUL OF NOISE

366 ACKNOWLEDGMENTS

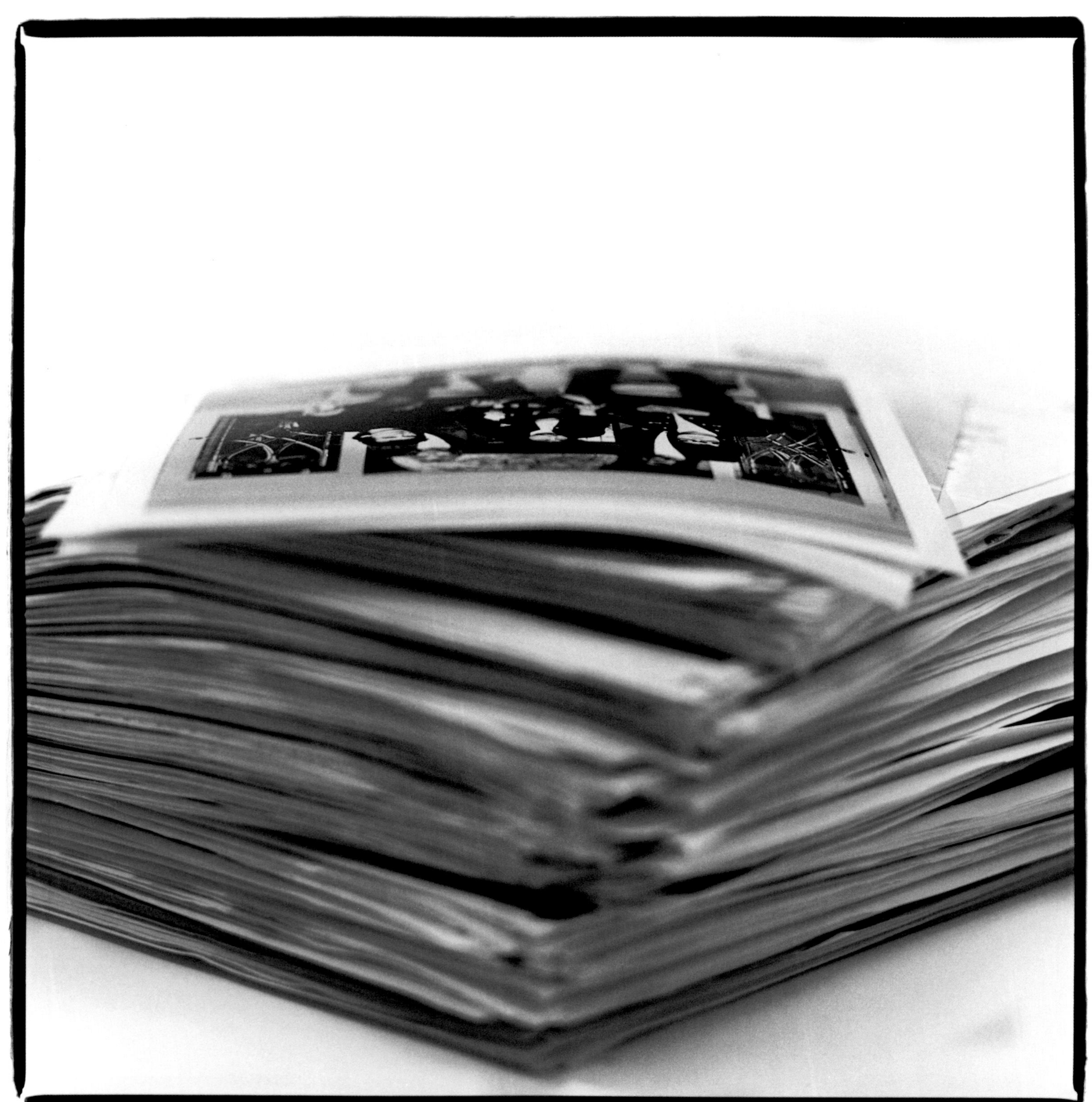

PHOTOGRAPH BY STEPHEN COLLECTOR

ON RECORD VOL.5 1988

MY JOB as a music writer sounds like nice work if you can get it, and I agree it's a blessed existence. The only better gig, I think, would be that of a travel writer. I got to hitch a ride on that gravy train once, in 1988, when a staff writer at *The Denver Post* declined a junket to Memphis for the 11th anniversary of Elvis Presley's death—a year removed from the hoopla that surrounded a decade without the King. So, the newspaper's travel editor contracted with me to go in his stead.

Elvis International Tribute Week had turned into a yearly nine-day Memphis celebration of Elvis. People came from across the country, taking part in dances and exhibits ranging from an Elvis impersonator contest to an Elvis 5K run. The entire commemoration was notable for a more spontaneous media circus—an "is Elvis alive?" hysteria, fueled by a book that claimed Elvis faked his death and rumors of sightings in Kalamazoo, Michigan, among other places.

Most of the Presley faithful seemed anxious for Presley's estate to debunk the controversy, but the late singer's representatives had sharpened their business acumen and begun to "control the marketing image of the deceased." The shops around Graceland and Memphis no longer carried tacky souvenirs like Elvis black velvet paintings or Elvis dashboard ornaments, only generic corporate merch like Elvis rugby shirts.

And that wasn't right. Granted, Elvis was the most popular entertainer in history, but the occupant of the maze of carpeted ceilings and mirrored walls known as Graceland mansion left himself open for parody. At least I found a shop on the outskirts of the city with a button that read, "Elvis Is Dead - But At Least He's Not Gaining Any More Weight."

The quietest event was the annual candlelight vigil service, when more than 6,000 Elvis followers walked single file from Elvis Presley Boulevard to the grave site. The mood was solemn and funereal, with no preponderance of Springolator shoes or beehive hairdos. It was simply a respectable cross-section of middle America, people who still felt the pangs of losing a friend. I learned that Elvis was still alive—in the hearts of his fans.

When I stepped up to the grave site, to quote from the movie *Animal House*, I thought the situation called for "a really futile and stupid gesture be done on somebody's part." So I snuck out my one-hitter and whispered, "King, I don't have any diet pills on me, but this one's for you."

Back in my role as music writer, I went to all the concerts and got all the new releases and press kits. CD sales zoomed that year, dominated by a heavy-metal explosion with Bon Jovi, Scorpions and Metallica cashing in. Michael Jackson's *Bad* album spawned five No. 1 singles, Bobby Brown's *Don't Be Cruel* was a blockbuster and George Michael made a stubble beard fashionable. Tracy Chapman was but one of a series of debuts by wonderful female singer-songwriters, ranging from Melissa Etheridge to Edie Brickell to Michelle Shocked. College radio discovered indie records by the likes of Dinosaur Jr, and Iceland's Sugarcubes, Jamaica's Ziggy Marley and Ireland's Hothouse Flowers checked in from around the globe. There were seminal albums by Public Enemy, the Traveling Wilburys, Jane's Addiction, Living Colour and many, many others. I was and am a very lucky boy. Please allow me to share. **— G. Brown**

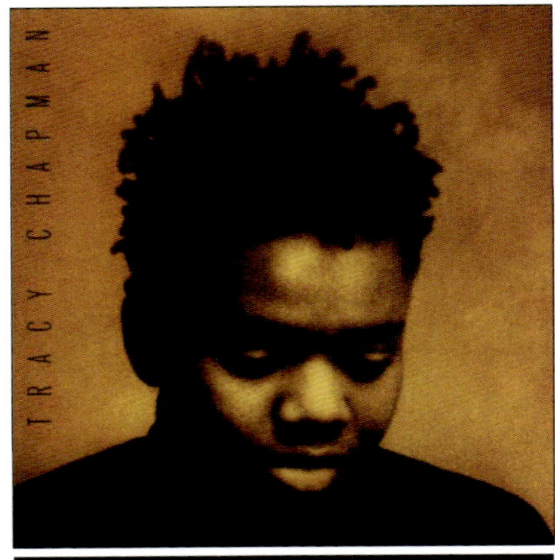

Billboard 200: *Tracy Chapman* (No. 1)
Billboard Hot 100: "Fast Car" (#6); "Talkin' 'bout a Revolution" (#75); "Baby Can I Hold You" (#48)

Young folk singer Tracy Chapman's talent and quiet charisma quickly grabbed the attention of the pop market.

IN APRIL 1988, a serious, uncompromising female singer-songwriter released her self-titled debut album to little fanfare. Three months later, *Tracy Chapman* had emerged as an astounding success story—platinum sales, six Grammy nominations (she eventually won three awards, including Best New Artist) and ringing endorsements from peers ranging from John Cougar Mellencamp to Jackson Browne. The surprise was that the 24-year-old Chapman's urban-folk tales weren't the usual fare for such commercial acclaim, a fact she was the first to acknowledge.

"Recording an album was just something I was going to look into once I got out of college," Chapman said. "I always assumed I'd be working on a very small scale."

Chapman spent a few years honing her songwriting and performing skills on the folk music scenes in Boston and Cambridge. Raised in Cleveland, she traveled to Tufts University in Massachusetts on a scholarship. "There are more colleges there than any other place in the country," she explained. "So I played a lot of schools, as well as coffeehouses and churches. I even played for quarters out in the streets on Harvard Square."

In 1986, Brian Koppleman, then a Tufts undergrad himself, brought Chapman to the attention of his father, Charles Koppleman, head of the high-profile SBK Songs, who helped her sign to Elektra Records for her recording debut. The album *Tracy Chapman* was a somber work filled with detailed songs and characters, narratives about concerns such as poverty, battered wives and racism. She wasn't as introspective as other folk-derived acts; she was more involved with making a specific connection with her audience.

"I'm not that conscious about where the songs are coming from in terms of point of view," she said of her muse. "And for that reason, they seem to come out in more universal key points rather than unique and personal ones."

The hit "Fast Car" served as a striking introduction to Chapman's well-crafted "thinking person's pop." Written in the first person, she observed a couple whose romance couldn't shield them from their economic prison. The singer was the pair's practical half, while her partner had a fast car but no job prospects or ambition. The song alternated between an optimistic aura when Chapman sang of the feelings of driving with him and a loss of momentum when she shifted to describing her dead-end daily life

The issue-conscious "Talkin' 'bout a Revolution" and "Baby Can I Hold You" gave further evidence of Chapman's songwriting skills, and she already had a retort for cynics who attributed the overwhelming acceptance of her musical humanism to yuppie guilt. "It doesn't concern me," she said. "You know, I don't know what a yuppie is anymore. It used to be great if you had a job and a relationship and you were happy. Now it's supposed to be a source of stress. But it's all of those people around me who are changing with my success. Things haven't changed for me. They're fine." ■

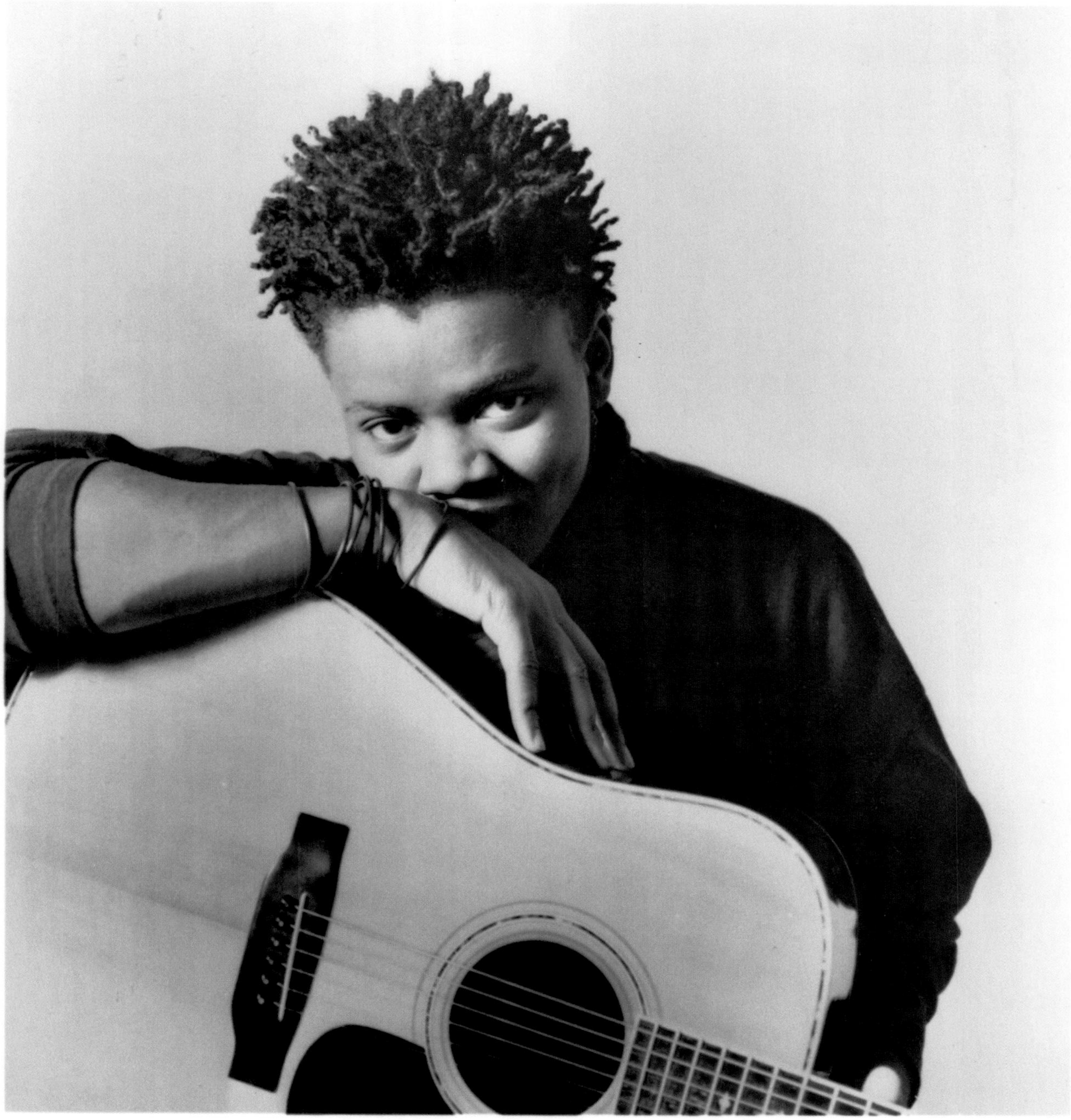

Photo Credit: Janette Beckman/1988

TRACY CHAPMAN

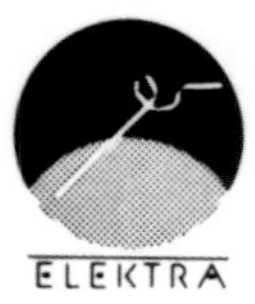

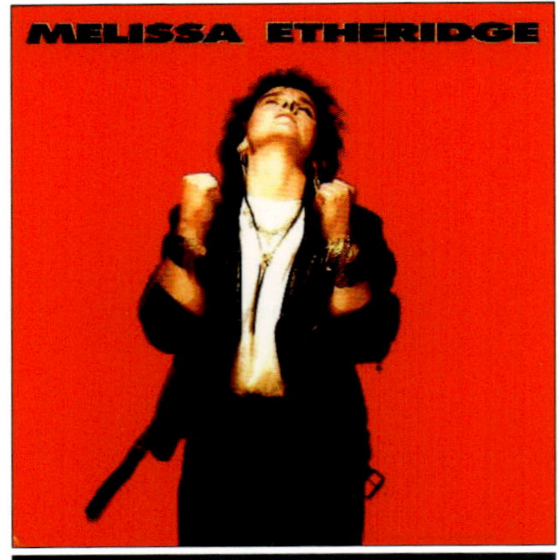

Billboard 200: *Melissa Etheridge* (#22)
Billboard Hot 100: "Similar Features" (#94)

In the recounting of her experiences, Melissa Etheridge's debut album concentrated on sincerity and substance.

EVEN WITH accolades pouring in about seemingly every new female singer-songwriter, Melissa Etheridge distinguished herself as a musical force. The emotionally charged single "Bring Me Some Water" introduced her unabashed vocal style and lyrical intensity as her self-titled debut album took solid steps up the charts.

Born in Leavenworth, Kansas, Etheridge left home at 18 to study guitar at the Berklee School of Music in Boston. "I'd been performing so long around Leavenworth in country bands, cover bands, solo," she said. "When I was underage, my father used to drive me to gigs and wait for me. Going to Berklee was my parents' idea—'If you're serious about this music thing, you've got to go to college'—and Berklee was the only college that would take me since I wasn't classically trained. But Berklee was just a chance to learn about 'life in the big city.' One can really learn a lot if they go in Berklee eager for what they have to offer. Myself, I was ready to take on the world. I didn't want to sit in a classroom and think about how you're supposed to write a song."

Etheridge was performing around Los Angeles when she got her first big break, a chance to write four compositions for the 1987 Nick Nolte film *Weeds*. Island Records founder and president Chris Blackwell had discovered her in a Long Beach club and, after seeing her for the first time, signed her "on the spot."

"That part happened fast, but the time from me getting to L.A. to the time when Chris walked into the bar where I was playing was four years of a lot of work, ups and downs, record companies interested and then not interested," she noted. "I guess the road along the way has been long but not that hard. I had an aunt I could live with when I came out to California."

Etheridge survived a false start recording her album with a large ensemble before going back to her acoustic arrangements. The bare-bones approach transformed *Melissa Etheridge* into an impassioned selection of pop-rock songs about obsessions with recent ex-lovers—"Chrome Plated Heart," "Similar Features" and "Bring Me Some Water." On "Like the Way I Do," she aggressively strummed her amplified 12-string Ovation acoustic guitar and offered a steamy, blunt description of a love affair gone bad.

"I write from a personal perspective, from an autobiographical point," she said. "I find that writing about what is happening in my life lends itself to a stronger song, one that people can relate to and grab hold of. There's nothing more powerful than the truth."

Of the inevitable comparisons—her gifted writing and energetic music recalled Janis Joplin, and her gravelly voice suggested Bonnie Raitt—she said, "It's how people communicate. I'm fortunate that all of the comparisons have been to strong women artists. When someone likens me to Joplin, that's great." ■

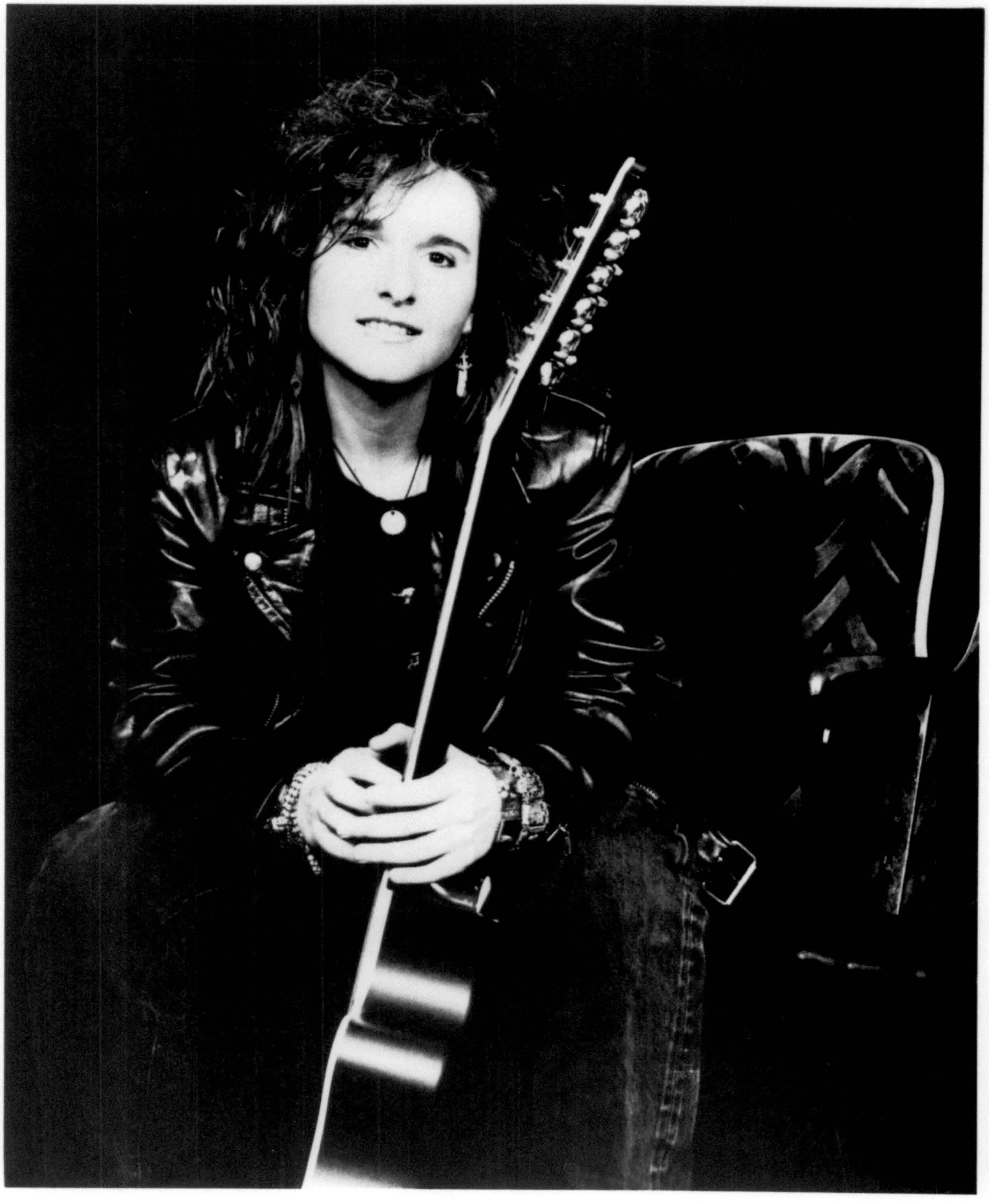

Photo Credit: Gary Nichamin

MELISSA ETHERIDGE

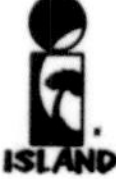

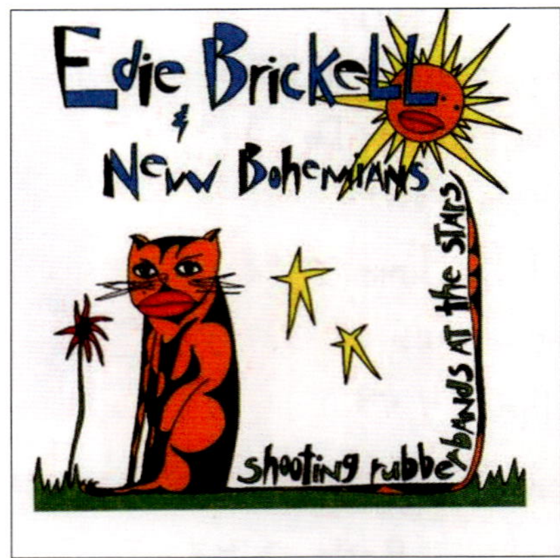

Billboard 200: *Shooting Rubberbands at the Stars* (#4)
Billboard Hot 100: "What I Am" (#7); "Circle" (#48)

Edie Brickell & New Bohemians had an unanticipated smash hit with the conversational fluidity of "What I Am."

SAVE FOR a fateful encounter, Edie Brickell might not have emerged as a bright new songwriting talent.

"Growing up, I always knew I wanted to be a singer, but I kept it my little secret," Brickell divulged. "I wanted to be creative, but I blew it off. I didn't have any courage, I didn't know any musicians, and I didn't know how to get started."

After high school, the bashful Brickell had enrolled at Southern Methodist University as an art major for lack of a better idea, and she quickly became depressed by her surroundings and inability to find her creative niche. One night in 1985, a girlfriend cajoled her into going to an after-hours club in Dallas.

"She gave me my first shot of Jack Daniel's—she said, 'You've got to loosen up and start talking to people,'" Brickell recalled. Playing in the corner were New Bohemians, at the time a ska-reggae instrumental group comprised of native Texans, and Brickell got "inspired. I walked over and started improvising with them, making up songs on the spot. It was real casual, but I realized right away that I wanted to be in a band with those guys."

Three years and sweeping personnel changes (bassist Brad Houser was the only original band member) later, *Shooting Rubberbands at the Stars*, Edie Brickell & New Bohemians' debut album, climbed into the Top 5 on the charts. Brickell described the work as a "musical kaleidoscope," but the focus was on her whimsically philosophical lyrics.

The single "What I Am" was a jaunty self-introduction that caught on in alternative music circles. Brickell's playful lyrical swagger ("Choke me in the shallow water before I get too deep") and winsome, breathy voice (which drew numerous comparisons to Rickie Lee Jones) was matched by New Bohemians' spare folk-pop and acoustic and light electric guitar embellishment.

Brickell claimed to be a shy young woman trying to keep fellowship with her bandmates and avoiding the invasion of privacy that came with rock celebrity. An issue of *Rolling Stone* magazine proclaimed her "Rock's Hip Hippie" on the cover.

"That's really not what I'm about—it's just because I dress comfortably," the fresh-faced singer shrugged. "I think it got started with the blue jeans (tight and faded) and long hair (brown and flowing). I figure if I had short hair and wore dresses but did the same songs with the same attitude, I wouldn't be called a hippie. I'm just a band member—there's a lot of focus on me because I'm singing, but the music itself represents the band."

In November, Brickell herself briefly lost focus when New Bohemians appeared on *Saturday Night Live* and she met another talented singer. "I kind of messed up the last chorus (of 'What I Am') because I saw Paul Simon standing there," she admitted, "and I just lost it." ■

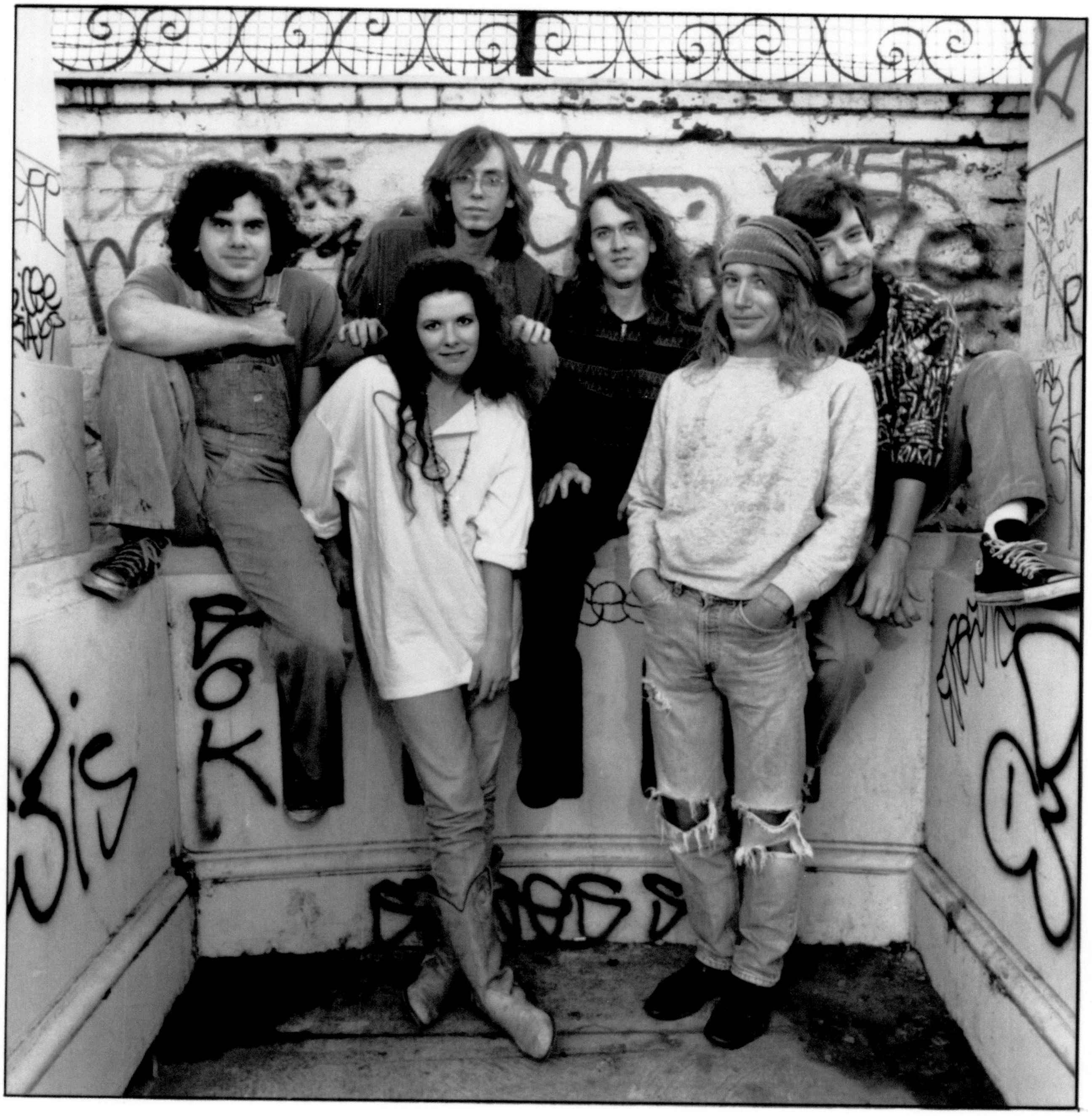

Photo Credit: Timothy White

Kenny Withrow

Edie Brickell

Wes Burt-Martin

Matt Chamberlain

John Bush

Brad Houser

Edie Brickell & New Bohemians

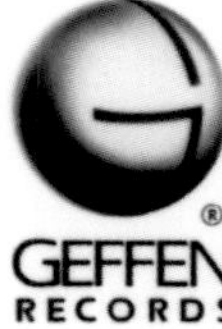

TANITA TIKARAM
ancient heart

Billboard 200: *Ancient Heart* (#59)

With the arresting "Twist in My Sobriety," Tanita Tikaram established herself as an exotic young star to watch.

TANITA TIKARAM'S deeply emotional, resonant voice was featured up front on "Twist in My Sobriety," an alluring and mysteriously mature smash that sold millions worldwide.

"It's funny—to me, that lyric was obscure. I liked it, but I didn't think it would make a lasting impression. It must have something to do with the haunting oboe part in the song," the 19-year-old singer-songwriter said.

"When I wrote it, I was preoccupied with a Philip Larkin poem called 'Poetry of Departures.' It was a very simple poem—essentially, someone is teasing himself in a way, saying 'Could I leave the sobriety and monotony of my ordinary life?'—and just the possibility that he could is enough to make him stay. That's what I was thinking. Now a lot of different ideas are going on in the song that can be generalized under this 'twist in my sobriety.'"

Tikaram grew up on the move, dominated by English culture with her mother (from the British protectorate of Sarawak) and her father (a Fiji Indian). Her music career began in earnest just months after she made her club debut in London.

"As a child, I didn't take an interest in music as much as I did in books and words," she explained. "My first songs were snappy observation pieces. Now I look forward to writing the songs, because you never know where your next one is coming from. It's always a surprise for me because I never understand a song until three months after I've written it, which is very perverse."

The song "Good Tradition," also complemented by Tikaram's husky, world-weary singing, was another highlight on *Ancient Heart*, her warm, folk-inflected debut album co-produced by Rod Argent and Peter Van Hooke. A European phenomenon, *Ancient Heart* was a No. 1 album on the German, Norwegian, Swiss and Austrian charts.

"I never think about the music in terms of how old I am, only in terms of what the songs demand," she said. "We just stumbled onto the sound we have when we did the album." ■

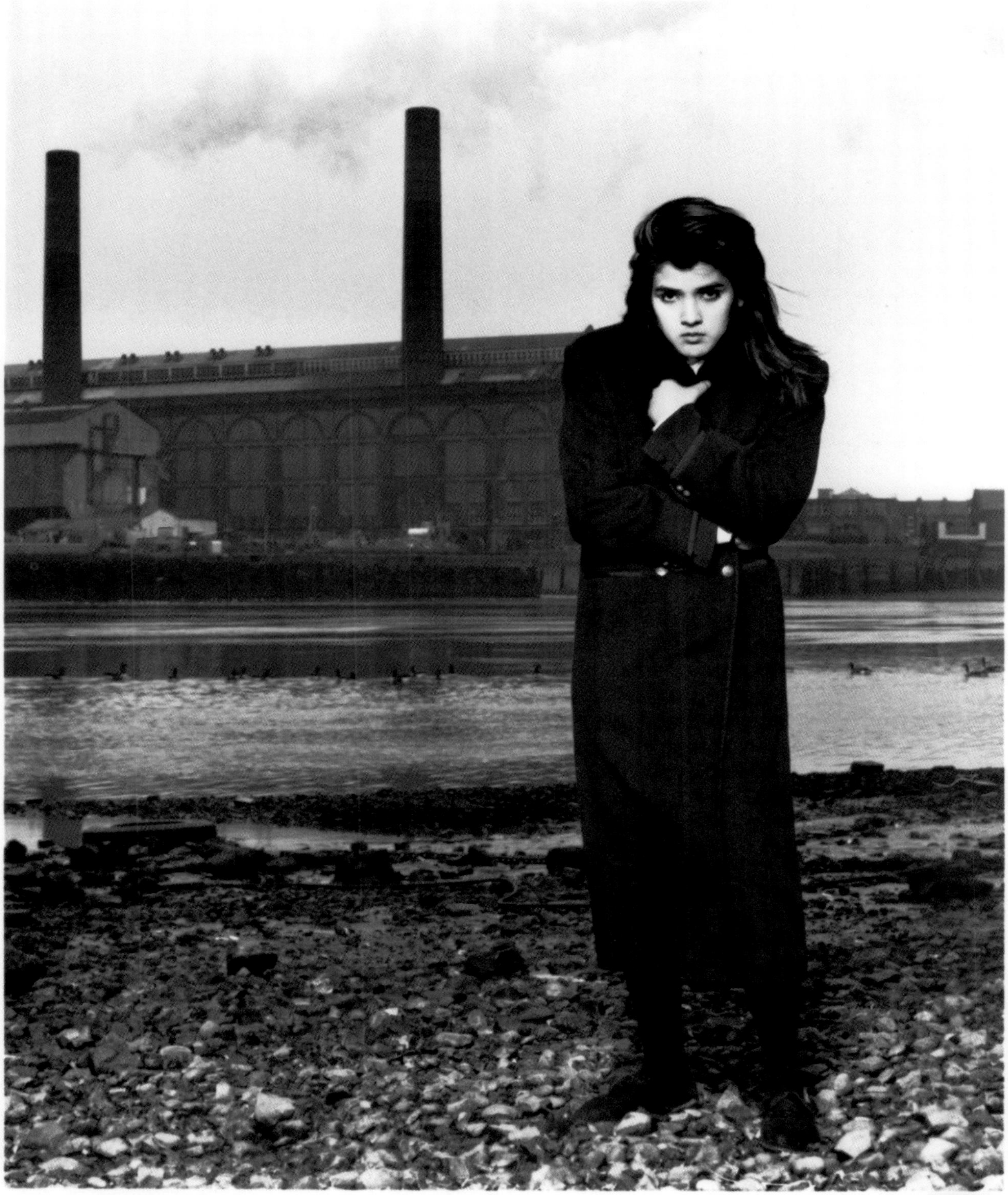

PHOTO CREDIT: TERRY O'NEILL

TANITA TIKARAM

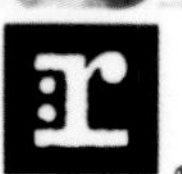

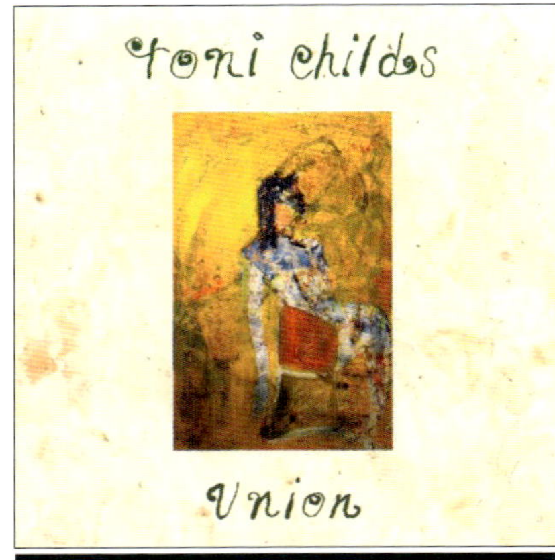

Billboard 200: *Union* (#63)
Billboard Hot 100: "Don't Walk Away" (#72)

The album *Union* and her sturdy vocal on the song "Don't Walk Away" started Toni Childs' path to self-discovery.

TONI CHILDS added her name to the list of female artists attracting attention with a significant debut album. *Union* was a remarkable work that presented her music in her stated goals –"sounds as colors, songs as environments, lyrics as emotions." Location hadn't been a constant in Childs' life—she grew up in various towns across America before traveling to London, where she had a song publishing deal and performed regularly. She formed a band called Nadia Kapiche, which implanted the intricate textures of world music in her.

"That was my first opportunity to stretch my songs left of center," the husky-voiced singer recalled. "But I never wrote songs with the intention of having anyone else perform them—I only wrote for myself."

After four years she returned to her native California with demo tapes she had made with British musicians. But she delayed plans to return to the UK when she met and became involved with David Ricketts, the writer, multi-instrumentalist and arranger of David + David (of "Welcome to the Boomtown" fame).

The collaboration was "inspiring—he understood what I was going for culturally, musically and texturally, matching up with the things I found beautiful," Childs enthused. "When you meet somebody and you're on the same wavelength, when you've never gone that deep or that far, you don't want to go on without that person."

On *Union*, Childs and Ricketts created a global sound by taking an amalgam of geographical influences—the record was recorded around the world, in London, Paris, Los Angeles, and even Africa, where Childs worked with vocal groups from Swaziland and Zambia. "That was something I've dreamed about for a long time—I've always loved African grooves and percussion," she said. "There're a lot of colors in the world, and a lot of sounds."

Union earned Childs two Grammy nominations, but the sudden acclaim for the album led to the demand for her first tour, which turned into an exhausting, sometimes exasperating experience.

"The powers-that-be want you playing yesterday," Childs mused. "All of a sudden, you're in a whirlwind, putting a band together on such notice. It's really shaky—it's had a lot of effect on my psyche. You're a writer, extremely inside yourself, working for years on childhood fantasies, and you don't realize that they've left you until success hits. Suddenly you're exposed and it's very scary, a roller coaster—'Turn it off!'" ■

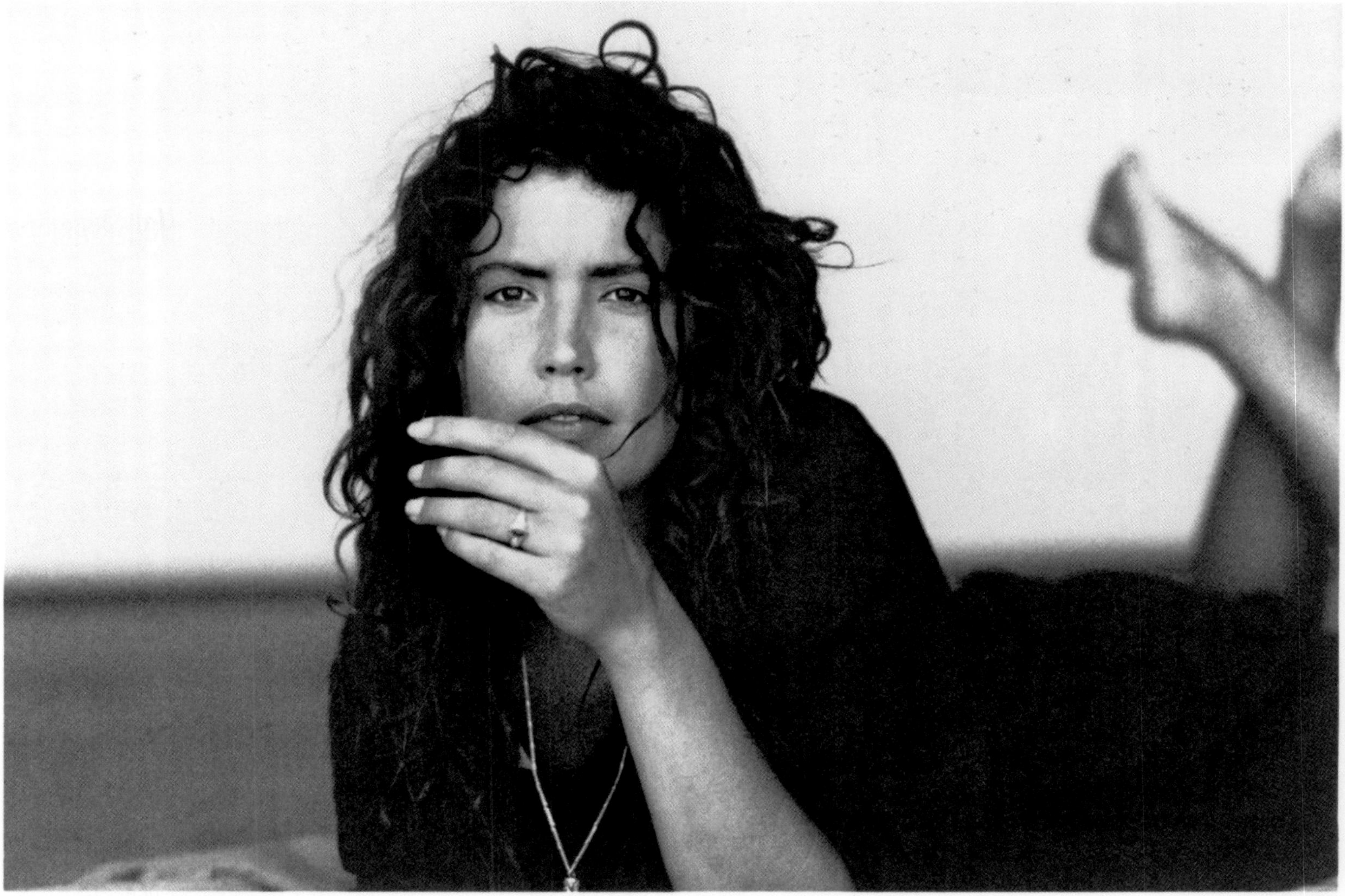

M.F.C. Management:
Peregrine Watts-Russell
(213) 204-5410

TONI CHILDS

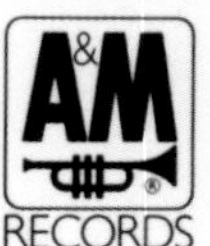

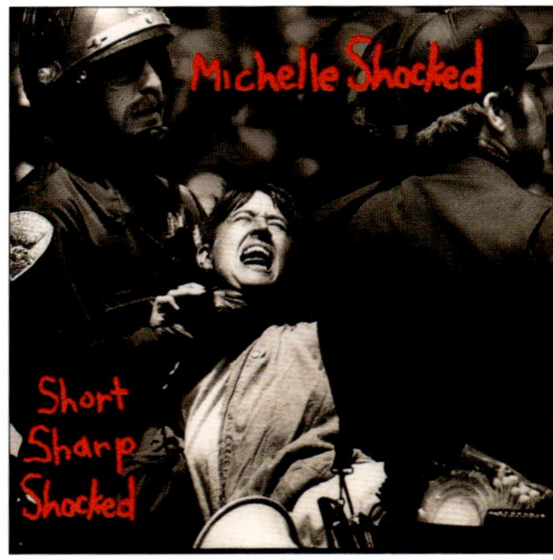

Billboard 200: *Short Sharp Shocked* (#73)
Billboard Hot 100: "Anchorage" (#66)

Michelle Shocked's *Short Sharp Shocked* was named one of the year's best albums by critics around the country.

FEW NEW contenders on the music charts were as enigmatic as Michelle Shocked. *Short Sharp Shocked*, her incisive debut studio album, won acclaim as a Grammy nominee in the Best Contemporary Folk Recording category, and the single "Anchorage" made it into the *Billboard* Top 100.

But Shocked resented being portrayed as part of the burgeoning breed of sensitive women singer-songwriters. She was legitimately more eccentric, as borne out by her list of self-descriptions: "feminist, anarchist, skateboard punk rocker, carpenter's apprentice, rape victim, storyteller." The cover shot on *Short Sharp Shocked* was a dramatic black-and-white news photo of her being dragged away in a police choke hold at a 1984 protest.

"It kills me that I'm drawing comparisons with other female artists on the basis that we're women," Shocked explained. "You're challenging yourself, making yourself better—and then you get in some ridiculous numbers game that measures quantity against quality. That's a trap that I'm trying to dance around."

Shocked preferred to place herself in two seemingly different camps. There was that of the Texas rootsy songwriter, as represented by Townes Van Zandt and Guy Clark. The other was of anarchist punk activists—after she fled her East Texas fundamentalist home at age 16, she fell into the San Francisco hardcore scene. She hitched to New York, becoming involved in squatter's rights and the politics of the homeless, and she was later committed to a psychiatric hospital in Dallas "until the insurance money ran out."

She was lifted away from her life of demonstrations and small folk festivals by an incident that became part of music industry lore. At the 1986 Kerrville Folk Festival in Texas, an impressed English observer recorded Shocked (and the local crickets) singing by a campfire on his Walkman, "like recording a conversation." Boom, a debut album (*The Texas Campfire Tapes*) and a leftfield hit in the UK that sent her stock soaring.

To produce *Short Sharp Shocked*, her US record company referred her to Pete Anderson, known primarily for his work with Dwight Yoakam. "I was so cynical after the debut album. I was afraid they'd trivialize it—'Okay, now let's make a real record.' So I did a lot of saber-rattling about not getting corrupted by the system, taking on the challenge of riding the tiger and not the other way around."

But Anderson's input was hardly formulaic, as he spiked Shocked's coffeehouse guitar sound with deft backing. *Short Sharp Shocked* opened with the surreal "When I Grow Up" and closed with a full-bore punked-out version of "Fogtown." "It's true to my nature that I assume the worst. Then, if I'm proven wrong, I beg forgiveness," she laughed. "Now that Pete has my trust, I'll work with him again." ■

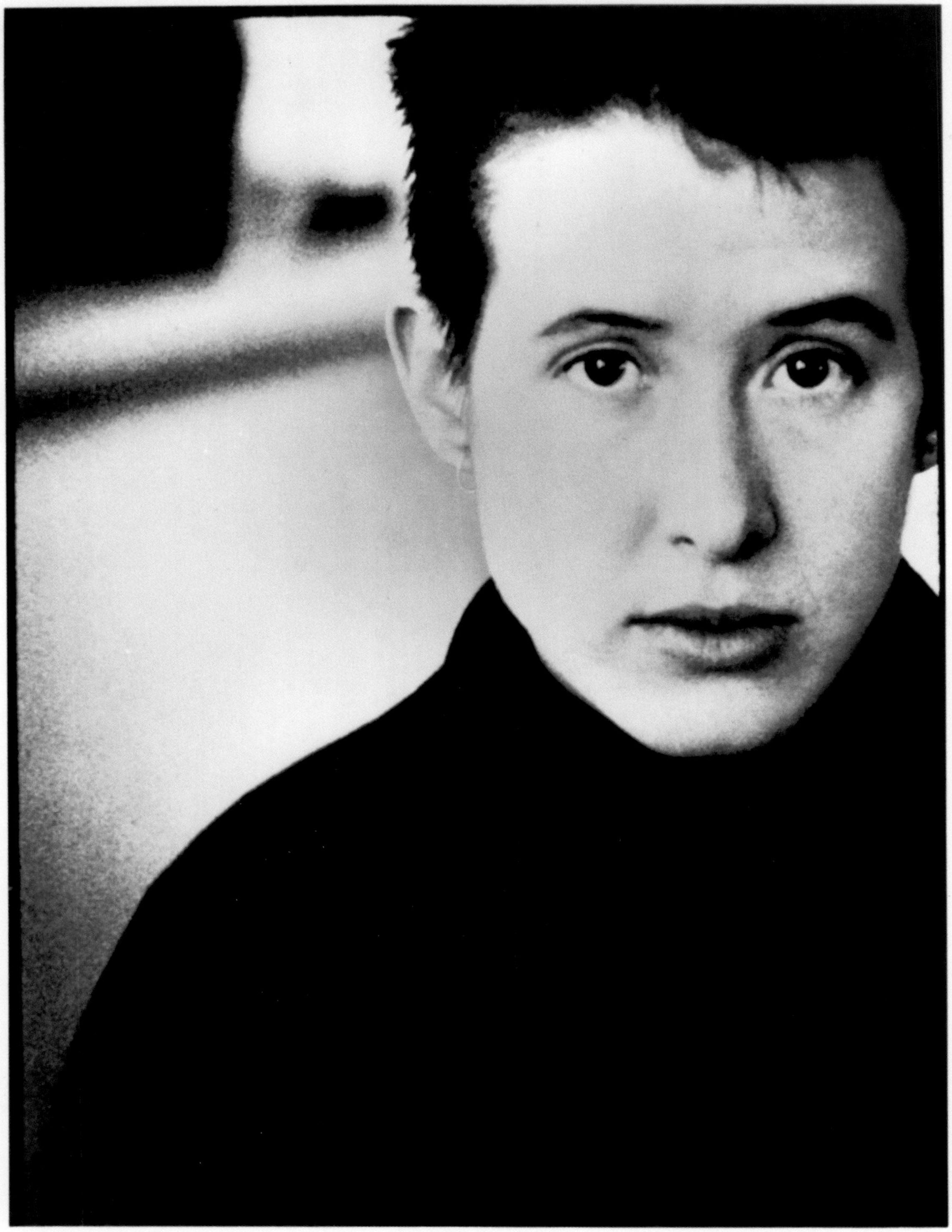

U.S. Management: A.I.R.
285 West Broadway Suite 300
N.Y.C. 10013 212-334-0001

Michelle Shocked

PolyGram Records

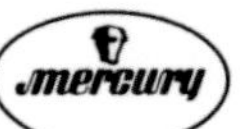

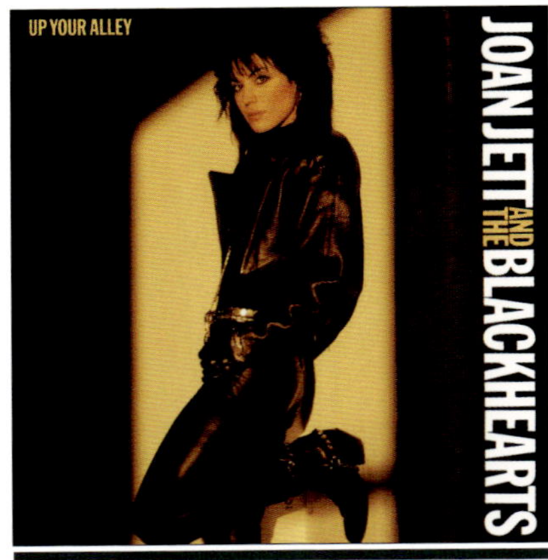

Billboard 200: *Up Your Alley* (#19)
Billboard Hot 100: "I Hate Myself for Loving You" (#8); "Little Liar" (#13)

Glam-rock drums and handclaps made "I Hate Myself for Loving You" another hit for Joan Jett & the Blackhearts.

JOAN JETT began her career at 15, joining the all-girl band the Runaways in 1975. With her first solo album in 1980, she emerged as the high priestess of the power chord. "I Love Rock and Roll" was a double platinum single (No. 1 for eight straight weeks in 1982), followed by the Top 10 "Crimson and Clover." Jett co-starred with Michael J. Fox in Paul Schrader's *Light of Day*, and while critics panned the film, her acting debut earned accolades.

The *Up Your Alley* album featured the expected down-and-dirty formula from Jett and her band the Blackhearts—anthemic hard-rock ditties packed with gritty three-chord riffs, topped off by Jett's eternally teenaged voice. The stomping "I Hate Myself for Loving You," a Top 10 hit, paid homage to one of her early heroes—Gary Glitter, whose "Rock and Roll Part 2" had become the bread-and-butter of football cheers.

"It's a certain style that's not hard to do, but I'm one of the only practitioners left," she explained. "I don't hear anybody else doing the hand claps or the gang vocals or the echo on the drums."

After years of interminable touring—she thought nothing of going out on the road for six to eight months at a time without a break—Jett had no need to justify her love for the music that changed her life. She was a disciple and a fan, one of the toughest, hardest-working women in music. And the guitar slinger with the sassy stage demeanor and no-nonsense hard rock sensibilities was still uncompromisingly committed to an ethical vision.

"I feel stupid sometimes saying this—it sounds cliched or sacrilegious—but rock 'n' roll is a sacred thing," Jett mused. "I've seen it in people's faces. When a fan in the audience looks me in the eyes during the show and knows that somebody out there understands—'You know what I'm feeling, thank you'—there's no way to describe it. That's what keeps me going. There are so many other bands out there that are totally full of shit in their leather jackets—all they think about is how much money they're gonna get. I know that's important—the bottom line is you've gotta pay your bills.

"But to me, that's a warped sense of what's fun. That's not why I got into this at all, to be rich and famous. Every once in a while, I wonder if I'm missing out on other things in my life. There's a tradeoff—I can't go out at night and hang out in clubs. I'm in a hotel room by myself." ■

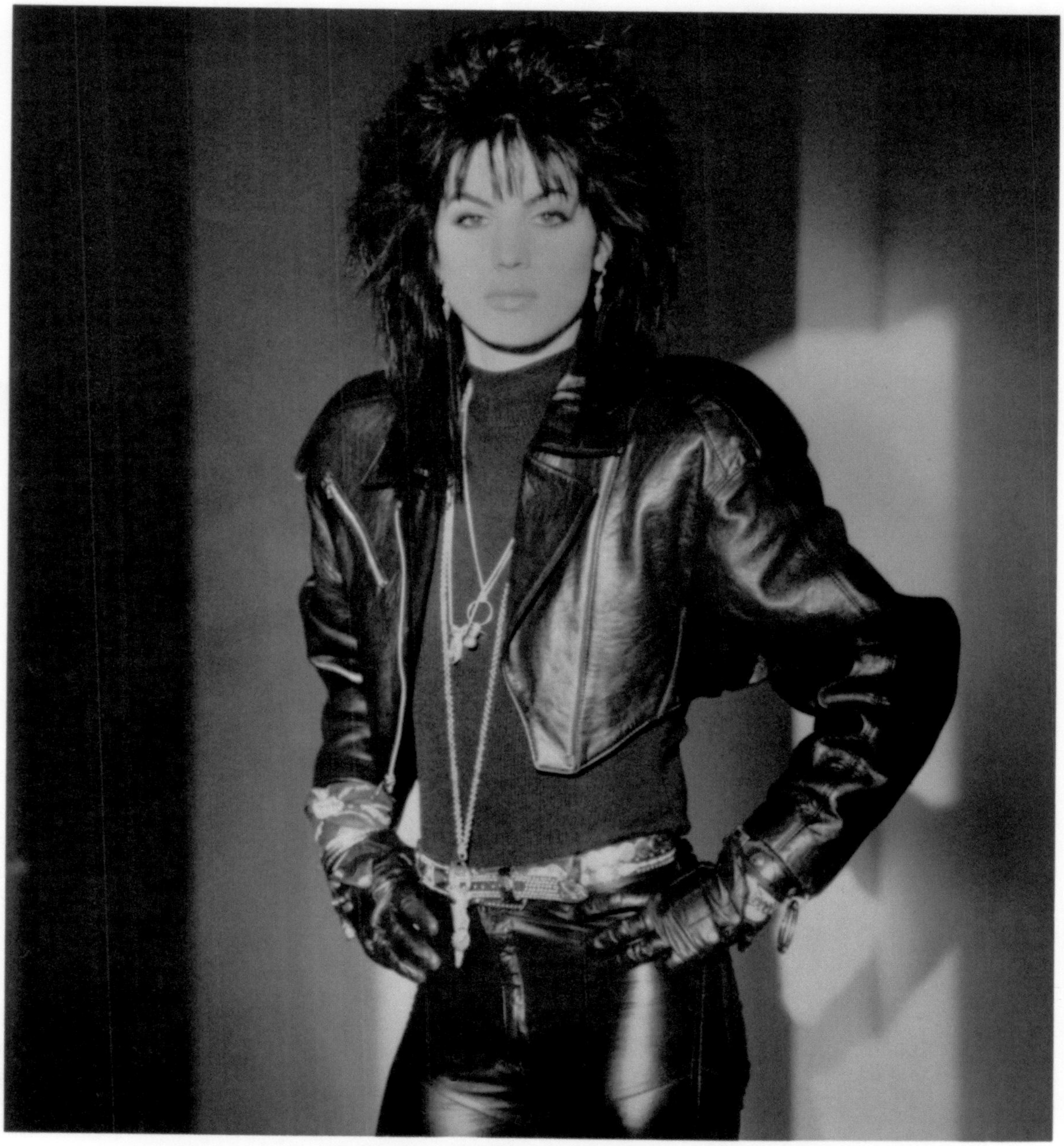

PHOTO: KEN NAHOUM

JOAN JETT AND THE BLACKHEARTS

8804

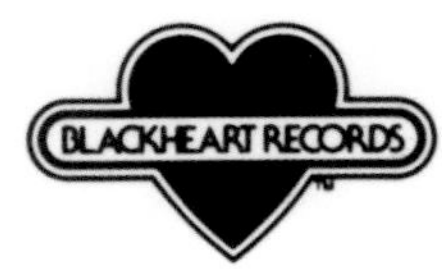

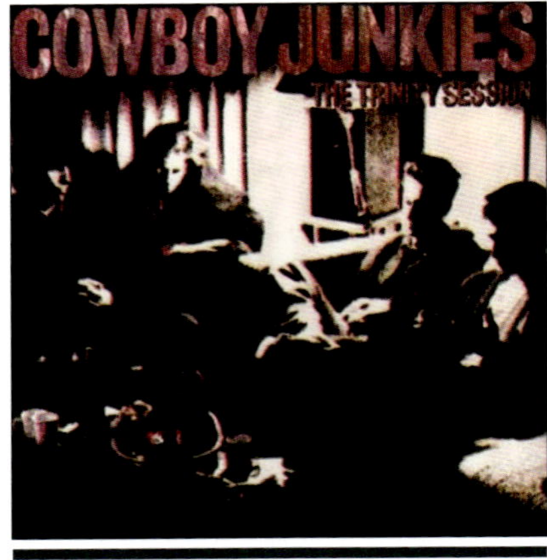

Billboard 200: *The Trinity Session* (#26)

The Trinity Session turned out to be the year's surprise underground sensation for Canada's Cowboy Junkies.

COWBOY JUNKIES earned rave reviews and substantial airplay for the slow-burn ebb and flow of *The Trinity Session*, the Toronto-based band's major-label debut album. The eerie, understated version of Lou Reed's "Sweet Jane" exploded on MTV and alternative rock radio outlets, and the somber tone of the idiosyncratic record was enthusiastically embraced as an intellectual alternative to the fluffy norm.

Such commercial fortune defied the odds, considering *The Trinity Session* was made in sparse contrast to production excess of the Eighties. It was recorded live with the band circled around a single microphone, captured on a digital two-track during a 14-hour session in November 1987 at Toronto's Church of the Holy Trinity, which was chosen for its pure acoustics.

"It should be stressed you don't have to do albums like U2 does albums," singer Margo Timmins said. "There was no overdubbing or post-production song edits on *The Trinity Session*. I don't think people understand, and I don't see how they could, unless they were there that day. Our cost was the rental of the church (about $100), a pizza and $25 to the caretaker who let us stay a little longer than we had planned. Our producer, Peter Moore, already owned the recording equipment, so we got out of it for less than $200, with a sound that we played rather than mixed."

Cowboy Junkies' gentle sound was a pared-down blend of country, blues and folk, built around Timmins' plaintive, slightly spooky voice and the simple, unhurried guitar work of her brother, Michael Timmins. Joining them were brother Peter (drums) and lifelong friend Alan Anton (bass). The slow, quiet music was described as "postmodern melancholy," and it bowled over audiences.

The advantage of being truly different contributed to the band's sudden success. The Junkies wrote brooding, anguished originals (notably "Misguided Angels" and "200 More Miles," a country-folk montage of life on the road), but some unique interpretations of other artists' songs attracted as much attention, such as a "death country" reading of Hank Williams' "I'm So Lonesome I Could Cry" and the hushed, desolate reworking of Reed's "Sweet Jane" (Reed himself referred to the cover as "the best and most authentic version I have heard").

"Music has always been important to us," Margo explained. "The six of us in the family all shared records, we always went to concerts, we all had our stereos and our parents never told us to turn it down. Mike and Alan have been in bands since 1980, and they came back from London three years ago wondering what to do next. Pete rented drums, and they asked me to do vocals. I never thought of myself as a singer, but I used to sing around the house, so Mike had an idea that maybe I could do it."

The Trinity Session proved to be a testament to the Junkies' singular style. "We asked that it be released as is, to show that the recording method was not inferior, that it was valid," Margo noted. "What we wanted out of a record company was faith and an understanding of our music, not 'Let's get a hairdo on her.'" ■

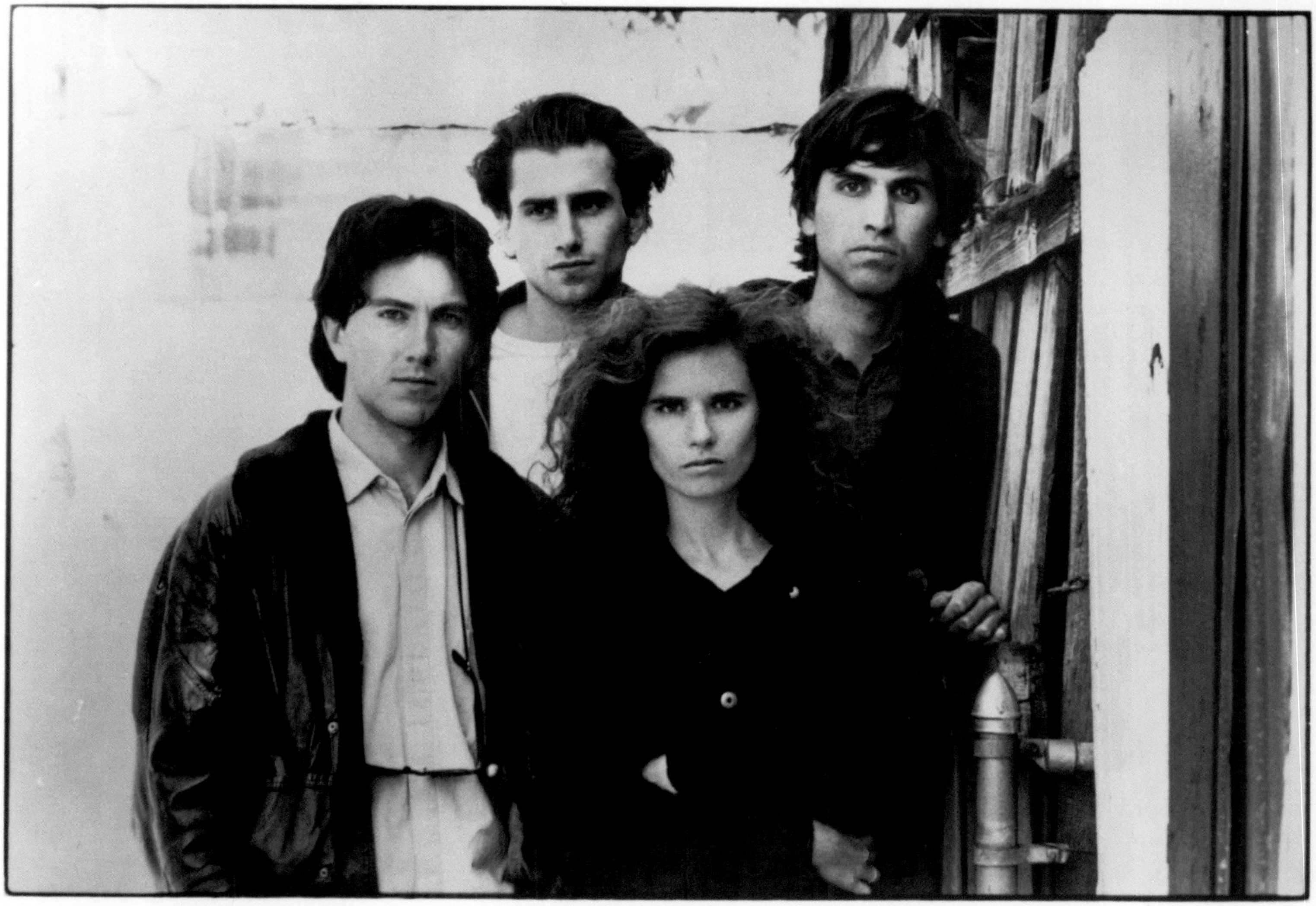

COWBOY JUNKIES

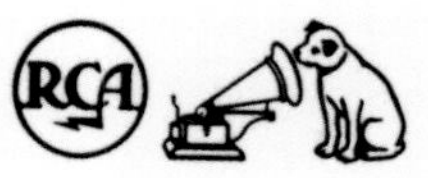

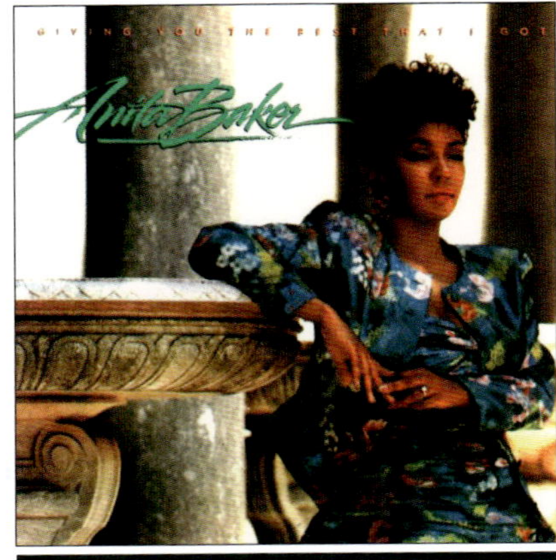

Billboard 200: *Giving You the Best That I Got* (No. 1)
Billboard Hot 100: "Giving You the Best That I Got" (#3); "Just Because" (#14)

Returning with *Giving You the Best That I Got*, Anita Baker perfected her sophisticated brand of romantic soul.

IN 1986, Anita Baker shot to No. 1 with *Rapture*, claiming superstar status among pop and Black music audiences with her Grammy-winning hit "Sweet Love." After that quintuple platinum debut album, Baker was back with its follow-up, *Giving You the Best That I Got*, which sold more than three million copies within two months of its release.

The title track, an audacious, semi-autobiographical love song, kept her at the top of the charts, and "Just Because" emerged as a wedding reception favorite. The emotional approach Baker brought to her phrasing gave the songs their elegance.

"Very early on, in my teens, I realized that I could move people," she explained. "But I was singing just to get a reaction to my range, displaying the three octaves that I have—I just got a primal feeling from popping a note and watching people go, 'Wow!'

"As I've gotten older, I've learned that there's more to this. Now I want to move people with the way I express the lyrics and not just pound them with note after note."

Baker described the album as "my intro to Jazz 101," bearing her trademark intimacy and sensuality. In disregard of superstar singer norms—being so divorced from the recording process that vocals were said to be "phoned in"—Baker was in the studio, singing along with the musicians as the basic tracks were cut, an old-fashioned technique more characteristic of singers in past decades.

"Sometimes the musicians don't want me in there," she acknowledged. "But I'm there. There is a relationship between singer, musician and the song you just can't get when the singer is alone in an isolated room.

"To me, a singer is somebody who can take any song and sing it. I can't do that. I have to personalize a song, fit it to me, fix it so I can take it from A to Z. It's got to have drama. Whether it's a quiet, understated melodrama or a slap-you-in-your-face drama, a song's gonna have moments." ■

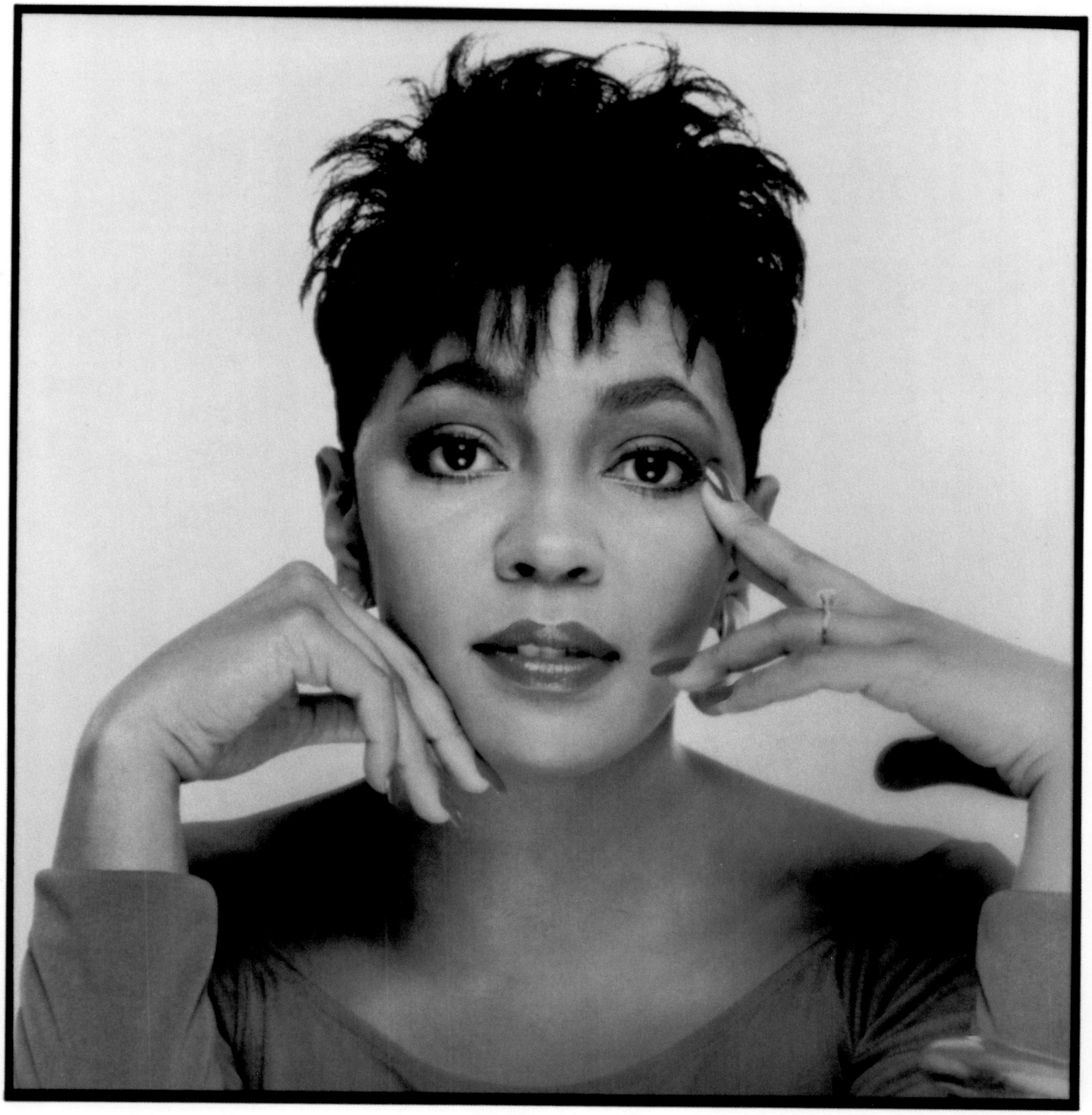

ANITA BAKER

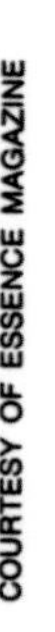

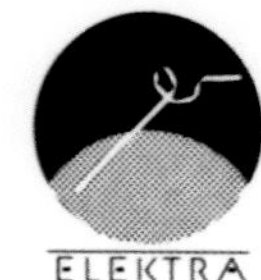

Billboard 200: *Get Here* (#49)
Billboard Hot 100: "Piano in the Dark" (#6)

Get Here emerged as Brenda Russell's greatest commercial success, spawning the single "Piano in the Dark."

ONE OF the year's most unconventional singles was Brenda Russell's "Piano in the Dark," a mature, literate tune concerning a troubled relationship. The moody pop ballad made the Top 10, despite the perceived impediment of a wistful, lingering piano solo.

"It's unusual these days, a real instrument instead of electronics," Russell said. "I believed in the song, but you never know what's going to happen with a record. You only know whether you did a good job or not. I knew if people got to hear it, it would do well."

The success of "Piano in the Dark" signified a career comeback for Russell, who had recorded other albums in the past decade that hadn't fared well commercially. She had to move to Sweden in 1984 to make her previous album, a work that she couldn't get released in America.

"It was a very rock 'n' roll record, and Black artists have a problem in the US when they're not doing R&B," she explained. "The labels said, 'Where's the urban hit?' So it was back to the drawing board."

However, Russell had amassed some impressive songwriting credentials. Roberta Flack, Anne Murray and Earth, Wind & Fire, among others, had recorded her songs, and Donna Summer scored an international hit in 1987 with her clever "Dinner with Gershwin."

Russell returned to A&M Records, and the *Get Here* album justified that decision with its sophisticated dance-floor grooves and gorgeously produced adult ballads. Russell gained the confidence to embark on her first tour.

"It's a great experience that I've wanted for a long time," she said. "It's fun once you get over that initial fear of doing it. It's not exactly like singing in front of a high-school auditorium." ■

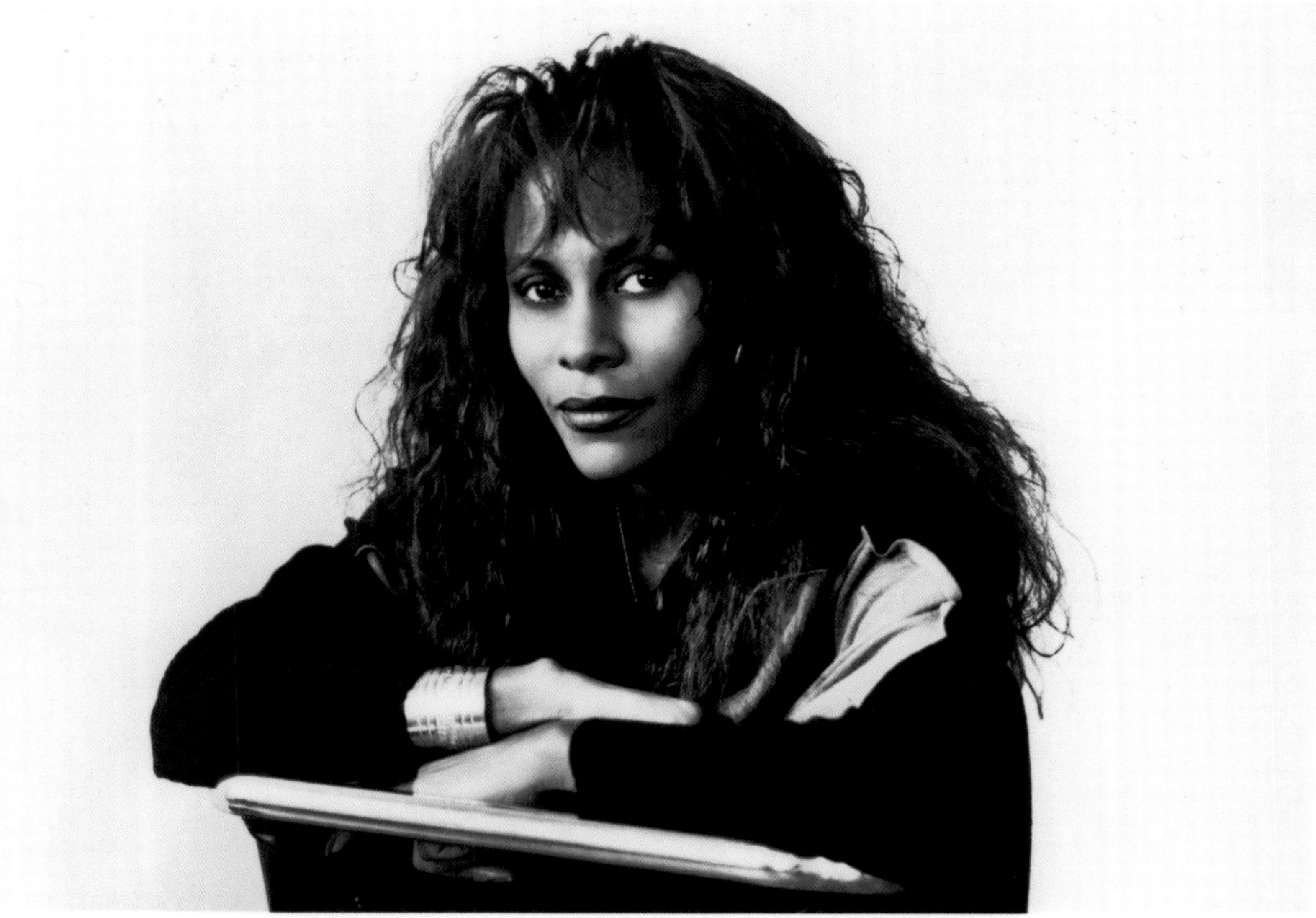

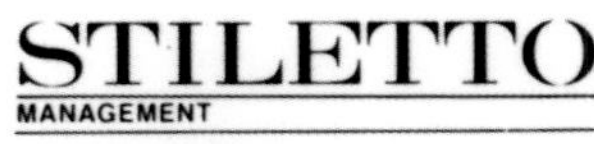

(213) 650-8560

BRENDA RUSSELL

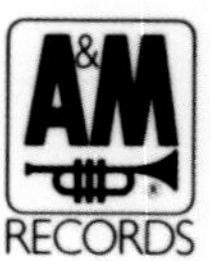

BILLY OCEAN
TEAR DOWN THESE WALLS

Billboard 200: *Tear Down These Walls* (#18)
Billboard Hot 100: "Get Outta My Dreams, Get into My Car" (No. 1); "The Colour of Love" (#17)

Billy Ocean soared straight to the top of the pop music charts with "Get Outta My Dreams, Get into My Car."

IN FOUR years, Billy Ocean had seemingly taken up residence on the American pop charts. The singles "Caribbean Queen (No More Love on the Run)," "Loverboy," "Suddenly," "When the Going Gets Tough, the Tough Get Going" and "There'll Be Sad Songs (To Make You Cry)" had all cracked the Top 5.

Ocean's *Tear Down These Walls* album featured another No. 1 single in the US and several other countries, "Get Out of My Dreams, Get into My Car." Ocean was quick to share credit for that hit with producer Robert John "Mutt" Lange, known not only for his projects with Ocean but also for his studio work with rock bands (AC/DC, Def Leppard, the Cars).

"The song came from Mutt," Ocean said. "He had the chorus, that 'get out of my dreams and into the back seat, baby' idea. He had recorded it with another band, which didn't work. So we worked together on different tempos, different melodies, different structures. Mutt is a very careful guy in the studio. Nothing goes on a record unless he thinks it's right. I knew it was a fairly special song when we were done with it."

The song's video wed real-life footage with animation, a concept popularized on a larger scale by the smash motion picture *Who Framed Roger Rabbit*?"

"I leave my videos to the professionals—my best contribution is to simply be open, flexible and attentive," Ocean said. "But even though I don't like to blow my own trumpet, I've felt proud. We came out with the 'Dreams' video before that film."

The 38-year-old vocalist, who was born in Trinidad and raised in London, had found success with Black, dance and adult contemporary audiences, a crossover situation he attributed to three factors. One is was his background. "Growing up in England, you can't help but approach music in a different way. There were such greats as the Beatles and the Rolling Stones, and I was getting soulful things from American music like Otis Redding. So I had great teachers."

Another was his powerful but warm voice. "It's a gift, but like anything else, if you don't take care of it, you lose it. It's a very valuable part of my body, so I rest, I exercise, I eat properly, I don't drink alcohol. Discipline of the mind, discipline of the body—everything affects everything else."

And Ocean had a strong belief in his talent. He found stardom only after years of dues-paying. "A song wouldn't be No. 1 if it wasn't good enough in the first place," he said. "Everything has come from my initial efforts. Now the payoff is going onstage, getting involved with an audience. It makes you feel human. When it's good, the industry can't take it away with petty nonsense." ■

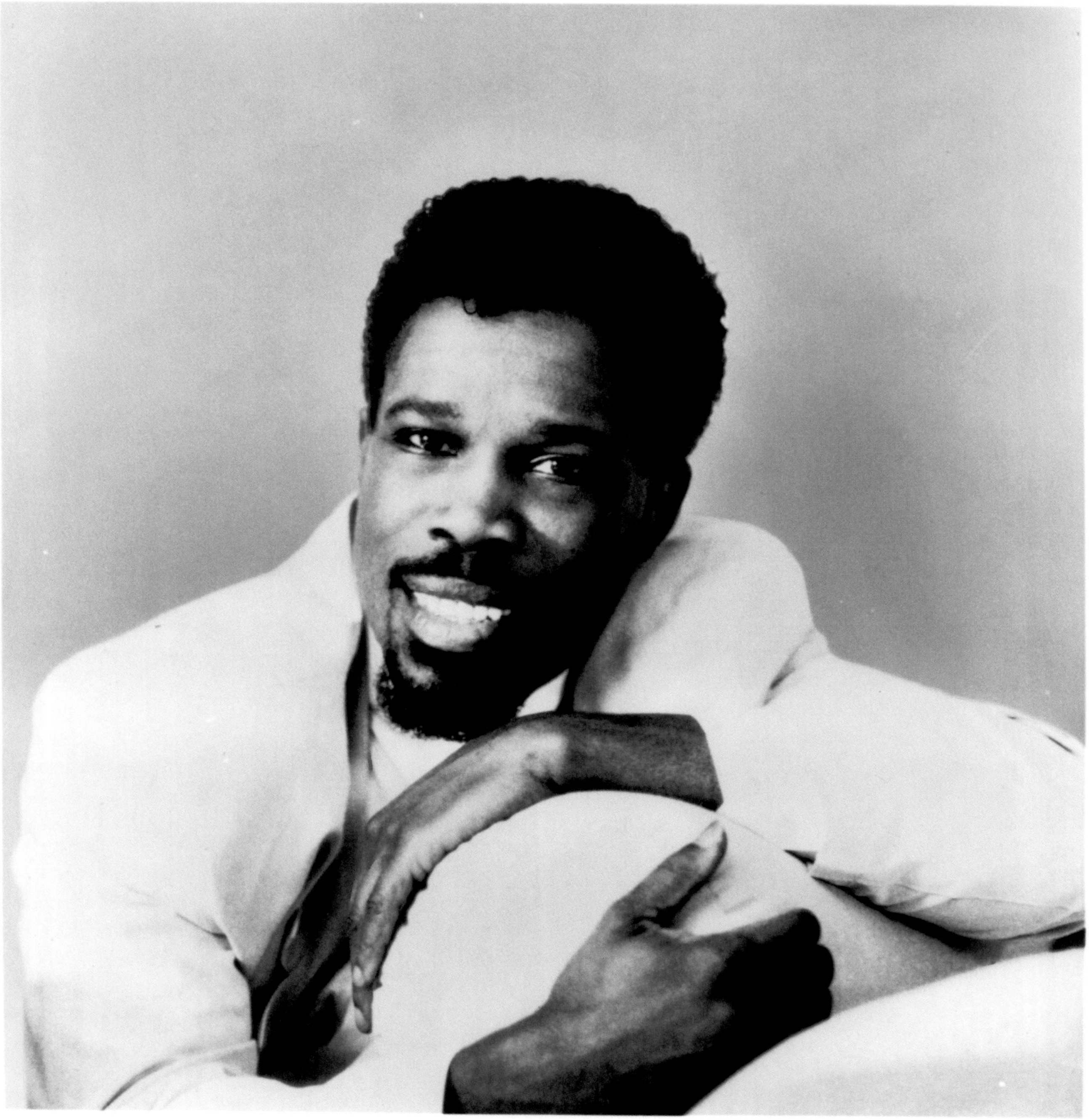

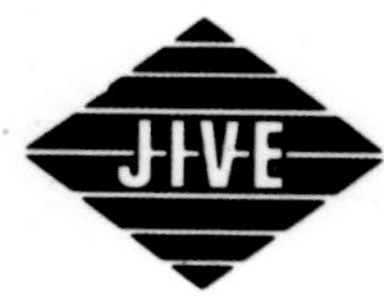

BILLY OCEAN

ARISTA™

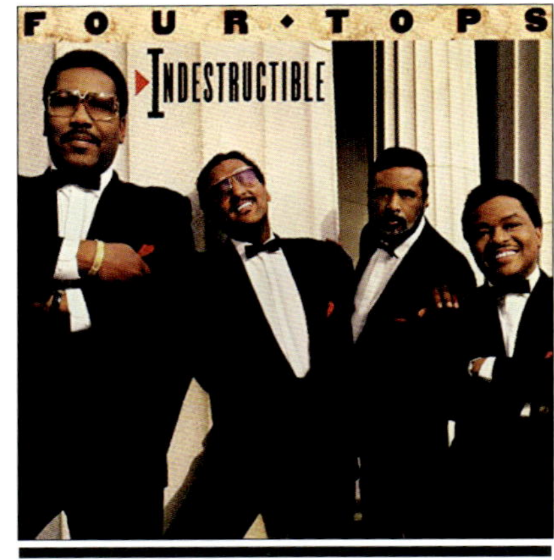

Billboard 200: *Indestructible* (#149)
Billboard Hot 100: "Indestructible" (#35)

The renowned Four Tops built upon their legacy with *Indestructible*, an album typifying their sound and style.

IT WAS a boast that no other pop group could make. The Four Tops had performed and recorded together for almost 35 years with their original lineup intact—Levi Stubbs, Abdul "Duke" Fakir, Renaldo "Obie" Benson and Lawrence Payton.

"We've known each other since we were little boys—kindergarten age—and we've been buddies all this time." Payton said. "We still live in Detroit. We've had our little ups and downs, but nothing enough to cause a divorce. A couple of the guys have been through several marriages, but we're still together. It's hard to keep a band together because every member has different things going on. We're fortunate. We're in the business of life together besides the music business."

The legendary Motown quartet had a long list of smash hit records to their credit, with Stubbs' huge, smoldering voice setting them apart from most other acts. "Reach Out I'll Be There," "I Can't Help Myself (Sugar Pie Honey Bunch)," "It's the Same Old Song," "Bernadette" and "Standing in the Shadows of Love" were some of the best sounds in Sixties soul music. And the Tops had remained great entertainers, too.

"We've always had a pride thing about performing," Payton said. "We never went into the business to take the money and run. We're there to make people happy. So we still give it our all, doing the same thing we did in the Sixties. We let it all hang out onstage, and then we come off and fight."

The Eighties had brought a number of firsts for the Tops. Stubbs made a critically acclaimed film debut as the singing and speaking voice for Audrey II, the man-eating plant in the 1986 movie version of the musical *Little Shop of Horrors*.

"And the main catalyst was the Motown 25th anniversary special (the 1983 celebration that appeared on NBC-TV)," Payton reminded. "That did a big number for everybody associated with Motown—Michael Jackson's career took off right after that. We did a 'battle of the bands' with the Temptations and we signed to tour internationally with them for four years."

The album *Indestructible* revolved around collaborations with Phil Collins (the UK single "Loco in Acapulco"), Aretha Franklin (the R&B and adult contemporary hit "If Ever a Love There Was)," Huey Lewis, Kenny G and producer Michael Narada Walden. The title track was a Top 40 hit. But the Tops were no longer heard on Motown.

"I thought Berry (Gordy, who discovered and signed the Tops to Motown in 1963 for an advance of $500) was a very nice guy with a lot of vision," Payton said of the departure. "I've heard that other people got raw deals out of the situation, but we turned our alright. It's exciting, because every day people say we're sounding better than ever. I say, 'Thanks—we've been around for a while.'" ■

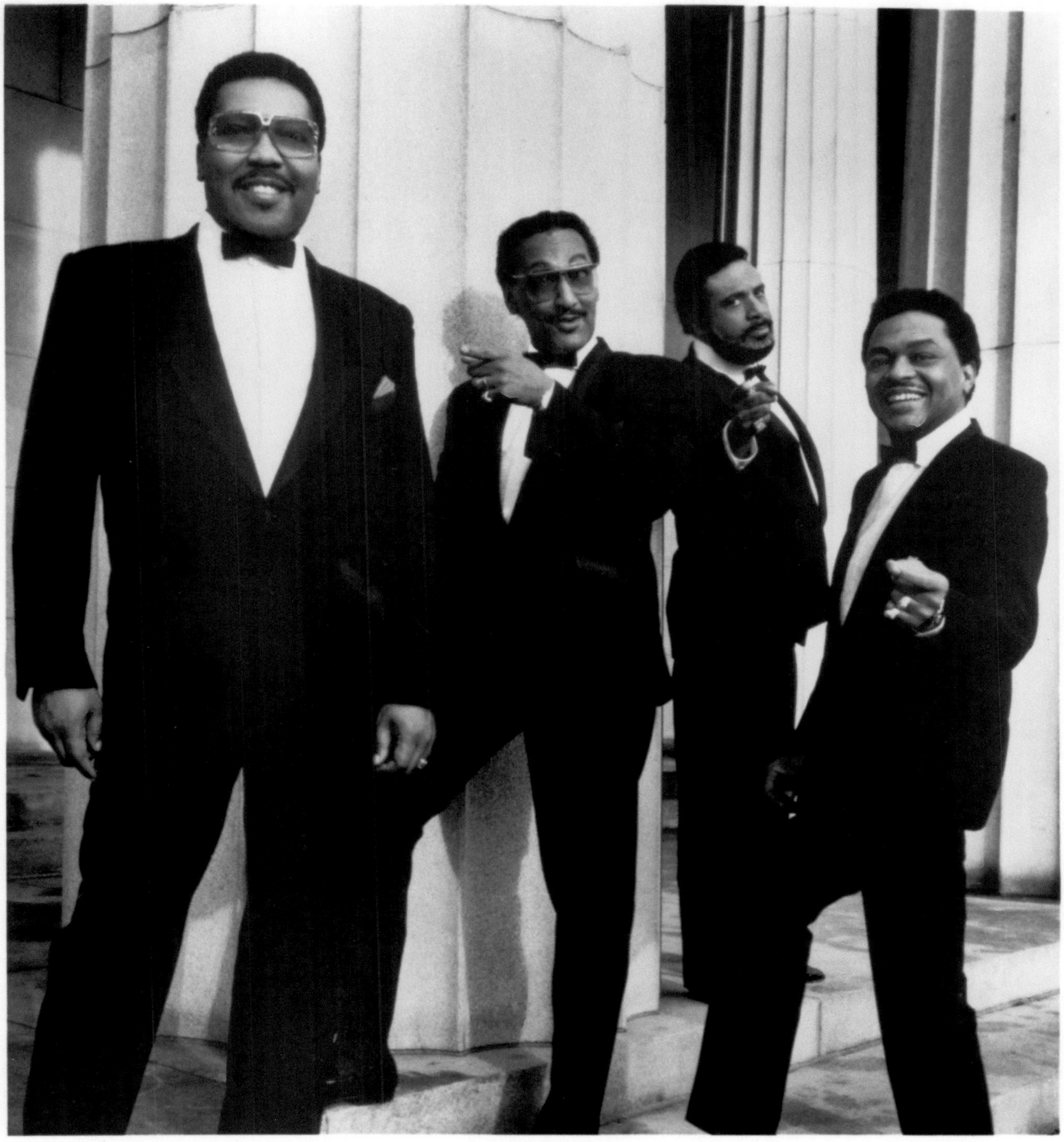

FOUR TOPS

AGENCY:

General Talent International
1700 Broadway
New York, NY 10019
(212) 245-3839

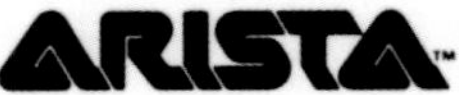

PUBLIC RELATIONS:

Burnham-Callaghan Associates, Inc.
357 West 55th Street
New York, NY 10019
(212) 245-7380

Billboard 200: *Traveling Wilburys Vol. 1* (#3)
Billboard Hot 100: "Handle with Care" (#45); "End of the Line" (#63)

The Traveling Wilburys' accidental origins gave birth to a supergroup and an album that stood the test of time.

A STAR-STUDDED band usually gets put together for a cause or a payday. The Traveling Wilburys, on the contrary, happened quite organically. It began with former Electric Light Orchestra leader Jeff Lynne producing Tom Petty's first solo outing without his band the Heartbreakers. When recording was interrupted to ready a B-side of a single for former Beatle George Harrison, suddenly Bob Dylan and Roy Orbison showed up.

The contributors had such a good time they stuck around to record as the Traveling Wilburys, for an album that climbed the charts in the United States and sold more than 4 million worldwide, winning the Grammy for Best Rock Performance by a Duo or Group.

"Pre-Wilburys, we would have such a good time sitting around at somebody's house all evening," Petty explained. "That's where the sound came from—everyone pulled out a flat-top guitar and played. The revelation was that we could sing together and make really nice harmonies. It was George's idea to form a group. At the time, none of us could foresee how well it was going to work out, but we enjoyed each other's company. They've become tremendous friends to me, which would be worth so much whether they played guitars or not. To make a successful record with them has been beyond my wildest dreams."

Traveling Wilburys Vol. 1 was remarkable for its short, catchy, modest songs, unencumbered by star-on-a-lark indulgences. "Handle with Care" and "End of the Line" hit the charts.

"It's playing, it's arranging, it's co-writing—it's getting everybody in the right place," Lynne said of the musical relationship. "I always mix my voice really quiet. Working with the other guys, I put them up as loud as I possibly can, because they're the singers. I've more or less run out of heroes."

The band members adopted tongue-in-cheek pseudonyms as half-brothers from a fictional Wilbury family of traveling musicians—Lucky (Dylan), Otis (Lynne), Lefty (Orbison), Nelson (Harrison) and Charlie T. Jr. (Petty). The Traveling Wilburys had made Orbison realize the benefits of his elder statesman of rock 'n' roll status. "I love it all, except the 'elder' part," he said with a laugh.

Tragically, Orbison died of a sudden heart attack in December, only a few weeks after the album's release.

"When Roy died, it took the wind out of our sails," Petty said. "We'd made plans to do so many things." ■

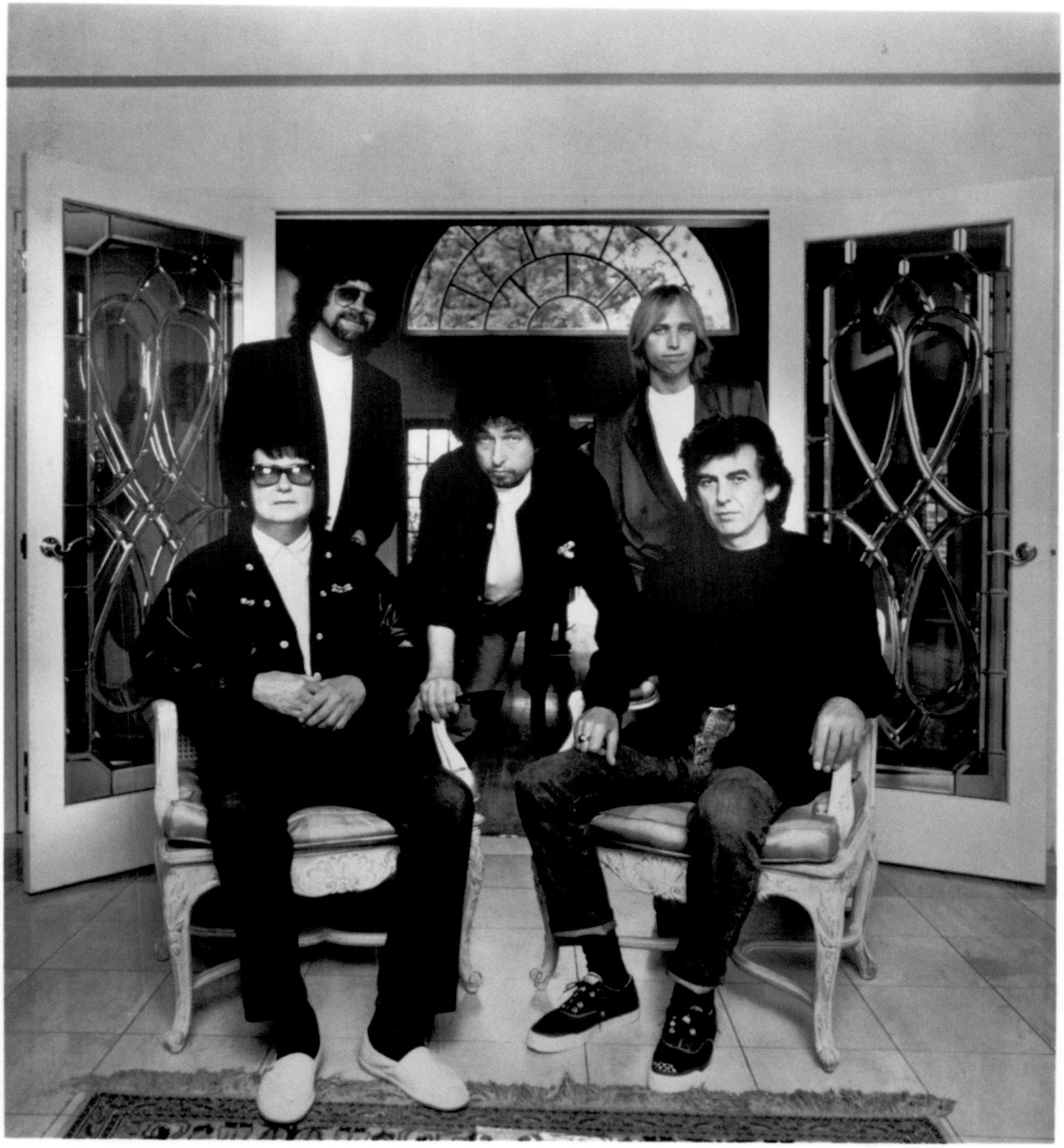

Photo Credit: Neal Preston

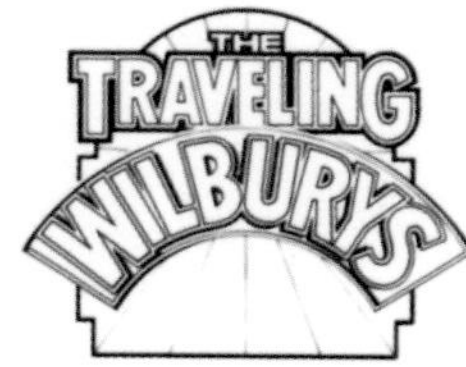

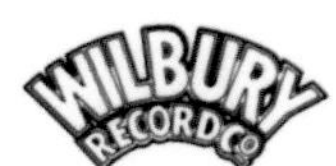

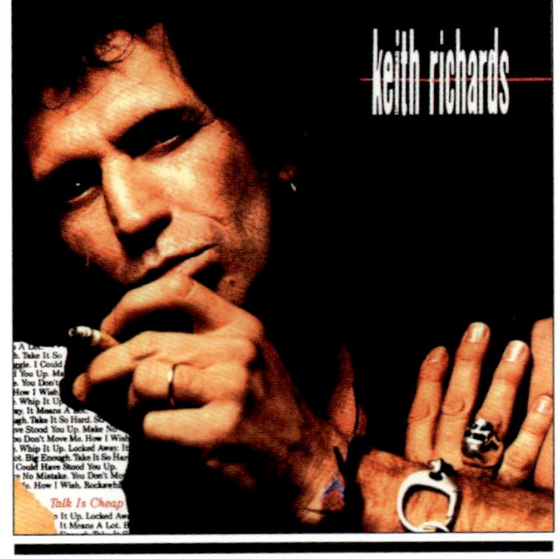

Billboard 200: *Talk Is Cheap* (#24)

During an ongoing quarrel with Mick Jagger, Keith Richards had fun generating a solo album, *Talk Is Cheap*.

STRONGLY COMMITTED to the Rolling Stones' good name and musical roots, Keith Richards would have been happy working for the rest of his life as he had lived it for the past quarter of a century—as the group's longtime guitarist. But after vocalist Mick Jagger refused to tour in 1986 in support of the album *Dirty Work* and was keen to promote his solo recording and pursue contemporary pop trends, Richards "reluctantly" began his own project.

"I never saw myself as anything but a Stone," he emphasized. "I felt perfectly content to create music as a Rolling Stone. I had no need to express myself in any other way. Unlike some other original rockers, I didn't have to get out there on my own to make my creative juices flow. They always flowed as a Stone.

"But it was time to get my ass into a recording studio and start making music. I could only play my record collection so many times, I could only sun in the Caribbean for so long, I could only make so many appearances as a sideman on other people's albums one more time."

Teaming up with drummer Steve Jordan as co-writer and co-producer (they had worked together on the Chuck Berry film *Hail! Hail! Rock & Roll*), Richards formed a backing band he dubbed the X-Pensive Winos. Members included guitarist Waddy Wachtel, saxophonist Bobby Keys, keyboardist Ivan Neville and Charley Drayton on bass. *Talk Is Cheap*, Richards' debut solo album, also featured Bernie Worrell, Bootsy Collins and Maceo Parker.

Richards was "ecstatic" over the results. "Take It So Hard," which passed for a tough Stones single, reached #3 on *Billboard*'s Mainstream Rock Tracks chart, and the album went gold—a bigger commercial success than Jagger's solo venture. ■

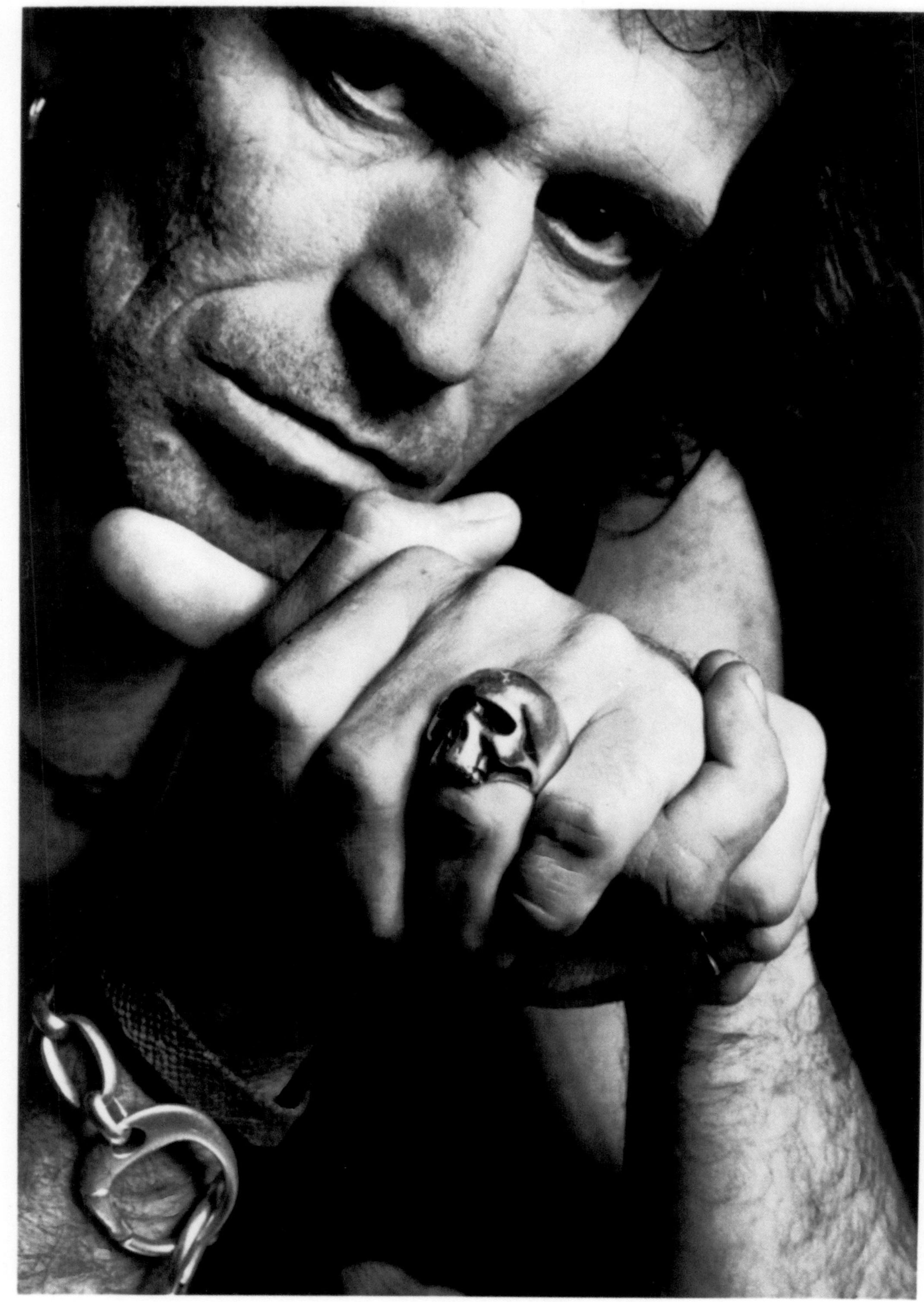

Photo Credit: Santé D'Orazio

KEITH RICHARDS

Virgin

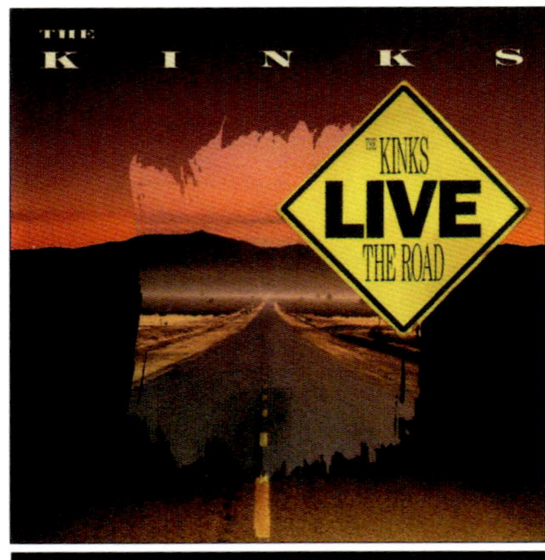

Billboard 200: *Live: The Road* (#110)

The Kinks' *Live: The Road* provided a sonic snapshot in celebration of an original and important rock presence.

THE KINKS deserved credit. While their contemporaries from the "British Invasion" of the Sixties were either disbanded, dead or as good as dead, the long-lived band continued to crank out decent albums. Ray Davies, the group's mercurial singer and songwriter, had established himself over the years as one of rock's most literate songwriters, a keen purveyor of social satire and topical wit. Davies described *Live: The Road* as "probably the most important work I've done." The live album, which spent a brief time on the charts, showed the Kinks at a vital stage of a turbulent career.

"The Kinks have never made a lot of money, but the overriding factor in sustain the band has been that we've constantly come out with new product," Davies said. "When people come to a Kinks concert, they don't just hear 'You Really Got Me' and 'Lola.' They hear a whole new catalog of music and ideas as well. That's what has kept us regenerating energy as performers and kept our fans interested. I don't like to write for a format. I'm luckier than Mick Jagger—Mick will always have to be Jumpin' Jack Flash, which is probably more difficult to do as he gets older. I write songs about subjects I feel strongly about, and when you're doing that for genuine artistic reasons instead of the latest fashion, it will work. I've got about six different characters I use to perform the songs in a show. I become a nonperson in a sense—I stop being Ray Davies onstage and become a rock 'n' roll actor."

The live material was introduced with one new studio recording, the title track. "I wanted one song that summed up the Kinks' career, so I wrote 'The Road' as a link piece," Davies said. "It's optimistic in places—I even mention Jimi Hendrix, saying, 'If we link up further up the road, that's all right with me.' But there's also a line, 'Some are survivors, some of us break.' Jimi broke. I think we've all been near the edge, where you say, 'Do I go over or do I withdraw?' I've been to the edge a few times."

Live: The Road then mixed into the sounds of the audience, heralding the tracks recorded on the band's American tour. The first was "Destroyer," which Davies described as "about someone who's got this mad will to succeed inside of a paranoid destructive element. I had that when I started. I really had the strong will to do well at something, but I wasn't doing well at art college—I would have ended up being a teacher or interior designer if I hadn't gone on tour with the band."

The album then collected past material that had become personal to Davies—"In the way they are sequenced, there is almost the story of the Kinks. It's turned into an autobiographical record, a statement, a watershed." The surprises came from the 1987 *Think Visual* album, the Bo Diddley-derived title track and the plaintive "Lost and Found." Guitarist and brother Dave Davies got the spotlight during a reading of his elegiac "Living on a Thin Line."

"When you're getting songs together, you don't think about making them for big arenas," Dave mused. "But I like good riffs—they make up the bulk of great rock 'n' roll tunes." ■

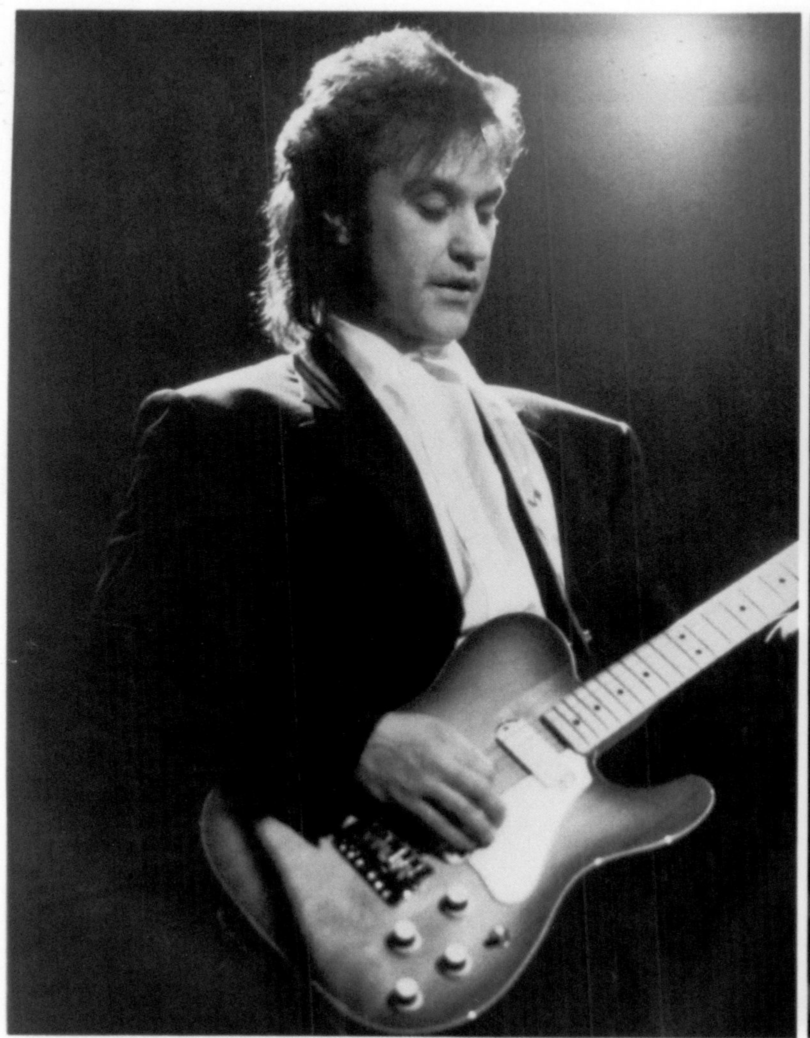

DAVE DAVIES

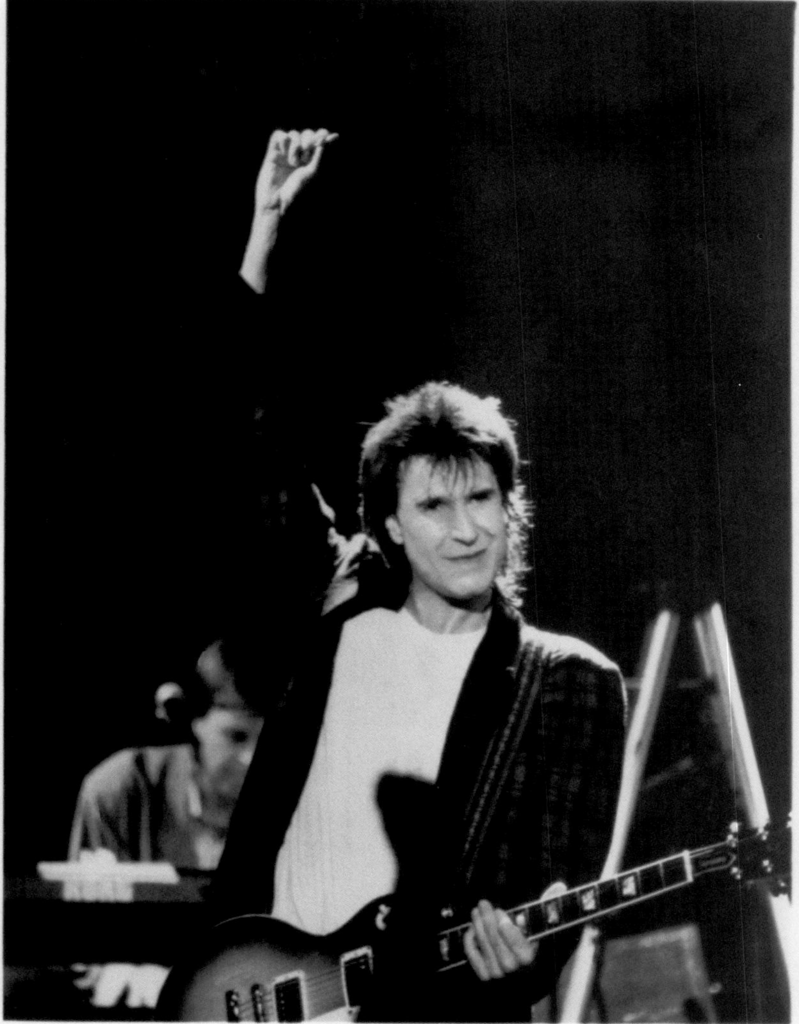

RAY DAVIES

THE
KINKS

MCA RECORDS

1/88

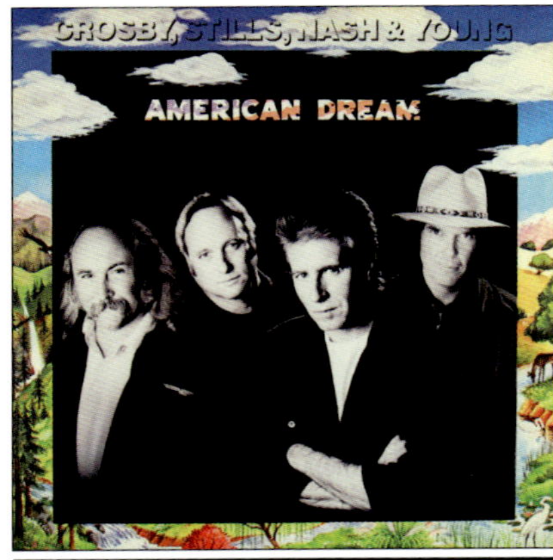

Billboard 200: *American Dream* (#16)
Billboard Hot 100: "Got It Made" (#69)

Crosby, Stills, Nash & Young reconvened to record *American Dream*, the band's first studio album in 18 years.

THE MUSICAL partnership of David Crosby, Stephen Stills, Graham Nash and Neil Young had formed and re-formed countless times since 1969. In various combinations, the seminal folk supergroup had loomed large as one of the rock music scene's most successful touring and recording acts. But as a quartet, celebrity had outweighed the quantity of the four often-fractious friends' recorded output.

In the mid-Eighties, Crosby's notoriety stemmed from his well-documented drug-abuse issues and the resultant paranoia that left him a shell of a performer. Young promised Crosby in 1983 that he would reunite with his erstwhile colleagues if Crosby could solve his problems and clean up his act.

A jail sentence stemming from drug and possession charges caught up with Crosby before death did. When he finally surrendered to authorities, by Crosby's own admission, he and girlfriend Jan Dance were consuming approximately seven grams of cocaine a day as well as a half a gram of heroin. Crosby beat his addiction while serving five months in prison at the Texas Department of Corrections in Huntsville during 1986.

"It seems that there's a tremendous amount of interest in how come I'm still alive," Crosby said. "I am beating the odds heavily. Most of the people who did as much drugs as I did are dead. I am such an egregious, outrageous archetype of how to mess it up totally. When people with good consciences and good hearts look at a drug addict, they almost always say, 'Why can't you just stop? You're dying, your family's gone, you can't work—stop!' They have no idea why a person can't do it. You always can, but you don't believe you can, and therein lies the tale. I thought I'd die if I stopped—that's part of it. It's the only disease I know that tells you you're fine and kills you at the same time."

True to Young's word, upon Crosby's release from prison, Crosby, Stills, Nash & Young assembled at Young's ranch in California to record *American Dream*, only the second album of original material by the four men. "I really think we've been together since we (first) got together," Young said.

The record made it to the Top 20 on the charts, but it was otherwise poorly received, and Young refused to support it with a CSNY tour. The compassionate Nash hadn't had it easy over the years, being in the middle of eternal squabbling.

"The feeling between us couldn't have stood a couple of months on the road," Nash said. "You've got to be close to do that." ■

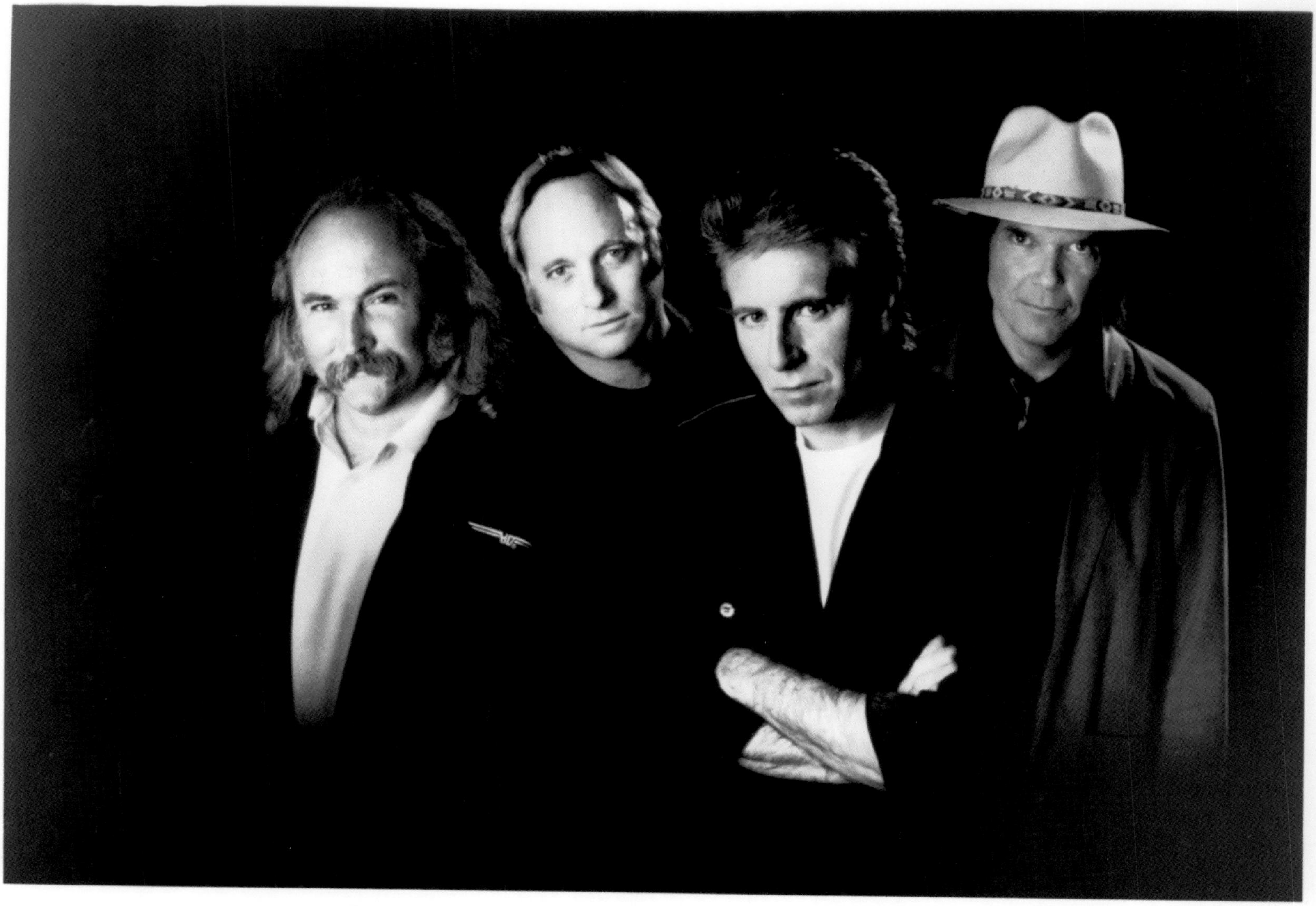

DAVID CROSBY STEPHEN STILLS GRAHAM NASH NEIL YOUNG

CROSBY, STILLS, NASH & YOUNG

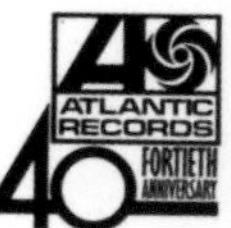

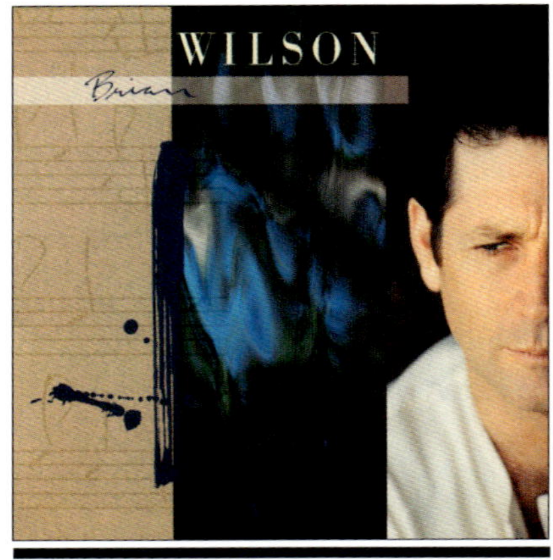

Billboard 200: *Brian Wilson* (#54)

One of pop music's most markedly distressed recluses, Brian Wilson reappeared with his debut solo endeavor.

THE CREATIVE force behind the Beach Boys, the world's most popular musical group at their Sixties peak, Brian Wilson seldom embodied the carefree, fun-in-the-California-sun persona of the group's sound. His ambitious work on the *Pet Sounds* album remained a landmark in the history of pop music production, but the burden of genius was too heavy for him. For most of three decades, he'd struggled with much-publicized mental-health problems.

"If I could have a wife and kids that loved me, an accounting job that I liked…I would still choose the life I've had, the emotional pain," Wilson said. "My art wouldn't have been brought out if I'd had a happy childhood."

Wilson described his father Murry, a failed songwriter and the Beach Boys' manager in the early days, as a viciously abusive parent whose violent mistreatment left his eldest son with permanent psychological scars and a predilection for substance abuse.

"He made me shit on a newspaper, he pulled out his glass eye and made me look in the empty socket," Wilson mused. "He once flogged me with a two-by-four—it caused deafness in my right ear. He also purposely dropped a motorboat on my hand. He was crazy."

The Beach Boys were thrust into the spotlight before Wilson was 20, and his musical talent outgrew his social abilities. Record company executives, his father and the other Beach Boys wanted him to churn out a surfing-cars-and-girls formula, but he began to draw inward, physically intimidated and incapable of asserting himself. Wilson drank heavily and, with the advent of the drug culture, began using "pot, LSD, uppers, downers, coke." It precipitated his descent into a living nightmare that almost cost him his life.

"I was stoned on such a broad scale, my head was so messed up," he recalled with a nervous laugh. "I hardly had a chance to get music out."

Wilson stopped washing himself and spent several years in his bed. In 1982, maverick therapist Eugene Landy intervened for the second time. It was rumored that Wilson had been brainwashed by Landy, and the relationship was unusual. Landy monitored Wilson twenty-four hours a day, and he went on to become a business partner and executive producer of Wilson's solo album. The single "Love and Mercy" exemplified *Brian Wilson*'s theme of spirituality, and fans were eager to latch on to any evidence that Wilson's musical genius was still intact. ■

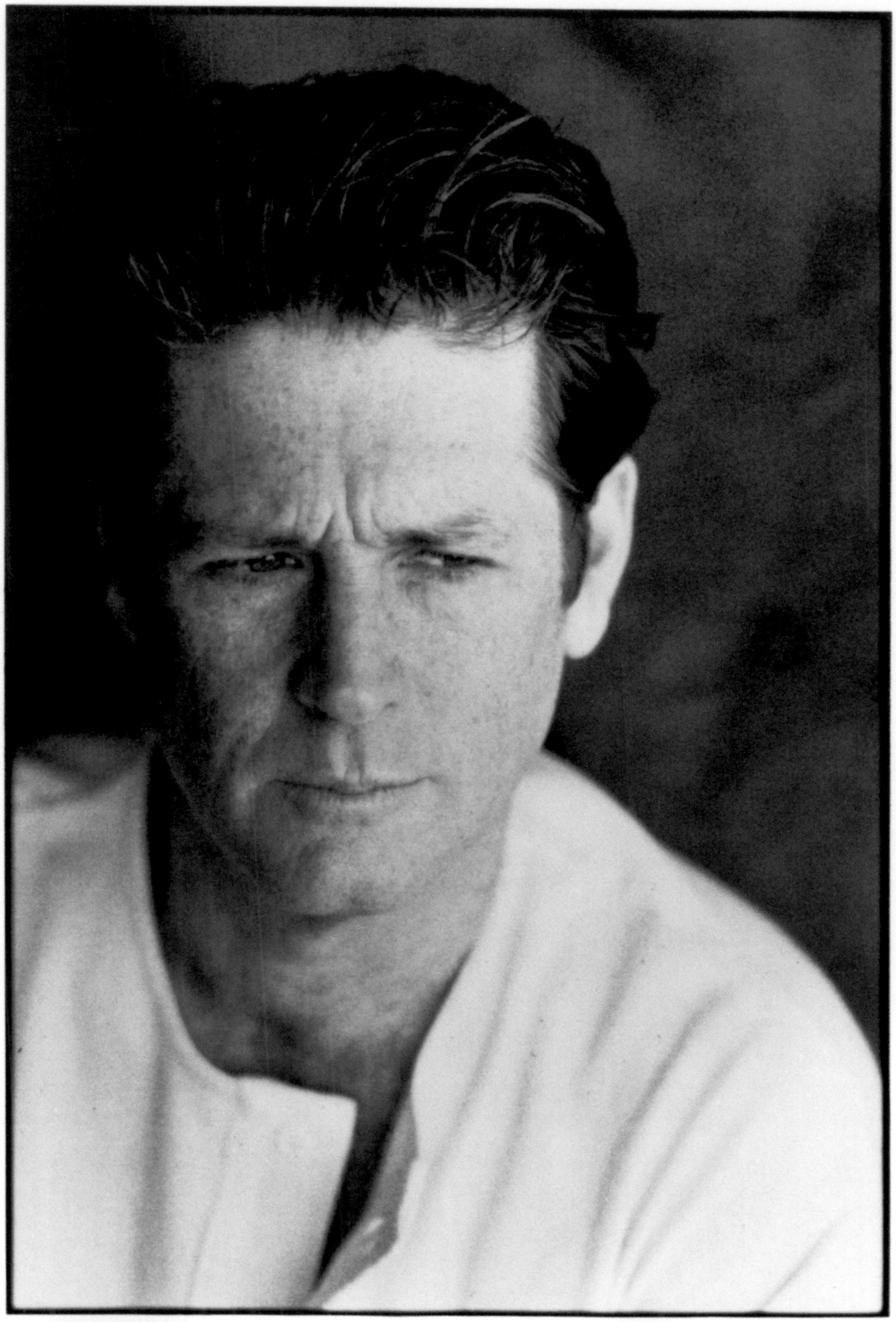

Photo Credit: Kamron Hinatsu

BRIAN
WILSON

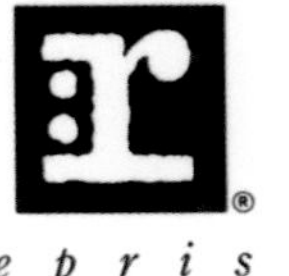

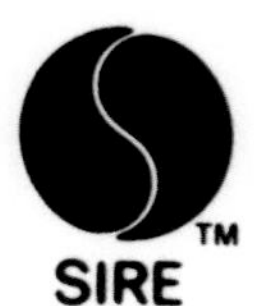

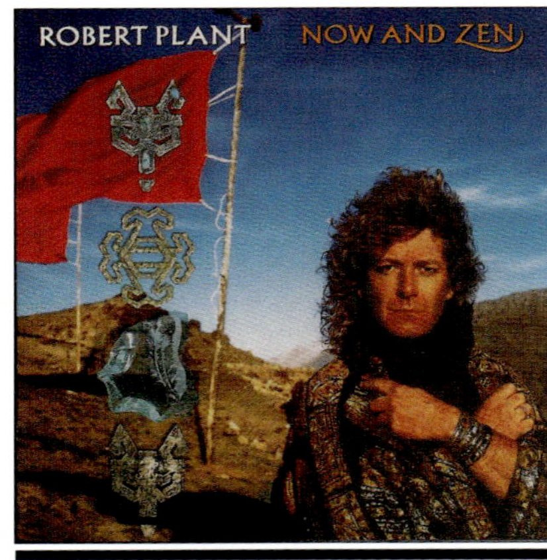

Billboard 200: *Now and Zen* (#6)
Billboard Hot 100: "Ship of Fools" (#84); "Tall Cool One" (#25)

With *Now and Zen*, Robert Plant found a renewed perspective on the sound that distinguished Led Zeppelin.

DELIVERING HIS fourth solo album, *Now and Zen*, Robert Plant focused some deserved attention on his solo career—a sizable accomplishment, considering he would always be the rock deity who sang in Led Zeppelin, the most influential and popular hard-rock band in history.

"I don't want to dissolve into the structure of happy middle age," the venerable vocalist stated. "I want to get through to kids who want to know what happened to that old guy who was the king of rock in 1971."

Of course, "the monster," as Plant affectionately referred to the Zep, was a one-in-a-million proposition, predicated as much on the drumming fury of the late John Bonham and the guitar frenzy of Jimmy Page as Plant's banshee wailing.

"When I started out (a solo career), I had to deny the whole thing," Plant explained. "But I know a lot of people are really disgusted every time I don't play Zeppelin stuff. If I have been stubborn, it hasn't been fair to people who come to my concerts."

Of course, Plant preferred to leave the task of resurrecting Zep riffs to youthful clones like Kingdom Come. He deserved credit for taking the streamlined sounds of his solo work to new settings instead of trading exclusively on his past. He assembled a solid, enthusiastic band of youthful players; keyboardist and songwriter Phil Johnstone, Plant's main collaborator, proved to be a particularly talented find.

The material featured a few Led Zeppelin samples, and Page was enlisted to play guitar on "Heaven Knows" and "Tall Cool One." Those tracks and "Ship of Fools" were all popularized by airplay on album-oriented rock stations, and *Now and Zen* was received positively by both fans and reviewers.

"Maybe what I'm playing is pretty good—not as good as Zeppelin, probably," one of rock's living legends concluded. "But it's far more important for my solo career to succeed than to tour with Led Zeppelin and get paid thousands of dollars." ■

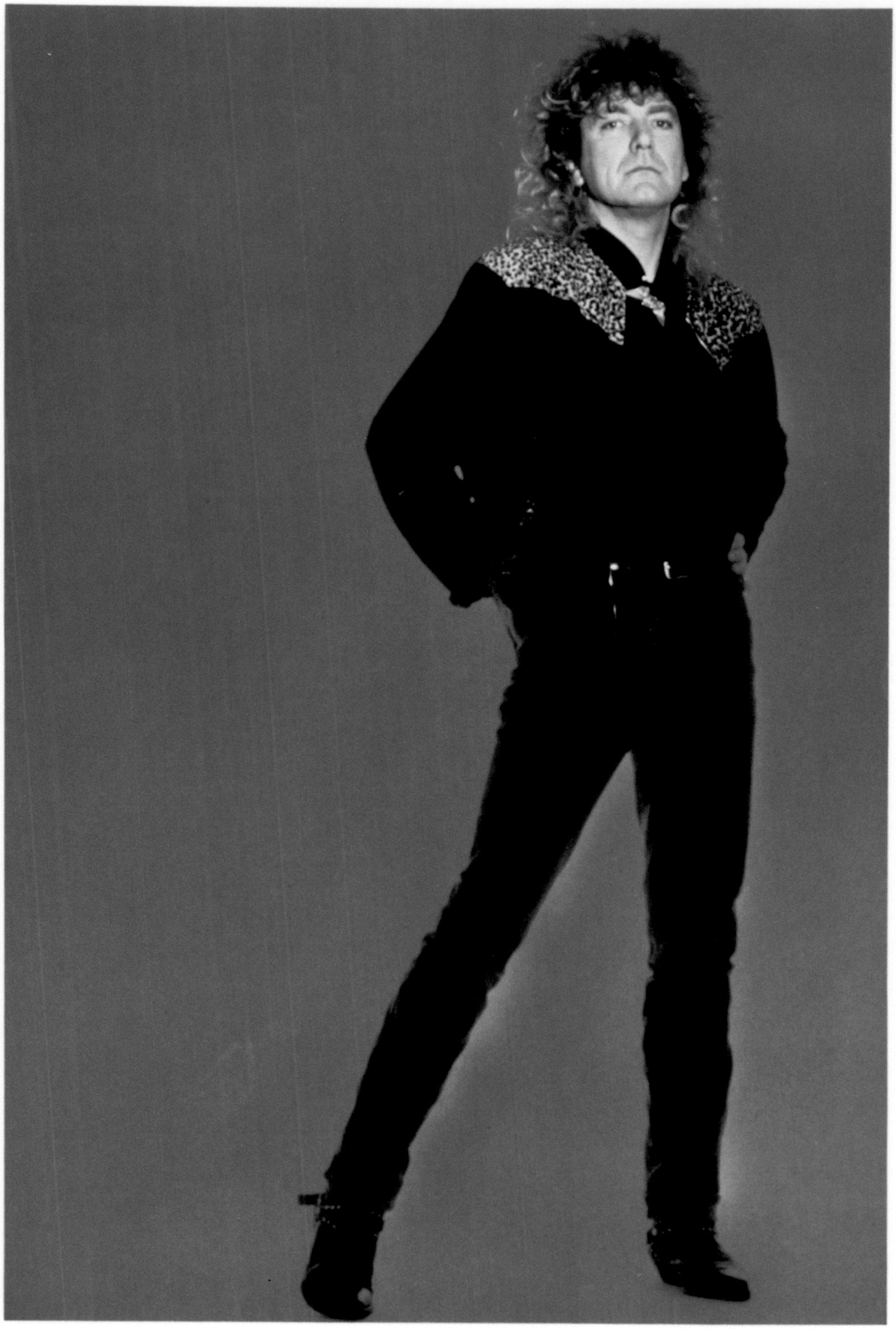

ROBERT PLANT

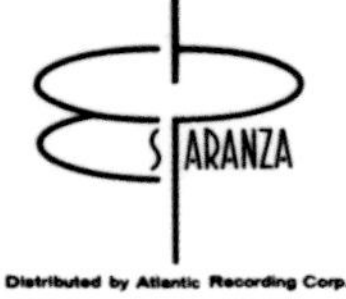

Distributed by Atlantic Recording Corp.

Billboard 200: *Dangerous Age* (#58)
Billboard Hot 100: "Shake It Up" (#82)

The release of *Dangerous Age* erased any doubt about the survival of Bad Company without singer Paul Rodgers.

THE ORIGINAL Bad Company attained instant celebrity in the mid-Seventies with "Can't Get Enough," the first of many hard-rock hits; "Feel Like Makin' Love," "Ready for Love" and "Rock ''n' Roll Fantasy" became album-rock radio staples. Drummer Simon Kirke (from Free) and guitarist Mick Ralphs (from Mott the Hoople) turned in the sparse, tight rhythms and riffs, but it was Paul Rodgers' smooth but explosive vocal talents that provided the transcendence.

The drain of touring was a significant reason for Rodgers leaving the British band in 1982, but Ralphs and Kirke relaunched Bad Company in 1986. Foreigner's Mick Jones introduced them to vocalist Brian Howe, who had previously worked with Ted Nugent. *Fame and Fortune*, Bad Company's first outing with Howe singing, had a dismal showing.

"There are a hundred reasons why that album turned out the way it did, but at the end of the day it was our fault," Howe said. "We had no name, and we made a record that appealed to the three of us, and when it was done, the record company reckoned that we should call ourselves Bad Company and be done with it—the band was still being heard on American radio a lot, and Simon and Mick had worked for that name as much as anybody. But we didn't sound anything like that."

Howe harbored some serious doubts about the band's ability to succeed with him out front, but the members set out to rectify some of the mistakes they had made. Howe co-wrote the majority of songs on the *Dangerous Age* album with producer Terry Thomas, the former Charlie guitarist, and the first thing they did was kick out the keyboards—Bad Company was back to a basic, tough, guitar-oriented sound. "I've seen Foreigner lose all their rock 'n' roll credibility by producing hit ballads," Howe noted. "We've learned from their error."

The success of *Dangerous Age*—album-oriented rock stations embraced "No Smoke Without a Fire," "One Night" and "Shake It Up"—assuaged Howe's concerns, but performing onstage was new to him since joining Bad Company, especially the Rodgers-era material he had inherited.

"It's strange what people expect," he said diplomatically. "I could copy Paul note-for-note—which is impossible for any singer to do—or I can sing the songs to my benefit. I still stick to the tunes, but I put my own interpretation on them. I would love to meet Paul and shake his hand, because he's one of my all-time favorite singers. Should I get the opportunity, I hope he doesn't hit me." ■

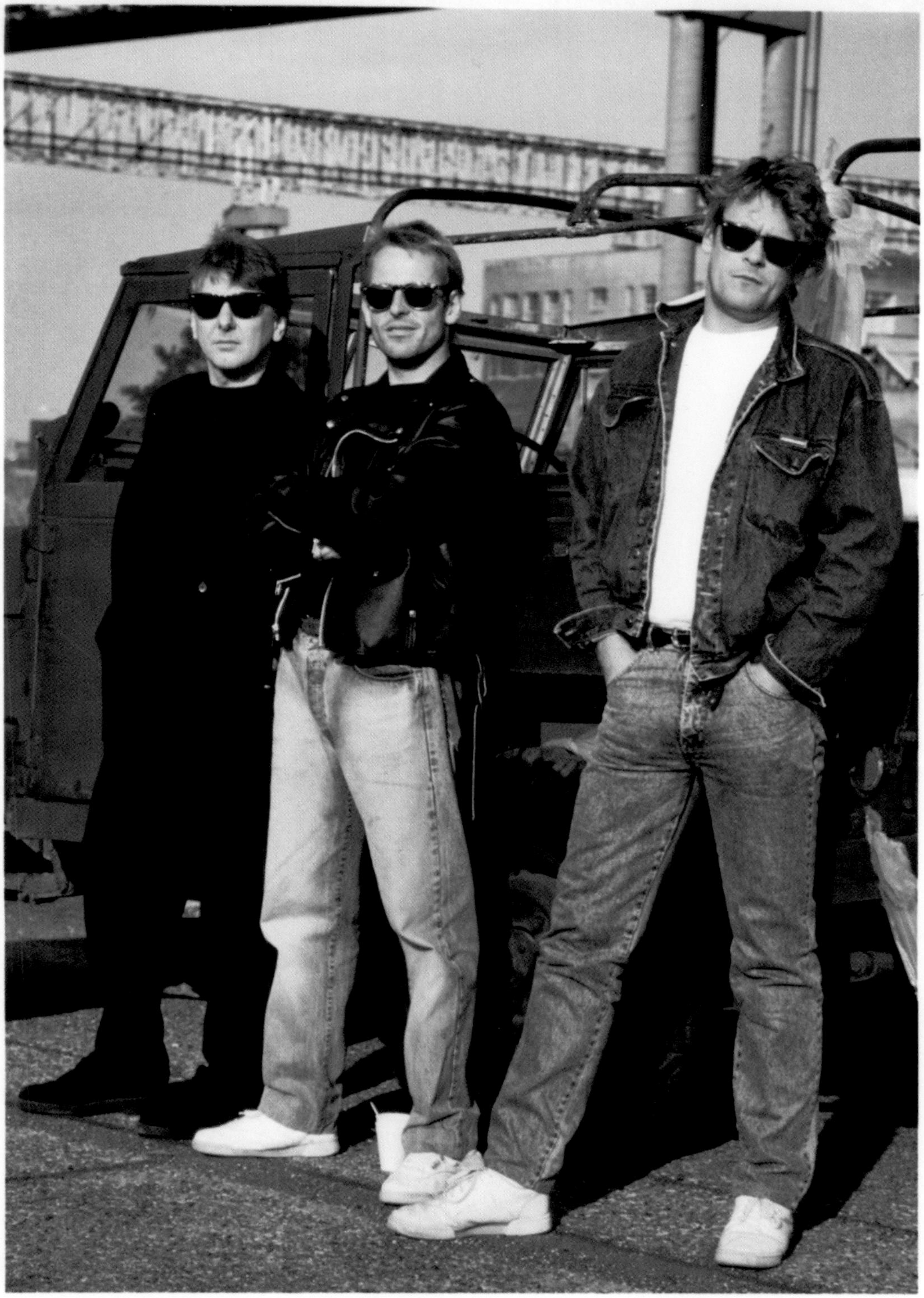

MICK RALPHS SIMON KIRKE BRIAN HOWE

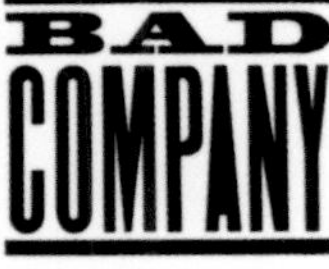

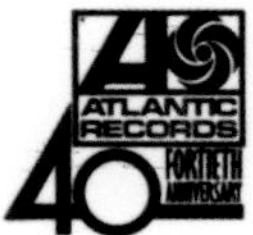

Billboard 200: *Sur la Mer* (#38)
Billboard Hot 100: "I Know You're Out There Somewhere" (#30)

The Moody Blues forged ahead, celebrating their veteran status with "I Know You're Out There Somewhere."

AS ROCK music rolled on through the years, more and more veteran acts were heralding their longevity in a notoriously ephemeral business. The Moody Blues marked a 20th anniversary with a new album, *Sur La Mer*.

"The common ground that's stayed the same in the band is a sense of old-fashioned decency," drummer Graeme Edge noted. "We were all raised in good families, so we don't like breaking up hotel rooms or throwing girls into vats of Jell-O. And musically, we share with millions of people that wonderful idealism of the Sixties, when we were going to change the world. We've kept that flame alive a little bit."

Edge acknowledged that the anniversary was based more on convenience than history. The Moody Blues originally formed in 1964 as local heroes out of Birmingham, England, and scored an international hit in 1965 with "Go Now!" The 20-year period being cited began with the release of 1968's *Days of Future Past* album and the splendor of the hit "Nights in White Satin."

"That earlier band was only around for 18 months, and it didn't include Justin (Hayward, guitar) and John (Lodge, bassist)," Edge said. "And Justin is the soul of this band."

Indeed, the "veteran cosmic rockers" became one of rock music's most dominant forces between 1968 and 1972 when such classic albums as *In Search of the Lost Chord* and *A Question of Balance* established their brand of orchestral rock. A six-year hiatus interrupted the band's career during the Seventies, but the 1986 hit "Your Wildest Dreams" had introduced the Moody Blues music to a new generation of young fans.

With *Sur le Mer* and the track "I Know You're Out There Somewhere," a thematic extension of "Your Wildest Dreams," the Moodies continued their MTV-era success. Yet the British group's Eighties output was criticized as more hit-oriented and less progressive than its early releases, and Edge admitted the band had lost a little spontaneity by exploring technology.

"On tour, the use of pre-programmed sections tends to ossify the arrangements, and I think *Sur la Me*r is a little too sanitized by sequencers," he allowed. "I want to hear more bacteria, more rock 'n' roll. But we're working to become virtuosos with this new stuff. I'm still the band's conductor—try to play together without a drummer! Drum machines? You can spill a beer on me and I still work. In fact, in the early days, you had to spill a beer in me to get me to work." ■

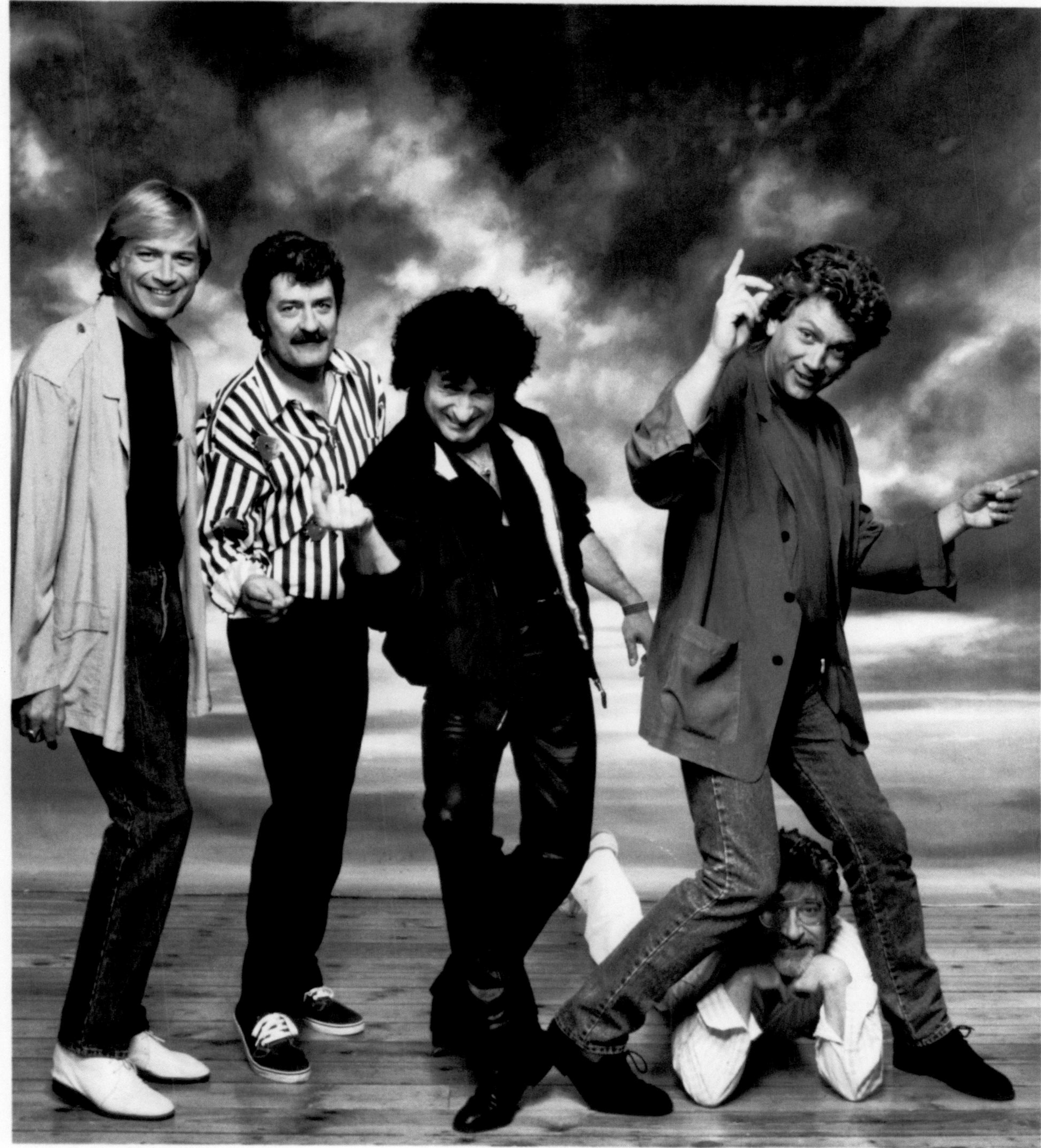

JUSTIN HAYWARD RAY THOMAS PATRICK MORAZ GRAEME EDGE JOHN LODGE

THE MOODY BLUES

polydor

PolyGram Records

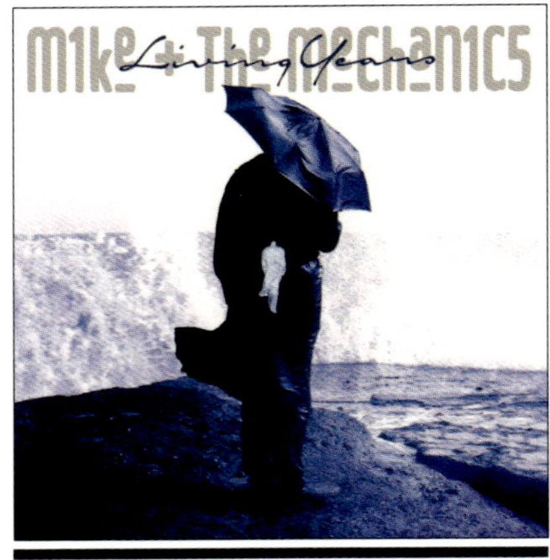

Billboard 200: *Living Years* (#13)
Billboard Hot 100: "Nobody's Perfect" (#63); "The Living Years" (No. 1); "Seeing Is Believing" (#62)

Mike + the Mechanics, Mike Rutherford's project outside of Genesis, earned a big hit with "The Living Years."

MIKE RUTHERFORD had taken a cue from Genesis bandmate Phil Collins—the guitarist and bassist kept busy with a hit-making side project, Mike + the Mechanics.

"It's very simple—I want variety, that's what we all want," Rutherford said. "It's not enough working with Phil and Tony (Banks), bless them, for 17 years. And they feel the same way, too. You need other people—a breath of fresh air, a bit of contrast. I've got a great combination in the Mechanics. And success does help—if the first album had bombed, I'd have thought it probably wasn't meant to be. But it's gone from strength to strength in its way. We went on tour, and it's been like a full-time part-time band since then."

In 1985, *Mike + the Mechanics* yielded a pair of Top 10 singles, "Silent Running" and "All I Need Is a Miracle." Having completed the *Invisible Touch* album and tour with Genesis, Rutherford reassembled Mike + the Mechanics—drummer Peter Van Hooke, keyboardist Adrian Lee, producer Christopher Neil and vocalists Paul Carrack and Paul Young returned to the lineup to produce the album *Living Years* in 1988.

"I have writer's ego—I want to do it all," Rutherford said. "This time around, I knew who was involved right from the beginning, so I was able to write songs with Paul Young and Paul Carrack in mind. It's fun music, looser than Genesis in a way. All of the best things I've done in my life have come easily, and this album came very easily."

Rutherford penned "The Living Years" with B.A. Robertson after both men mourned the loss of their fathers and while Rutherford's wife was about to give birth to their son. Buoyed by Carrack's soulful vocal, the song, which addressed a son's regret over unresolved conflict with his deceased father, hit No.1.

"It's about how you can never say the things you want to say to your father," Rutherford explained. "And how in turn you can never give your children the benefit of your knowledge. That's such a strange position." ■

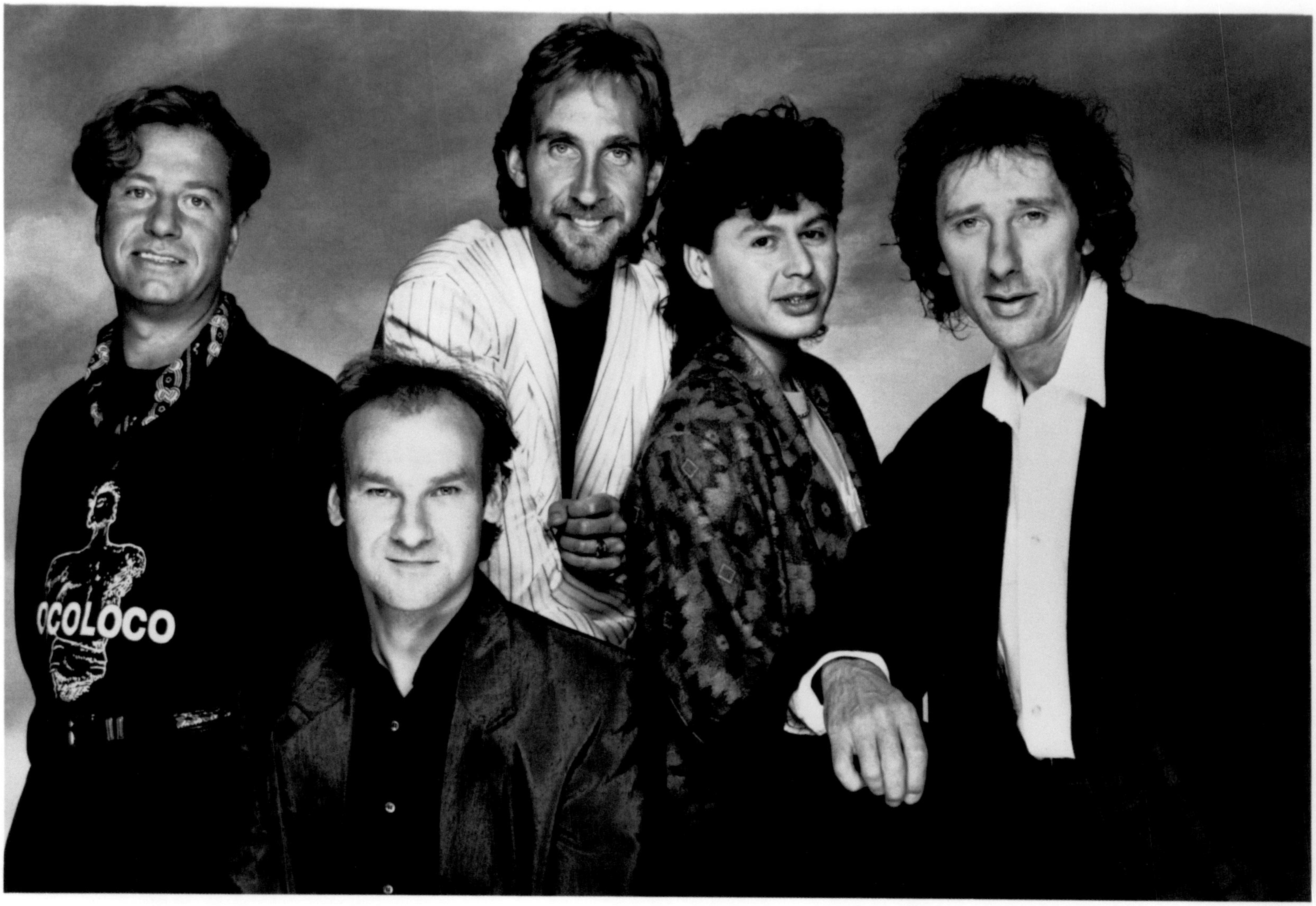

PAUL YOUNG PAUL CARRACK MIKE RUTHERFORD ADRIAN LEE PETER VAN HOOKE

MIKE + THE MECHANICS

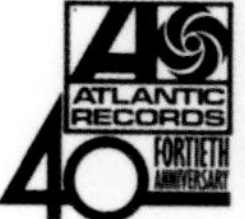

Billboard 200: *...To the Power of Three* (#97)

3, a decidedly old-wave trio, was a short-lived spin-off incorporating former Emerson, Lake & Palmer members.

THE BAND 3 had also been dubbed Emerson, Palmer & Berry—the latest incarnation of Emerson, Lake & Palmer. The original group had spearheaded the progressive-rock sounds of the Seventies before musical pretentions began outweighing the legendary virtuosity of the members. The group broke up in 1980, with keyboardist Keith Emerson pursuing movie soundtracks and drummer Carl Palmer joining Asia.

In 1985, a brief ELP reformation featured former Rainbow drummer Cozy Powell (not chosen because of his initials). Then Emerson teamed with Palmer and newcomer Robert Berry, a vocalist and guitarist from San Jose. How did a 31-year-old American wind up with a couple of British rock veterans?

"I owned my own recording studio, and I was doing what a lot of local musicians do—sending demo tapes to the record companies in Los Angeles," Berry explained.

A label executive passed a tape to Palmer, who liked the material enough to track down Berry, and Emerson eventually came on board to arrange the tunes. *...To the Power of Three*, 3's debut album, was an attempt to update the progressive-rock genre, Berry said.

"Carl and I wanted to apply a song format to those epic musical values. We wanted to say in seven minutes the things ELP used to say in 20 minutes. Keith is still the main instrument—he plays solos with both hands as if he was two completely individual people, and there aren't many other people in rock who do it like that.

"The first thing Keith says about his past is that ELP was an institution, and people expected him to live up to that. That's why he wanted to get into this band, to have some fun with music. If it sounds like ELP, it's because his hands were such a big part of that.

"There's a local musician like me in every town we'll play in. I hope that inspires them—look what happened to me. Local boy makes good."

...To the Power of Three was a commercial failure, and 3 split up. ■

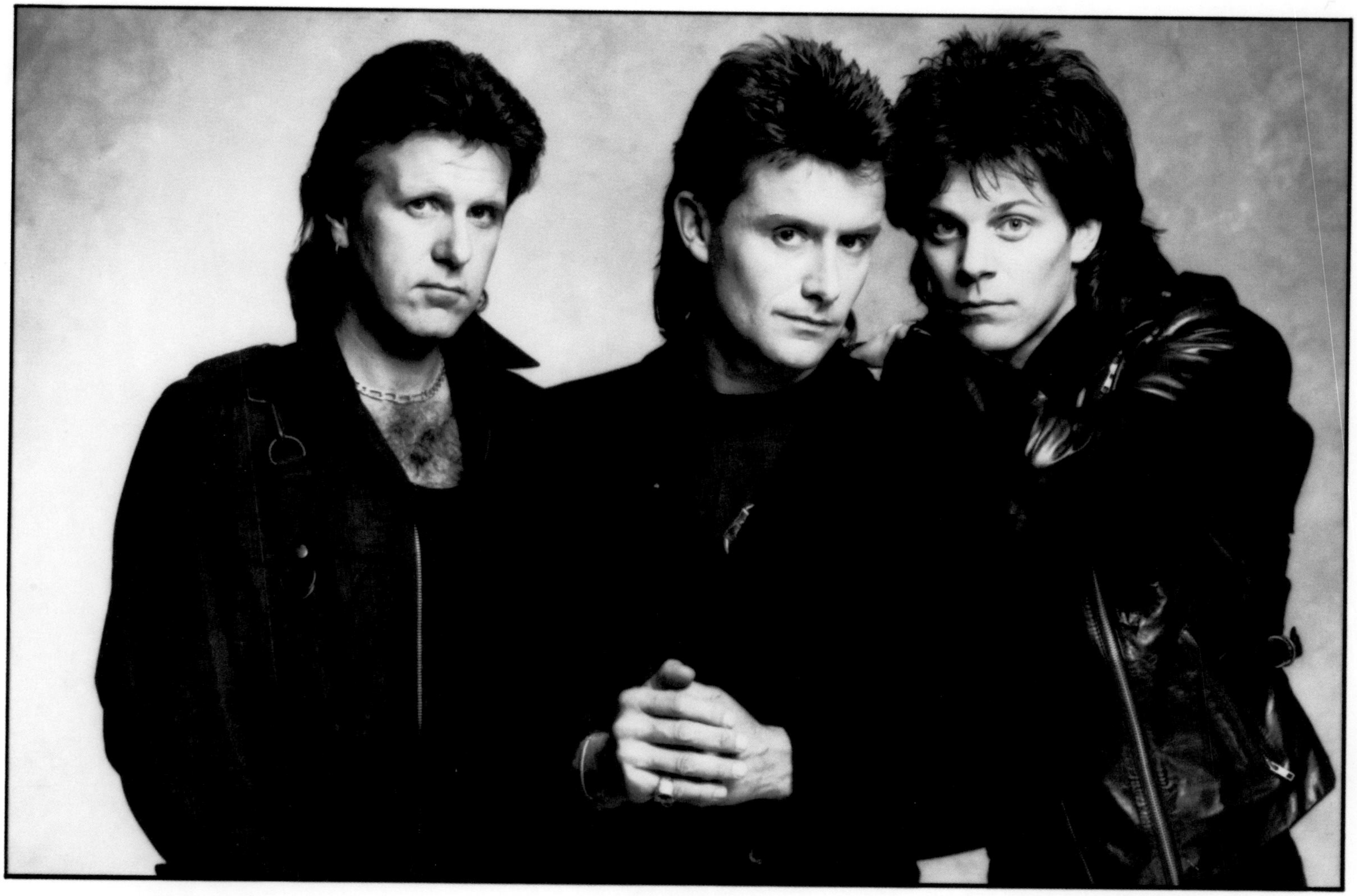

KEITH EMERSON

CARL PALMER

ROBERT BERRY

Photo Credit: Randee St. Nicholas

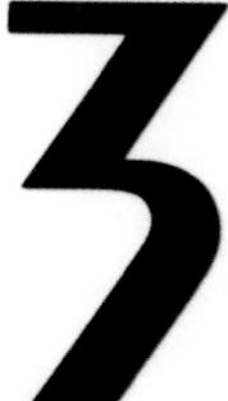

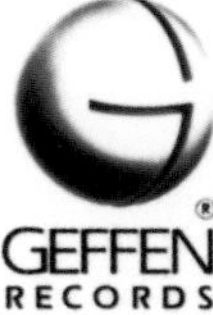

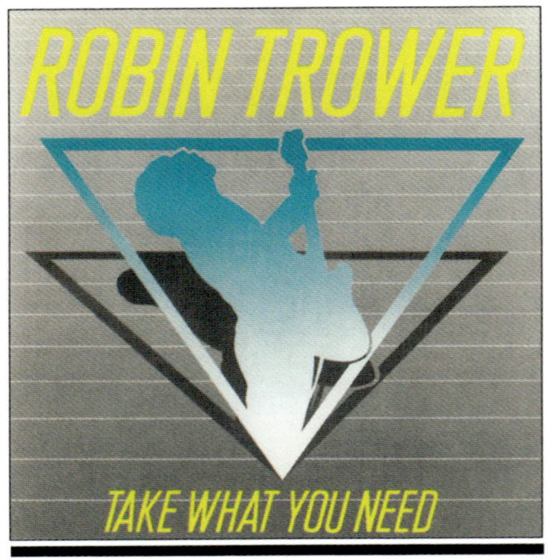

Billboard 200: *Take What You Need* (#133)

British rock guitarist Robin Trower's *Take What You Need* brought his thick, creamy tone back to the forefront.

HARDCORE ROCK guitar fans had appreciated Robin Trower's strong playing with Procol Harum in the Sixties, and then again as the leader of his own power trio. 1974's *Bridge of Sighs* was perhaps his most famous album, his inspired blues-rock lyricism fashioned from Jimi Hendrix's style into a softer, understated approach. Yet the British guitarist then removed himself from commercial consideration for most of the Eighties.

"I'd succeeded at one thing in the Seventies, but I felt I'd come to the end of what could accomplish in that style," Trower said. "So I just took some time off to re-evaluate, to concentrate on becoming a proper songwriter instead of a guitarist."

When Trower was ready to return to the rock wars, he assembled a band featuring vocalist Davey Pattison (formerly with Ronnie Montrose's band Gamma), bassist Dave Bronze and drummer Pete Thompson. But his sabbatical had cost him the attention of the music industry. "We just couldn't get the interest when we started looking around (for a record deal)," Trower said. "I found you've got to prove something to them."

So he did, releasing 1987's *Passion* album on the independent GNP Crescendo label. Such songs as "No Time" and "Caroline" re-established the classic Trower guitar sound on FM radio, and he was snapped up by Atlantic Records. The songs on *Take What You Need*, including the single "Tear It Up," marked a departure for Trower—more beat-conscious, not as dreamy and atmospheric as his previous material.

"I definitely set out to make a rock 'n' roll album in my own terminology, which probably doesn't fit anybody else's," he said. "I don't think you can sit down and write music to order, but I selected the songs that I felt would make the most rocking album."

Take What You Need was evidence that Trower was committed to stripping down his sound in the musical climate of high-tech overkill.

"I went through that stage 10 years ago," he said. "I was messing around, synthesizing the guitar with a whole bank of effects pedals, just changing the sound beyond all recognition. If you listen to albums like *In City Dreams* and *Caravan to Midnight*, it sounds like there are keyboards, but it was actually all done with guitars. It was a nice experiment, fun and all that, but I'm a guitarist, and I love the sound of the guitar. So I've reverted to using as natural a guitar sound as possible."

That approach restored his status as a guitar hero in America, but he continued to be ignored in his homeland. "It's a different ballgame in England, you know—it's much more of a fashion, come-and-go thing. I've struggled in the past when I've tried to break out in Europe. There's a market for what I do, but it's difficult to reach it because there's no radio exposure. So I prefer performing in America, because the audiences are more in tune with what I do. I feel I've found my natural home." ■

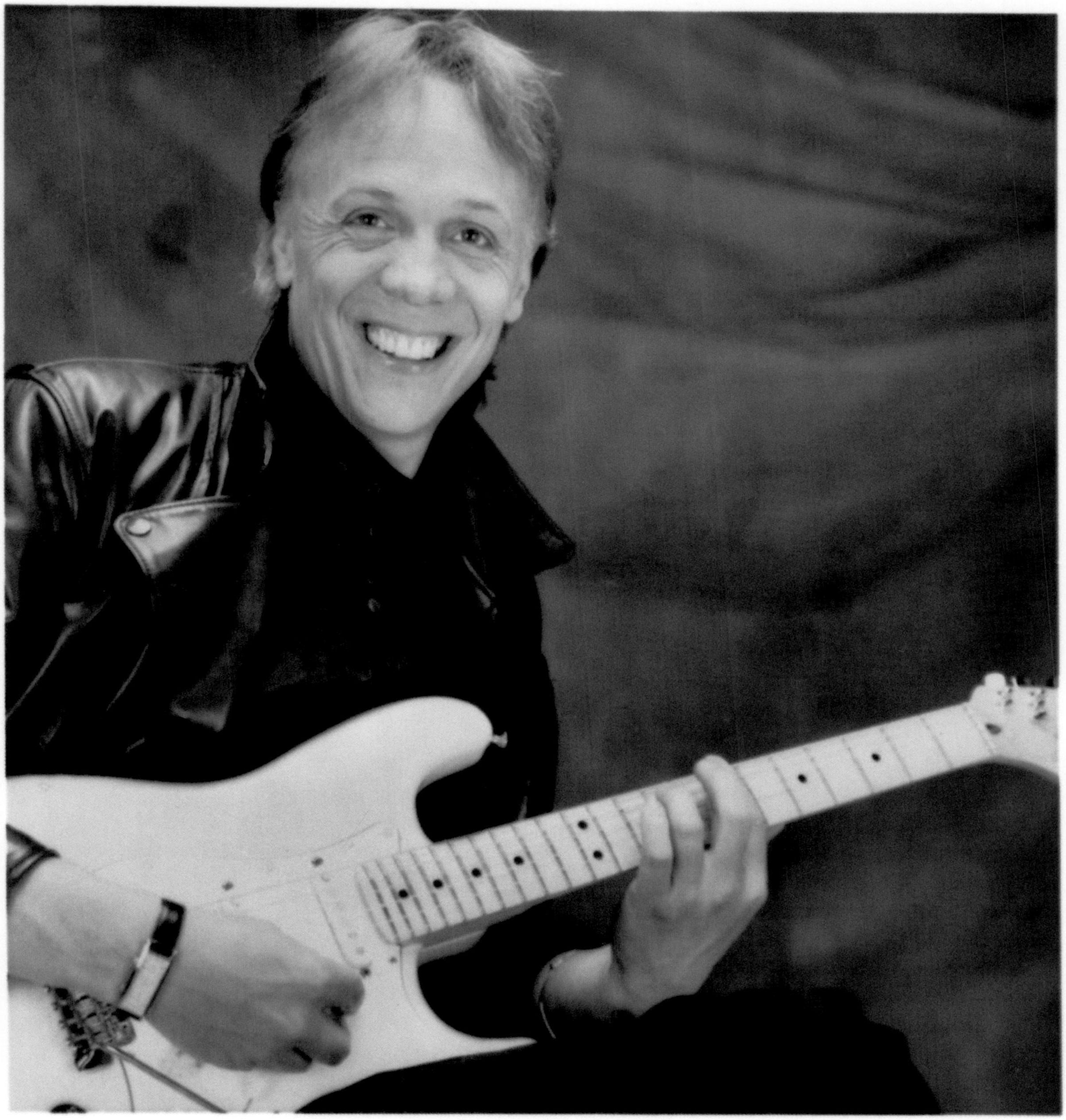

ROBIN TROWER

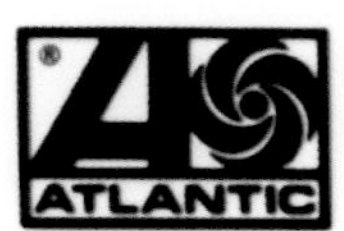

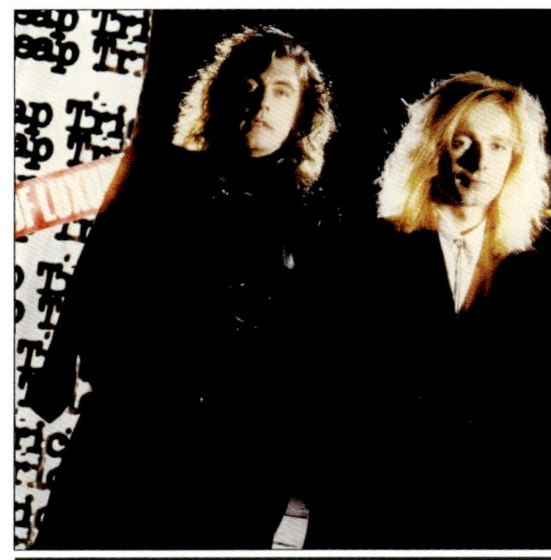

Billboard 200: *Lap of Luxury* (#16)
Billboard Hot 100: "The Flame" (No. 1); "Don't Be Cruel" (#4); "Ghost Town" (#33); "Never Had a Lot to Lose" (#75)

As "The Flame" sat atop the charts, rock music pundits accorded the year's comeback honors to Cheap Trick.

CHEAP TRICK peaked in the late Seventies with such power-pop hits as "Surrender" and "Dream Police"—tunes that melded Who-like clarity with Beatles-esque harmonies. But the Eighties hadn't been as commercially potent for the Midwestern band until the release of "The Flame," a stirring mid-tempo power ballad showcasing a dramatic Robin Zander vocal. Taken from the *Lap of Luxury* album, it became the first No. 1 single of Cheap Trick's career.

It also marked the group's rare use of outside songwriting sources, but guitarist Rick Nielsen assured that Cheap Trick called its own musical shots. "Nobody could tailor-make this band into anything," he said. "Everybody just took a realistic approach to this album. The record company said, 'Look, we want you guys to have hits, and if you can write them all, great.' Sure, I wish we'd written 'The Flame.' To tell the truth, the first time I heard it, I hated it." ("He ripped the songwriters' cassette out of the player and threw it on the floor," drummer Bun E. Carlos noted.)

"But down deep, I knew it was a good song," Nielsen continued. "But we had to make it sound like us—Robin's voice, Tom (Petersson)'s 12-string bass. I suppose anybody could have done the song and it would have been a hit, but ours is a good *band* version. The fact that it's our first No. 1 doesn't mean much, just that we're able to put out another single."

That other single was a Top 5 metal-rockabilly remake of the Elvis Presley standard "Don't Be Cruel," the latest in a string of smartly executed cover versions by the Tricksters.

"It's a good summertime tune," Nielsen enthused. "To take somebody else's song and turn it into your own is a cool thing. 'Ain't That a Shame' (a late Seventies hit for the band) was more of a copy of the John Lennon version than the Fats Domino original. We added a drum solo and the guitar breaks to make it our own. 'Don't Be Cruel,' same thing—if that sounds like Elvis instead of Cheap Trick, I'll wear Spandex."

During their hiatus from the charts, when record sales and concert audiences had diminished—the kind of popularity drop that caused many acts to splinter—the members of Cheap Trick continued to tour hard in small theaters and clubs, weathering the changing winds of pop music with the perseverance of professionals.

"I know some of the songs we've had in recent years—'If You Want My Love,' 'Tonight It's You'—were worthy of No. 1," Nielsen said. "But it's the right song at the right time, a lot of work and a little luck. A lot of kids must think *Lap of Luxury* is our first album, but I can't expect them to go back five years. It was hard to stick together. It would have been easy to give up. But I've always had a positive attitude, and we like what we do too much to quit." ■

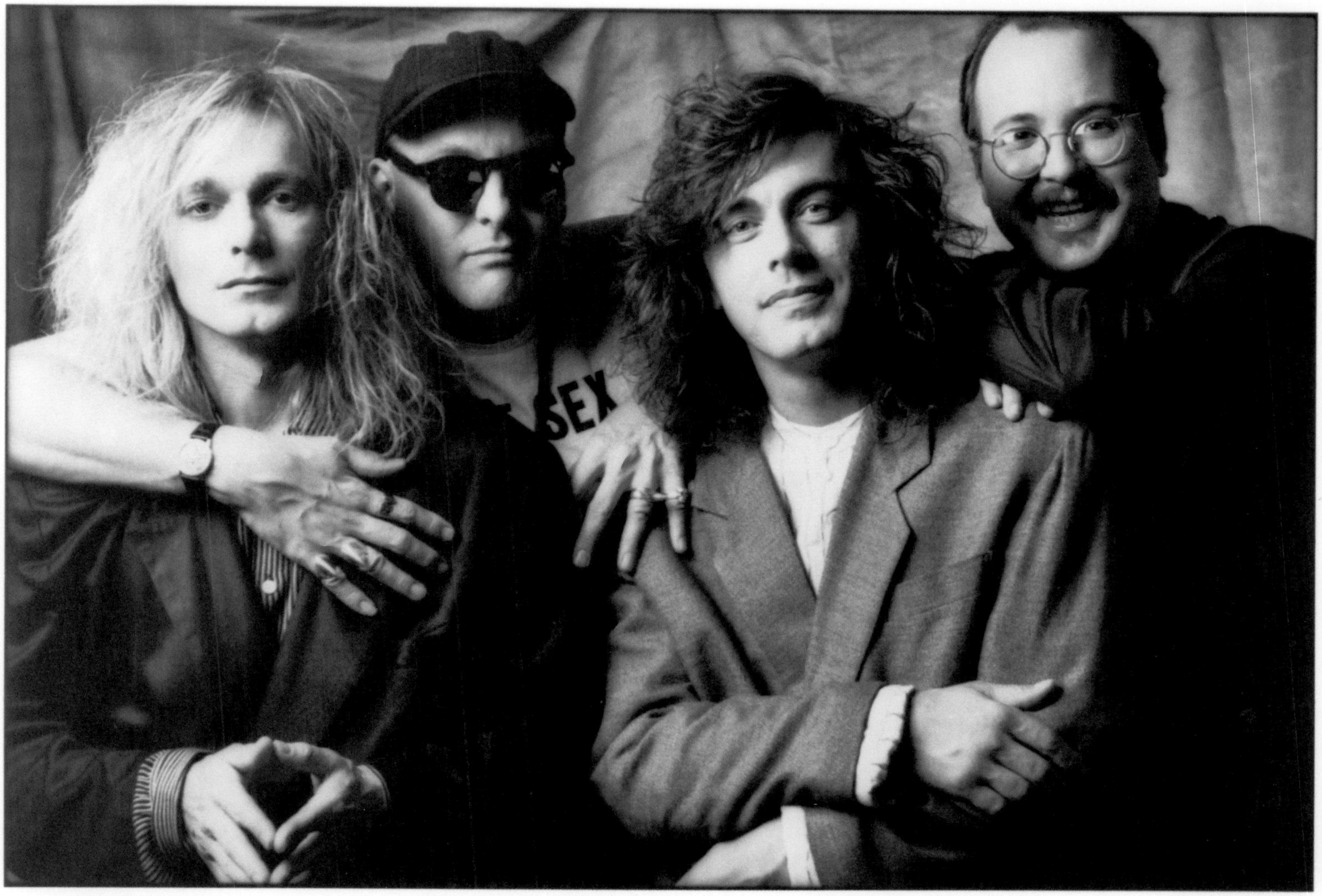

ROBIN ZANDER RICK NIELSEN TOM PETERSSON BUN E. CARLOS

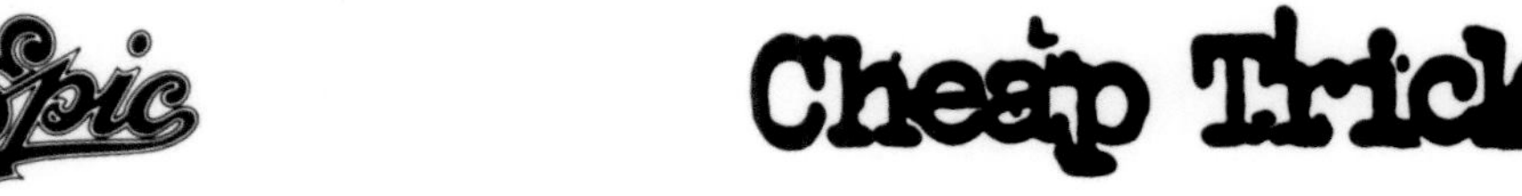

PHOTO: NORMAN SEEFF

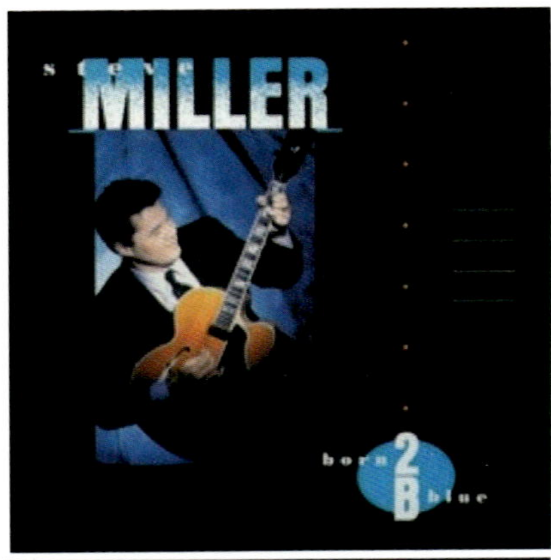

Billboard 200: *Born 2 B Blue* (#108)

Steve Miller's inaugural solo effort and final Capitol Records release corresponded with his first tour in years.

IN ONE year, the Steve Miller Band's *Greatest Hits 1974-78* album generated sales of one million units worldwide in one year—1988, a decade after its release. "It's a testament to a lot of things—some good tunes, the popularity of classic rock radio formats and budget-line prices so young people can buy the cassette for $3.99," Miller said.

Miller had honed his craft in the Sixties playing grand-scaled progressive blues-rock. He didn't break out as a mainstream superstar until his eighth album, 1973's *The Joker*, when the title track became his first No. 1 hit. The durable performer reached the pinnacle of his success in 1976 and 1977, when he made multiplatinum millions from his crisp, melodic guitar rock. *Fly Like an Eagle* and the follow-up *Book of Dreams* stood as textbook examples of commercial radio pop; most of the tracks could be heard daily on both AM and FM stations around the country.

Following a four-year hiatus, Miller returned with an unsuccessful album, but then he again demonstrated his resiliency with 1982's *Abracadabra*. The title track became the Steve Miller Band's third No. 1 single and the No. 1 selling song in the world that year.

"I have to work so hard to write those hits," Miller insisted. "All Paul McCartney has to do is say 'hello' and it sounds like a hit. 'Abracadabra' took me three years and 15 minutes. It was a totally different song that I discarded and did over. It's so tough for me, but you always try to make it look real easy."

Miller had spent the rest of the Eighties sequestered on his Oregon spread, offering an occasional album. He released *Born 2 B Blue*, a solo set of blues and jazz standards interpreted in a more modern context, including a version of "Zip-a-Dee-Doo-Dah" and a cover of Lee Dorsey's "Ya Ya." He then hit the concert trail for the first time in six years.

"I was a dinosaur—I didn't think people still cared about my music," Miller said. "I went out with to do a jazz-blues tour with (longtime friend) Ben Sidran, and I had this idea that sophisticated, older people would be my audience, but there are no adults at all at the concerts. The screaming level is bizarre, like the state high school basketball championship. It's little kids all excited, knowing every word to 'Jungle Love' and 'Jet Airliner'—there's a whole new audience aged 10-20 who have discovered what I'm doing. It's great party music—it's positive, there's good playing, the songs aren't as simple as they seem but they're real easy to take in.

"And things got damaged by MTV. It ended up with a lot of sampled music being performed by actors and models, all that 'attitude' stuff. When those people hit the stage, they stink." ■

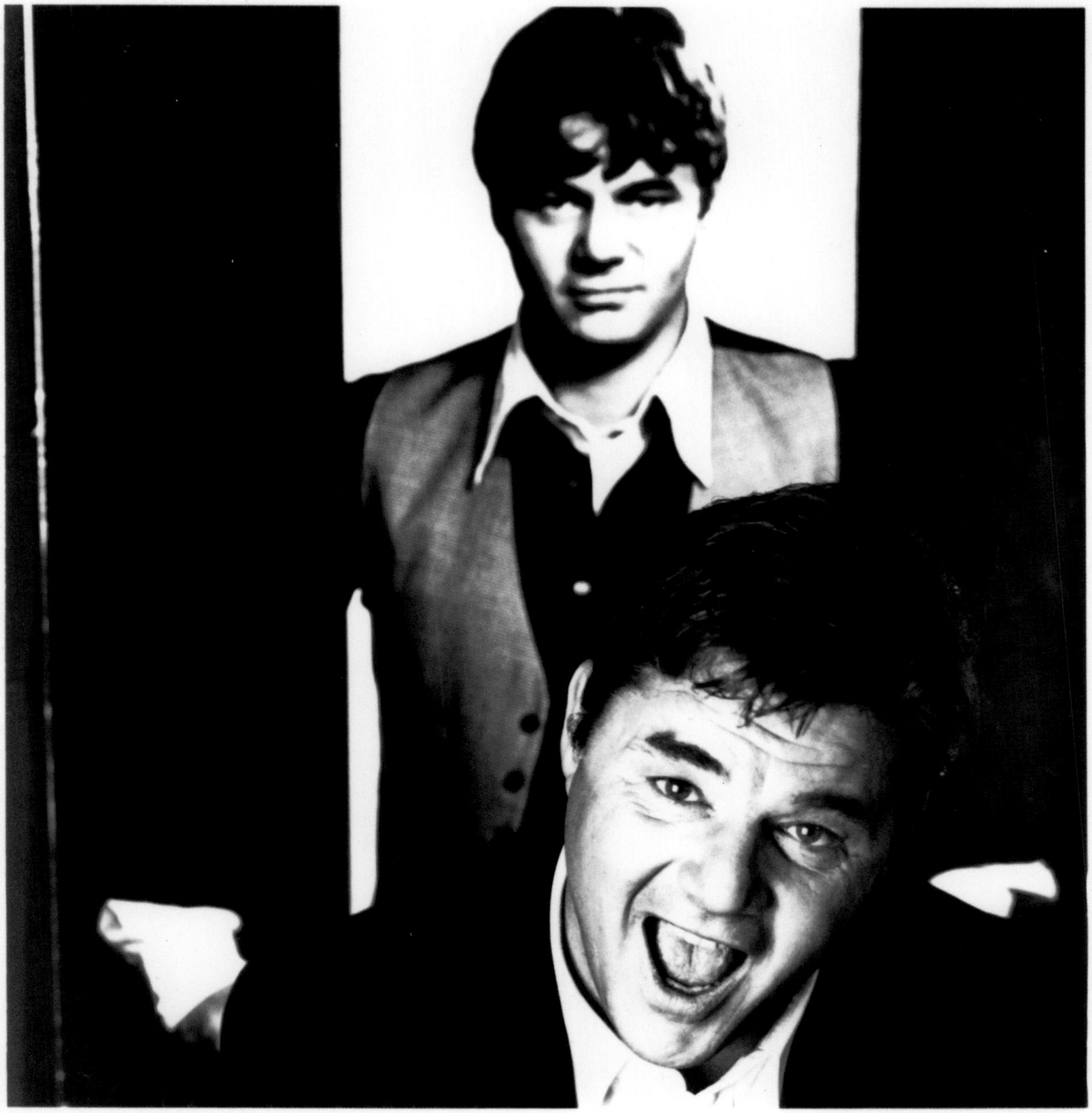

Photo: Lynn Goldsmith / 1988

STEVE MILLER

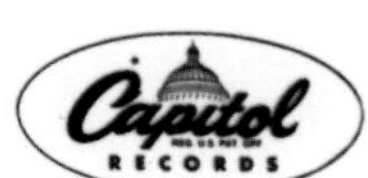

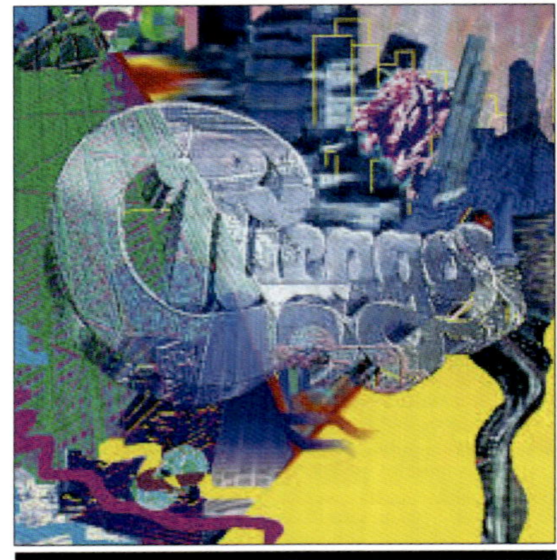

Billboard 200: *Chicago 19* (#37)
Billboard Hot 100: "I Don't Wanna Live Without Your Love" (#3); "Look Away" (No. 1); "You're Not Alone" (#10); "We Can Last Forever" (#55)

With *Chicago 19*, Chicago extended its easy-listening audience at the expense of the band's early rock following.

CHICAGO BEGAN recording in 1969 as Chicago Transit Authority, one of the first groups to synthesize jazz and rock with blasts of brass. By the *Chicago X* album of 1976, the band had scored its first No. 1 single with a romantic ballad, "If You Leave Me Now," written by bassist Peter Cetera. At that point, Chicago had avoided any major personnel changes.

With the accidental shooting of lead guitarist and founding member Terry Kath in 1978, everything changed. Deeply shaken, the septet went on a brief hiatus before regrouping, but between 1978 and 1982, none of Chicago's five singles made the Top 40. Looking for a spark, the group eventually recruited keyboardist Bill Champlin and producer David Foster, and with the new, trimmed-down sound, Chicago reasserted its position as one of rock's most popular acts. "Hard to Say I'm Sorry," another Cetera ballad, went to No. 1, and the revitalized band tapped a whole new generation of "Chicagophiles" who were discovering the music for the first time.

"They identify with the radio ballads," keyboardist Robert Lamm said. "They're unaware of the band's history. They hear a classic and go, 'Oh, that was you guys! I didn't think you were such a rock band.' They're surprised."

Then in 1985, frontman Cetera made the decision to pursue a solo career, a potentially crippling situation. But the remaining members of Chicago merely took stock and set new objectives. "We wouldn't have survived the personality clashes and unhappiness if Peter had stayed in the band," Lamm explained. "Finding a bass player who could sing tenor and contribute songs was really tough, but just facing that challenge put the band in a renewed frame of mind."

Indeed, in the what-have-you-done-lately world of pop music, Chicago hadn't missed a beat with new recruit Jason Scheff. The group's *Chicago 18* in 1986 boasted the Top 5 single "Will You Still Love Me," and *Chicago 19* arose as a platinum success, yielding three Top 10 singles—"I Don't Wanna Live Without Your Love," "You're Not Alone" and the No. 1 smash "Look Away." Yet despite the commercial acceptance, Lamm, who often contributed pointed commentary to early Chicago works, was somewhat frustrated that Chicago had become such a mainstream band.

"It's fine to write about love or breaking up—those are emotions that we all experience and relate to," he said. "But once Cetera's ballads became the signature Chicago songs, the words were sacrificed for the texture of the lyrics and melody. I'm the agitator. I hate consistently denying the roots of where Chicago came from. We haven't been deep enough on songs that speak of social and political conditions. It's an idealistic position to take. The band is propelled more and more by outside forces—the record company, the booking agency, the management, the radio programmers—and we've had a lot of success in the Eighties doing it that way.

"But sometimes I feel that we're sacrificing some musical adventure for the sake of maintaining an audience, a career. So I'm gonna continue to rock the boat." ■

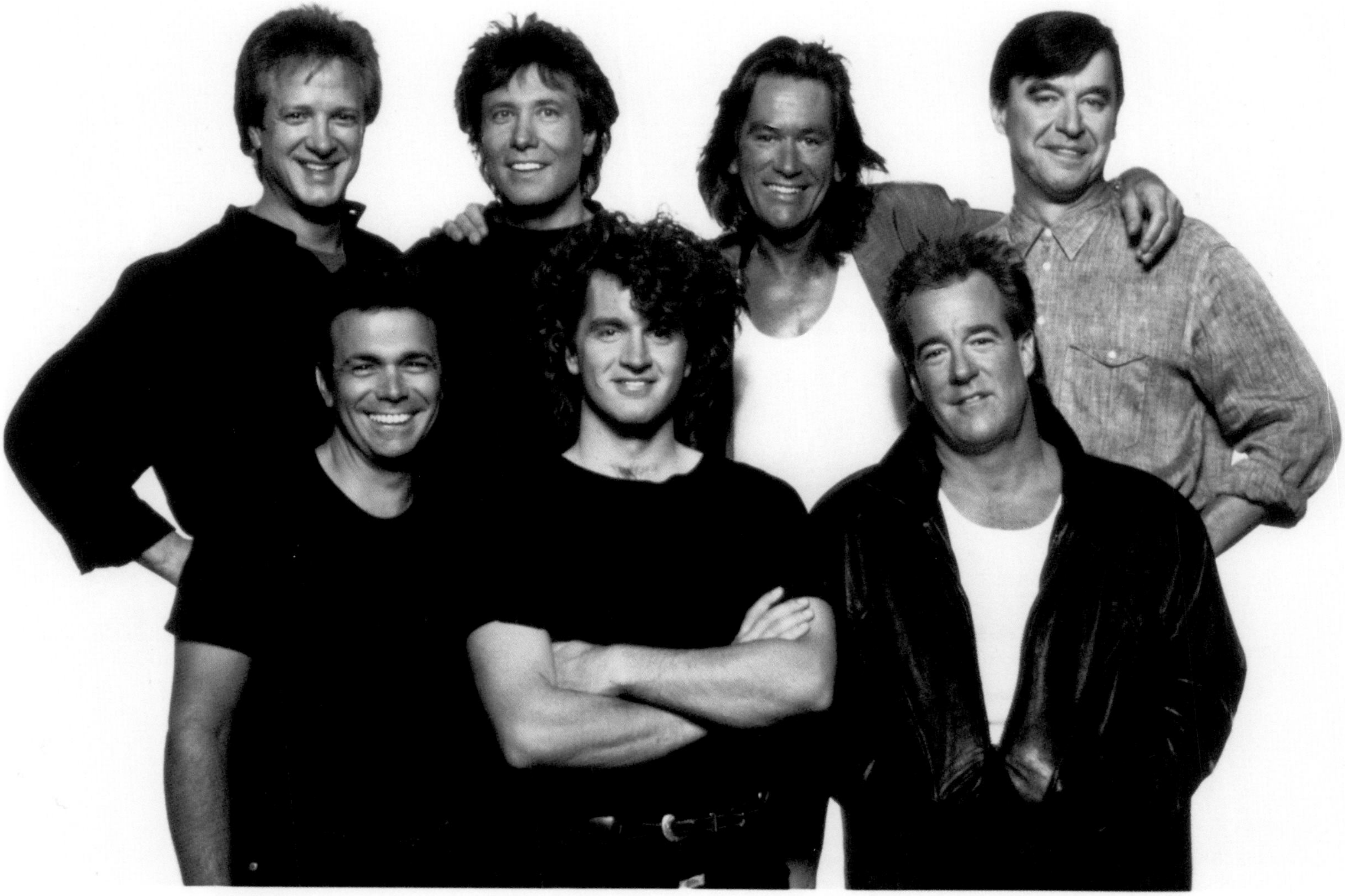

LEE LOUGHNANE
DANNY SERAPHINE
ROBERT LAMM
JASON SCHEFF
BILL CHAMPLIN
JAMES PANKOW
WALT PARAZAIDER

Photo Credit: Stephen Danelian

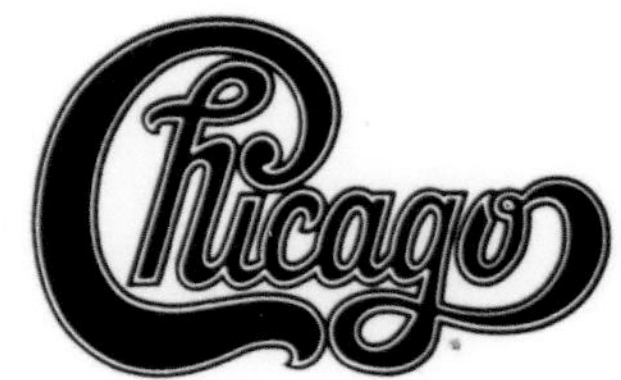

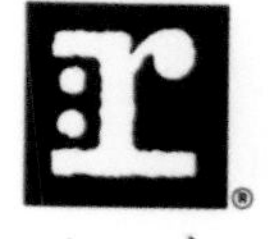

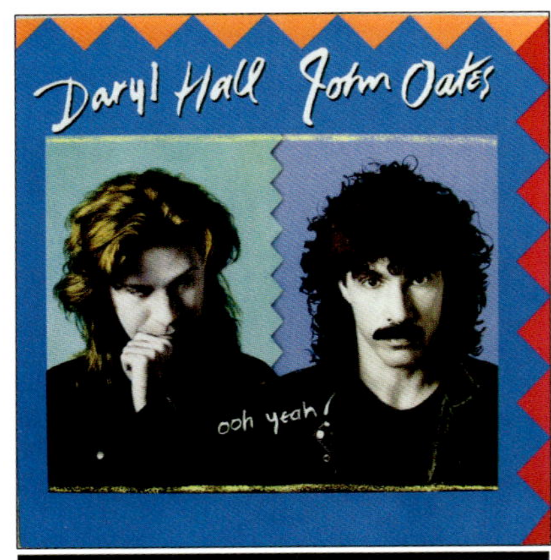

Billboard 200: *Ooh Yeah!* (#24)
Billboard Hot 100: "Everything Your Heart Desires" (#3); "Missed Opportunity" (#29); "Downtown Life" (#31)

Daryl Hall & John Oates peaked in the Top 10 for the final time with the hit "Everything Your Heart Desires."

THE MOST successful duo in the history of recorded music, Daryl Hall & John Oates' era of chart dominance was coming to an end.

"Starting in the early Seventies, we worked with a constant cycle of recording and touring—it's never really stopped," Hall said. "After doing it for so long, it was time to reassess and move to another phase of our creative lives."

Hall & Oates signed with Arista Records when their RCA obligation ran out. *Ooh Yeah!*, their first release for the label, had the unmistakable Hall & Oates magic, a seamless blend of rock backbeats, Philly soul and folk-pop. The single "Everything Your Heart Desires," their sixteenth Top 10 hit, pushed the album to platinum status. The tall blond guy with the edgy voice and the short dark guy with the warm voice could still sing rings around contemporary artists.

But *Ooh Yeah!* was regarded as a disappointment, charting lower and selling fewer copies than previous albums.

"I don't really think that being successful in pop music has that much to do with talent—it has to do with timing, just being in sync with the way people think," Oates said. "Certain groups do it at certain times and fall out. We've been really lucky and had a long run. We don't do too much differently from what we did through the Seventies, but we got on a roll. We seemed to almost dictate the sound of radio and people were playing catch-up to us. You can't predict it or plan on it. It either happens or it doesn't. Our strong point isn't chasing someone else's tail. We just want to do the best version of Hall & Oates that we can." ■

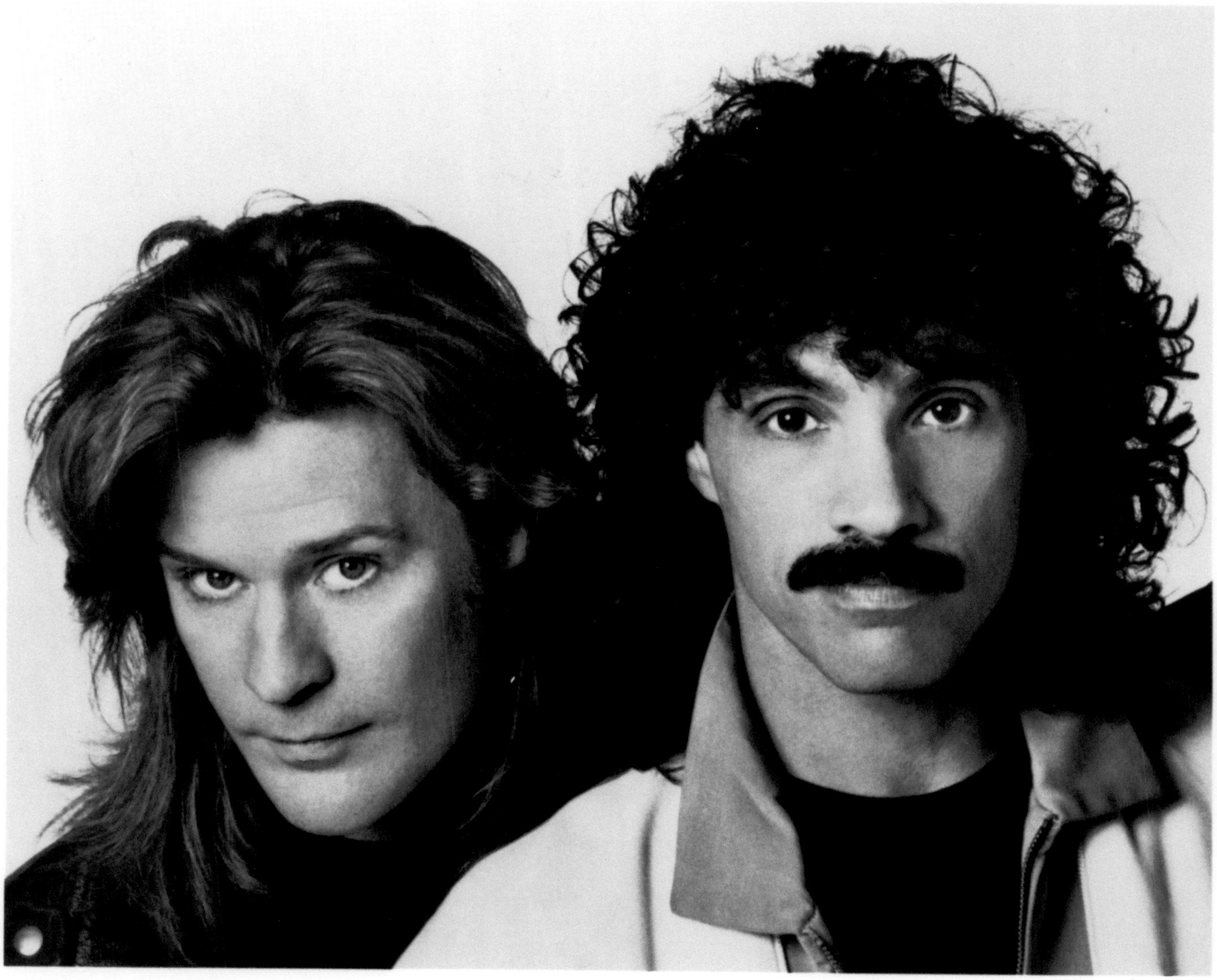

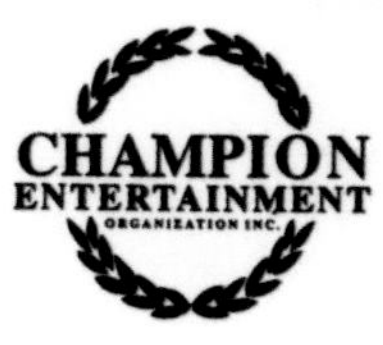

Daryl Hall John Oates

ARISTA™

Billboard 200: *Let It Roll* (#36)

One of America's best-loved groups of the Seventies, Little Feat was revived with the popular *Let It Roll* album.

IN THE early Seventies, Little Feat emerged with the extremely inventive but largely ignored albums *Sailin' Shoes* and *Dixie Chicken*, yielding good reviews but little commercial impact. *The Last Record Album* in 1975 gave the Feat its first hint of chart action, but the group was never fully appreciated for its amazing scope of blues rock, jazz fusion, R&B, country and acoustic music. The group was funky but loose and unpredictable, factors that lent a terrific sense of spontaneity to its performances—captured on 1978's *Waiting for Columbus*, the last album before leader and founder Lowell George died of a heart attack a year later.

The other principals—guitarist Paul Barrere, drummer Richie Hayward, bassist Kenny Gradney and percussionist Sam Clayton—figured they could not go on as a unit without their leader; they kept their chops up playing with such artists as Robert Plant.

And Bill Payne rated as the most in-demand session keyboardist on the West Coast, earning recording and touring credits with Linda Ronstadt and Bonnie Raitt, among others.

"But I'd forgotten how much I was able to stretch out as a player in Little Feat," Payne said. "I had the idea to put it back together, even though I'm the one who said I'd never do it. But we had a jam session in 1986. I couldn't remember any of the songs—playing 'Time Loves a Hero' was like singing a Christmas carol. But it felt great. We were dying to play our own stuff again."

After a tour with Bob Seger, Payne got serious about resurrecting Little Feat. He found management, began writing tunes and set about finding a singer to replace George. The choice was Craig Fuller, the original vocalist in Pure Prairie League before that band became a pure country act. Fuller had toured with Little Feat in the late Seventies as an opening act with songwriter Eric Kaz, and Payne had almost formed a band with Fuller upon the Feat's demise.

Let It Roll, the reunion album, was an unexpected, delightful pleasure. With deft, sure playing and an extensive musical vocabulary, the reconstituted Little Feat cross-pollinated genres and rhythms with ease. The band garnered a Grammy nomination, the title track went to No. 1 on the album rock charts and the response to the group's return to performance was rabid.

"It's made quite an impression on us, from the standpoint of taking the Little Feat legacy seriously." Payne said. "It was great to be in an enigmatic group, but now people should see how this thing works. We have to put ourselves out there and let people make a decision." ■

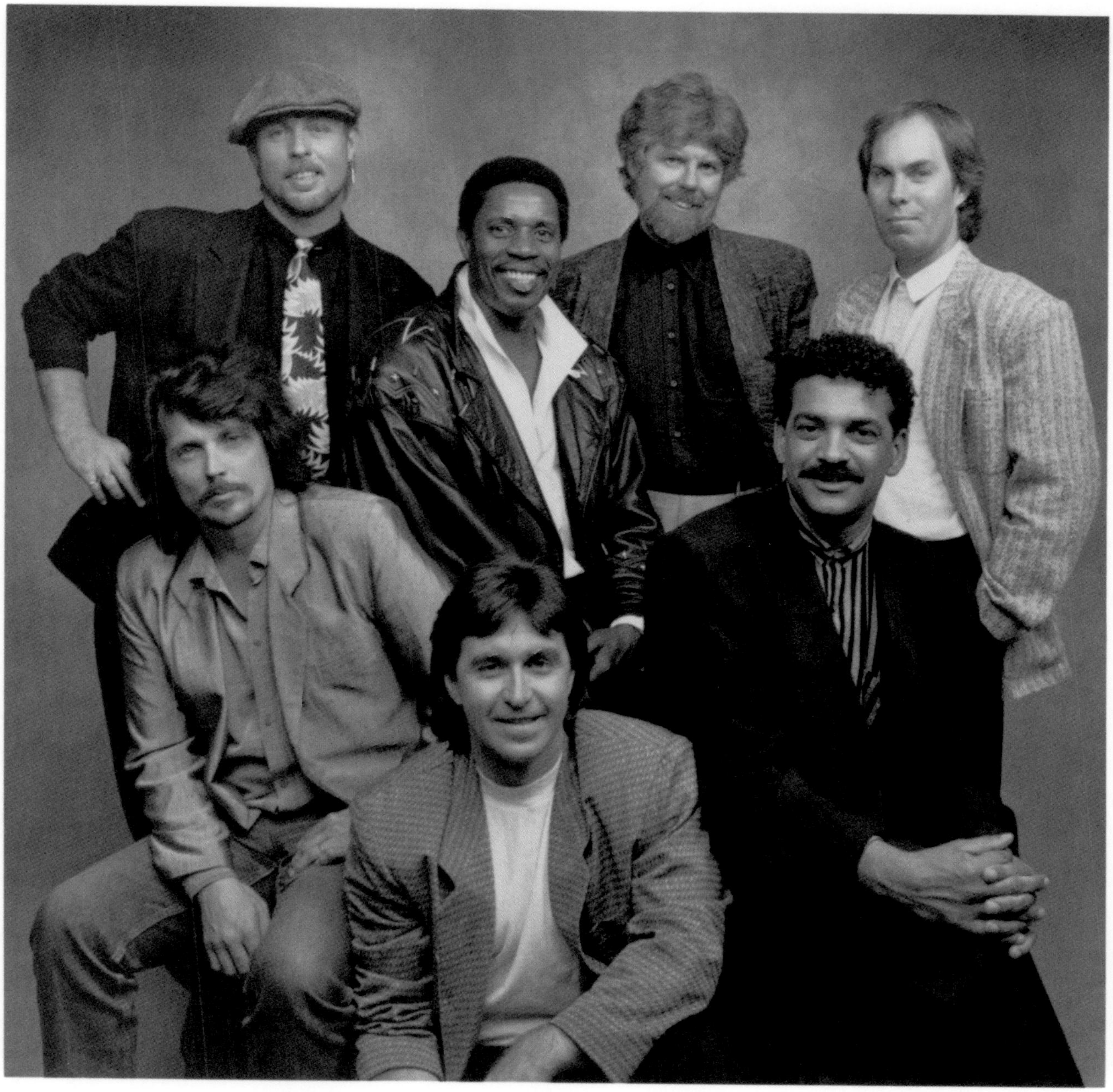

Photo Credit: Jim Shea

Paul Barrere   Sam Clayton   Fred Tackett   Bill Payne

Richie Hayward   Craig Fuller   Kenny Gradney

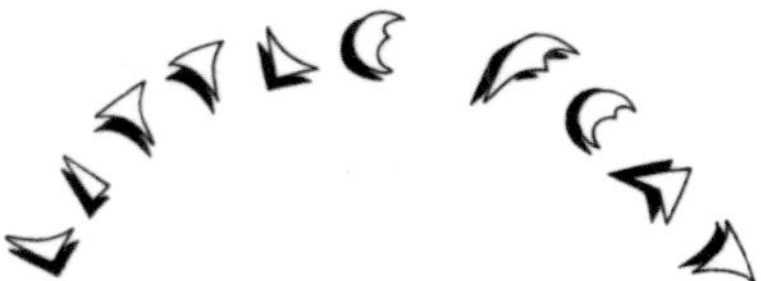

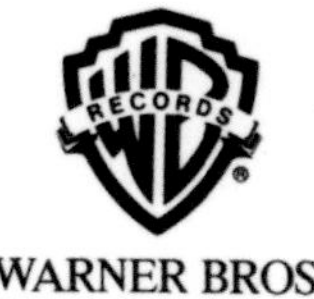

WARNER BROS.

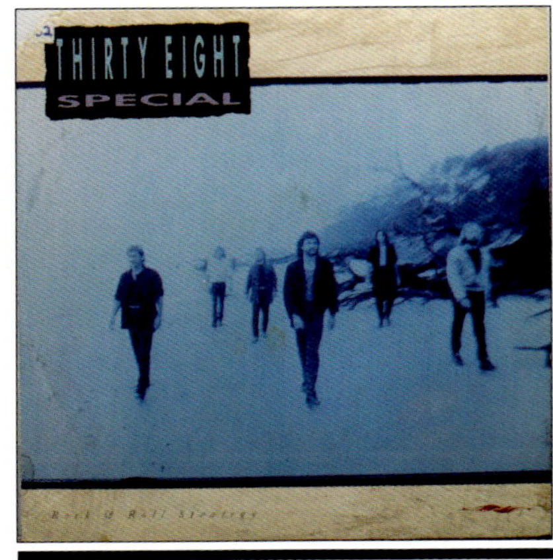

Billboard 200: *Rock & Roll Strategy* (#61)
Billboard Hot 100: "Rock & Roll Strategy" (#61); "Second Chance" (#6); "Comin' Down Tonight" (#67)

A less guitar-heavy sound made the rock ballad "Second Chance" an adult-contemporary smash for 38 Special.

OVER THE course of 14 years and seven hit albums, 38 Special had matured from a soft-focus Lynyrd Skynyrd into one of Southern rock's finest products. But a personnel change occurred in the band for the first time in a decade, as Don Barnes—the singer on such hits as "Caught Up in You" and "Hold On Loosely"—departed for a solo career. A new 38 Special lineup debuted on the *Rock & Roll Strategy* album, and the musical catalyst was vocalist and keyboardist Max Carl, previously the lead singer for Southern California favorite Jack Mack & the Heart Attack, a nine-piece R&B group.

Carl, a sports fan, likened his status to that of a "free agent." Several solo albums and the stint with Jack Mack lacked commercial success, but Carl had always been considered a major talent among his peers—Frank Zappa, Little Feat, Tower of Power and Southern Pacific all tendered offers before he accepted 38 Special's invitation.

"I had gone through a period where my confidence was shaken," Carl admitted. "But I had a lot of support—I'm lucky to have friends who are superstars, like Bruce Hornsby. They called to help me through, to tell me to hang in there. I was nervous about joining 38—I was an R&B guy trying out for a Southern rock band. But we got along as personalities—we're a cross between Monty Python and *The Andy Griffith Show.* And underneath it all, everyone had a gut feeling that the music was going to work."

Guitarist Danny Chauncey, who wrote Eddie Money's hit "I Wanna Go Back," was also solicited, and Carl, the Los Angeleno from Nebraska, started writing about the South. His songs put a spark back into the band and yielded the most versatile album of 38 Special's career.

"I've always written stories," Carl mused. "Some of them have been fantastic, others have been real. To make this record, I was commuting from L.A. to Jacksonville and Atlanta, and it seemed like every time I made a trip, I had a great experience that ended up in a song."

Carl wrote "Little Sheba," one of his most evocative and hilarious contributions, after a night in a Florida bar where he ate alligator and watched girls wrestle in gelatin. He also collaborated with singer Donnie Van Zant on the title cut. The stunning ballad "Second Chance" became the band's biggest smash, charting on pop, mainstream rock and adult contemporary radio formats.

"There's a real festive feeling when we play now," Carl concluded. "There are so many bands that are so serious about what they do. 38 Special is still a band that lights up. 'Hey, they actually pay us to do this—let's crank it up!'" ■

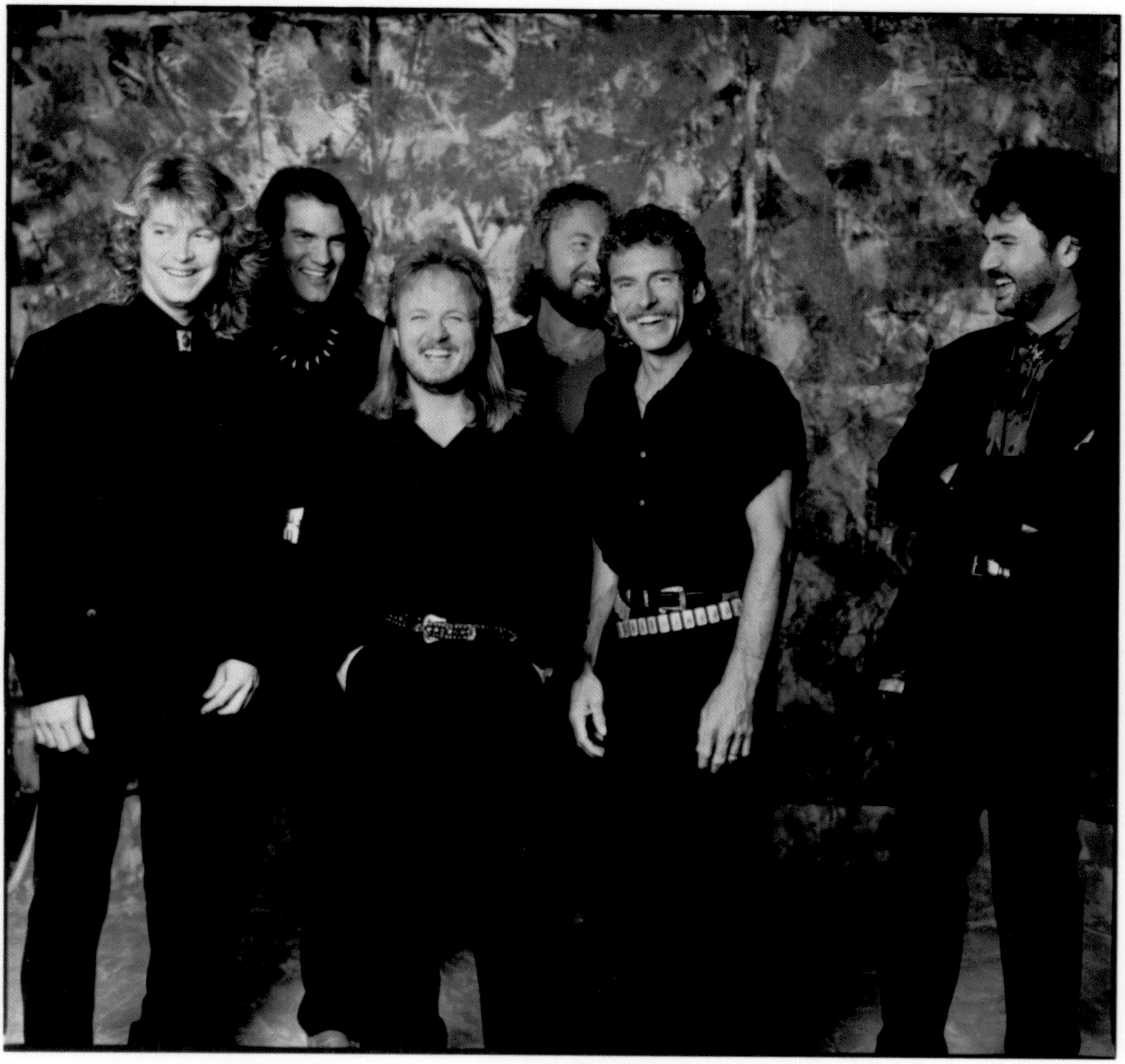

MAX CARL

LARRY JUNSTROM

DANNY CHAUNCEY

DONNIE VAN ZANT

JACK GRONDIN

JEFF CARLISI

Management:
The Mark Spector Company, Inc.
(212) 315-1410

38 SPECIAL

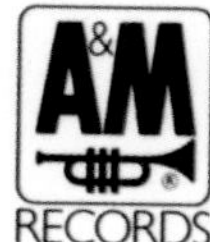

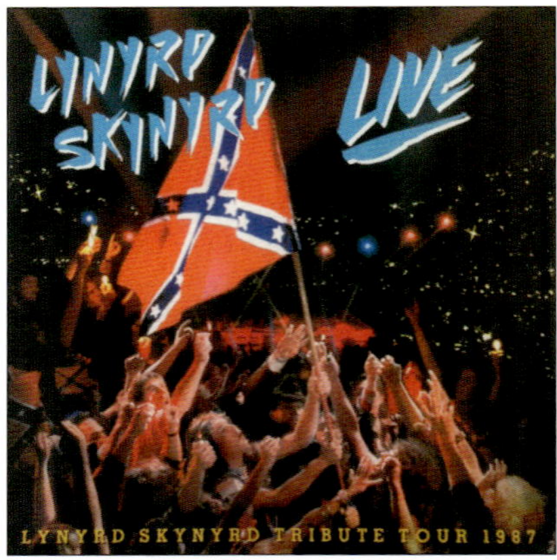

Billboard 200: *Southern by the Grace of God* (#68)

Southern by the Grace of God resurrected Lynyrd Skynyrd's career a decade after an overwhelming disaster.

LYNYRD SKYNYRD formed during the late Sixties in Jacksonville, Florida, taking its name from the members' authoritarian P.E. teacher, Leonard Skinner. The group was discovered playing Southern bars and clubs by producer Al Kooper and quickly became established as America's most celebrated rock 'n' boogie band of the mid-Seventies, drawing from British hard rock influences instead of the country roots favored by most Southern acts. The powerful three-guitar lineup debuted on the *Pronounced Leh-nerd Skin-nerd* album, which included "Free Bird," the group's anthem. Lead vocalist Ronnie Van Zant's reputation as a rabble-rousing hero was further solidified with the Top 40 hits "Sweet Home Alabama" (the famous riposte to Neil Young's scathing "Southern Man") and "Saturday Night Special."

But on October 20, 1977, the rock music world shook when Lynyrd Skynyrd was silenced at its peak. The band's rented single-engine plane crashed in the swamps near Gillsburg, Mississippi, en route to Baton Rouge, taking the lives of Van Zant and guitarist Steve Gaines.

After a decade of silence, five members of the surviving Skynyrd members reunited in the fall of 1987 in celebration of the original band, performing at the Charlie Daniels Volunteer Jam. Guitarist Gary Rossington reteamed with Billy Powell (keyboards), Leon Wilkerson (bass), Artimus Pyle (drums) and Ed King (guitar). He also recruited guitarist Randall Hall and Johnny Van Zant, Ronnie's younger brother, as vocalist.

"It was a hard decision for all of us whether or not to play, but it finally got to the point where it was time to do it," Rossington said. "Once we got up there, it just fell into place."

Lynyrd Skynyrd then embarked on a tribute tour, releasing the live album *Southern by the Grace of God.*

"I'm sure there are people who think it's wrong, and I felt like that until this year," Rossington said. "I didn't ever want to go back out as Lynyrd Skynyrd without Ronnie Van Zant and Allen Collins (Collins survived the plane crash but was paralyzed from the waist down in a 1986 car accident). I always felt Skynyrd was the three of us, and without those two, the band was gone for me. But this tour is being done for the memories and the people involved. It's been hard sometimes bringing up the old emotions, but it's also been fun. We just try to somehow let those bad feelings go and have the good ones take over. The last thing we did was have a plane crash together. Now we're having a good time together." ■

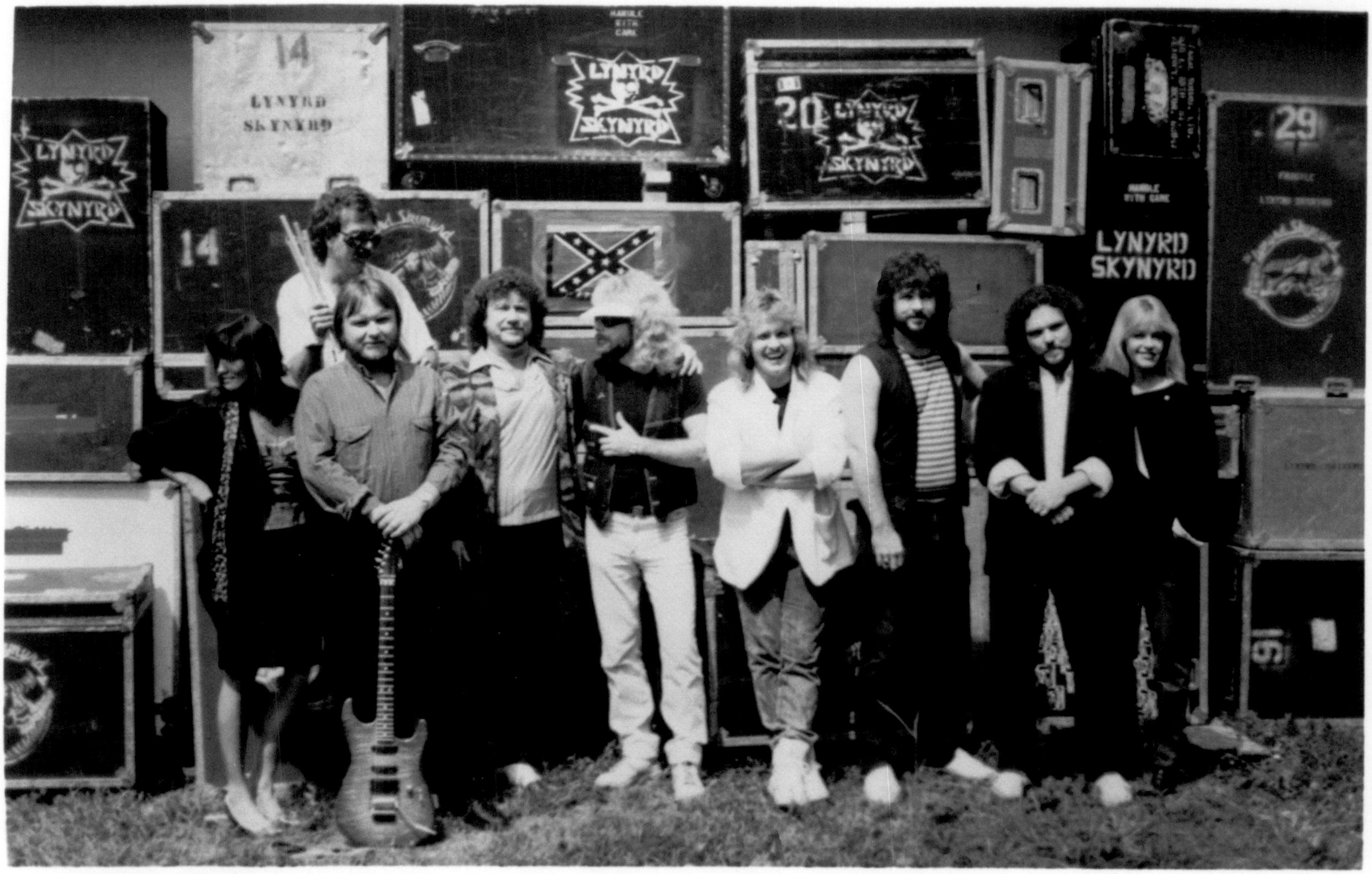

Left to right:

Carol Bristow, Artimus Pyle, Ed King, Billy Powell, Leon Wilkeson, Johnny Van Zant, Randall Hall, Gary Rossington, Dale Krantz Rossington.

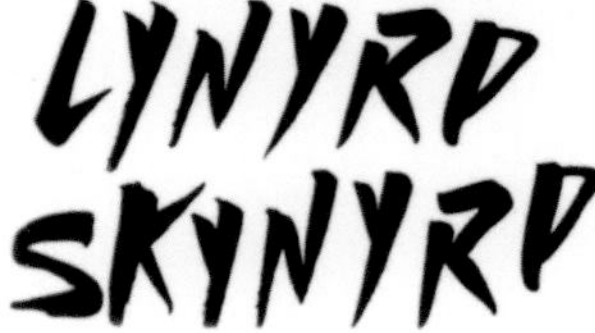

MCA RECORDS

Billboard 200: *Hot Water* (#46)

Earning more revenue from his shows than his albums, Jimmy Buffett delivered *Hot Water* to his fervid fan base.

WHAT WENT through Jimmy Buffett's mind when he looked out at his concert audience and saw a sea of "Parrotheads"—adult party animals garbed in Hawaiian shirts having the best time possible?

"I don't even try to analyze it," he laughed. "It started mushrooming a few years ago. Through word-of-mouth, everybody realized they could come to our shows and be part of a carnival. You can be the president of the bank or work at the 7-Eleven—on that day when I come to town, if you're a Parrothead, you can act pretty insane. And get away with it."

Such fandom ensured that tropical rocker traditionally played to sellout crowds, despite the lack of a hit record in the Eighties. "I've always considered myself to be more of a performer and writer than a musician and singer, and I've stuck with what I know best," he explained. "It's paying off more today because the essence of what I do is on stage. It's more fun the longer we do it."

Not that Buffett's recording career had languished. *Hot Water*—his 16th album and first in two years—rated as his most eclectic work to date, courtesy of guest contributors ranging from Steve Winwood to Memphis legend Steve Cropper. The album was mostly recorded at Buffett's new Shrimpboat Sound Studios in Key West.

"I'd been building a friendship with Ralph McDonald (who produced three tracks)—I don't think anybody else has a hand on the pulse of what's happening in contemporary Caribbean music like Ralph does," he said. "And I took advantage of my geography. People like Winwood wound up coming down to Key West to work. It's not really hard to get people to Florida in January through March, and it was so comfortable I rode my bicycle to work. The most important thing I did on this record was living at home."

Many fans assumed that Buffett was the laid-back, carefree character portrayed in his songs, but the protean talent qualified as an author, environmentalist, clothing designer and restauranteur. The "son of a son of a sailor" also added a new element to his lifestyle by piloting his own seaplane. He wrote the single "Homemade Music" on a long trip from Key West to Tallahassee, while composing the closing "That's What Living Is to Me" in a little village on the north coast of Haiti when he returned to explore the places he didn't get to see on his boat.

"Flying gives you total freedom," he said. "I haven't given up sailing, but when you're up there, you can really let go of things. The plane's opened up—pardon the pun—a lot of horizons for me. I love the romanticism of flying a seaplane, too. It goes with nature, and I have that flair. I guess these days you could call me an airborne sailor!" ■

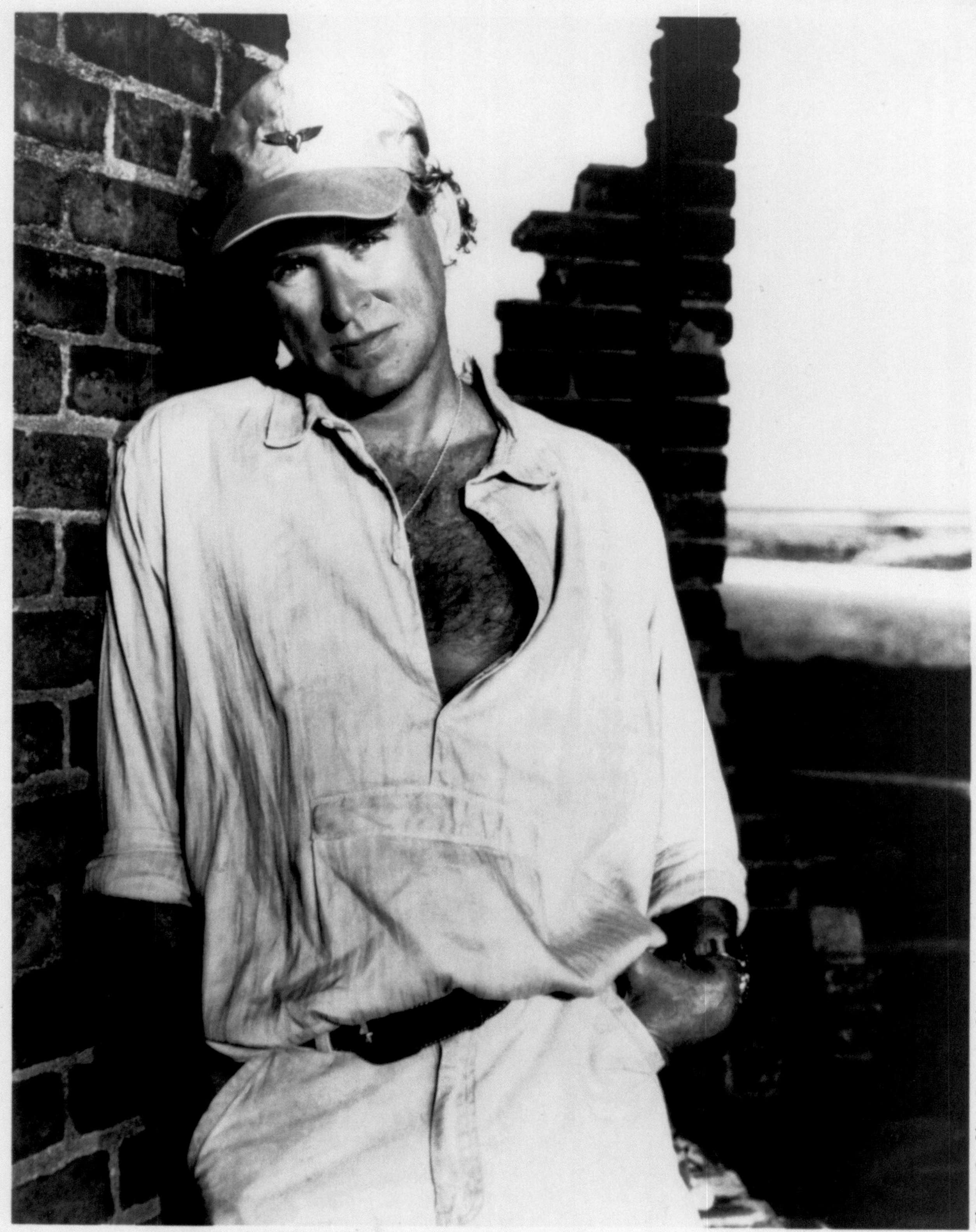
Photo Credit: Jean Pagliuso
JIMMY BUFFETT
.MCA RECORDS

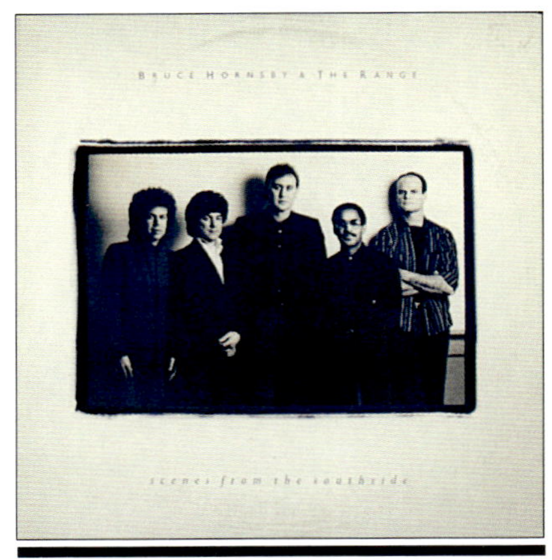

Billboard 200: *Scenes from the Southside* (#5)
Billboard Hot 100: "The Valley Road" (#5);
"Look Out Any Window" (#35)

Another set of Bruce Hornsby & the Range's rich piano-based stylings carved out a high spot on the pop charts.

BRUCE HORNSBY knew that his evocative, piano-driven Americana was out of step with the synthesized sounds that dominated pop music.

"Basically, I'm a keyboard player who doesn't like keyboards," he laughed. "With all of the current technology, it's so easy to make a record sound 'modern' just by buying the latest synthesizer and putting the next hot new sound on your record before the next guy does. But to me, that approach dates a record. So I go for the most generic, ordinary, B-flat sound that I can, one that doesn't have any connotation. That lets the songs speak."

The down-home elegance of Hornsby's music was good for selling two million copies of *The Way It Is,* his 1986 debut album. He earned acclaim for introducing jazz piano stylings to mainstream rock, but the artist admitted to being a "late starter" musically. The 6-foot-4 Hornsby was a self-described jock, playing basketball for his high school team in Williamsburg, Virginia. At 17, he became enamored of Elton John's "Levon" and Leon Russell and renewed an earlier interest in the piano.

"I just got real intense with it," he explained. "I went to music school and got my degree. The degree hasn't done me anything, but the discipline has. I spent seven years practicing five or six hours a day, even Christmas. If you go about it in a methodical, intelligent way and don't get hung up on trivial matters, you can get it together on a musical instrument quickly."

Hornsby then began concentrating on songwriting, and Michael McDonald of the Doobie Brothers encouraged him to move to Los Angeles in the early Eighties. Hornsby spent years writing formulaic pop songs for a publishing company while sending out his own music on demo tapes. Rejection notices piled up, but when he was finally afforded a chance to record, the results were amazing. *The Way It Is* spawned three hit singles ("Mandolin Rain," "Every Little Kiss" and the title track) and earned Hornsby a Grammy for Best New Artist.

New artists were often hard pressed to come up with songs for a follow-up album, and Hornsby initially felt a sense of pressure. But the excitement of his success "got me jacked up and the creative juices flowing." His second album was conceived as the musical equivalent of a book of Southern short stories, "evocations of things from our home area. We called it *Scenes from the Southside* to draw attention to the fact that it's a collection."

A majority of the album's material was co-written with his younger brother John, a lawyer—"He helps with lyrics," Hornsby said. "The Valley Road," a story-song of a rich-girl poor-boy romance set on a plantation, reached the Top 10 with a McCoy Tyner-meets-rock arrangement. The stately "Look Out Any Window" addressed pollution in a socially alert way. And Hornsby's own version of "Jacob's Ladder" had already been a hit for Huey Lewis & the News in 1987. ■

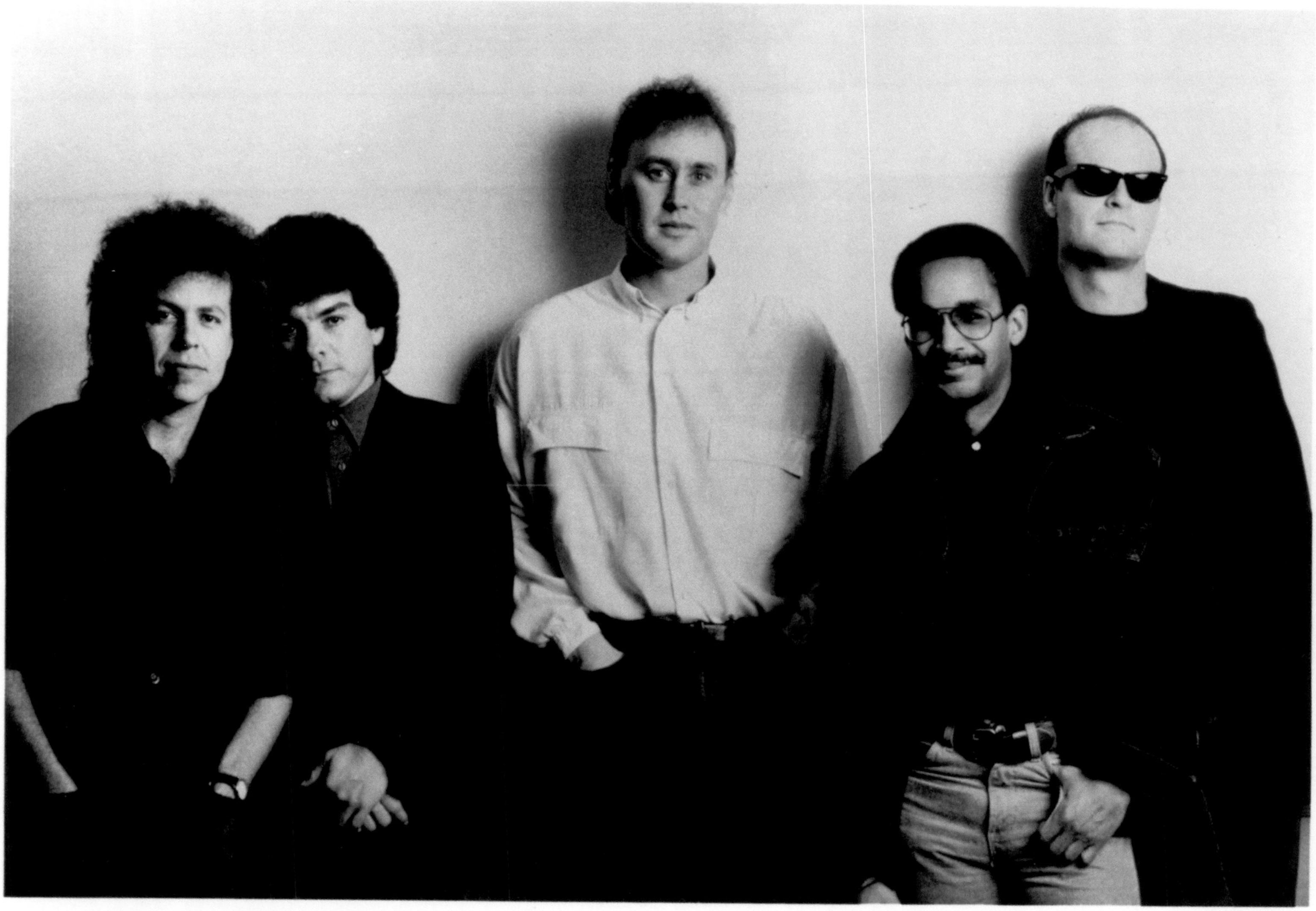

BRUCE HORNSBY
AND THE RANGE

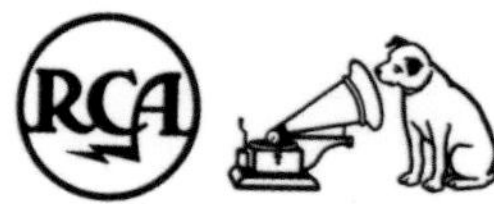

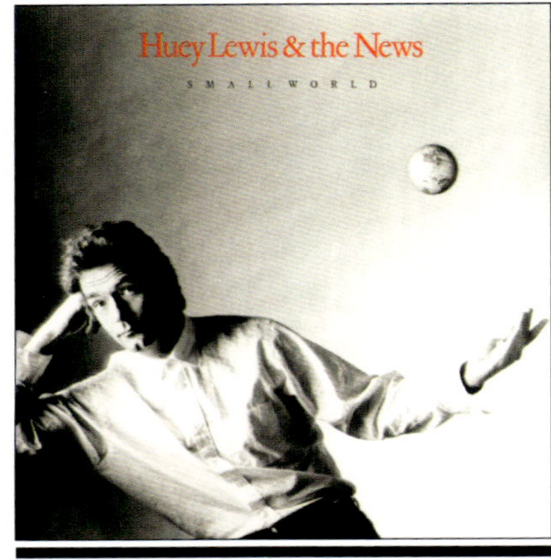

Billboard 200: *Small World* (#11)
Billboard Hot 100: "Perfect World" (#3);
"Small World (Part One)" (#25);
"Give Me the Keys (And I'll Drive You Crazy)" (#47)

Having found commercial favor, Huey Lewis & the News' *Small World* expanded the reach of the band's music.

FOLLOWING THE success of the No. 1 *Sports* and its follow-up *Fore*—sales of the two albums totaled over 15 million worldwide—Huey Lewis & the News hatched a plan.

"We were going to get out of people's faces," Lewis explained. "We've been at this for nearly a decade nonstop, and we figured it was time for a break, for us and our fans."

But things didn't work out that way. "We got together just to write and play after a few months off, and we had a lot of ideas," Lewis said. "The stuff just poured out, and it felt different. I didn't expect a record, but it was too much fun, too easy to ignore. Before we knew it, we'd done an album."

The relaxed attitude surrounding the creation of *Small World*, the group's fifth album, led to some new directions. Lewis and his cohorts—Chris Hayes (guitar), Bill Gibson (drums), Sean Hopper (keyboards), Johnny Colla (guitar, sax) and Mario Cippolina (bass)—made many observations while club-hopping on tour in Europe, and they wound up incorporating crosscurrents of jazz, reggae and ska into *Small World*.

"Perfect World," the first single, was written by Alex Call, a former Clover band member with Lewis. His song carried through the album's sense of social relevance, the opportunity to "Keep on dreamin' of livin' in a perfect world." Legendary jazz musician Stan Getz performed the sax solo on Part 2 of the title track. Lewis first met Getz when he and his father, a former jazz drummer, attended a benefit for the late Zoot Sims.

"Getz came up and introduced himself to me," Lewis recalled. "My dad is dumbfounded that Getz is talking to his kid. He's saying, 'Hey, why don't you let me play on some of your stuff? I can play that too, ya know.' He gave me his card—it said, 'Stan Getz: Have Sax, Will Travel.' When we cut the 'Small World' track, we broke it down for Getz to blow on the end. And he came in and killed it. He used dynamics that rock 'n' roll doesn't have to begin with—he'd dip down underneath the track sometimes where you could barely hear him, laying back against the pushy, aggressive horn licks we'd already put down. It was really educational."

The only sour notes emanated from the corporate world—Lewis sensed that he'd been labeled a subversive due to the previous year's MTV Video Music Awards.

"They were running all those Pepsi ads," Lewis recalled. "We were waiting backstage, and every time they cut away it was another Pepsi commercial—especially that Tina Turner and David Bowie one, 'Here's two old hookers for Pepsi.'

"And I'm sorry, but I couldn't resist it—when I went onstage, I said, 'I've gotta say it, I like Coke. I'm not trying to be a wise guy, nobody's paying me, but I just think it tastes a little bit better, alright?' And apparently Pepsi is still livid to this day—they almost pulled their sponsorship from MTV—and everybody's a little afraid of me now. Isn't that ridiculous? Lou Reed is doing ads and they're scared of Huey Lewis." ■

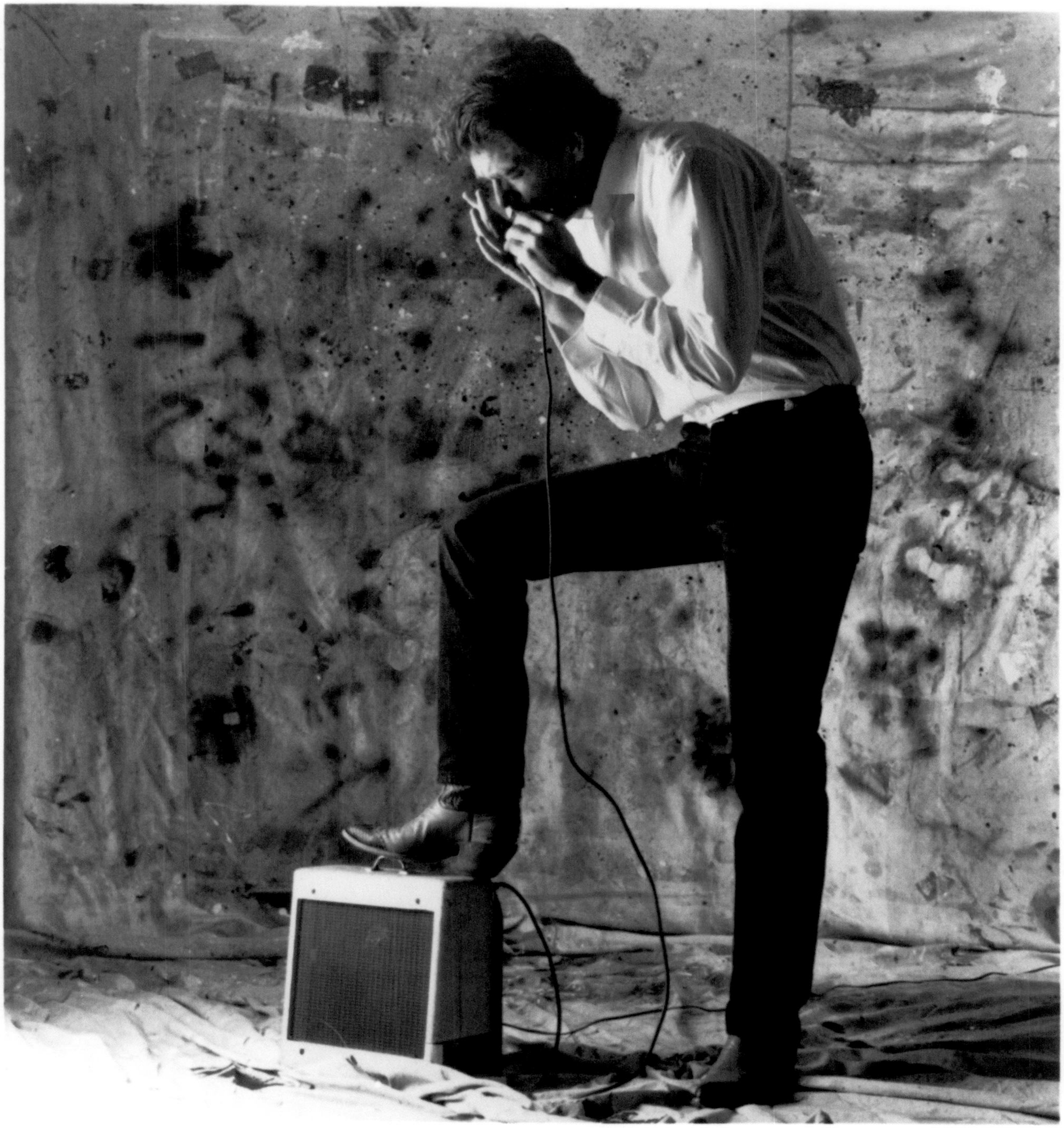

Photo Credit: Jock McDonald

HUEY LEWIS

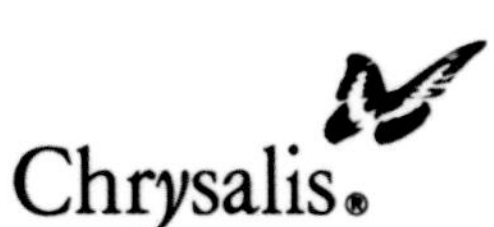

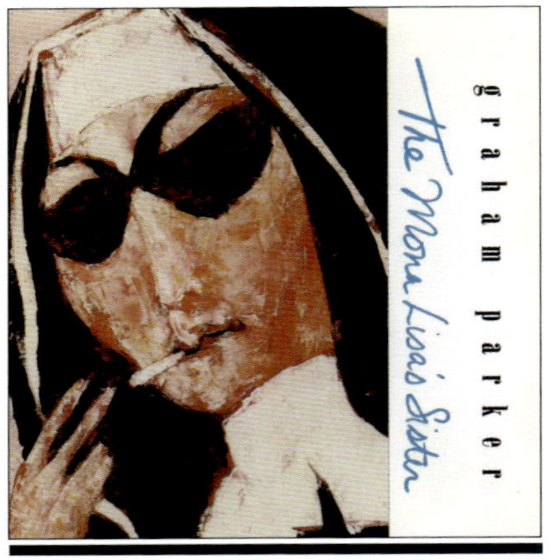

Billboard 200: *The Mona Lisa's Sister* (#77)

With *The Mona Lisa's Sister*, the gritty, soulful Graham Parker finally converted critical approbation into sales.

"I USED to be rock's angry young man," Graham Parker said. "Now I suppose I'm rock's slightly-grumpy-in-the-morning, getting-on-to-middle-age man."

Among rock music cognoscenti, Parker had been considered a major talent since he exploded out of the British pub-cock scene in 1976. Supported by the Rumour, a razor-sharp band headed by guitarist Brinsley Schwarz, the wiry singer and songwriter fused the working-class frustration of punk to the soulfulness of R&B on several substantial albums. His debut, *Howlin' Wind,* and 1979's exuberant *Squeezing Out Sparks* were recognized in *Rolling Stone* magazine's "100 Best Albums of the Last Twenty Years" issue.

But while Parker's work had drawn critical acclaim, career momentum and a commercial breakthrough had not been forthcoming. "I'm the best-kept secret in the West," he once complained in a song.

That status changed with *The Mona Lisa's Sister,* his best album of the Eighties. Based in upstate New York, where he said he'd been learning to ski since his last album, 1985's *Steady Nerves,* Parker had also spent the hiatus embroiled in a battle with his former record company. He insisted on producing his next album himself after working with seven different producers.

"I didn't know what they wanted from me," he said. "They didn't want my songs or my production. They said they wanted somebody else. So I said, 'Get somebody else.'"

The Mona Lisa's Sister then surfaced on another label, featuring an intimate sound based on Parker's acoustic guitar. The compelling themes and musical nuances vindicated his desire to seize control of the record. "Get Started. Start a Fire," a college radio hit, boasted a simmering guitar break and vocal, while the closing cover of Sam Cooke's "Cupid" revealed a deeply felt commitment to the ideals of romance.

Yet it was "Success," an emotionally dense treatise about artistic integrity, that served as the album's cornerstone. How did Parker, a man who was still looking to win the audience he deserved, measure success?

"By the amount of records you sell and the amount of money you make, of course," he laughed. "But seriously, I've been a success since I signed my first record deal. I've been rolling in money compared to the days when I was pumping gas. Success is really revenge, making this record after some people didn't think it was strong enough and having it be accepted, even critically. I could bullshit about peace of mind is being successful, but I still don't know what peace of mind is. If I have it, it lasts about five minutes and I'm on to the next worry." ■

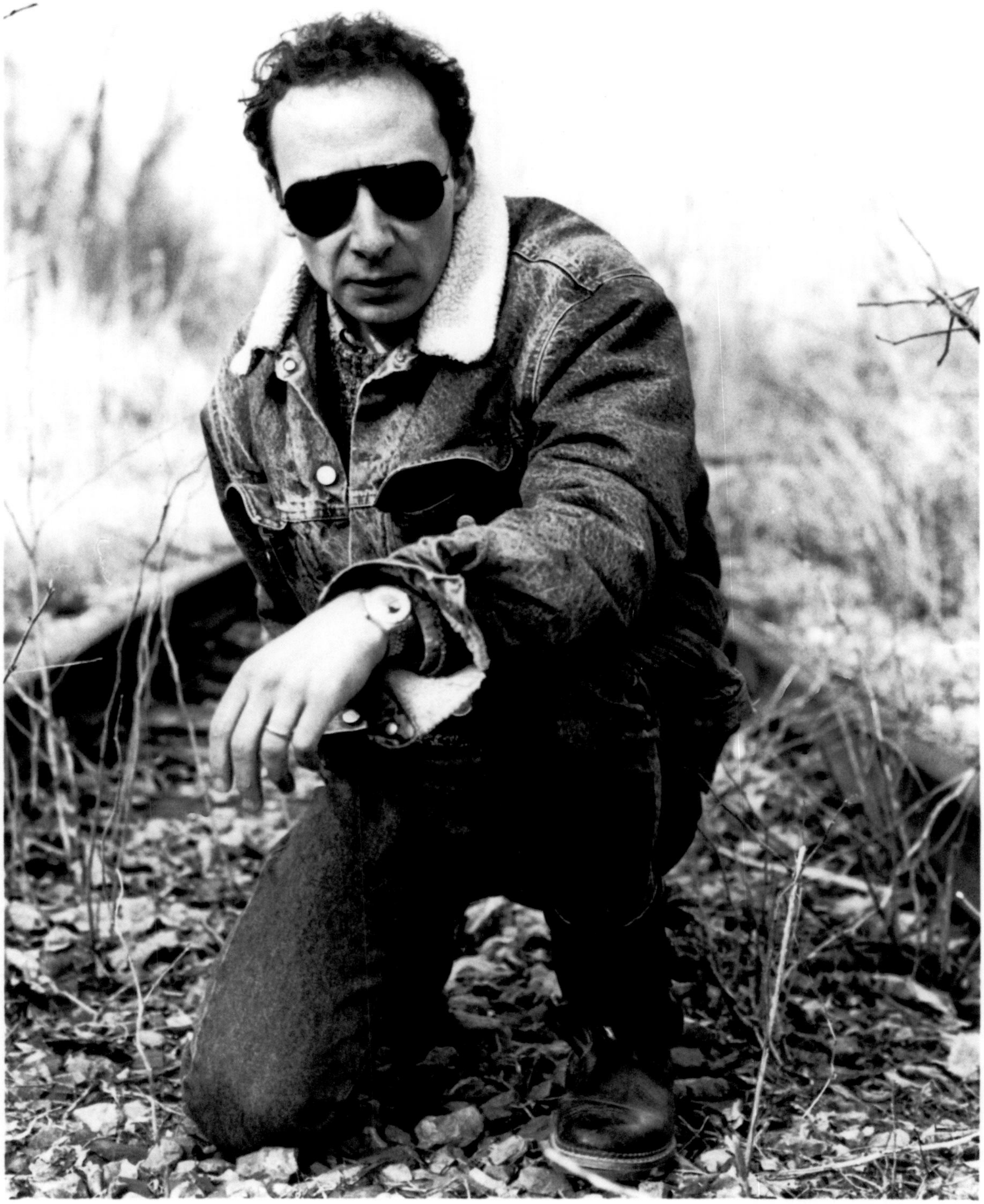

Photo Credit: Jolie Parker

graham Parker

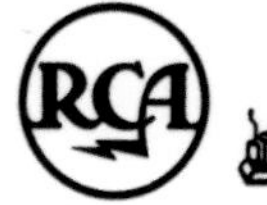

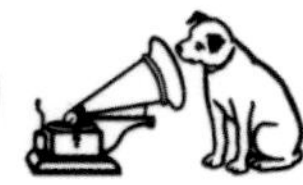

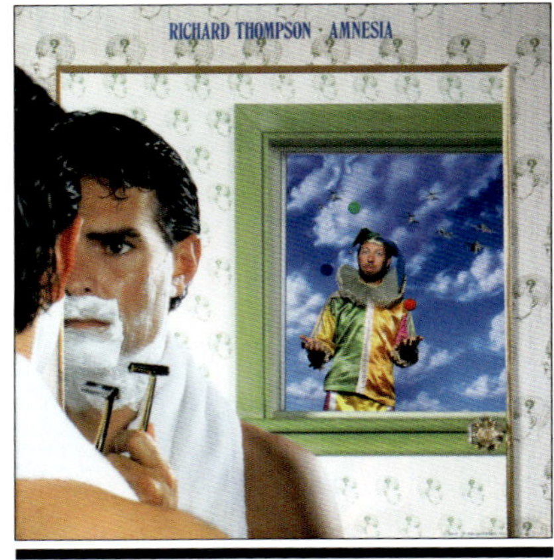

Billboard 200: *Amnesia* (#182)

Amnesia placed the traditional English music of Richard Thompson's background against classic guitar work.

RICHARD THOMPSON had never lacked for critical acclaim. In the late Sixties, he founded Fairport Convention, the most distinctive and satisfying of British folk-rock groups. He went on to record several albums with his wife Linda, and 1982's *Shoot Out the Lights* rated as their masterpiece. The songwriting, singing and his extraordinary guitar playing combined for some majestic music. Naturally, when mainstream recognition was imminent, the Thompsons dissolved their marriage and musical partnership.

"My sticky divorce was quite fun, because my ex-wife's a singer as well. So, every line from every song for years after that, it was, 'You know he's writing about her and she's writing about him.' People take it very personally when you're writing the song and singing it at the same time—they say, 'It's him, poor fellow, he really has got the blues. He is going to put his head on the railroad track.' People won't accept that you're writing from another persona; they want the song to be your life. They want you to be this Merle Haggard figure who's spent five years in prison for manslaughter. I think it should be both. I'd hate to limit songwriting to looking inward or outward. The best songs are the ones that have both things in them."

Thompson had pursued a solo career, and the *Amnesia* album showcased a return to traditional instrumentation. "Turning of the Tide" peaked at #30 on *Billboard*'s Alternative Rock chart.

"I think it's one of the most aggressive records I've made," he said. "You should be getting more creative as you get older. I still feel too old for rock 'n' roll in one sense. It's really a young market, it always has been. But now rock music is so broad a category, it can support boring old farts like me, and it also incorporates areas of jazz and classical music, all kinds of things. It'd be nice to be like the old blues guys like B.B. King, to still be playing at 60-plus. That's be very good. Hell, Shakespeare was just hitting his stride at 40." ■

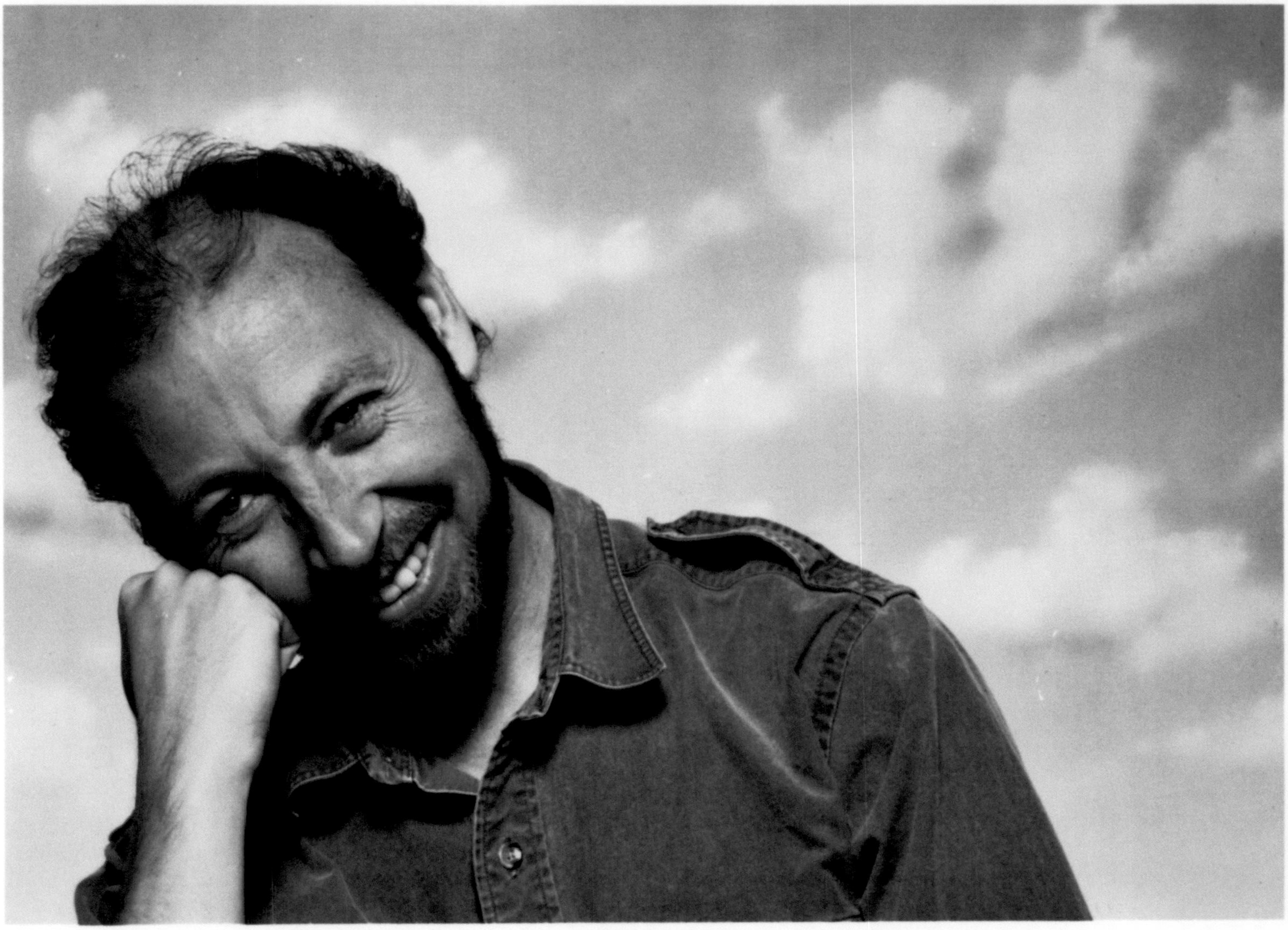

RICHARD THOMPSON

Photo: Hugh Brown/1988

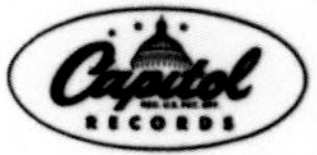

Guitarist Leo Kottke circled back to the studio and recorded *Regards* from Chuck Pink, a set of instrumentals.

FOR NEARLY 20 years, Leo Kottke had been heralded as the world's foremost steel-string acoustic guitar master. *Regards from Chuck Pink* sustained his career renaissance as a "new age" artist, if only because he recorded for the instrumental Private Music label.

"The company has promoted itself in that arena, so I might as well add new age to my list," Kottke said. "Over the years, I've been in the folk bin, the jazz bin, the country bin, the rock bin and the blues bin—they're all okay with me. At least new age is broader than most labels—it leaves room for a lot of instrumentalists to sneak in."

The problem with the categorization was that Kottke had included vocal selections in his past repertoire. Yet he found other parameters to explore on *Regards from Chuck Pink*.

"I don't connect to what I suspect are commercial trends because they don't interest me," he said. "Making a record is simply a matter of curiosity for me. This time around I wanted to work with small string arrangements, and I wanted to use more synthesis but not keyboard synthesizer, because that's been done to death."

So Kottke availed himself of an EWI (electronic wind instrument), a guitar synthesizer and "living, breathing human beings playing them." The self-taught guitarist pushed himself as well.

"I practice more than I ever have," he said. "I always used to play like a little pig; I could never get enough guitar. But it was just dabbling in whatever I was interested in at the time. Nowadays I'm playing harmonic scales, trying to get a more inclusive grasp of the fingerboard."

The lively "Busy Signal" was nominated for a Grammy, but for all his fine recordings, it was in concert that Kottke excelled, as fans came to experience his personality and laid-back sense of humor as much as his amazing technical facility on guitar.

"I get as many requests for stories as I do for songs," he said, citing the namesake of his album. "There was a fry cook at Pink's Hot Dog Stand in Los Angeles around 1969 who was a dead ringer for Chuck Berry, and he was a real pain in the neck. So he became the first Chuck Pink, and it went from there to become a metaphor for the guy you don't want to hear from." ■

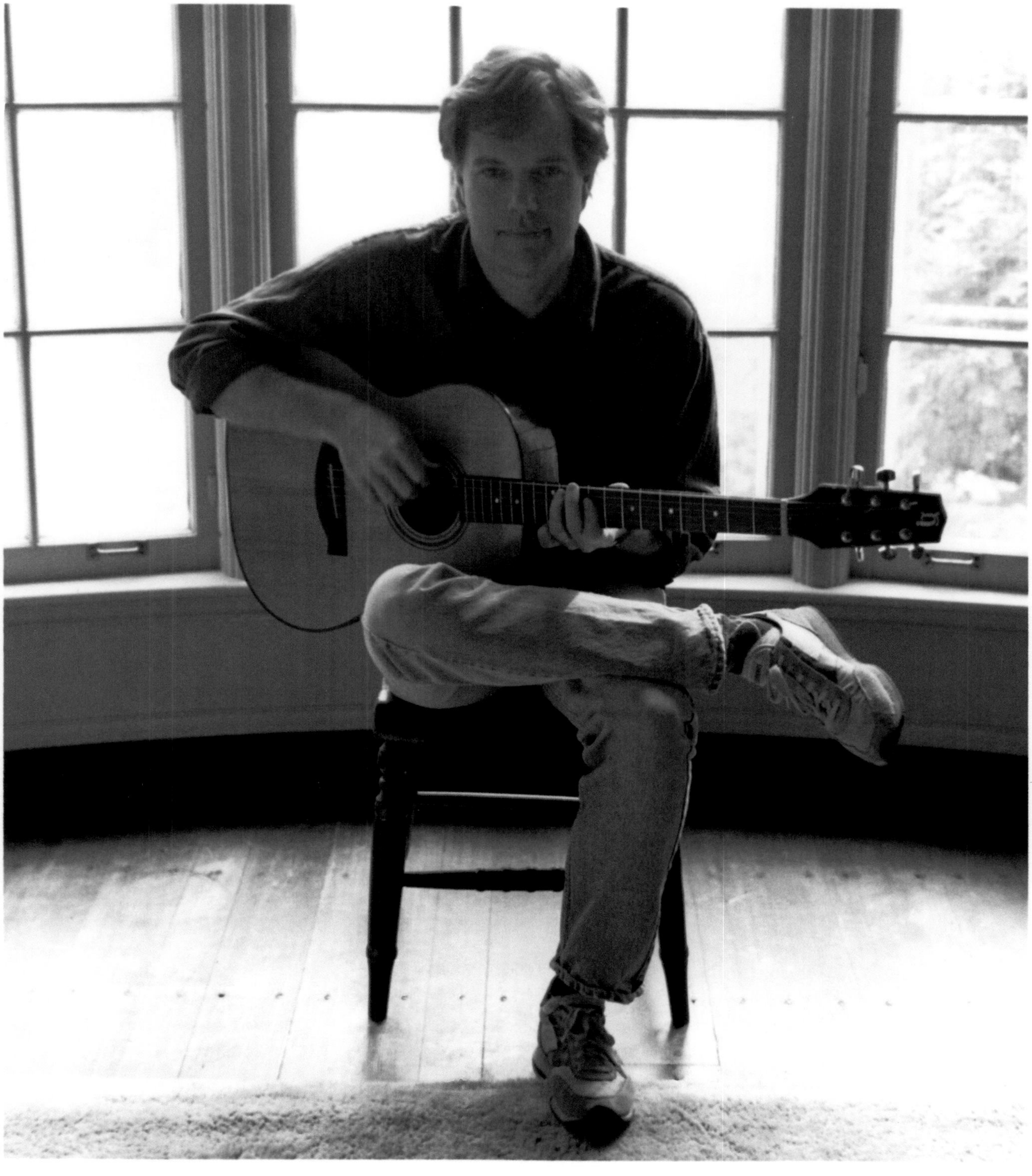

LEO KOTTKE

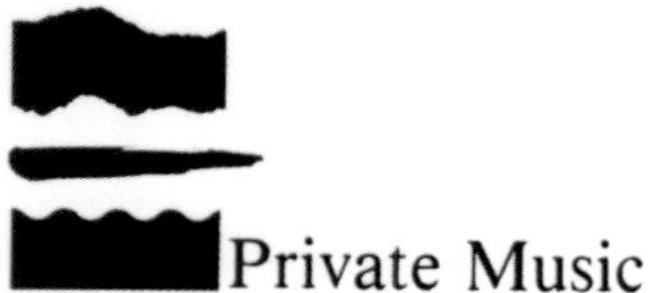

Photo Credit
Tom Berthiaume

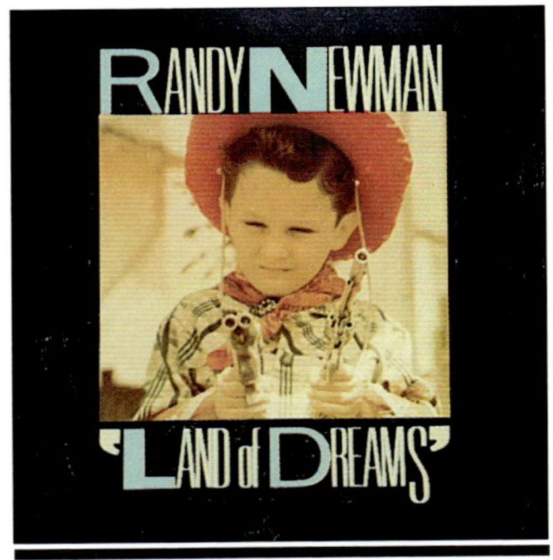

Billboard 200: *Land of Dreams* (#80)
Billboard Hot 100: "It's Money That Matters" (#60)

Land of Dreams was another entry in a long line of Randy Newman's meticulously formulated masterstrokes.

FOR LISTENERS to come to terms with his wry, uningratiating style, Randy Newman had waited two decades.

"See, I like the idea of the untrustworthy narrator," he said. "A lot of my characters are insensitive—they're generally exaggerations, they don't know how they indict themselves. What they say and think is colored by who they are. When a song works, the audience understands the character's point of view, and they don't mistake it for mine."

Yet the complex, self-effacing songwriter's biggest hit single, 1978's "Short People," offended plenty of people for the wrong reasons—many mistook the satire on bigotry for bigotry itself. In another career twist, "I Love L.A.," Newman's 1983 attack on the yuppification of Los Angeles, brought him widespread exposure with a witty video.

"And now the song is used as this knee-jerk anthem that gets played during the fourth quarter at Lakers (basketball) games," he said. "A lot of my songs could get me in trouble, but big hits reach people who are used to having my words mean what they absolutely have to mean."

Newman's *Land of Dreams* album expanded the public perception of his musical tableaux. The facetious wisdom of "It's Money That Matters" was underscored by a rollicking guitar lick contributed by Dire Straits' Mark "Money for Nothing" Knopfler, who produced seven of the album's twelve tracks. As usual, the song reflected an attitude for which Newman "hasn't any sympathy at all," which made it all the more remarkable for its accuracy.

"And there's been no trouble. I'm waiting for the banks to want to use it, but I doubt they will," Newman laughed. "Ironically, the lyrics are problematic. My heart is with the public radio and bookstore people, but unlike most of my songs, it may be true that 'it's money that matters'—you can't avoid it in this country."

"It's Money That Matters" rose to the top of *Billboard*'s Mainstream Rock chart, but Newman worried about the skewered smugness of "Roll with the Punches"—"I don't know whether people on the whole are going to get the song, know that I really don't think that a little black kid should have to live in filth and roll with the punches." "Follow the Flag," a tribute to patriotic doom, was equally difficult with its utter lack of irony.

Never a prolific artist, *Land of Dreams* was Newman's first album in four-and-a-half years. He didn't make any excuses, even though his life had been complicated by Epstein-Barr virus, a disease that resulted in generalized malaise and fatigue.

"I never should have mentioned that to anybody, but I'm the one who brought it up," he noted. "If it exists at all—there's some doubt about it—then I had it. But it's the perfect disease for me. Nothing but bed rest is prescribed, and it's always been my goal to lie down." ■

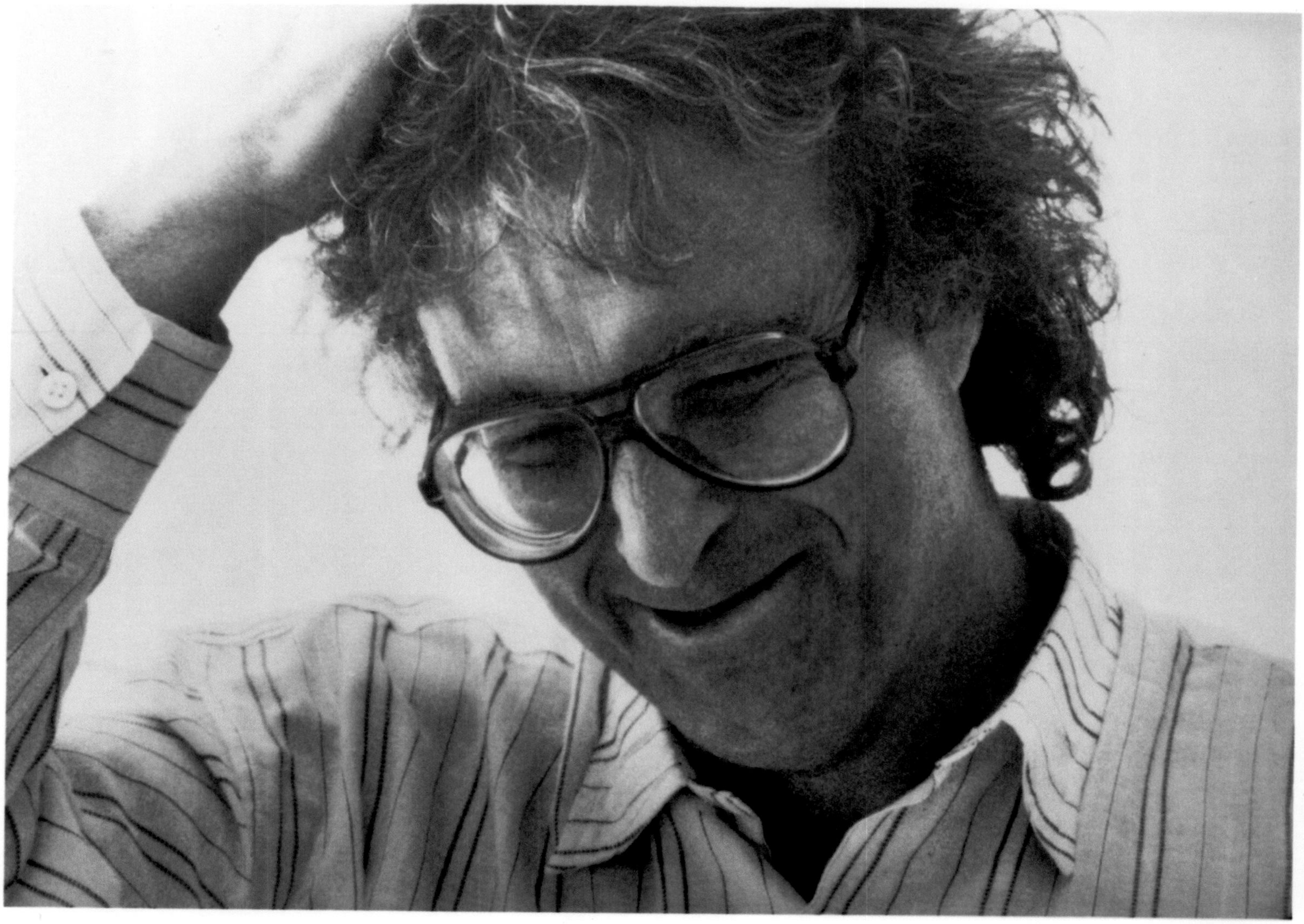

Photo Credit: Melodie Gimple

RANDY NEWMAN

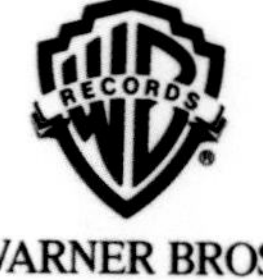

WARNER BROS.

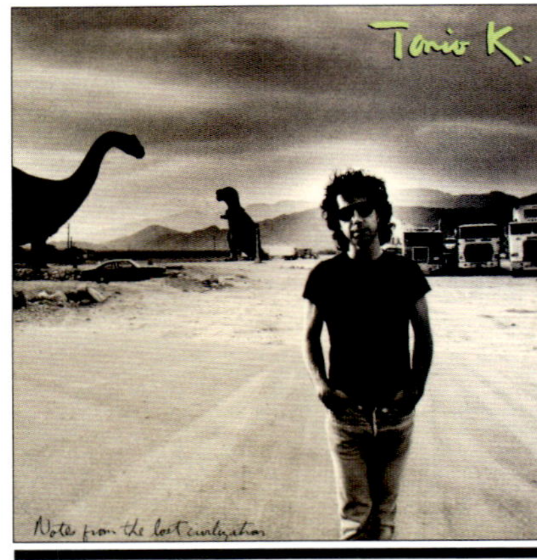

Acclaimed for years as "the funniest serious songwriter in America," mellow Tonio K. wasn't cranky anymore.

ON HIS 1979 debut album, *Life in the Foodchain*, Tonio K. emerged as an angry young man with a sense of humor, howling about life's indignities from his Los Angeles vantage point. His lyrical sensibilities were on full display in "H-A-T-R-E-D," which featured an immortal couplet:

Yes I wish I was as mellow
As for instance Jackson Browne
But 'Fountain of Sorrow' my ass, motherfucker
I hope you wind up in the ground

Tonio K. (born Steve Krikorian—he adapted his professional name from *Tonio Kröger*, a Thomas Mann novella) continued his cranky albeit funny moralizing on ensuing records, such as the acerbic "Mars Needs Women" ("Maybe you should apply," insisted the refrain).

"It was all sort of a game—change your name and wear dark glasses," the mercurial K. said. "I figured it was my turn to do that—confuse the issue as much as possible and have fun."

But within a few years, K. transformed from a foul-mouthed cult favorite into a nearly mellow guy. The material on *Notes from a Lost Civilization* revealed a married man newly sensitive to women's viewpoints, a Christian who had replaced his angst with guarded optimism. He sounded downright affectionate on "Stay," an actual love song—"a new angle on an old theme set to the original music," K. said. "Without Love," which marked K.'s first video airplay on MTV, peaked at #42 on *Billboard's* Mainstream Rock Songs chart.

But K. wasn't mistaken for the typical mewling singer-songwriter. No one else could have hatched the alternative anthem "I'm Supposed to Have Sex with You," a song he'd written for an unmade movie that surfaced on the soundtrack to the comedy *Summer School*. "It's obviously one big goof from beginning to end," he said. "Maybe 65 percent of the people who've heard it have gotten the joke. The other 35 percent take me for the foremost advocate of random sex in the Eighties." ■

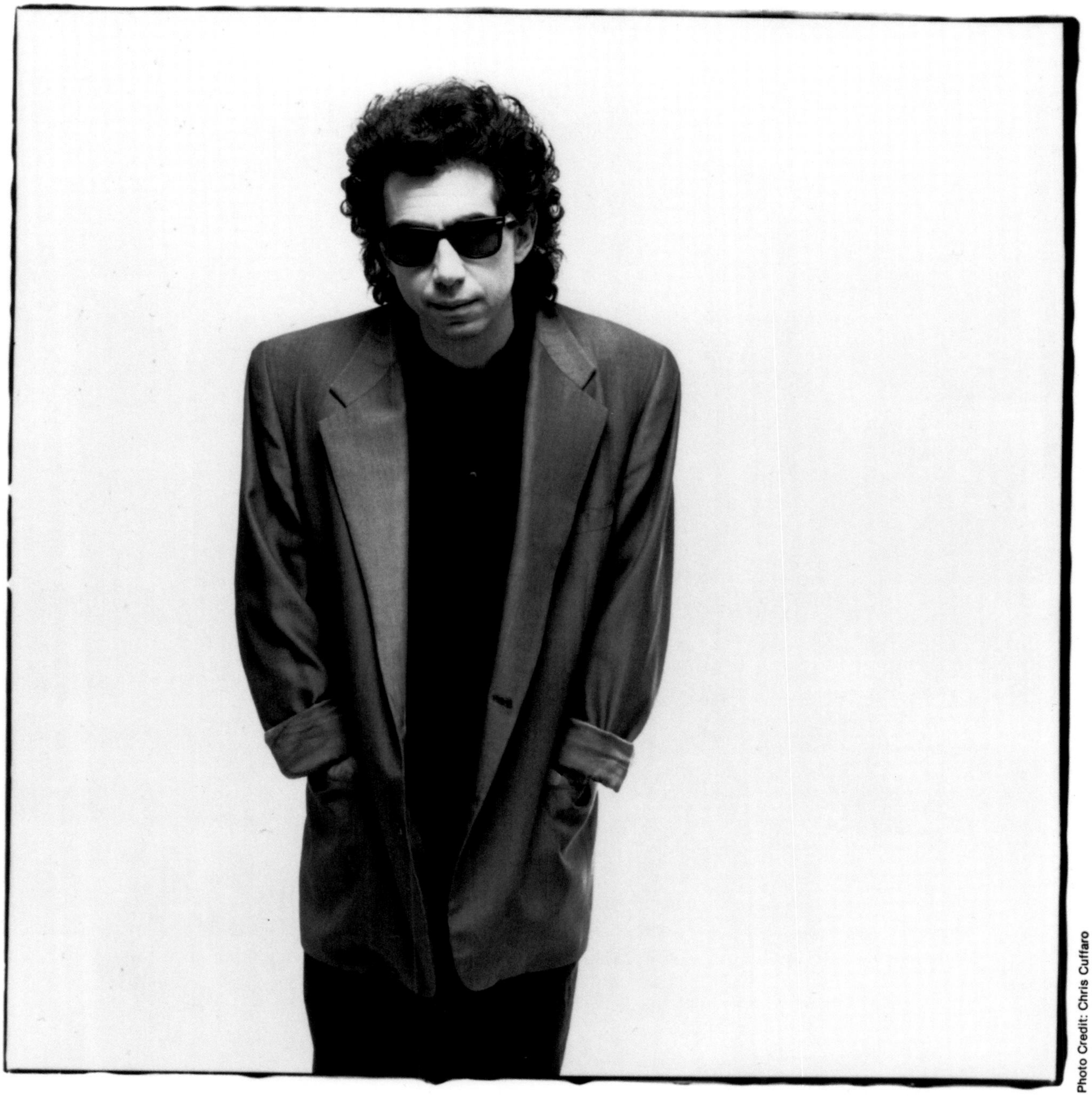

Photo Credit: Chris Cuffaro

TONIO K.

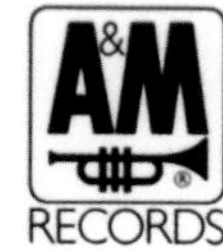

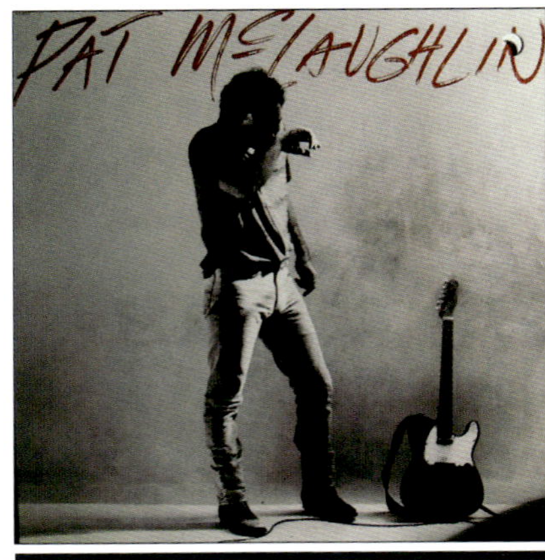

Pat McLaughlin issued his first major-label solo album, a showcase for his unique, soulful and clever songs.

ONE OF the year's biggest publicity pushes was focused around a down-home performer—members of the rock media were inundated with paraphernalia ranging from Pat McLaughlin baseball caps to Pat McLaughlin jigsaw puzzles. That type of hype was usually reserved for the latest haircut bands from England, because they needed the help. But in this case, the center of attention was a 38-year-old singer-songwriter based in Tennessee who professed to be the last person to know what the fuss was all about.

"I really don't know how my record is doing," the self-effacing McLaughlin shrugged. "If anything good happens, I figure someone will tell me. You know, I've been at this a long time—I've been a carpenter just as long as I've been a musician."

McLaughlin was discovered playing in a Nashville club by Steve Berlin (of Los Lobos fame), who helped him assemble a band and spread the word about his songwriting talent. McLaughlin became the subject of a bidding war among several record labels, with Capitol Records earning the right to release *Pat McLaughlin*. The album was produced by Mitchell Froom (Crowded House, Los Lobos), who surrounded McLaughlin with the finest Los Angeles session players.

The album showcased McLaughlin's wry tunes, which usually elicited a yeah-I've-been-there-too reaction from listeners. His song "Lynda" reached No. 1 on the country charts when Steve Wariner covered it. In concert, his everyman demeanor permeated his material, revealing his gentle humor and thoughtful turns of phrase. In an age when music was often equated with fashion, he looked more like a bass fisherman than the next big thing.

McLaughlin's vocal and composing skills were enough to ensure that his days of holding down a day job were over. And he had the last word on the hype. "I'll tell you what," he grinned. "Next, maybe they'll come out with Pat McLaughlin pen holders to protect my pockets." ■

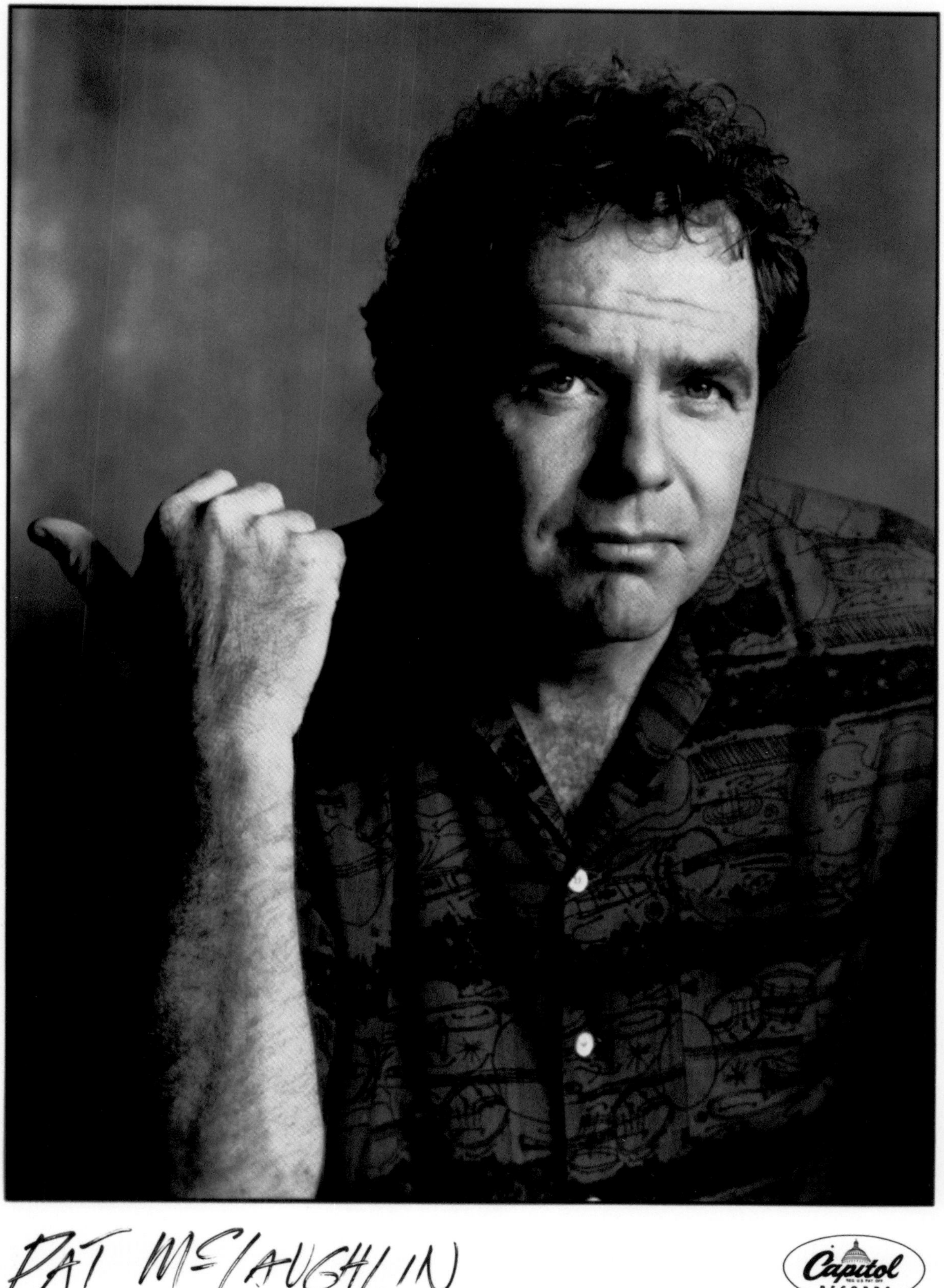

PAT McLAUGHLIN

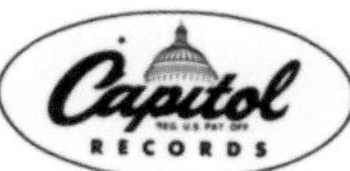

Photo: Greg Gorman / 1988

Billboard 200: *Back to Avalon* (#69)
Billboard Hot 100: "Meet Me Half Way" (#11) "Nobody's Fool" (#8); "I'm Gonna Miss You" (#82); "Tell Her" (#76)

Soft rocker Kenny Loggins employed a wide variety of collaborators to strengthen his *Back to Avalon* album.

KENNY LOGGINS had always actively sought out collaboration opportunities with other artists, from his early days with Loggins & Messina ("Your Mama Don't Dance") through his hits as a solo artist—"Whenever I Call You 'Friend'" in 1978 (a duet with Stevie Nicks of Fleetwood Mac) and "Don't Fight It" in 1982 (with Journey frontman Steve Perry). He co-wrote "What A Fool Believes" and "This Is It" with Michael McDonald of the Doobie Brothers.

Loggins was also known for a string of soundtrack contributions, and *Back to Avalon*, his first solo record in three years, included "Meet Me Half Way" (from the movie *Over the Top*) and "Nobody's Fool" (from *Caddyshack II*). But the album was also noteworthy for Loggins' pairing with an array of noted songwriters, producers—Peter Wolf (Starship), Patrick Leonard (Madonna), Richie Zito, Dennis Lambert, Giorgio Moroder and Richard Page—and musicians including Dann Huff, Mickey Thomas, Siedah Garrett, Mike Baird and others.

"I've always viewed collaborations as periods of growth," he explained. "You learn from the people you write with. Everyone has their own relationship with their muse. I read the biography of George Kaufman, the great Broadway writer who was nicknamed 'the Great Collaborator,' and it impressed on me that I have a particular talent for collaboration. You have to have the temperament for it, to know how to give and take."

Back to Avalon was Loggins' first solo album to miss gold certification, marking a commercial decline.

"I've started to redefine my borders and see that I can't be the workaholic I used to be," he said. "I'm not really trying to say anything to anyone but me." ■

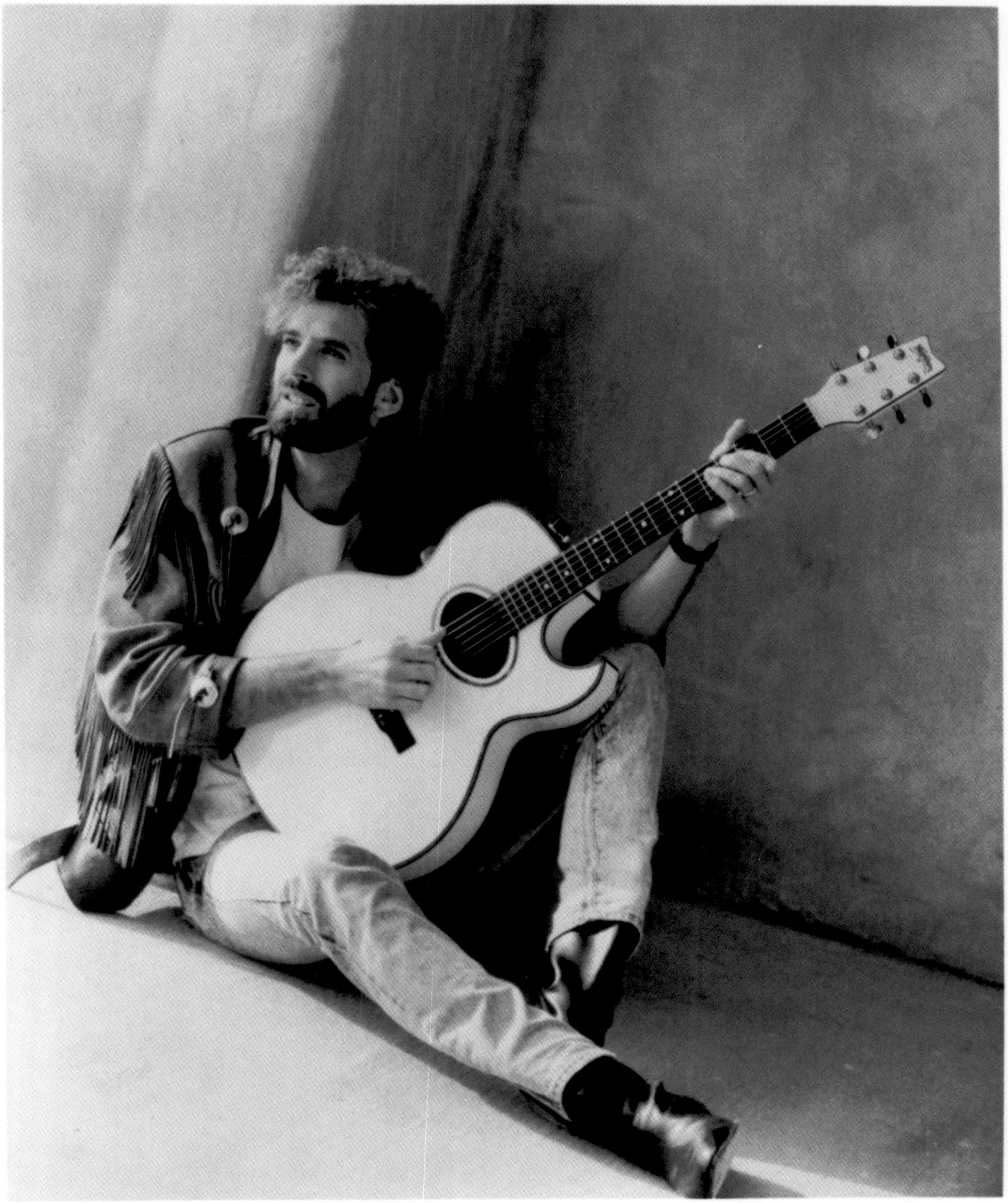

PHOTO: VICTORIA PEARSON

MANAGEMENT:
Larry Larson & Assoc.
P.O. Box 10905
Beverly Hills, CA 90213
(213) 271-7240

KENNY LOGGINS

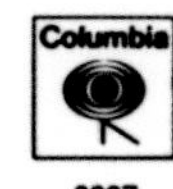

8807

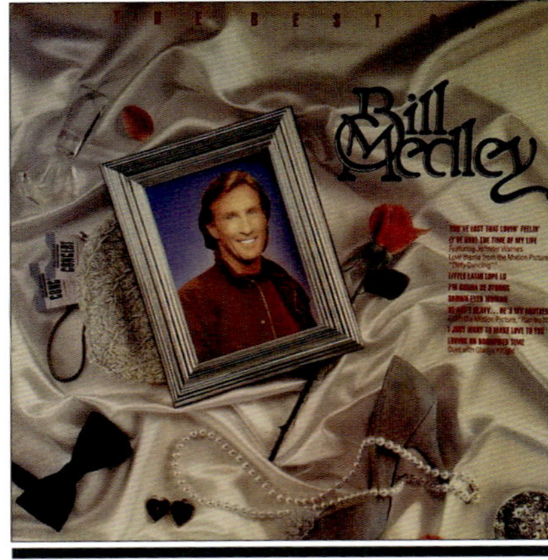

Bill Medley's career had been resurrected, thanks to his soundtrack contribution to the movie *Dirty Dancing*.

THE STATISTICS spoke for themselves—*Dirty Dancing* rated as the country's hottest entertainment phenomenon. That might have come as a surprise to some people, given the movie's relatively innocuous premise of a young girl coming of age during a 1963 Catskills vacation and becoming mesmerized by the hotel dance instructor and the uninhibited movements of "dirty dancing." But since its release, *Dirty Dancing* had grossed more than $100 million at the box office, and more than 400,000 *Dirty Dancing* videocassettes had been sold as well.

Known for his emotionally charged baritone, Bill Medley was one-half of the Righteous Brothers, the blue-eyed soul duo that scored such classic hits as "You've Lost That Lovin' Feelin'," "(You're My) Soul and Inspiration" and "Unchained Melody" in the mid-Sixties. "(I've Had) The Time of My Life", his duet with Jennifer Warnes from *Dirty Dancing*, hit No. 1, won a Grammy and collected an Oscar for Best Original Song.

Not that Medley had any expectations for the film's love theme.

"I'd like to tell you that I've been a genius at selecting songs, but I didn't have a clue with that one," he laughed. "I backed into it. They came to me, thank God. And I was cold to the idea because I thought my last duet ('Loving on Borrowed Time' with Gladys Knight, from the Sylvester Stallone film *Cobra*) would be a hit. It wasn't."

Medley released both duets on *The Best of Bill Medley*, which also included the new studio efforts "He Ain't Heavy, He's My Brother" (which charted in England) and a remake of Gene Pitney's 1964 classic "I'm Gonna Be Strong" ("It's like the way Pet Shop Boys redid 'Always on My Mind,' a pop-dance record," Medley said).

He also redid "You've Lost That Lovin' Feelin'." The Righteous Brothers' original version had risen again thanks to its inclusion on the *Top Gun* soundtrack. On stage, Medley was amazed to see 12-year-olds in his audience singing along when he performed the classic—"These kids know every word!" ■

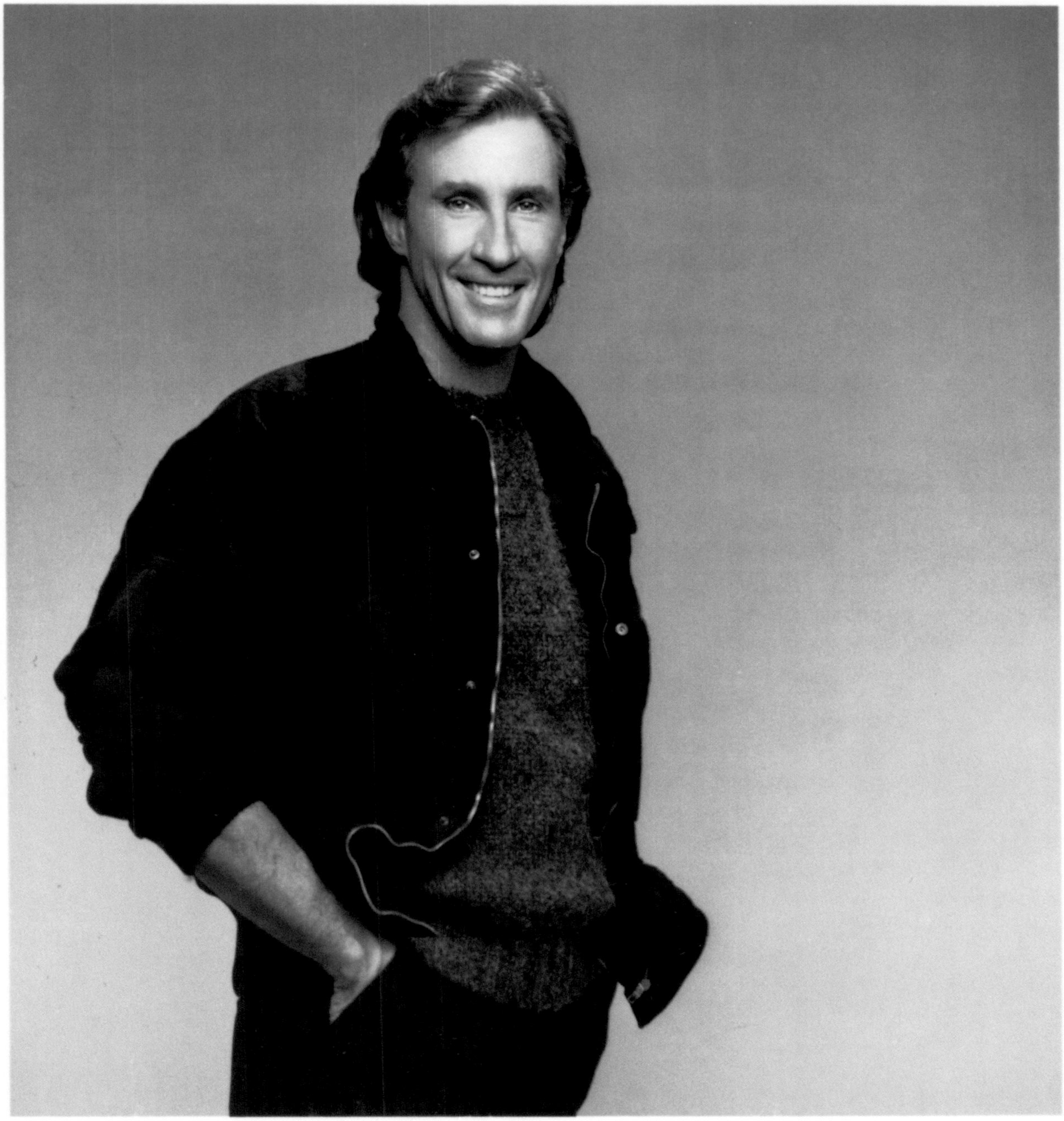

Photo Credit: Greg Gorman

BILL MEDLEY

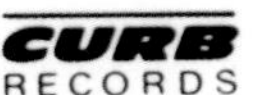

Billboard 200: *Reg Strikes Back* (#16)
Billboard Hot 100: "I Don't Wanna Go On with You Like That" (#2); "A Word in Spanish (#19)

With the hit "I Don't Wanna Go On with You Like That," Elton John made the scene as a reborn pop singer.

ELTON JOHN'S album *Reg Strikes Back* (the "Reg" referred to his birth name, Reginald Dwight) marked a commercial return to form, spurred by the hit "I Don't Wanna Go On with You Like That," which became his highest-charting single in a decade. And he'd acquired a new non-camp image. Every gaudy stitch of his old outlandish stage clothing was piled into a giant heap for the album's cover photo. Sotheby's in London auctioned off the costumes and other artifacts—"like the Duchess of Windsor, except I'm still alive," John said.

"You get to the point where you become a parody of yourself. I've just done that whole thing to death. The last tour was the last glittery one I'll do. I still want to play concerts—I just don't want to go on stage looking ridiculous anymore. I want it to be theatrical, but more in a staging than a costume sense."

Once again, John worked with longtime collaborator Bernie Taupin on *Reg Strikes Back.*

"Bernie and I have never stopped working as a team, but we've never actually written anything together, never sat down to work in one place—I think I'd kill him," John allowed. "It must be frustrating for him to see me take his lyrics, go off with them and come up with a song. But he never complains. This year will make 21 we've been together. We know each other backwards and forwards."

John's throat surgery the previous year hadn't dulled his vocal style.

"I lost my falsetto completely after the operation and it took me about five months to get it back—it was just worn out," he said. "But I'm singing better than ever. I regard myself now as a singer who plays piano rather than a piano player who sings. For the next twenty years, I should be able to sing my ass off." ■

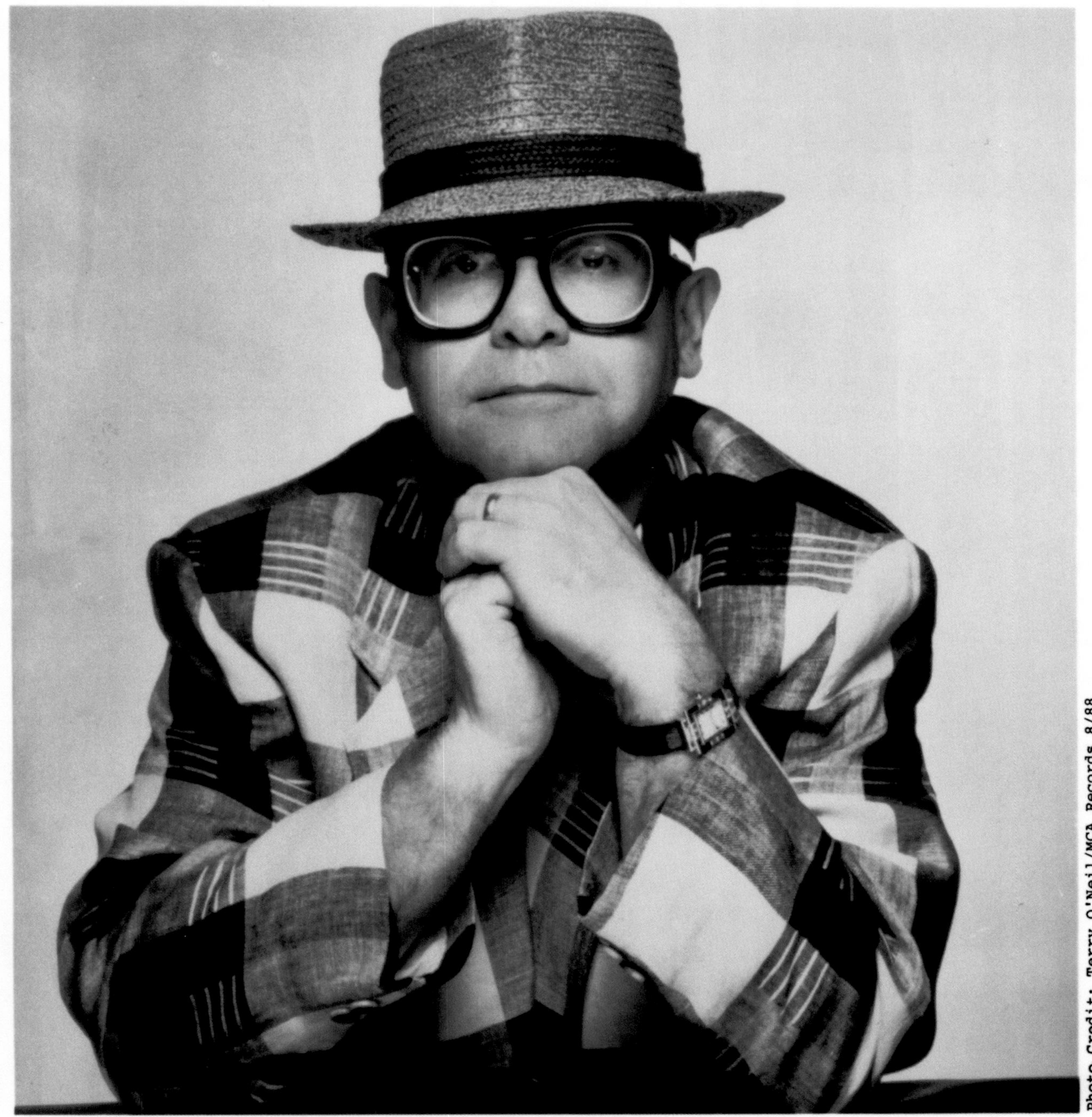

Photo Credit: Terry O'Neil/MCA Records 8/88

ELTON JOHN

.MCA RECORDS

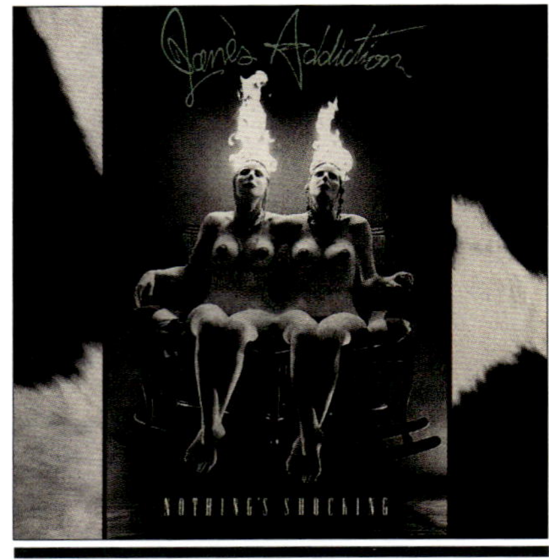

Billboard 200: *Nothing's Shocking* (#103)

Releasing the landmark *Nothing's Shocking*, Jane's Addiction shaped the alternative nation's spirit and sound.

PUTTING A freaky turn on hard-rock riffology, Jane's Addiction's intense brand of "psychodramatic" music was calculated to get attention. The songs on the major-label debut album *Nothing's Shocking* ranged from anguished (the sex-is-violent ranting of "Ted, Just Admit It…," about serial killer Ted Bundy) to confused (the delicate neo-folk rock of "Jane Says").

Perry Farrell played the role of the shaman/father figure, dallying with sexual imagery and fiercely sermonizing on individual automony. "I'm willing to get a reaction any way I can," the audacious and outspoken frontman said. "But it's been a struggle. I had to lie my way into this business. At first, I couldn't get into a band. I'd answer ads in the Los Angeles music papers—'Into: Joy Division, Psychedelic Furs, the Cure.' And I'd go to audition and they'd say, 'You don't sound anything like them.' Everybody was looking for their hero. Something fresh, something not already accepted, was considered a little bit strange."

Jane's Addiction's abrasive sound and aggressive attitude pushed many industry, media and consumer buttons, yet the latest darlings of the L.A. club scene were hotly pursued, and Warner Bros. won the bidding war. The four members—Farrell, bassist Eric Avery, drummer Stephen Perkins and guitarist Dave Navarro—started to transcend any resistance, and *Nothing's Shocking* got a nomination in the brand-new Grammy category of Best Hard Rock/Metal Performance—"a contest we never entered," Farrell smirked. "I'm sure our music gets people off, but at this point, everybody has some big story they'd rather talk about. There's so much activity that surrounds us that people tend to be gossip hounds more than music fans."

Farrell cited the attention focused on the controversial cover art for *Nothing's Shocking,* a sculpture of two nude conjoined twin women with their hair on fire that Farrell made using body castings of his girlfriend. The album was banned by eight of the biggest record retailers in the country.

"I was asked to consider coming up with another cover," Farrell said. "But I was too naïve to consider the repercussions if I refused. I figured, 'If people want the record, they can find it.'" After Farrell convinced the outlets that his sculpture was art, not porn, they agreed to carry the album.

And the band's first video, "Mountain Song," included just enough full-frontal nude footage of Farrell's girlfriend to keep it off MTV. Predictably, Farrell maintained that he would never consent to an edited version of any Jane's Addiction video in order to receive airplay on any broadcast channel. MTV then agreed to air "Mountain Song" with black censor bars.

"To me, *decadence* is a word invented by people who don't like what I do," Farrell concluded. "Decadence isn't shooting your mouth off about how crazy you are. It's personal, what you can get away with in a country that's taking away our freedoms every year with a new law." ■

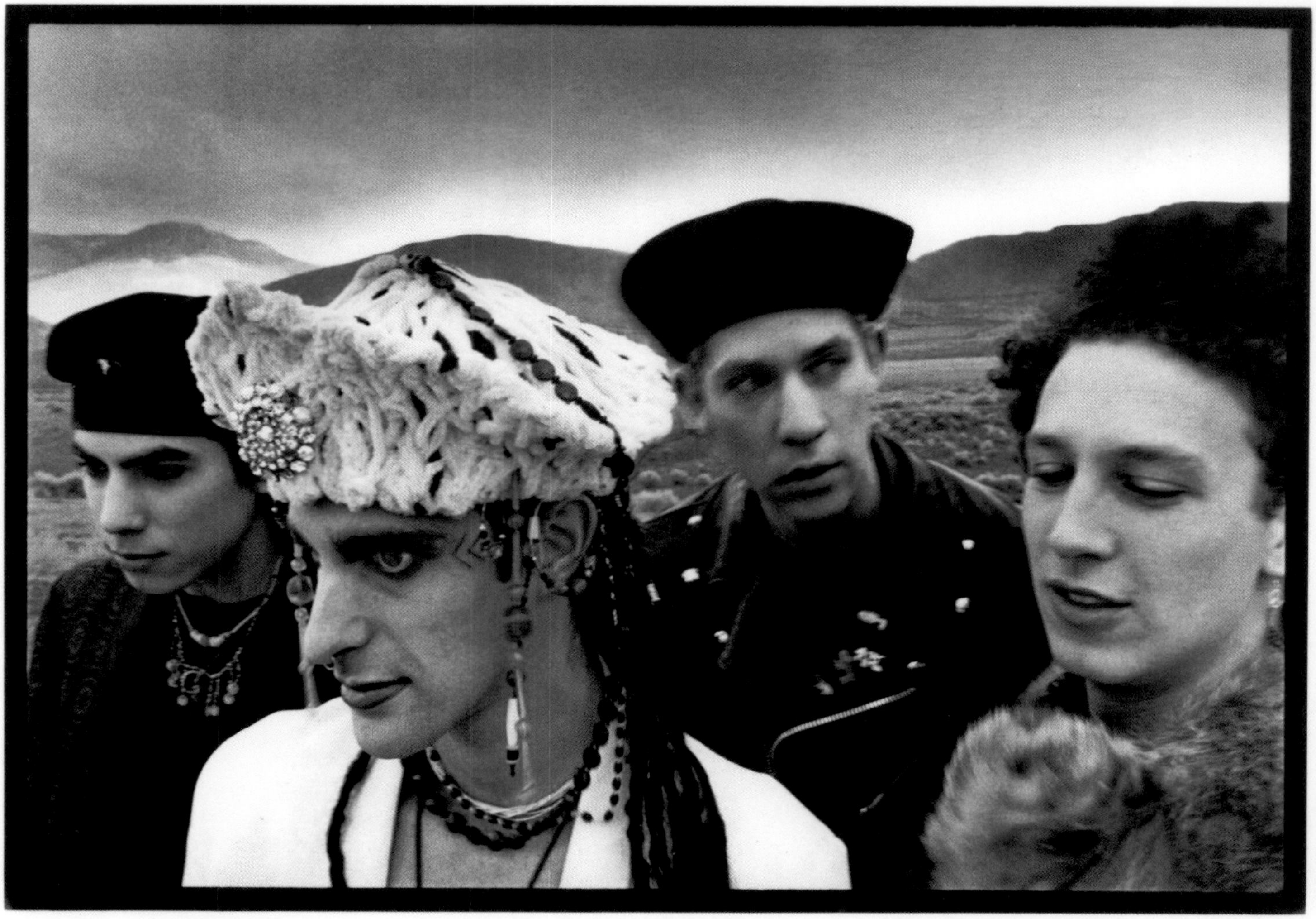

Photo Credit: Kevin Westenberg

DAVE NAVARRO PERRY FARRELL ERIC AVERY STEPHEN PERKINS

Jane's Addiction

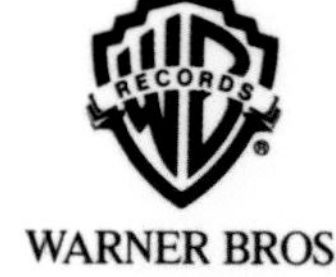

WARNER BROS.

Billboard 200: *Life's Too Good* (#54)

The Sugarcubes broke out of Iceland to startling international fame with the debut album *Life's Been Good*.

THE SUGARCUBES hailed from Iceland, a remote base for rock music. Yet several adventurous and arty singles—the signature hit "Birthday," "Coldsweat" and "Deus"—all topped the British independent charts, and the debut album *Life's Too Good* made major inroads at colleges and alternative outlets in America.

"People don't know that our country exists, so they've ignored it," singer and trumpeter Einar said. "We are little, but don't ignore us. Ignorance is our worst enemy."

Despite their cultural isolation, the five Sugarcubes had emerged with an intriguing repertoire. In the past, Iceland's music scene was patterned on a mishmash of American and British pop, rarely straying from the accepted international models.

"It's difficult to explain why we started," Einar mused. "Music is like a disease to us—it's something in us that we have to do. We've always been in bands, rehearsing and putting on concerts, just to have something to do. When we would sit around at home, we always got into trouble."

The Sugarcubes wound up fostering an eccentric sound that was mysteriously compelling, a reflection of the deeply rooted spiritual beliefs of their countrymen. High-energy post-punk textures merged with the band's main instrument—the incredible howling alto of petite femme fatale vocalist Björk.

"We've always said the musical development of people is not up to scratch," guitarist Thor said. "People always say, 'Why does she sing like that? Why do you have to play such weird music?' We say it's not weird—it's just a different version of pop. We're just playing the music we want to hear, and if it's valid, then we deserve to be heard on American radio."

The fresh, innovative sound of *Life's Too Good* won the band extensive media attention and generated excitement.

"But too many conclusions have been made about our music," Thor said. "It's not the overproduced American sound, it's not the street English sound, but we don't have a 'native Icelandic sound.' We have personal songs which are a little naïve."

"We just want to go out and play and have fun," Einar concluded. "We don't want to do badly in America, but if we do well it might become too much for us." ■

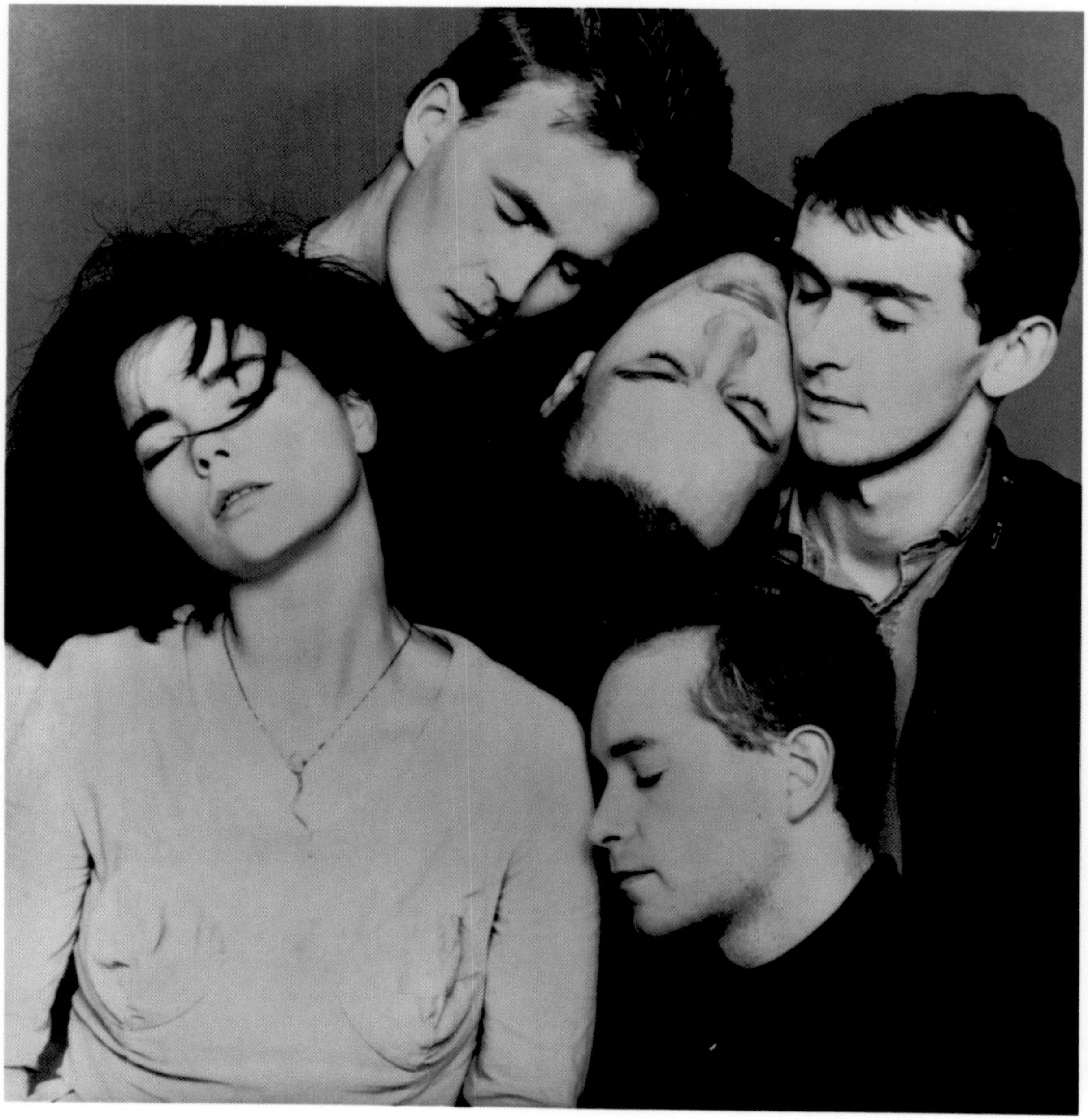

PHOTO CREDIT : PAUL COX

the sugarcubes

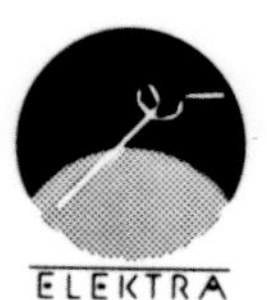

Billboard 200: *What Up, Dog?* (#43)
Billboard Hot 100: "Spy in the House of Love" (#16); "Walk the Dinosaur" (#7); "Anything Can Happen" (#75)

"Walk the Dinosaur" and "Spy in the House of Love" substantiated the imaginative funk of Was (Not Was).

SINCE DEBUTING in 1981, the slightly unhinged rock-funk music of Was (Not Was) had enjoyed critical rather than public acclaim. But the iconoclastic band finally reached the Great Un-Wased. The groove monster "Spy in the House of Love" topped the dance charts, and the *What Up, Dog?* album cracked the US Top 100 album chart.

Was (Not Was) operated under the beat-crazy baton of producer-writer-musicians Don Fagenson and David Weiss, a.k.a. Don and David Was. The Detroit natives presided over an ensemble made of the Motor City's best musicians.

"I've known David since we were 12," Fagenson said. "One recreational device was to sit with a tape recorder and write songs. We accumulated experience and now it's our business, but we never intended anything more than to make the next tape better than the last one."

Was (Not Was)' bizarro soul was first evidenced on the disco hits "Out Come the Freaks" and "Tell Me That I'm Dreaming" (which included mutilated vocals from Ronald Reagan himself). The clever tracks bridged the gap between white and Black music, a wild amalgam of dance, rock, pop and jazz rhythms. Fronted by veteran R&B vocalists Sweet Pea Atkinson and Sir Harry Bowens, Was (Not Was) offered a funny, offbeat commentary on American life.

"But the label felt we had a lead singer identity crisis," Fagenson explained. "David and I were two white guys, and they wanted us to be a rock band. But we have two Black vocalists—they aren't young cute kids with high voices, they're traditional soul singers. The label wanted us to replace them, but missed the point—we're a family."

It took nearly three years for Was (Not Was) to get free of the contract, at which point the group set sights on Europe. "We thought we would do better there even though we lived in America," Fagenson said. "Soul music is held in much higher esteem."

Instead of hiding behind off-the-wall concepts, Fagenson and Weiss focused on writing songs. *What Up, Dog?*, the first Was (Not Was) album in five years, yielded "Walk the Dinosaur" and "Spy in the House of Love," hits in Europe and the US. Yet the music had remained a backdrop for Weiss' peculiar lyrical perspective.

"Our subject matter goes deeper than what you usually hear over dance music," Fagenson noted. "David's lyrics are more likely to be coming out of a guy who sounds like Bob Dylan than Wilson Pickett. We've consciously placed them in an unconventional setting to showcase them that much more. The irony of mixing the two things is the fun of it—that's where it becomes homemade soup as opposed to Campbell's." ■

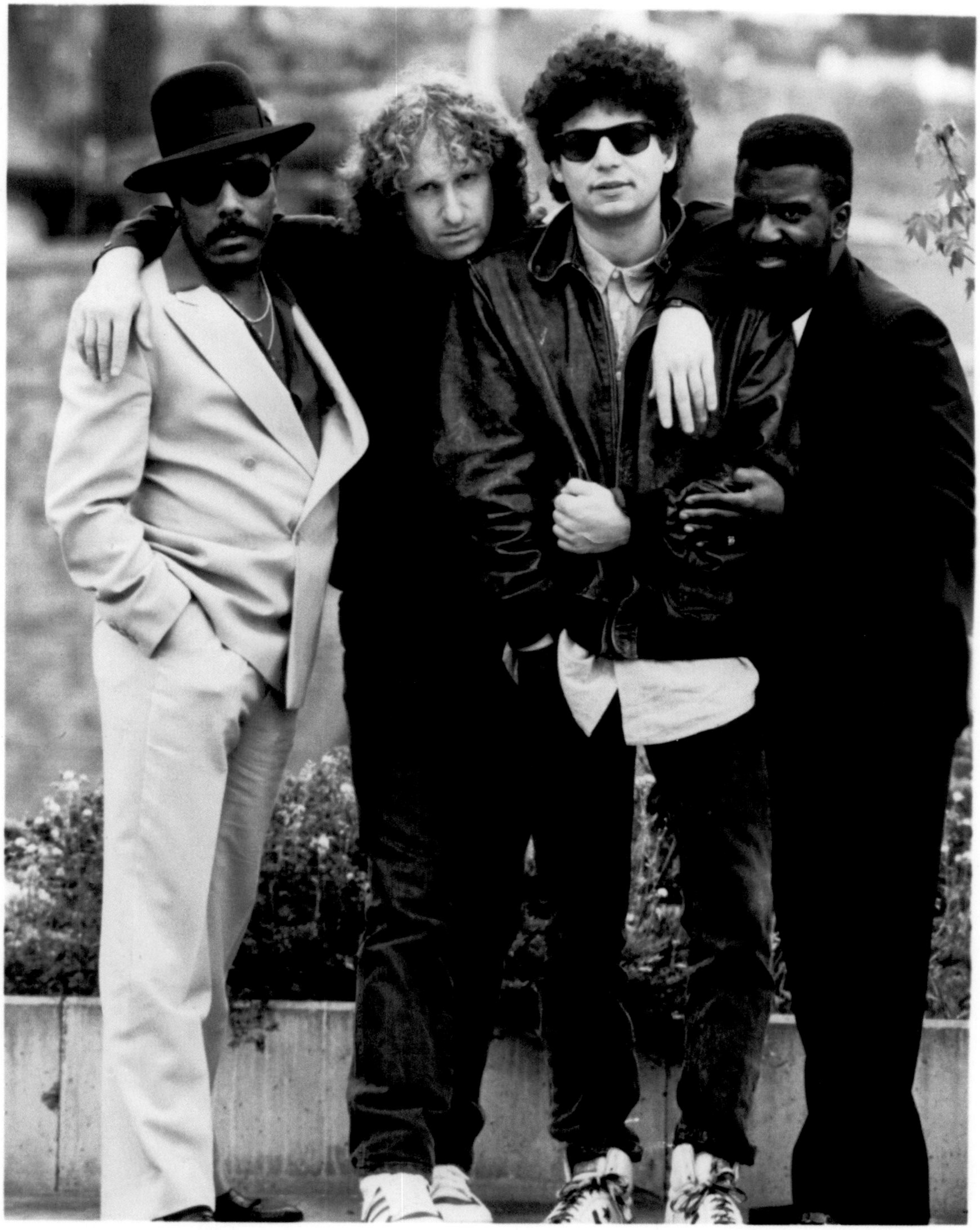

L to R: Sweet Pea Atkinson, David Was, Don Was, Sir Harry Bowens

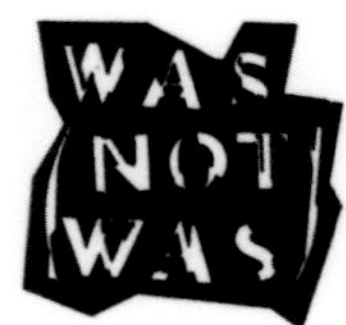

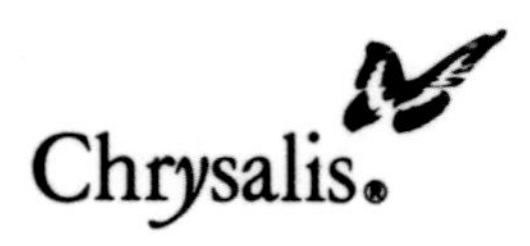

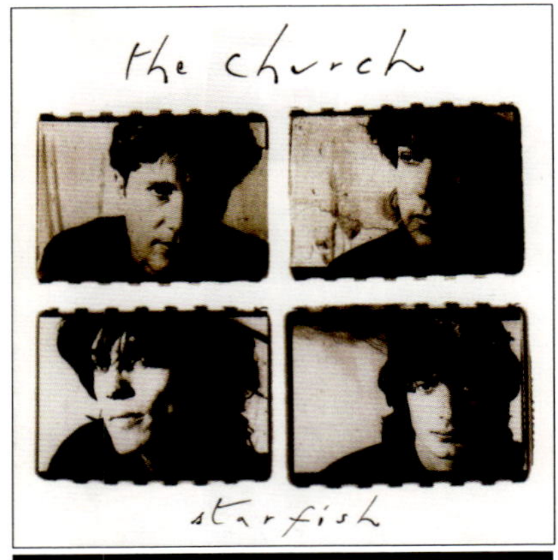

Billboard 200: *Starfish* (#41)
Billboard Hot 100: "Under the Milky Way" (#24)

The Church's illusory, atmospheric guitar-based rock broke through with the single "Under the Milky Way."

WITH THE shimmering hit single "Under the Milky Way" from the album *Starfish*, the Church turned the neat trick of peaking at #2 on the mainstream rock charts. The attention was deserved if somewhat belated. In 1981, the Church had released an exceptional single in "The Unguarded Moment," and the Australian band seemed primed for success. But *Blurred Crusade*, the group's superb second album, was never released in America.

"If I knew why that happened, I'd be a very happy man," guitarist Marty Willson-Piper said. "Back then, it was a mixture of things. We had an inexperienced manager, the band wasn't that good live yet, Australia hadn't taken off as a relevant musical center. But by the same token, the opposite of those elements is what has made *Starfish* successful."

The Church recorded *Starfish* in Los Angeles with producers Waddy Wachtel and Greg Ladanyi, both veterans of the Los Angeles studio scene. The band's brand of ethereal pop—largely based on Willson-Piper's hypnotic, jangly guitar arrangements and singer and bassist Steve Kilbey's cryptic, disaffected lyrics—found mass appeal without compromising its artistic vision. "I'm not scared of being commercially successful," Willson-Piper said. "People like U2 and Peter Gabriel have made great music that also got played on the radio."

Starfish, a Top 30 album, and "Under the Milky Way" re-established some international career momentum. Ironically, the band's status in Australia wasn't as lofty as the new stateside profile indicated.

"Australia's always had a funny relationship with us because we're not pure rock 'n' roll," WIllson-Piper said. "We did come up through the pub circuit, and that's why the Church is pretty powerful live, but we're an aesthetic, esoteric group. We just took our artistic inspiration and played to these suburban audiences of drunks. The hybrid of the two situations created what we are today."

Volatility among members was key to the Church's chemistry, and Willson-Piper alluded to the occasional band wars. "We're likely to scream at each other," he allowed. "But then we forget about it." ■

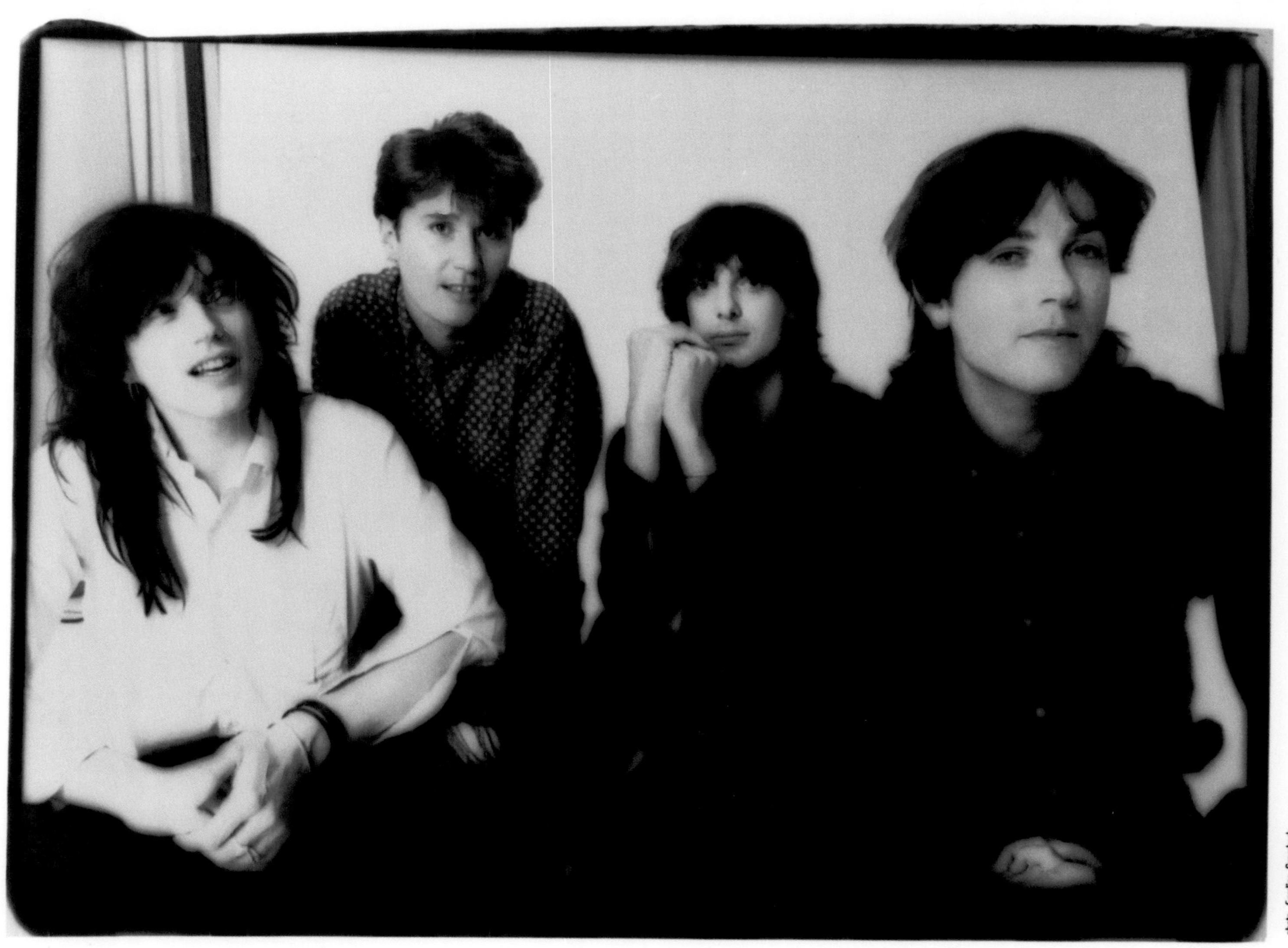

photo: Caroline Greyshock

ARISTA

the church

Mike's
ARTIST MANAGEMENT LTD
225 west 57th street/suite 301/new york ny 10019/(212)765-9610 telex: 497-0554

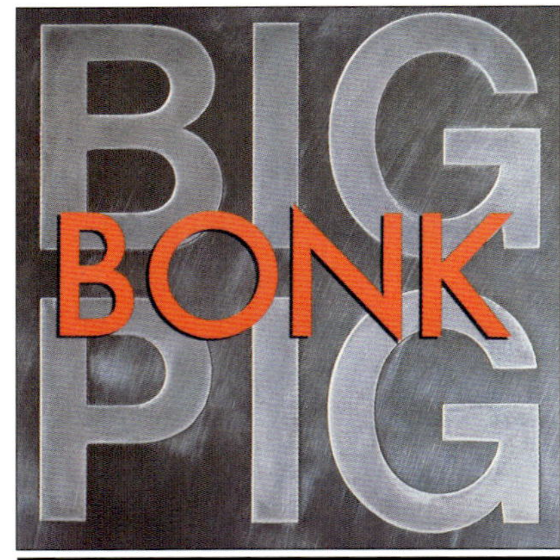

Billboard 200: *Bonk* (#93)
Billboard Hot 100: "Breakaway" (#60)

A quirky brand of tribal-pop was showcased to great effect on the track "Breakaway," Big Pig's finest hour.

FOLKS WITH an eye and ear out for rock music's next big thing noticed Australia's Big Pig. The septet's instrumentation: no guitars or bass, just three drummers, two percussionists, a harmonica and keyboards, with singer Sherine wailing over the top.

Oleh Witer formed the group in 1984 after tiring of the standard rock band format. After witnessing a performance by Kodō, the Japanese taiko drumming ensemble, he realized the traditional role of drums in pop bands was too confining.

He conceived "an amalgam of the a cappella gospel sound from the Thirties with a lot of energetic drumming and some funk for its rhythm and feels." Witer struggled initially with a Big Pig framework that included eight drummers.

"I first saw them in London, and they were a bit unwieldy," Sherine said. "The first lineup included people who were enthusiastic about the idea rather than specifically talented. So Oleh went back to Melbourne and re-formed the group."

Sherine joined at that point, along with a harmonica player and keyboardist for commercial considerations. Her aggressive, gospel style emerged as a cornerstone of the Big Pig sound.

"It's different to sing in such a rhythmic context," she said. "In the beginning, there was so little to bounce off melodically—it was just me carrying the lyrics. Now the sound has developed much more."

The debut album *Bonk* featured "Breakaway," a cover of R&B singer Chuck Jackson's song "I Can't Break Away." The eye-popping video was played on MTV, and the song was featured in an episode of the TV cop drama *Miami Vice* and in the opening sequence of the comedy film *Bill & Ted's Excellent Adventure*.

Big Pig's appearance was also noteworthy. Onstage, the members wore identical ankle-length black aprons to convey the blacksmith-like effort put into making the music (one reviewer laughingly called the uniforms suggestive of "an Albanian gymnastics team").

"When we play live, it's incredibly physical, really hard work," Sherine said. "The only way to pull it off is to be energetic, otherwise the whole performance falls flat." ■

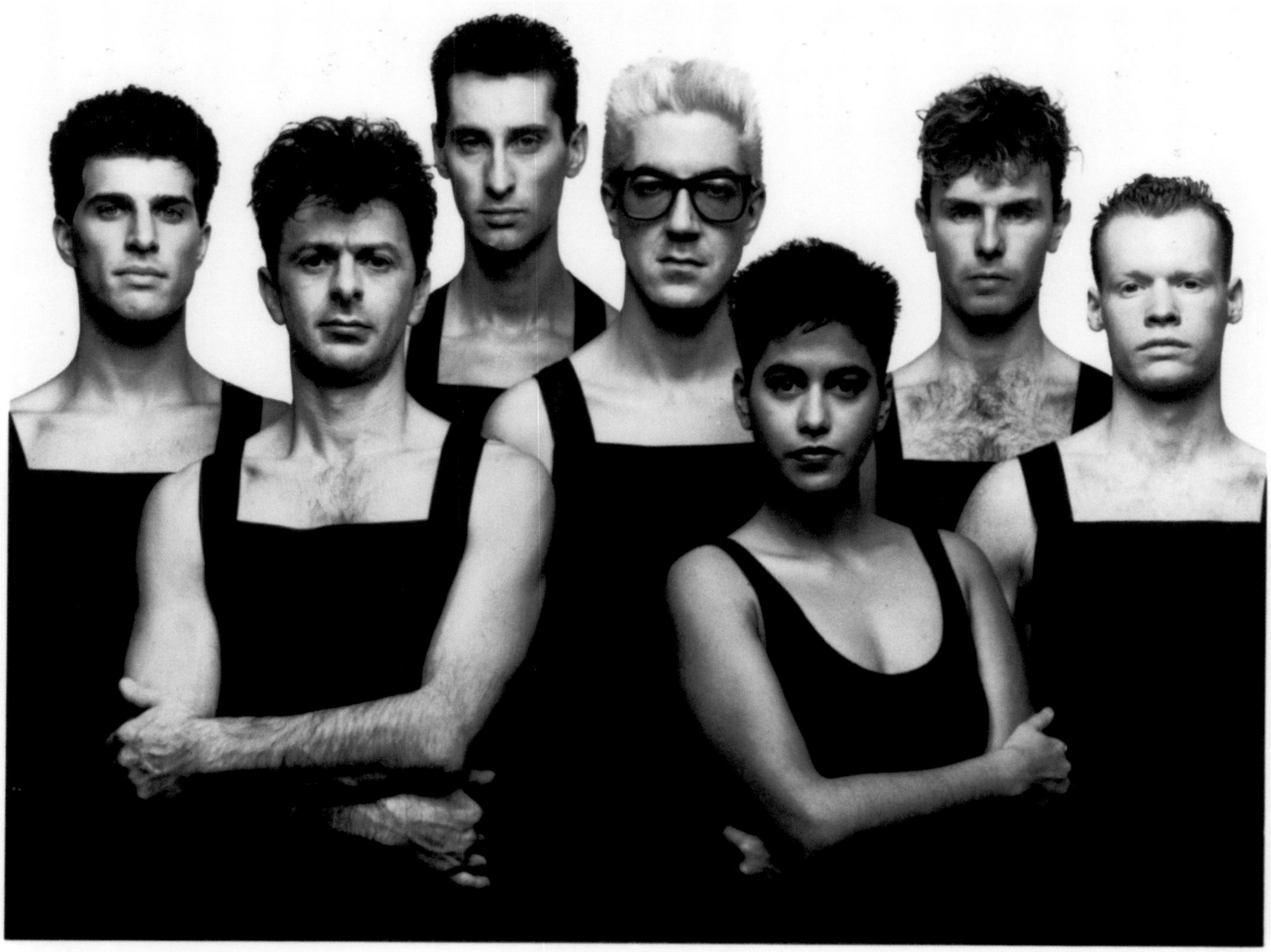

ADRIAN SCAGLIONE
TONY ANTONIADES
TIM ROSEWARNE
OLEH WITER
SHERINE
NEIL BAKER
NICK DISBRAY

BIG PIG

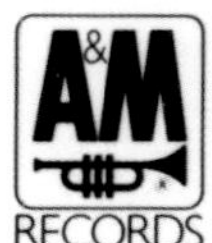

Under the Sun, Paul Kelly & the Messengers' second album, showed off the frontman's storytelling prowess.

HE STILL awaited his commercial breakthrough on American shores, but reviewers had lavished praise on Australian Paul Kelly's two albums, *Gossip* (1987) and *Under the Sun.* Kelly's talents were obvious—a crack band in his Messengers who capably worked in any number of styles, from blues to country to folk to hard rock, and an intelligent, sensitive songwriting streak that drew comparisons with such rock greats as Bob Dylan, Ray Davies, Elvis Costello and Lou Reed.

Kelly was philosophical about the notices. "It's inevitable," he said. "I'll just wait until they're comparing someone to me. In my career, things have happened gradually. I'm not going anywhere."

The albums were part of a much larger catalog in Australia. Kelly formed his first group in 1979, and he assembled the Messengers in 1984 after moving to Sydney to make a solo album. *Gossip* was released as a double LP in Australia; it was pared down to 15 songs to introduce Kelly in America. *Under the Sun* further revealed Kelly's songwriting strengths—"more songs on sex, death, memory, family and friends"—and the musical vocabulary of the Messengers. "Dumb Things" peaked at #16 on *Billboard's* Modern Rock chart and was included in the soundtrack for the Yahoo Serious film *Young Einstein.*

Kelly aimed to be the first artist out of a new echelon of Australian acts (i.e., ex-Saints member Ed Cooper, the folk-based Weddings Parties Anything) to establish a foothold in the US and make a mark on the concert scene.

"It's tough—I see myself as having two jobs," Kelly said. "The qualities required for songwriting and the qualities required for performance are opposite things. Performing people have a lot of confidence, but a lot of writing songs is doubting things, private. You do it by yourself with your own time. And the whole business of being in a band is meeting a lot of people and having the nerve to sing in front of crowds, being public. I've always felt very schizophrenic, because it's never been natural to get up in front of people. But with the songs doing well, I'm relaxing a little bit." ■

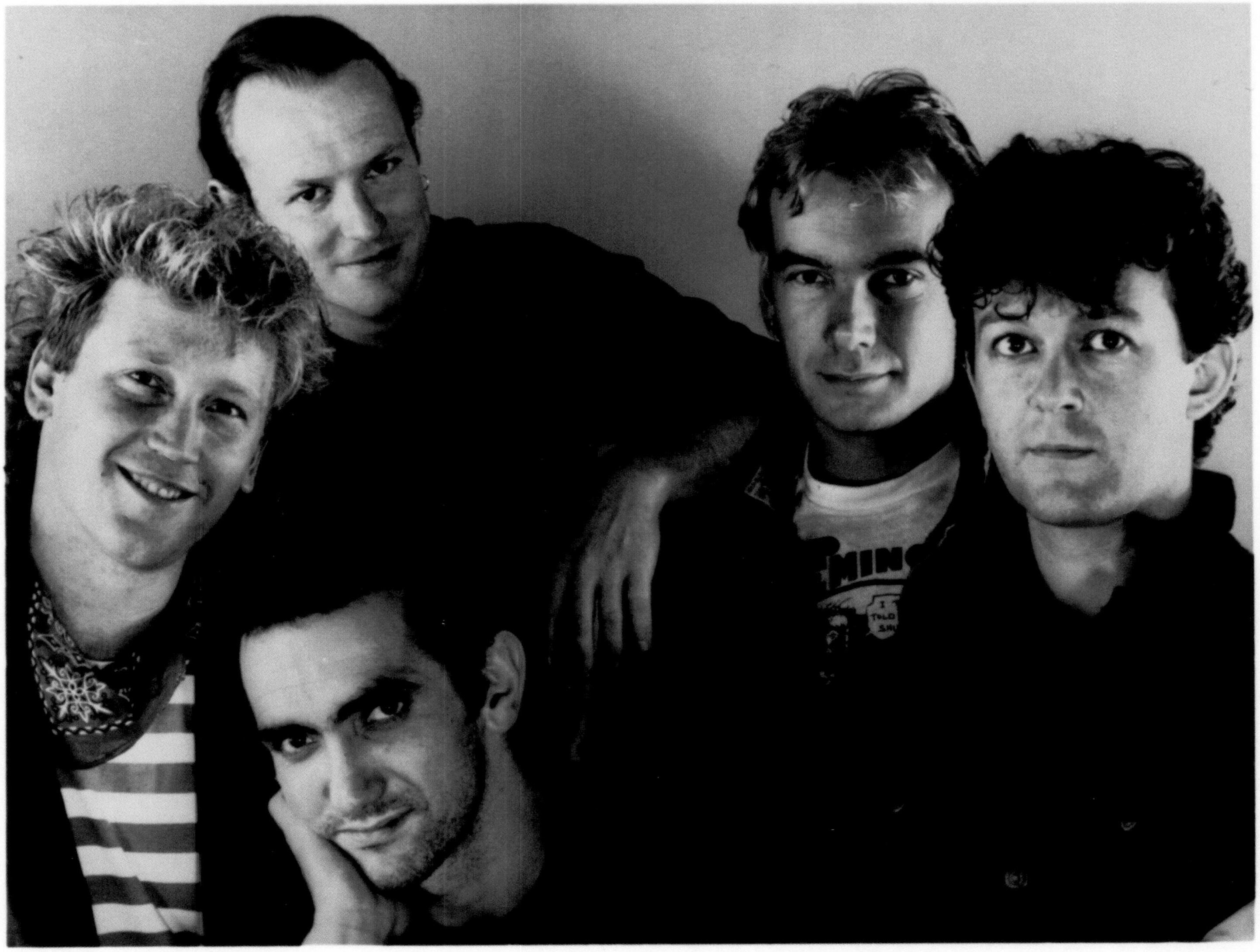

PETER BULL

MICHAEL BARCLAY

PAUL KELLY

JON SCHORFIELD

STEVE CONNELLY

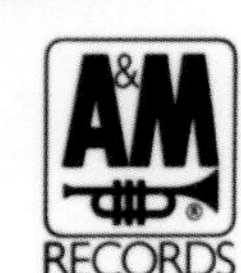

PAUL KELLY AND THE MESSENGERS

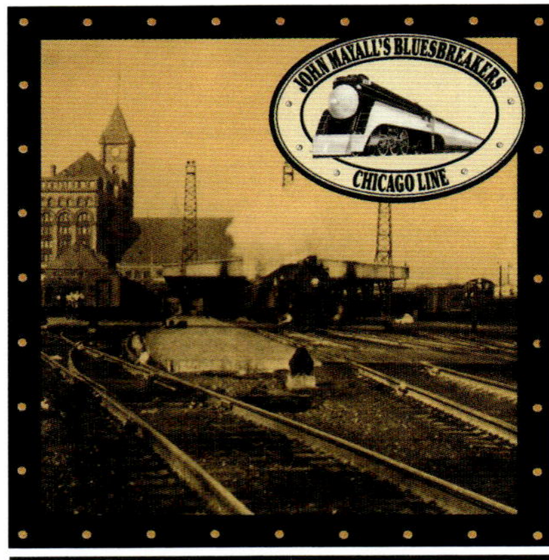

Restoring the name Bluesbreakers for his band enhanced interest in John Mayall's *Chicago Line* recording.

HE EARNED the title nearly two decades earlier, but John Mayall remained "the grandfather of the British blues scene." His career had spanned 25 years and more than 30 albums—"So far back, I'm surprised anyone bothers to count," the musician laughed.

Yet Mayall seemed destined to be remembered more for the people he groomed for stardom than for his own contributions to the development of rock music. In the mid-Sixties, his successive bands of Bluesbreakers virtually served as a finishing school for many of Britain's leading instrumentalists. The original lineup, considered the first important British blues band, featured Eric Clapton on guitar. Peter Green, John McVie and Mick Fleetwood (later of Fleetwood Mac), Jack Bruce (of Cream), Mick Taylor (who replaced Brian Jones in the Rolling Stones) and Andy Fraser (Free) were a few of the future stars who graduated from the Bluesbreakers.

But Mayall harbored no regrets that many of his alumni became better known than he did. "I've never looked at my bands in the same way other people have. I'm not training musicians out there like a coach who trains athletes to go out for the Olympics. I put bands together for the enjoyment of all of us."

Mayall moved to America in 1969 and during the Seventies worked increasingly in a jazz-blues style. He assembled a refurbished Bluesbreakers lineup in 1984. On the *Chicago Line* album, two hot and hungry soloists—guitarists Coco Montoya and Walter Trout—provided the creative energy. The band averaged more than 100 shows a year. "This is the longest any lineup of the Bluesbreakers has been together—seasoned blues players becoming more seasoned by the minute," Mayall enthused.

While blues was "on the map," Mayall recalled Sixties Britain, when the music was just gaining a foothold, as young bands such as the Rolling Stones covered material by American blues greats Muddy Waters and Jimmy Reed.

"Pop wasn't played in the clubs—traditional jazz had ruled there for almost ten years," Mayall said. "But there were a few elements of blues, small quartets, within some of the trad jazz bands. And the blues grew out of that and replaced the trad jazz scene."

Mayall's name soon became synonymous with classy British blues, even though the singer, keyboardist and harmonica player was 30 years old before he put his first band together. "It's not where you come from that's important, it's what you hear in your head and what you put out through your instrument," he said. Indeed, for a time Mayall battled a reputation as a frugal eccentric, as he had once lived in a tree house. "But the motivation was the opposite of being a recluse," he explained. "I lived in a crowded house with a large family, and I wanted my own room, so I built it up a tree. Of course, I used the house for the main facilities. I've never been like Jesus lost in the wilderness, but if anyone want to think that's eccentric, fine." ■

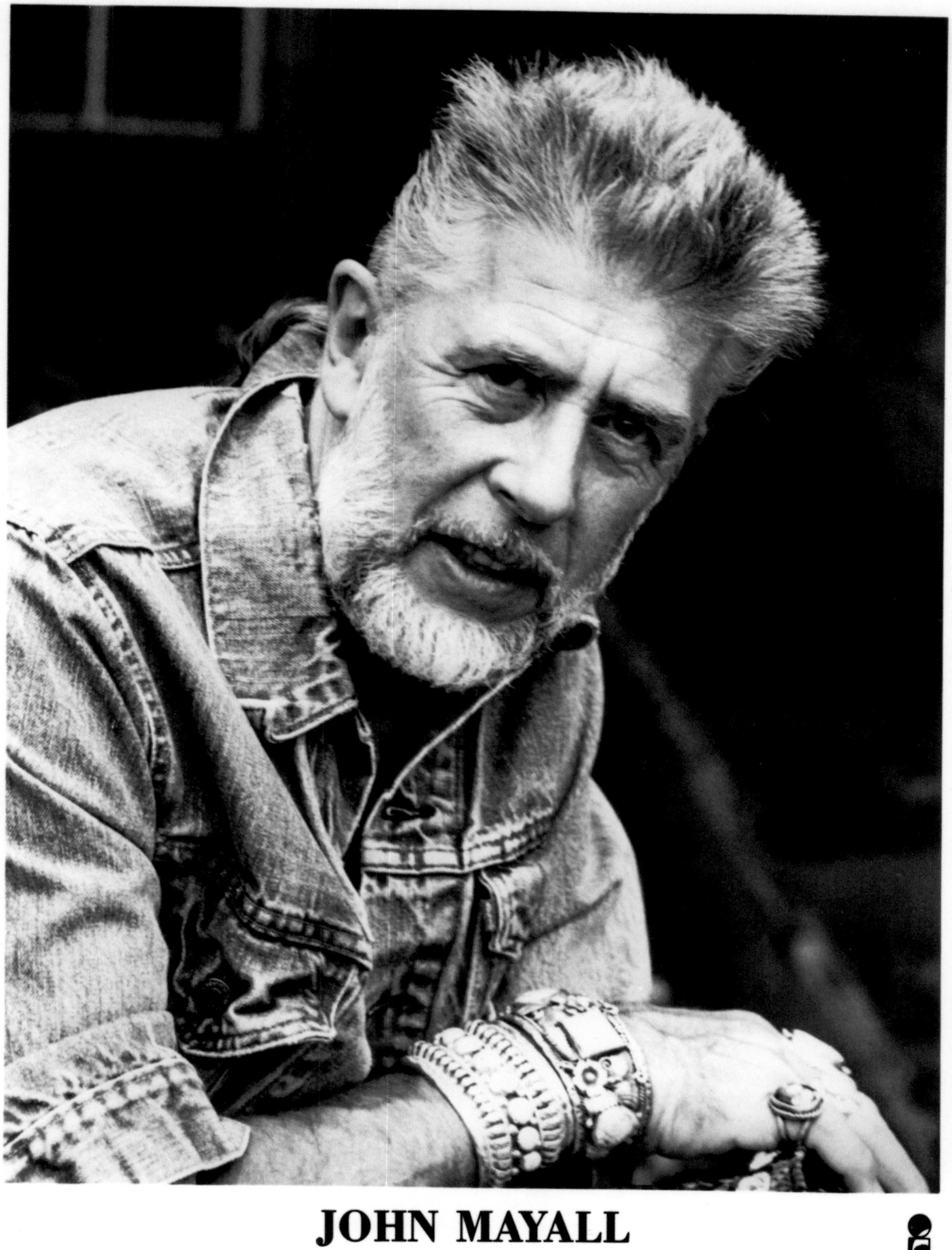

Photo Credit: Gary Nichamin

JOHN MAYALL

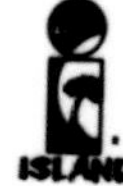

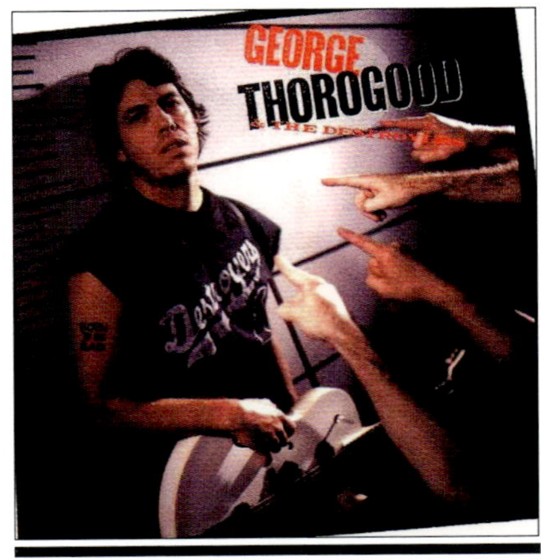

Billboard 200: *Born to Be Bad* (#32)

Born to Be Bad distinguished George Thorogood & the Destroyers at their hard-charging, house-rocking best.

THE TITLE track from *Born to Be Bad,* a mock-boasting number, allowed George Thorogood to step out and swagger, sticking to his recipe of high-energy, blues-based rock with a dash of earthy humor.

"But when I put the song together a long time ago, it had different lyrics—the original title was 'Born in the USA,'" he said. "It was all ready to go, but I had to wait out this guy from New Jersey. And it's worked out better. 'Born to Be Bad' is closer to what people think of me. It's the difference between *Rocky* and *Raging Bull.* One is American-hero-makes-good, the other is an obnoxious pain in the ass."

After nearly 15 years of one-night stands, Thorogood's first love remained performing live, but the hard-working bluesman's enthusiasm had been buoyed by the response to *Born to Be Bad.* The album captured Thorogood and his Destroyers' upbeat mix of blues, R&B and classic rock 'n' roll, balancing straightforward versions of classics (Elmore James' "Shake Your Moneymaker") with original material ("You Talk Too Much," a tongue-in-cheek jab at a domineering female played for laughs in the Ralph Kramden tradition).

"It's the sound I've been shooting for ever since I got started," he insisted. "People say that rock 'n' roll is supposed to change, that you're supposed to be innovative. The musicians that started with the blues in the Sixties became the rock legends of today, so everybody is expected to create accordingly.

"I say, why? Why tamper with something that's working for me? Yes, we might throw in a country song or an acoustic piece, but in general our style was developed years ago. It's like we built a Chevy in 1975, and we're still driving that same car, but now we've got it honed down exactly the way we want it."

Thorogood had earned a faithful following without catering to Top 40 radio or studio trickery, pursuing his three-chord rock and slow tough-guy blues. So while he had moved up from bars to arenas, the singer and guitarist planned on sticking to the basics.

"We worked hard to get where we are, and I just want to sustain it, not expand on it," he reasoned. "I just want to get everybody worked up with a great rock 'n' roll tune—anything beyond that is beyond me." ■

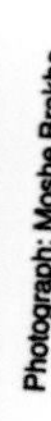

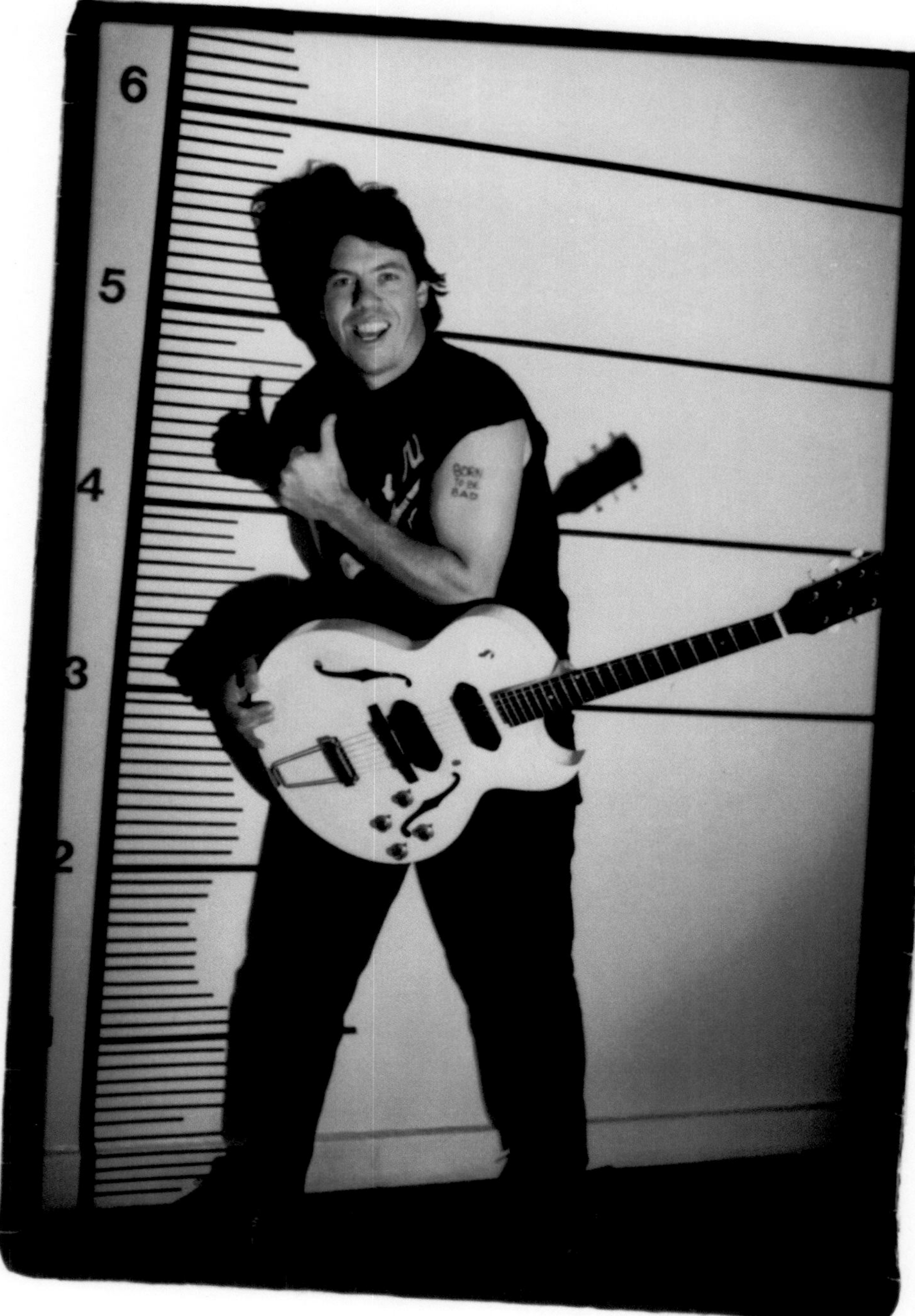

GEORGE THOROGOOD

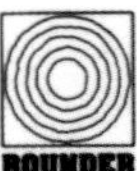

EMI MANHATTAN®

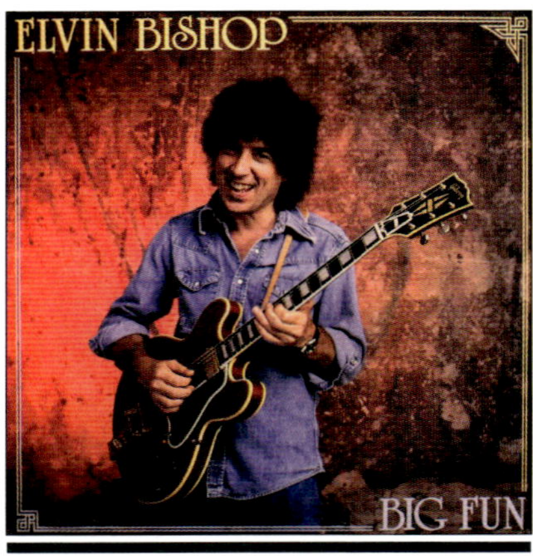

Guitarist Elvin Bishop was back with *Big Fun*, a means to express his good-time brand of blues and roots music.

HOOKED ON the blues as a teenager, Elvin Bishop chose the University of Chicago, with a campus tucked in the middle of the South Side ghetto, because it was close to the music he loved.

"The first thing I did when I got there was make friends with the guys working in the cafeteria," he recalled. "Within 15 minutes, I was into the blues scene."

As a member of the original Paul Butterfield Blues Band, Elvin Bishop was considered one of the best young guitarists of the late Sixties, bringing authentic Chicago blues to a rock and folk audience—as the band developed, he and Mike Bloomfield pioneered the extended twin-guitar jamming that became a force in rock music. He left the Butterfield band for a solo career and emphasized a country boy persona as "Pigboy Crabshaw," complete with straw hat and overalls.

Bishop eventually hit the jackpot in 1976 with "Fooled Around and Fell in Love," a "change of pace" tune with vocals supplied by pre-Jefferson Starship vocalist Mickey Thomas.

"I had this 'cute' series of licks and decided to put words to them, but this was in 1971," he said. "I wasn't until four years later that we had a spot on an album for one more song, so I flashed back on 'Fooled Around.'"

Bishop appreciated the "good money" he made as the writer and publisher of the #3 pop hit, but that smash turned his band's focus away from his blues-oriented guitar playing and redirected it toward a more commercial sound.

"And then the folding of Capricorn Records in 1979 put me out of a contract," Bishop said. "I was just in the frame of mind where I didn't care whether I made any records or not."

Bishop laid low for nearly a decade. He forsook the pleasure of alcohol and stimulants and started a family in California. He spent a lot of time in his garden and at the fishing hole, and he also gigged regularly on the West Coast.

He then signed with Chicago-based Alligator Records, Bruce Iglauer's independent blues label. *Big Fun* found Bishop putting his personal stamp on songs, particularly a slide instrumental version of Jimmy Reed's "Honest I Do."

"It's just what I wanted out of each track,' Bishop said. "I made no compromises. You know, a lot of people—not my fans—think that I can just play the 'rough and rowdy' music. And of course I can! But that's not all I can play." ■

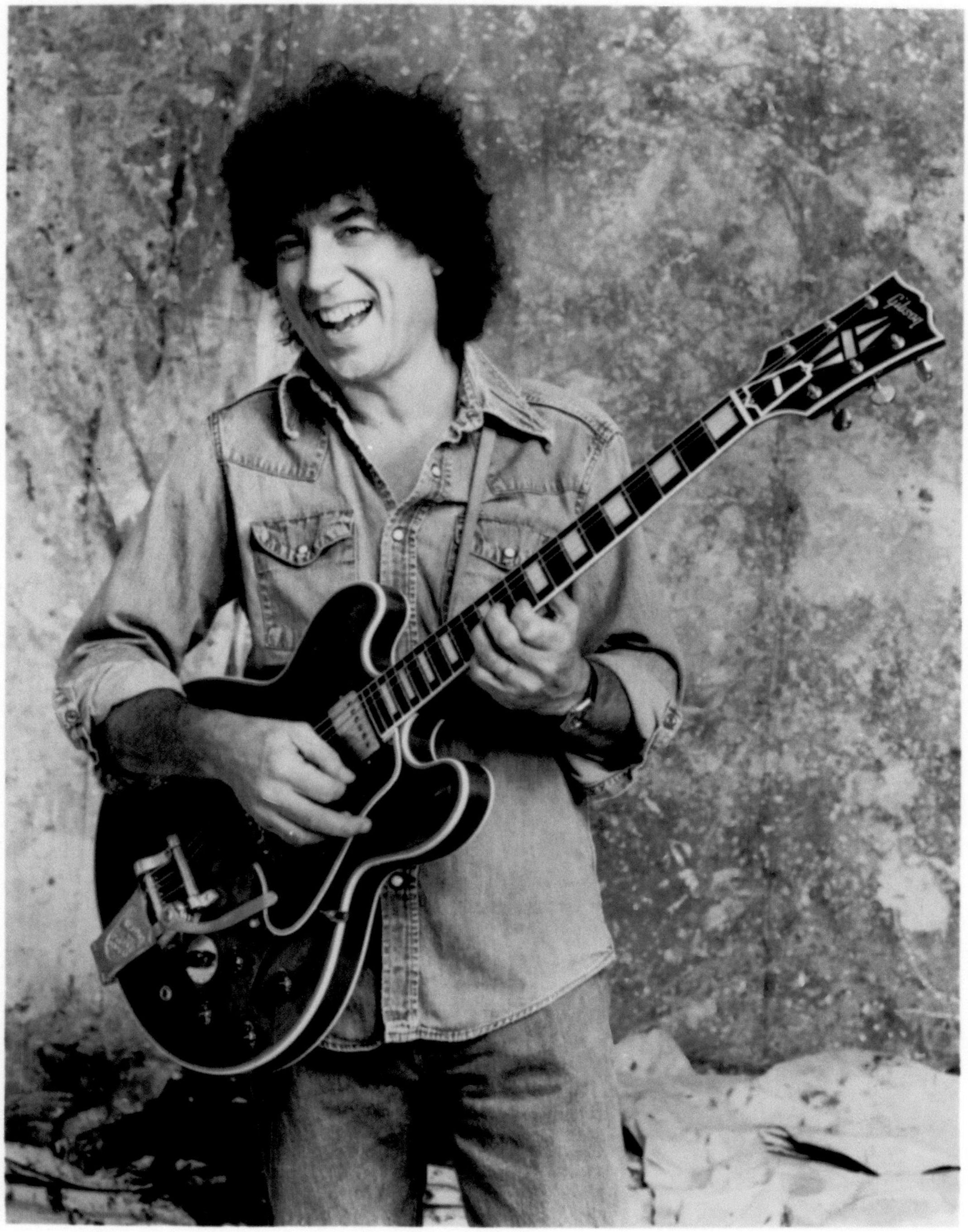

PAT JOHNSON

ELVIN BISHOP

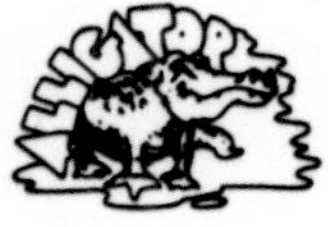

ALLIGATOR RECORDS
Box 60234
Chicago, IL 60660
(312) 973-7736

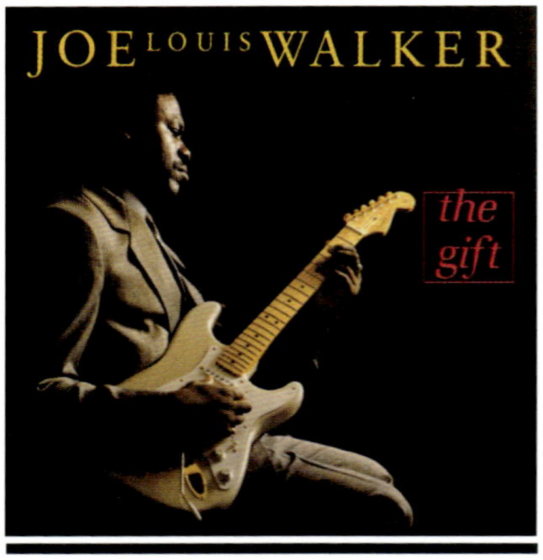

Joe Louis Walker's burst of talent moved the guitarist to the verge of stardom in the competitive blues scene.

AS HE sang of himself in "My Main Goal," Joe Louis Walker had "come a long way in a short amount of time." Certainly the bluesman had attained recognition at a rapid pace that belied his 25 years of performing. Just three years earlier, Walker was a sideman in a gospel group. On the basis of his *Cold Is the Night* and *The Gift* albums, the 37-year-old guitarist had emerged as the most promising talent on the contemporary blues scene since Robert Cray.

Walker got sidetracked by gospel music by accident. "I used to be sowing my wild oats, hanging out and partying all the time," he said. "But in 1975 I went through some heavy changes at a time when a gospel group was after me to play. I showed up at rehearsal and started playing guitar. What started as two weeks wound up being 10 years."

In 1985, Walker attended the New Orleans Jazz & Heritage Festival and was inspired by the variety of acts on hand. "I heard a lot of music, and I saw my potential to play. So when I came back home to northern California, I put a little group together, and one thing led to another."

In his tightly crafted songs, smooth vocals and uncluttered guitar work, Walker blended time-honored blues paradigms with reworkings of Memphis-style soul in the Stax/Volt tradition of his idol, Otis Redding.

"That whole era was genuine American music—Black gospel and white country without any other influences," he said. "Music nowadays is good, but it's more thought-out. The music back then was more of a feeling, played by people with instruments instead of sounds and effects."

A heavy touring schedule abroad had established Walker as the toast of the international blues circuit, and he'd received advice from a previous generation of blues greats.

"B.B. King, Albert Collins—they just tell me to play what I play and find my own identity. I mean, I'm not going to play it any better than Muddy Waters played it."

Walker was already cautious regarding notices heralding him as "ready to cross over to the rock world" as did his labelmate Cray.

"Robert went through the same thing," Walker said. "But he went in and played the same type of music he always played. The million people who then bought his album came to his sound, not the other way around. If I get the same chance, I won't be crossing some imaginary line with new music. I guarantee I'll be doing the same thing I am now." ■

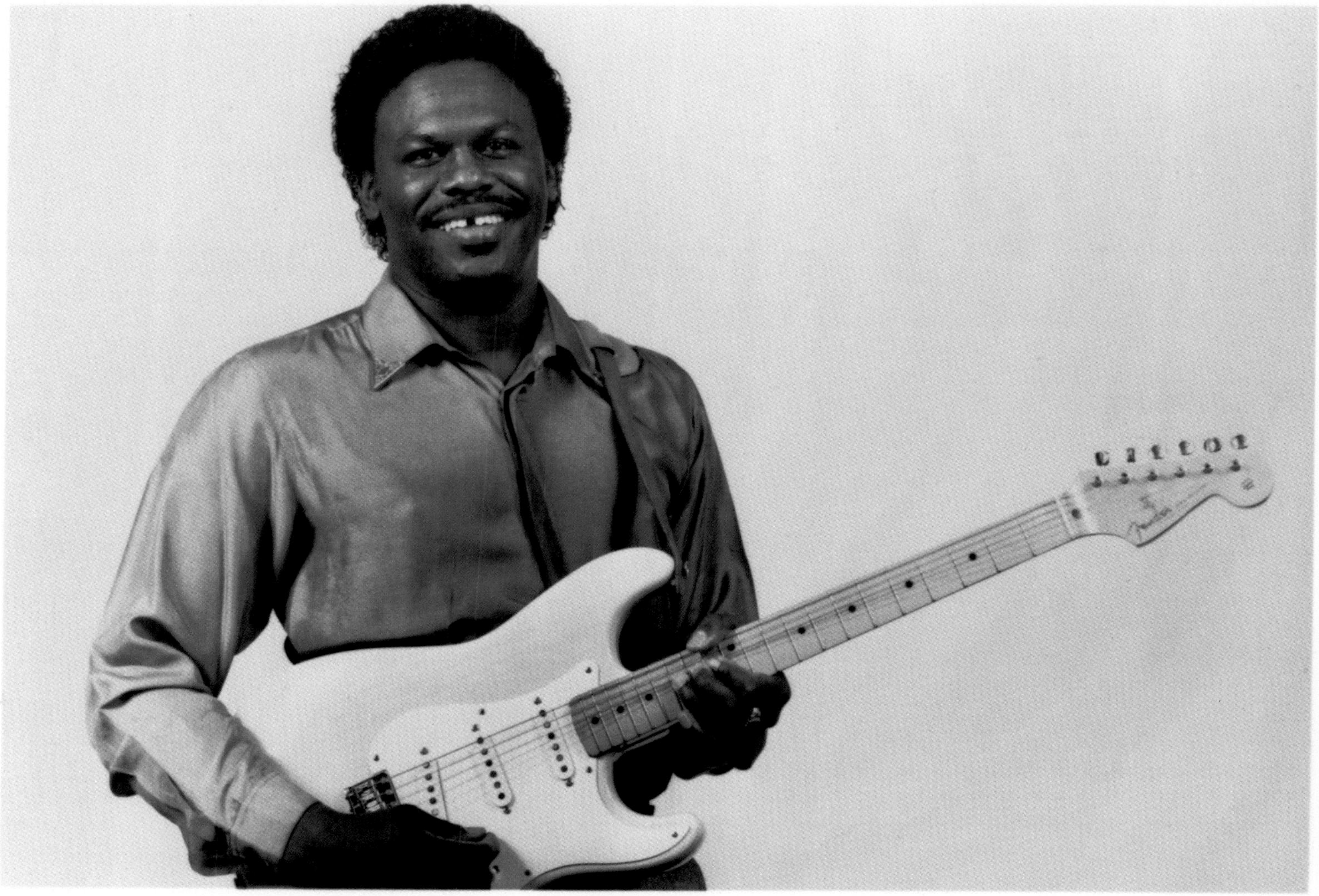

Photo by: JOHN DE LEON

Joe Louis Walker

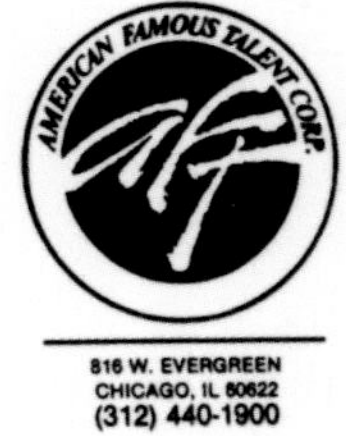

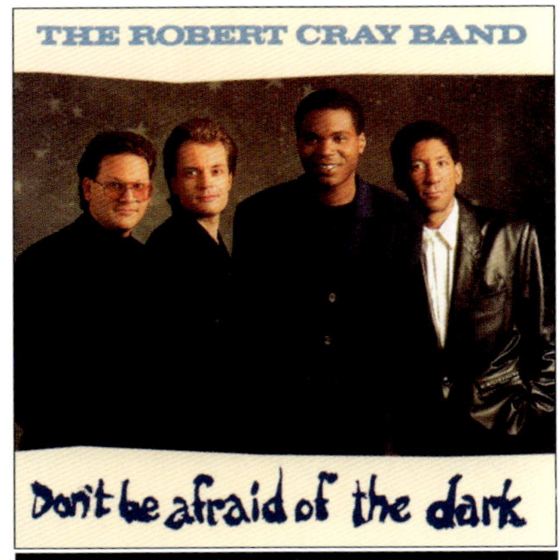

Billboard 200: *Don't Be Afraid of the Dark* (#32)
Billboard Hot 100: "Don't Be Afraid of the Dark" (#74)

The Robert Cray Band's *Don't Be Afraid of the Dark* album didn't vary stylistically from its platinum precursor.

WHEN BLUESMAN Robert Cray broke through the mainstream with the hit "Smoking Gun" and scored a Grammy for his sizzling 1986 album *Strong Persuader*—which followed over a dozen years of playing on the road—he found himself being hailed as the B.B. King of the Eighties, acclaimed for reviving a moss-backed genre. Cray had "the whole package," as Eric Clapton put it—good looks, smooth vocals and a biting guitar style.

Yet some blues purists balked at the universal appeal Cray had found with a new generation. They noted that blues music had a basic integrity, a power that represented the triumph of the human spirit over personal defeat. And they questioned whether Cray's hit-bound work was his "life expression" or simply a commercial vehicle.

But Cray had always been open-minded musically, so his brand of blues reflected a bit more soul, funk—and, yes, pop—than traditional blues did. And he didn't apologize for the taste of his material or the resulting dividends.

"I'm not a walking encyclopedia of the blues," Cray admitted. "But when I talk with other blues musicians, their input is always positive. My situation has helped out the blues in general and their careers as well. I don't think about the success thing. We just come up with some new things, rehearse, record, and hope people like them. It's that simple."

The Robert Cray Band was still composed of players who had known him for a decade or more—Richard Cousins (bass), David Olson (drums) and Peter Boe (keyboards)—and he was still produced by his perennial collaborators, Bruce Bromberg and Dennis Walker.

"There's not pressure commercially—we're doing what we want to do," Cray said. "I consider it a luxury to have a team that's stayed together for so long.

Don't Be Afraid of the Dark contained the usual complement of up-tempo boogie numbers ("Acting This Way"), but it was when Cray sang about "lyin' and cheatin'" that he was at his most bluesy. The steamy title track, punctuated by the Memphis Horns, was marked by his sincere delivery of sexy lines—"Put on some music, Marvin Gaye's real nice." It continued his penchant for real-life lyrics that adults could relate to. "I like singing songs like that," he enthused. "A lot of stuff goes on that people don't talk about."

Lest anyone thought carnal attractions and desires were the extent of Cray's inspiration, "Night Patrol" served as a stunning example of topical, contemporary blues

"You travel around, you get to witness what the homeless go through in this country," he mused. "We've been seeing it on the streets for a long time, watching people with no place to go. The Cray Band's music is about real feelings and real situations, and the songs say that for us. Now we're just seeing them get to more people." ■

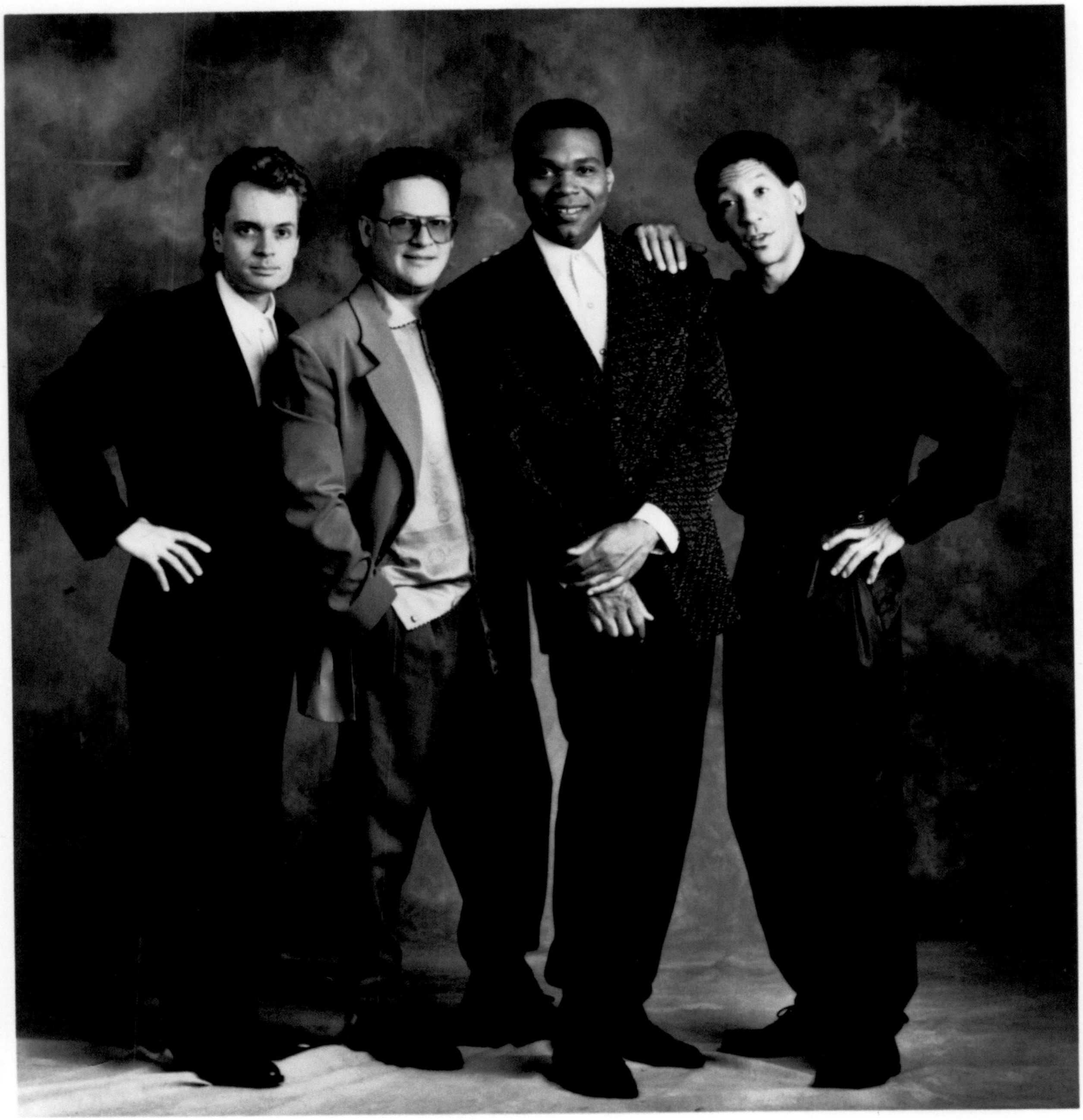

PETER BOE DAVID OLSON ROBERT CRAY RICHARD COUSINS

ROBERT CRAY

Mercury

PolyGram Records

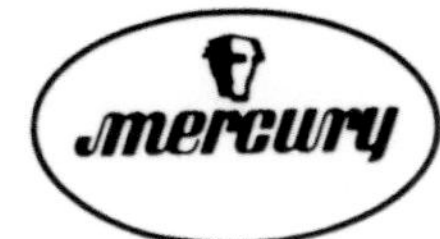

Billboard 200: *See the Light* (#22)
Billboard Hot 100: "Angel Eyes" (#5)

The Jeff Healey Band leaped out of the Toronto bar circuit and into the forefront of the musical landscape.

CANADIAN MUSICIAN Jeff Healey's story read like a Hollywood script. Born with eye cancer, he lost his sight at age 1. When he got a guitar—a toy one at 3, a real one at 11—he taught himself an unorthodox method. No guitar great had ever played like Healey, hunched over with his black Stratocaster on his lap. In particular, his left-handed work set him apart—with all of his fingers spidering up and down the fretboard, he got different types of vibrato; with his thumb bending on the treble strings, he hit notes above and beyond where guitarists could normally reach.

One night in 1985, Healey wound up on a stage with Albert Collins, and his prowess was soon proclaimed in reverential tones around professional circles—Stevie Ray Vaughan circulated a quote, "Man, he is going to revolutionize the way the guitar can be played." Critics, fans and peers were all uncharacteristically enthusiastic about Healey's power trio (featuring bassist Joe Rockman and drummer Tom Stephen).

"I don't think I'm necessarily playing anything I haven't heard before," Healey said. "It's just a matter of imagination."

See the Light, Healey's highly acclaimed debut album, sold nearly two million copies worldwide. The country-tinged smash hit "Angel Eyes" went Top 5 on the pop charts, "Confidence Man" became a Top 10 album rock hit (both were John Hiatt songs) and "Hideaway" received a Grammy nomination for Best Rock Instrumental Performance. The tonal fireworks, the blistering dexterity, plus his sweet, bluesy voice and blond, blue-eyed looks (which weren't covered by dark glasses)—Healey seemed destined for a long creative run, but he didn't believe the hype.

"I've tried playing guitar the normal way, but I can't play a lead that way for anything," he countered. "I'm not trying to break new ground—I'm just trying to be comfortable."

While the band was recording *See the Light*, the members were also filming the Patrick Swayze movie *Road House*. And Healey, who essentially played himself, gave people a good reason to see the flick.

"The script called for the house blues band (at the bar where Swayze's bouncer character worked) to have a blind guitarist who plays on his lap," Healey explained. "I found out later that the guy who wrote the screenplay was from my hometown, Toronto. He had based it on us." ■

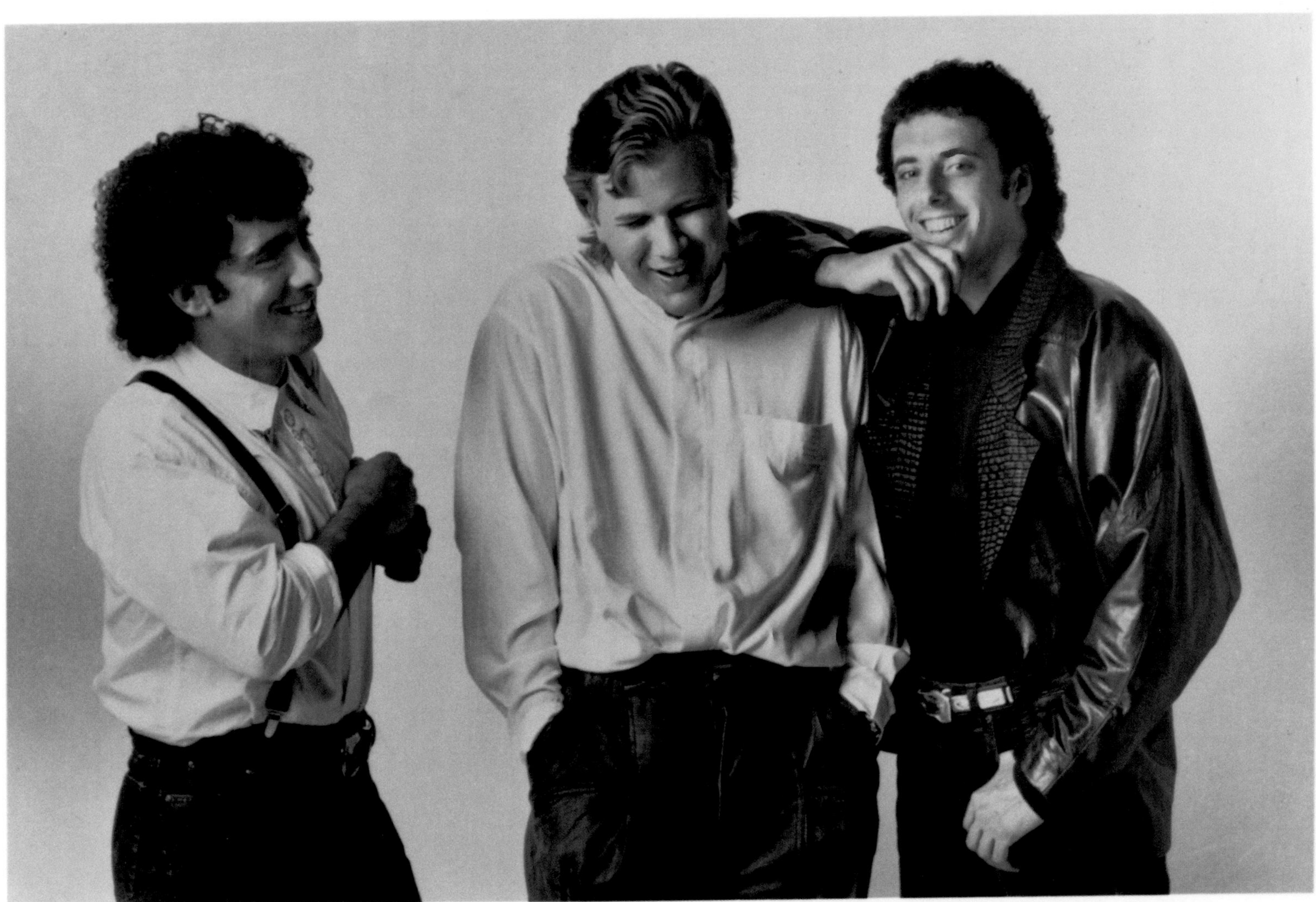

Management:
Forte Records & Productions
326½ Howland
Toronto, Ontario
Canada M5 R3 B9

THE JEFF HEALEY BAND

ARISTA™

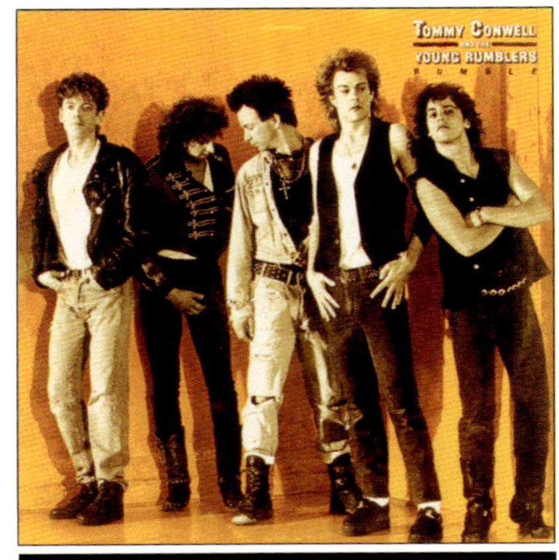

Billboard 200: *Rumble* (#103)
Billboard Hot 100: "I'm Not Your Man" (#74); "If We Never Meet Again" (#48)

The chipper "I'm Not Your Man" emerged as a radio and video hit for Tommy Conwell & the Young Rumblers.

SEEMINGLY COMING out of nowhere to seize the musical moment, Tommy Conwell & the Young Rumblers' debut single was a No.1 mainstream rock hit, holding off such big-name competition as U2, Steve Winwood and Bon Jovi. "I'm Not Your Man" was based on fundamental values—some hot guitar work, an infectious hook and Conwell's raspy voice. The band's simplicity of presentation came from early rock 'n' roll and the blues.

"Blues is the roots, the rest is the fruits," Conwell grinned. "Robert Cray has been successful with cool, smooth blues, and Stevie Ray Vaughan has gotten across Hendrix-style blues. I'm trying to get in more of a raw blues thing like Hound Dog Taylor—I like that street-corner shouting that's at the beginning of 'I'm Not Your Man.' And what a kick, when the music that you're into makes it."

Conwell and the Young Rumblers were Philadelphia's pride, having achieved a degree of stardom in the trenches of the mid-Atlantic bar band circuit since forming in 1984. An independently released album titled *Walkin' on the Water* sold 70,000 copies and attracted attention from major labels. Conwell and his band were primed for national prominence on the strength of their debut album *Rumble*, produced by Rick Chertoff (whose credits included Cyndi Lauper and the Hooters).

The joyous, self-deprecating "I'm Not Your Man" packed a certain wallop and conviction that set Conwell above the general cluster of new acts, although comparisons to Bruce Springsteen and George Thorogood abounded. The follow-up single was a soulful interpretation of Jules Shear's "If We Never Meet Again."

In concert, Conwell bashed away on a guitar that got as much ink as his music—a 1969 Guild X500 with signatures carved into it, autographs he started collecting when his act began opening for big names.

"But it's the way I play that's important—a lot of our sound is based on it," Conwell said. "We're a hard-working band—we're rowdy, we sweat, we do some redneck rock 'n' roll. And we usually get you by the end, no doubt." ■

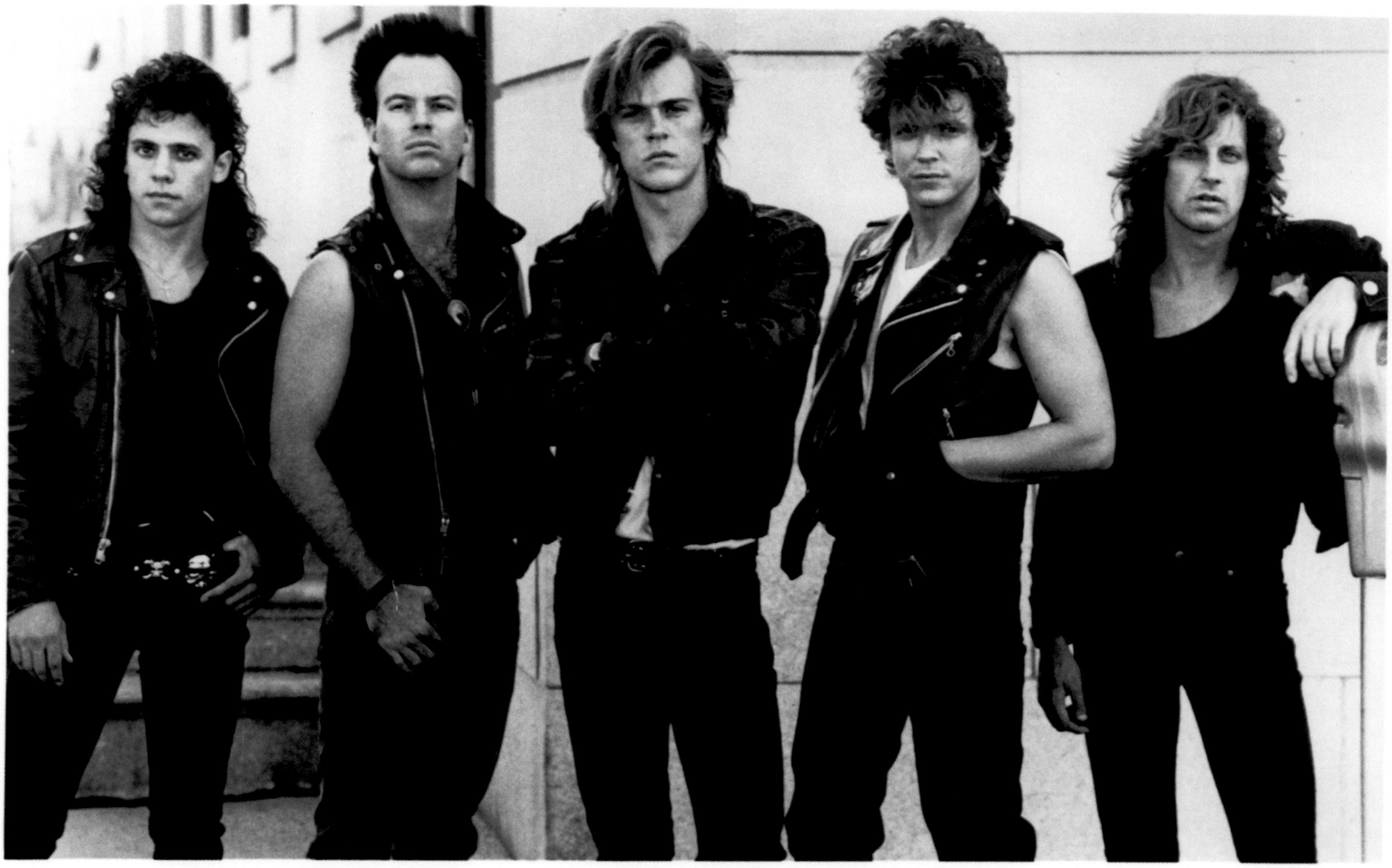

From left. CHRISTOPHER DAY, PAUL SLIVKA, TOMMY CONWELL, ROB MILLER, JIM HANNUM.

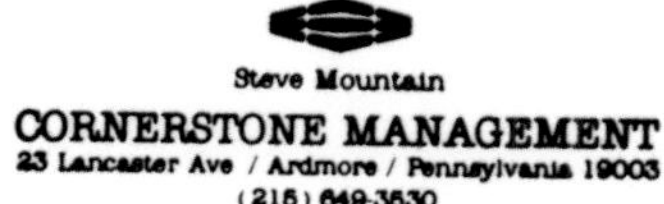

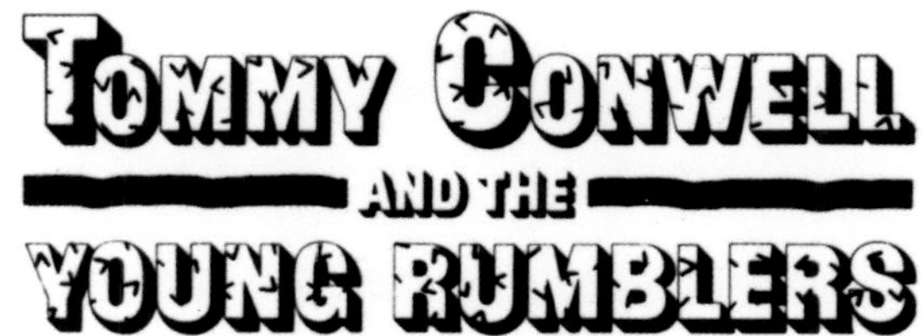

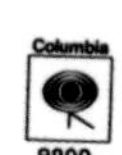

PHOTOGRAPH: PATRICK HARBRON

HENRY LEE SUMMER

Billboard 200: *Henry Lee Summer* (#56)
Billboard Hot 100: "I Wish I Had a Girl" (#20);
"Darlin' Danielle Don't" (#57); "Hands on the Radio" (#85)

Indiana native Henry Lee Summer set the rock airwaves on fire with the feel-good track "I Wish I Had a Girl."

"I WISH I Had a Girl" became a Top 20 debut single for Henry Lee Summer, a springtime hit inspired by a stay in Louisville, Kentucky.

"Specifically, it was a red-light district—you know, where you put a quarter in and watch the girls dance," Summer recalled. "Now, I was just walking by. I didn't have no quarters that day, anyway. But a couple of dancers came over and started sashaying all over the place. I started saying, 'I wish I had a girl who walked like that.' They turned around and called me a jerk."

Summer then headed to a club and wrote "I Wish I Had a Girl," a song reflecting the soulful sound of the American heartland. "The first time I played it, someone came up and told me the chords were the same as Bruce Springsteen's 'I'm Goin' Down.' But those have been used on every song in the world. I play standard R&B-derived rock, just like folks from Springsteen to Creedence Clearwater Revival to Bob Seger. We all have the same chords and we all hit the snare drum real hard."

Summer hailed from Indiana, and his "overnight success" had resulted from years of steady gigging at every club, ballroom, high school, college and fair around his Midwest home turf. He had parlayed his earnings into the learning experience of independent recordings—he got his product into neighborhood stores, schmoozed with local radio programmers and ultimately sold 50,000 albums.

"I've always had fun playing music," he stressed. "And we were gonna put out records no matter what. When the doors closed on a record deal, it was just time for plan B, to do it ourselves."

The Hoosier pop-rock singer's persistence eventually paid off with a self-titled album on a major label. He was touted as "not just another tall, lanky kid from Indiana," a reference to John Cougar Mellencamp. Kicking off with a joyous howl, a re-recorded version of "I Wish I Had a Girl" hit No. 1 on *Billboard*'s Mainstream Rock Tracks chart.

"Any song that's any good, I probably wrote in two or three minutes," Summer said. "I'm a regular kind of person, and I know for damn sure there's a lot of regular people out there who relate to my music." ■

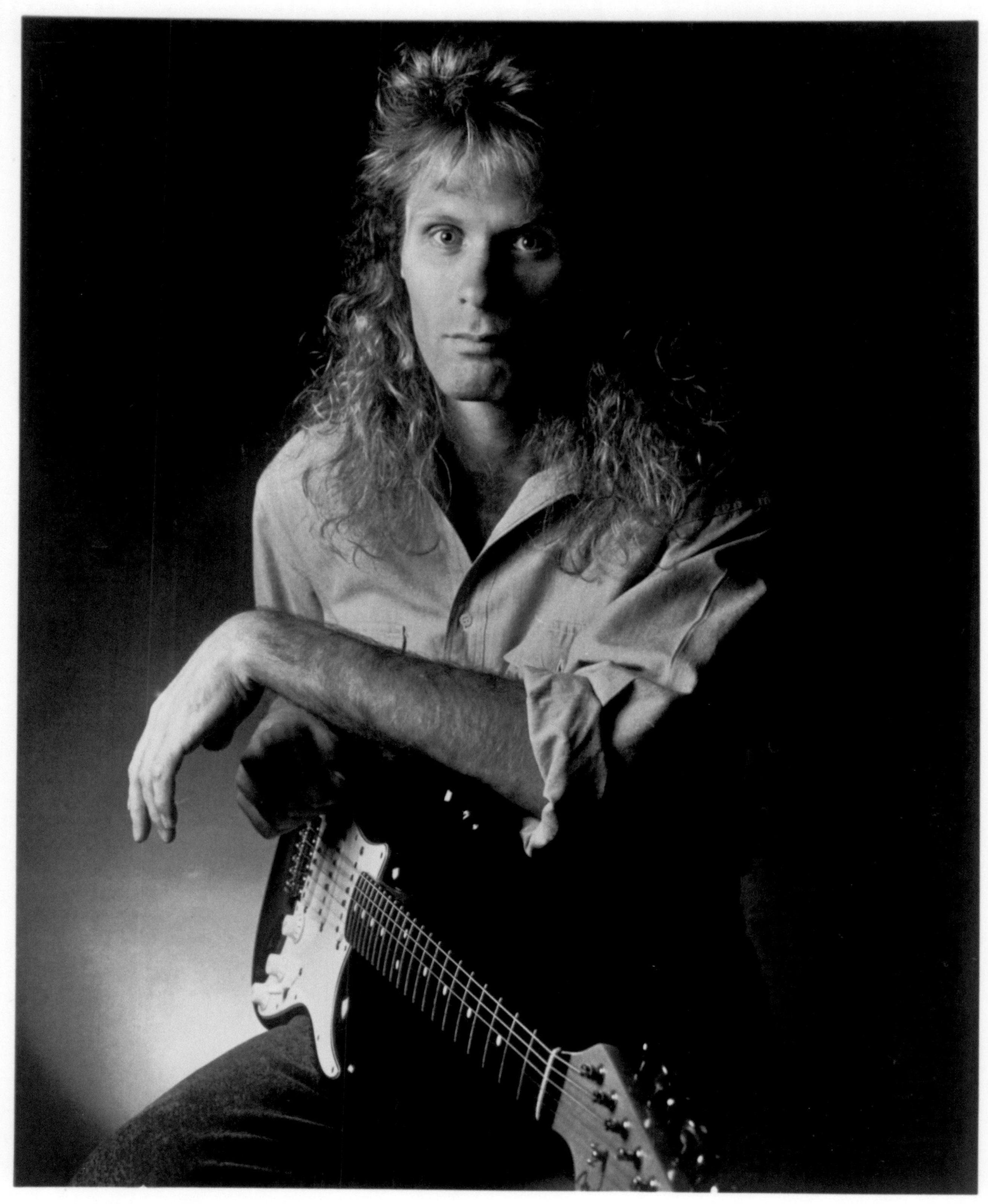

HENRY LEE SUMMER

JAMES BOGARD ASSOCIATES
317 849 3203

CBS ASSOCIATED RECORDS

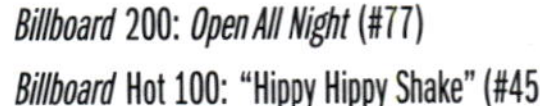

Billboard 200: *Open All Night* (#77)
Billboard Hot 100: "Hippy Hippy Shake" (#45)

The Georgia Satellites came out with *Open All Night*, their loud and proud follow-up to a surprise smash hit.

PLASTIC DANCE sounds, slick poseur metal and introspective pop had conquered the charts in the latter half of the Eighties, but the Georgia Satellites scored a triumph for down-home American rock 'n' roll with a 1986 debut album and the smash "Keep Your Hands to Yourself."

"I was just proud to make a really good rock 'n' roll record that we could stand behind," leader Dan Baird said. "I was going, 'God, please let it sell enough so we get to make another one.'"

The album *Open All Night* continued in a hard-driving vein. The title track was a chugging roadhouse rocker, and "Mon Sheri" captured the lustful, wonderfully sloppy spirit of the Faces—three tracks were complemented by the barrelhouse piano of Ian McLagan, a founding member of the legendary English band.

"It was his idea," drummer Mauro Magellan said. "We hung out with him in California, and we got along without any weirdness. I hate to sound like a hippie, but the vibes were there."

The scraggly bar band from the South simply advocated three-chord rock 'n' roll basics laid down by Chuck Berry and the early Rolling Stones.

"You don't have to be on the cutting edge artistically to be emotionally affecting," Baird said. "But you can't let the music get safe. It has to have an edge, those elements of danger, recklessness and adventure that make for great rock 'n' roll."

The Satellites kept their edge sharp by choosing oddball songs to cover. "Hippy Hippy Shake," a rousing remake of the Swinging Blue Jeans' 1964 hit, appeared on the hit soundtrack to the movie *Cocktail*.

"They edited the movie to the Swinging Blue Jeans' track, so we had to play along with the record," Baird revealed. "That's why there's a little tempo hesitation at the bridge—'You shake it to the left,' et cetera—the original drummer slowed down a hair, and we had to follow that."

If there was an x-factor, it was the fat sound offered by guitarist Rick Richards. "It's a Sixties feel with a Seventies sound," he readily agreed. "I was definitely influenced by Berry and the Stones, but I didn't start playing lead until I got turned on to Eric Clapton. And that was during the era of big amps."

The Georgia Satellites never revealed enough unique traits to assure them of continued interest from the public. "We're just another band with three chords," Magellan admitted. "But we can only be ourselves." ■

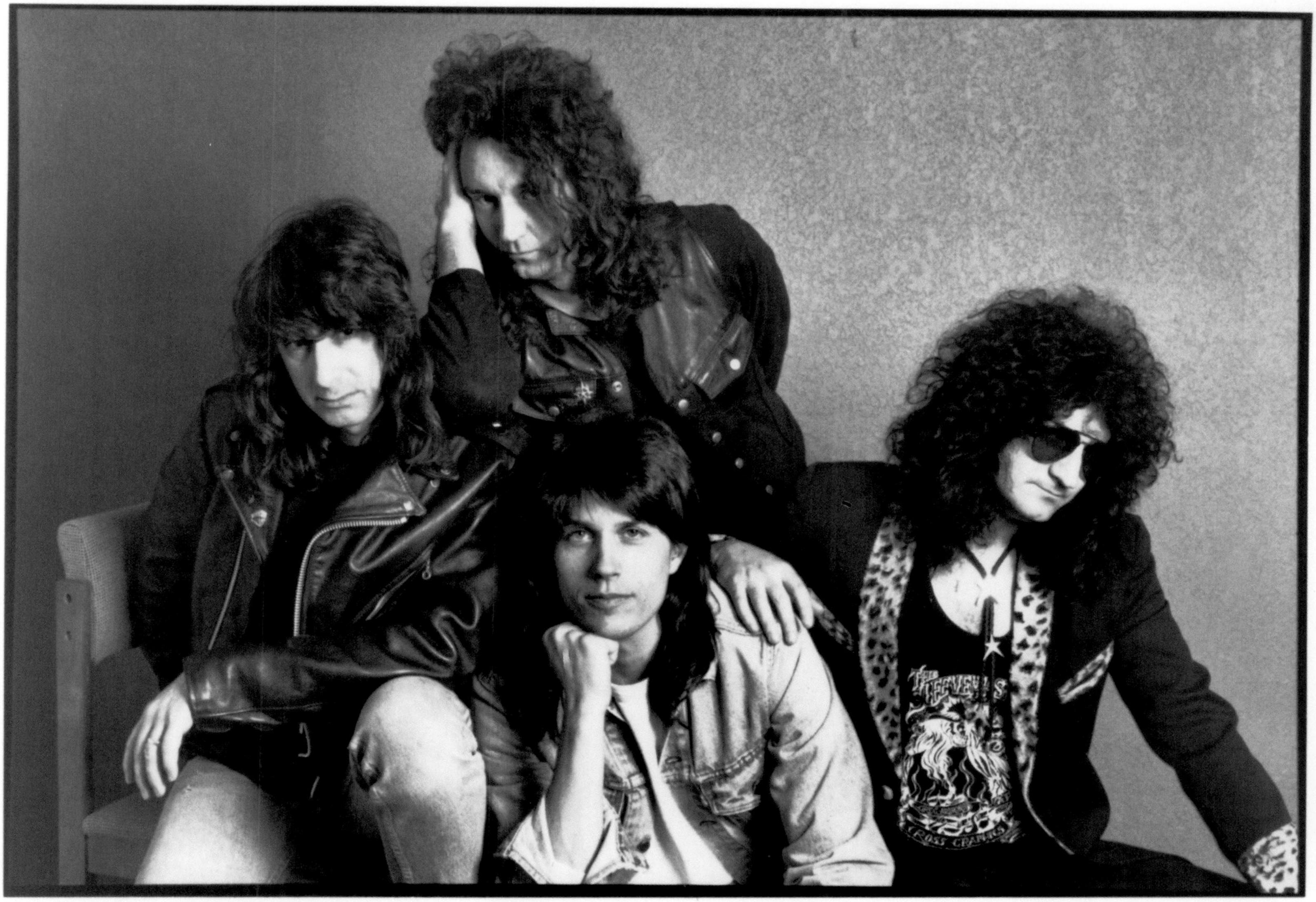

PHOTO CREDIT: LAURA LEVINE/1988

MAURO MAGELLAN RICK PRICE DAN BAIRD RICK RICHARDS

THE GEORGIA SATELLITES

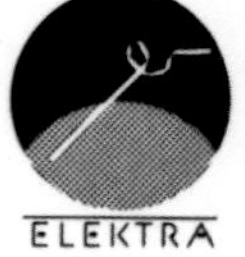

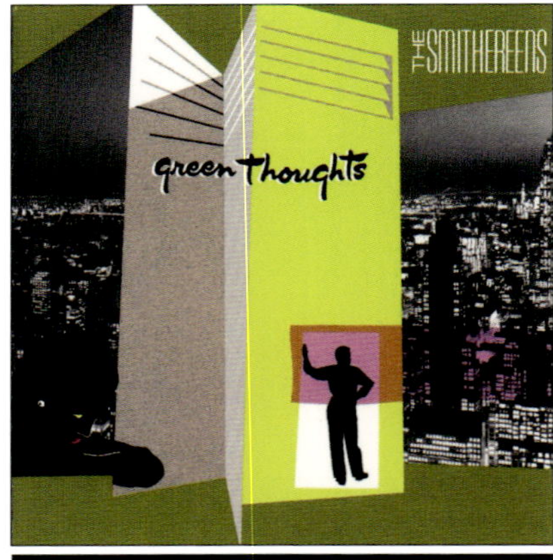

Billboard 200: *Green Thoughts* (#60)
Billboard Hot 100: "Only a Memory" (#92)

The Smithereens topped the album-rock charts with "Only a Memory," a brooding single written by Pat DiNizio.

FANS AND critics had taken to the Smithereens simple but clever reworkings of echoey Sixties British Invasion tunefulness and garage rock crunch—all of it hinging on singer and guitarist Pat DiNizio's knack for crafting fantastic three-minute guitar-driven power-pop songs.

"We're lucky," DiNizio said. "We're on MTV, we're on the radio—and we're the only guitar-oriented band that has found a niche in a pop context. There are other bands who have done it—R.E.M., U2—but are they rock 'n' roll in the traditional sense? Not by my definition."

The Smithereens' exuberant, edgy sound paired with to DiNizio's out-of-love lyrics. "I'm generally a fairly happy-go-lucky guy," he countered. "I've never pretended to be a tortured artist. I'm just a guy from New Jersey who used to be a garbageman who picked up a guitar."

Holed up in his apartment, DiNizio composed the entire *Green Thoughts* album in four weeks, and the group again enlisted Don Dixon to produce. The New Jersey-based quartet's style evinced itself on the tracks "Only a Memory" and "House We Used to Live In." But DiNizio discovered that, in the post-video rock era, the Smithereens risked becoming known more for his facial hair than the music. "I meet people and they want to touch the beard, which is officially known as a Chesterfield in the trade," he said. "Then they ask me why I grew it. Well, it was a joke, which has apparently had the last laugh on me. It gets tiresome at times, but it's become the visual focal point of the band." ■

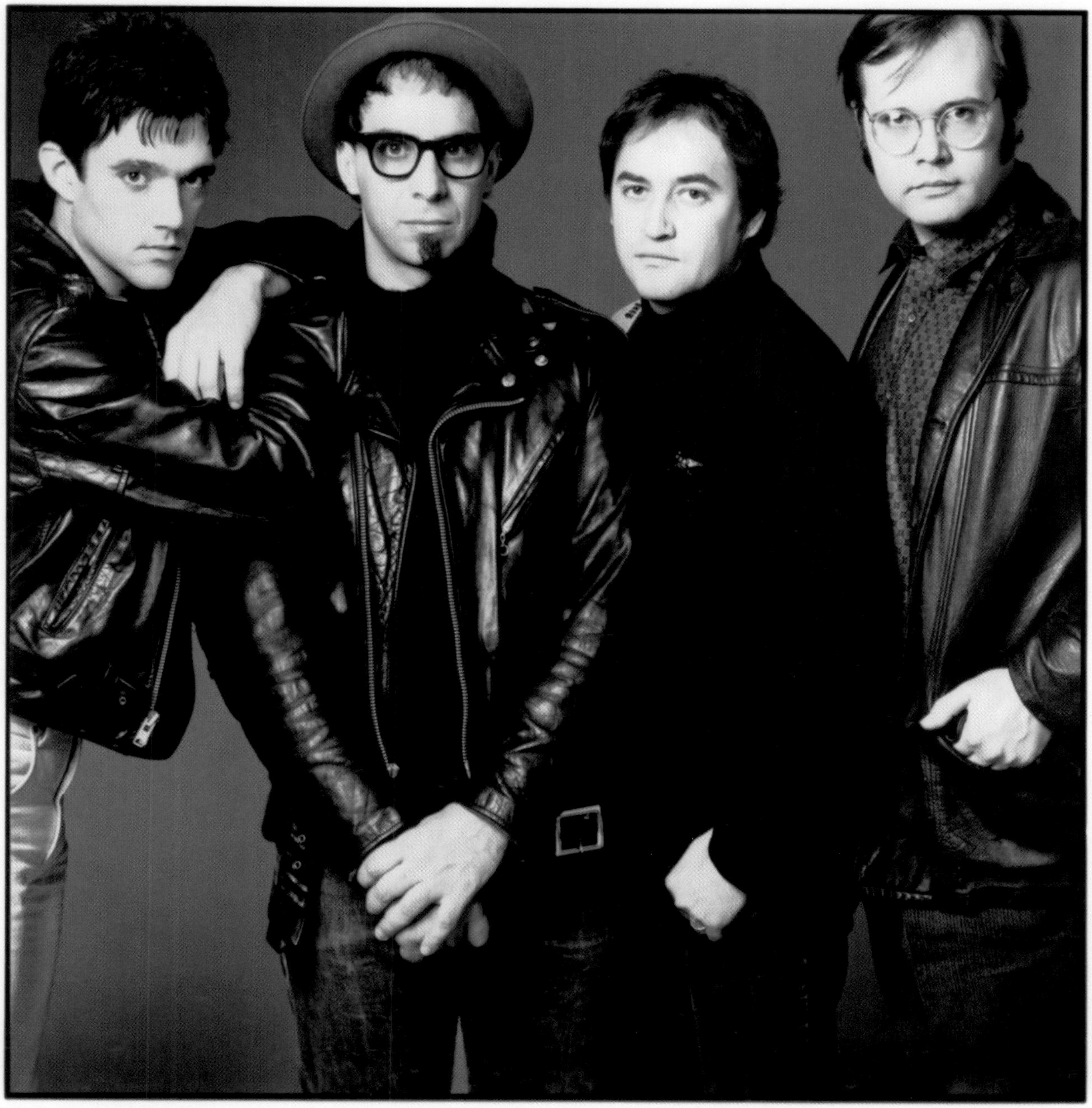

Photo: Deborah Feingold / 1988

Mike Mesaros | Pat DiNizio | Jim Babjak | Dennis Diken

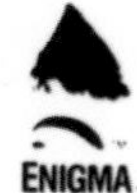

THE SMITHEREENS

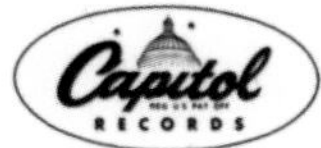

Billboard 200: *Treat Her Right* (#127)

Treat Her Right's roguish "I Think She Likes Me" caused a commotion on the US college charts and in the UK.

THE QUARTET Treat Her Right was considered Boston's best-kept secret until the blues-rock band recorded its self-titled debut album independently and got it released in England. Only then did a major US label pick it up. "I Think She Likes Me" emerged as one of the best oops-she's-married songs since Lynyrd Skynyrd's "Gimme Three Steps."

After graduating from the University of Massachusetts, guitarist and vocalist Mark Sandman had worked a variety of blue-collar jobs where he would often earn considerable overtime pay. This allowed him to take leave of work and travel outside of New England to places such as rural Colorado, the setting for a number of his songs, including "I Think She Likes Me." Sandman sang about the confusion of walking into a bar and being approached by a woman whose husband later makes an unwelcome appearance:

She'd told me things about her life
She'd never told me she was someone's wife
The man with the gun says, "Why'd you buy her a drink?"
I said, "I think she likes me that's what I think"

"I will remain mute about the specifics, but I maintain it's true," Sandman said of the incident.

The stripped-down, blues-tinged sound—Sandman played "low guitar," only the bass strings—was typical of Treat Her Right (the name came from a 1965 hit by Roy Head), whose other members came from across the country and had varied musical backgrounds.

"We're not revivalists or purists," Sandman said. "But we do have an aesthetic—keep it simple at all costs. Resist the temptation to add. If you're going to do something to a song, subtract." ■

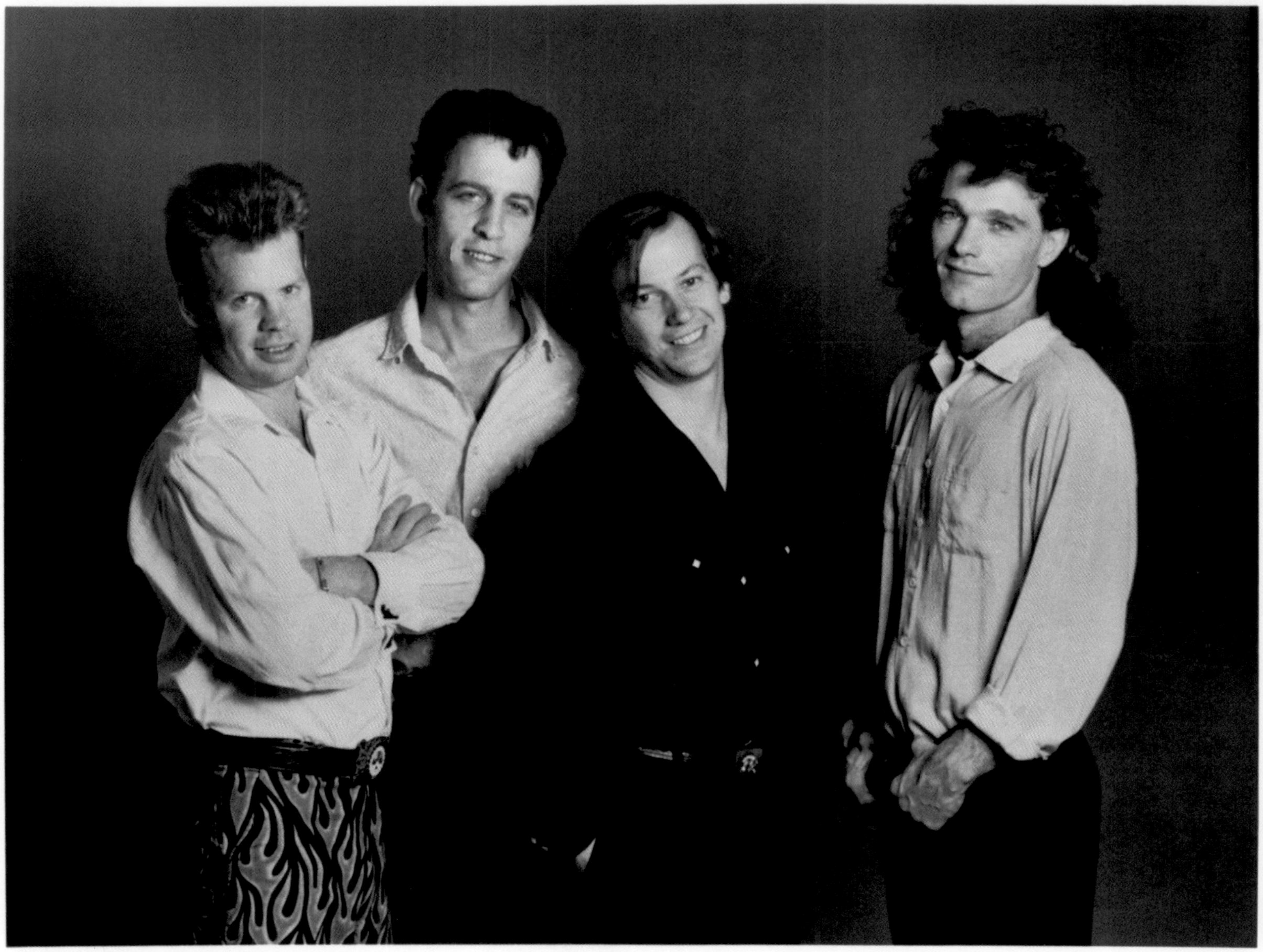

TREAT HER RIGHT

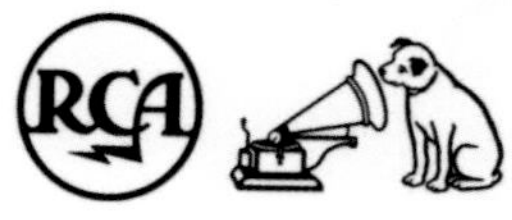

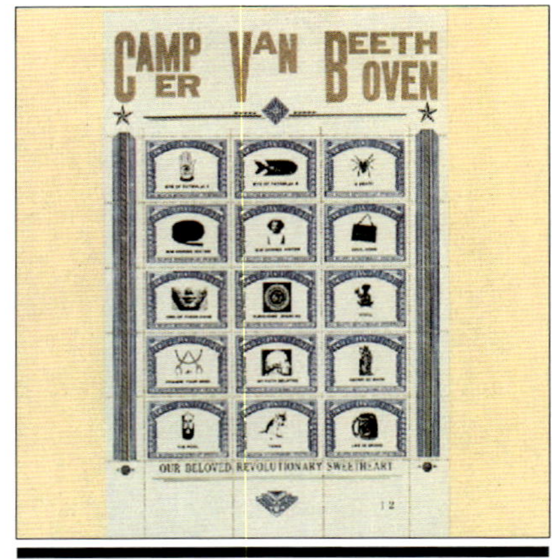

Billboard 200: *Our Beloved Revolutionary Sweetheart* (#124)

Indie rockers Camper Van Beethoven courted mainstream appeal with *Our Beloved Revolutionary Sweetheart.*

FOR SEVERAL years, the five members of Camper Van Beethoven had reigned as the darlings of the alternative music market. The group endured various descriptions—bassist Victor Krummenacher said that "wacky" and "hyphen-hyphen ethno-everything" had been applied most tiresomely. And CVB's music certainly rated as an eclectic fusion of various exotic forms. The band attempted everything from arcane instrumentation to mocking but affectionate performance versions of songs by Pink Floyd and Ringo Starr.

But lead guitarist Greg Lisher insisted his bandmates didn't describe themselves as "surrealist absurdist folk" just to be weird. "We just don't like to be pigeonholed for doing one thing or another," he explained. "Everyone has very different styles as far as what they listen to and what they play. And they overlap in Camper. We interpret styles that we're not necessarily familiar with, like country music. That's how we get a sound."

Formed in 1984 in Santa Cruz, California, Camper Van Beethoven soon debuted on the underground scene with the album *Telephone Free Landslide Victory*. College radio picked up on "Take the Skinheads Bowling," a simple folk-punk tune about skate rats that unexpectedly became a huge hit among new music fans.

"We had no idea that song would take off like it did," Lisher admitted. "But then people thought we were a novelty band, a joke band, and jokes get old. You don't keep doing the same joke over and over. So each record since has had its own style and sound."

Two subsequent independent albums sold well and received critical acclaim, which led to *Our Beloved Revolutionary Sweetheart*, the band's first record for a major label. The single "Eye of Fatima"—described by singer David Lowery as "kind of the closest thing to a Creedence Clearwater song we could come up with"—even received scattered mainstream airplay.

The shape-shifting smart alecks had taken a more polished course, but Camper Van Beethoven retained its strange side, covering Buzzcocks' "Harmony in my Head" and Herb Alpert & the Tijuana Brass' "Wade in the Water" in concert. If longtime fans thought the group's higher commercial profile constituted a betrayal of its iconoclastic beginnings, Lisher said they were missing the point.

"We have no regrets," he said. "This is a step we've been thinking about for a long time. None of us wanted to mill around the independent scene any longer. We want to sell some records." ■

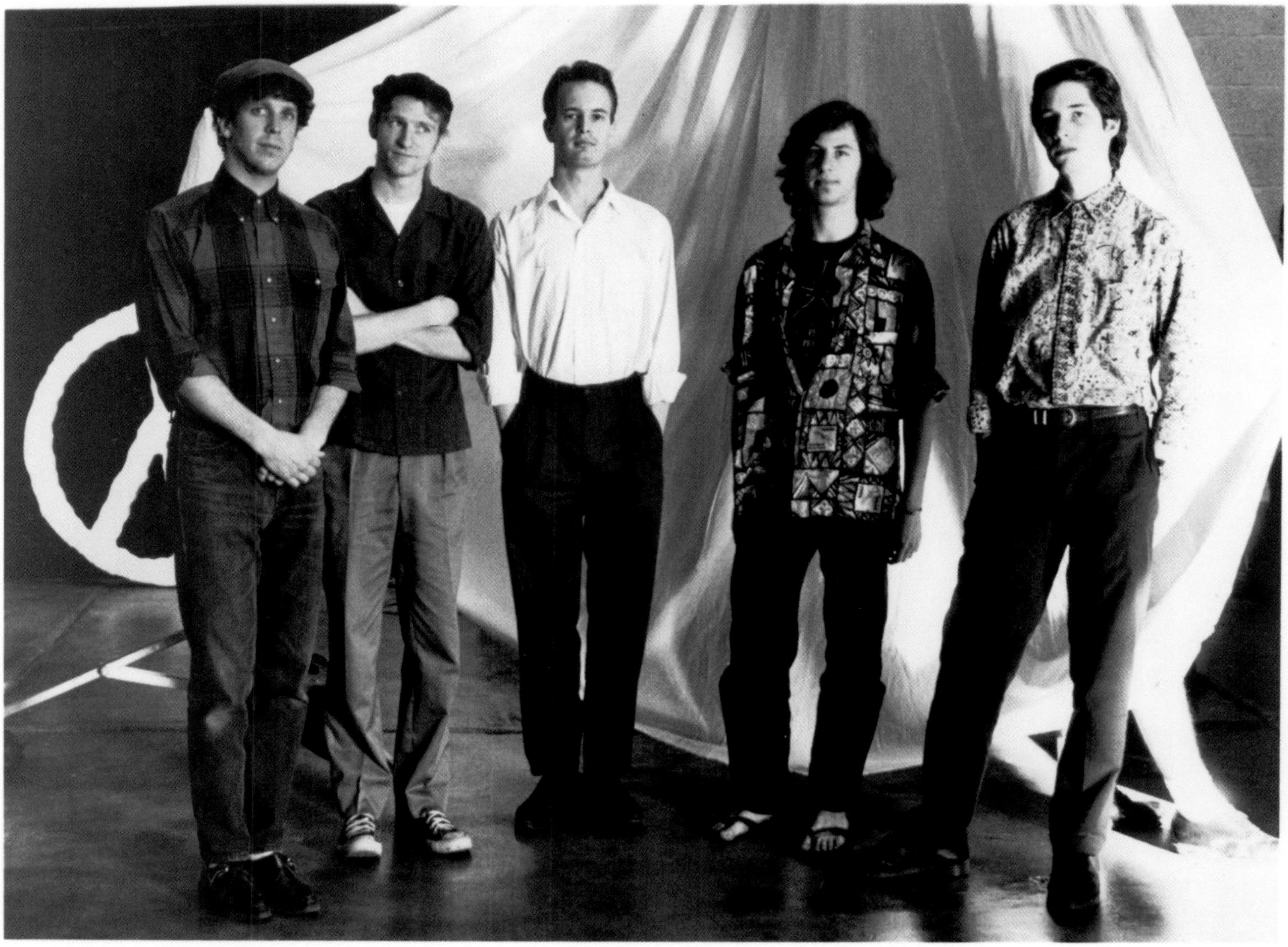

Photo Credit: Melanie Nissen

CAMPER VAN BEETHOVEN

Virgin

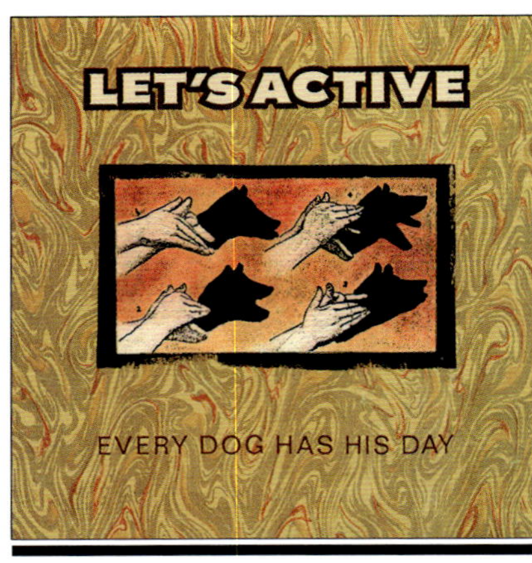

Let's Active's *Every Dog Has His Day* became a labor of love for the band's frontman, producer Mitch Easter.

MITCH EASTER had gained notoriety for his producing talents. At the Drive-In Studio, located at his parents' house in Winston-Salem, North Carolina, he'd handled such acts as R.E.M., Suzanne Vega, Marshall Crenshaw, Velvet Elvis and Game Theory. But Easter was also a bandleader, masterminding the twists and turns of Let's Active's evolving career.

While previous Let's Active releases had centered on Easter's individual vision of moody, ringing jangle pop, establishing him as an eclectic instrumentalist, *Every Dog Has His Day* featured a real band providing dense, muscular grooves. Easter was joined by Angie Carlson on keyboards, guitars and vocals, with Eric Marshall on drums and John Heames on bass.

"The group's other three members play well, but that's secondary to knowing the social and musical connotation of things—we could get a bass player who plays 128th notes, but the music wouldn't jell if we couldn't talk about it," Easter said. "Like if you made a reference to Montrose, everybody would laugh at it the same way or not laugh at it the same way. That's the big test."

"Every Dog Has His Day" peaked at #17 on *Billboard*'s Modern Rock Tracks chart.

"I enjoyed that fast-cheap-and-efficient ethic that popped up in the early Eighties, but now those kinds of records aren't doing anything—there are a lot of hits by supposedly underground bands that are done mostly with machines and studio musicians, and I don't know where I fit into that scene," Easter mused. "Records are equal parts triumph and heartbreak, and hopefully the triumph wins out. In some ways, you're always trying to reach a wider audience, but in another you're just trying to reach yourself all over again and make sure you should still be doing this." ■

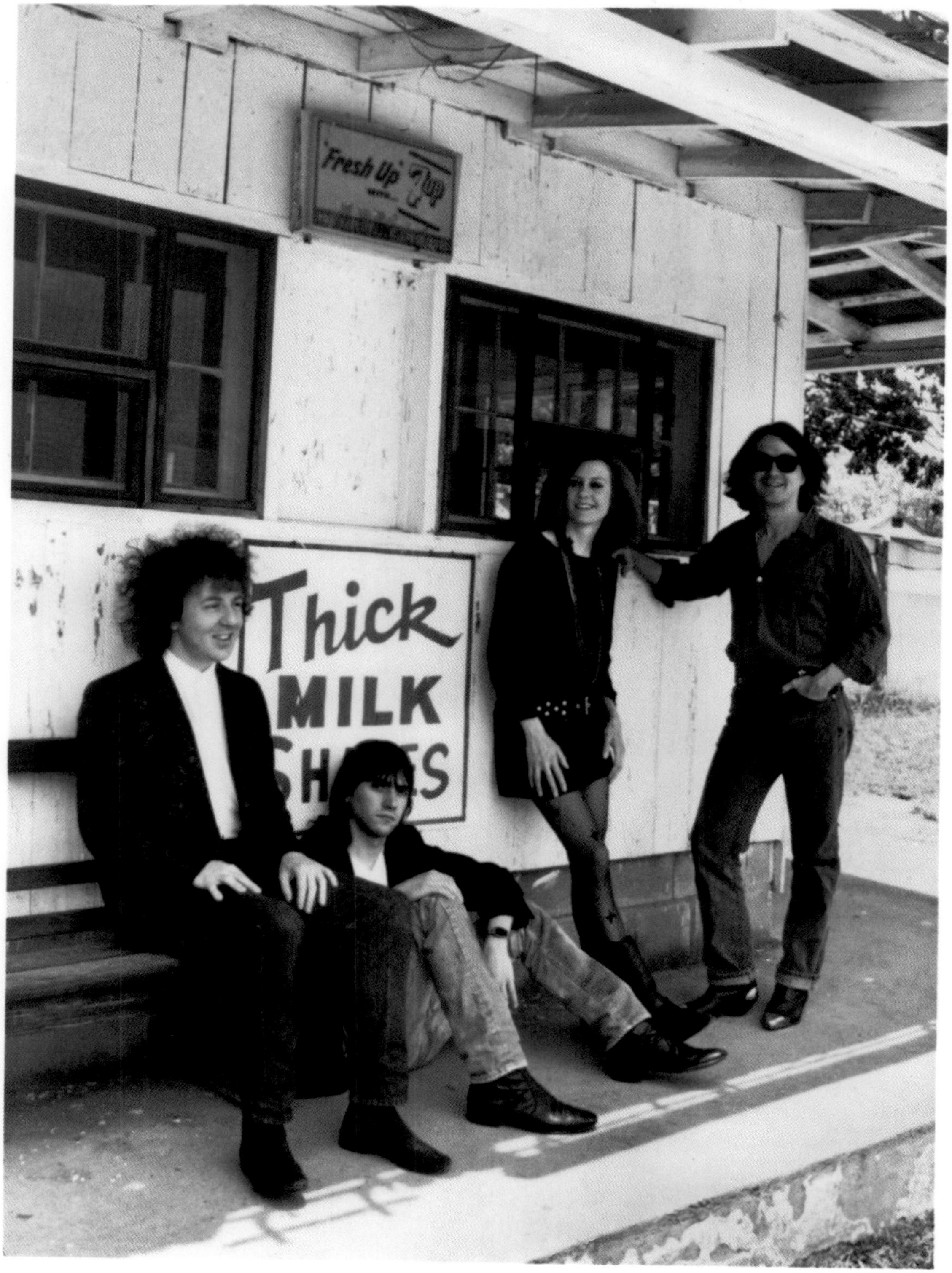

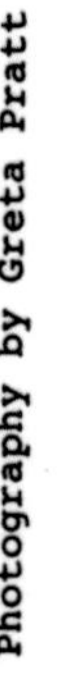

"WOOF"

MITCH EASTER
ANGIE CARLSON
ERIC MARSHALL
JOHN HEAMES

LET'S ACTIVE

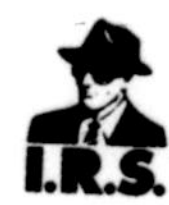

Billboard 200: *Only Life* (#173)

The Feelies made a sound based on simple guitar phrases constantly in flux, captured by the album *Only Life*.

IN THE wake of the 1980 debut album *Crazy Rhythms,* the Feelies got tagged as an odd cult band. The members, who hailed from suburban New Jersey, dressed like nerdy, nervous preppies—"a glasses band," as guitarist Glenn Mercer recalled. The reclusive, subdued mystique belied some sophisticated rhythmic concepts—the Feelies drew their inspiration from the Velvet Underground, emphasizing the interplay and textures of their electric guitars while vocals and lyrics took a back seat. They confined themselves to holiday-only performances.

The group had actually disbanded in 1981 and evolved into a collective, with members involved with at least three different bands simultaneously. One, the Willies, was a solely instrumental outfit.

"It was experimental—we formed it with the idea of changing every time we performed," Mercer said. "Initially we accompanied tapes, and then the tapes accompanied us, then we phased the tapes out. Instead of a left-right stereo mix, we'd do a front-rear mix. It was just a low-key do-anything-you-want-to-do forum."

The Willies involved into another incarnation of the Feelies, and by 1986, the Feelies rated as quasi-legendary new wave survivors. R.E.M.'s Peter Buck produced the nervously pastoral *The Good Earth*, and the band enjoyed an association with film director Jonathan Demme, who directed their videos and cast the band in the movie *Something Wild* (playing the Monkees' "I'm a Believer" in a high-school reunion scene).

Only Life marked the Feelies' major label debut and only the third album in the quintet's 11-year existence. A typically hypnotic, subconscious listening experience, *Only Life* revolved around the spare but multilayered guitar drones of guitarists Mercer and Bill Million.

"The way we play guitar is based in folk music, using as many open strings as we can instead of barre chords," Mercer said. "That gives the music a ringing quality—people are always telling us that they can hear vocal parts that aren't there. They're frequencies that the guitars have created."

The early Feelies sound had been tempered by percussion and more prominent lyrics and melody, but the mesmeric strains of the Velvet Underground remained—*Only Life* contained a cheerful version of the Velvets' "What Goes On." The frenetic, joyous "Away" peaked at #6 on *Billboard's* alternative songs chart, and Demme put the tune "Too Far Gone" on the soundtrack to his *Married to the Mob*. "There is no better band," Demme said, "maybe because they are so studiously uncareerist."

"As long as we don't have to work 9 to 5 and still make a living, we remain unthwarted by the business of music," Mercer said. "We don't have a master plan—we don't look ahead a month or two. The surprise of not knowing what's going to happen is what keeps it interesting." ■

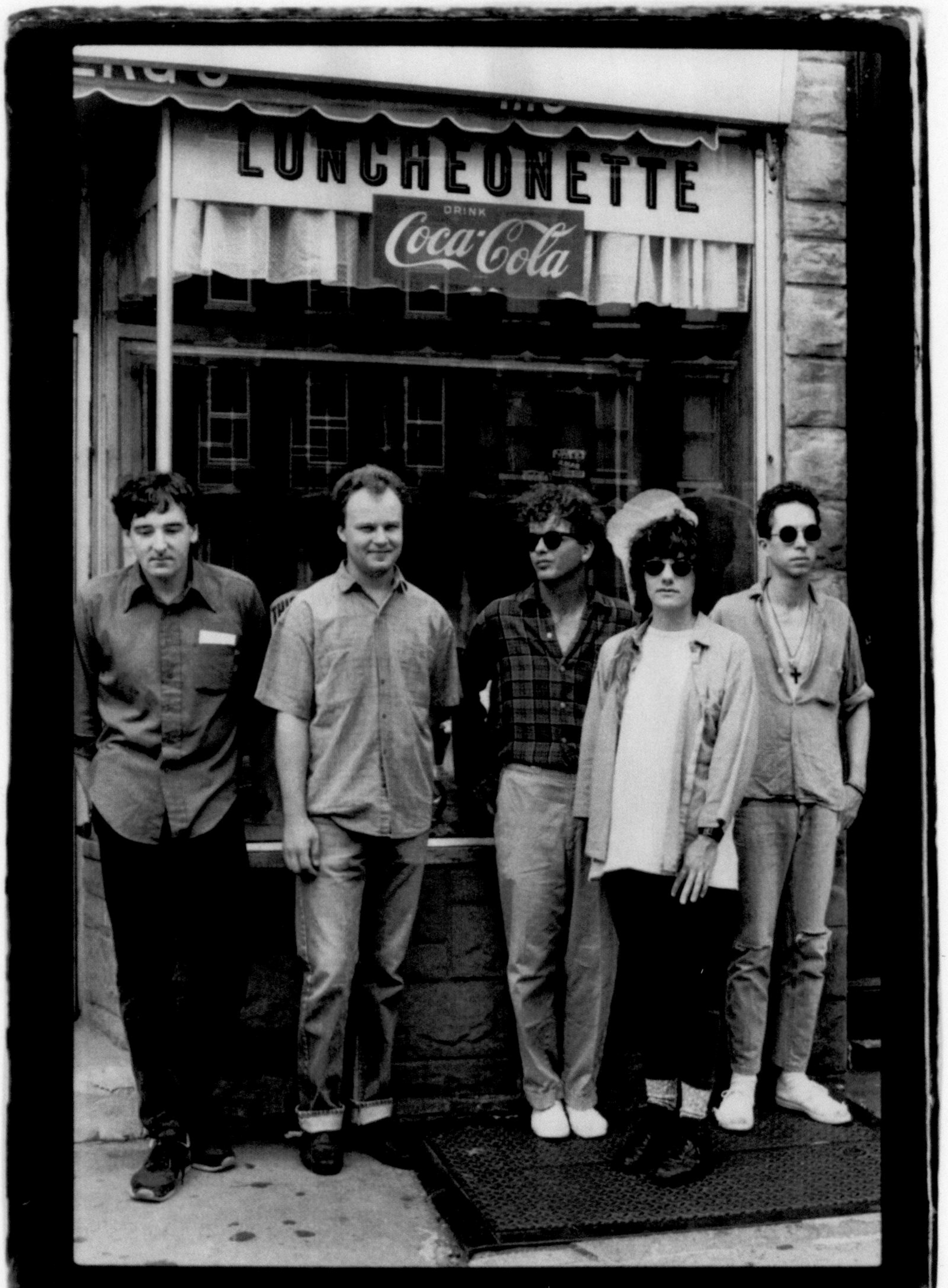

Dave Weckerman Stanley Demeski Bill Million Brenda Sauter Glenn Mercer

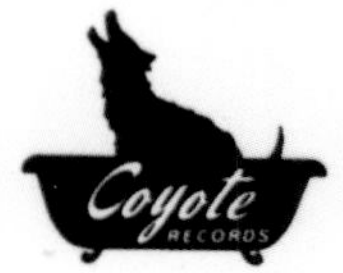

THE FEELIES

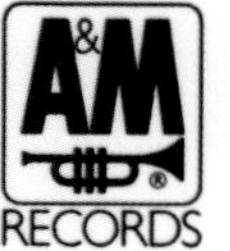

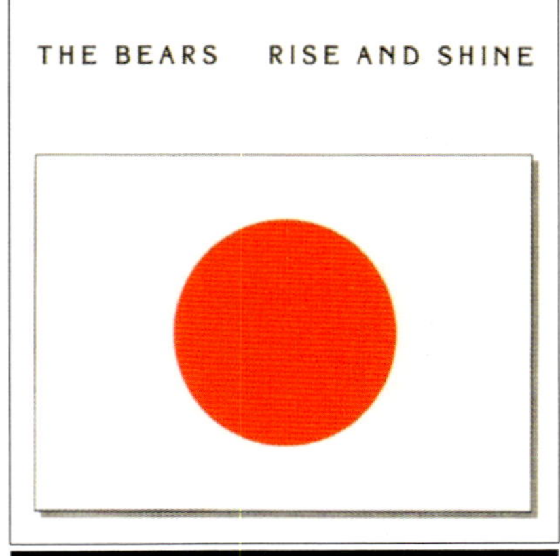

Billboard 200: *Rise and Shine* (#159)

The Bears served up a program of melodic pop, calculated weirdness and Adrian Belew's stunning guitar work.

ADRIAN BELEW'S prolific career had included stints with many famous associates—Talking Heads, David Bowie, Frank Zappa and the revived King Crimson, among others. But for several years, the avant-garde guitarist had based himself in Lake Geneva, Wisconsin, to play with the Bears, a dizzyingly diverse bunch.

"It's a plan that I've had for a long time," Belew explained. "I never saw myself as a studio musician, but those opportunities came up when someone I respected called, like Paul Simon or Laurie Anderson. But I never felt comfortable in that role. I always thought what I did needed complete attention to write, record and produce the songs. Now there's more of that feeling instead of my coming in to put solos or interesting sounds on someone else's records."

With his fellow Bears—guitarist Rob Fetters, bassist Bob Nyswonger and drummer Chris Arduser—Belew had set up a number of musical parameters to work in. "We said, 'Okay, the Bears sound like this to us—two-part vocals, exotic guitar overtones.' And ever since then, we've been seeing how we can fit things into that mold."

On their self-titled 1987 debut album, the four Bears spiced up their Beatles-esque tunefulness with ethnic musical motifs, an approach they dubbed "East meets Midwest." The *Rise and Shine* album incorporated everything from sunny tropical rhythms ("Save Me") to Belew's guitar imitation of a Turkish zurna on "Nobody's Fool."

"From my role in the band, I saw us going further into a more natural, acoustic type of music," Belew noted.

Unfortunately, a corporate decision undermined the exposure of *Rise and Shine*—Primitive Man Recording Company (PMRC), the Bears' record label, was disbanded by its parent company in the middle of the four-man pop outfit's tour. ■

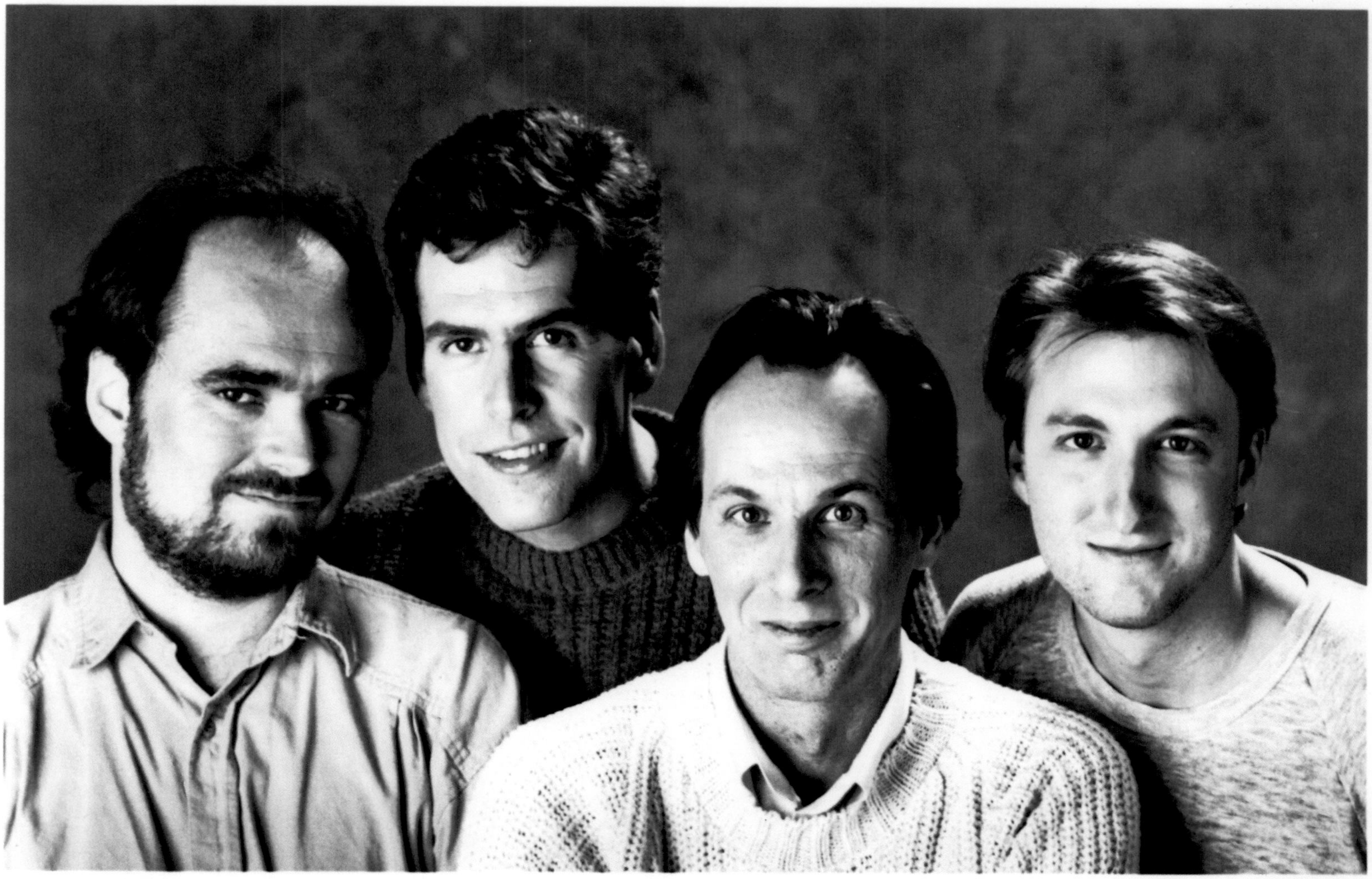

Bob Nyswonger Rob Fetters Adrian Belew Chris Arduser

Photography • Sandy Ostroff

THE BEARS

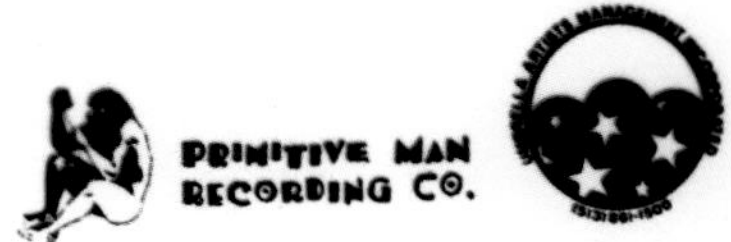

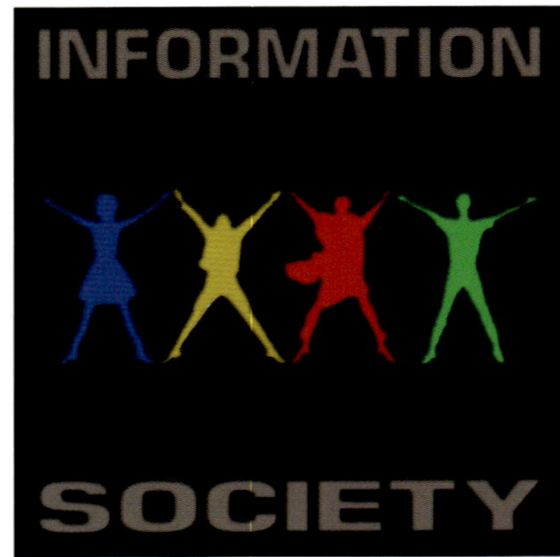

Billboard 200: *Information Society* (#25)
Billboard Hot 100 "What's on Your Mind (Pure Energy)" (#3);
"Walking Away" (#9); "Repetition" (#76);
"Lay All Your Love on Me" (#83)

"What's on Your Mind (Pure Energy)" by Information Society hit the dance clubs and then reached the charts.

A TOTALLY electronic group from Minnesota, Information Society scored a smash single with "What's on Your Mind ("Pure Energy)"—the first pop hit to feature Latin hip-hop beats.

"That kind of syncopation is very unusual—most dance music that makes it onto the pop charts has a four-on-the-floor beat," bassist James Cassidy said.

The dance hit "Running" had launched Information Society's career, and the band's eccentric performances at clubs in New York City and Miami—"track shows," using a mixing board and effects as instruments the way other musicians used keyboards and drums—gained unexpected success. With the crossover pop triumph of "What's on Your Mind," InSoc relocated to NYC to rehearse a live band.

The debut album *Information Society* meshed synthesized samplings of funk rock with hip-hop beats, and the grooves benefited from the pop sensibilities of producer Fred Maher (a member and co-producer of Scritti Politti). The band members monitored a library of more than 1,000 homemade samples, cutting and pasting snatches of pop culture. "What's on Your Mind (Pure Energy)" included a vocal sample from Leonard Nimoy as *Star Trek*'s Mr. Spock, saying "pure energy."

"We sampled excerpts from a lot of television stuff that we grew up listening to as kids," Cassidy said. "But we've been sampling in our music since before there were samplers, using tape recorders. We were some of the first people to sample James Brown's voice as a piece of percussion, and now that's a huge sensation. And many of the samples on the album are five-year-old recordings of anvils being struck from my father's machine shop." ■

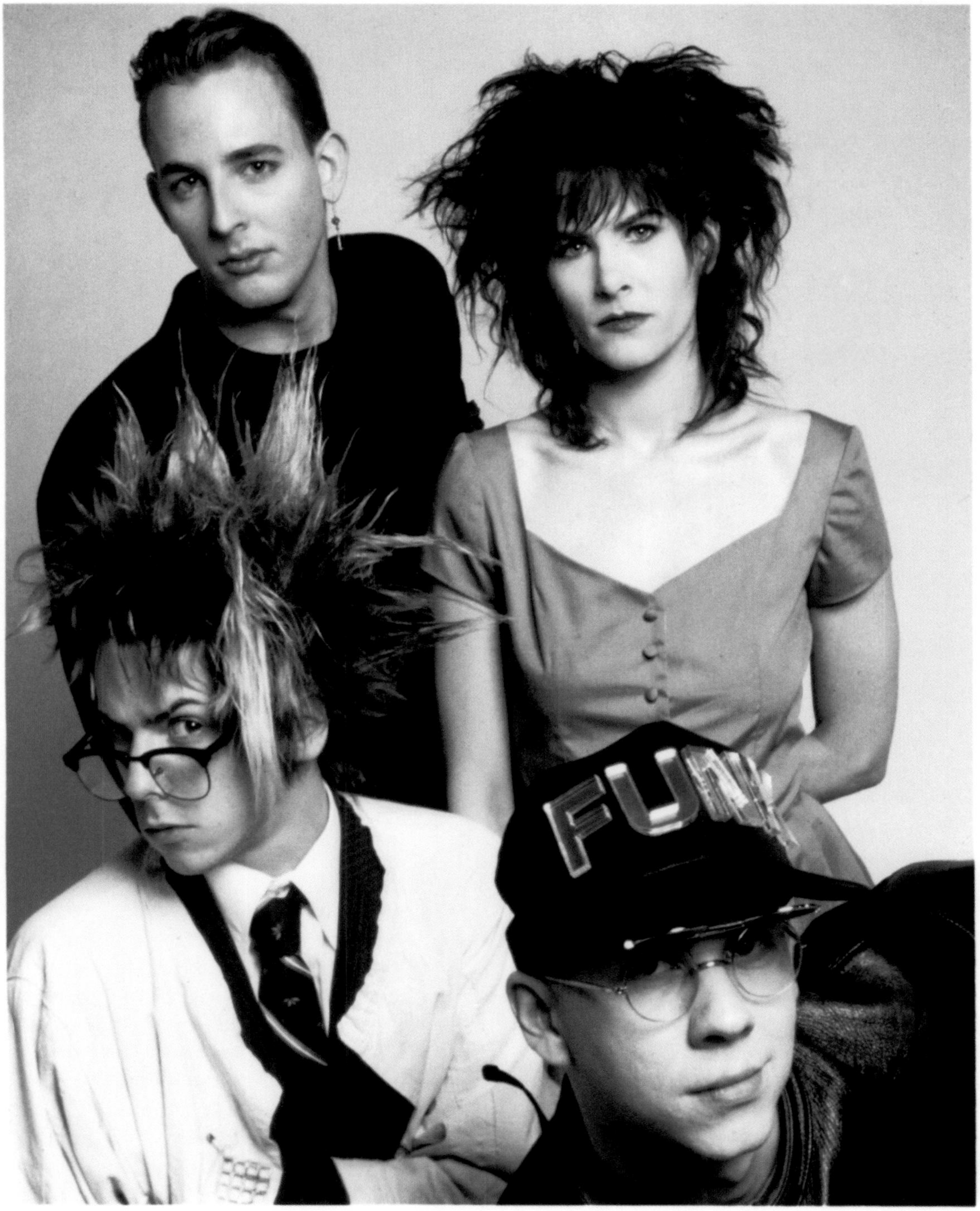

Photo Credit: Isabel Snyder

James
Kurt

Amanda
Paul

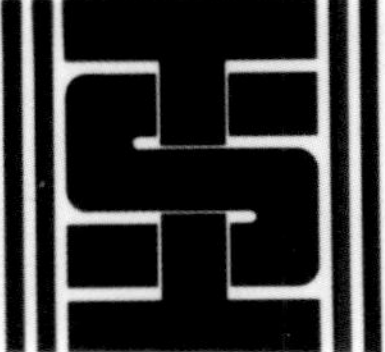

INFORMATION SOCIETY

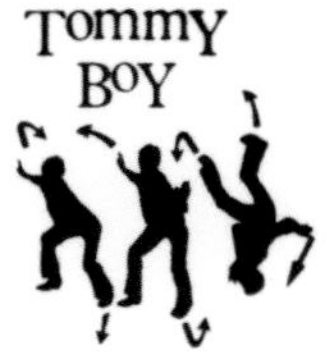

GARY CLAIL'S
TACKHEAD
SOUND
SYSTEM

Members of the Tackhead collective cultivated sundry collaborations at the cutting edge of industrial music.

THE CORE of Tackhead—Doug Wimbish (bass), Skip McDonald (guitar) and Keith LeBlanc (drums)—previously served as the house band on rap label Sugarhill Records' best releases (DJ Grandmaster Flash's "The Message" and "White Lines"). An unusual creative setup, Tackhead fused elements of hip-hop, funk and electronics into post-modern dance music. But instead of collaborating on musical ideas, the principals of the New York-based outfit simply passed their individual input on to the next person.

The trio provided a sonic anchor for British producer Adrian Sherwood, who used a mixing board as another instrument, stripping down and manipulating the hard-edged funk output with radical echo, reverb, digital samples and tape collages. And over that harshly edited product, fellow Brit Gary Clail offered his freehand vocal experimentation, adding singing and speaking color commentary in his ongoing individual performances as Gary Clail's Tackhead Sound System.

"I take the outtakes made by the band and dub them live through a P.A. mixing deck while other rhythms and sound effects play simultaneously," Clail explained. During the mixes, Clail tried to express himself by shouting and ranting on a megaphone through a microphone. The response to the Tackhead Sound System gave Clail the confidence to perform with Tackhead live, the most visible figure in the group's hierarchy

"I've got no musical background—I don't play an instrument, and I didn't buy records as a kid," the vocalist said. "So I'm fresh, not influenced by anything else. I try to incorporate true-to-life stuff. I work for a living when we're not playing—I've got a scaffolding business with my father back home. In the evening, I go drinking with the workers, and those guys give me the best lyrics without even knowing it—it's just the way they see life. I could try to be an artsy type and come up with trendy thoughts that sound good to analysts, but that's a waste of time."

The impact of *Tackhead Tape Time* on other musicians exceeded its public acclaim, but Clail wasn't concerned. "Trying to shock somebody anymore is so boring," he mused. "With Tackhead concerts, we've incorporated the down-to-earth street credibility of the band with the madness of Adrian's live shows. People's mouths are open for the first 20 minutes. Even if people say it's not their cup of tea, they go away saying that this band is different from anything else they've seen. An airline attendant came to a show and told me that she heard 'industrial strength hip-hop with a touch of Jimi Hendrix.' And to me, that sums it up." ■

TACK»HEAD

GARY CLAIL
KEITH LE BLANC
ADRIAN SHERWOOD
SKIP MC DONALD
DOUG WIMBISH

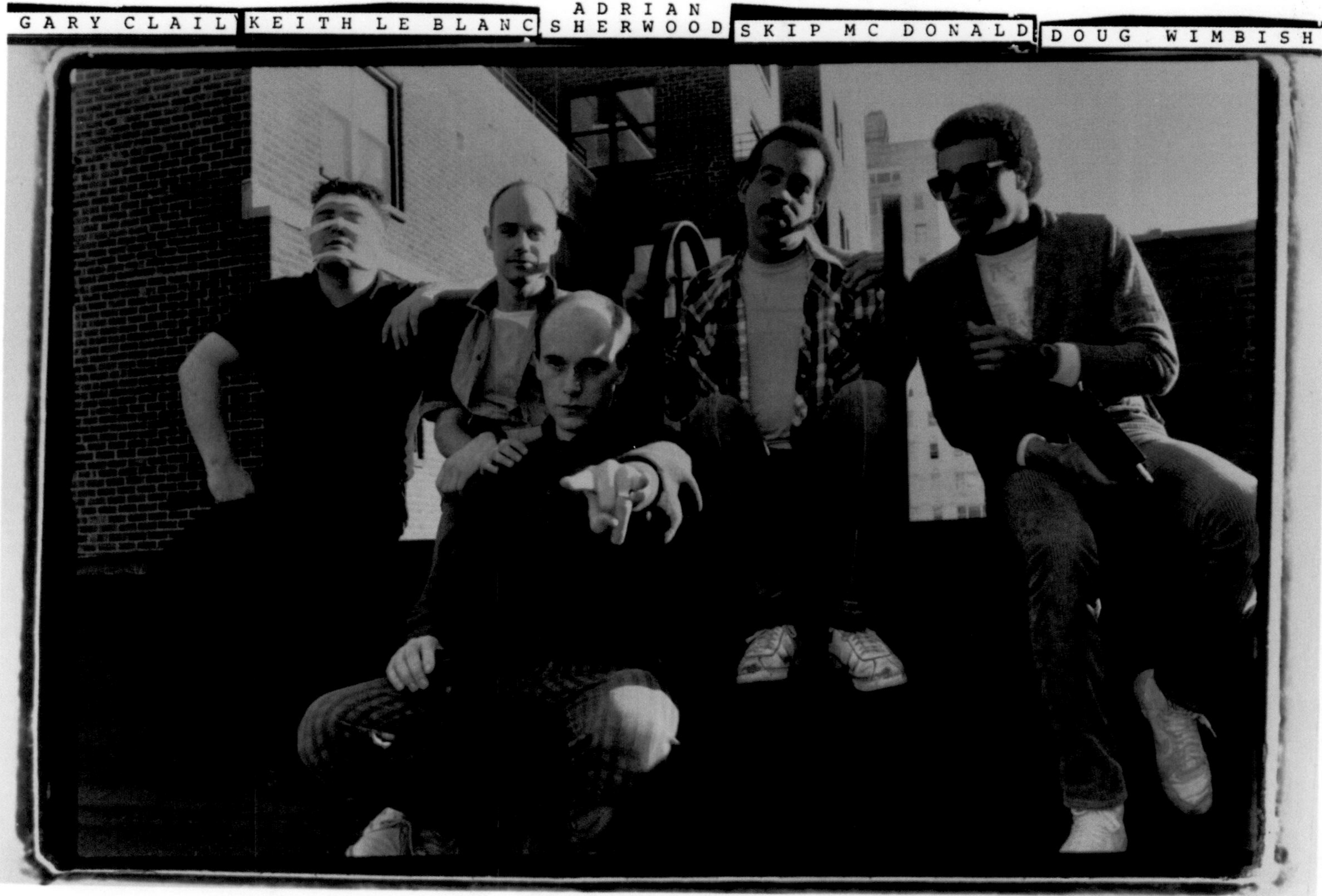

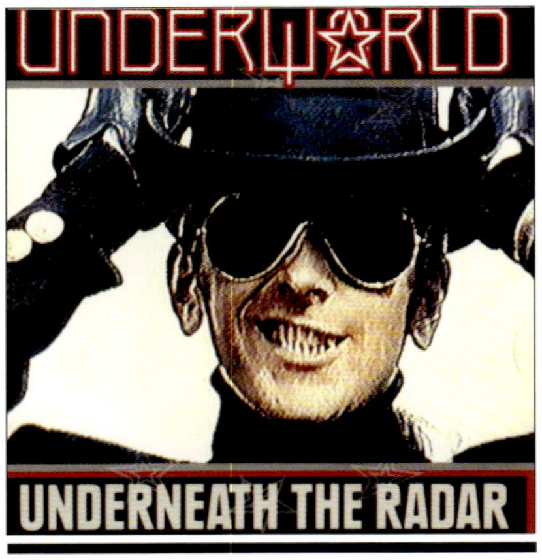

Billboard 200: *Underneath the Radar* (#139)
Billboard Hot 100: "Underneath the Radar" (#74)

Underneath the Radar by Underworld navigated to success in South Africa, Australasia, Canada and America.

THE NUCLEUS of the English band Underworld—Karl Hyde (guitar), Rick Smith (keyboards) and Alfie Thomas (guitar)—had collaborated for eight years, always based on the propostion of resisting prevailing musical styles.

"When we first started working together, England was in the middle of the New Romantic movement and the Blitz scene—the fashion was long black coats and short hair," Thomas said. "So of course we took to wearing bright plastic coats and coloring our hair."

As Freur, the trio managed to score a massive European hit with "Doot-Doot," but the group didn't sustain success. "We were onstage one night and it just didn't feel right anymore," Thomas said. "So we mutually agreed to put it aside to go on with something else."

Although Freur had ceased to inspire the threesome, their collective creative spirit hadn't waned. Within a month they'd reunited, intent on a fresh start. They became Underworld along with drummer Bryn Burrows and bassist Bas Allen, and their demos became the basis for the *Underneath the Radar* album. Produced by Rupert Hine (Tina Turner, the Fixx), the project gained attention for the way it was recorded.

"All of the tracks were played live, with no overdubs—the whole band was in the studio at the same time," Thomas said. "It has almost become a promotional gimmick, because it seems to be a unique way of working in 1988. Instead of synching up to the machines and synthesizers, we looked each other in the eye while we played. Maybe more bands will follow through and capture that spirit of recording live."

The dense textures and massive drum sound of the title track harked back to the glam-rock sound of the Seventies, but Underworld wasn't simply the musical flavor of the month from England—the album hadn't even been released in the band's native country. "For some reason, they just don't care about us," Thomas said. "Our audience is in America."

And Thomas' clean-shaven pate had also proven advantageous. "No one can call us the latest haircut band from the UK," he noted. "I've taken care of that right off." ■

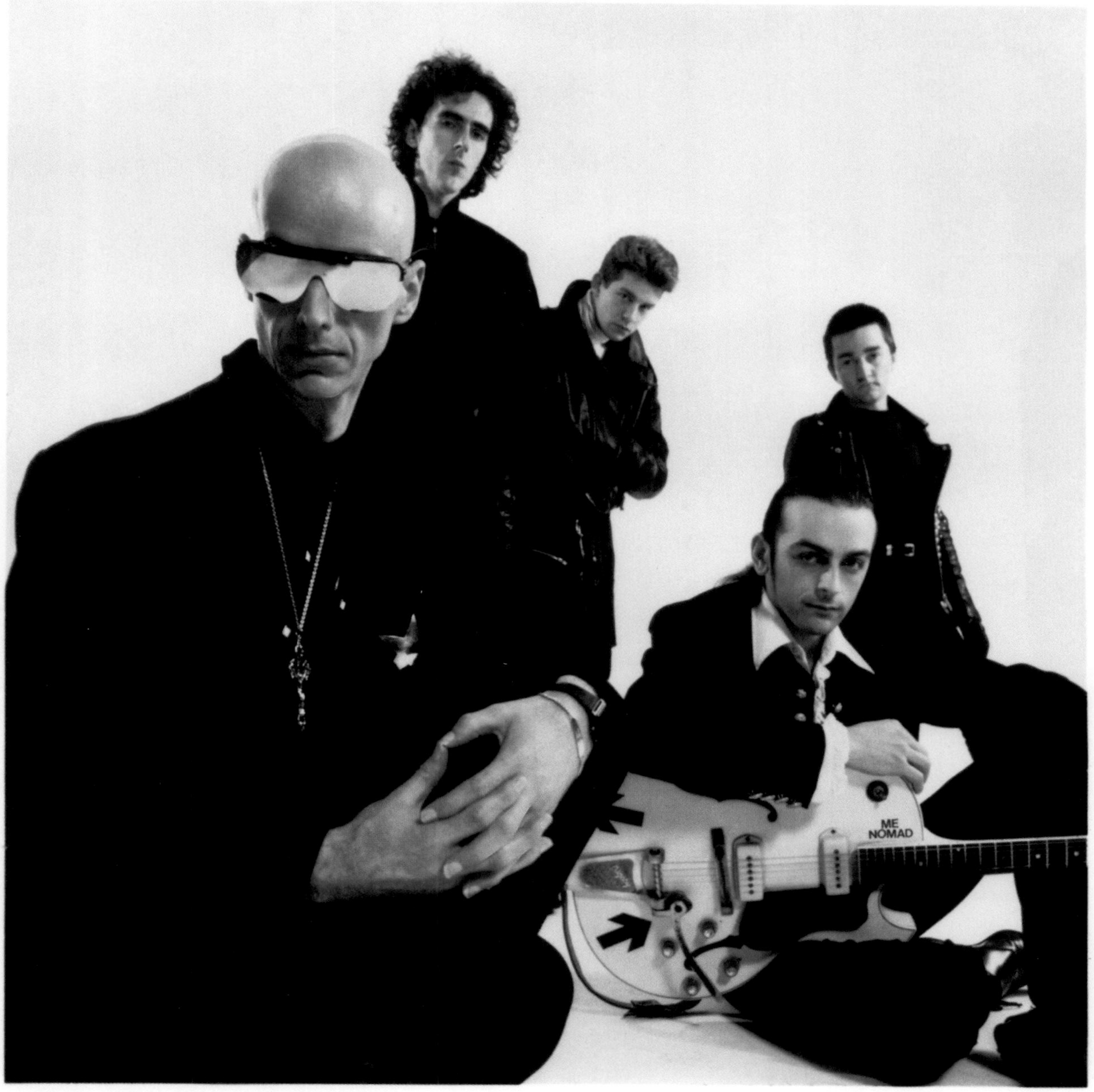

Photo Credit: Simon Fowler

ALFIE THOMAS RICK SMITH BAZ ALLEN KARL HYDE BRYN BURROWS

UNDERWORLD

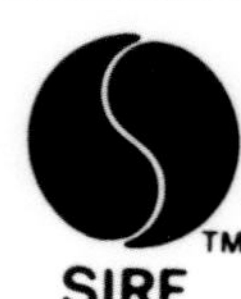

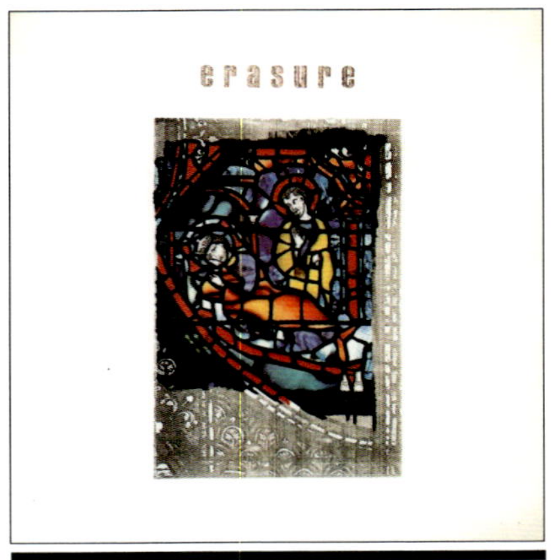

Billboard 200: *The Innocents* (#49)
Billboard Hot 100: "Chains of Love" (#12); "A Little Respect" (#14)

The English duo Erasure racked up a couple of Top 20 hits in the US, "Chains of Love" and "A Little Respect."

SONGWRITER AND keyboardist Vince Clarke was a founding member of Depeche Mode and half of the group Yaz. Andy Bell was an unknown vocalist when he answered a music newspaper ad in 1985 and hooked up with Clarke. Together, they formed Erasure—and quickly chalked up hits in the UK.

Theirs was a curious chemistry between opposites—Bell, the flamboyant, melodically tremulous singer, and Clarke, the shy studio-centered technician whose simple, synthesized dance music was cleverly arranged and instantly memorable.

The Innocents became the team's mainstream breakthrough album in the US, a staple on the dance club scene with the singles "Chains of Love" and "A Little Respect." For the lavish live performances, Bell created a larger-than-life campy persona, with a penchant for sequined jackets, tutus, tights and abbreviated costumes. With a theatrical flair for melodrama, he mugged and pranced merrily.

"When we first started performing, Andy didn't say a thing, didn't move a muscle—he just stood there in the middle of the stage," Clarke said. "His whole persona has taken him years to develop. The audiences are really into it. I think people warm to you if you look silly."

"I feel part comedian onstage, like the cabaret," Bell said. "I'm into presenting pop as a joke. People like Paula Abdul rely on choreography and backing tracks and video, and they're hailed in the US as artistic visionaries. It's a joke."

Referring to his openly gay identity, Bell noted of American reviews, "One guy said it's possible to like Erasure and hate homosexuals. That's like saying you can be into Michael Jackson and hate Blacks."

Erasure marked Clarke's longest connection to a band or recording project. "You have to be a diplomat to be a singer—I'm easygoing," Bell said. "Vince had a different attitude—he'd cut people off. He's a very commercial writer, and I've encouraged him to be more open and to try things. We just do what we do, writing pop songs and using synthesizers to make the music. We're not going to start making jazz records." ■

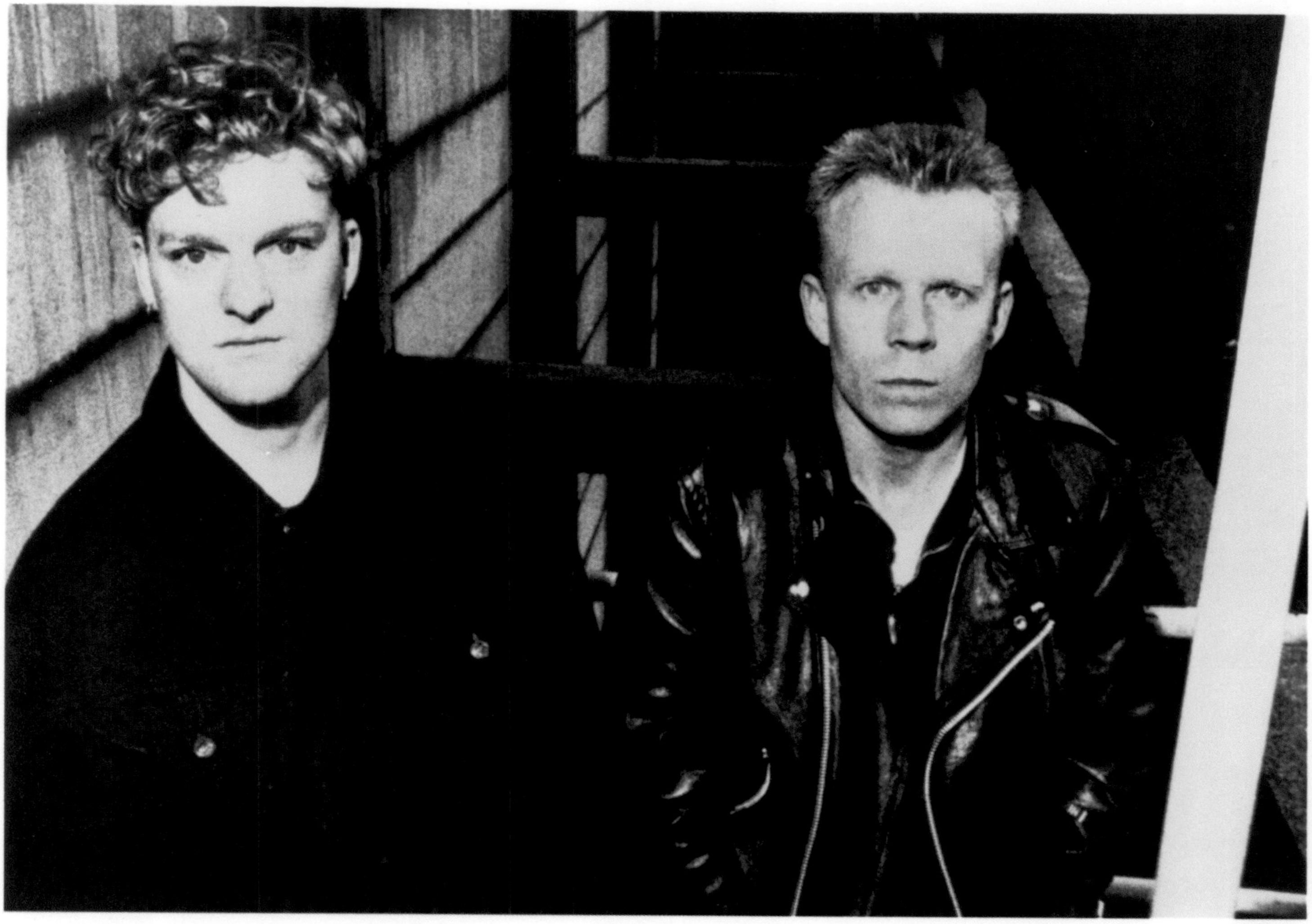

Photo Credit: Richard Houghton

erasure

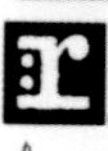

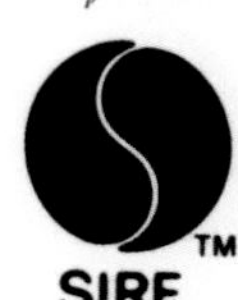

SIRE

Billboard 200: *Lovely* (#106)

The Primitives' exuberant "Crash," a former No. 1 single in England, arose as a top alternative track in the US.

AN APPEALING mixture of gloss and grunge, the Primitives contrasted Tracey Tracey's sweet vocals with a fuzzed-out rock 'n' roll sound. The band's simple pop-with-a-twist songs were instantly accessible, and its killer "na-na-na-na-na" chorus made the breezy hit "Crash" was a perfect summer single.

"None of us expected that song's success," the waifish Tracey admitted. "It was written within the first five weeks the band came together back in 1986; it was two years before we did something with it."

The British indie pop band formed in Coventry, England. Tracey joined after a handful of gigs, and the group built its brand of pop around what was described as her "sexy indifference."

As evinced on the *Lovely* album, the Primitives' music had the cheery exuberance of Blondie and the Go-Go's, but Tracey described the comparisons as annoying.

"They get to be a pain. I know every band likes to think they're unique, but after several years people should recognize our own sound. Looking at the British charts, it's all synthetic, has no substance and is quite forgettable. It's full of rubbish, except for a few bands like the Primitives. We just want the basics in our songs—guitars, bass, drums and a nice melody." ■

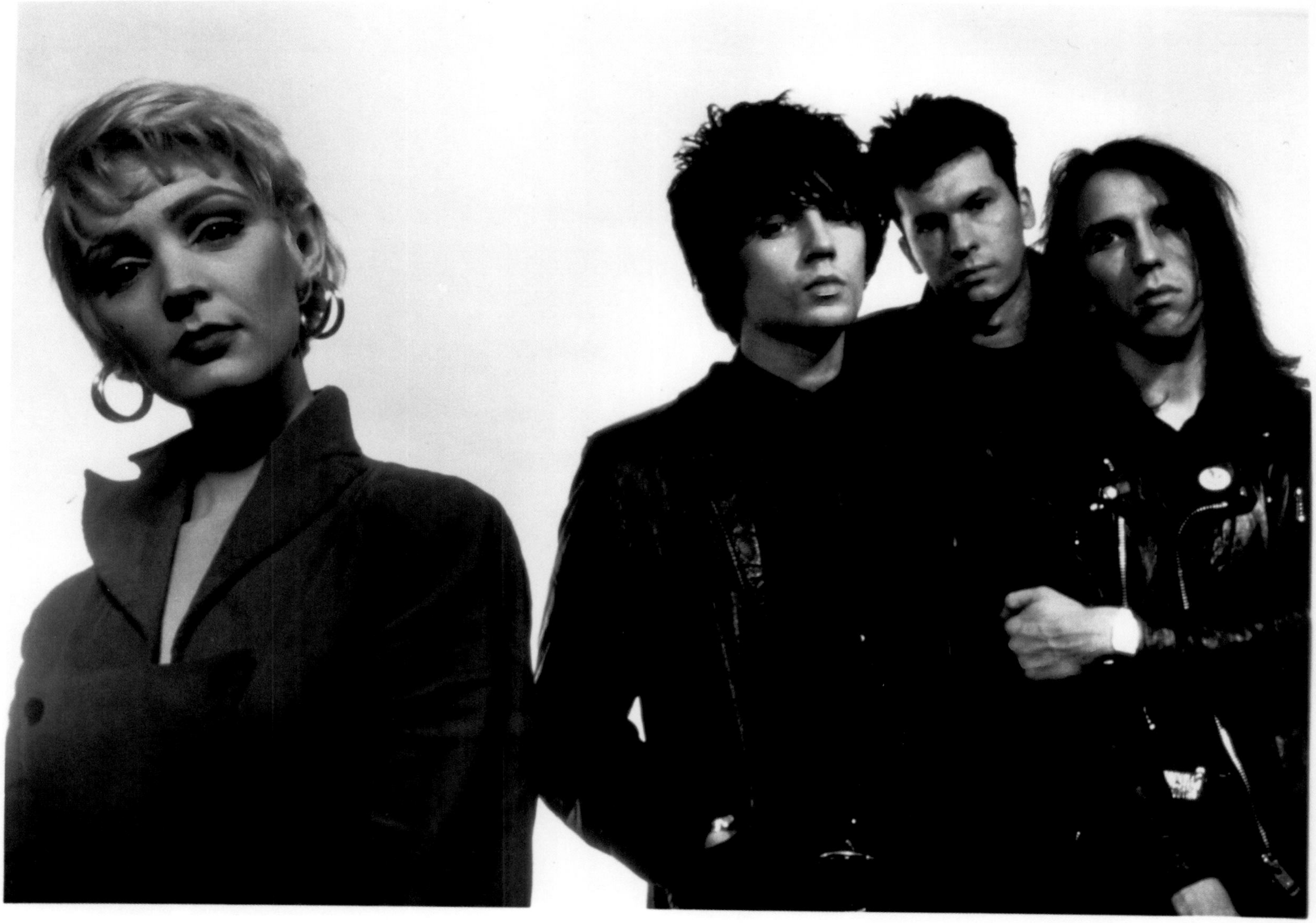

THE PRIMITIVES

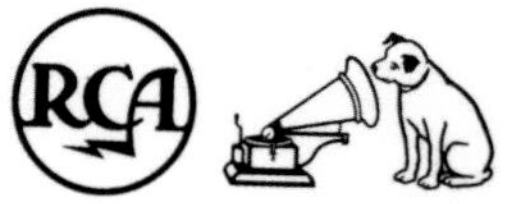

Billboard 200: *Sunshine on Leith* (#31)
Billboard Hot 100: "I'm Gonna Be (500 Miles)" (#3)

The Proclaimers attained an international smash with the exuberant, captivating "I'm Gonna Be (500 Miles)."

IDENTICAL TWINS Charlie and Craig Reid grew up in Leith, Scotland, and began playing American rock and country tunes in their early teens. Punk killed off any lingering interest in formal education, and the pair began performing acoustic sets as the Proclaimers in 1983. Their fortunes took a turn for the better in 1986 after a fan sent a Proclaimers demo (with no contact address) to the Housemartins, a chart-topping British band. That group eventually managed to track down the siblings and gave the Proclaimers the opening slot on its British tour, which in turn led to a recording contract.

"Throw the 'R' Away," a defense of their almost impenetrable accents, was a highlight of *This Is the Story*, the Proclaimers' 1987 debut featuring the spare acoustic sound of the brothers' vocals and Charlie's guitar. "Letter from America" led the British music press to label the Reids as a "political" act, but they disagreed with such tags, citing their equal concern for romance and their sense of humor. They later re-recorded "Letter from America" with electric backing, and the single's success in England gave Charlie and Craig the confidence to record with outside musicians—their second album, *Sunshine on Leith*, found the pair's impassioned folk-country-pop blend backed by a full band.

"We always thought that we would pursue a couple of albums with just the guitar and two voices," Craig said. "But we reached an obvious stage where we were not fulfilling the potential of the songs. We can put them over better with a band."

It was appropriate that the unlikely pop stars (with their short-haired, thick-rimmed glasses persona) then set their sights on the United States.

"We live in Scotland, USA," Craig said. "Certainly the Proclaimers could nae exist without such Yanks as the Everly Brothers, Elvis Presley, Eddie Cochran and Johnny Cash. We've always said America was our No. 1 priority, because anybody who heard American music growing up in Scotland was influenced by it. One of the most remarkable things about Scots is the way they become obsessed with American forms of music, like soul and country. If you go to a big country-and-western club in Glasgow, it'll be full of guys with holsters and guns."

Sunshine on Leith went platinum in the United Kingdom, and the Proclaimers were acclaimed as a post-punk Everly Brothers, most famous for the wildly catchy "I'm Gonna Be (500 Miles)." The punchy call-and-response song also reached No.1 in Iceland, Australia and New Zealand, and it eventually conquered the American charts five years later, becoming a belatedly massive hit following its inclusion on the soundtrack to the movie *Benny & Joon*. ■

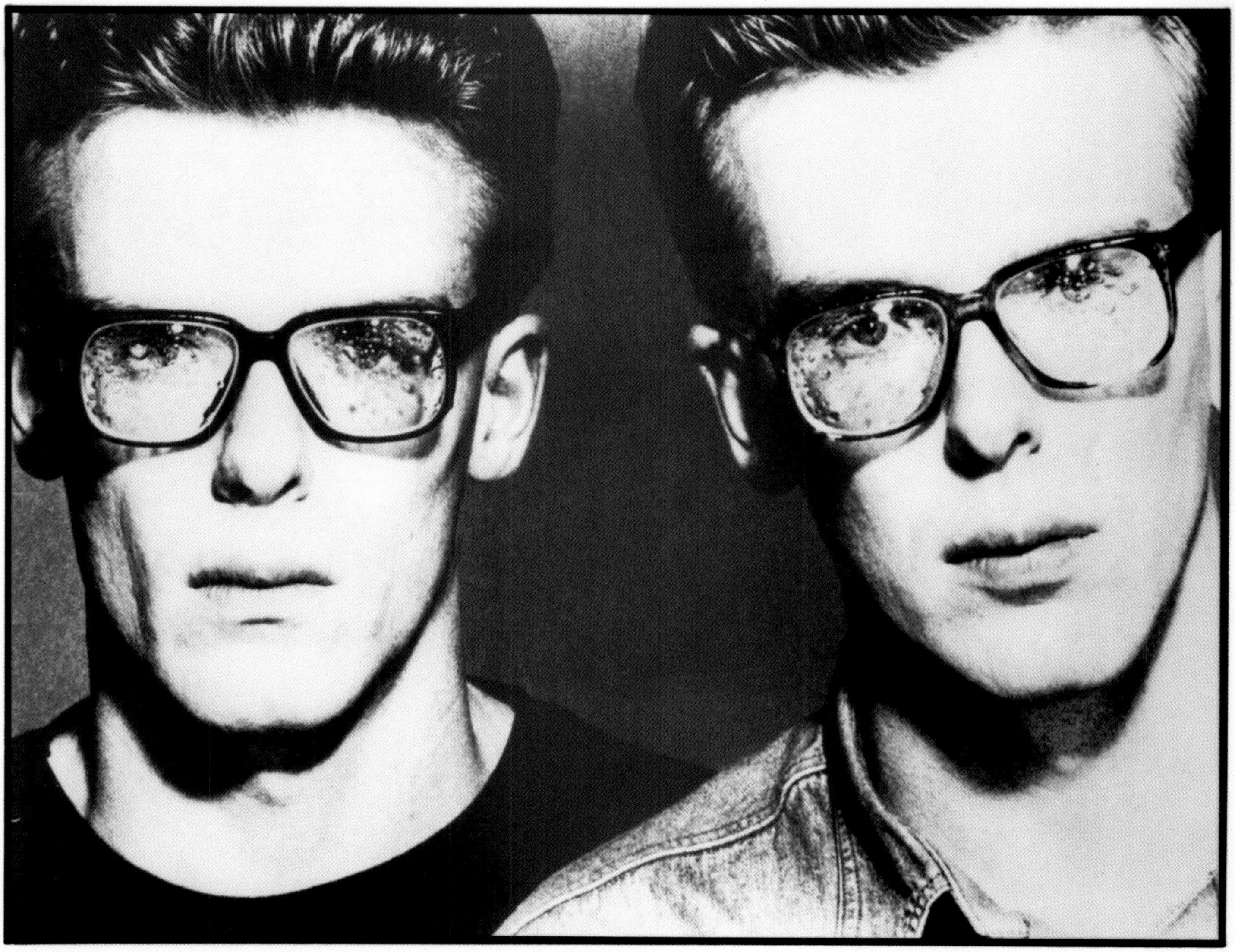

THE

PROCLAIMERS

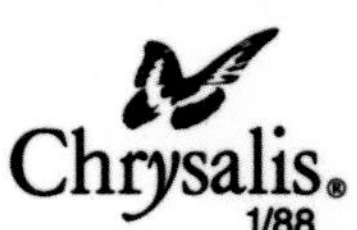

Billboard 200: *Irish Heartbeat* (#102)

Two of the Emerald Isle's institutions, Van Morrison & the Chieftains, teamed up for the album *Irish Heartbeat*.

BY PERFORMING a foot-stomping legacy of Ireland's jigs, airs and reels, the Chieftains had attained celebrity status across the world. After 16 albums and countless collaborations, the group's brand of acoustic music had come to be enthusiastically appreciated by a rock audience. Indeed, members of the group had recorded or performed with pop stars ranging from Eric Clapton to the Grateful Dead to Dan Fogelberg.

Celebrating 25 years as the best-known purveyors of Irish folk music had brought a "circus of activity," as leader Paddy Moloney put it. Another feather in the Chieftains' green caps came in the form of *Irish Heartbeat*, a long-awaited collaboration with Van Morrison. The Irish-born performer returned to his roots, the soulful sounds which had influenced him throughout his life, including the children's song "I'll Tell Me Ma."

"We've co-produced old Irish folk songs with a new approach," Moloney said. "The first time we ever touched bases (with Morrison) was at a concert in Edinburgh—he had seen the BBC special on the making of the James Galway & the Chieftains' *In Ireland* album (a film broadcast by PBS in America). Now we've worked like the devil on this album."

Moloney had also worked on *Primitive Cool*, Mick Jagger's solo album, where he performed on the track "Party Doll," and he called in markers with such friends as Jackson Browne, Don Henley, Art Garfunkel and Paul McCartney in the silver anniversary year. While he indulged in rubbing shoulders with popular music's biggest names, Moloney was also willing to collaborate with lesser-known talents.

"It's still Chieftains music after all this time," he said of his band's refusal to adapt its style to meet commercial demands. "And we'll continue to play what we're best at. We have a saying in Ireland—'Ta gach rud to hiontach,' which loosely translated means 'Everything is great.' And that's how we feel." ■

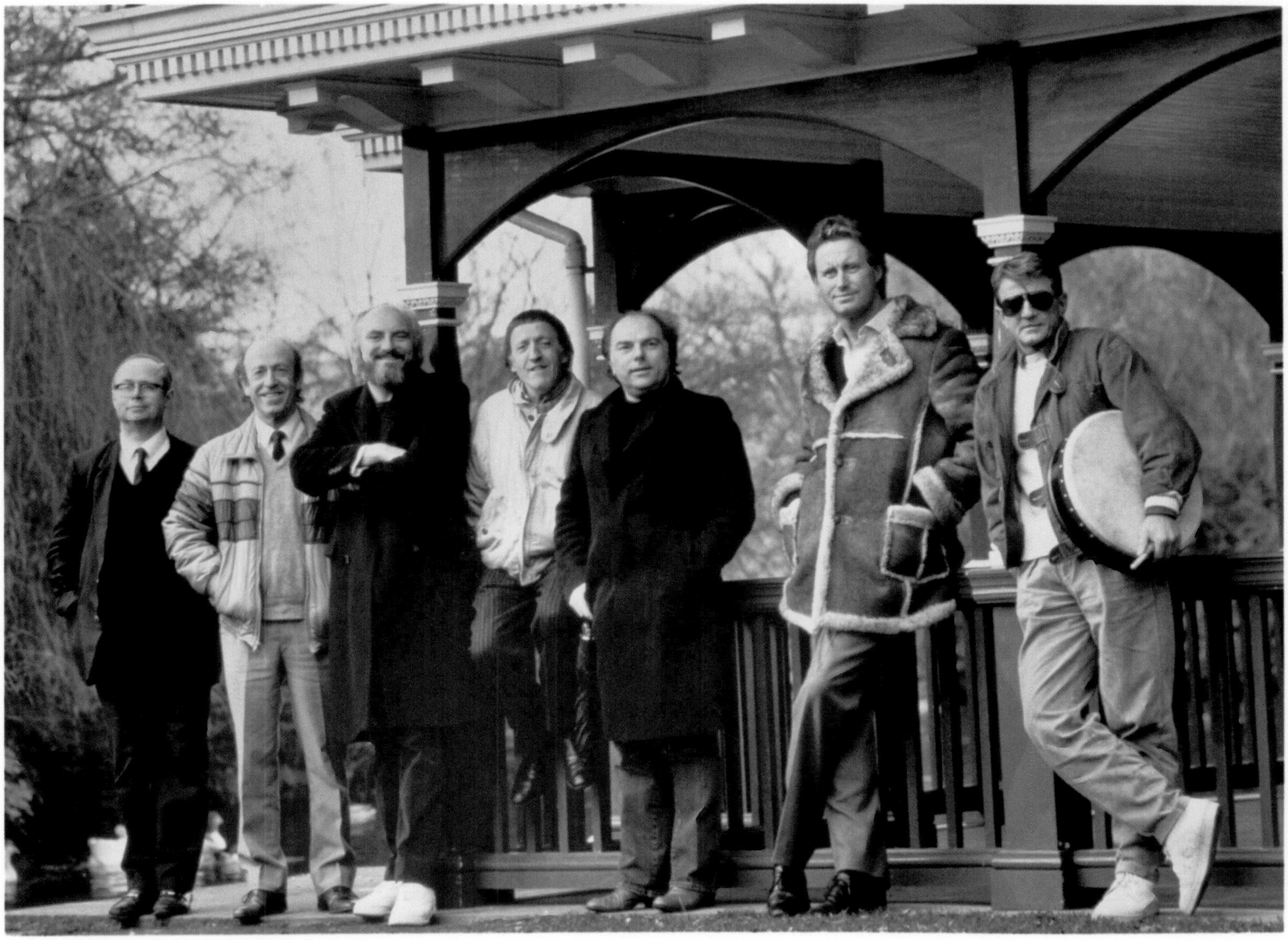

Van Morrison And The Chieftains

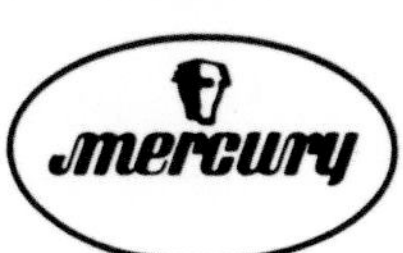

PolyGram Records

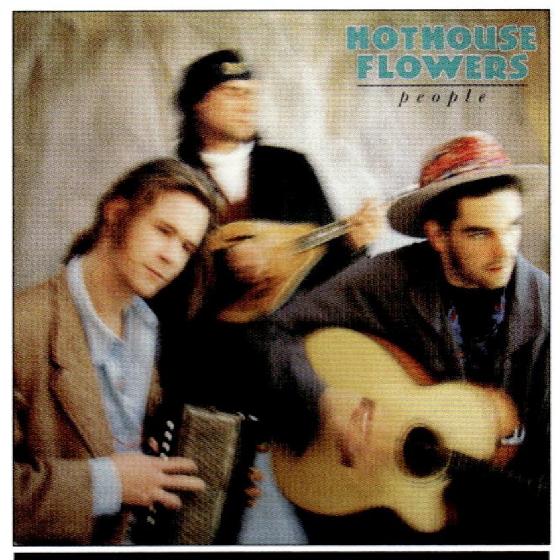

Billboard 200: *People* (#88)

People, the debut album from Hothouse Flowers, got to No. 1 in the band's native Ireland and #2 in the UK.

HAILED AS the pop world's hottest new Irish export, Hothouse Flowers had won a sizable trans-Atlantic audience with a rootsy musical approach that differed from anything else on the charts, combining traditional Gaelic influences with echoes of American soul and gospel. *People* incorporated bouzouki, mandolin, harmonica and bodhran (a goat-skinned tambourine) alongside guitars, bass and drums.

"We didn't consciously decide to sound quintessentially Irish, but we were brought up on traditional Irish music as well as rock 'n' roll," guitarist Fiachna Ó Braonáin said. "It's in our blood, so it comes out. We're all able to play more than one instrument, so we use them to give our records lasting interest."

The young Dublin quintet was the result of a longstanding partnership between Ó Braonáin and keyboardist Liam Ó Maonlaí, who met at an all-Gaelic-speaking school where their music classes included training on traditional Irish instruments. They later took over the street corners of London, busking in record shops and wherever anyone passing by would listen "for pocket change and fun." They eventually assembled a band that built a considerable local following, causing mayhem in the British press with their fresh-sounding "Gaelic blues."

Hothouse Flowers gained more notoriety in 1986, when *Rolling Stone* magazine pegged the eclectic group as "the hottest unsigned band in Europe." U2's Bono gave the members their first recorded shot when Mother Records, the independent record company his band had founded, released their debut single, "Love Don't Work This Way." That led to a deal with a major label, and the release of *People*.

When the melodically buoyant "Don't Go" became a massive European hit, Hothouse Flowers emerged from U2's formidable shadow. "We're both Irish, but there aren't any musical similarities," Ó Braonáin mused. "As far as we're concerned, U2 has been a great help from a career point of view. They offered us our first single, and we opened for them in front of 40,000 people in Dublin. They've never lost interest in up-and-coming bands—they're always encouraging and helping people along." ■

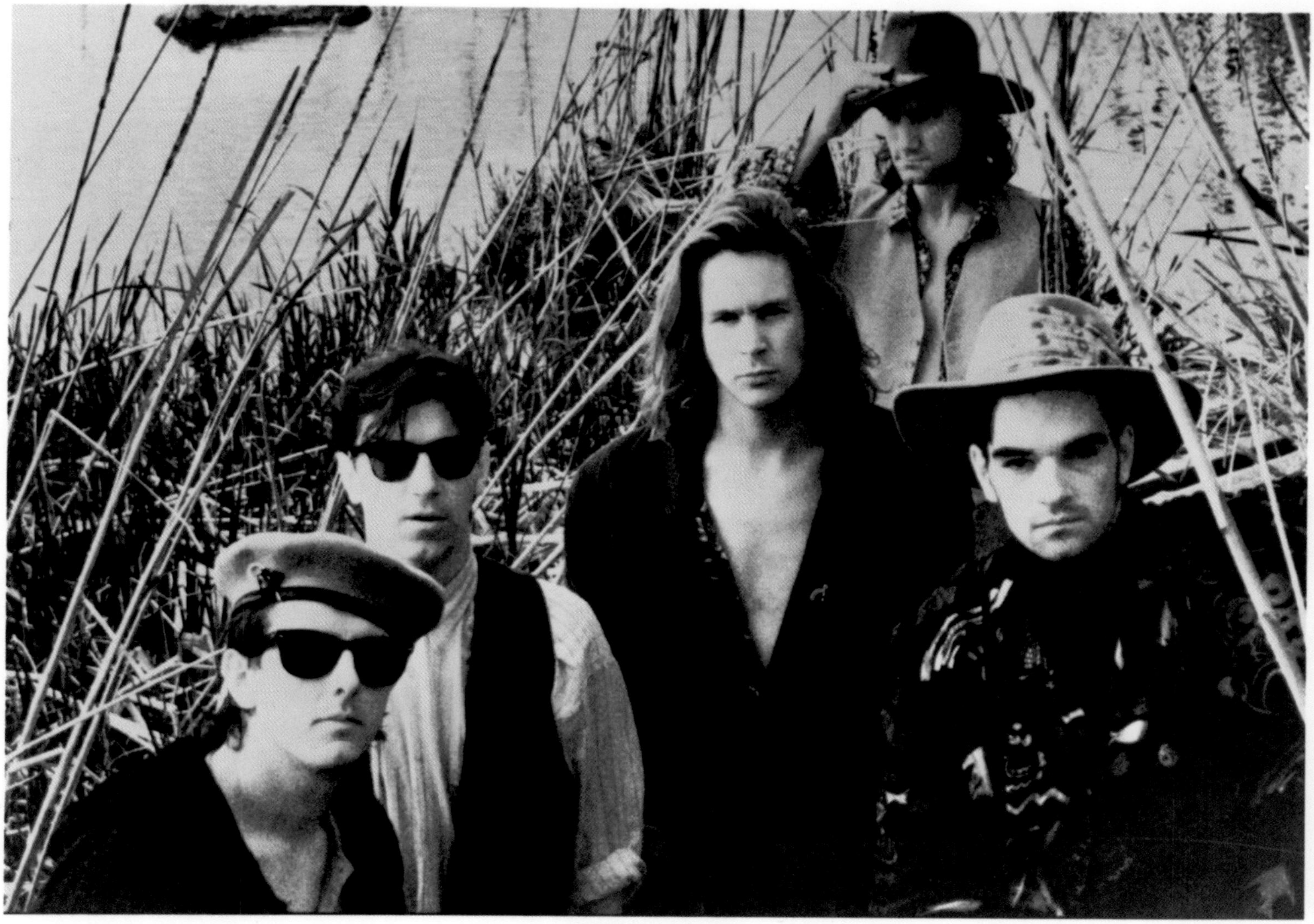

HOTHOUSE FLOWERS

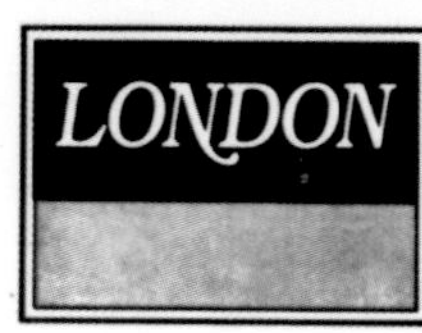

PolyGram Records

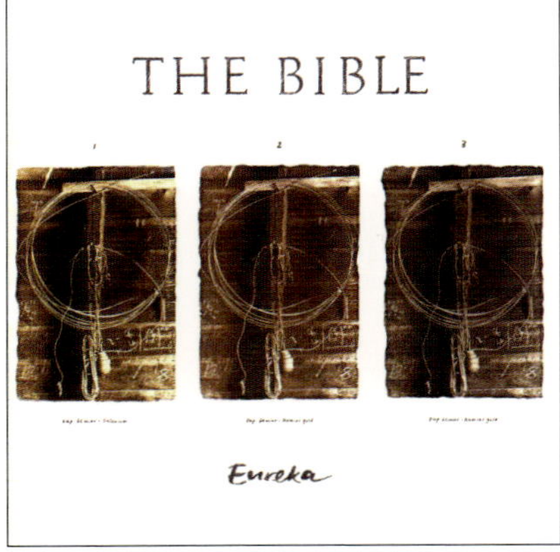

The Bible, a band from East England, spread the word about *Eureka*, a US recording produced by Steve Earle.

THE BIBLE was formed in 1985 when singer and lyricist Boo Hewerdine teamed up with keyboardist Tony Shepard and eventually joined with drummer Dave Larcombe and guitarist Neill MacColl—the son of folk legends Ewan MacColl and Peggy Seeger, and brother of pop star Kirsty MacColl.

On the strength of an independently-released disc that made a substantial splash in the UK, a contract with Ensign followed—also the home of the Waterboys, World Party and Sinéad O'Connor. *Eureka,* the English band's debut American album, provided a chance for "Bible study" among new music pundits.

In a surprising collaboration, *Eureka* marked the first outside production effort by Steve Earle, the up-and-coming country rock star. Earle had heard the band's independent UK-only album and offered his assistance.

"We weren't sure how we'd get on. We're rural Englishmen, and he's... well, he's a Texas lunatic," MacColl laughed.

"We'd been working with English producers, and we found that they were very slow, because they were used to producing bands that couldn't play," Hewerdine explained. "We wanted somebody who would let us play the whole thing in one go—that's the way Steve makes records in Nashville, so he was perfect. He really got the performances out of us."

On *Eureka*, the Bible worked elements of various musical genres (jazz on "November Brides," MacColl's folk roots in general) into a sophisticated blend. Hewerdine's aloof British vocals packed an emotional punch, and "Honey Be Good" rated as an atmospheric Sixties-style piece. "Crystal Palace," the most pop-oriented tune on *Eureka*, displayed Hewerdine's sense of wordplay, but the song that best represented the Bible's approach was the lovely "Skywriting."

Yet in spite of good reviews, *Eureka* failed to find an audience.

"We've all been in bands on major labels before, and it's taken a long time for all of us to find a band as comfortable as this," Hewerdine observed. "But pop music has become a lot like the film business—everything has to be huge. The individual thing has been forgotten." ■

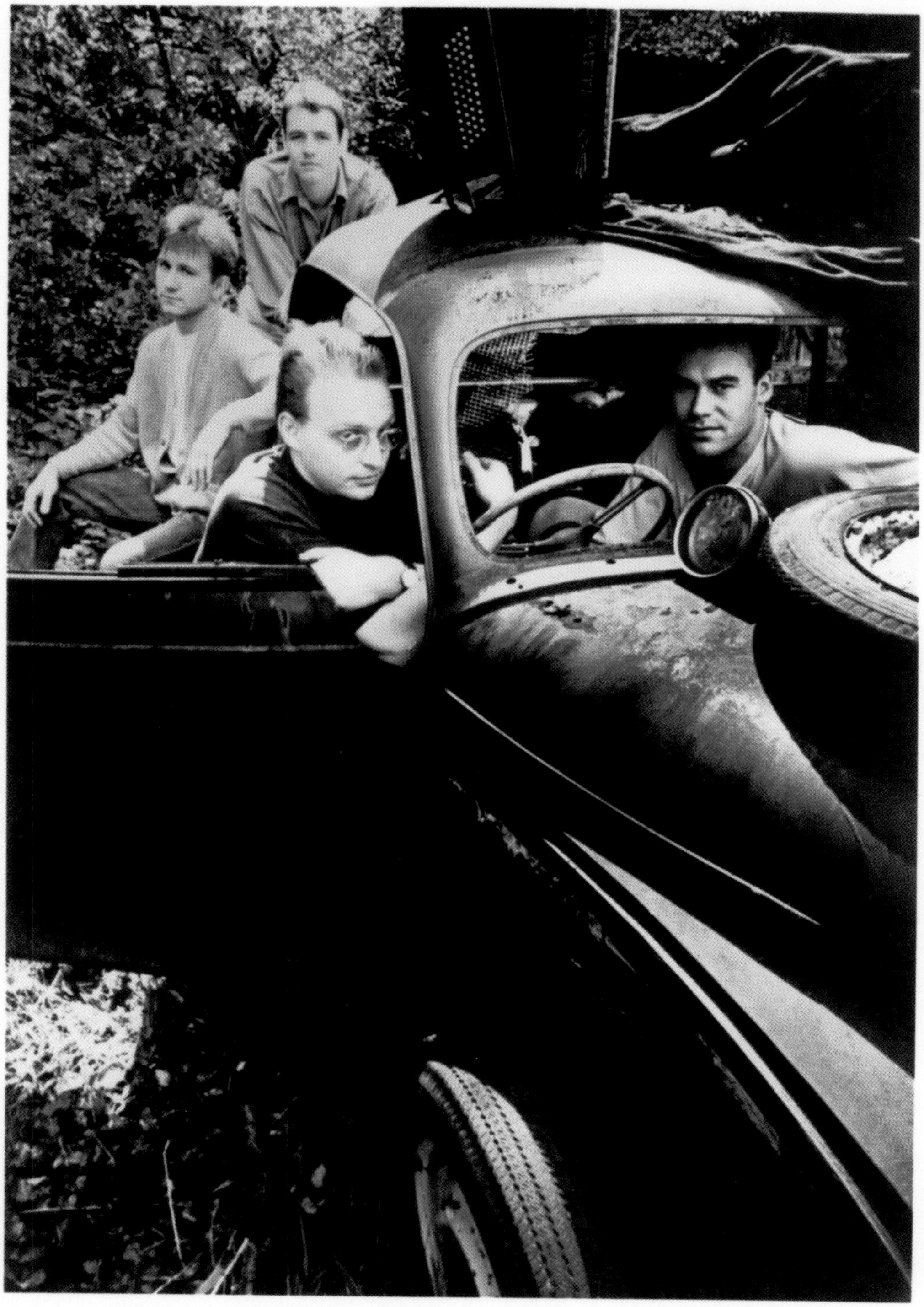

Clockwise from top: Neill MacColl, Tony Shepherd, Boo Hewerdine, Dave Larcombe.

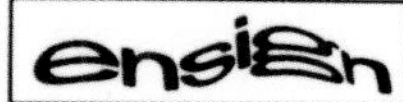

THE BIBLE

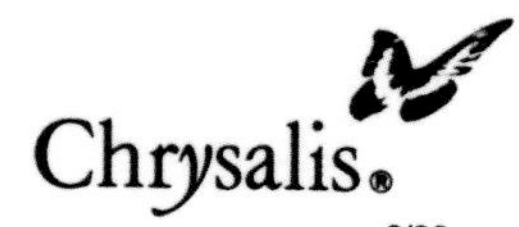

Chrysalis®

6/88

TIM & MOLLIE O'BRIEN TAKE ME BACK

Take Me Back proved that nothing could beat Tim & Mollie O'Brien's tight, near inseparable sibling harmonies.

RAISED IN Wheeling, West Virginia, Tim O'Brien was the youngest in a family of five children. At the age of 12, he got his first guitar—"I saw the Beatles on *The Ed Sullivan Show*, and that looked like a lot of fun"—and decided to take up music with his older sister Mollie. Both continued to study and perform as a duo at school and church functions and local coffeehouses through their teens, surrounded by the rich musical heritage of the day. "Pop radio had Peter, Paul & Mary, Roger Miller and the Singing Nun, all in one," he recalled.

Tim eventually moved to Colorado in 1974 and became part of the state's music scene, playing swing music with the Ophelia Swing Band, then forming Hot Rize (and its comic alter-ego, Red Knuckles & the Trailblazers) in 1978. The quartet gained widespread fame as one of America's most innovative and entertaining bluegrass bands, becoming festival mainstays, making national TV appearances and playing the Grand Ole Opry in 1982. "And there was Beef 'n Bean Day up in Milliken, Colorado," O'Brien noted.

Having earned recognition as one of the best singers, mandolin players and songwriters in roots music, Tim expanded his repertoire as a duo partner with Mollie. "Mollie was always singing—she was in musical theater—but then she was dormant with for a while. After I'd been living in Colorado for several years, she came out and we briefly lived together."

In 1984, a promoter who had heard their harmonies convinced them to reunite for a Mother's Day concert in Denver, and they continued to perform together regularly as an Americana duo. Their dazzling duets were captured on *Take Me Back*, an album of old-timey country songs released on Sugar Hill Records. "Down to the Valley to Pray" had a nifty fiddle, mandolin and clawhammer banjo accompaniment. John Prine's "Unwed Fathers" was a powerfully sung contemporary ballad. Nick Forster of Hot Rize added accompaniment on a variety of acoustic instruments, including slide guitar on the bouncy "Papa's on the Housetop."

"Mollie and I started singing again, doing whatever music we wanted to do," Tim said. "How great it was to get that going again." ■

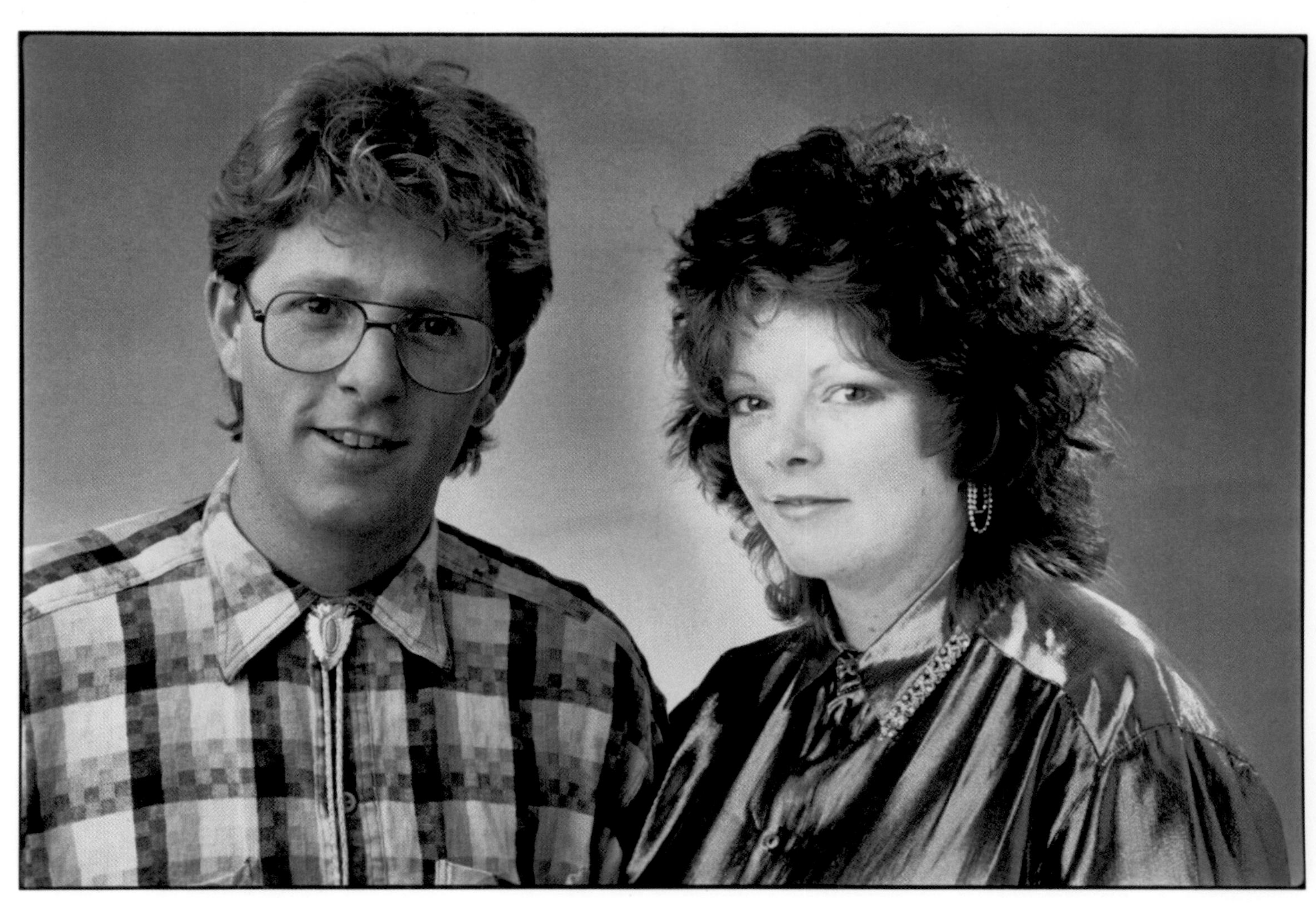

Tim & Mollie O'Brien

Justifiably hailed as a vital talent, **Sam Phillips** fired up an engaging pop event titled *The Indescribable Wow.*

SAM PHILLIPS' first forum for performing her songs was her local church, and in 1986 she made *The Turning* (under her given name Leslie) for a contemporary Christian label. But the singer-songwriter grew disenchanted with the genre's closed-minded lyrical constraints (and her label's description of her as "the Christian Cyndi Lauper").

While her music still conveyed an undeniable spirituality, her secular debut album, *The Indescribable Wow,* rated as an intelligent, ingratiating pop treasure. Every song was placed in an upbeat, colorful setting with Sixties pop references—catchy choruses, ringing guitars.

"When T Bone (Burnett, her beau) was producing the album, he'd ask me about backwards guitars and harmonies, and I'd say, 'Give me more, more, more,'" Phillips said.

"I grew up hearing all of the old Forties songwriters—Irving Berlin, Rodgers & Hart. And the Beatles continued that tradition of melody, so of course I tip my hat to them. I heard them when I was three and loved stuff like the harpsichord. But it's not because I want to be the Beatles—nobody ever will be again. They're so widely referenced by people whose songwriting is closer than mine. Maybe everyone notices because I'm a woman doing it.

"Plus growing up in Los Angeles was like a Raymond Chandler novel made into a Fellini film with a Ventures soundtrack."

Phillips was praised for her bewitching warble and her delicate, compelling song sense. "Holding On to the Earth," infused with one of the coolest organ sounds since the classic oldie "Incense and Peppermints," peaked at #22 on *Billboard*'s Modern Rock Tracks chart, and "I Don't Know How to Say Goodbye to You" and the arty "What Do I Do" would have been smart, baroque hit singles in a perfect retro world.

"The things that I write about might be complicated, but I don't think my lyrics are highfalutin—I don't think I'm a poet; Dylan is a poet," Phillips said. "I've expected my record company to say, 'Give us a bunch of radio songs or say goodbye.' Instead, they're open to my being extreme. There's the 'spectacle' end of the business—Michael Jackson, Madonna, the heavily marketed stuff—and there's music. I hope there'll be a format for music." ■

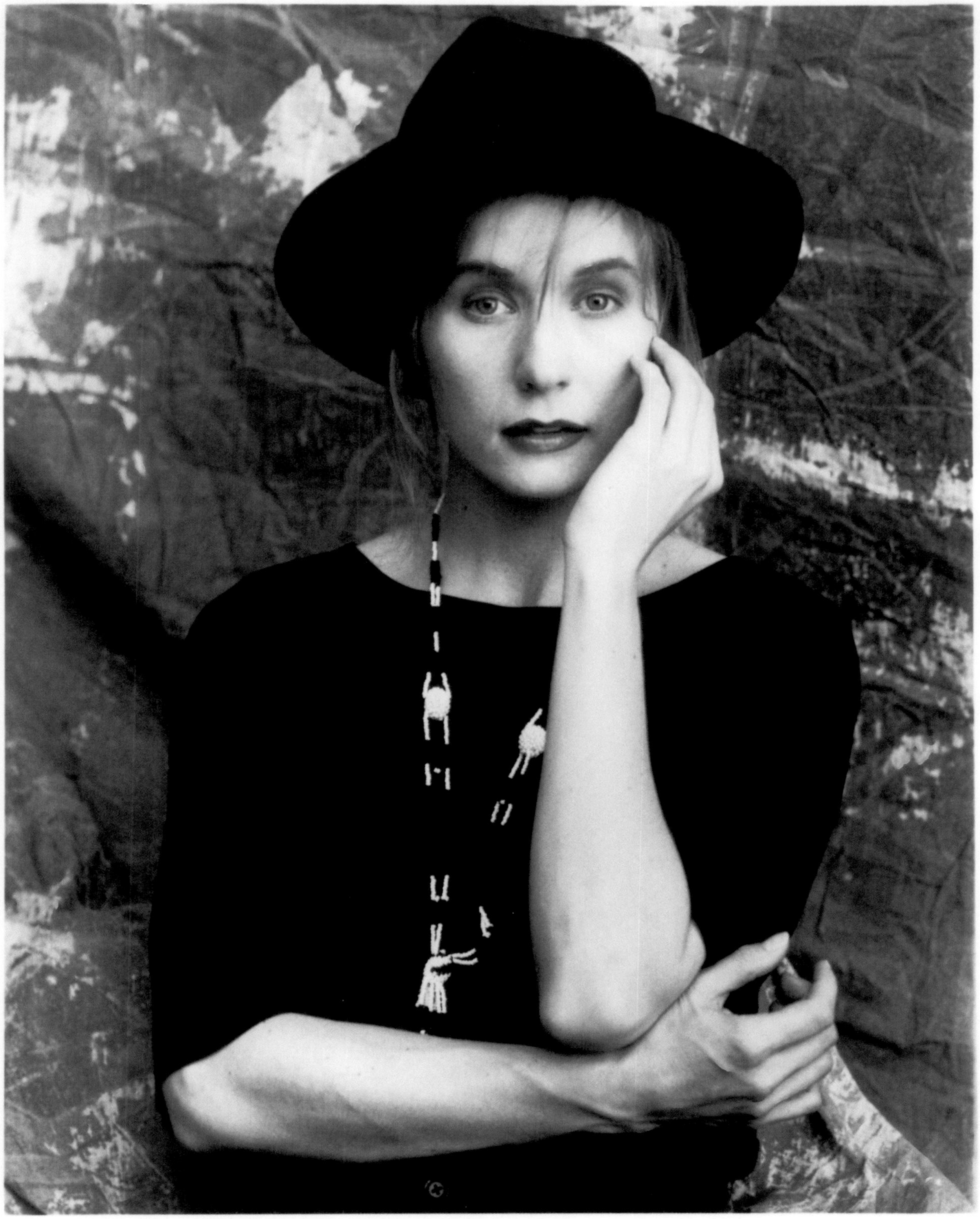

Photo Credit: Taylor King

SAM PHILLIPS

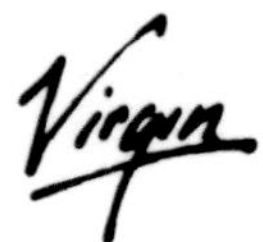

Dubbed "the Voice" for her powerful, flexible singing, gospel singer Sandi Patti arrived at national acclaim.

AS HER string of Dove and Grammy awards suggested, Sandi Patti ranked as one of gospel music's most popular female performers. In her nine-year career, the gently sincere vocalist had reached Christians across the country through recordings as well as performing nearly 100 concerts annually in America's major auditoriums and arenas.

The assumption was that Patti, the daughter of a music minister, was singing for people who already knew about Jesus. "I call my audience the 'church family,'" she said. "Most of them have come across a Christian lifestyle. But the same problems found in schools and businesses are also found in the church. We're not immune to drug and alcohol abuse or marital difficulties. So I hope that what I share can be of encouragement to those struggling with something major in their lives."

In past decades, the term "gospel music" meant Black gospel or Southern gospel. But in the late Eighties, different musical styles that shared the same message all fell under that heading or the modified "contemporary Christian music" tag.

"Jesus didn't talk to the fishermen in the same way He talked to a tax collector or the same way He talked to a Pharisee," Patti noted. "Yet His message was the same. I think that is where the Lord is leading us in music. We need to share with people in a way they can understand, yet we've got to be sure the message stays the same."

As evidenced by her *Make His Praise Glorious* album, Patti's music fell into a conservative category. "It's adult contemporary, or middle-of-the-road—it sounds the same as secular music, but that's not to belittle it," she said. "When people come home from a hard day at work, they're not going to put on music that challenges their values and examines their priorities."

Yet Patti knew the inspirational content of her lyrics would keep her from recognition in the mainstream pop market. "My very strong Christian lyrics are appropriate for those I am singing for, but I would have to soften them to get any kind of secular radio airplay," she admitted. "That just isn't something that I'm willing to do. I understand that my music isn't accepted by a lot of people, and that's fine. I'm very comfortable with what I'm doing." ■

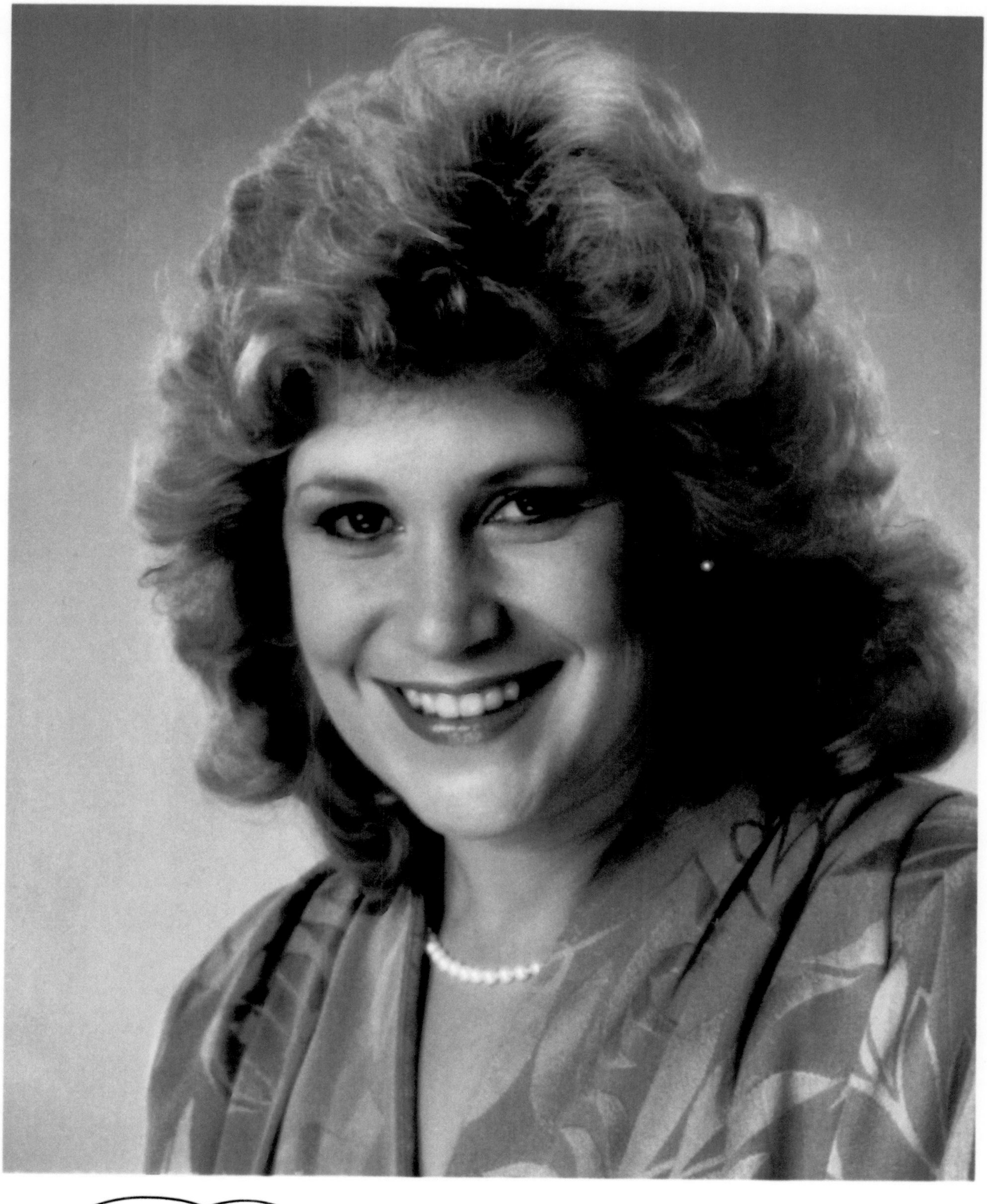

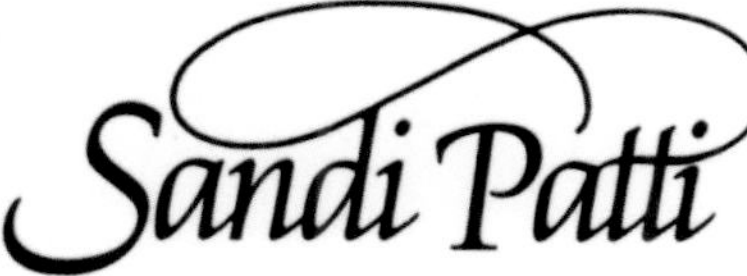

Management & Booking:
The Helvering Agency
2200 Madison Square
Anderson, IN 46011
(317)642-0017

Billboard 200: *In God We Trust* (#32)
Billboard Hot 100: "Always There for You" (#71);
"I Believe in You" (#88)

Christian metal band Stryper's *In God We Trust* made a move toward a larger, more orthodox pop audience.

AFTER PAYING dues on the Los Angeles club circuit, Stryper's popularity as confirmed-Christians-yet-hard-rocking-dudes had continued to spread over five years' time. Heavy metal's God squad was making big bucks from a large, ready-made audience of Christian kids who could not or would not listen to secular rock music. The 1986 album *To Hell with the Devil* sold over a million copies, earned a Grammy nomination and exposed the band to a whole new audience with the Top 40 single "Honestly."

Stryper's *In God We Trust* release shipped gold, music biz lingo for a half-million units in advance sales. The album of friendly arena rock offered a few keyboard-oriented ballads, lyrical treatises on money and mankind, and a harmony-laden sound that drew comparisons to Styx. The act's motives were calculatedly canny—Stryper brought its faith and optimism to a community alienated by mainstream Christianity, yet they did it as a rock band, not a religious agency.

But because they wore makeup, silly yellow-and-black costumes and poofed-up hair, the members of Stryper took a monumental amount of abuse from fundamentalists. And in the wake of the scandals that brought down virtuous televangelists Jim Bakker and Jimmy Swaggart, drummer Robert Sweet and his cohorts had to endure religious life in the limelight, fielding perpetual questions about being an elaborate con job. Sweet noted that the band preferred to take the heat now, rather than in the afterlife.

"With success, it's getting even harder in some ways," he said. "Now people expect too much sometimes, that we should be able to drop everything to talk for an hour about our faith, or that we're pushovers. That's not really what Stryper is about. Nobody's perfect. We're just trying to be an example of something good, trying to encourage people to look at God. We've always tried to write songs about hope."

"We are singing about something that is a little bit different than what most rock bands sing about," Robert's brother, guitarist Michael Sweet, added. "How can being positive create so much controversy?" ■

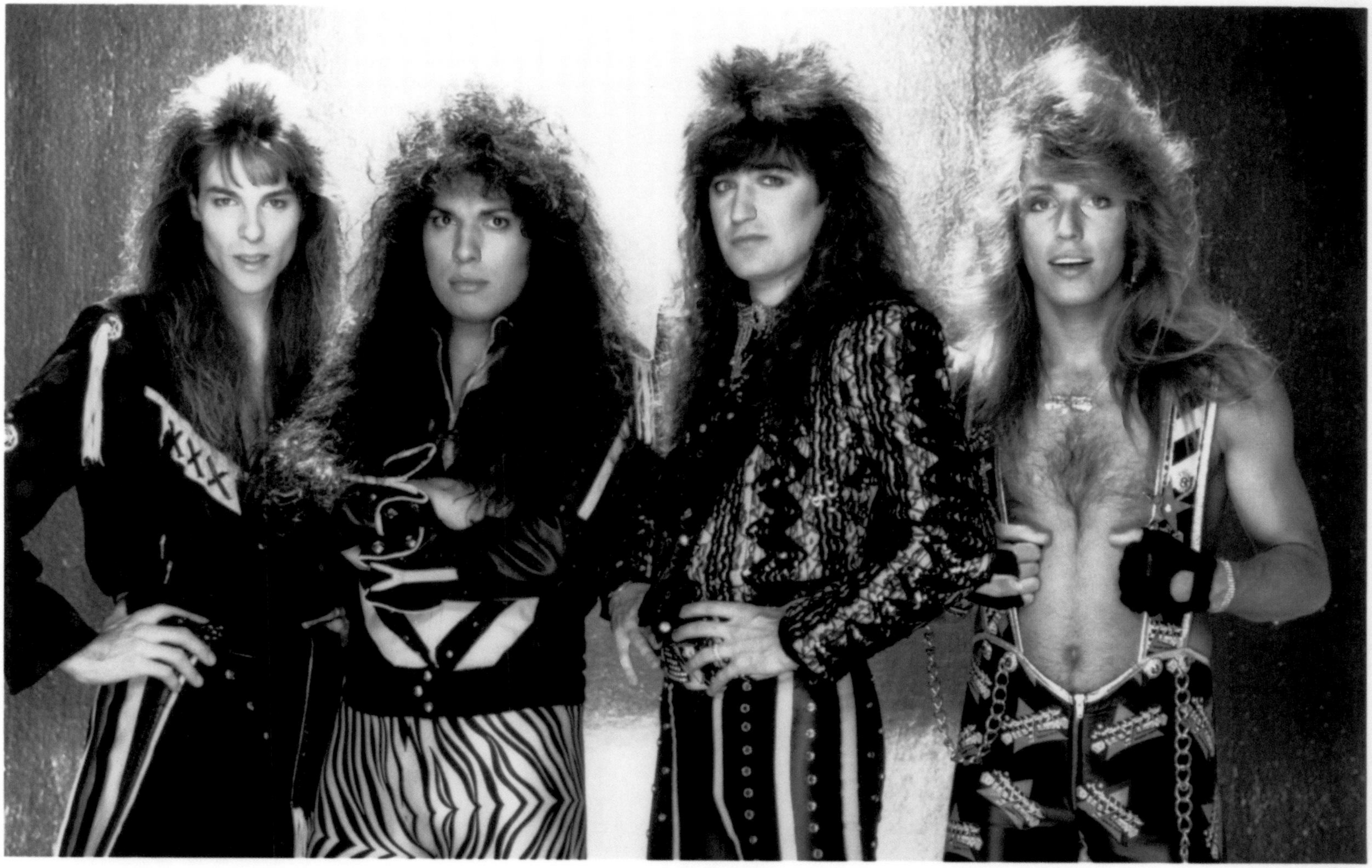

L to R: Tim Gaines, Oz Fox, Michael Sweet, Robert Sweet

Photo by Neil Zlozower

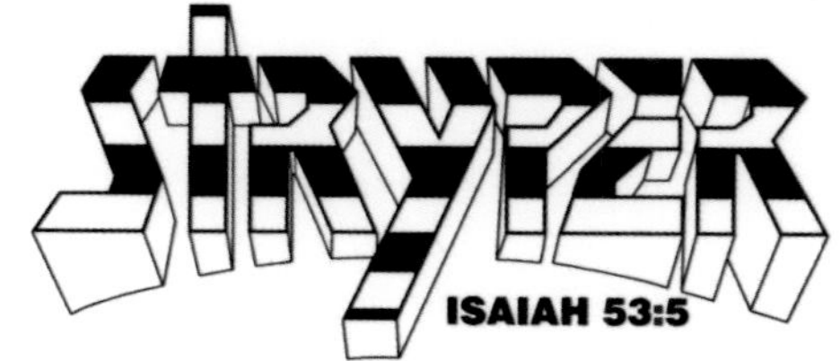

ENIGMA

ENIGMA RECORDS
El Segundo, California 90245-2428
213/640-6869
ENIGMA CANADA
2183 Dunwin Drive, Mississauga, Ontario L5L 3S3
416/828-612

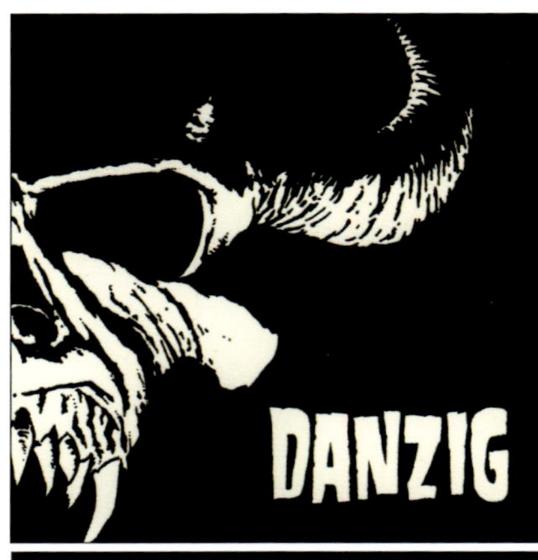

Billboard 200: *Danzig* (#125)

Formerly the leader of the Misfits and Samhain, Glenn Danzig found another means of expression in Danzig.

TO CASUAL observers, Danzig might have appeared to be another doltish metal band from the realm of inverted crucifixes and cow skulls, churning out primitive riffs while singing the praises of Satan.

But the malevolence was professional and focused, dominated by Glenn Danzig's trademark voice—his Elvis-from-hell delivery was too goofy to be scary, but it was entertaining, nonetheless. His tasteful, precise band (guitarist John Christ, bassist Eerie Von, drummer Chuck Biscuits) referenced the best classic rock—Black Sabbath, Led Zeppelin and the Doors. And while Danzig's lyrics reflected his fascination with Celtic paganism and Black Mass, he maintained his interest in such matters was purely scholarly.

"If someone asks me if I believe in Satan and I say yes, then I'm branded a Satanist," Danzig mused. "People never ask me if I believe in God as well. In the doctrine of God, He created Satan, who was a fallen angel—but narrow-minded types are going to think what they want no matter what I say. They're set in one mode."

Producer Rick Rubin (of the Cult, Beastie Boys and Run-D.M.C. fame) chose Danzig to be the flagship for his new Def American record label, and on *Danzig* he sharpened up the group's sound substantially. But the spooky, brooding feeling of the music remained.

"I approach things from a historical perspective—I won't write or say anything unless I know what I'm talking about, unlike other musicians who spew out anything that comes to mind," Danzig said. "There's a lot of personal stuff in my music, but the basis is always in reality. My views come after that."

"Mother" was the band's most successful tune—"Mother, tell your children not to come my way," Danzig bellowed. Formerly of the punk bands the Misfits and Samhain, he considered himself a misinterpreted artist, not a demonic stud with a Nautilus-developed chest. "I have a sense of humor," he insisted. "But a lot of people don't like me or what I'm about, and that's the shot they take—I'm humorless. Well, yeah—when people confront me, why shouldn't I be serious?" ■

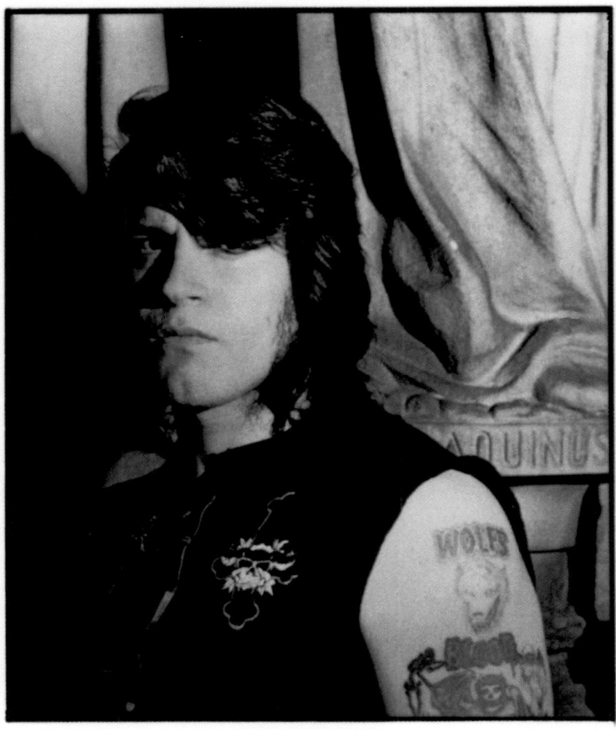

Glenn Danzig

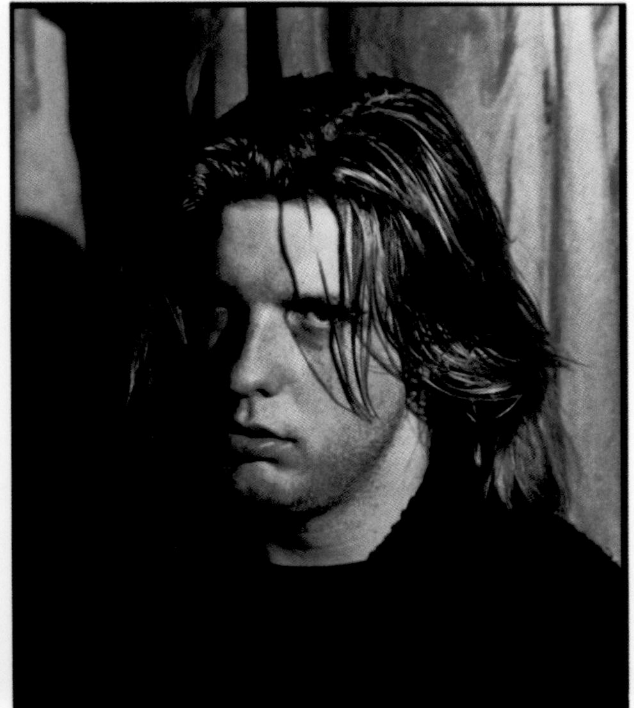
Chuck Biscuits

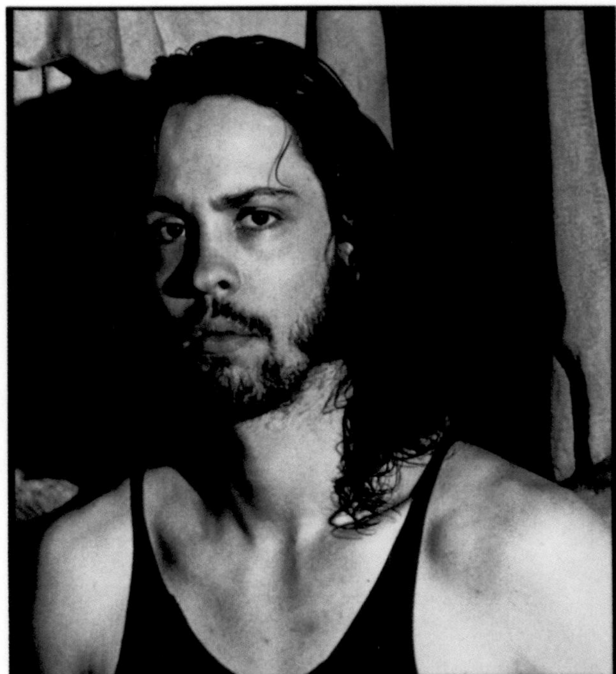
Eerie Von

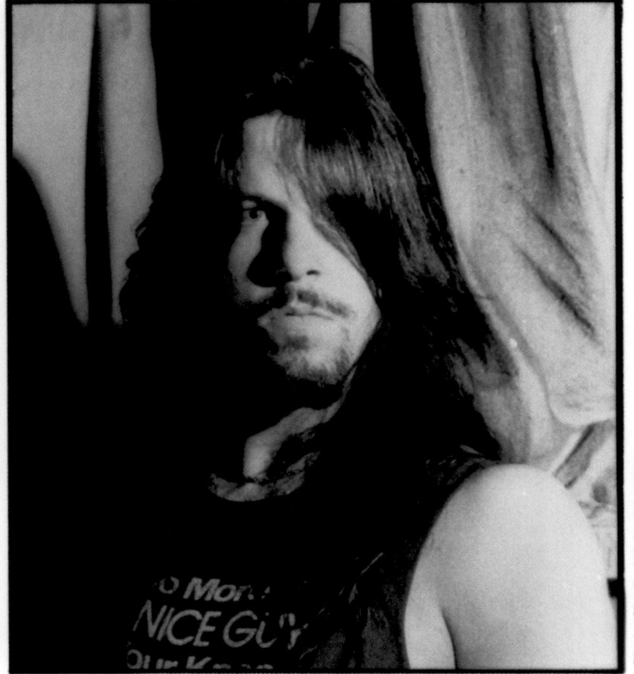

John Christ

Photo Credit: Michael Lavine

DANZIG

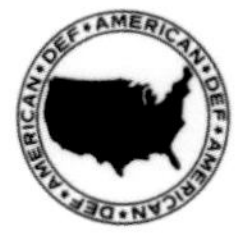

Distributed exclusively by Geffen Records.

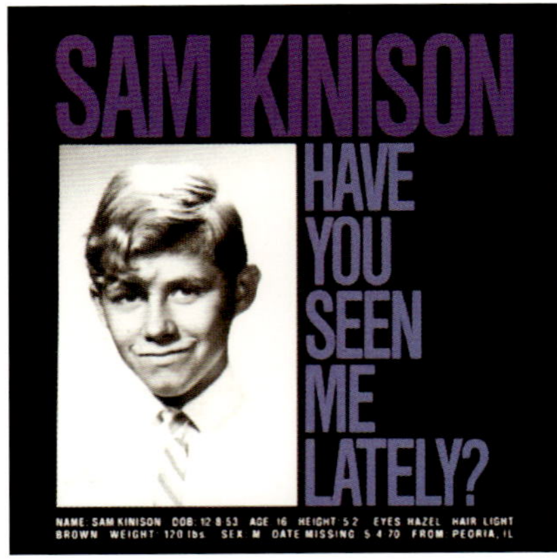

Billboard 200: *Have You Seen Me Lately?* (#43)

Stand-up comedian Sam Kinison shouted a novelty cover version of "Wild Thing," a hit music video on MTV.

WILDMAN COMIC Sam Kinison's controversial topics, bellowed outbursts and signature scream had won him fans of all types, particularly from the heavy-metal set. So Kinison combined his two greatest loves, comedy and rock 'n' roll, on his *Have You Seen Me Lately?* album, making his singing debut on a raunchy rendition of the Troggs 1966 classic "Wild Thing."

Not surprisingly, Kinison revamped the lyrics as only he could for his broken-man persona: "Wild thing/You made me trust you/Then you stuck the knife in my heart, you lying, unfaithful, untrustable tramp…"

"When I was 15 years old, I was a rocker with an electric guitar," he said. "So I set out to do a song on my album for the identification. I don't know any other comic who's really been accepted into the metal-rock scene other than myself."

Kinison embarked on his adventurous singing career at the Universal Amphitheater in Los Angeles, when some guys from Billy Idol's band and Mötley Crüe came onstage. "We did an impromptu version of 'Wild Thing' because it only has three chords, so everyone could play," he recalled. "Then my record company suggested that I record it since I couldn't get any radio play with the spoken-word stuff on my album. And once we got in the studio, we got crazy."

The remake reached #18 on *Billboard*'s Album Rock Tracks chart, thanks to the interest generated by the video version. The clip, which Kinison described as "everything I always wanted to be in high school," was a who's who of hard rockers from Bon Jovi to Poison to Whitesnake, Aerosmith, Guns N' Roses and other bands. It also featured the notorious Jessica Hahn (whose sexual tryst with Jim Bakker had led to the televangelist's downfall) as the "Wild Thing," and a special appearance by comedian Rodney Dangerfield.

The other part of *Have You Seen Me Lately?* was filled with Kinison's outrageous, no-taboos-left-unchallenged comedy monologues—"Parties with the Dead," "Lesbians Are Our Friends," "Robo-Pope." "Rubber Love" caused a controversy with his comments on AIDS.

"I haven't set out to make any enemies—I really do try to entertain," the ex-preacher allowed. "I'm not trying to see how many groups I can get to protest my shows or how many letters I can get written to my record company—'Have him stopped! He's like Hitler at a Jew rally! Kill him! Beat him! *Aauuugh!*'" ■

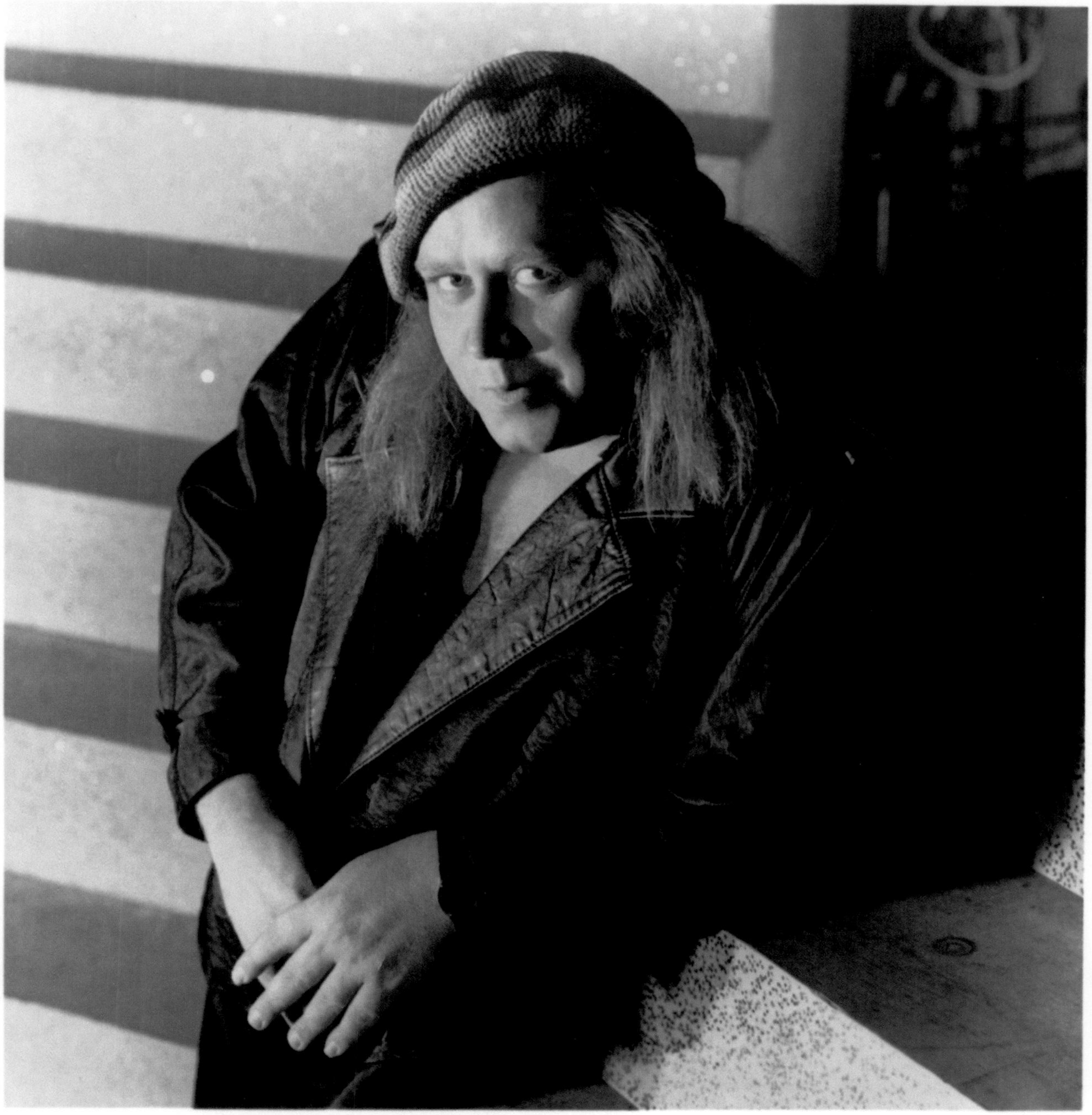

SAM KINISON

Photo Credit: Raul Vega

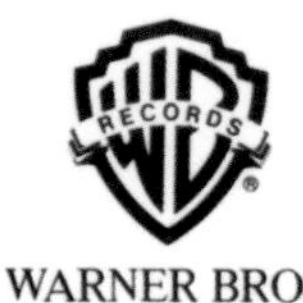

WARNER BROS.

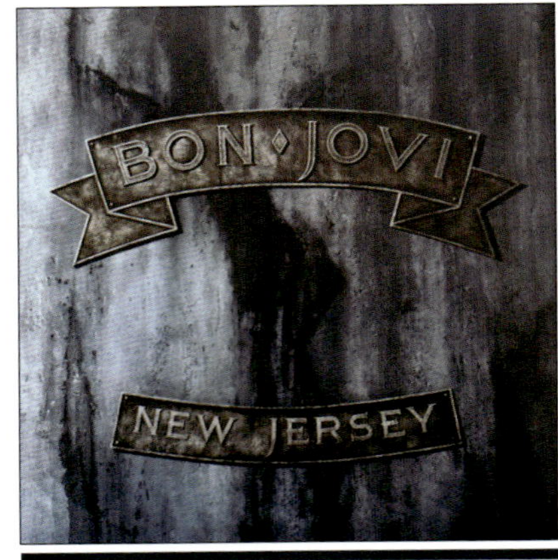

Billboard 200: *New Jersey* (No.1)
Billboard Hot 100: "Bad Medicine" (No. 1); "Born to Be My Baby" (#3); "I'll Be There for You" (No. 1); "Lay Your Hands on Me" (#7); "Living in Sin" (#9)

New Jersey captured Bon Jovi's frame of mind upon returning home from a world tour to unpack and write.

FOR FIVE years, Bon Jovi had grown up in the public eye. The most spectacular spurt came with the phenomenal success of *Slippery When Wet*, the No. 1 album that established the band as one of the biggest rock acts of the decade, propelled by the No. 1 hits "Livin' on a Prayer" and "You Give Love a Bad Name," as well as the Top 10 "Wanted Dead or Alive." Naturally, the group felt pressure to repeat that success.

"We set out to make a strange record," singer Jon Bon Jovi explained. "But unfortunately, when we played those songs for people, they thought we were going to lose a lot of our fans. Instead of bridging the gap, we had just jumped over the water."

So the group got back on track, recorded *New Jersey* and achieved similar global success. The singles "Bad Medicine" and "I'll Be There for You" went to the top of the charts, and "Born to Be My Baby," "Lay Your Hands on Me" and "Living in Sin" cracked the Top 10.

"I put out *New Jersey* with the idea that I had to have another big successful record so no one could deny that we could do it," Bon Jovi said. "And it's done just fine."

The band remained the same as always, five friends from New Jersey—Bon Jovi, Richie Sambora (guitar), David Bryan (keyboards), Alec John Such (bass) and Tico Torres (drums). But this time around, they looked a little rougher around the edges, not quite so video-groomed. Bon Jovi didn't want to be thought of as a pretty boy.

"I've had to take all this 'He's so good-looking, blah, blah,' and it makes me want to throw up," he insisted. "All I ever wanted to do was play in a rock band. I didn't think of myself as a pinup. That stuff threw me for a loop from day one. I've tried to downplay anything to do with that. Other bands say they want to look good, but I could never see myself wearing lipstick. In New Jersey, you get beat up for that."

As a certified superstar, Bon Jovi was frequently a focal point for attention. Headlines ranged from his marriage (he tied the knot in a surprise ceremony at the Graceland Chapel in Las Vegas to bride Dorothea Hurley) to an arrest (he was caught ice-skating at a closed rink at 3:30 in the morning in New York City and charged with trespassing).

"But the media attention on my personal life is nothing compared to what it could be—I don't deal with it a quarter as much as Madonna and Michael Jackson," he noted. "This isn't a business you complain about, because you're lucky just to be in it. And I enjoy it too much to be uncomfortable."

While the music had obviously struck a major chord with a young audience, critical acclaim was in fairly short supply. Not that it bothered Bon Jovi. "Your fans are the ones most critical of you—they're the ones who let you know when they think you're screwing up," he laughed. "That's why we thought about calling our album *Same Old Dudes in New Shoes*. We still think of ourselves as being the kids' band." ■

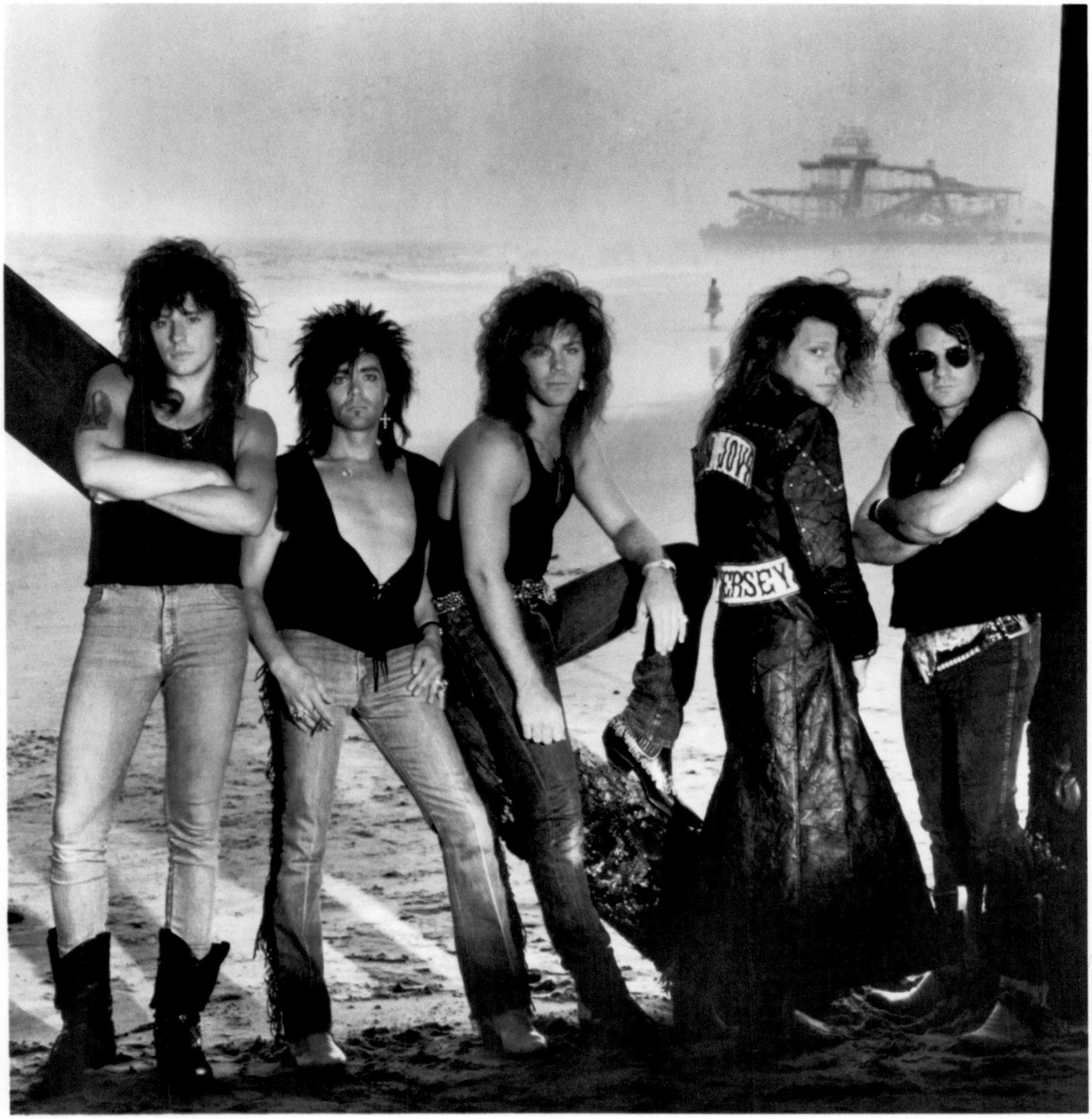

RICHIE SAMBORA ALEC JOHN SUCH DAVID BRYAN JON BON JOVI TICO TORRES

BON JOVI

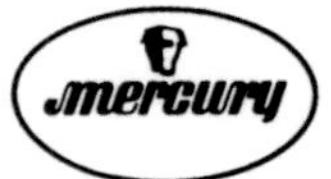

PolyGram Records

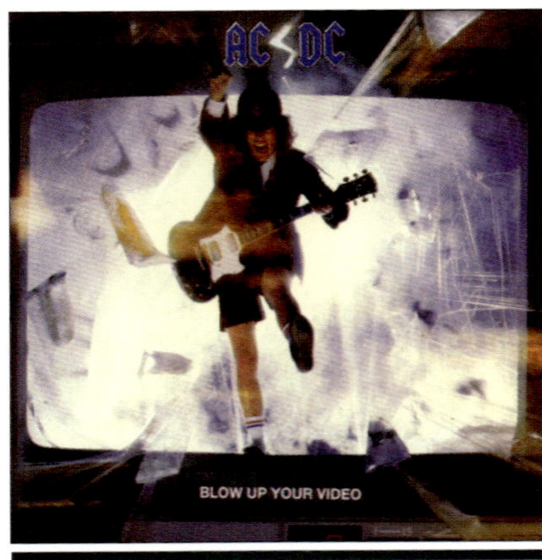

Billboard 200: *Blow Up Your Video* (#12)

A commercial winner, *Blow Up Your Video* reunited AC/DC with the antipodean rockers' original producers.

FOR MORE than a decade, AC/DC had set the pace in international hard rock circles. Led by guitarists Angus and Malcom Young, the Scottish-born brothers who formed the Australian band in 1974, the group blew the musical world into submission with their relentless 12-bar boogie and crushing guitar onslaughts.

Much of AC/DC's rebel image grew out of the antics of singer Bon Scott, who died in 1980 and was replaced by Brian Johnson. But the band had never taken the macho image of heavy metal too seriously. Nothing typified that more than Angus' mad-dog stage romps in his trademark sweaty uniform of schoolboy cap, blazer and short pants—the customary striptease, the ritualistic lowering of the shorts, the "full moon" from the riser.

"I'm a rotten guitar player if I'm standing still," Angus said.

AC/DC struck early-Eighties platinum on the strength of tight songs ("You Shook Me All Night Long," "Back in Black") and the meaty production of hitmaker Robert "Mutt" Lange. But the excellent *Blow Up Your Video* album reunited the archetypal metal merchants with the famed production team of Vanda & Young—Angus and Malcolm's older brother, ex-Easybeat George Young, and his partner, Harry Vanda, who carried AC/DC's aggressive image to record on the band's first three albums in the Seventies.

"Harry and George have always had that fun attitude with us, and we feel loose and relaxed in their company," Angus explained. "They also like to work fast, as we do. We like to get in there, get a sound, and get out."

Blow Up Your Video featured the highlights "Heatseeker" and "That's the Way I Wanna Rock 'n' Roll," and AC/DC remained a popular concert draw. Malcolm Young had decided to take some time off to cope with a drinking problem, and he wasn't present on AC/DC's tour of the United States. But with nephew Stevie Young filling in for Malcolm, AC/DC continued to play some of the most ferocious rock music to pour off a stage.

"There's a whole new excitement about this band these days," Angus concluded, "and there's a whole new generation of kids to be won over." ■

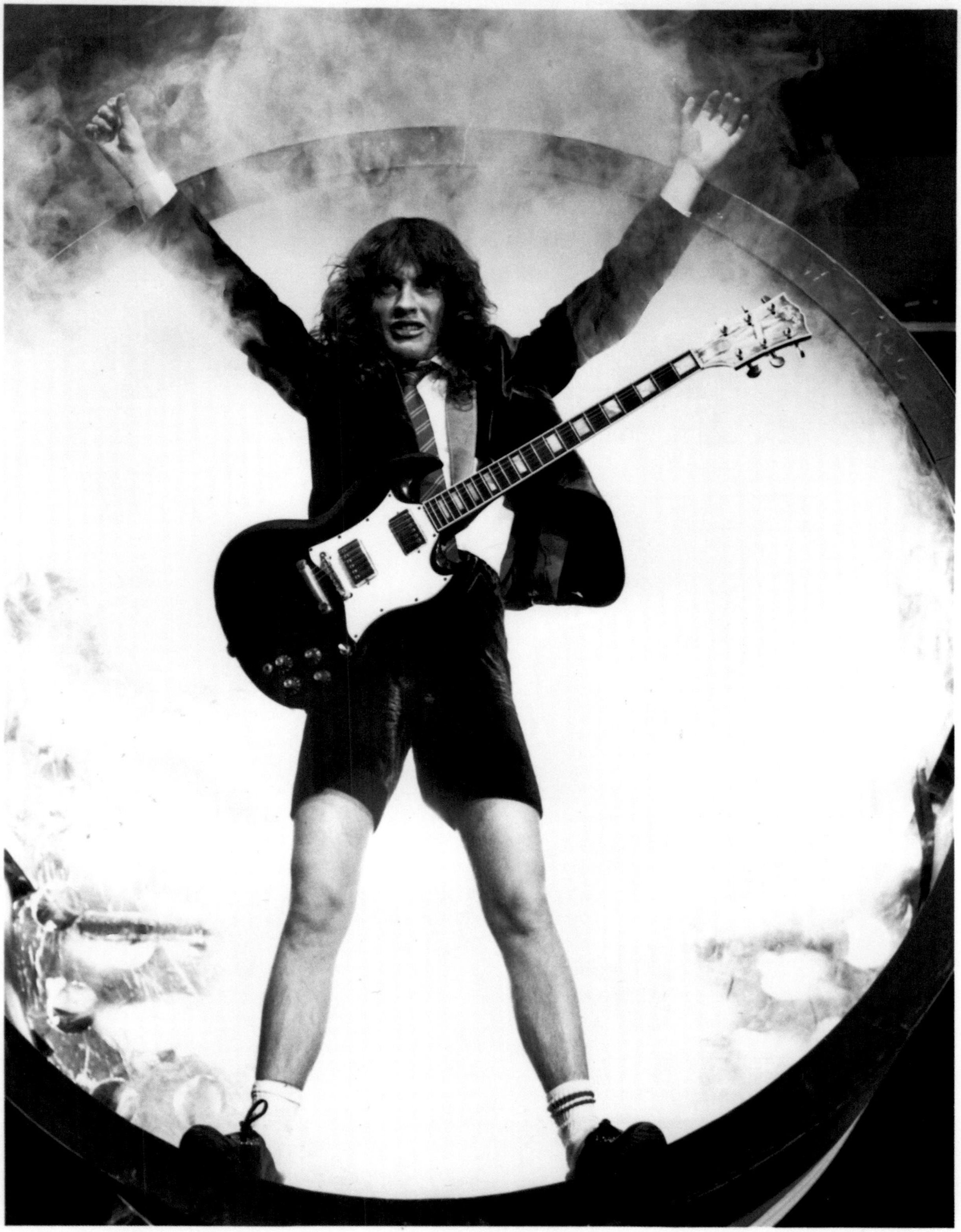

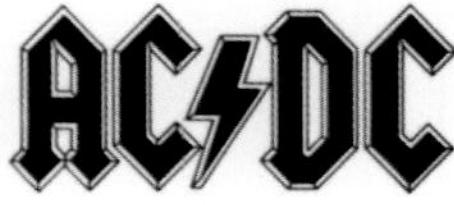
AC/DC

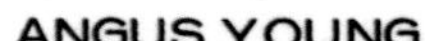
ANGUS YOUNG

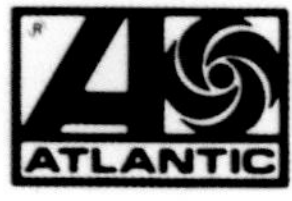
ATLANTIC

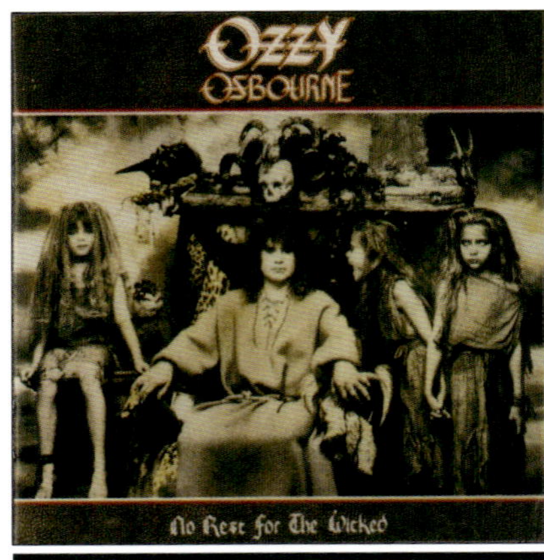

Billboard 200: *No Rest for the Wicked* (#13)

In "Miracle Man," Ozzy Osbourne ridiculed the adversaries who had excoriated him as an agent of the devil.

OZZY OSBOURNE, the always outrageous godfather of heavy metal, celebrated a rite of passage with his *No Rest for the Wicked* album. "Ozzy has become a man this year—21 years in the music biz," he crowed. "Now all I want is to be left alone to do my work."

Which was easier said than done—as Osbourne's career had taken him from obscurity to mega-success, his maniacal antics had earned him a reputation as a part-time loon. *No Rest for the Wicked* perpetuated the raucous style he'd developed as lead singer with Black Sabbath.

"But there's no black magic, there are no satanic messages—it's just tongue-in-cheek fun," he insisted. "I fail to understand why people still think I'm a devil worshipper after all this time. I try to ignore it and hope it goes away, but somebody always comes up with a weird interpretation of my songs. Now there's a group accusing me of enticing my audience to have baby sacrifices. Apparently, I'm doing this on stage—it's news to me. I don't know where they get their information."

No Rest for the Wicked kicked off with "Miracle Man," which took a shot at the money-hungry, Bible-thumping capers of disgraced television evangelists. "I got a bit of a smile on my face when Jimmy Swaggart and Jim Bakker got caught with their groupies and their fun on the side," Osboune admitted. "It's true hypocrisy, the likes of those people condemning me! They ought to sweep up their own backdoor before they start cleaning up after me. I've watched their programs over the past 10 years where they've shown my album covers and said that I'm Satan, that I should be banned. But they're not doing any better themselves, are they?"

But Osbourne wasn't above taking a close look at himself—he had spent a second stint in an alcohol treatment program, and he tackled his personal problems in "Demon Alcohol." "It really is a demon—at least it is for me," he said. "But I'm getting better and stronger as each day goes by. If anybody is sick and tired of being sick and tired, there's more help in this country than anywhere else in the world if you're prepared to stick it out. Since I stopped drinking six cases of beer a day, I've dropped 18 pounds, I have more energy and my attitude is good most of the time."

Zakk Wylde kept Osbourne's track record for discovering fiery young guitarists intact, but it was Osbourne's voice, that eternally teenage wail, that drove *No Rest for the Wicked.*

"What I hear these days are so many cliched singers, screeching and screaming the same boring shit over these pounding high-speed rhythms," he mused. "I don't know one from the other—everybody sounds like Ronnie James Dio. I just sound like Ozzy." ■

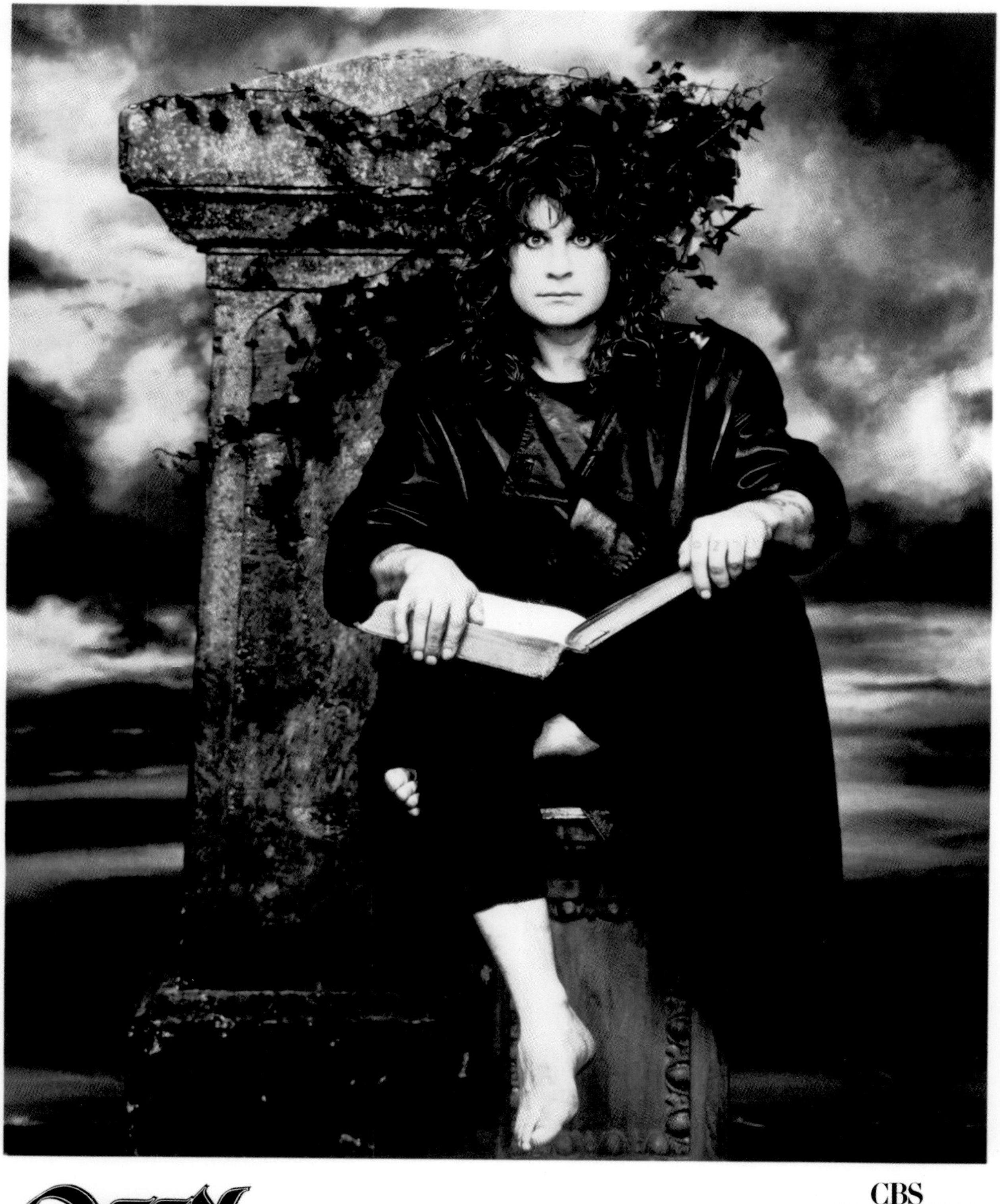

PHOTO: BOB CARLOS CLARKE

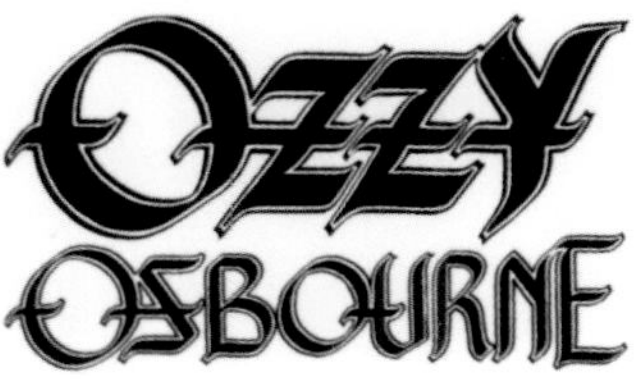

CBS
ASSOCIATED

8810

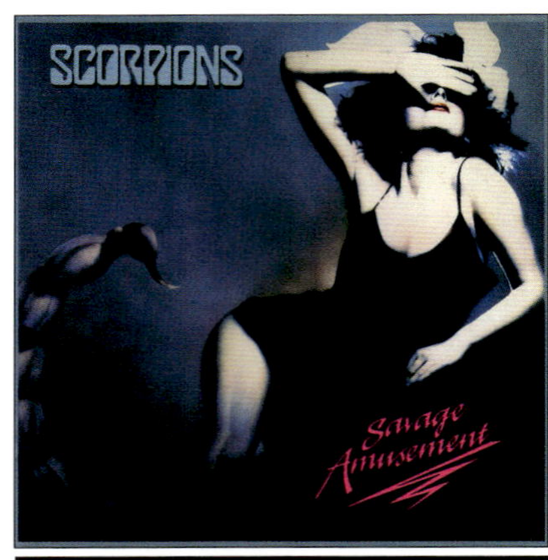

Billboard 200: *Savage Amusement* (#5)
Billboard Hot 100: "Rhythm of Love" (#75)

Scorpions presented a more polished charm on *Savage Amusement*, the West German rockers' tenth album.

THE WAY Scorpions had it figured, a grueling tour schedule provided more opportunity for adventure. It provided inspiration for the *Savage Amusement* album, on which the songs focused on the physical and emotional temptations that entertained the German rock stars on extensive world treks.

"You tour the world playing to 20,000 people in different cities every night and new countries ever few weeks," vocalist Klaus Meine said. "You relax and just let go—there are some places where you simply walk into the hotel and you can smell that there will be an amazing backstage party."

"The way we live our lives, we stay awake until the early-morning hours, and when we're tired, we sleep," drummer Herman Rarebell mused. "So we never feel jet-lagged!"

The lifestyle reflected founder and guitarist Rudolf Schenker's long-term commitment to music.

"I started Scorpions as a school band in 1966, but the current band didn't start until Klaus joined in 1970," he explained. "There are not many bands who have had their names for as long as we have had ours. Other bands change their names, looking for new luck to make it big. I thought, 'Scorpions is a good name, why change it? If we make better music, we'll make it.'"

And ever since "No One Like You" became a No. 1 album rock track in 1982, the band's albums had gone platinum and its reputation had spread as far as Thailand. Schenker got the credit for constructing Scorpions' efficient power riffs, and *Savage Amusement* struck an impressive balance between hard rock aggression and the pop accessibility that Def Leppard and others had popularized; the power ballad "Rhythm of Love" brought the group another hit.

Scorpions made a historic 10-concert appearance in Leningrad, the first time the act had played the Soviet Union. "It was amazing—the kids were just the same as they are here," Meine said. "Rock 'n' roll is the international language." ■

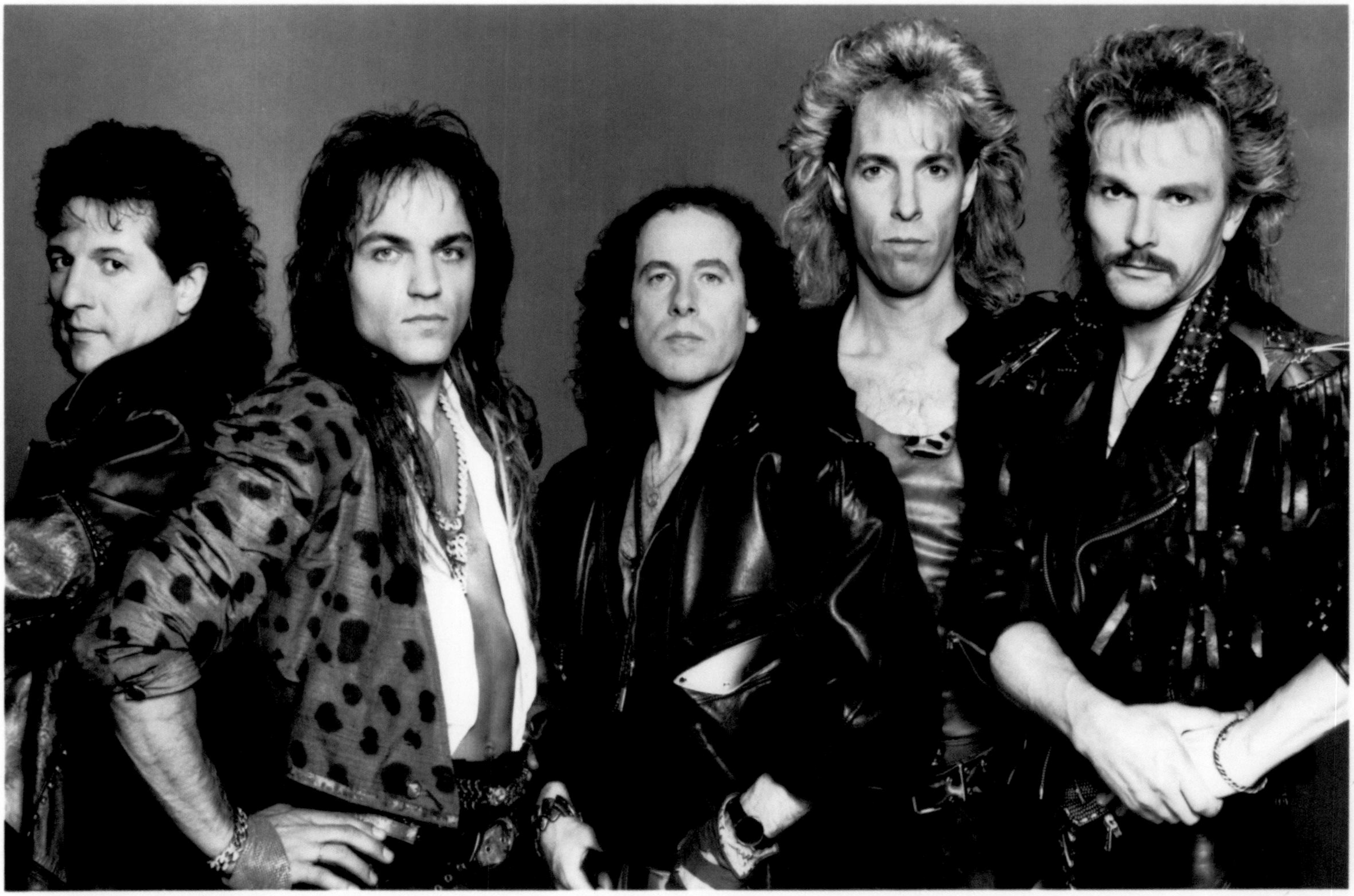

HERMAN RAREBELL MATTHIAS JABS KLAUS MEINE FRANCIS BUCHHOLZ RUDOLF SCHENKER

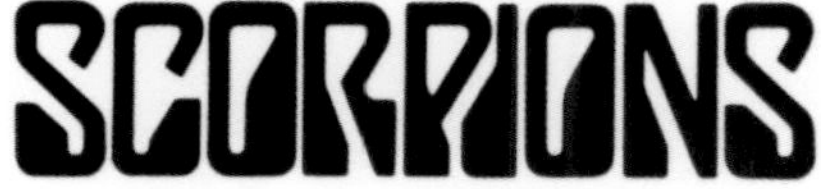

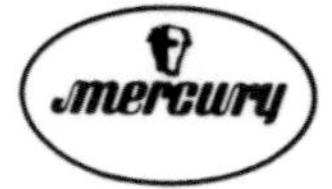

PolyGram Records™

Billboard 200: *Ram It Down* (#31)

The title of the *Ram It Down* album said everything when it came to Judas Priest's heavy-metal zealousness.

AFTER 12 years of bashing out head-banging classics on the heavy-metal treadmill, Judas Priest became mercenaries on 1986's *Turbo* album.

"*Turbo* went to extremes—it expanded on the commercial, catchy side of the Priest," guitarist K.K. Downing said. "After that, we thought, 'Right, that's it, we'll never make another concerted effort to make a multimillion-selling album. We'll just be the Priest.'"

And so the British outfit had returned to some "take-no-prisoners" rock on *Ram It Down*, the 11th Priest studio album. "We certainly haven't taken any steps forward with it," Downing laughed. Nine tracks of metal madness pitted the ear-splitting caterwauling of singer Rob Halford and the double lead-guitar assault of Glenn Tipton and Downing. There was also a remake of Chuck Berry's rock 'n' roll standard "Johnny B. Goode," which was featured in the teen-flick *Johnny Be Good*.

"The producers of the movie *Top Gun* had wanted to use a song from *Turbo*, and we said no, we wanted to keep it for our album," Downing said. "Of course, the soundtrack went on to sell five million copies. So we thought, 'Hey, we can't let this slip by again.' We were skeptical about doing a classic. It was like trying to do the American national anthem, but it's heavy enough for us."

Still, the song didn't garner the expected radio airplay. "That's the way it goes," Downing said. "Moms and dads still haven't learned to accept Judas Priest. They think we have a devil-worshiping, drug-taking image that they don't want their kids to associate with."

Regardless, the band returned to US concert stages, its reputation for spectacular stage productions intact. Previous tours had featured Metallian (the heavy metal monster that jumped from the cover of 1984's *Defenders of the Faith*) and Hellion (the birdlike creature introduced on the *Screaming for Vengeance* album).

The new special effects culminated with Halford rising 100 feet above the audience in a laser "disintegrator cannon" just before the destruction of his ever-present Harley-Davidson Low Rider and a good portion of the stage. ■

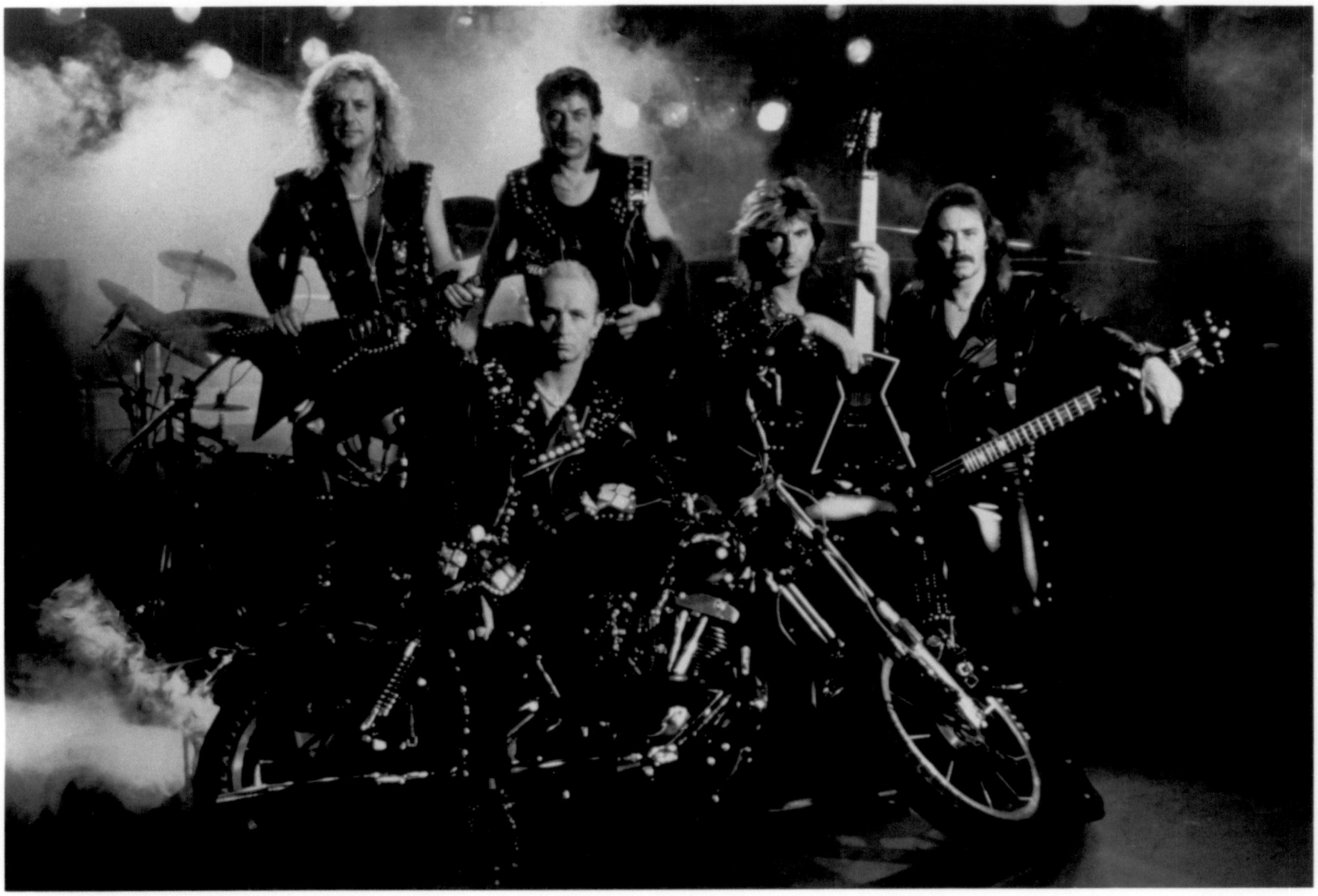

PHOTOGRAPH: TONY MOTTRAM

JUDAS PRIEST

Columbia
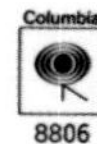
8806

Billboard 200: *Seventh Son of a Seventh Son* (#12)

Iron Maiden's string of uncommon metal albums continued with the powerful *Seventh Son of a Seventh Son.*

ONE OF metal music's great success stories, Iron Maiden enjoyed devoutly loyal fans and worldwide sales in excess of 20 million albums. *Seventh Son of a Seventh Son*, the English band's seventh studio release, was a concept album dealing with "the fight for the soul of the mystical Seventh Son" and featuring the band's first experimentation with keyboards and synthesizers. In something of a twist, this departure coincided with the ascendancy of young thrash bands who were first inspired by Iron Maiden.

"The music scene has changed around us," lead singer Bruce Dickinson said. "A lot of thrash and speed metal bands play simplistic stuff really fast without a lot of melody. We also have lots of energy and fire, but we make it technically difficult to play as well. We try to build challenges into every album, and there's a lot of heavy-duty stuff on this one."

The swashbuckling Dickinson wasn't quite the subhuman life form that many people associated with the heavy-metal genre. He prowled stages like a warrior-poet of old, his go-for-the-jugular screaming over the din of his bandmates: "A lunge and a feint, a parry too late/A cut to the chest and you're down." The lyrics reflected another aspect of the shrewd, likable Dickinson's lifestyle. An accomplished fencer, he taught the sport and searched for tournaments during his days off. The activity helped diffuse the band's punishing touring schedule.

"When we're on the road, I get two or three days a week when I can train," Dickinson said. "I'm currently lurking around in the Top 20 ranking of domestic fencers, and that's fairly respectable, considering how hard I work at my singing job. I try to do my best and enter a lot of competitions. It's quite fun to get out and meet different people, at any rate. But all of this talk that's surfacing about being world champion next year is a load of rubbish. At some point you come up against the fact that the people you're trying to beat have been professionals for 10 to 21 years." ■

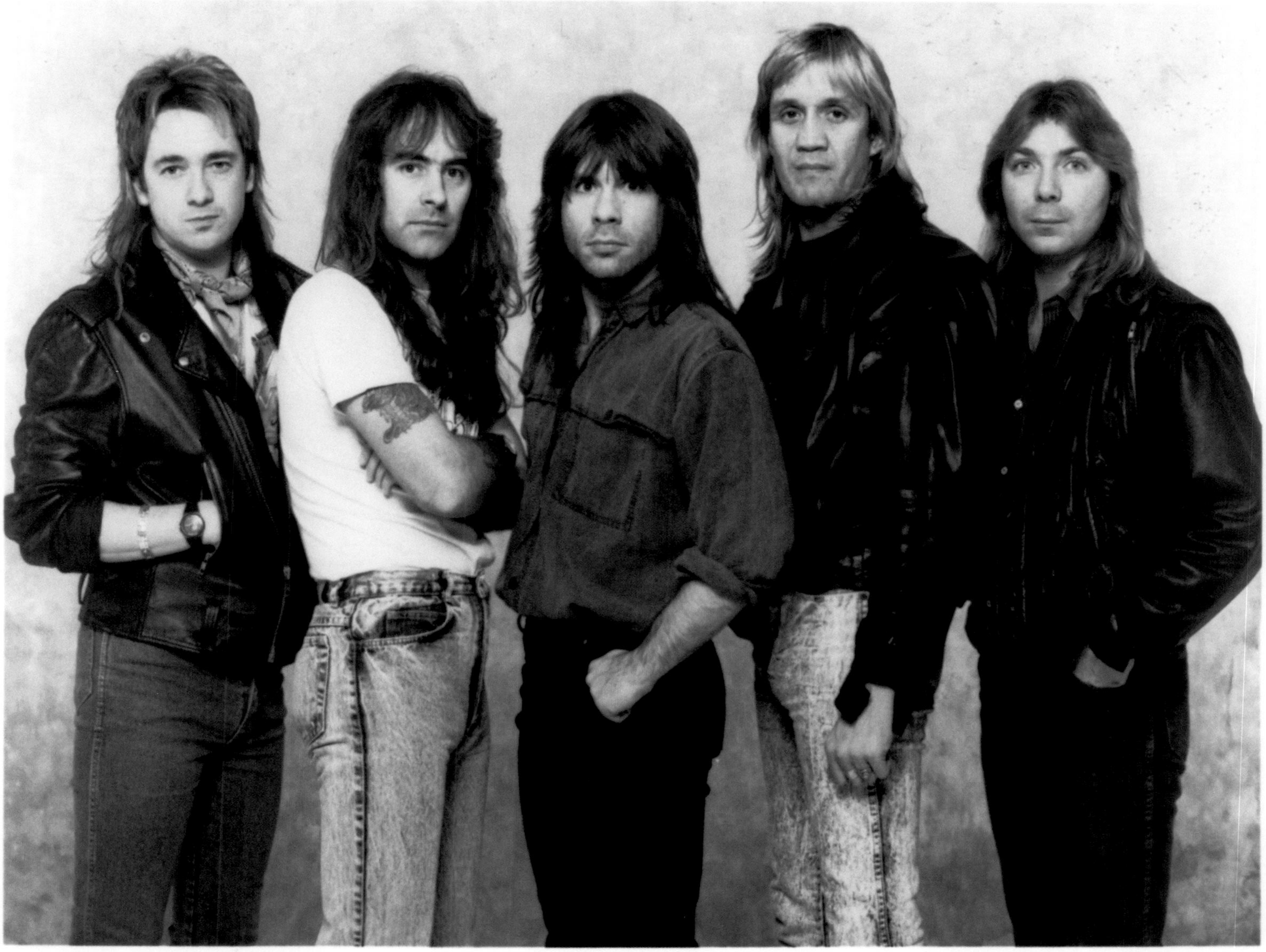

IRON MAIDEN

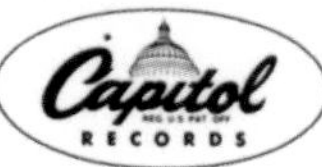

Photo Credit: Ross Halfin/1988

Billboard 200: ...*And Justice for All* (#6)
Billboard Hot 100: "One" (#35)

...*And Justice for All* was the first Metallica album after bassist Cliff Burton was killed in a tour bus accident.

BLARING GUITARS, crashing drums, howling vocals—heavy-metal music seemingly existed to annoy parents as much as to rally teenaged fans. Yet the bulk of heavy metal was formulaic and stylized. Bands put on makeup, spiked their hair, sang about sex and driving fast cars—and sold two million records.

However, where most metal acts played up to the media, Metallica had refused to package itself for mass consumption since forming in 1981. The band's high-speed music pursued equal parts punk energy and hard-rock bombast, and the lyrics shifted from metal's usual braggadocio. The group hadn't concocted an image—the four cohorts wore the same T-shirts, jeans and sneakers onstage and offstage. Metallica had never made a promotional video clip, and the albums weren't played on commercial rock radio stations.

But Metallica scored some surprising achievements. Each of the band's three albums had sold more than 500,000 copies, and ...*And Justice for All* was a million seller—the record entered the Top 10 of the *Billboard* chart in its third week. ...*And Justice for All* contained 65 minutes of music spread over nine first-person monologues addressing censorship, pollution, paranoia and suicide.

"A lot of acts sell albums on the strength of a hit song, and those types of fans aren't as loyal," drummer Lars Ulrich noted. "When we sell a million albums, there are a million people who know every note of every song. Our fans are unbelievably devoted."

In concert, rather than timing their songs to accompany lasers and pyrotechnics, the members simply flung their shoulder-length hair to the beat as their fingers flew.

"Stamina is the key," guitarist Kirk Hammett said. "Our songs take a lot of chops—there's a great physical demand to play at the speed and intensity that we do. We play two hours and three encores, for as long as we can every night. So we can't be overweight or debauched by intake of alcohol."

Even on their first headlining tour of US arenas, the men of Metallica wanted to be different from the rest of the music business. The staging included a thematic backdrop based on the album cover, an unsubtle depiction of injustice. "But it's different from your standard heavy-metal show—it's not a fucking circus act," Hammett insisted. "We wanted to be creative with the opportunities that have been put in front of us. We've done tours that have been simple enough—just our amps or a scrim in the background. Now we've augmented the music."

And not only did Metallica release singles—"One" became the band's first Top 40 hit in the US—but the members filmed videos. "We had never wanted to do one because we had to do one or because it was time to do one," Hammett said. "We just want to put it out and see what it does. Like Lars says, we want to do what we feel good about, what's right for us. If you like it, you're invited along. If you don't—well, there's the door." ■

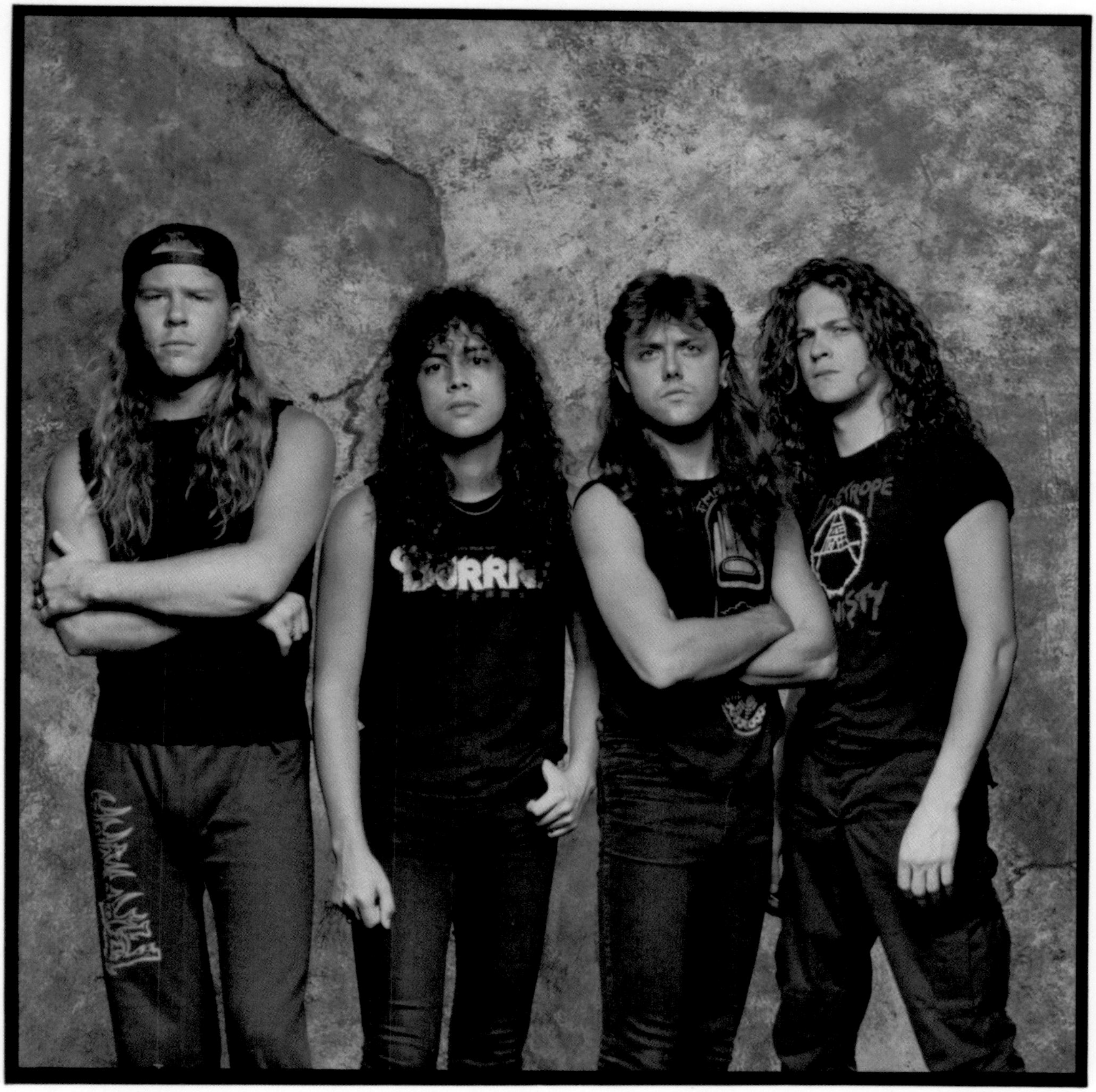

PHOTO CREDIT: ROSS HALFIN/1988

JAMES HETFIELD KIRK HAMMETT LARS ULRICH JASON NEWSTED

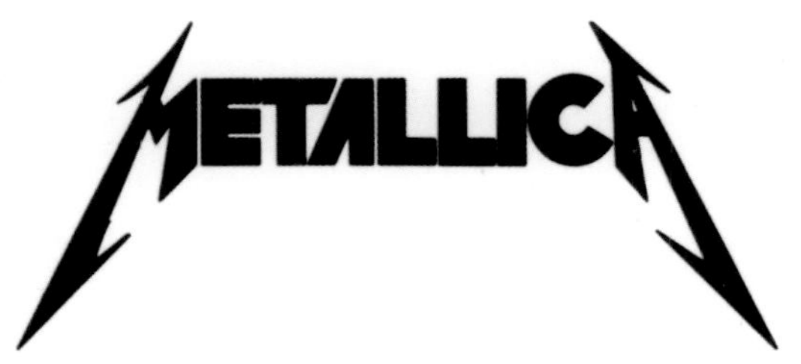

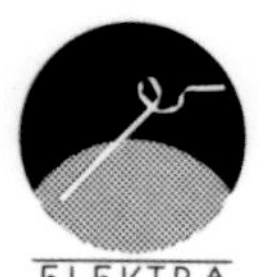

Billboard 200: *So Far, So Good...So What!* (#28)

Created by a new lineup that wouldn't survive, Megadeth launched the kinetic *So Far, So Good...So What!*

ALTHOUGH MEGADETH proudly reigned as a premier band, the band's meltdown sound, described by bassist Dave Ellefson as "a very aggressive, power-metal style," didn't seem conducive to commercial success. Megadeth had never received radio airplay, and video exposure was minimal.

Yet the Los Angeles-based band claimed a Top 30 album with *So Far, So Good...So What!* Touring had been the key to the breakthrough—when Ellefson and Dave Mustaine formed Megadeth in 1983 (after Mustaine's dismissal from Metallica), the group immediately embarked on a national tour.

"We didn't want to just do the L.A. club scene, we wanted to build a legion of fans around the world," Ellefson said. "A heavy cult following is what metal music has always been built on. Megadeth has never been based on a hit single. I think hit singles can hurt a band, because you're only as good as your last one."

So Far, So Good...So What! found Mustaine and Ellefson joined by new recruits Jeff Young (guitar) and Chuck Behler (drums), and the record captured the bruising, thrashing energy of the band's shows. Megadeth even covered the Sex Pistols' "Anarchy in the U.K." with altered lyrics, and the group's attitude was further displayed on "Hook in Mouth," a direct (and surprisingly clever) swipe at the Tipper Gore-led Parents Music Resource Center.

"It's aimed at censorship in general, any religious or parental groups that don't have a clue to what rock music is all about," Ellefson said.

Indeed, even with a cover sticker that warned of lyrics that "may be considered offensive by some audiences," the album sold. It didn't hurt that Megadeth was a good-looking band that attracted girls in a scene that was geared for male teens.

"Our philosophy is us being us, not being puppets or a fictitious overblown rock-star trip," Mustaine said. "People can see that there are no meat byproducts in Megadeth. When it comes down to our music, there's no cereal filler. We're the real gravy train." ■

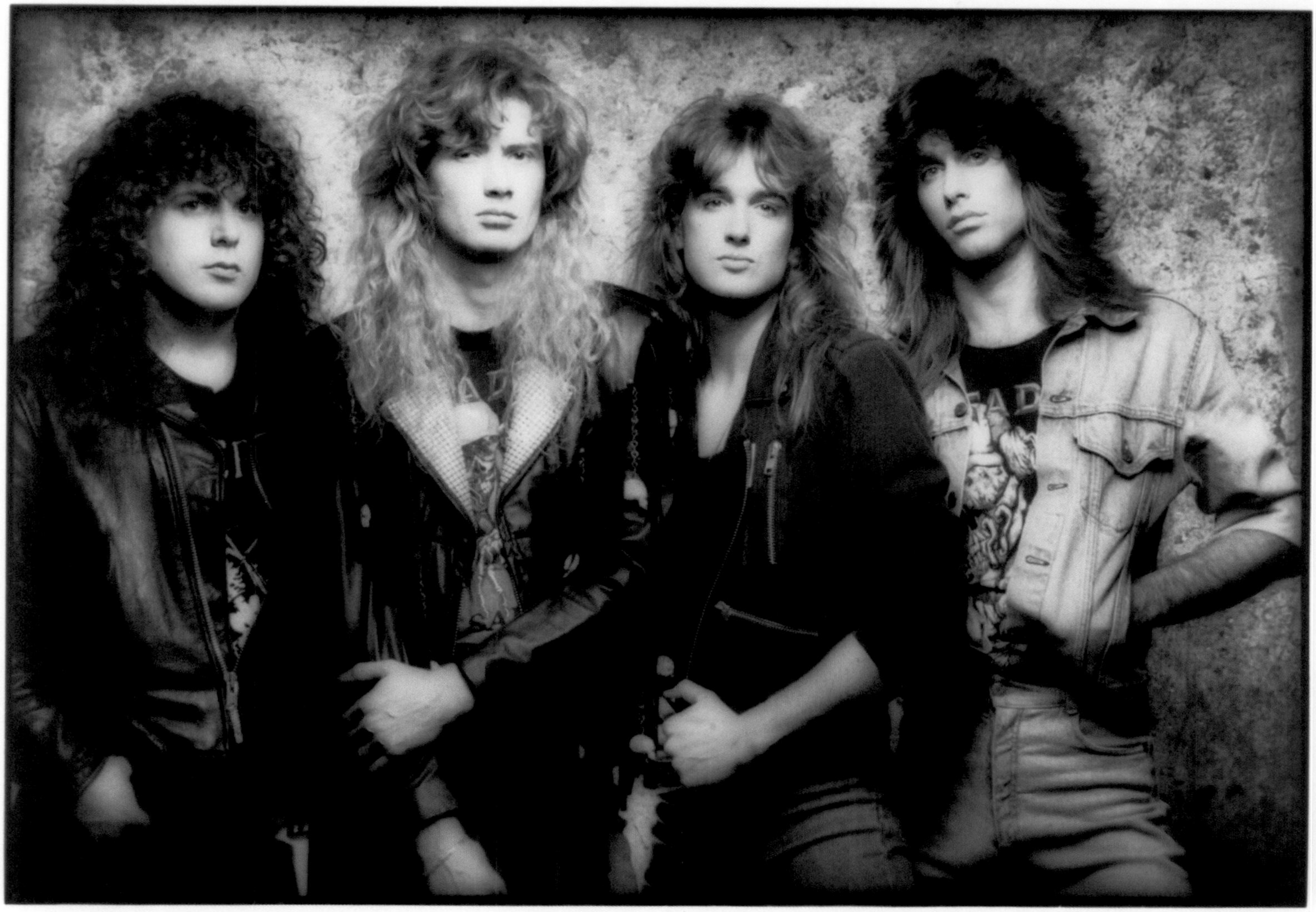

Photo: Neil Zlozower / 1988

Chuck Behler Dave Mustaine Dave Ellefson Jeff Young

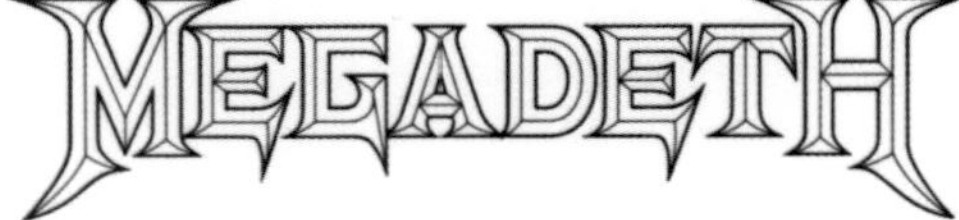

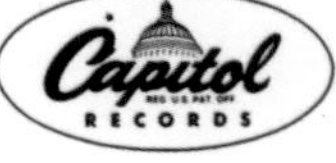

Billboard 200: *Operation: Mindcrime* (#50)

Operation: Mindcrime promoted Queensrÿche's reputation as one of metal's most adaptable, inventive acts.

BEING SMART could be a liability in the heavy-metal business—many bands relied on big hair rather than strong musicianship to sell their songs—but Queensrÿche was hailed by the hard-rock world for providing intelligent high ground for the genre. Conceived in the early Eighties, the Seattle-based quintet was labeled everything from glam to thrash during its years of underground cult status, but *Operation: Mindcrime* stood out as epiclike in delivery—an ambitious, complex "aural film."

"Every song works like a chapter in a story," guitarist Chris DeGarmo said. "The lyrics are an extreme vision of reality that could occur in late Eighties America."

The themes on *Operation: Mindcrime* centered on psychological manipulation, anarchy and rebellion. The 15-track album outlined an alleged governmental conspiracy plot engineered by the Reagan administration in an intelligent albeit aggressive manner. Plot characters and between-song dramatic segues told the story of three characters created by lead singer Geoff Tate: Doctor X, the instigator of a violent underground revolutionary movement; Nikki, the street kid who became the victim of mind manipulation (Doctor X capitalized on his drug problem and got him to carry out political assassinations); and Sister Mary, a prostitute-turned-nun who doubted her faith.

"In the past, some of our stuff's been kind of vague and mystical-sounding," Tate explained. "I tried to approach this whole album with a modern feel. Personally, I'd like to see more originality and adventure in metal. The music should move with the times, with different instrumentation and lyrical approaches, even different haircuts."

"We're not science-fiction fans, but we're media buffs," DeGarmo added. "In our travels, we're constantly scouring newspapers and television. We try to be an objective mirror of society without putting limits on our songwriting. We took a chance and did what we wanted—a heavy concept album with cynical overtones." ■

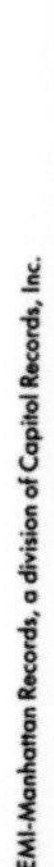

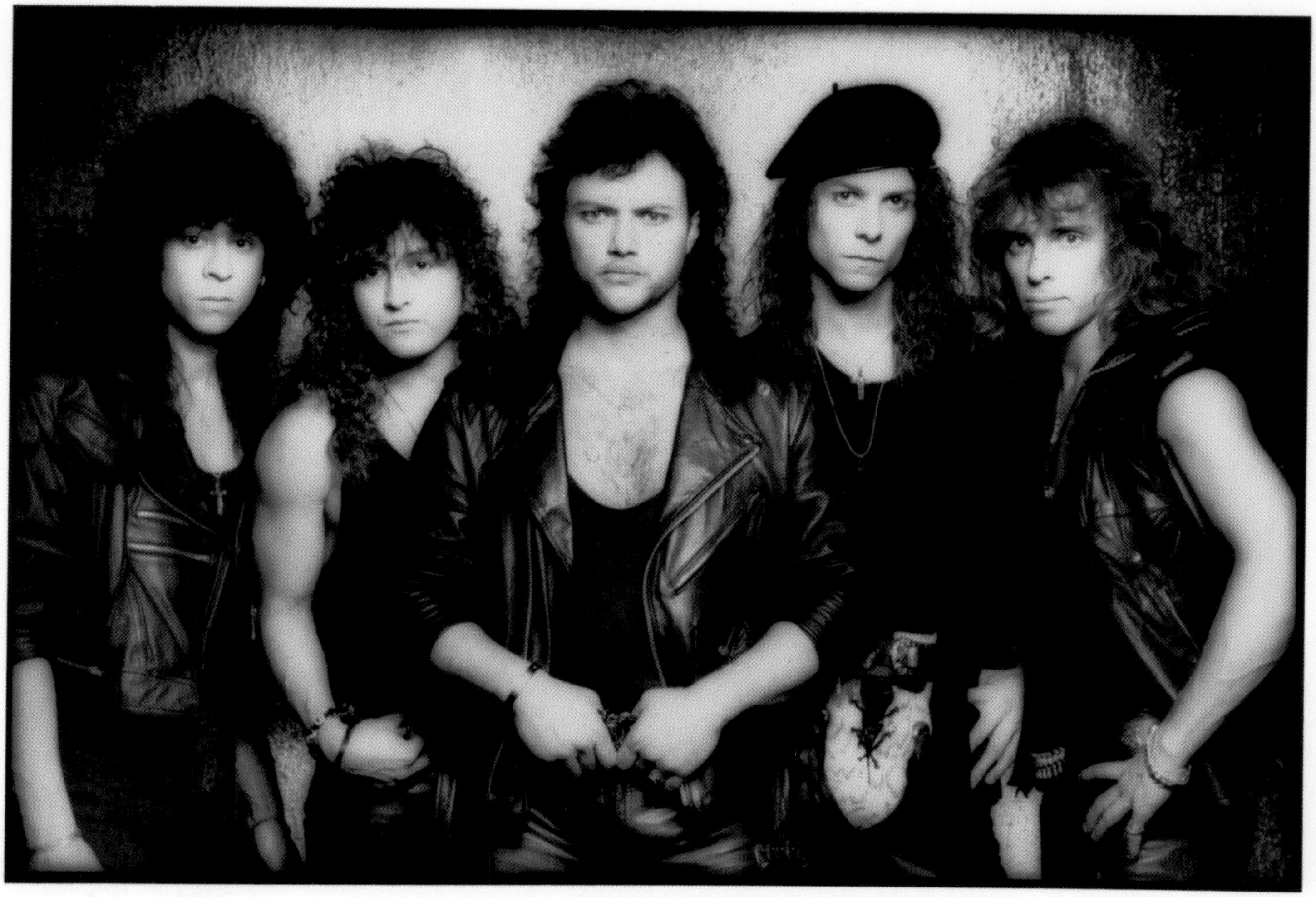

Queensrÿche

Left to right:
Eddie Jackson, Michael Wilton, Geoff Tate, Chris DeGarmo & Scott Rockenfield

EMI
MAN
HAT
TAN®

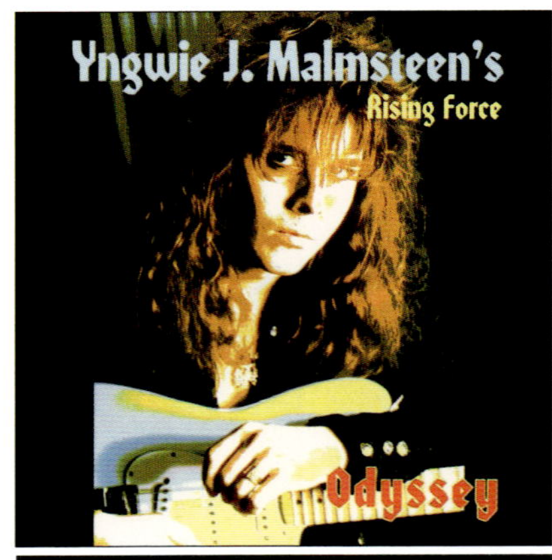

Billboard 200: *Odyssey* (#40)

While rehabilitating from a car accident, guitarist Yngwie Malmsteen formulated some radio-friendly material.

SINCE HIS arrival in America in 1983, Yngwie Malmsteen had garnered acclaim in heavy-metal circles for his warp-speed solos and flawless technique.

"When I was teaching myself to play, I was listening to a lot of classical music," the Swedish guitarist explained. "I learned the pieces and absorbed that way of composing. I imposed that in a hard-rock context—using heavy drums and guitars, but within the same melodic framework as a classical piece. Of course, guitar fans are like a reverent army. There seems to be this enormous curiosity about what I do and how I do it. But I don't think about it—I pretty much just play."

Yet Malmsteen's burgeoning career was nearly cut short when he smashed his Jaguar into a tree.

"It was very serious—I was in a coma for a week," he recalled. "Being able to play a guitar was sort of secondary at that point." Malmsteen had to rehabilitate his right hand, which was paralyzed. "I couldn't even hold a glass of water. But now I'm fine—you can judge that from the album."

Odyssey, the fourth album with his band Rising Force, found Malmsteen tempering his legendary intensity with the awareness of his own mortality. "For those first few months after the crash, I was just happy to be alive. I started looking at things differently. I don't write lyrics, but in general, I worked on material that had spiritual, metaphysical themes."

Odyssey teamed him for the first time with singer Joe Lynn Turner of Rainbow fame, and the collaboration expanded Malmsteen's audience. The pop-metal tune "Heaven Tonight" had more radio airplay than any previous Rising Force track.

"The reason Joe is in the band is because I think he's a good singer, not because I thought it would be a good commercial move," Malmsteen insisted.

Yet Turner's vocals certainly added an accessible element to the virtuosic guitarist's searing fretwork. While Malmsteen had worked with singers before, he'd always been known more for his solos than his songs, filling every available space with a volley of guitar notes. With Turner in tow, songcraft balanced his neoclassical metal riffing, and he hoped to have smash singles along with his instrumental workouts.

"This is still very much my band," he said. "I want to reach a lot more people. I know I'm a very good player—now I'd like a big hit record." ■

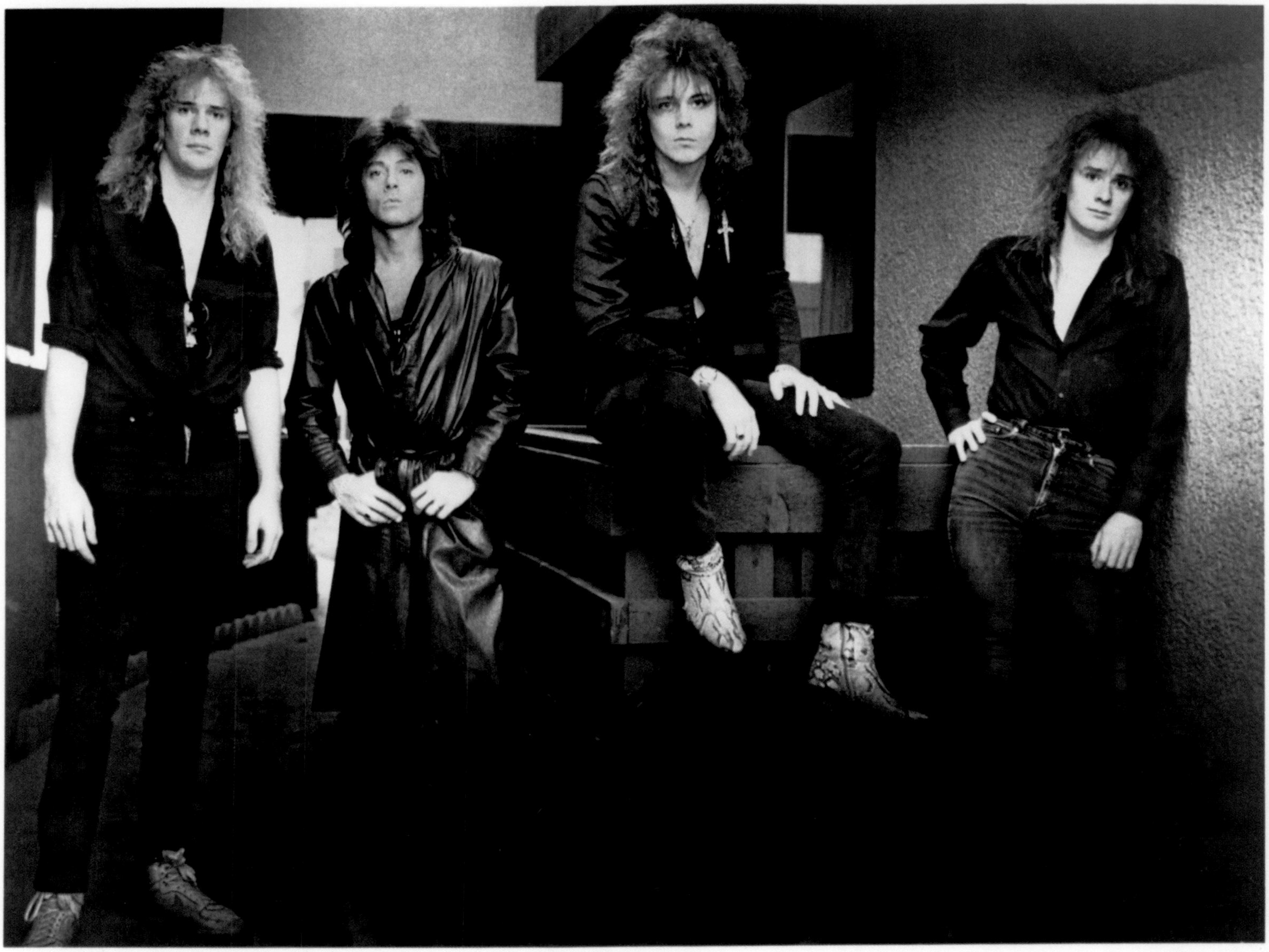

YNGWIE MALMSTEEN

PolyGram Records

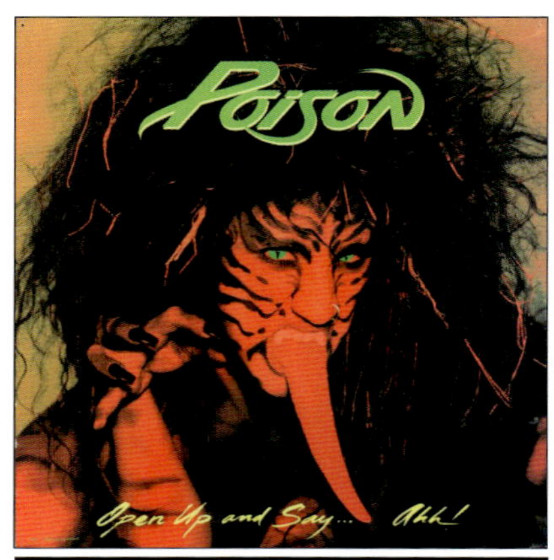

Billboard 200: *Open Up and Say...Ahh!* (#2)
Billboard Hot 100: "Nothin' but a Good Time" (#6); "Fallen Angel" (#12); "Every Rose Has Its Thorn" (No. 1); "Your Mama Don't Dance" (#10)

Hearing health wasn't on the minds of devotees requiring a second dose of Poison, *Open Up and Say...Ahh!*

WHEN POISON first broke out of the Los Angeles club scene in 1986, the visually garish band was ridiculed as a bad joke. Many felt they had stumbled into the big time through blind luck or accident. But the self-styled bad boys were feeling pretty good, thanks to their multiplatinum second album, *Open Up and Say...Ahh!* Singer Bret Michaels was enjoying life at the top of the glam-rock heap.

"We've heard criticism that we can't play, that we're all makeup and hair spray, that we're a B-rated sex act, but it's worn off," he said. "Do I like to look weird and go out onstage? Yes—I don't argue that. But we're doing what we want, we're enjoying it and we're successful at it, and that makes people jealous." Poison achieved commercial legitimacy by landing a No. 1 hit with the poignant "Every Rose Has Its Thorn."

"I wrote it before we recorded our first album, but I was leery and insecure," Michaels said. "Most rock bands have a power ballad that kicks in big, but 'Thorn' is just an acoustic guitar song. I thought it would do the opposite of what it did, but then I found out how many people related to it."

"Your Mama Don't Dance"—a remake of the 1972 Loggins & Messina hit—cracked the Top 10.

"I did that song in a cover band years ago," Michaels recalled. "I brought it up at a Poison sound check and it turned out good, so we put it on the album. A lot of kids don't know that it was a song before that—they think Loggins & Messina are fake names in the band. Their original version was done real light and funky on keyboards, but a great song is a great song no matter who does it. The record company said, 'Nobody's going to understand why you did this'—covering an old Alice Cooper or Deep Purple song would have been better for us. But we've always stepped left of center, so we did it our own way. We Poisoned it."

Live, the band earned the dubious distinction of being called "the Club Med of rock 'n' roll."

"We're still fans ourselves—we pay money to see other bands, so we know what the kids want to see," drummer Rikki Rockett noted. "They know they'll get excitement at our shows, not highbrow art. We don't make art—we make hamburgers!" ■

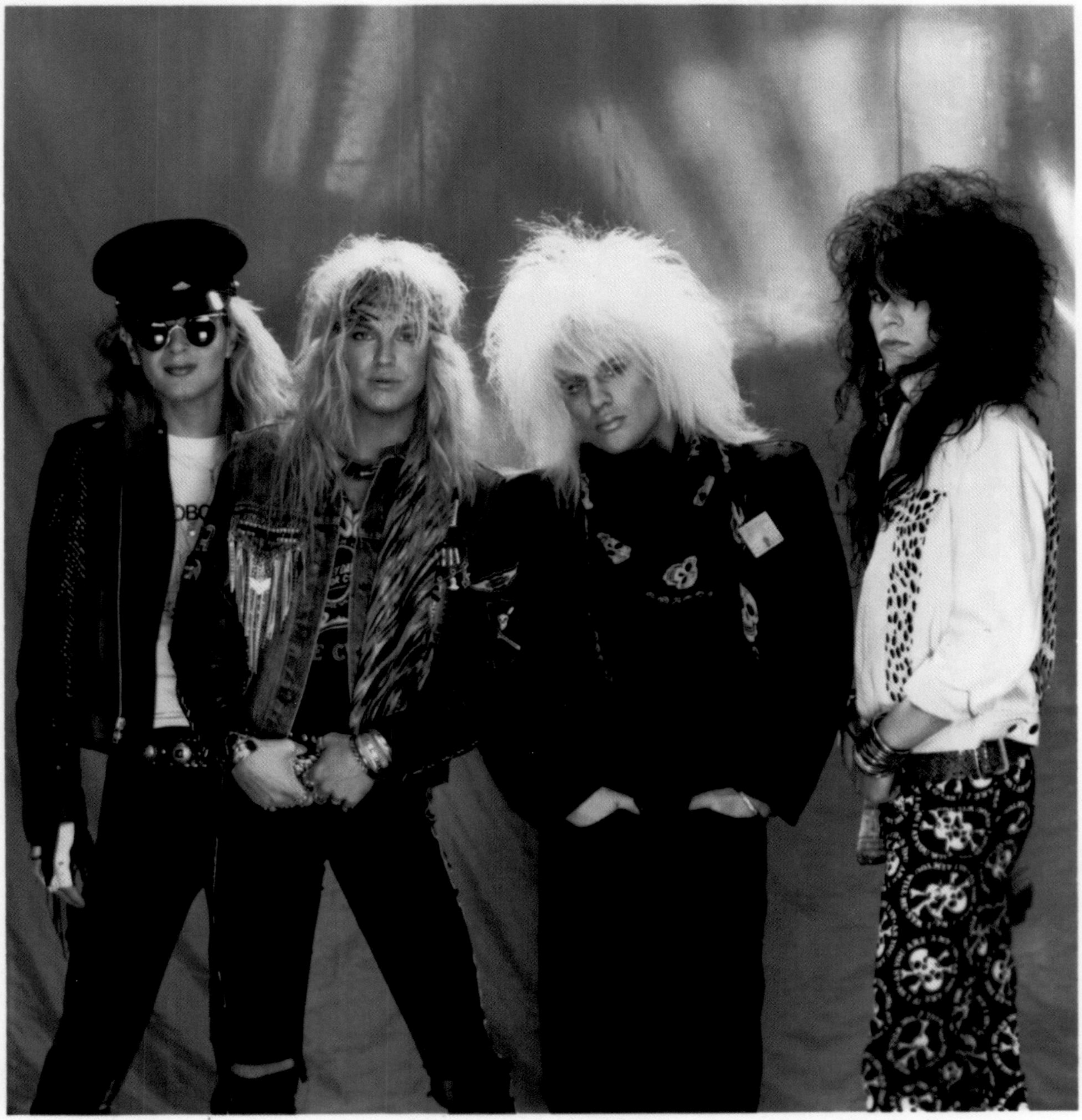

Photo: William Hames / 1988

Rikki Rockett | Bret Michaels | C.C. DeVille | Bobby Dall

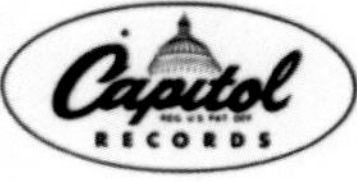

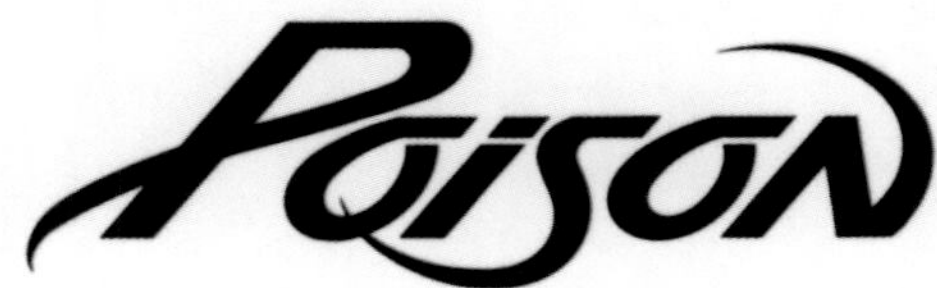

Billboard 200: *L.A. Guns* (#50)

Veterans of the Hollywood hard-rock scene, L.A. Guns discharged a rambunctious eponymous debut record.

IN THE world of heavy metal, the kingpins of a subgenre best described as "Los Angeles sleaze-rock" were Guns N' Roses, whose *Appetite for Destruction* album rated as a surprisingly potent look at life in the dirty-ass musical underbelly of the City of Angels.

Competition was sure to follow with the band's success, and sure enough, L.A. Guns attempted to make national waves as well. While songs like "Sex Action" and "Bitch Is Back" were expected to play in Southern California, it remained to be seen how they would fare in Middle America.

"But there's definitely a scene out there," guitarist Tracii Guns enthused. "A lot of kids come dressed like us—they got big hairdos."

L.A. Guns had a convoluted genesis. Guns and Axl Rose of Guns N' Roses were once bandmates in Hollywood Rose, and then Rose sang with Guns in L.A. Guns, then Guns was in Guns N' Roses with Rose. Eventually, Guns split and reformed L.A. Guns. The last addition was vocalist Philip Lewis, who was known for his work with the British band Girl (which also spawned Def Leppard's Phil Collen). "I knew when I was 15 that he was the guy I would want in my band," Guns said. "But you never think anything like that can happen."

What they did on *L.A. Guns* was "very raw without being total metal. It's a lot more direct than other people's albums. We tried to write some commercial songs and keep them as heavy as we could. There's a friendly competition with Guns N' Roses. Everybody's talking about the both of us, and we're both striving to be the best,"

With exposure, the members hoped to corner the sex-booze-and-tattoos market.

"We're lucky—we have an image," Guns said. "We're all the same kind of people; we look the same offstage as we do onstage, I think a lot about what we can do to be different from the other bands, but we never end up using my good ideas." ■

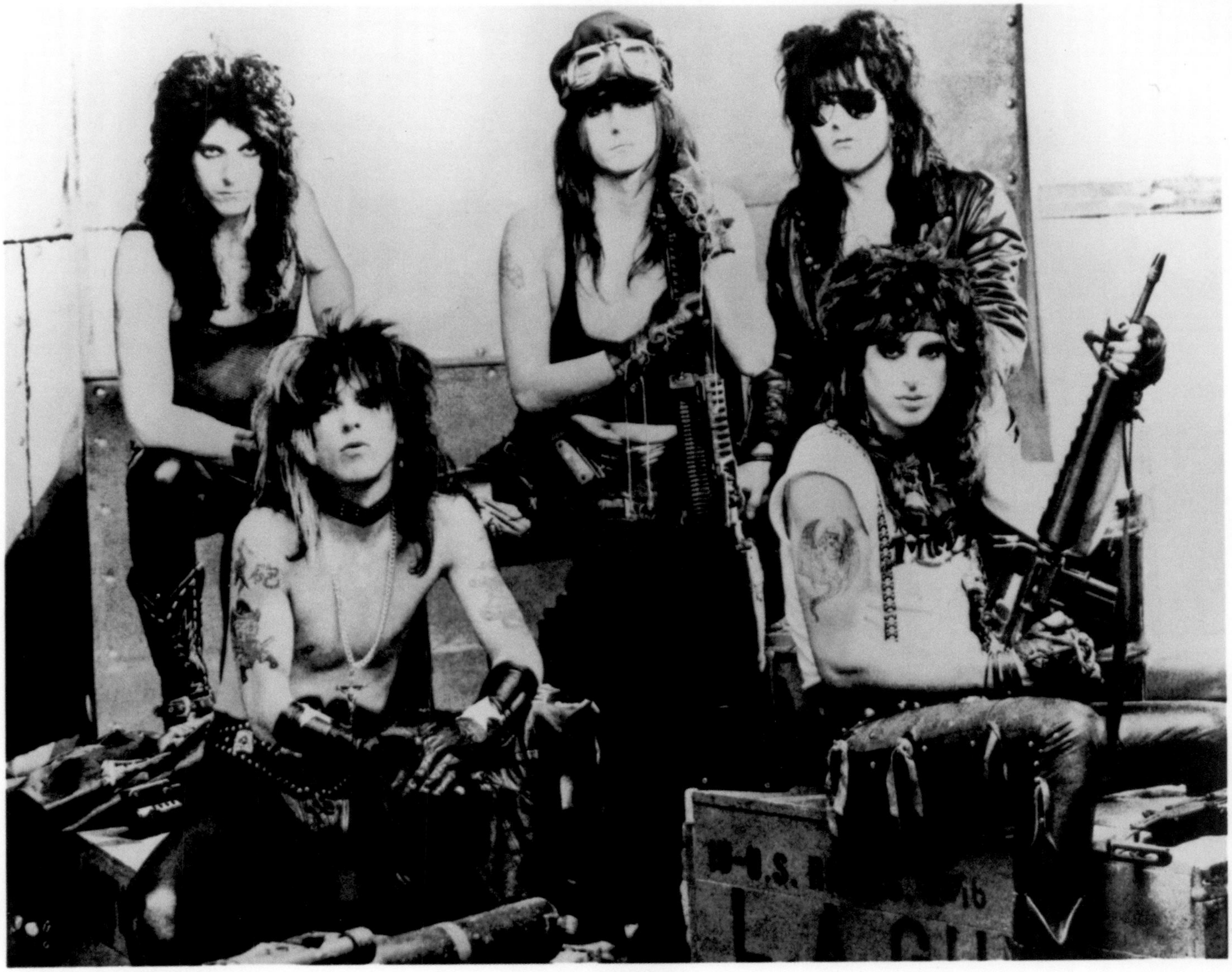

L.A. GUNS

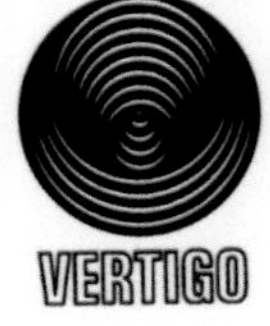

PolyGram Records

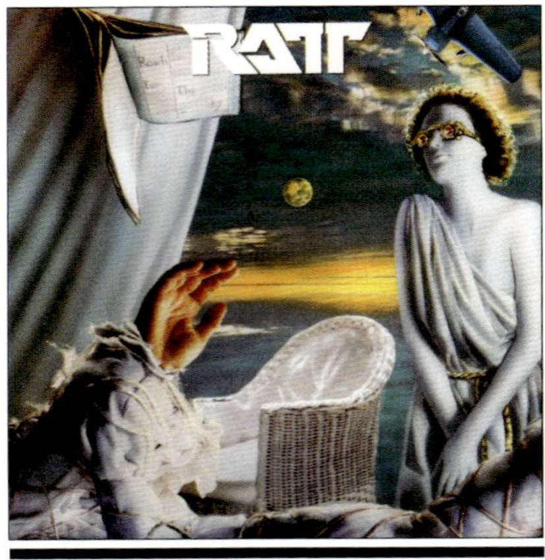

Billboard 200: *Reach for the Sky* (#17)
Billboard Hot 100: "Way Cool Jr." (#75)

Sticking it out in the hair-metal genre, Ratt ratified its ingrained pop crossover potential with "Way Cool Jr."

A PREPONDERANCE of hard-rock bands got comprised of scrawny little guys, but the members of Ratt were generally big, athletic types. Guitarist Robbin Crosby picked up the guitar in fifth grade but dropped it not too long after when he became obsessed with baseball.

"I was a surfing maniac, and I had a chance to go to college and play ball," Crosby said. "But I decided to rock 'n' roll instead."

Crosby then formed Ratt with some fellow "land-gypsy gladiators, cement pirates" from the Los Angeles rock scene, and the lineup had remained the same since. *Reach for the Sky,* Ratt's fourth album, was cut with long-time producer Beau Hill, and the typically sharp track "Way Cool Jr." rated as a worthy addition to the "Ratt 'n' roll" repertoire.

A general misconception was that the band had had only one hit record, but all five of Ratt's albums had been certified platinum at the least. More accurately, the quintet had had only one hit song, 1984's "Round and Round."

"That was a grand moment, and I wouldn't change a thing, but the song cast a shadow on the band—we're not really a singles group," Crosby said. "We're a survivor from that metal wave of 1983 and 1984." ■

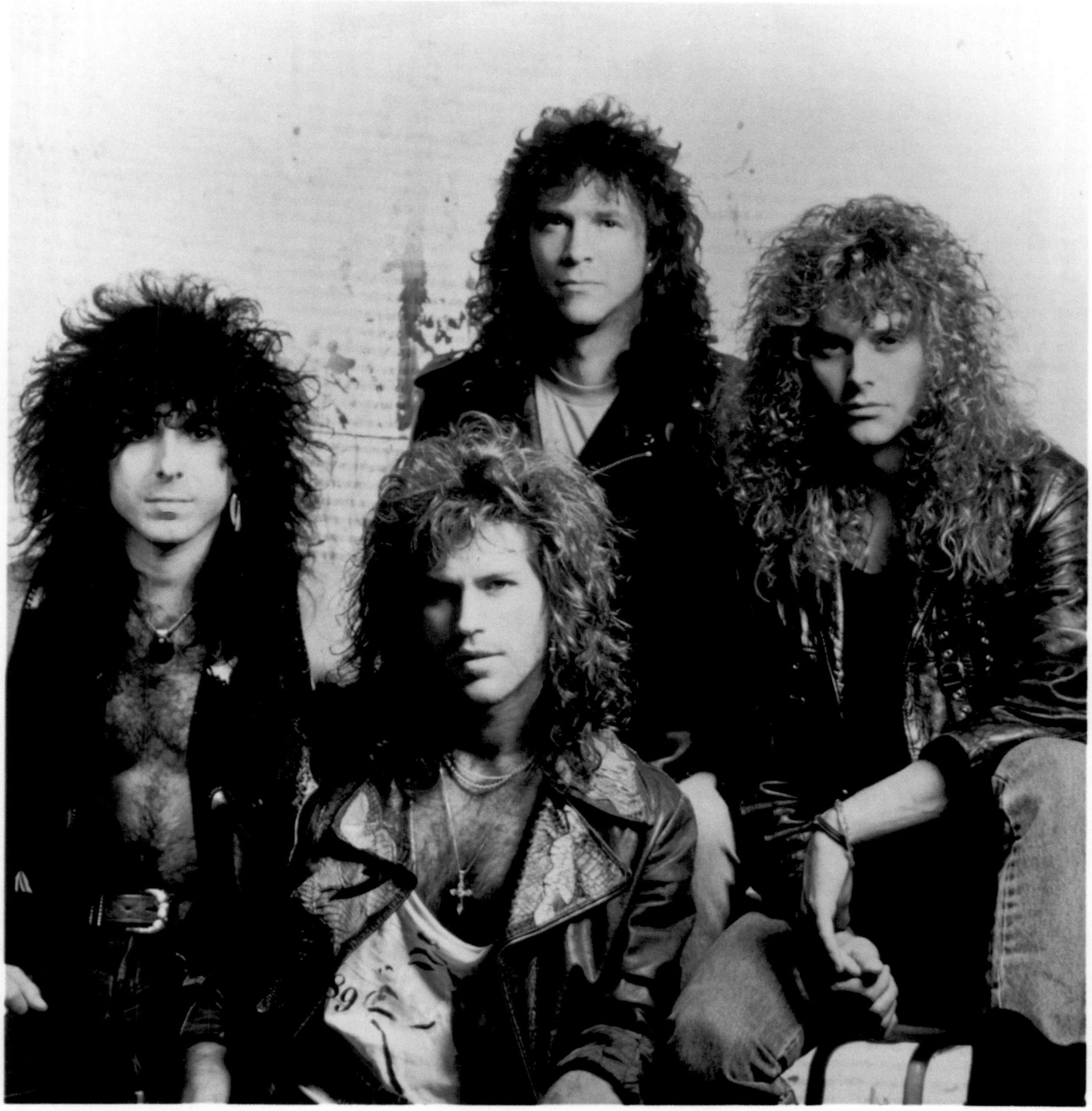

photo: Steven Selikoff

PAUL TAYLOR KIP WINGER ROD MORGENSTEIN REB BEACH

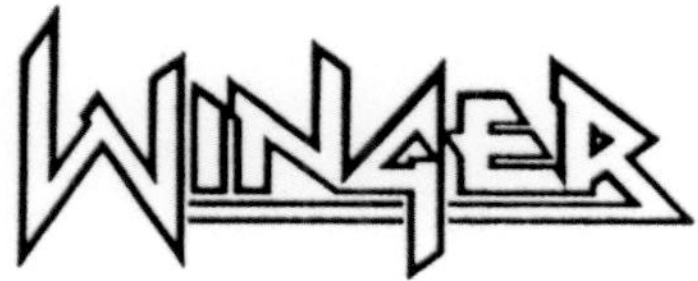

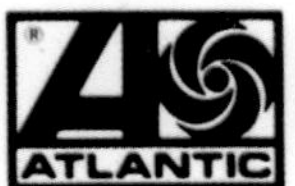

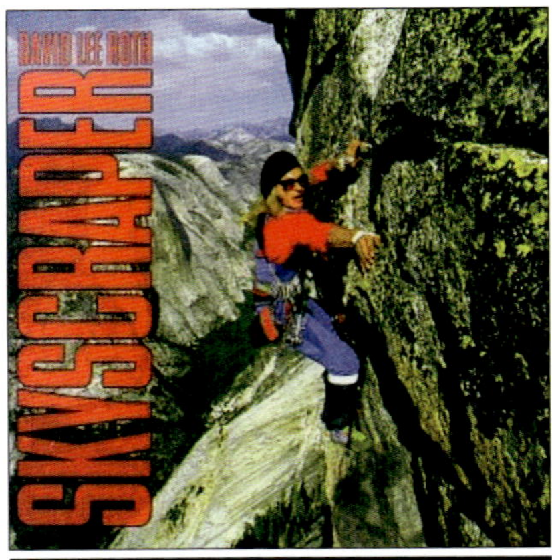

Billboard 200: *Skyscraper* (#6)
Billboard Hot 100: "Just Like Paradise" (#6); "Stand Up" (#64)

Doing everything a little bit larger than life, dashing David Lee Roth swaggered his way through *Skyscraper*.

WHEN VAN Halen became one of the world's most popular hard-rock bands, nimble-fingered guitarist Eddie Van Halen proved to be the musical standout. But it was the charismatic David Lee Roth, with his flowing blond mane, onstage kicks and flair for unabashed showmanship (oh, and those Spandex trousers) who established the group's party-hearty image.

After more than a decade together, the hyperactive vocalist had a falling-out with the other members in 1985. He kicked his mouth into overdrive, returning with his trademark bravado, canny self-awareness and the expected ribald wit and trash-talkin' jive. Some people thought the hyperactive singer's act was ready for irrelevance, the kind of self-impressed clowning they scoffed at.

But the EP *Crazy from the Heat* and the album *Eat 'Em and Smile* had gone platinum.

"Just because I was miserable didn't mean I wasn't having a great time," Roth said. "I was one of the architects of one of the most familiar Americana sounds in the history of the genre. My voice and the sound of Eddie Van Halen's guitar are as well-known as the McDonald's arches. Even if you've never owned a record of mine, you're intimate with it tearing out of a flatbed in front of you at the drive-thru at Burger King.

"What we were serving up was a new hybrid of unusual references. Mine started primarily in Black music because of the schools I went to when they started integrated busing—I was in the front row of the first bus. I was with 90 percent black and Spanish-speaking kids from junior high to junior college, hearing Motown all the way through the dance music craze. Combine that with what the other guys were putting together, and you had Viking thug-pop with the Four Tops on every chorus—it was a horse of a different color. And it was laced with my sense of humor, which is gleefully sarcastic and obviously enthusiastic."

Roth had assembled a virtuoso band for *Skyscraper,* his first endeavor as a co-producer (with guitar hero Steve Vai). The video for his hit single "Just Like Paradise," as well as the album cover, featured a harnessed Roth climbing the granite face of Yosemite's fabled Half Dome.

"All the world is a party—but I say that with a co-conspiratorial chuckle, not a belly laugh," the notorious frontman said. "A great deal of my image has been conditioned by my imitators, some of whom are very successful. In one sense, I'm flattered. In another, I feel like a guy driving past a car wreck and feeling lucky that no one was killed!" ■

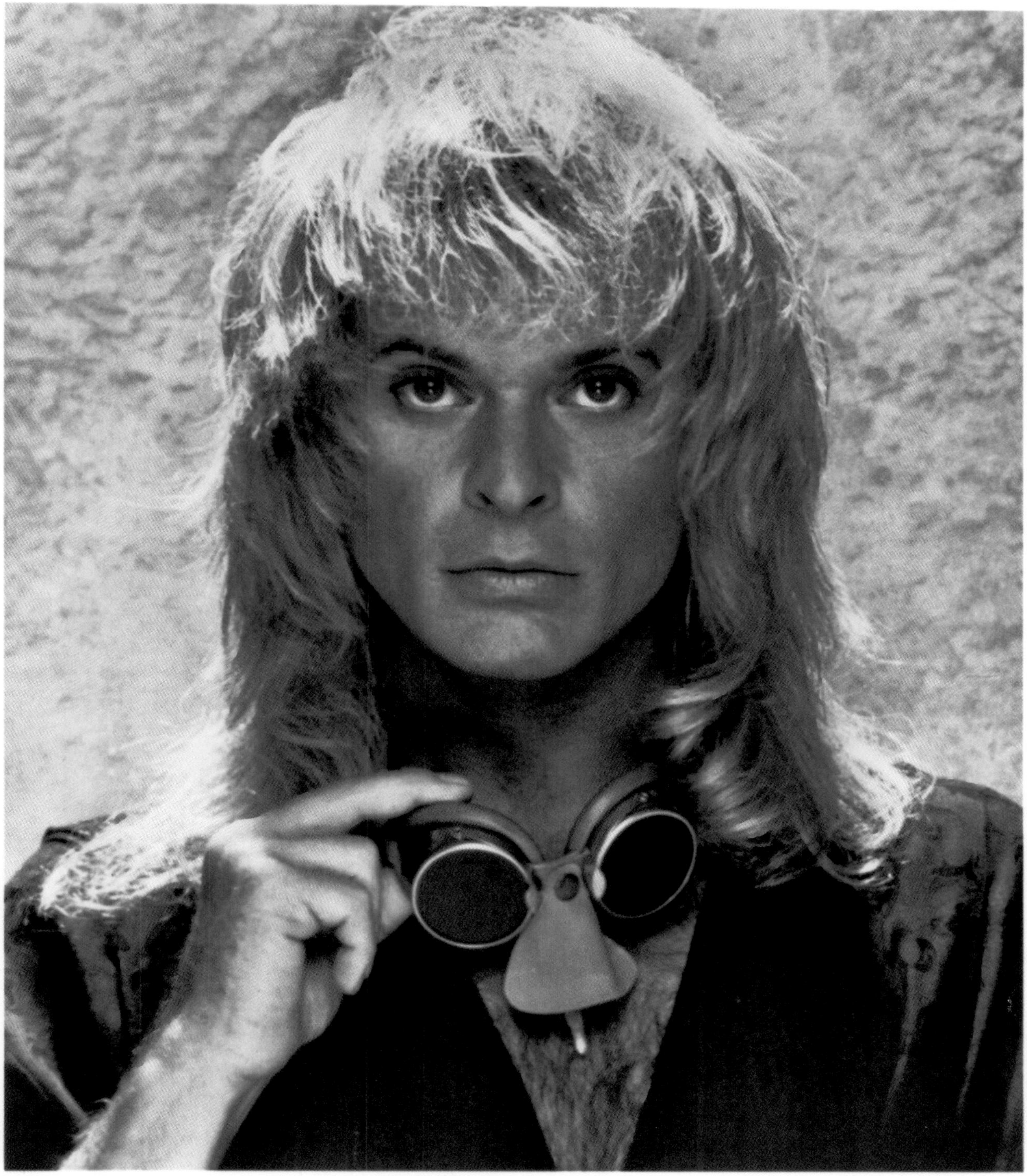

Photo Credit: Neil Zlozower

DAVID LEE ROTH

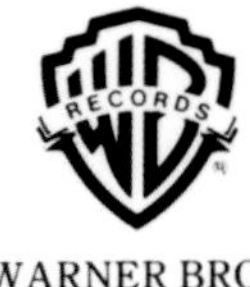

WARNER BROS.

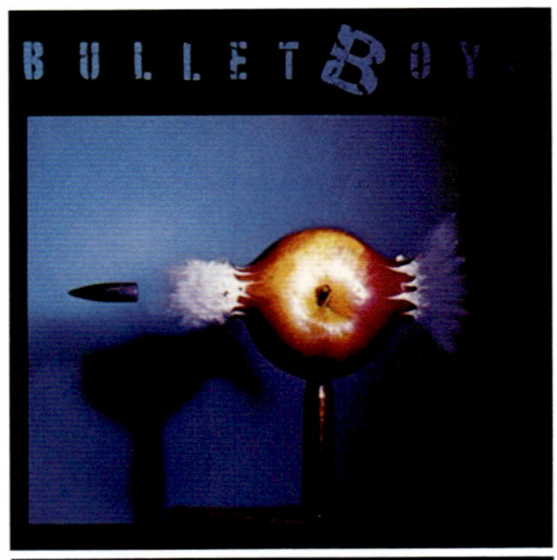

Billboard 200: *BulletBoys* (#34)
Billboard Hot 100: "Smooth Up in Ya" (#71);
"For the Love of Money" (#78)

During the last wave of the pop-metal scene, BulletBoys managed to squeeze out a gold-selling debut album.

ON THEIR self-titled album, the four members of the Los Angeles-based BulletBoys benefited from the superstar production expertise of Ted Templeman—the "power groove rock" of "Smooth Up in Ya" and a glam-metal cover of the O'Jays' "For the Love of Money" recalled the energy of Templeman's early work with Van Halen.

Indeed, some press coverage had BulletBoys pegged as Van Halen's heirs apparent—as if raw punch, major attitude and a sense of humor were the only criteria. After all, flamboyant singer Marq Torien had obviously spent the majority of his Wonder Bread years in front of the bedroom mirror emulating David Lee Roth's strutting, mugging and preening.

"I feel we're going to have an era like Van Halen did, like Led Zeppelin did, like Aerosmith did," Torien bellowed. "I'm a strong believer in fate and in playing to destroy people. We look at this as a football game—you don't go out there to lose or draw, you go out there to win. That's our format as far as rock 'n' roll is concerned."

The members had convened in a condemned building, aptly named "the Piss Room," to jam and write songs. Two months later, a demo tape brought them to Templeman's attention. "We didn't bang the clubs—we got our tunes together and brought people in to see us to get our record deal," Torien assured. "We're not stars or personalities, we're musicians. I used to be up there in the nose-bleed heaven of big arenas watching bands. Now we're the ones rocking hard, and anyone that isn't going to rock as hard as us better get out of the way." ■

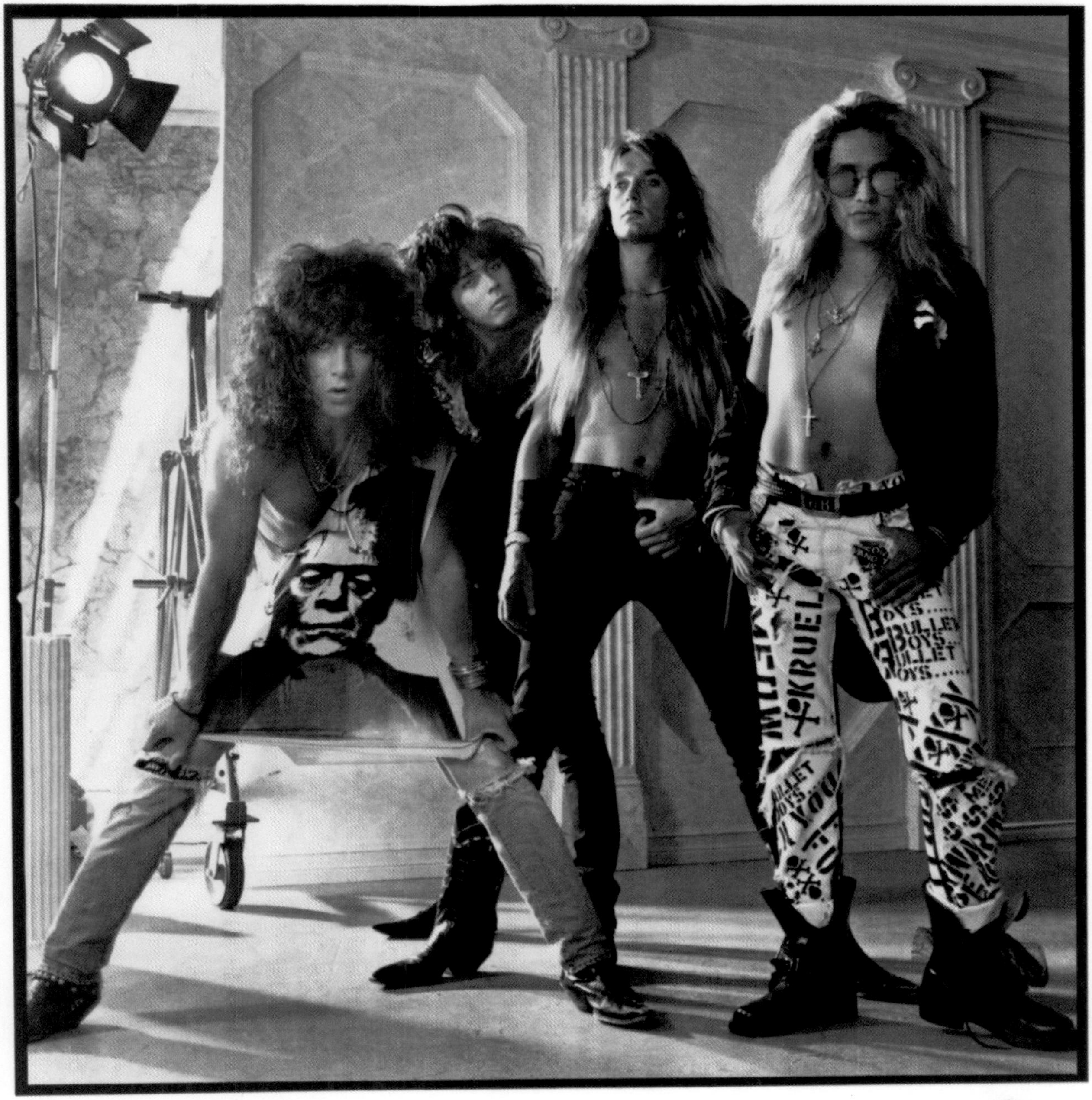

Photo Credit: Aaron Rapoport

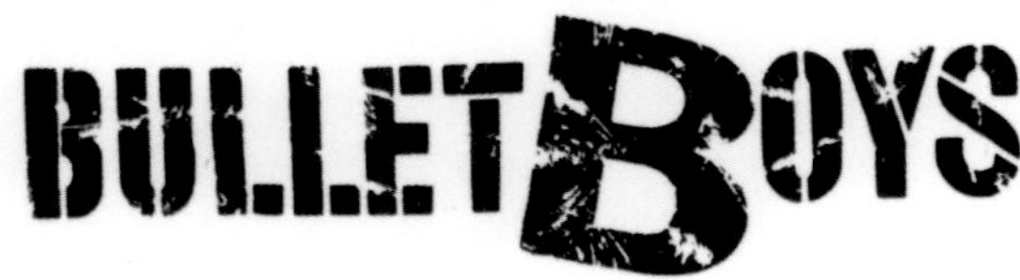

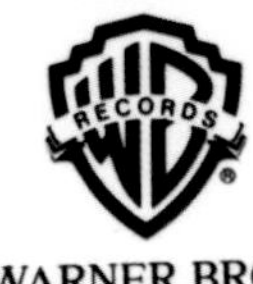

WARNER BROS.

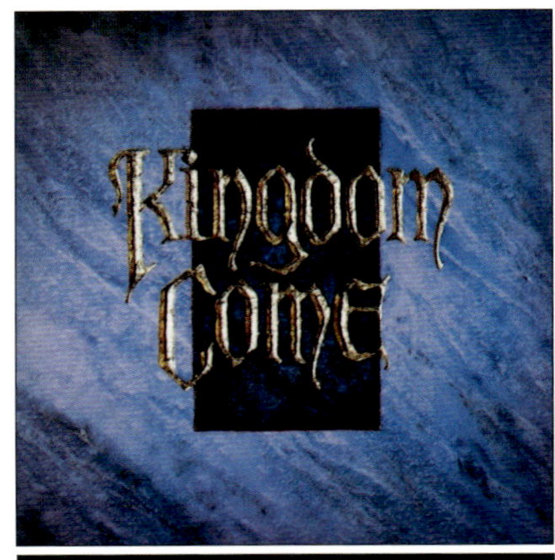

Billboard 200: *Kingdom Come* (#12)
Billboard Hot 100: "Get It On" (#69)

Forging an aural likeness to Led Zeppelin, Kingdom Come generated a hefty amount of buzz with "Get It On."

THE MOST talked-about new rock band of 1988, Kingdom Come stirred up passions, pro and con, regarding its Led Zeppelin-like sonics. Was singer Lenny Wolf exploiting a classic sound, or following a great tradition? Some in the press derisively dubbed the band "Kingdom Clone," but plenty of fans who were too young to celebrate Zeppelin in its early Seventies heyday subscribed to the latter theory—the band's self-titled debut album sold a million copies.

"I'm not justifying it anymore," Wolf said. "The first three weeks, I was very flattered to be compared to Zeppelin. But after three months, I was tired of hearing about it."

Wolf grew up poor in Hamburg, Germany, and came to America with his rock 'n' roll dreams at age 21. He formed Stone Fury in 1984, singing lead and playing guitar, but the group broke up after two albums.

"Musically, we weren't on the same level," he said. "I like snobby, bluesy, street rock 'n' roll, and my partner was into experimental keyboards."

Wolf put together Kingdom Come with manager Marty Wolff, who leaked the single "Get It On" to radio stations around the US, generating speculation about the "mystery" band, even "Zeppelin reunion" rumors. "Get It On" was a hit, reaching #4 on *Billboard*'s Album Rock Tracks chart, and the band was chosen to open the "Monsters of Rock" tour supporting Van Halen, Scorpions, Metallica and Dokken. "It was like being born and learning how to run before you could even walk," rhythm guitarist Rick Steier said.

"We got a hard time from some people, but all of that actually challenged us even more," Wolf added. "I've finally found my style—a Seventies feel with an Eighties sound." ■

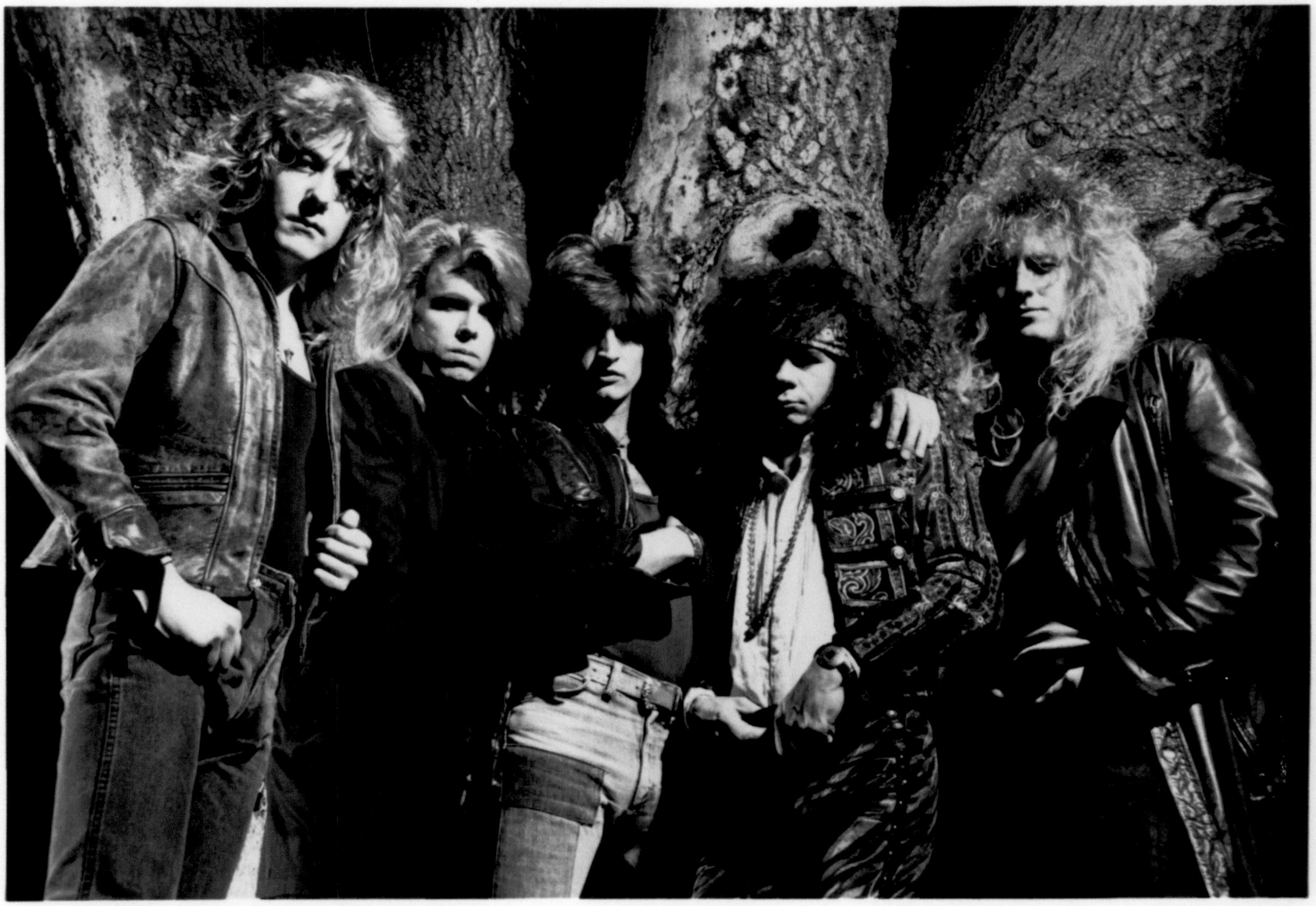

James Kottak | Johnny B. Frank | Lenny Wolf | Danny Stag | Rick Steier

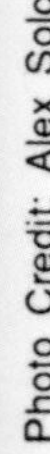

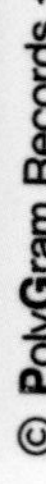

KINGDOM COME

PolyGram Records

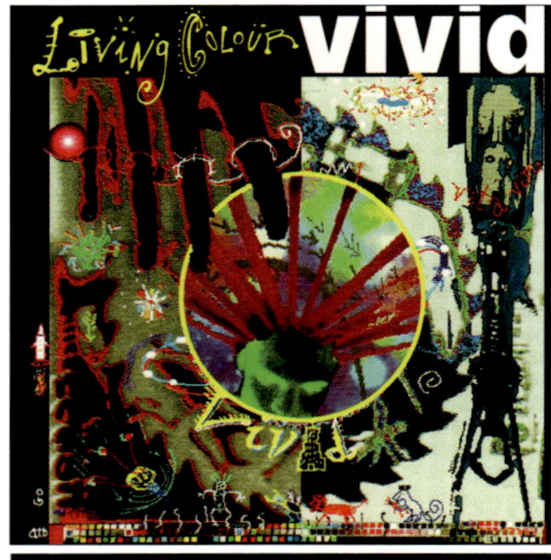

Billboard 200: *Vivid* (#6)
Billboard Hot 100: "Cult of Personality" (#13);
"Glamour Boys" (#31); "Open Letter (To a Landlord)" (#82)

The smart *Vivid* and its anthemic single, "Cult of Personality," left Living Colour's Black mark on hard rock.

THE MEMBERS of Living Colour accomplished what no Black musicians had done since the days of Sly Stone and Jimi Hendrix—they broke rock's color barrier, reaching the same white adolescents that other heavy-metal bands reached. The media proclaimed the lifting of rock's color line, but the band continued to wage a battle over image.

"There's so much more to talk about in the music," vocalist Corey Glover said. "But everyone asks about three things—is racism a problem, why are four Black men playing rock 'n' roll, and what was it like playing with the Rolling Stones?"

Vernon Reid, the band's founder and guitarist, had spent nearly six years running into a wall of indifference, paying immoderate dues as a sideman as he crusaded for his right to rock. Many Black artists had successfully "crossed over" from the R&B charts to the pop charts, but rock radio, the key format for young rock bands, had been slow in recognizing the Bus Boys, Mother's Finest and other past Black rockers. And traditionally Black radio had been even slower to play Black rock.

Reid formed Living Colour in 1984. First a power trio, the band eventually added a singer—Glover, an actor who played Francis, the smart-mouthed soldier in Oliver Stone's Oscar-winning *Platoon*. By 1986, the lineup was set with bassist Muzz Skillings and drummer William Calhoun.

Concurrently, Reid co-founded the Black Rock Coalition, dedicated to combating racial stereotypes in rock and pop music, and Living Colour was both his personal outlet and the Coalition's flagship ensemble. Mick Jagger caught the band on the New York club scene in 1987 and recruited Reid for his solo album, *Primitive Cool*, which led to Jagger producing two tracks for the group. After an extended run of demo-shopping, Living Colour was signed by Epic Records.

"We were in a very strange position because of who we are and what we do," Glover said. "It was Catch-22. There were Black folks on the album cover, so white stations wouldn't play it, but when the needle hit the groove, Black stations wouldn't play it. The state of rock 'n' roll has to do with ignorance—there's no sense of history. Rock 'n' roll was supposed to be this polyglot of music, a bit of this and that. They called it rock 'n' roll for lack of a better word, and that whole attitude became the cornerstone of where the industry is at today—give it a label. Yes, we're 'Black rock' because we are Black. But it's music that's made for everybody. It's about what touches you, not what color you are."

Originally given a lukewarm reception, the band's message eventually got through to America. *Vivid*, the debut album, a hard-rock blizzard of fuzzed-out guitar flurries and funk flavorings, went to #6 on the pop charts and hit platinum. The diamond-hard "Cult of Personality," based around a deceptively simple, Led Zeppelin-ish riff, received heavy exposure on MTV and album rock radio formats and won a Grammy for Best Hard Rock Performance. Following the album's release, Living Colour opened for the Rolling Stones on the American dates of the Steel Wheels tour.

"We're Black. We play rock 'n' roll. Now maybe everybody could give that a rest," Glover said. "We'd like to move on from here." ■

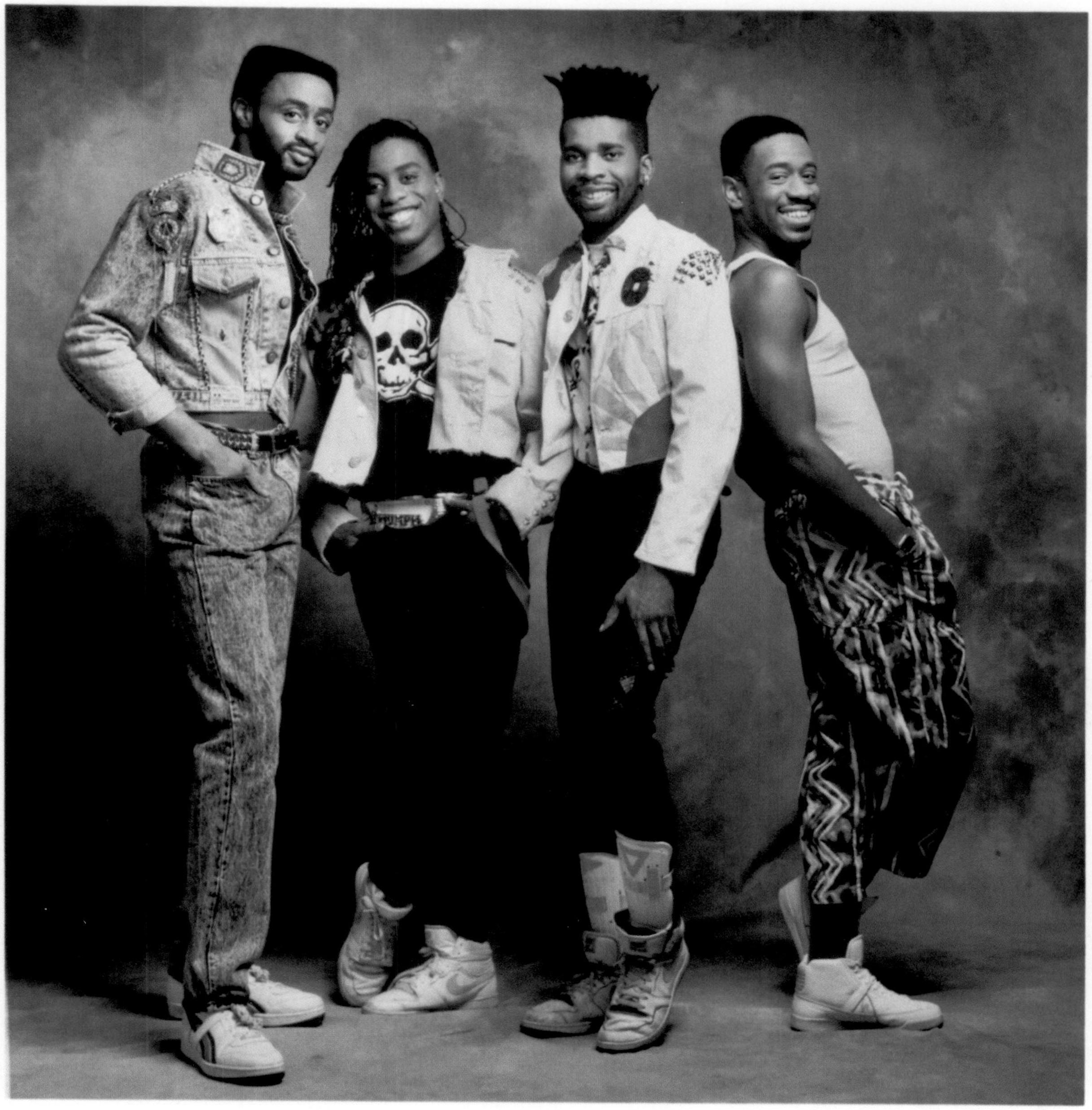

PHOTO CREDIT: DEBORAH FEINGOLD

Living Colour

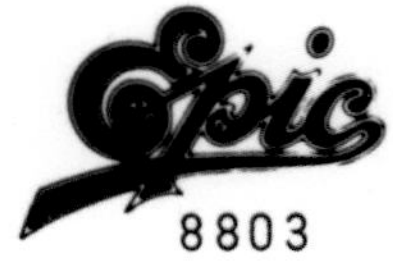

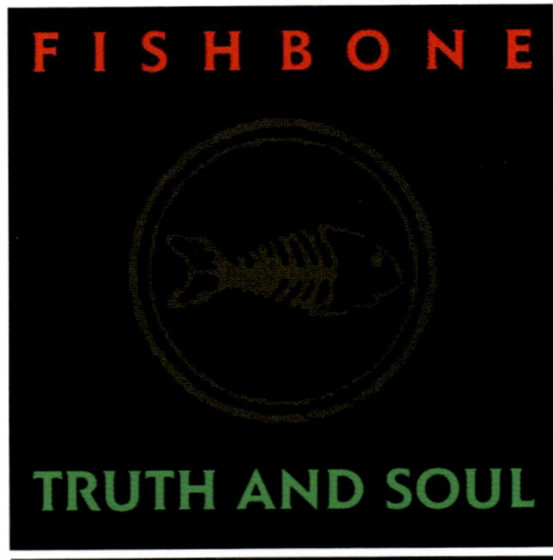

Billboard 200: *Truth and Soul* (#153)

With the album *Truth and Soul*, Fishbone added left-leaning social analysis to its ska and funk-metal styles.

FOR A decade, Fishbone had become known for onstage chaos and an uninhibited blend of horn-driven R&B and speed metal. But the six Black members had then reached young adulthood, and the ambitious *Truth and Soul,* the band's second album, focused on an instrumental precision and an unexpected lyrical maturity behind the breakneck beats.

"The record is about life in general, and the government and the shit that happens in your neighborhood in particular," singer Angelo Moore said.

A hard-rocking remake of Curtis Mayfield's "Freddie's Dead" addressed the drug menace, and the music video became the band's first hit on MTV. But the members wrote all the other songs. "Slow Bus Movin' (Howard Beach Party)" was an indictment of the social climate that permitted the Brooklyn racial incident, and Moore's "Ma and Pa" was a tale of divorce told from a kid's point of view.

"I wrote that song in one day," Moore explained. "For a long time, I went through child custody with my parents—they went to court, and I saw them act like kids. I love them, but I couldn't believe they were fighting over me like I was a lollipop. I felt like I was the adult, on the outside looking in."

Yet Fishbone remained a party band. The dance tune "Bonin' in the Boneyard" proved that the band had lost none of its irreverent playfulness, balancing serious points with good-times anarchy. "Life is a ballet, man," Moore concluded. "You've got to laugh. You can't be totally negative or depression will screw you up. You have to look for hope." ■

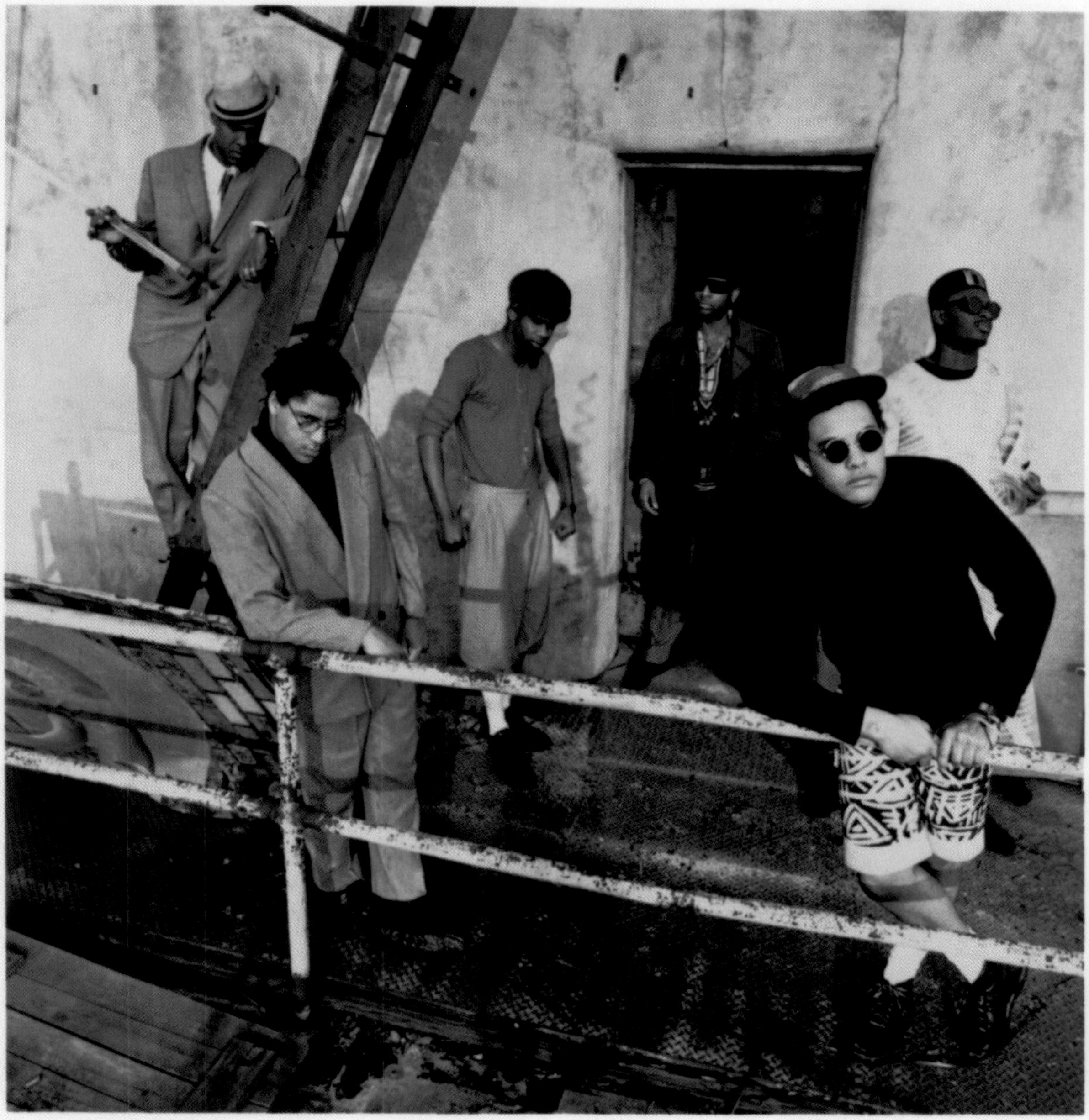

PHOTO: JOHN SCARPATI

WILLIAM MORRIS AGENCY

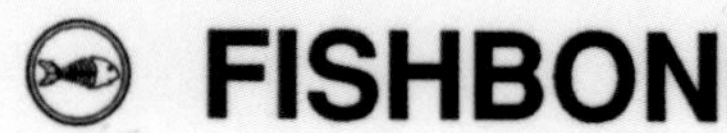

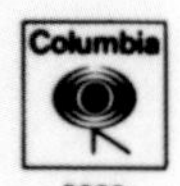

8808

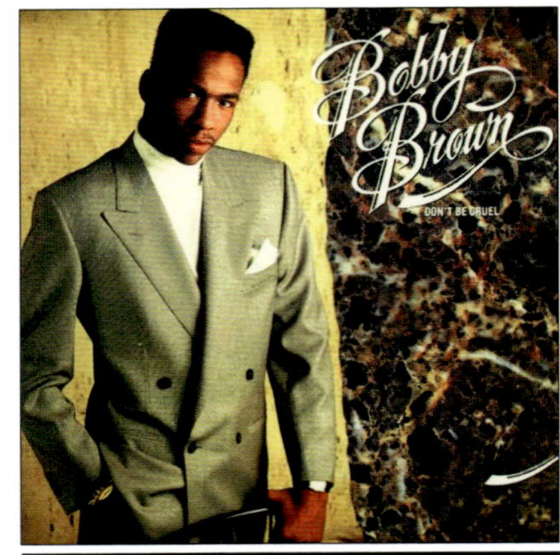

Billboard 200: *Don't Be Cruel* (No. 1)
Billboard Hot 100: "Don't Be Cruel" (#8); "My Prerogative" (No. 1); "Roni" (#3); "Every Little Step" (#3); "Rock Wit'cha" (#7)

Bobby Brown's daring new jack swing approach crossed over to pop patrons with the megahit *Don't Be Cruel*.

NEW EDITION had its beginnings in 1981 among five friends growing up in the projects of Boston who found an escape in singing. Bobby Brown, the co-lead vocalist, was the teen quintet's youngest member at 12. In 1983, "Candy Girl" launched a string of pop hits ("Cool It Now," "Mr. Telephone Man") and two platinum albums for the bubble gum soul champions.

But in 1985, Brown left New Edition. The split could have resulted in a dilution of talent, acrimony among the two factions and legions of betrayed fans. But Brown and New Edition were the apparent happy exceptions—Brown said he hated the thought of competing with his childhood friends, and they went on a national tour together.

"We've all known what we've wanted to do from the beginning," Brown said. "So once I made the move to go solo, they accepted it. That's why it's worked out relationship-wise."

Brown happily noted that both he and his former bandmates had prospered commercially in the wake of his departure. New Edition replaced Brown with singer Johnny Gill and hired producers Jimmy Jam and Terry Lewis to update and harden their sound.

And Brown had done even better. "My Girlfriend" introduced him as a solo act in 1987, and that ballad from his debut album *King of Stage* became a No.1 record on the R&B charts. Brown began working with Babyface and Antonio "L.A." Reid, the top R&B producers and songwriters of the budding new jack swing movement. *Don't Be Cruel* launched five Top 10 pop smashes, including "Every Little Step," the title track and the No. 1 "My Prerogative."

"I want to sell records," Brown admitted. "I don't want to be an artist making music to please myself. My songs are straight grooves and rhythms with some vocal lines on them, with a rap at the beginning or the end. I incorporate rap because that's what kids want to hear. Rap is the backbone of black music right now."

The savvy still-young singer tempered his mercenary attitude by noting that stardom wasn't as glamorous as it might appear. "Fans don't see the late nights or the early mornings, or the pressures to get your record to No. 1 and stay there, or the energy it takes to get onstage every night to perform. You always have to watch out behind your back and look over your shoulder to see what your manager is doing. You have to sacrifice having companions, because you don't know who's your friend and who's not. It's not an easy business. But I started young, and I still love what I do. So it's gonna be my business for the rest of my life. I'm never gonna quit." ■

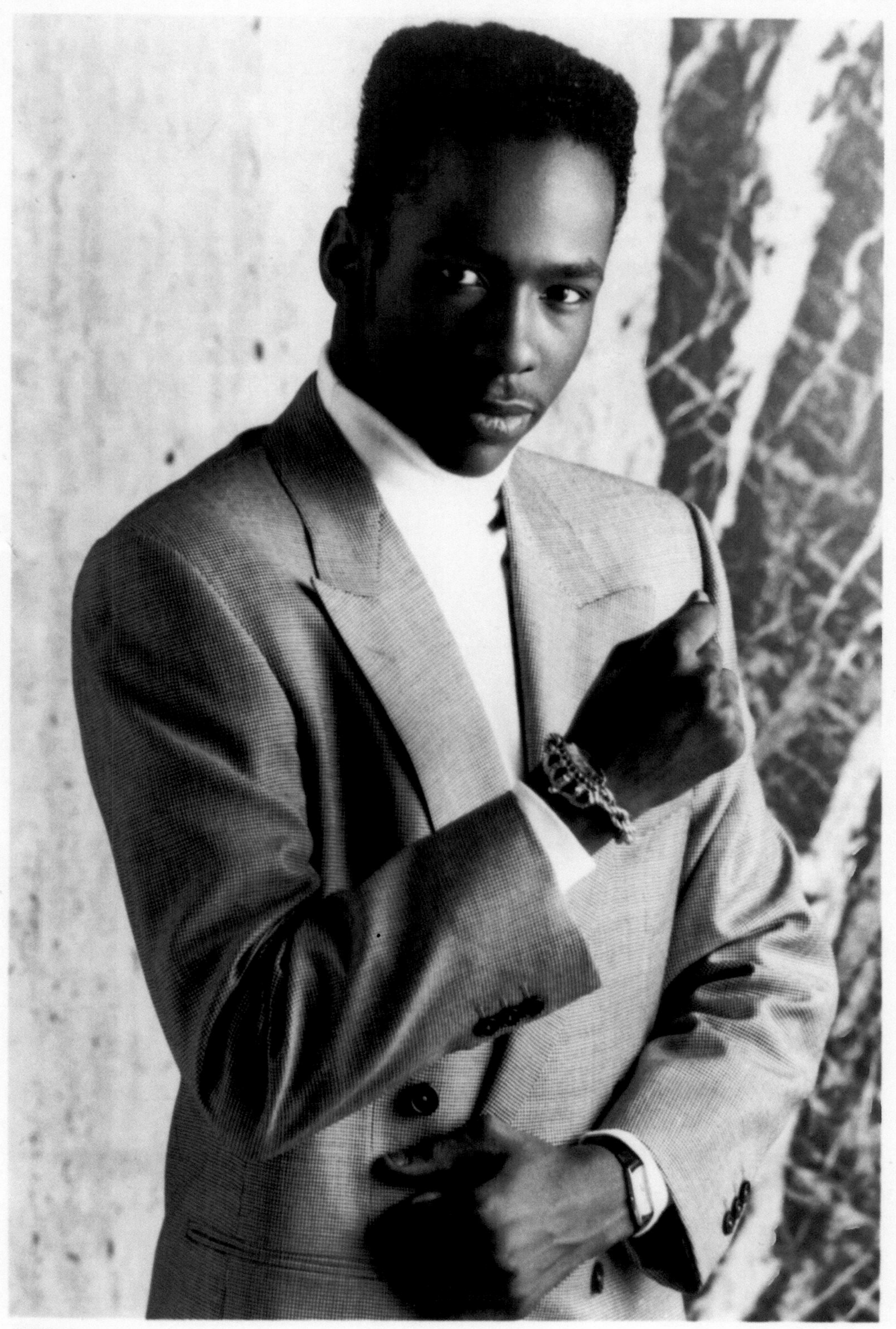

Bobby Brown

MCA RECORDS

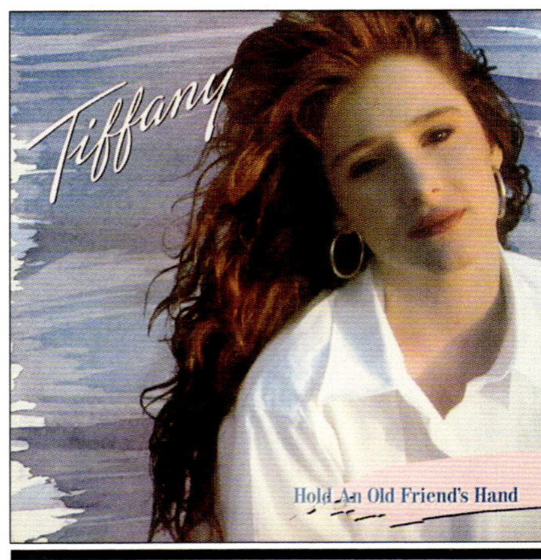

Billboard 200: *Hold an Old Friend's Hand* (#17)
Billboard Hot 100: "All This Time" (#6); "Radio Romance" (#35)

Despite legal issues, teen-pop singer Tiffany delivered *Hold an Old Friend's Hand*, a more mature collection.

SOME FANS and music insiders had the idea that teen acts were little more than puppets of their record companies and managers, their success based on image, not talent. Tiffany, the 17-year-old "princess of pop," had been hounded by that perception since she burst into the limelight with her four-million-selling 1987 debut album. Being a teenage celebrity had put her through the emotional wringer. Her adult detractors derided her as a mere tool of her manager, George Tobin, whose control over her career was considered excessive. His share of her royalties was 50 percent after expenses, exceeding the norm.

So Tiffany's mother and stepfather took Tobin to court over control of Tiffany's career, which led to Tiffany petitioning to become an "emancipated" minor and no longer under her mother's legal guardianship. Tiffany, whose last name was Darwish, conceded that the court battle left a bad taste in people's mouths. "I'm sure a lot of people feel like a teenage artist is supposed to be the girl next door, and that was, and is, my image. But the girl next door isn't supposed to go to court and sue her mother."

Tiffany's emancipation petition was actually a way to keep her stepfather out of her financial affairs and have her money put in an account that couldn't be touched until she was an adult. The court rejected her emancipation but granted her the account. Her relationship with her mother, she said, was critical in her life.

"We always had somebody in the middle interpreting how we felt. We weren't able to talk to each other, and the courtroom wasn't the best place to change that. Now I'm not living with her, but we've been through counseling and we're talking for the first time, about how I feel and why I'm doing things. My mom and I always loved each other. That will never change, and with that love we can work things out. You don't know what a big thing it is for a teenage girl to say that."

Her image somewhat tarnished, Tiffany's second album, *Hold an Old Friend's Hand*, didn't come close to the success of her debut. It showcased a more mature sound and image, and sales exceeded a respectable 1.5 million, but there wasn't much of a buzz. The tender ballad "All This Time," the first single, went Top 10 on the pop chart, but "Radio Romance," the second single, fizzled in the 30s.

"The music business has made me grow up a little faster," Tiffany said. "I don't think I'm more mature than anyone else in my age group, but that's what happens to kids in show business. There's been a lot of criticism in the last year, but I've learned from it. I want to understand the business."

A high-school senior in Southern California, Tiffany traveled with a tutor while on the road. "I'm missing out on high-school life," she admitted. "But I'm getting something great in return—a chance to travel, a chance to be a star." ■

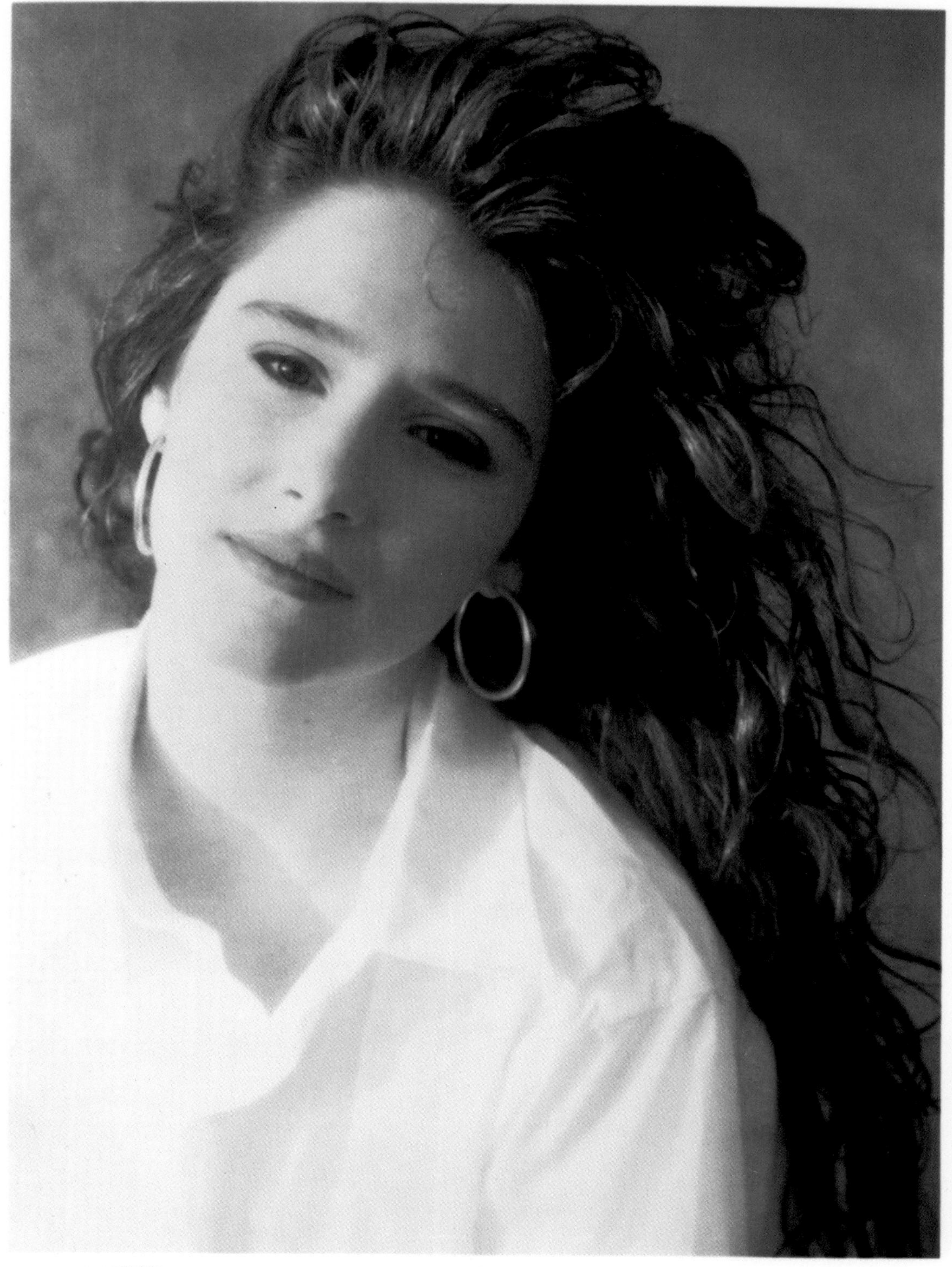

Tiffany

MCA RECORDS

Billboard 200: *Hangin' Tough* (No. 1)
Billboard Hot 100: "Please Don't Go Girl" (#10); "You Got It (The Right Stuff)" (#3); "I'll Be Loving You (Forever)" (No. 1); "Hangin' Tough" (No. 1); "Cover Girl" (#2)

Teenage stars New Kids on the Block unleashed a youthful hysteria with their second album, *Hangin' Tough*.

THE MEMBERS of New Kids on the Block, a Boston-based boy band with a breakthrough album, *Hangin' Tough*, found it offensive that some fans and industry insiders assumed they were all image and no talent.

"People underestimate us," 18-year-old Donnie Wahlberg insisted. "When you're young in this business, people have the preconception that you can't have a mind of your own. I wonder if these are the same people who, when they were kids, didn't like anyone trying to tell them what to do. New Kids on the Block are puppets on nobody's string. When you see us performing on stage, you're seeing the five guys who make the decisions, who sit down for hours at a time talking about what we want to do."

The five adolescents who made up the group—Wahlberg, Jon Knight, Jon's brother Jordan, Joe McIntyre and Danny Wood—were chosen by producer and songwriter Maurice Starr in 1984 after six months of auditions. Starr was interested in starting a streetwise group that could rap as well as sing bubblegum tunes. Earlier in the decade, Starr had put together New Edition, the popular teenage group from which Bobby Brown emerged. Wahlberg, a rapper and dancer from a family of nine kids, was the first chosen.

"Being from Boston isn't like being from Hollywood or New York—I never dreamed of making it because I thought the chances were crazy," he said. "I was going to school on the subways, trying to survive. Maurice helped me believe in myself. He knew from my personality that I had what it took, that I wasn't going to let anything stand in the way of what I believe in. But it bothers me when Maurice is described as the Svengali behind New Kids. He had me put the rest of the group together. Maurice is our guidance, but he's not our leader. What we do every day is our vision. We can't live our lives for anyone else."

The danceable R&B, pop and rock of *Hangin' Tough* took NKOTB beyond the self-described "kid funk" of their 1986 debut album, climbing to multiplatinum status and spawning five Top 10 singles. The quintet reached No.1 with "I'll Be Loving You (Forever)" and the title track. The band members were careful about their image, emphasizing the importance of being good yet streetwise by performing at various anti-drug rallies.

"We present a positive message by example," Wahlberg said. "We don't have to bog down our songs by saying 'Don't do drugs, stay in school and keep away from crime.' It's our choice to do those things. Our songs are out there to make people happy, and when they look beyond the music, they see a group of kids who make them dance, who have energy and excitement, who are still cool. That's why they relate to us." ■

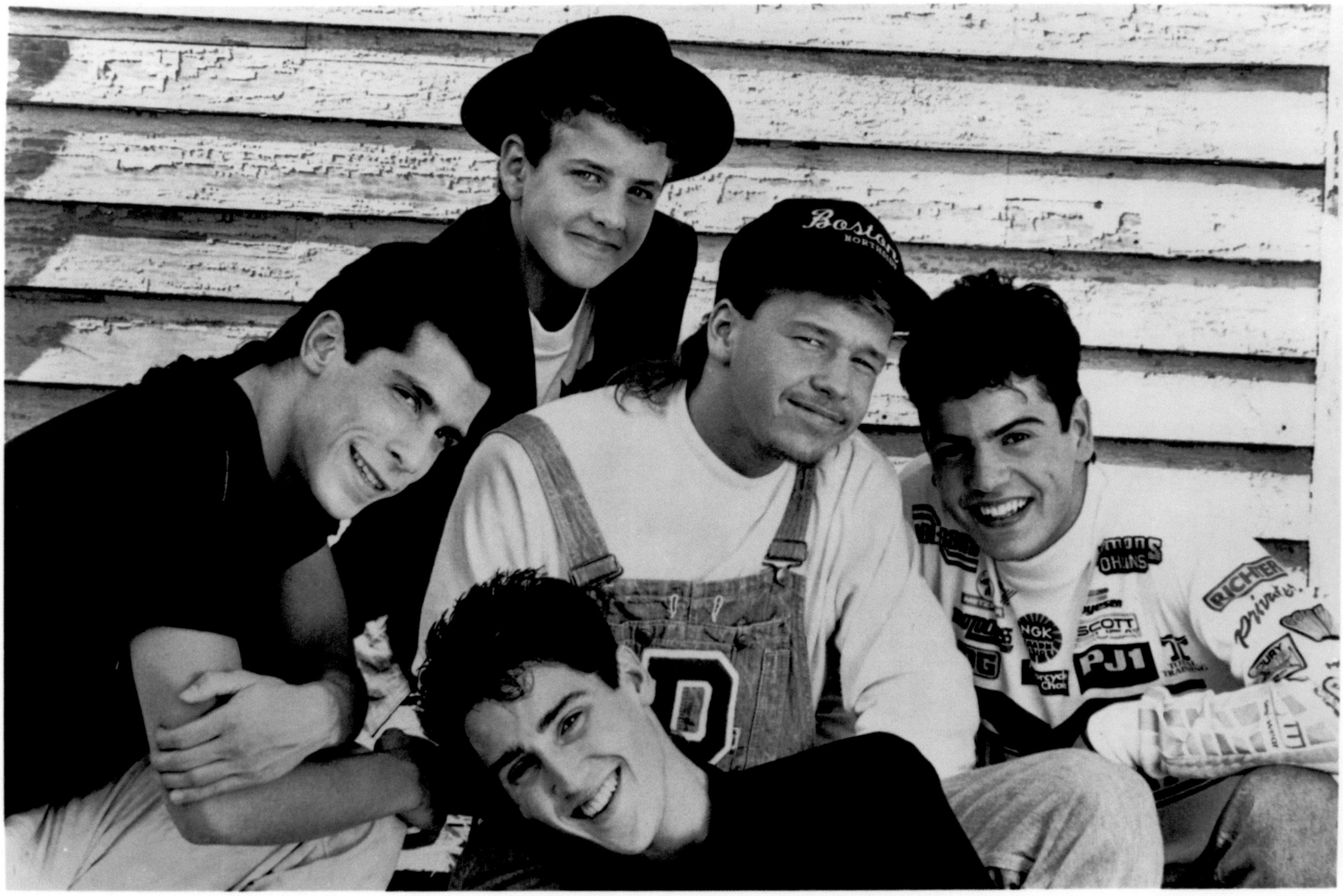

From left. DANNY WOOD, JOE McINTYRE, DONNIE WAHLBERG, JORDAN KNIGHT, and (bottom) JON KNIGHT.

PHOTOGRAPH: LYNN GOLDSMITH/LGI

NEW KIDS ON THE BLOCK

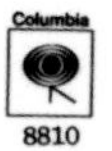

8810

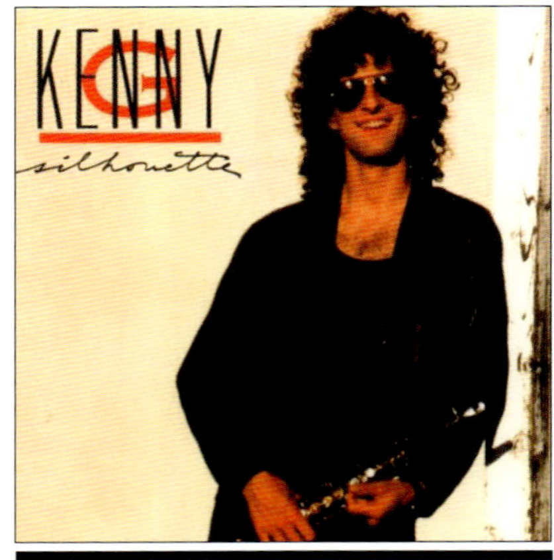

Billboard 200: *Silhouette* (#8)
Billboard 200: "Silhouette" (#13); "We've Saved the Best for Last" (#47)

With *Silhouette* riding high on the charts, sax man Kenny G endured a bombardment of criticism and mockery.

FROM HIS perch atop the jazz and pop worlds with *Silhouette*, Kenny G would have appreciated a little credibility as well. He'd had it in 1982, when he began a four-year stint playing saxophone in the progressive Jeff Lorber Fusion band. He distinguished himself to the point where he landed his own solo recording deal, and his first three albums sold primarily in the jazz and R&B markets.

But in 1987, Kenny G (nee Gorelick) became an industry phenomenon with the rapturous ballad "Songbird." It was rare for a jazz or instrumental track to reach hit status, yet "Songbird" became only the sixth instrumental single to crack the Top 10 in the Eighties, and only the second not associated with a film or television show. Kenny G performed "Songbird" on *The Tonight Show* on three different occasions, and it ranked as a Top 5 video of the year on the soft-rock cable television station VH-1.

Still, despite the mainstream acclaim, Kenny G had become the target of some critics who claimed he played the jazz equivalent of Muzak, or "yuppie jazz." However, the enthusiastic woodwind player still took his smooth, melodic pop music seriously.

"'Songbird' was written as a sincere expression of love for a woman who changed my life—it wasn't contrived as a would-be instrumental hit," he said. "But now the jazz traditionalists give me a hard time—they're offended that what I'm doing is sometimes labeled as jazz. But I'm not supervising the comments, and I don't encourage people to label the music, and I don't have to pay attention to criticism about what I'm doing. I've been playing live for ten years, and I've seen the reaction most people have to my sax playing. It's opened doors. A lot of people wouldn't listen to instrumental music before."

Silhouette went well past platinum. It became one of the Top 10 albums in the country just a little over a month following its release, and *Billboard* named it the No. 1 Jazz Album of the Year. The instrumental title track emerged as a multi-format smash.

"We've Saved the Best for Last" featured the sultry voice of Smokey Robinson, but Kenny G noted that he only recorded vocal songs to complement his instrumentals.

"I can't guess what people are going to like—I just know that when I put an instrumental song together in the studio, I make sure I'm not boring people with my arrangements," he said. "I make the melody flow a certain way, then open up a solo section where I can improvise, then return to the melody. That way I have a sense of starting and finishing in my songs, and I like that. A lot of instrumentals I hear start somewhere and keep going and going until the song fades out, and I feel like I went on a ride and didn't come back to the start again. So I'm proud of my music. And I'll let it speak for itself." ■

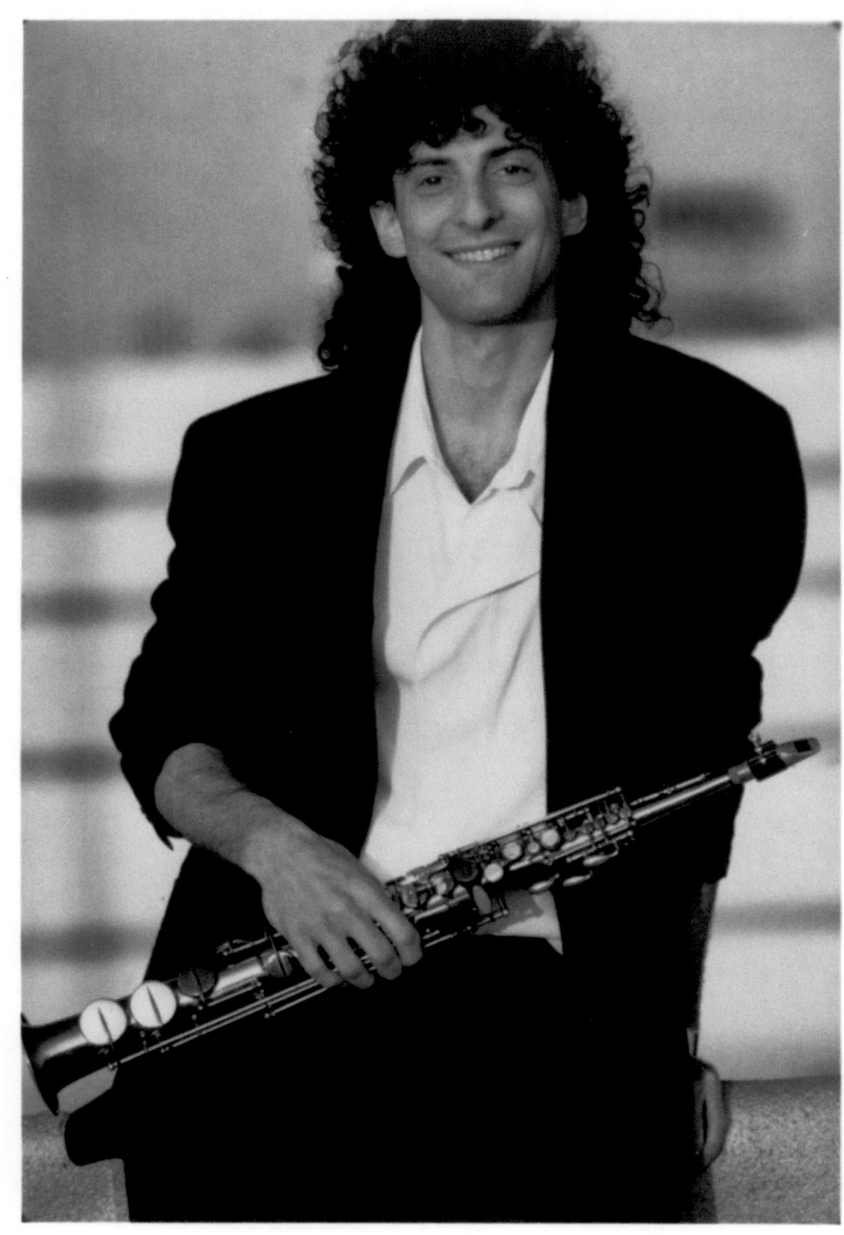

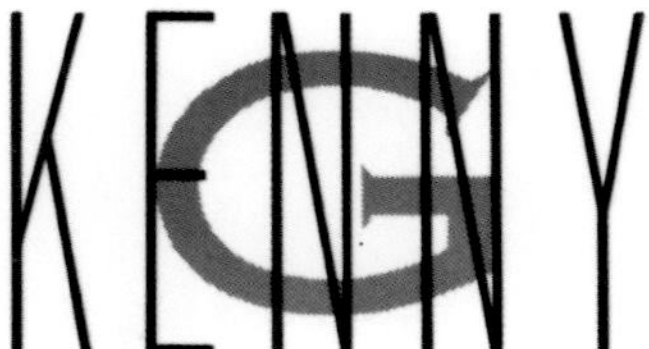
KENNY G

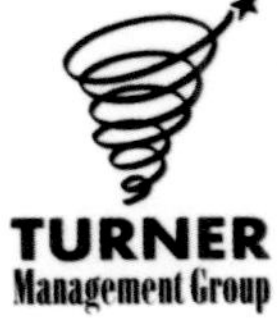
TURNER
Management Group

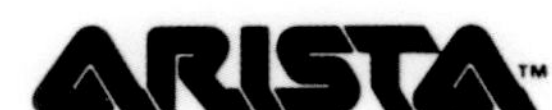
ARISTA™

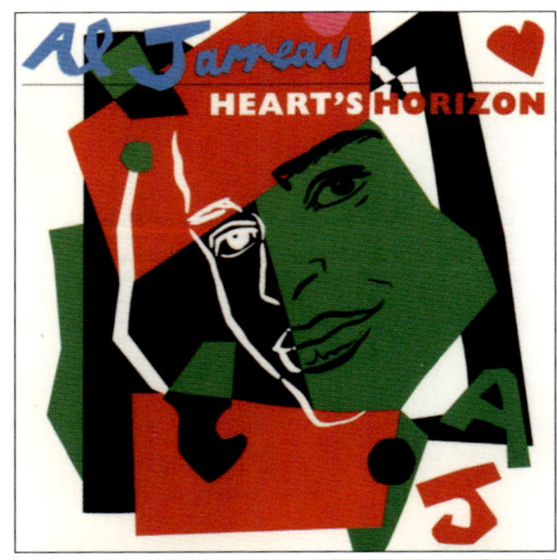

Billboard 200: *Heart's Horizon* (#75)

After scoring a hit with "Moonlighting," Al Jarreau soon assembled material and talent for *Heart's Horizon*.

AL JARREAU had stayed secure in his status as a distinctive, four-time Grammy-winning jazz vocalist. But until the title theme from the television series *Moonlighting* became a Top 40 single in 1987, he had a problem with pop radio.

"They're a bit subject to categories—they don't listen to enough Jarreau music to conclude that there's real pop stuff on my albums," Jarreau said. "But 'Moonlighting' had the effect of loosening up radio, encouraging them to start thinking that I do have songs with pop appeal."

"Moonlighting" wasn't Jarreau's first entry on the pop charts—1981's "We're in This Love Together" and 1983's "Mornin'" managed the same feat—but it became the most popular song of his career. *Heart's Horizon*, his first recording since "Moonlighting," reflected his desire to blur elements of three different musical genres as dictated by radio—jazz, R&B and pop. "I want the biggest commercial success I can have," Jarreau stated. "I think I can do that and still maintain my integrity."

Jarreau desired special attention be paid to the track "10K Hi," a funk-rock interlude written and produced by newcomer Phillips Saisse featuring live and sampled bites of Jarreau playing "98 percent" of the backing music and vocals.

Heart's Horizon peaked at No. 1 on the contemporary jazz albums chart, and the single "So Good" made #2 on the R&B charts. But another TV series was still directly responsible for introducing Jarreau to more pop listeners than any of his recordings—he performed the theme song of ABC-TV's *Murphy's Law*, a short-lived sitcom. ■

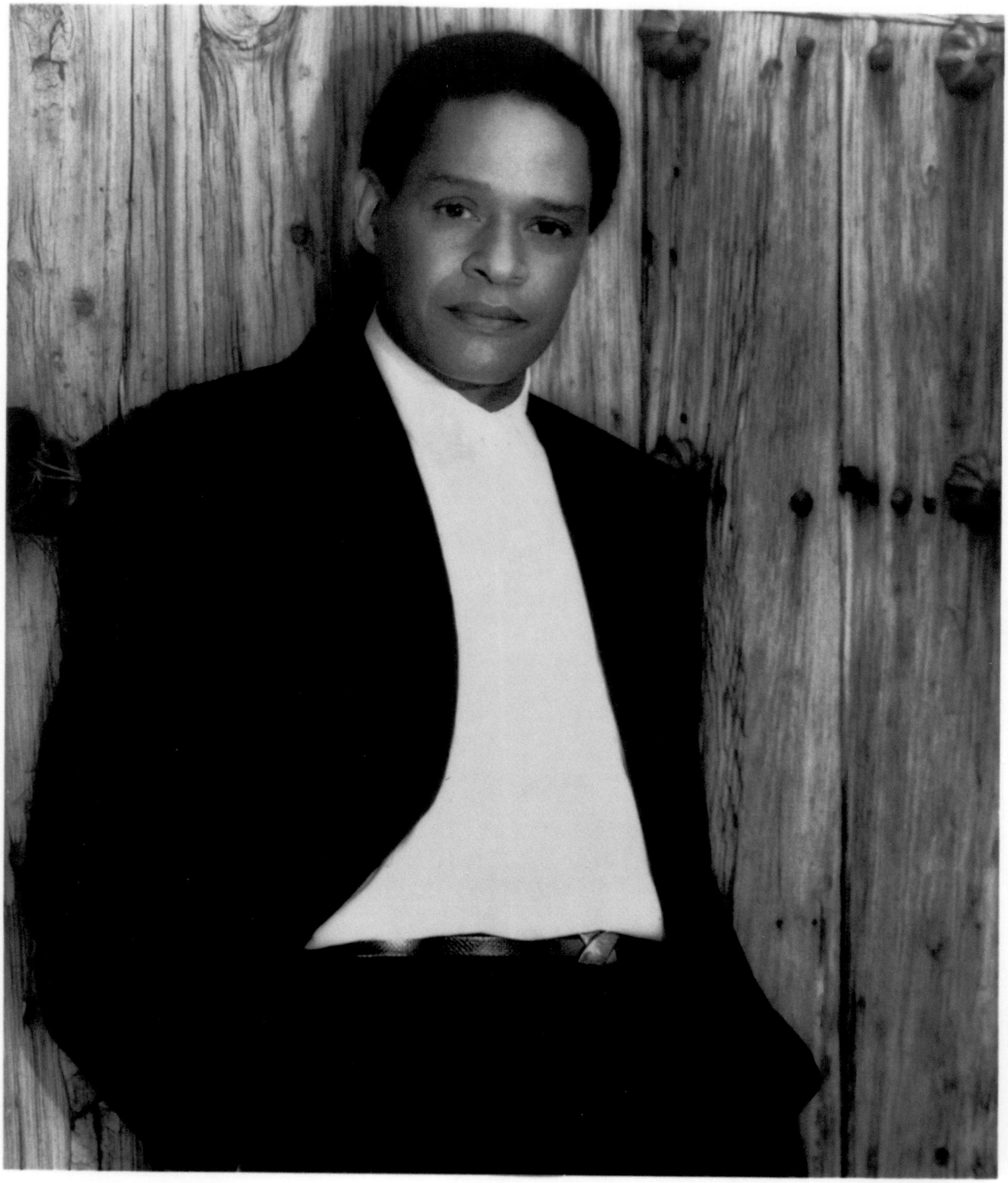

Photo Credit: Freddie Lopez

Al Jarreau

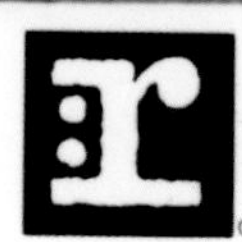

reprise

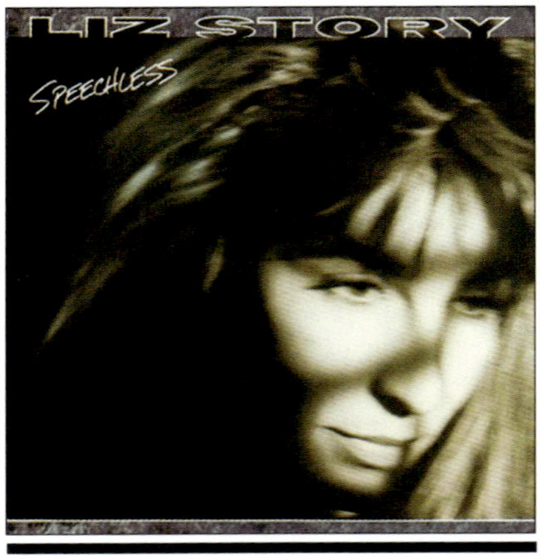

Holding out against the "new age" tag, Liz Story probed the myriad capabilities of the piano on *Speechless*.

SHE HAD four albums to her credit, but first and foremost pianist Liz Story considered herself a performer.

"My ultimate goal is to play my music beautifully, and I just look at the recording process as allowing me to be on stage to do a show," Story said. "One only needs a record to sell so one can have an audience so a promoter can be convinced to bring one to town for a concert, which is all I want to do. Those other steps along the way have been the biggest surprise for me in this business, but I'm dealing with it."

Story first studied piano at New York's Julliard Music School and continued across town at Hunter College. She had also learned from jazz legend Sanford Gold and attended the Dick Grove Music Workshops. *Speechless* was a return to solo piano pieces after a foray into eclectic arrangements involving other instruments.

"I'm still studying classical piano to increase my palette and create flexibility in my hands," she explained. "In a way, your musical vocabulary is what you've already done. When you sit down to work on a piece of Mozart or Bach or Chopin, it's like switching languages. It makes completely different techniques available to you."

Peaking at #13, *Speechless* was Story's debut on *Billboard*'s New Age Albums chart. While she had trouble summing up her music in a few words ("It's a pretty non-verbal process, is the point"), new age wasn't even in the running.

"I can't be bothered with terms," she said. "I'm in a business where music is marketed and promoted, and a hook is needed, but on an artistic level, it has little to do with the music. It's an old, old crisis that has been going on since the Baroque period. Artists are held accountable for the terms somebody else comes up with. I've been called jazz, just because *Billboard* put my second album (1985's *Unaccountable Effect*) on the jazz charts, and then impressionistic, which shows very little knowledge of what that term really means. And now I'm supposed to be new age, which most people are unaware of what it means historically. It's strange that I'm supposed to explain it."

Actually, Story's favorite metaphor for her music was drawn from her days as a left-handed fast-pitch softball sensation in high school. "In pitching, there was a kind of concentration and focus that was a performance," she said. "In a sense, that's when performing really began for me, out there on the mound. It required incredible intensity over and over again. It put me on the spot." ■

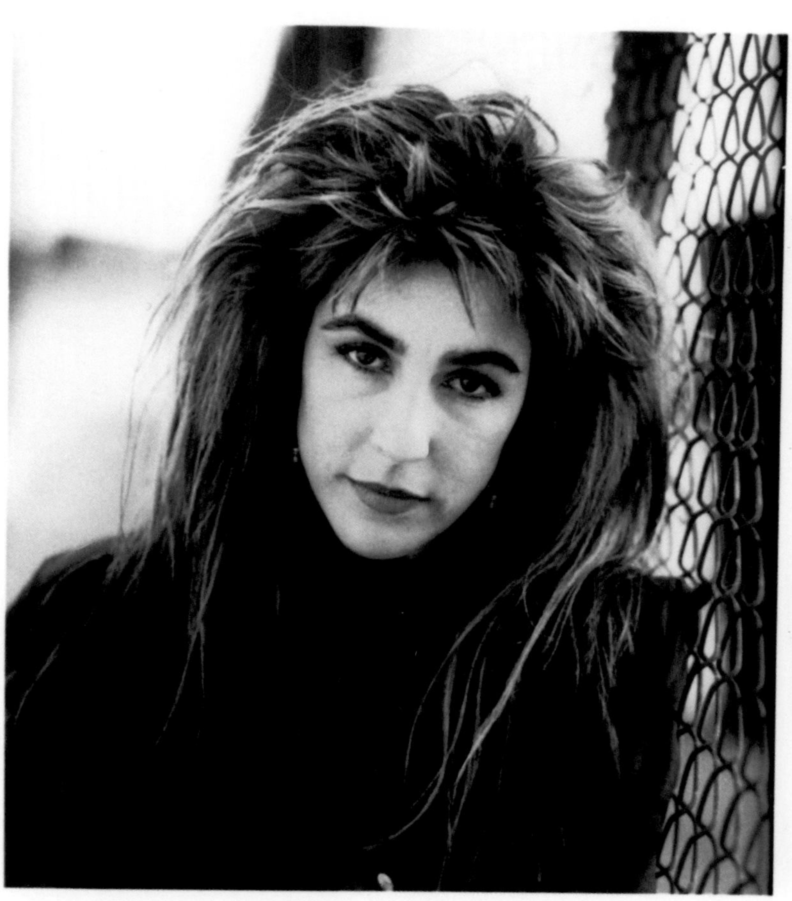

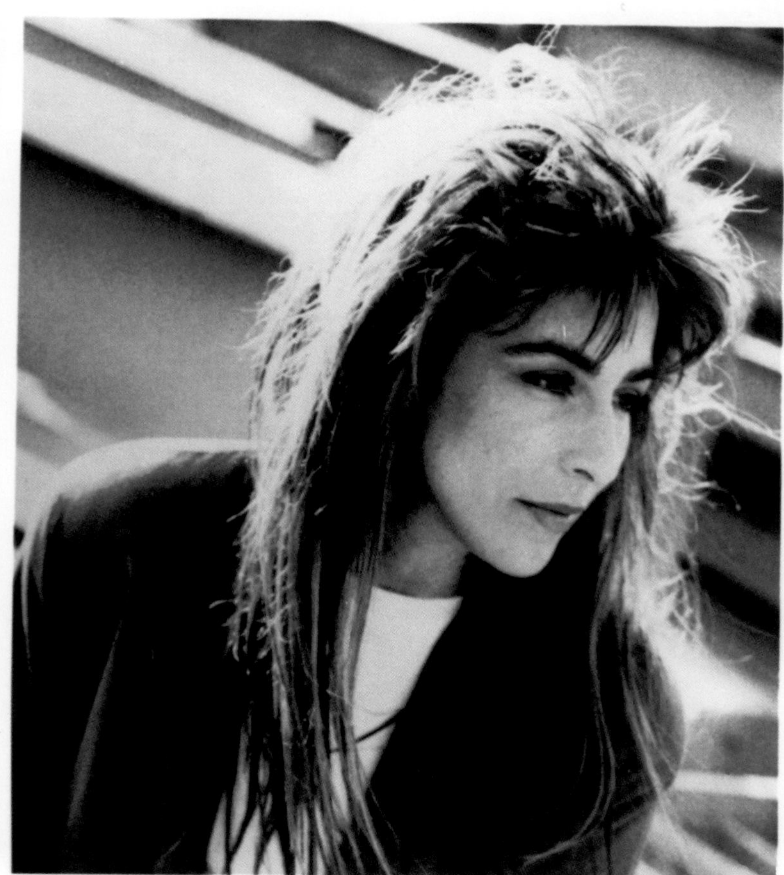

LIZ STORY

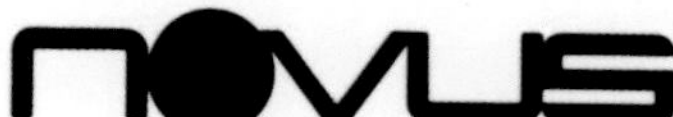

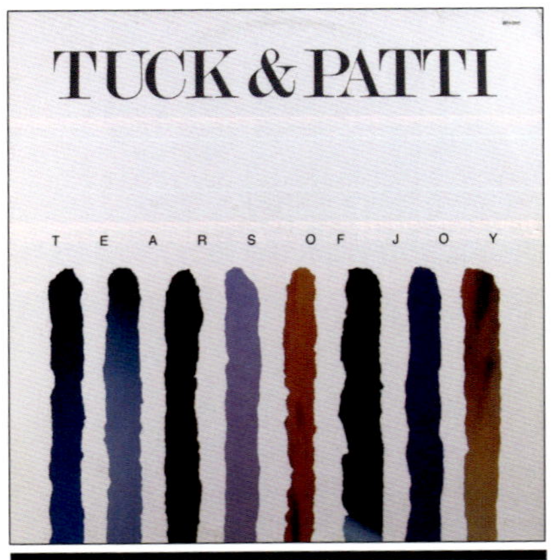

Enthusiasm and intimacy made the jazz duo Tuck & Patti all the rage among an attentive, upscale audience.

PATTI CATHCART was a singer possessed of a deep, rich, almost operatic vocal control. Tuck Andrews was a guitarist who had mastered a lyrical, darting touch. Together they were Tuck & Patti, whose debut album *Tears of Joy* stood as an ebullient, elegant testimony to their teamwork and interplay.

Both principals had experience playing in large jazz and rock ensembles—the couple met in 1978 while auditioning for a Las Vegas show band that never got off the ground, but, as Cathcart said, it was "musical love at first sight." They initially formed as a duo as a way to earn money to start a group, but they quickly became committed to exploring the boundaries of what could be done with one female voice and one guitar.

"Coming from band backgrounds, a duo was a whole new thing," Cathcart explained. "In a band, there's always a battle to get space in the music. Suddenly, with only two people, those spaces were like the Grand Canyon. When we approached a tune in the beginning we said, 'What are we gonna do? We're missing bass and drums—how do we cover up what's not there?'

"But it was just a matter of changing our heads, learning not to be afraid of that. We're not making up for the loss of something, we're just taking pieces and using them."

Tuck & Patti sealed their personal and professional lives by getting married in 1981. They always had enough gigs to avoid economic pressures, seasoning their musical partnership with nearly a decade of working in small clubs on the Monterey Peninsula before recording *Tears of Joy.*

"We've been approached by record companies ever since we started performing, but we haven't felt ready to record until recently," Tuck said. "We had real high standards. We wanted to get better technically."

Conventional wisdom might have dictated the use of a backing ensemble or an elaborate production approach, but the album's liner notes insisted that no sidemen or overdubs were used. While most guitar-vocal duos found themselves in the folk category, Tuck & Patti were marketed in jazz circles because they were fearless improvisers, pushing each other without encroaching.

"Now that we've played together so long, there are all kinds of safe paths to take that are very attractive," Andress said. "But we keep reminding each other to take chances." ■

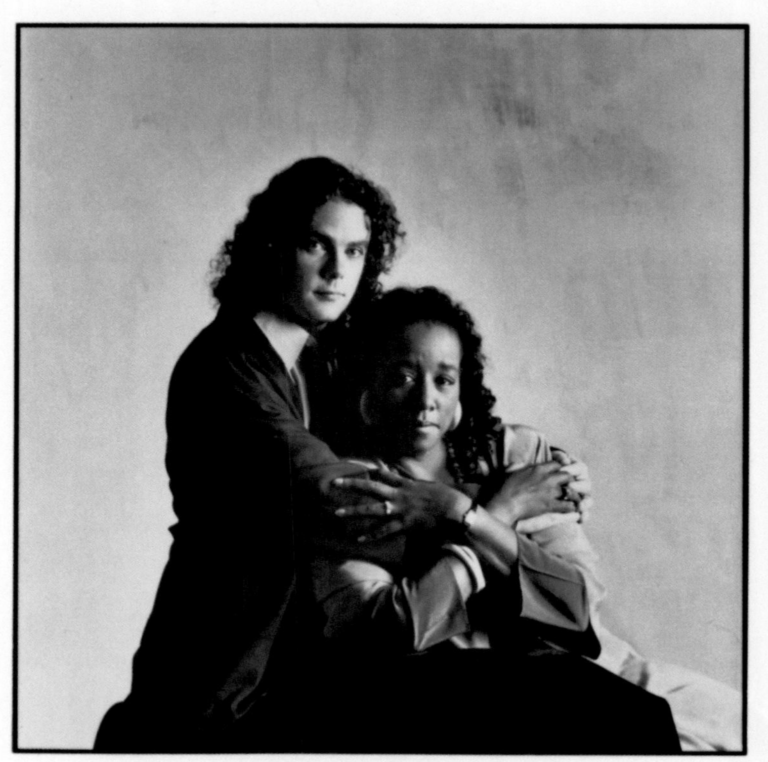

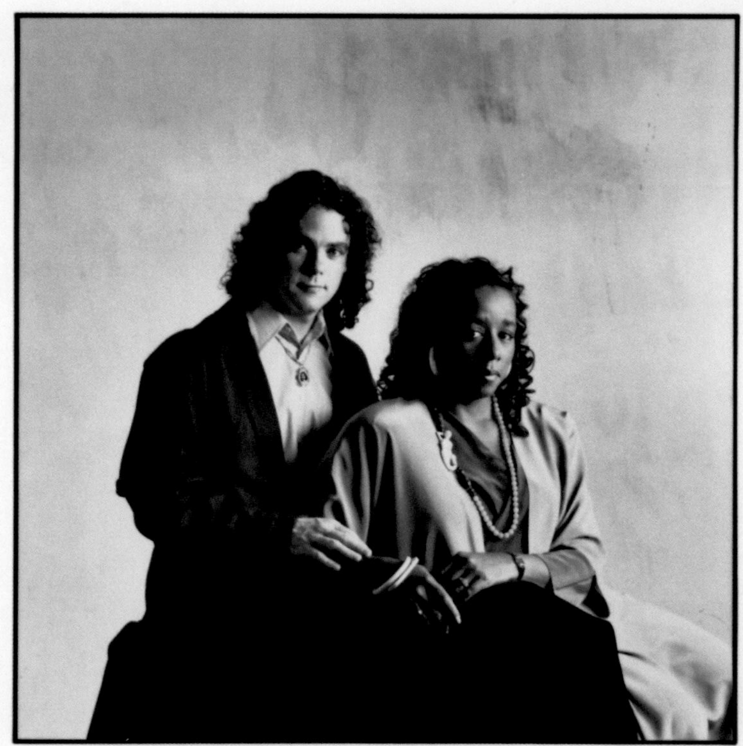

Photo by Fred Stimson

Windham Hill Jazz Recording Artists

Tuck & Patti

Windham Hill Records, Box 9388, Stanford, CA 94309 (415) 329-0647

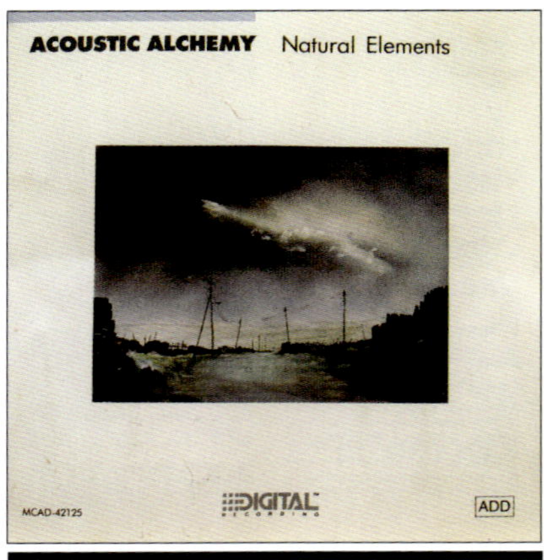

English-born Nick Webb and Greg Carmichael harmonized their two guitars to formulate Acoustic Alchemy.

WITH A mood-setting chemistry on acoustic and classical guitars, Acoustic Alchemy emerged as a best-selling act in the burgeoning "new age" genre. The band's songs were a popular item on WAVE playlists (the new-age-formatted radio stations), and *Natural Elements,* the second Acoustic Alchemy album, topped the New Adult Contemporary charts recently created by the music trades.

Yet Acoustic Alchemy had never performed its music in America. The group, a British duo consisting of guitarists Greg Carmichael and Nick Webb, came to the US for a few select concerts.

"We hadn't even been to the States except to get a record deal," Webb said. "The term 'new age' came from the States, and now it's filtering its way back. It hasn't taken off as much in England, but I think it's here to stay. Maybe not the name. The feeling in England is that 'new age' is a very strange title for instrumental music."

Webb, the group's founder, had a passion for finger-style steel-string guitar and cited British folk-rock giants John Renbourn, Bert Jansch and John Martyn as mentors. Carmichael's expertise was nylon-string, classical guitar, and the sophisticated instrumental sound generated between the two, blended with synthesizers and sequencers, had roots in pop and jazz as well.

"Coming from Europe, we're incorporating influences that haven't seeped through to American new-age acts," Webb noted. "That works in our favor. We were making this brand of music for our own enjoyment long before America coined new age. I think a lot of the music's popularity has a lot to do with the sudden increase in the quality of recorded sound. It's allowed people to present instrumental music in a fresh, clear way."

The *Natural Elements* material was written in marathon sessions with the beauty of nature surrounding the two principals. They secluded themselves in a small cottage in the New Forest near the south coast of England.

The quick acceptance of the album in America surprised them. "I didn't know that there were radio stations that played this style of music," Webb said. "We hit the nail on the head commercially, but it was totally an accident." ■

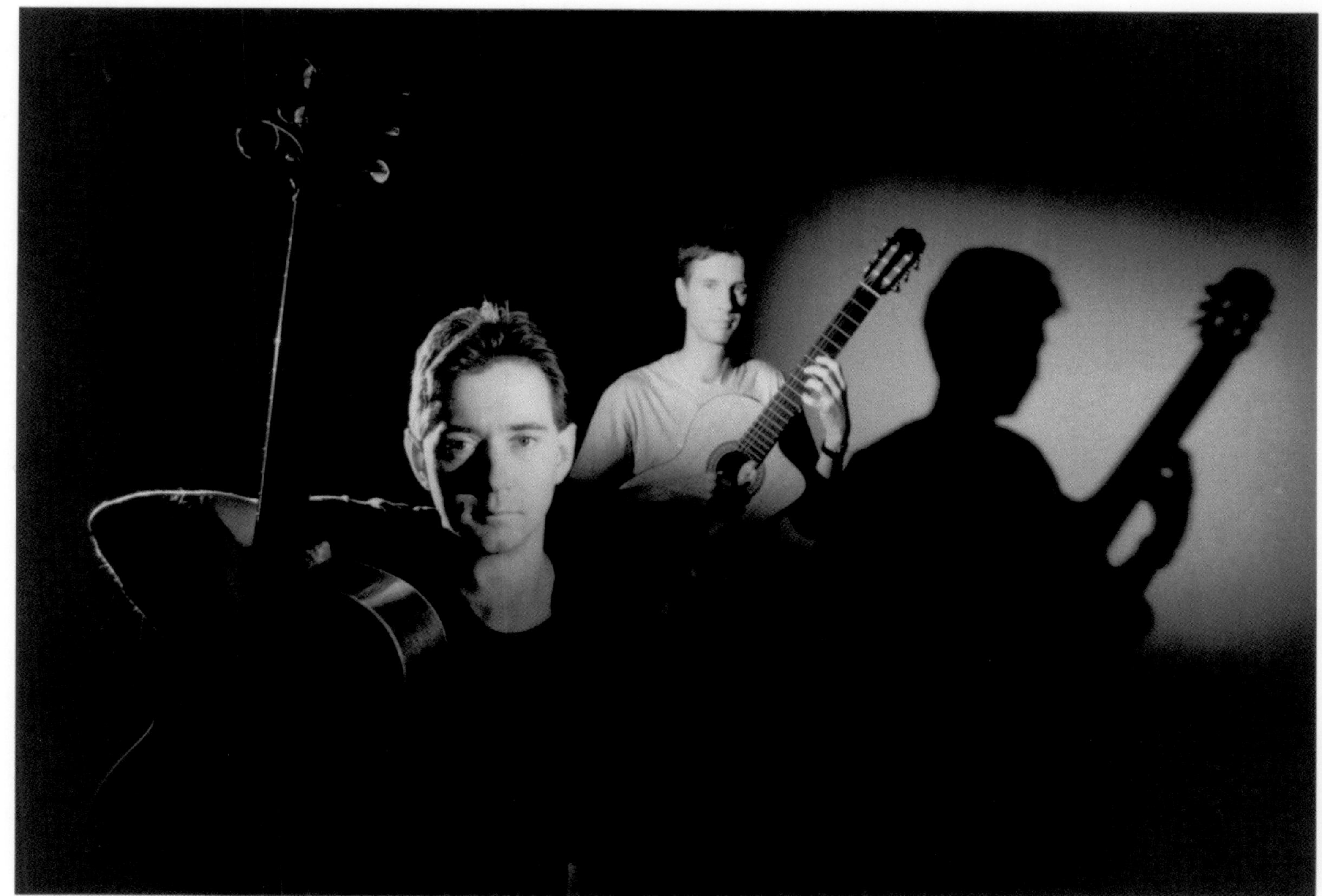

photo: Paul Cox 0288

ACOUSTIC ALCHEMY

MCA
MASTER SERIES™

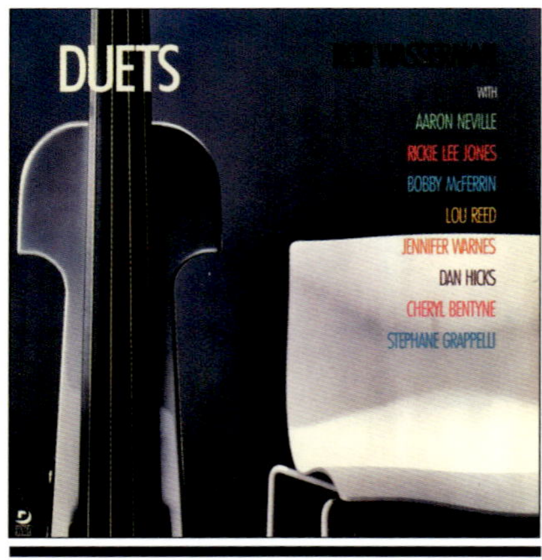

Rob Wasserman considered *Duets* part of an overall plan to explore the purview of the bass in popular music.

ROB WASSERMAN proved his ability to turn off-the-wall projects into reality with his 1984 debut album, *Solo*, featuring songs for acoustic bass. The Bay Area musician then conceived of pairing acoustic and electric upright bass with diverse singers of great stature. He approached Aaron Neville, Bobby McFerrin, Lou Reed, Rickie Lee Jones, Jennifer Warnes, Cheryl Bentyne (of the Manhattan Transfer), Dan Hicks and jazz violinist Stephanie Grappelli. The result was *Duets*, exploring different pop-jazz genres.

"I wanted this to be a music record, to show the bass could be a solo instrument, like piano or guitar," Wasserman explained. "Each song showed different ways of doing that. There's no technology on it—it could have been recorded at any time over the last 20 years. The only rule was that it just be two musical forces doing whatever they could do, and the selling point was to let the singers have complete freedom. Most people suggested standards, and it worked because it was a collaborative process, not just name artists showing up to sing some chart that they didn't really care for. Everybody got a chance to get away from formulas, get away from themselves."

Neville sang "Stardust." "He's loved that tune ever since he heard the Billy Ward & the Dominoes' doo-wop version in his youth," Wasserman noted. "I recorded some parts mixed far in the background with his vocal part to give it an eerie psycho-acoustic quality. Then Aaron proceeded to go crazy overdubbing a jigsaw puzzle of voices."

Reed's raspy rendition of "One for My Baby (And One More for the Road)" redefined the Frank Sinatra classic. "Lou hates the Sinatra version, but we hit it off right away in the studio."

Wasserman started on his path at age 20, when he began playing bass after stopping violin lessons eight years earlier. Within a year he was studying at the San Francisco Conservatory of Music and playing with jazz drummer Charles Moffett; he then toured and recorded with Jerry Garcia, Van Morrison and Rickie Lee Jones. The Grammy-nominated *Duets* continued Wasserman's crusade to convince people that the bass—both his acoustic and his Clevinger electric six-string upright—could fulfill a wide melodic role.

"People may not buy this record for the bass—I'm probably the least-known person on it—but I was the glue," he said. "I think we proved you didn't have to have a band. It's great to be able to hear a voice sputter a little—and really hear the bass in a broader light. It's funny, because when people think they're hearing flute on this—or mandolin, or a synthesizer—it's bass. It can sing, too." ■

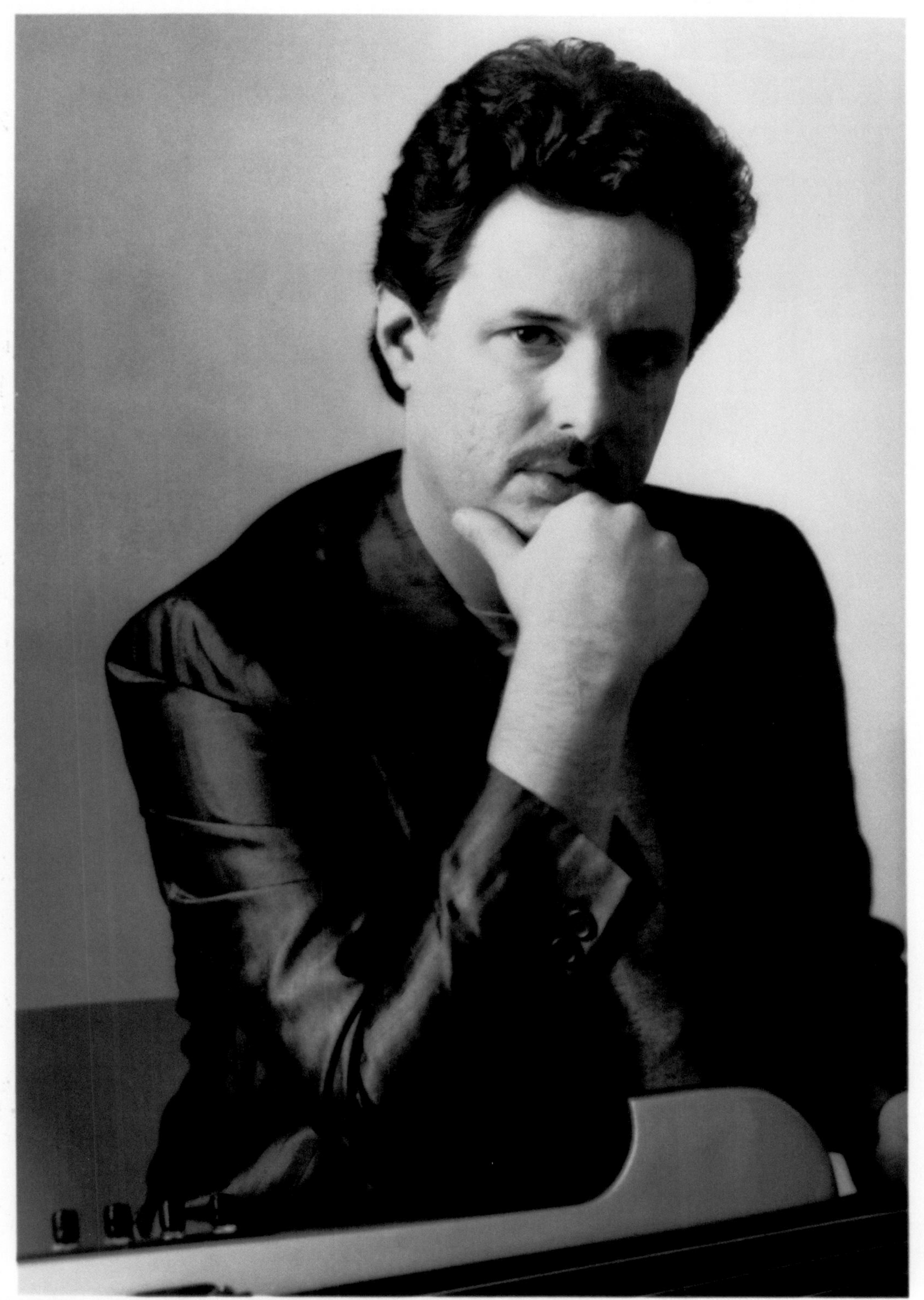

ROB WASSERMAN

MCA RECORDS

Billboard 200: *Folksongs for a Nuclear Village* (#168)

The Lyricon, a "woodwind synthesizer," became the central element of Chuck Greenberg's band, Shadowfax.

KNOWN FOR what member Chuck Greenberg called "world music," the band Shadowfax formed in Chicago in 1972 and played steadily in the area until 1978, when the disco era forced a three-year hiatus. Greenberg moved to Los Angeles and made an album with Alex DeGrassi for the Windham Hill label. When offered a recording deal, he told the label about the band, and Shadowfax ultimately recorded four albums for Windham Hill.

Folksongs for a Nuclear Village was the group's debut on Capitol Records, a move Greenberg hoped would distance Shadowfax from the new age tag that had become synonymous with Windham Hill.

"That 'new age' thing is a problem for us," Greenberg said. "We're a band that doesn't like to be categorized—we were doing our music long before the term was coined. There's going to be a huge granola backlash, and I don't want to be around when it comes."

Still, *Folksongs for a Nuclear Village* won the Grammy Award for Best New Age Performance. Greenberg, who played woodwinds and the Lyricon—an analog electronic wind instrument he helped engineer—had a vision regarding the future of live music.

"It's not going to be, 'Let's go out and see a band play,'" he said. "There's nothing new about doing a tour anymore—there are too many bands out. We want to combine different forms of art into a unique experience, something that would make people want to come out from in front of their TVs and go to a live show."

So Shadowfax teamed with Momix, a free-wheeling Connecticut-based troupe of pliant, acrobatic dancers. "Momix is pretty futuristic—they defy description," Greenberg said, noting the troupe's use of outsized props such as skis and stilts. "We met them three years ago on a failed movie project, and they choreographed some of our tunes in their show. I think there's a common ground between their outlook on dance and our outlook on music. We've always felt our tunes were visual." ■

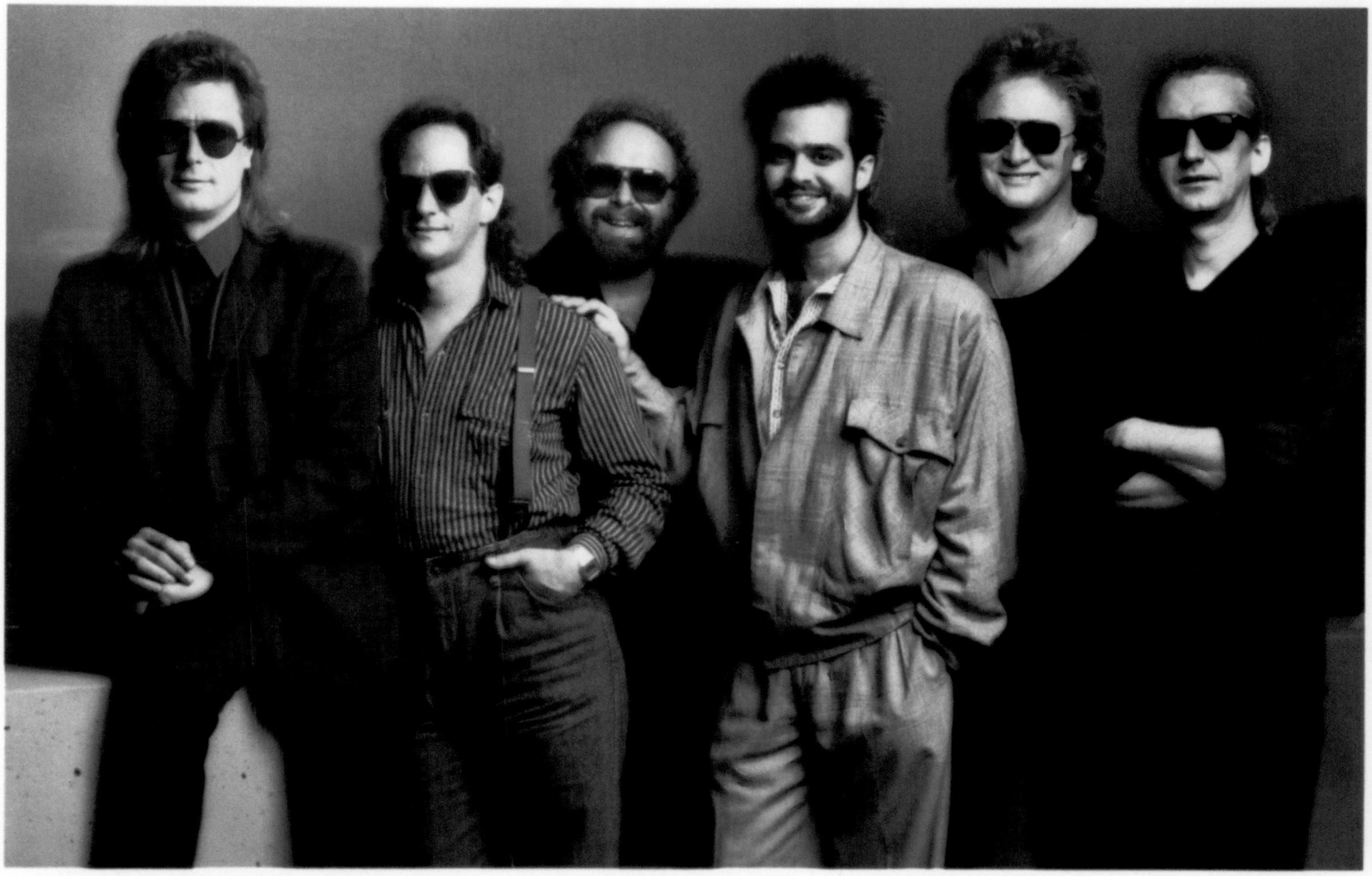

Photo: Jay Buchsbaum / 1988

Phil Maggini | Stuart Nevitt | Chuck Greenberg | Charlie Bisharat | David Lewis | G. E. Stinson

SHADOWFAX

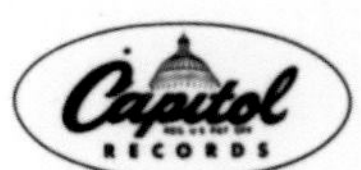

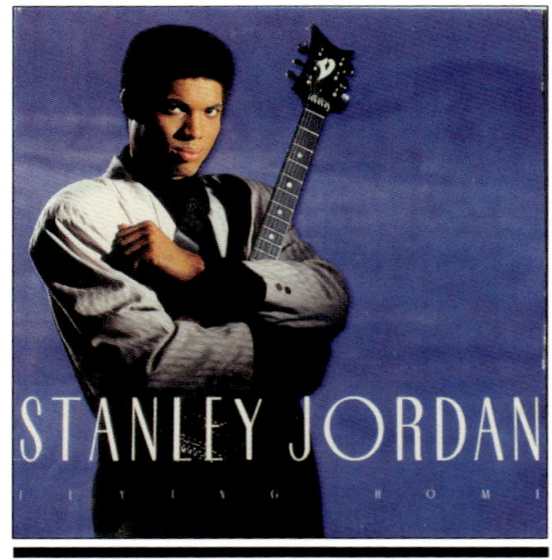

Billboard 200: *Flying Home* (#131)

On *Flying Home*, accomplished jazz guitarist Stanley Jordan switched to funkier, poppier modes of expression.

NO ONE had ever made the guitar sound quite the way Stanley Jordan did with his innovative "touch" technique. Rather than strumming with one hand and fingering notes with the other in the conventional manner, Jordan tapped out notes with both hands on the fretboard, his fingers striking the strings much as a pianist struck a keyboard.

His revolutionary approach completely altered the function of his instrument—by sounding chords and covering bass lines with his left hand while he played rapid-fire melody with his right, he often sounded like two or even three guitarists at work compared with the average player whose hands acted sympathetically.

"Basically, all of my fingers are like little percussion mallets," the soft-spoken virtuoso explained. "I wanted to be able to play guitar in a more contrapuntal style, like a piano. What I'm doing now is a final stage following experiments with all kinds of approaches. I was involved with bands as a teenager, but I spent more time by myself. There were things I was doing that didn't fit in with a band."

Jordan's clear, distinct sound had earned him Grammy nominations, and his recordings enjoyed lengthy stays on the jazz charts. 1986's *Standards, Vol. 1* featured solo performances of music he grew up with.

But *Flying Home* was a departure. Jordan wrote or co-wrote most of the songs, and the project was more pop and mainstream in nature. Jordan called the commercial-sounding album his favorite because it combined "the fun of rock, pop, jazz and R&B with the serious discipline of classical music."

His incredible picking technique was displayed on an instrumental treatment of Led Zeppelin's rock classic "Stairway to Heaven." "Maybe some people only care about the technique, but my own attention isn't on it," Jordan said. "I've been playing this way for a dozen years, so I don't even think of it as strange anymore. Now I want to develop my direction, make all of the variables involved in making music come out right." ■

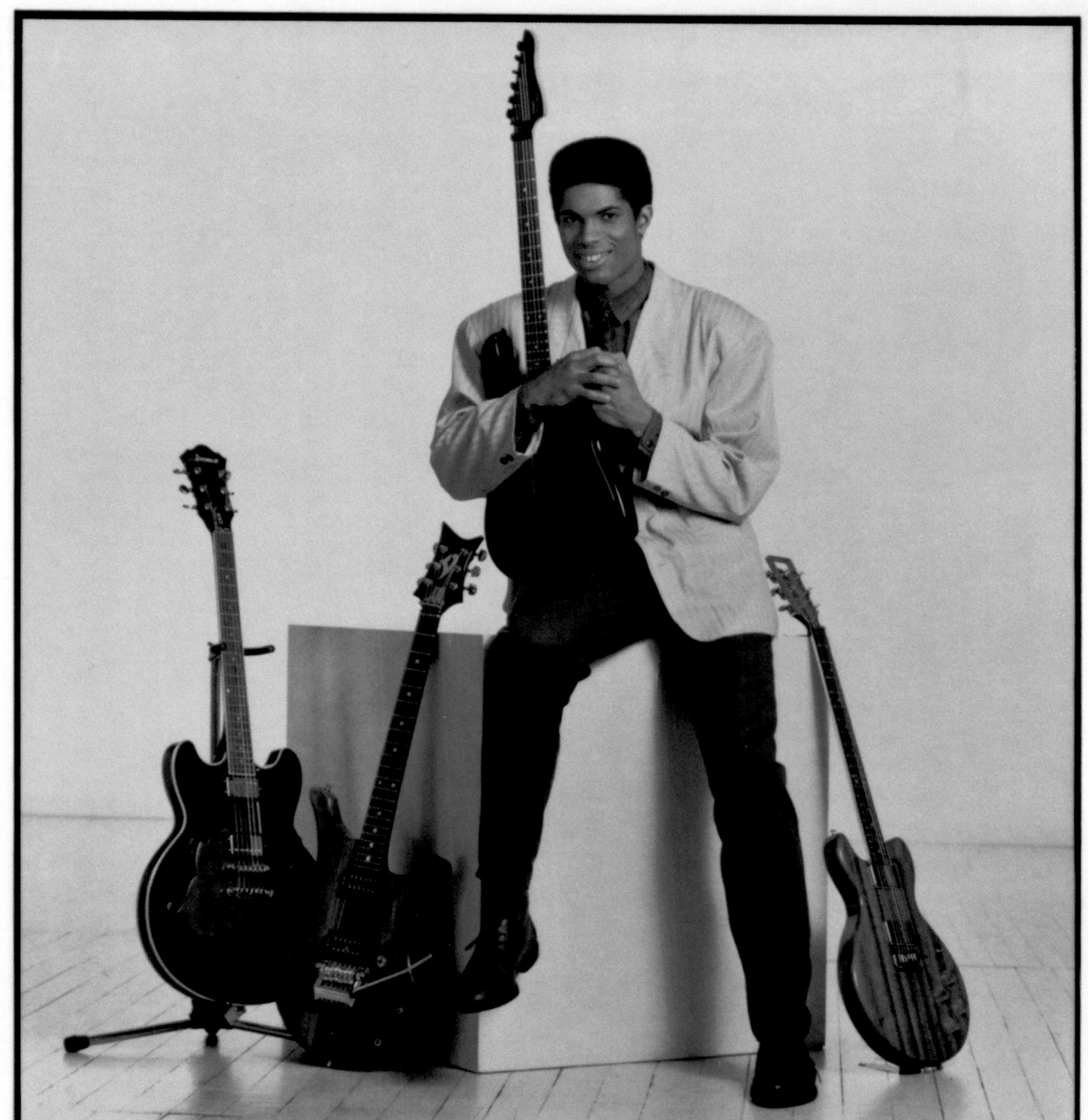

Photography: Timothy White

STANLEY JORDAN

EMI
MAN
HAT
TAN®

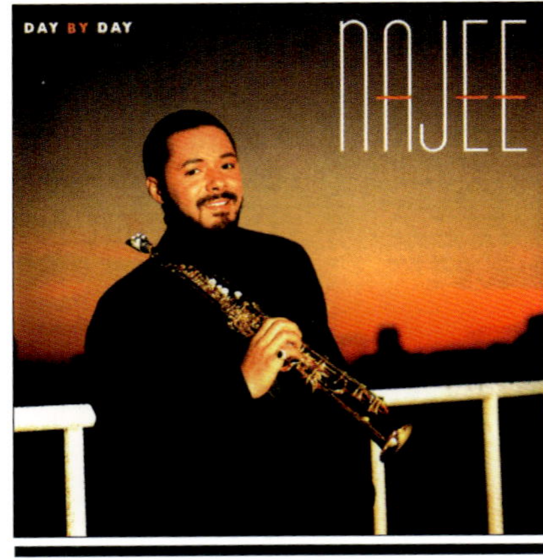

Billboard 200: *Day by Day* (#76)

Jazz newcomer Najee's engaging *Day by Day* was positively received by his peers within instrumental music.

SAXOPHONE SENSATION Najee had splashed onto the scene in 1987 with *Najee's Theme*, a debut album which earned a Grammy nomination for Best R&B Instrumental Performance and was certified gold. Striving for commercial airplay on smooth jazz radio, his follow-up, *Day by Day*, climbed the national jazz, R&B and pop charts.

"I've tried to be strategic on my first two albums," the instrumentalist admitted. "My objective was to establish my name in the industry and sell as many records as possible."

Najee made a career following his musical intuition, but his path hadn't been typical. The New York City native was raised by his mother; his father passed away at a young age. "She loved jazz and West Indian music, and she particularly liked having a lot of saxophone records around." He started studying the clarinet in elementary school because "all the saxophone chairs at St. Mark's Lutheran School had already been assigned," but he switched to sax, and his mother further fueled his interest by surprising him one day with his own instrument.

"I had no idea I would become a musician," Najee allowed. "In fact, I was mostly interested in traveling at the time, so I naturally gravitated towards careers where travel was a prime consideration. For instance, I went to high school for aviation, not for music."

Music, however, became his ticket to see the world. Living in a neighborhood that teemed with local bands, he performed on a USO tour of military bases with a group called Area Code. After a year on the road, he returned home and attended Bronx Community College before going to the New England Conservatory of Music in Boston. After a year, he got an offer to go on tour with singer Chaka Khan and subsequently got his own recording contract.

Najee was trying to differentiate himself from the horde of fusion saxophonists out there.

"Because some people heard Kenny G first, they think I'm an imitator," he mused. "That's not the case, yet to say either one of us is an innovator would be inaccurate as well. We both came up during a time when Ronnie Laws, David Sanborn and Grover Washington, Jr. were the prominent voices of the saxophone. We've patterned a style after those players." ■

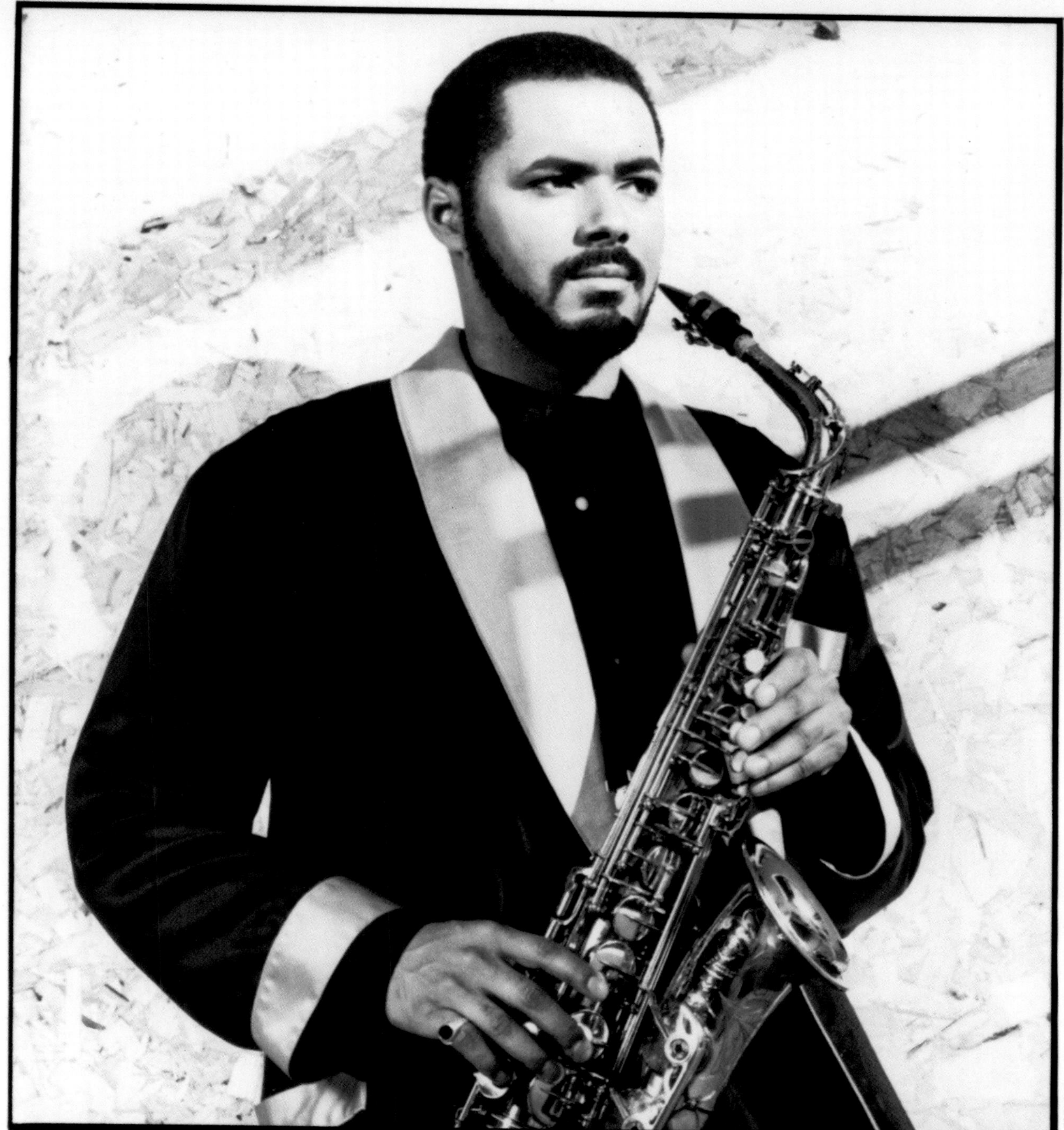

Photography: Carol Weinburg

NAJEE

EMI
MAN
HAT
TAN®

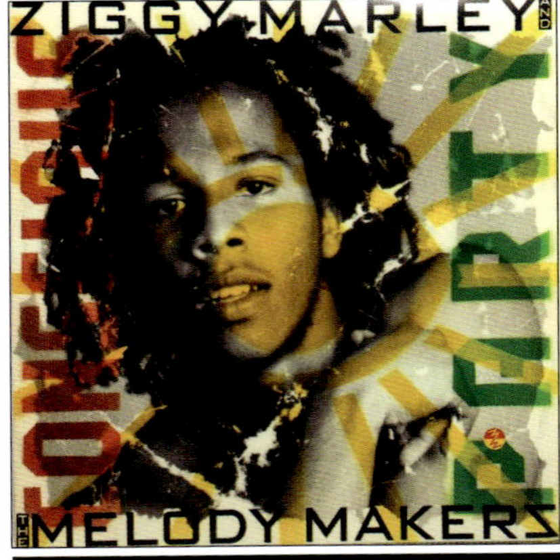

Billboard 200: *Conscious Party* (#23)
Billboard Hot 100: "Tomorrow People" (#39)

Ziggy Marley & the Melody Makers' *Conscious Party* carried off the Grammy Award for Best Reggae Album.

WHEN THE legendary Bob Marley died of brain cancer in 1981 at age 36, it seemingly doomed the future of reggae music outside of Jamaica—no artist since had matched his eloquence at stating the Third World's struggles for self-expression and freedom. But a new Rastafarian musical hope emerged from the reggae scene—Marley's eldest son, Ziggy, and his *Conscious Party* album became the subject of a big US marketing push.

It was easy to ascertain why Ziggy's career advisers were excited to pin the tag of reggae's redeemer on him—physically and vocally, he was a near ringer for his late father. But while the comparisons to his dad's legendary music undoubtedly were burdensome, the 19-year-old acknowledged the cultural and spiritual aspects of reggae music that his dad fostered.

"I don't want people to think of me as larger than life—I'm just a normal man with a talent he's trying to use," Marley cautioned in his Jamaican patois. "But I want other people to see they can also listen to the law of God and fulfill their lives. You always have people talking and singing, but it's you who's listening who must make the difference. We've been talking about freeing people, and it's not happening. When that happens, I'll be happy."

Ziggy was no novice to the music biz—he'd recorded and performed with his siblings (younger brother Stephen and sisters Sharon and Cedella) as the Melody Makers since 1979. On *Conscious Party,* produced by Chris Frantz and Tina Weymouth of Talking Heads, he adeptly balanced a sound commercially acceptable to white audiences with the full range of reggae's rhythms and instrumentation. "Tomorrow People" became the first "reggaefied" US chart hit in years.

Ziggy reconciled the legend of his father, knowing it was a burden, a boon—and a blessing.

"Like father, like son—that is the history of the world, and there is no way I can escape that," he mused. "People can only see us in my father's shadow. They must try and understand—I am not trying to follow my father. I am trying to follow the entity that my father followed, the only father of all of us—which is the Almighty. My father was like the Old Testament. I am the New Testament, part of a new generation. In time, people will realize that." ■

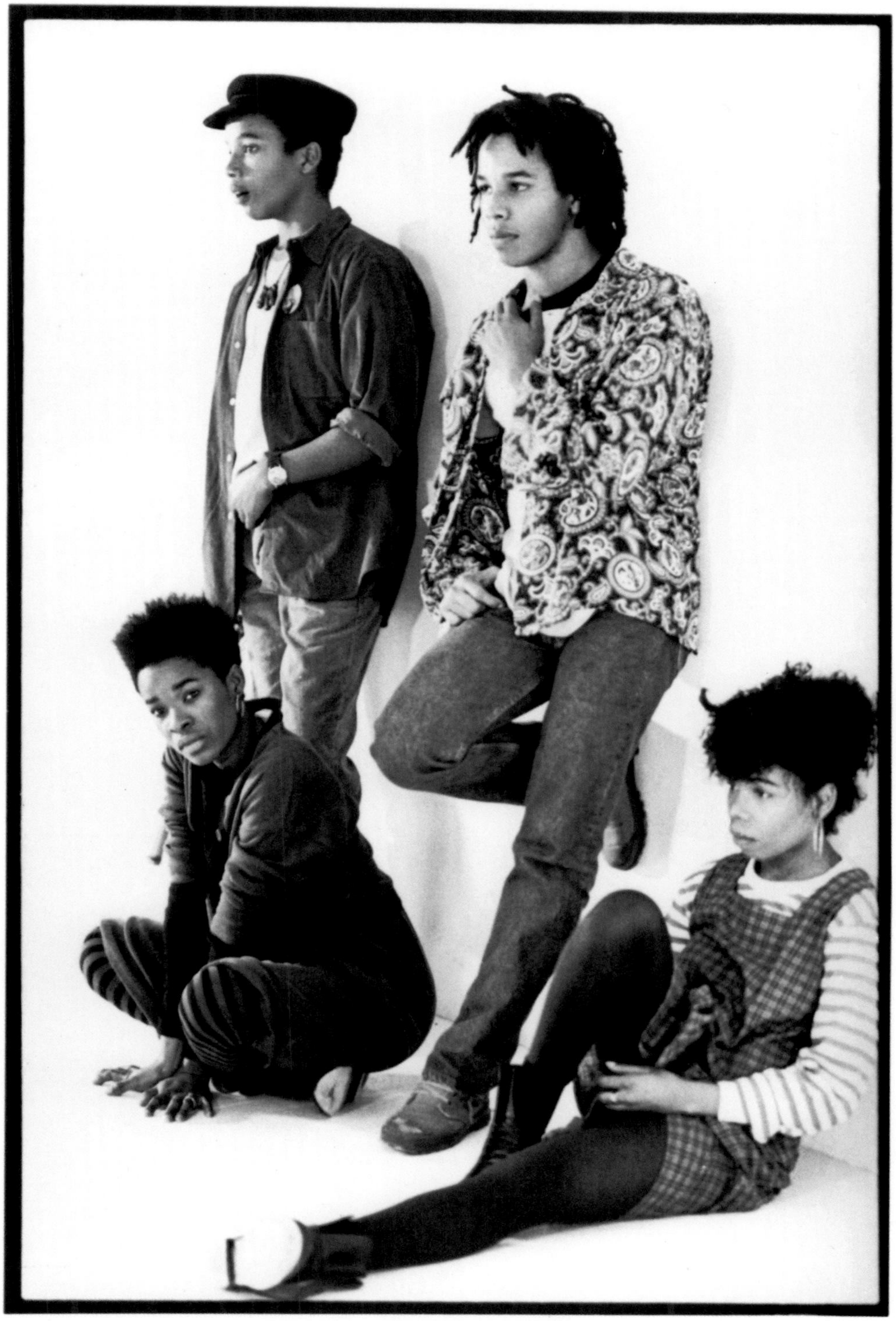

Photo Credit: Arthur Elgort

Management/Direction:
Jim Golden
(213) 204-4412

ZIGGY MARLEY
and
THE MELODY MAKERS

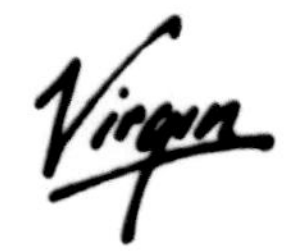

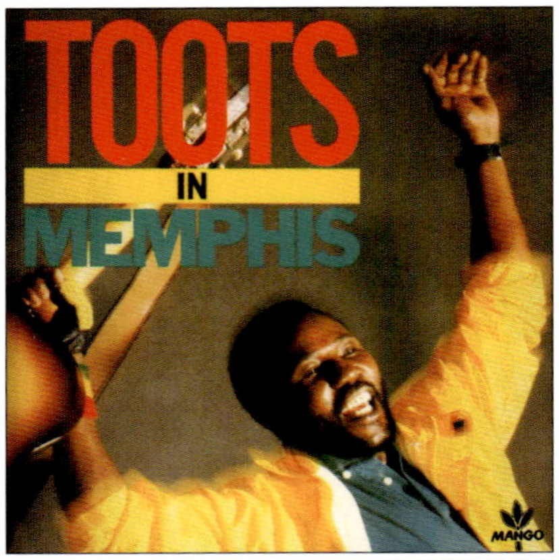

Legendary reggae singer Toots Hibbert proffered *Live in Memphis*, his unfeigned tribute to classic soul music.

SPANNING THE development of Jamaican music from ska through rocksteady, Toots Hibbert first got together with the Maytals in 1968. Their energetic, straight-from-church style animated the single "Do the Reggay"—the first song to use the word *reggae*—and the classic "Pressure Drop" gained them notice outside of their home country.

Of all Jamaican singers, Toots took his main lesson from American R&B stars, a style compared to Otis Redding and other soul icons. Following the 1981 live album *Knock Out!*, the Maytals broke up, and Toots continued as a solo artist. Inspired to give back some American soul, he recorded *Live in Memphis* with both top reggae musicians (the powerhouse Jamaican Riddim Twins, Sly Dunbar and Robbie Shakespeare) and session players from Hi and Stax Records, including Andrew Love (of the Memphis Horns) and Eddie Hinton on guitar.

"I had the idea for years, and the record company agreed to do it," Toots said. "I take the reggae and soul roots, twist them around, turn them upside down and make them be mine. It was easy, because we are all from one family."

Recorded with producer Jim Dickenson at Ardent Studios in Memphis in just 10 days, most of the album's final tracks were first or second takes. For material, Toots delved into the catalogues of such Memphis luminaries as Redding ("Hard to Handle"), Al Green ("Love and Happiness") and Eddie Floyd ("Knock on Wood").

Toots in Memphis was nominated for a Grammy Award in the category of Best Reggae Recording. ■

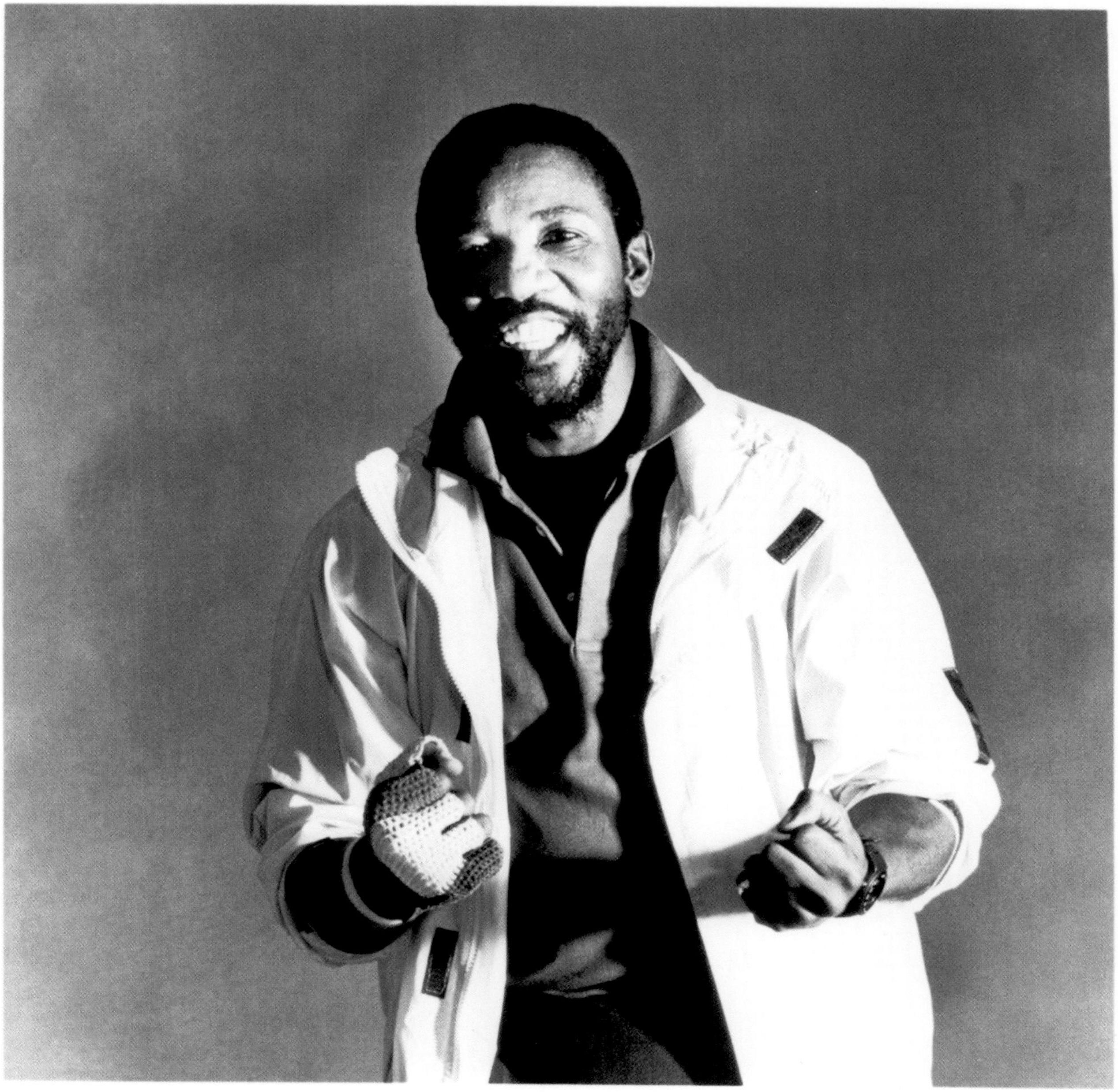

Photo Credit: George DuBose

Mango®

TOOTS

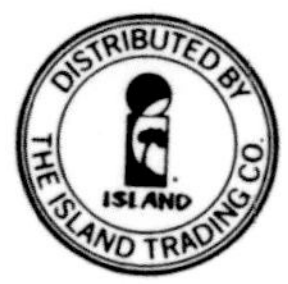

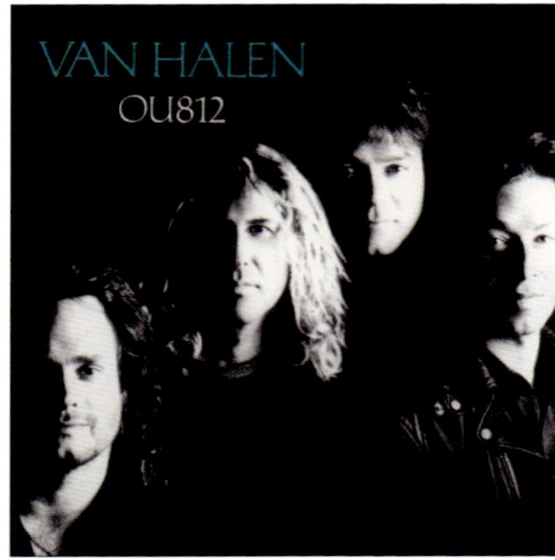

OU812, the second **Van Halen** album with Sammy Hagar as vocalist, reached No. 1 and launched the hits "When It's Love" and "Finish What You Started."

Billboard 200: *OU812* (No. 1)
Billboard 120 Hot 100: "Black and Blue" (#34); "When It's Love" (#5); "Finish What Ya Started" (#13); "Feels So Good" (#35)

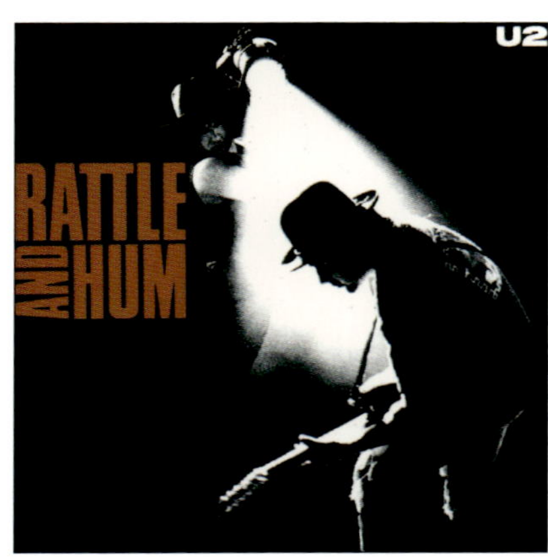

Featuring nine new songs and six tracks recorded throughout the Joshua Tree tour, *Rattle and Hum* captured **U2**'s "discovery" of American roots music.

Billboard 200: *Rattle and Hum* (No. 1)
Billboard Hot 100: "Desire" (#3); "Angel of Harlem" (#14); "When Love Comes to Town" (#68); "All I Want Is You" (#83)

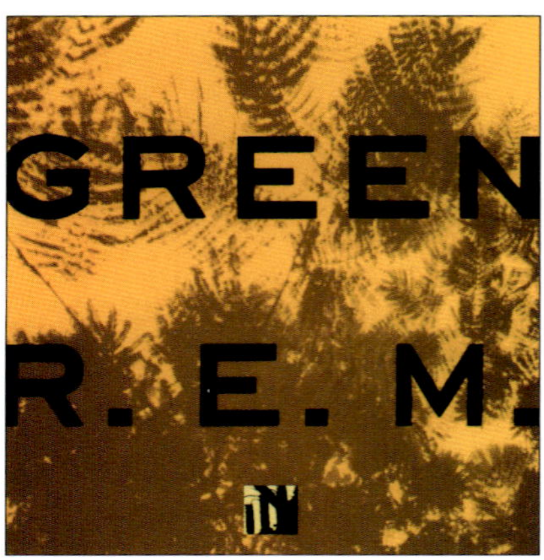

Having transitioned from an underground phenomenon to a worldwide sensation, **R.E.M.** reasserted its formidable musical capabilities with *Green.*

Billboard 200: *Green* (#12)
Billboard Hot 100: "Stand" (#6); "Pop Song 89" (#86)

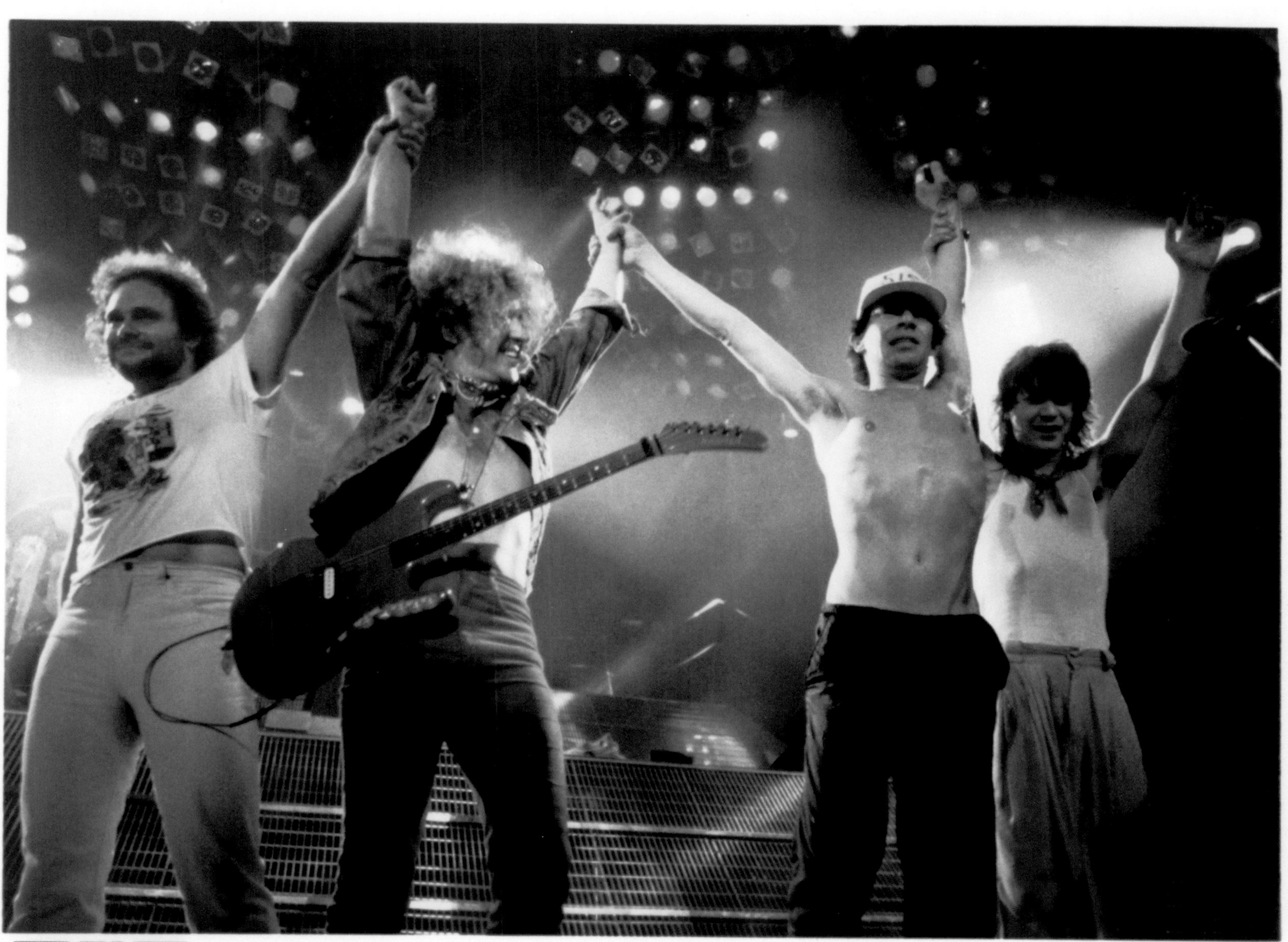

VAN HALEN

PUBLIC RELATIONS
SOLTERS/ROSKIN/FRIEDMAN, INC.
5455 WILSHIRE BOULEVARD
LOS ANGELES, CA 90036 (213) 936-7900
45 WEST 34TH STREET
NEW YORK, NY 10001 (212) 947-0515

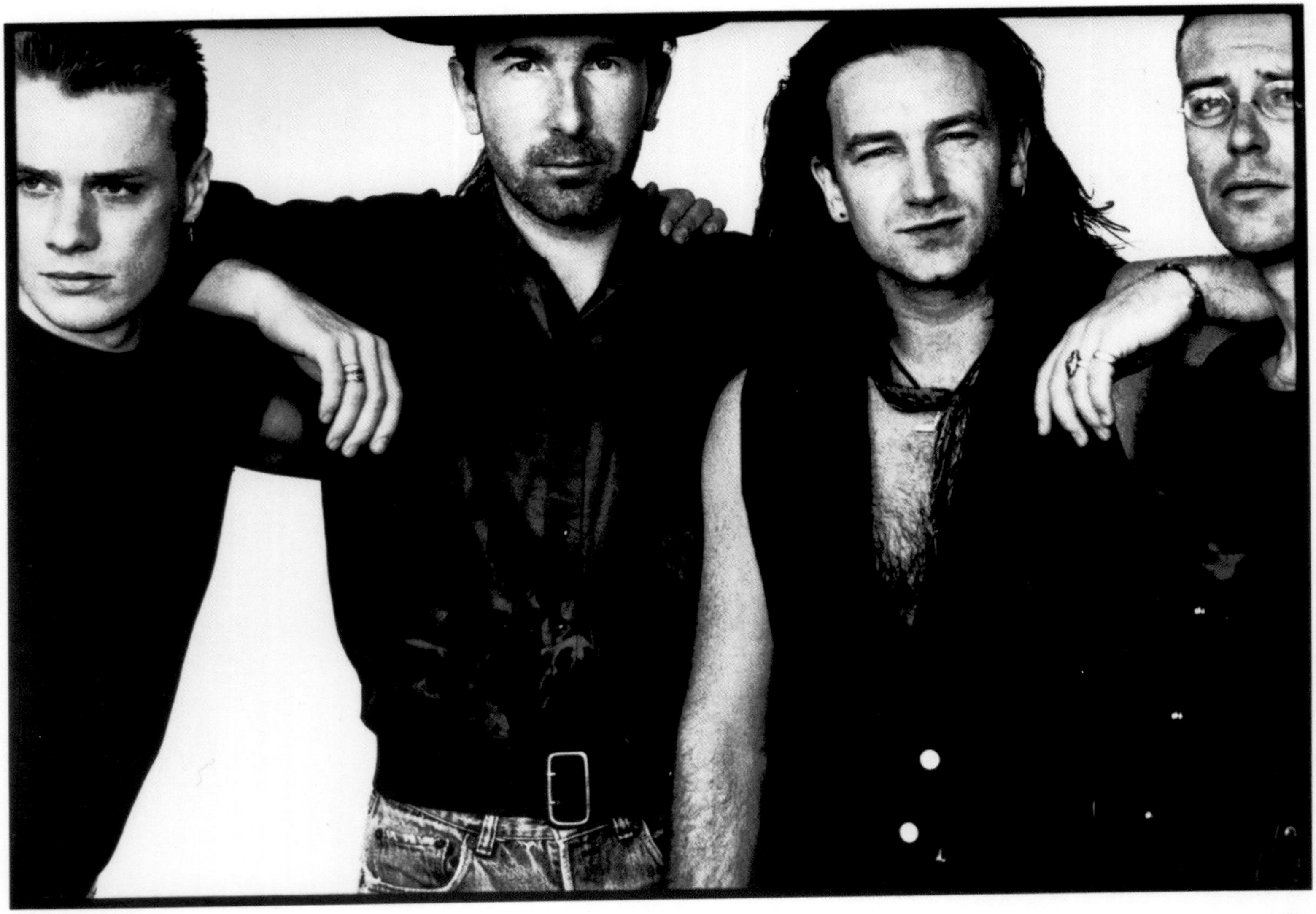

Photo Credit: Anton Corbijn

U2

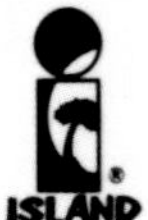

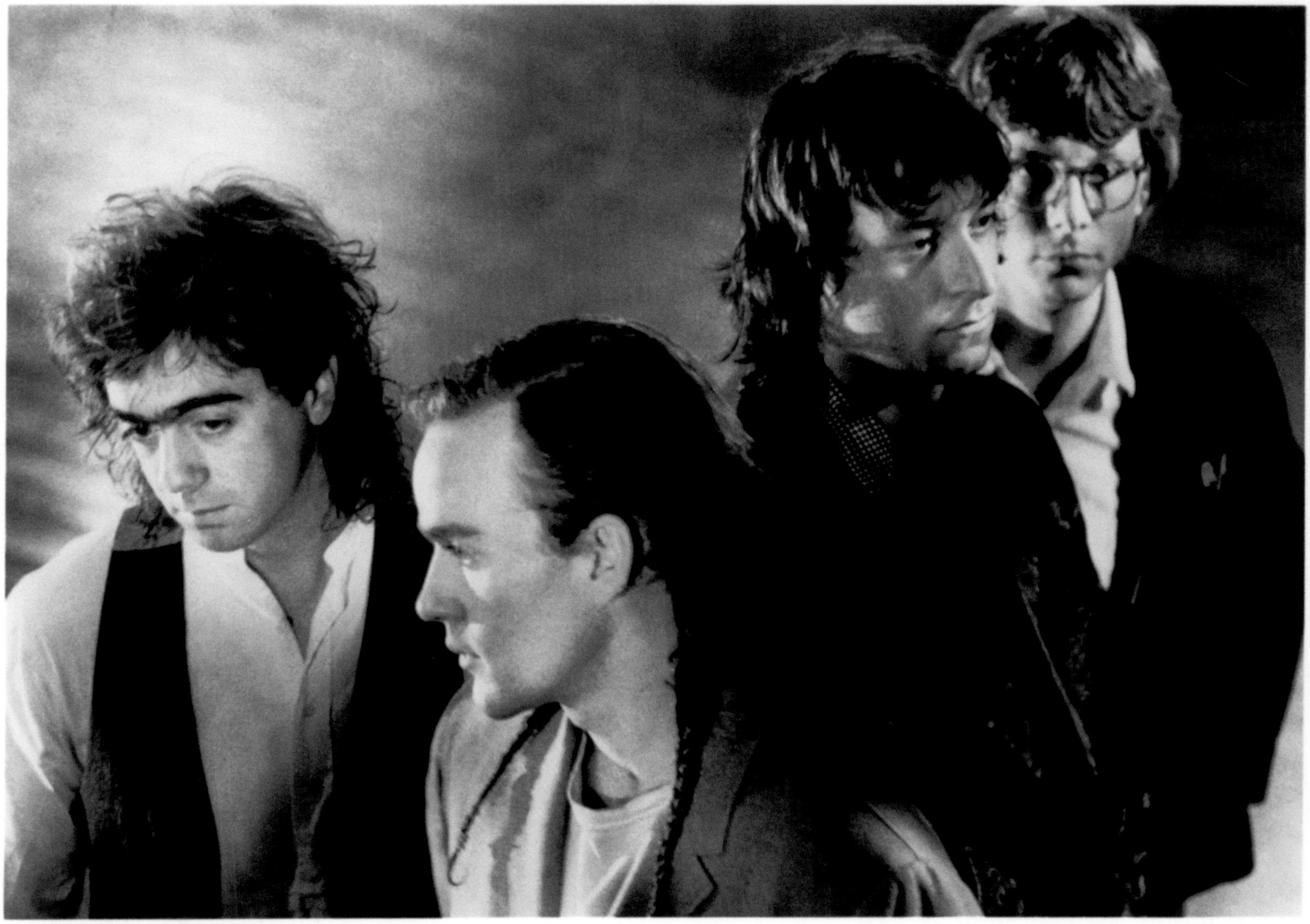

Photo Credit: Michael Tighe

R. E. M.

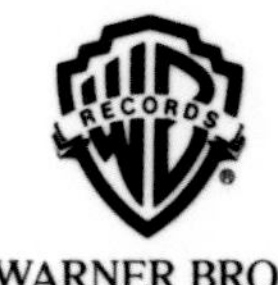

WARNER BROS.

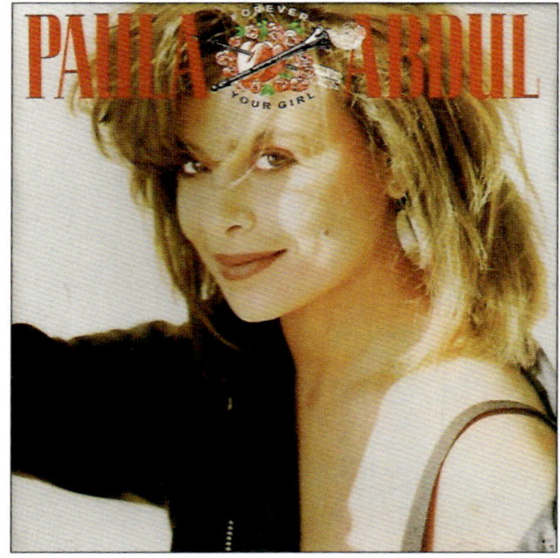

Successful choreographer **Paula Abdul** launched her music career as the hit-packed *Forever Your Girl* began a record 64-week climb to No. 1 on the charts.

Billboard 200: *Forever Your Girl* (No. 1)
Billboard Hot 100: "Knocked Out" (#41); "(It's Just) The Way That You Love Me" (#3); "Straight Up" (No. 1); "Forever Your Girl" (No. 1); "Cold Hearted" (No. 1); "Opposites Attract" (No. 1)

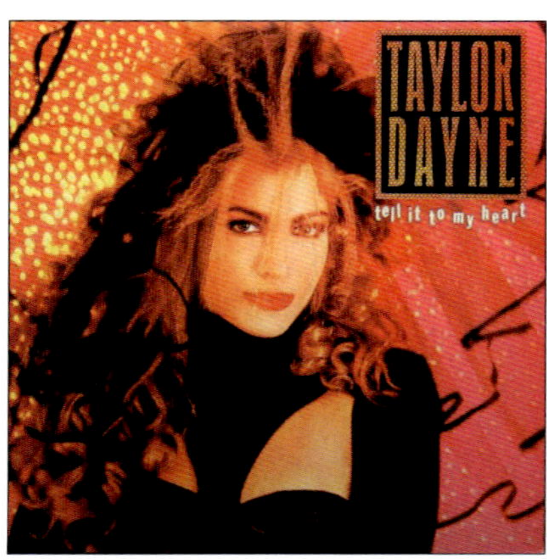

Taylor Dayne rose to fame with a debut album featuring four Top 10 hits, including the dance-pop smash "Tell It to My Heart" and "I'll Always Love You."

Billboard 200: *Tell It to My Heart* (#21)
Billboard Hot 100: "Tell It to My Heart" (#7); "Prove Your Love" (#7); "I'll Always Love You" (#3); "Don't Rush Me" (#3)

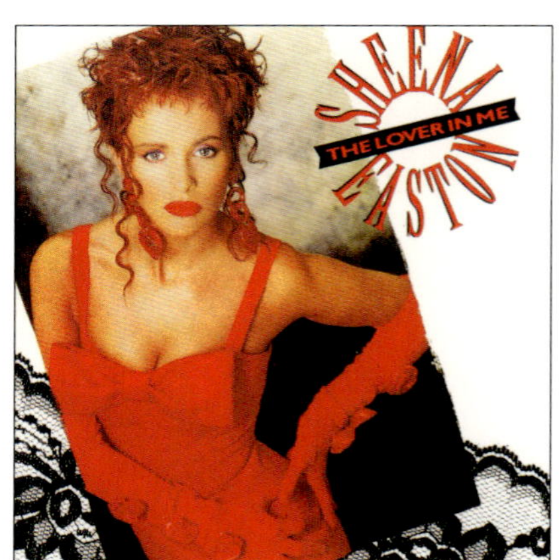

Working with the potent production team of L.A. Reid & Babyface, **Sheena Easton** scored a huge hit with the big-beat title track from *The Lover in Me*.

Billboard 200: *The Lover in Me* (#44)
Billboard Hot 100: "The Lover in Me" (#2)

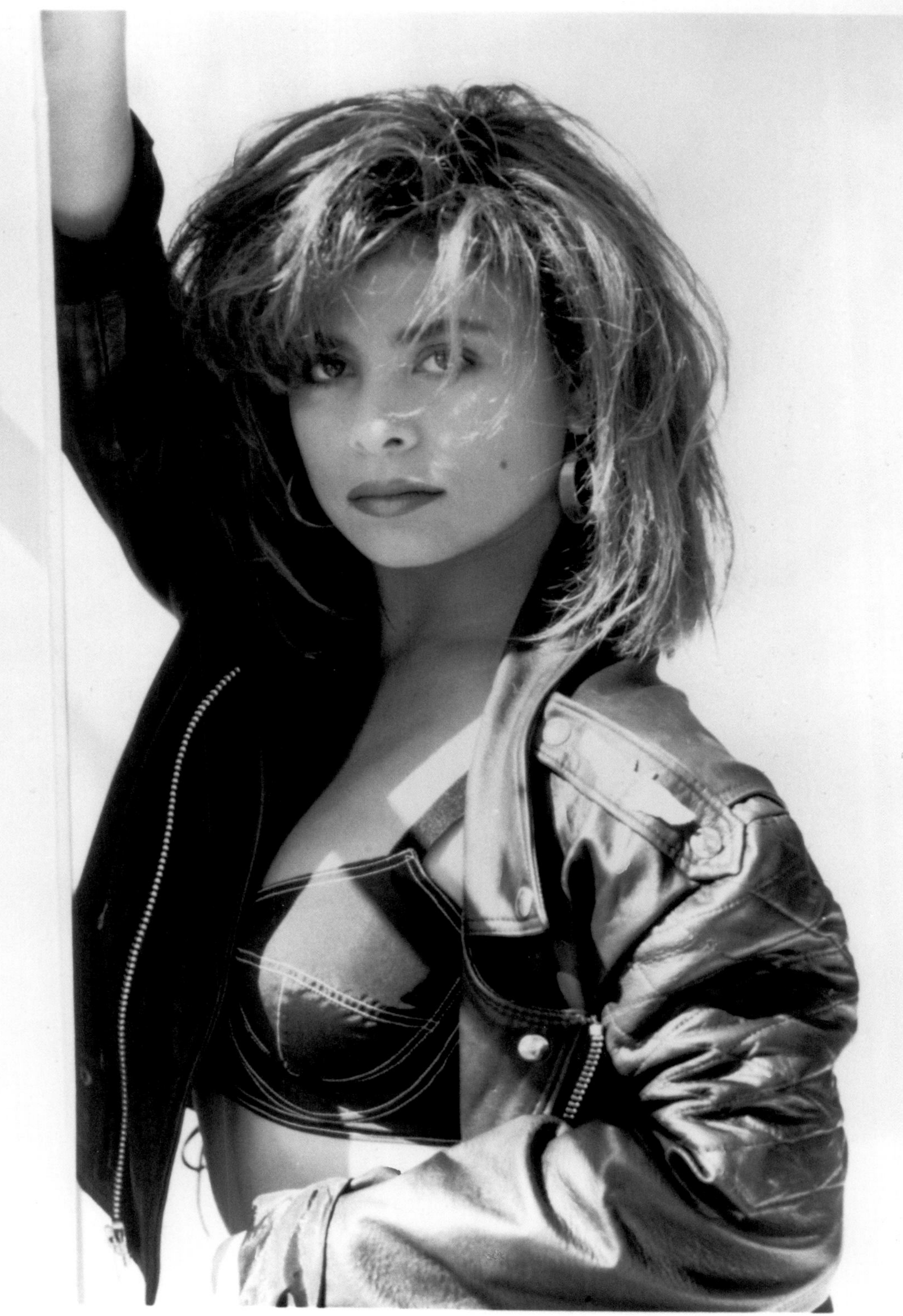

Photo Credit: Alberto Tolot

Paula Abdul

Virgin

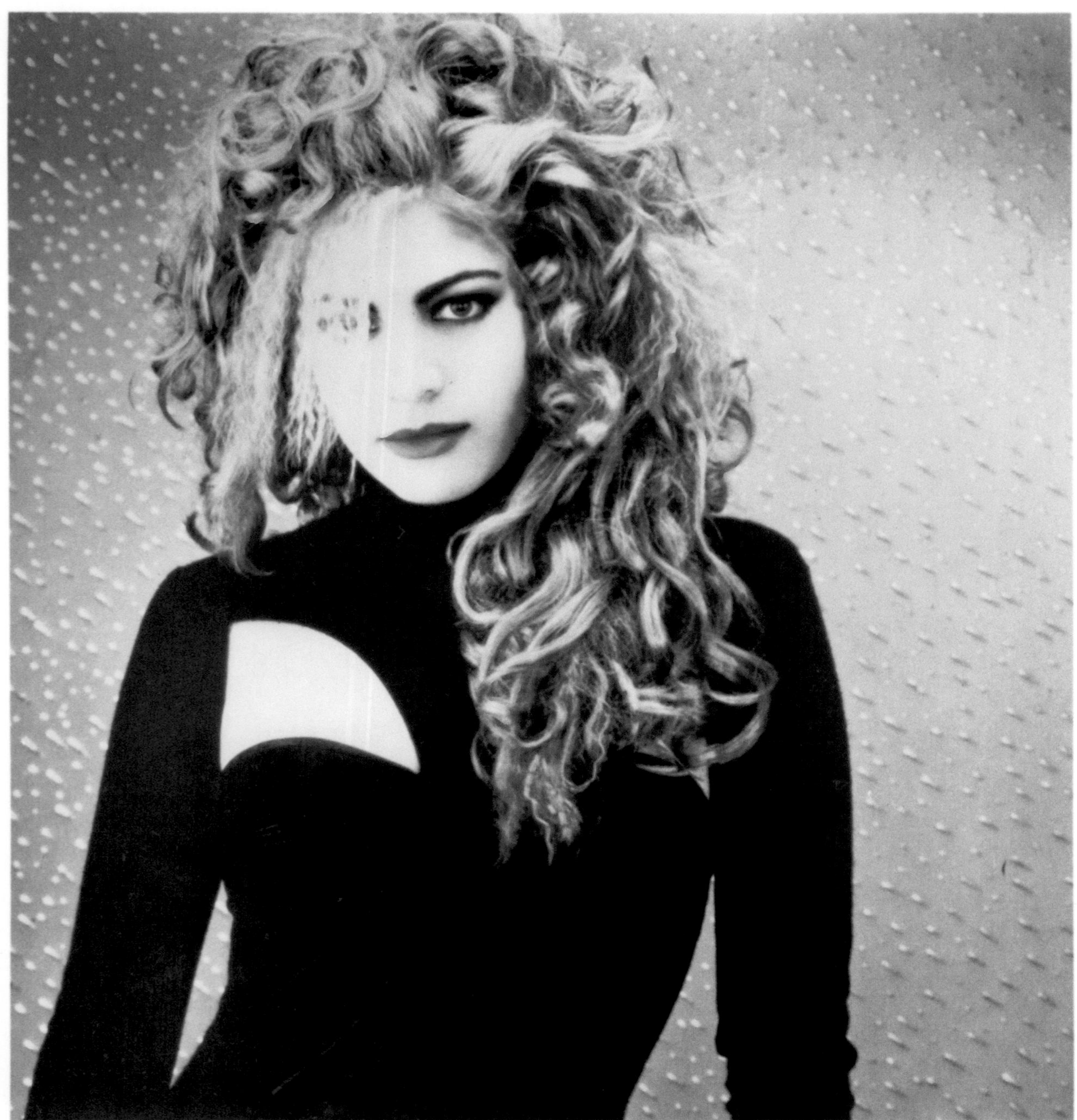

Management:

Tony Abbate
ABBATE & MEGALE
2288 Jerusalem Avenue
N. Bellmore, NY 11710
(516) 221-0909

Taylor Dayne

ARISTA™

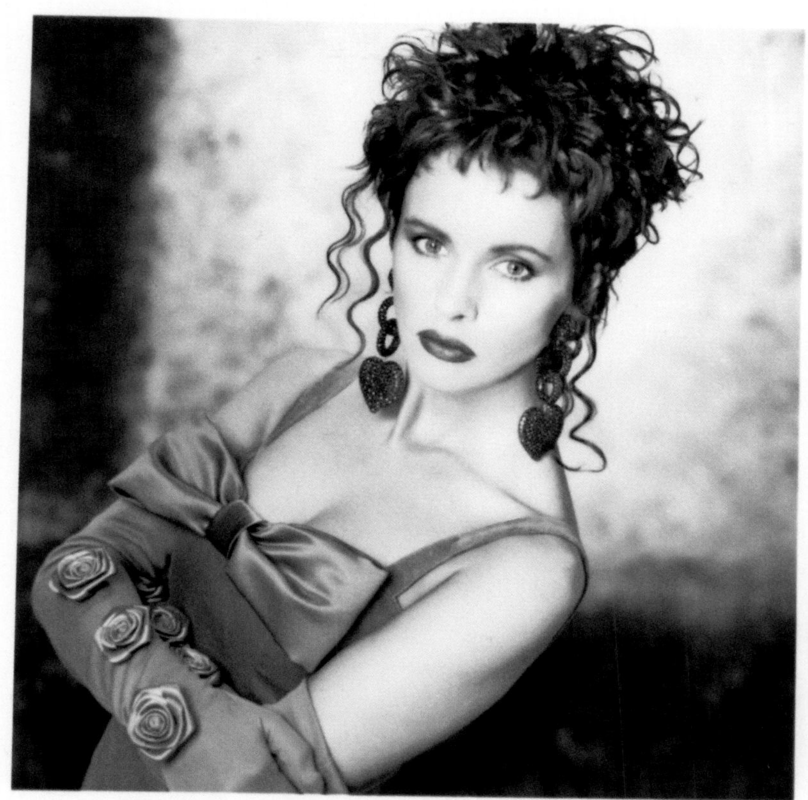

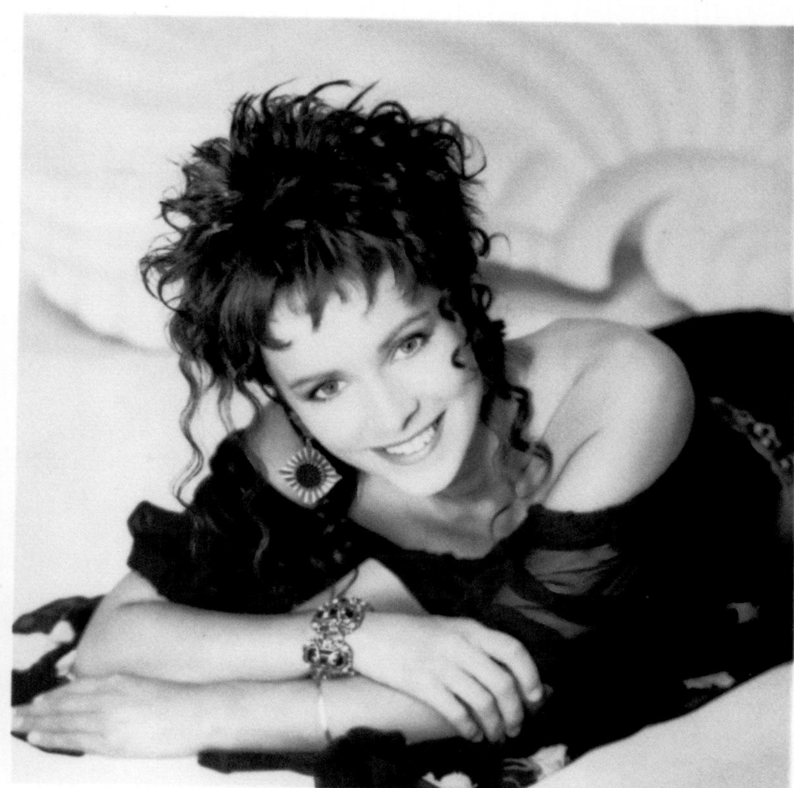

Photo Credit: Randee St. Nicholas/MCA Records

SHEENA EASTON

MCA RECORDS

Rod Stewart bounced back with *Out of Order*, which featured four hit singles and a Grammy-nominated adaptation of Bob Dylan's "Forever Young."

Billboard 200: *Out of Order* (#20)
Billboard Hot 100: "Lost in You" (#12); "Forever Young" (#12); "My Heart Can't Tell You No" (#4); "Crazy About Her" (#11)

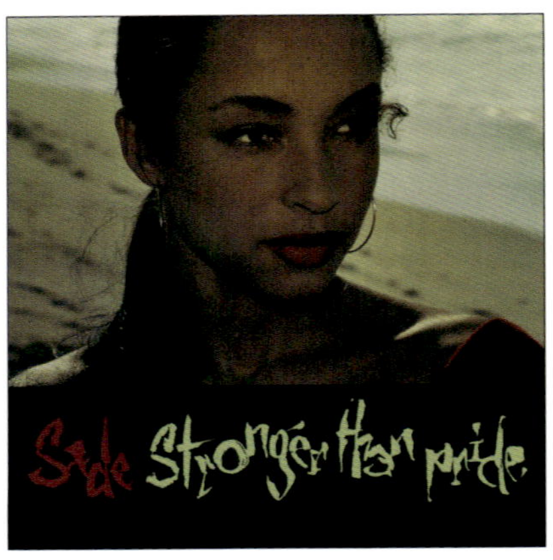

Stronger Than Pride, **Sade**'s third straight multiplatinum album of unmistakable jazz, soul and Latin elements, starred the signature hit "Paradise."

Billboard 200: *Stronger Than Pride* (#7)
Billboard Hot 100: "Paradise" (#16)

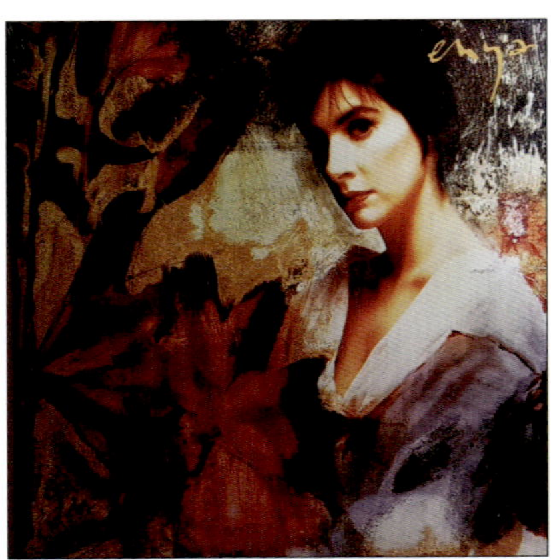

Rooted in Celtic traditions, yet accessibly modern, *Watermark* thrust Irish musician **Enya** to global fame, highlighted by the hypnotic "Orinoco Flow."

Billboard 200: *Watermark* (#25)
Billboard Hot 100: "Orinoco Flow" (#24)

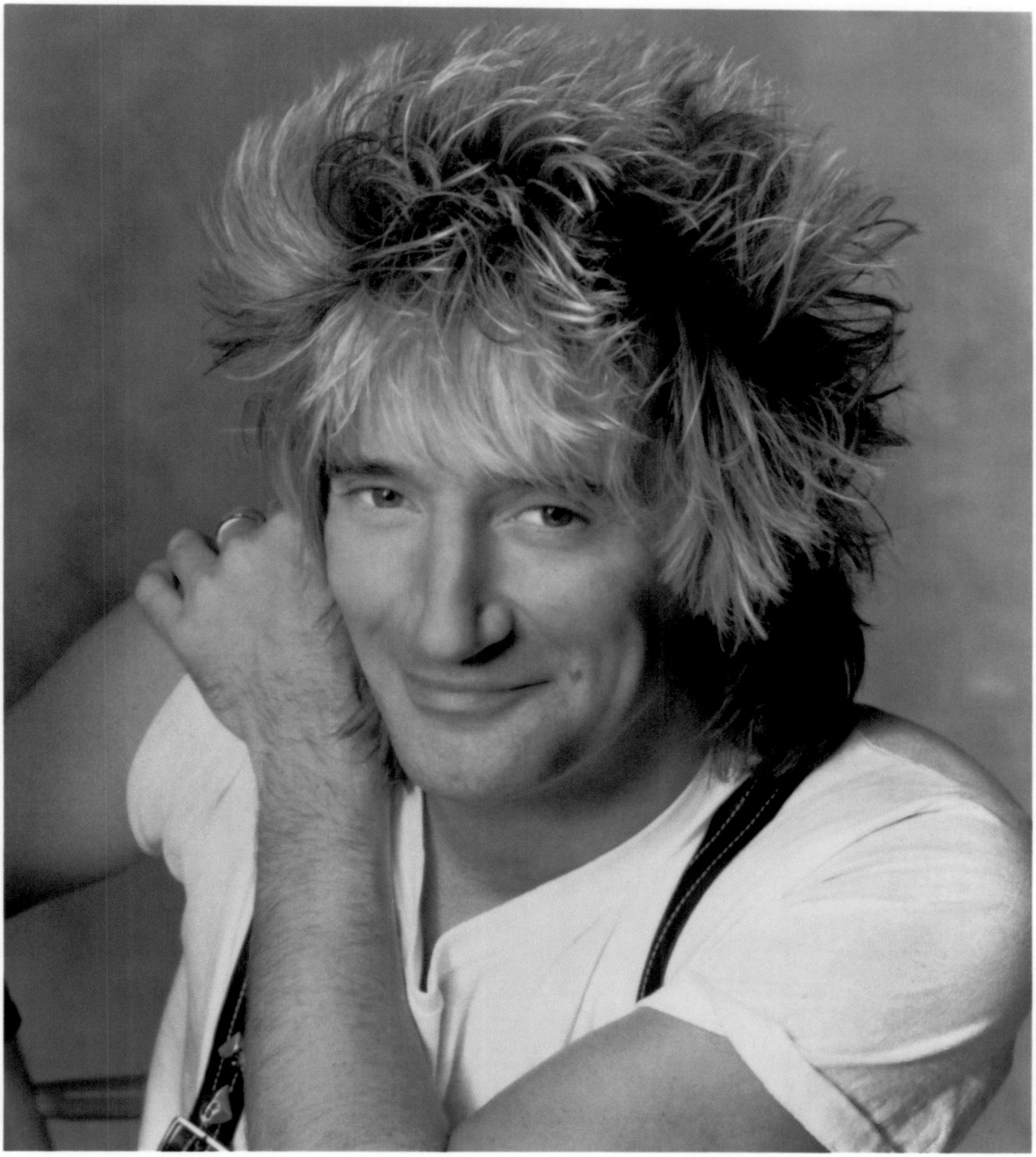

Photo Credit: Randee St. Nicholas

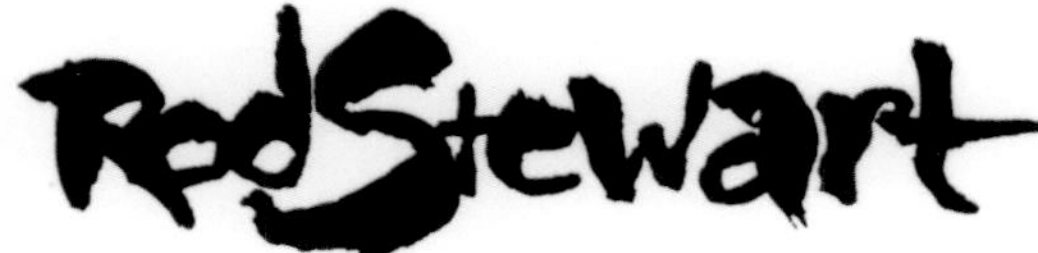

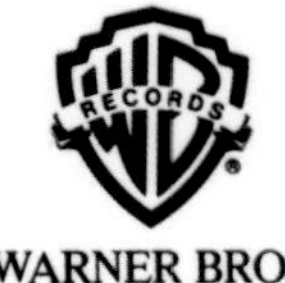

WARNER BROS.

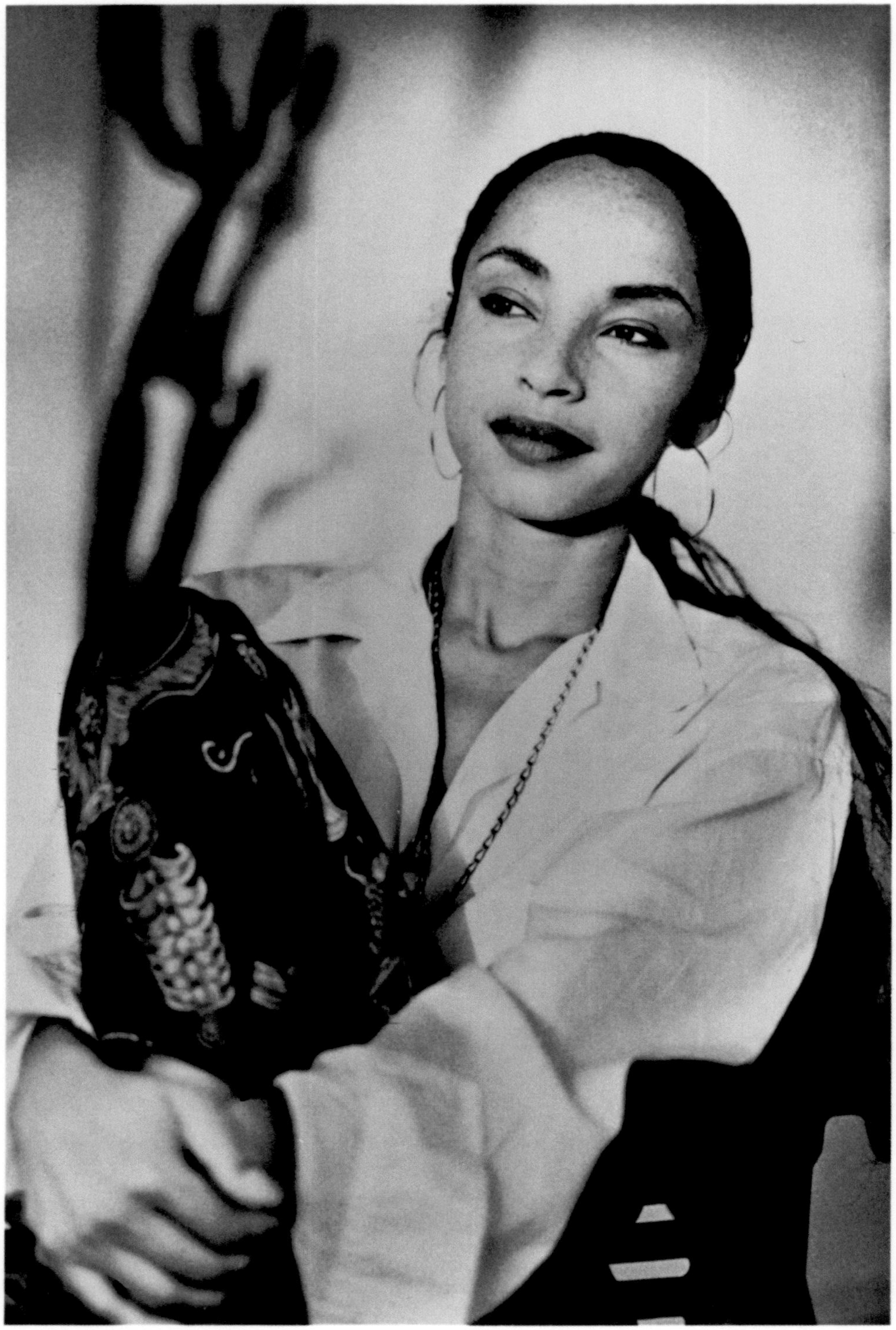

PHOTOGRAPH: CHRIS ROBERTS

SADE

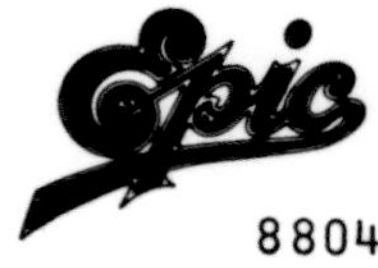

8804

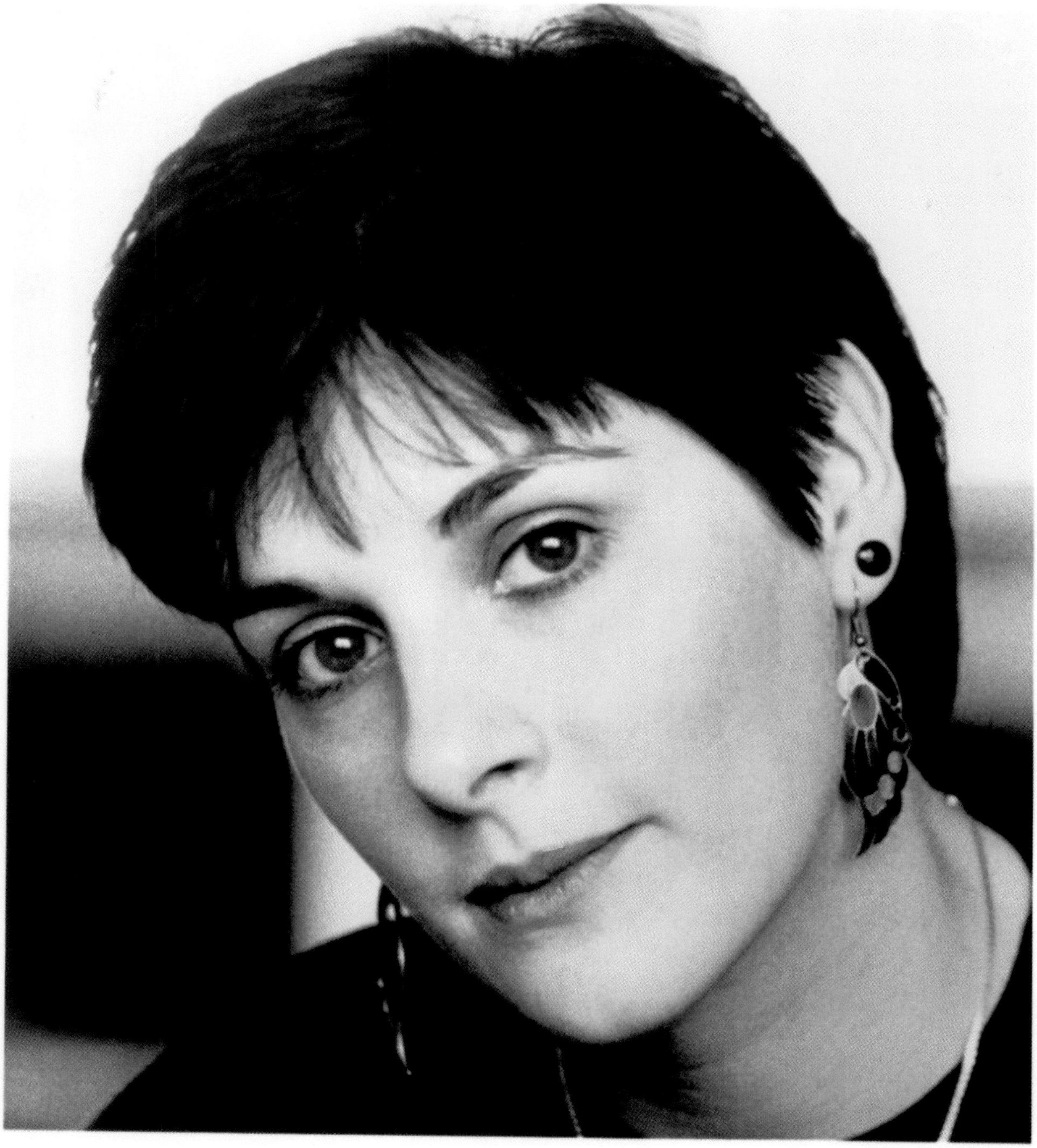

ENYA

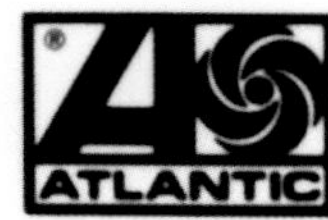

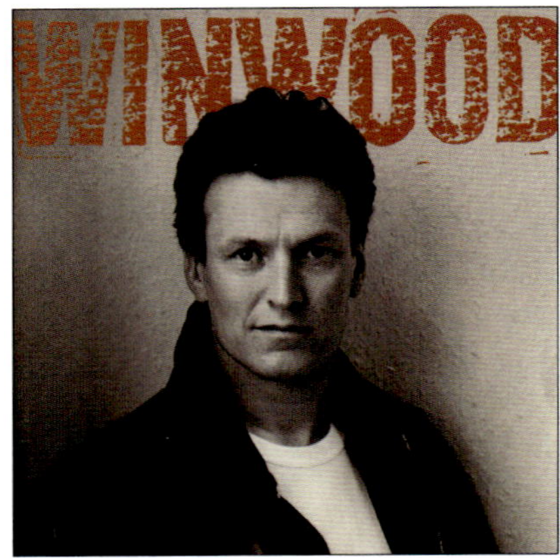

Roughly 25 years after his debut with the Spencer Davis Group, **Steve Winwood** rose to No. 1 with *Roll with It* and the title track, his biggest hit ever.

Billboard 200: *Roll with It* (No. 1)
Billboard Hot 100: "Roll with It" (No. 1); "Don't You Know What the Night Can Do?" (#6); "Holding On" (#11); "Hearts on Fire" (#53)

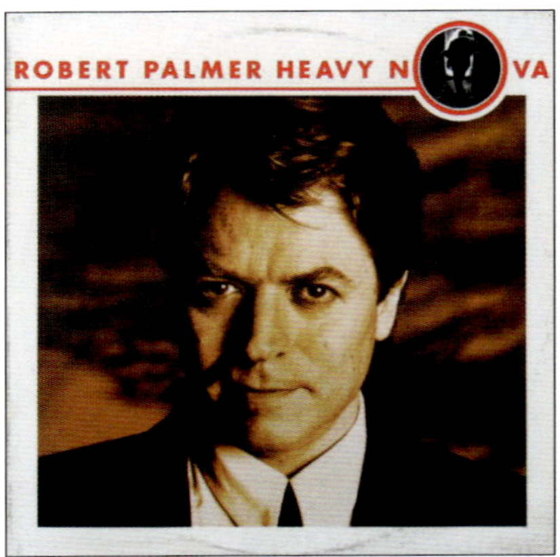

Robert Palmer scored another hit, "Simply Irresistible," the iconic video showing the suave singer beset by a troupe of mysterial, leggy female models.

Billboard 200: *Heavy Nova* (#13)
Billboard Hot 100: "Simply Irresistible" (#2); "Early in the Morning" (#19); "Tell Me I'm Not Dreaming" (#60)

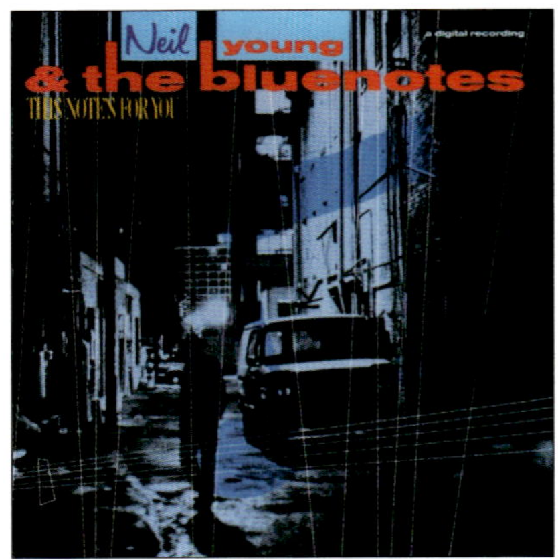

Neil Young & the Bluenotes' *This Note's for You*, a foray into blues and R&B, got noticed for the title track's video lampooning corporate sponsorships.

Billboard 200: *This Note's for You* (#61)

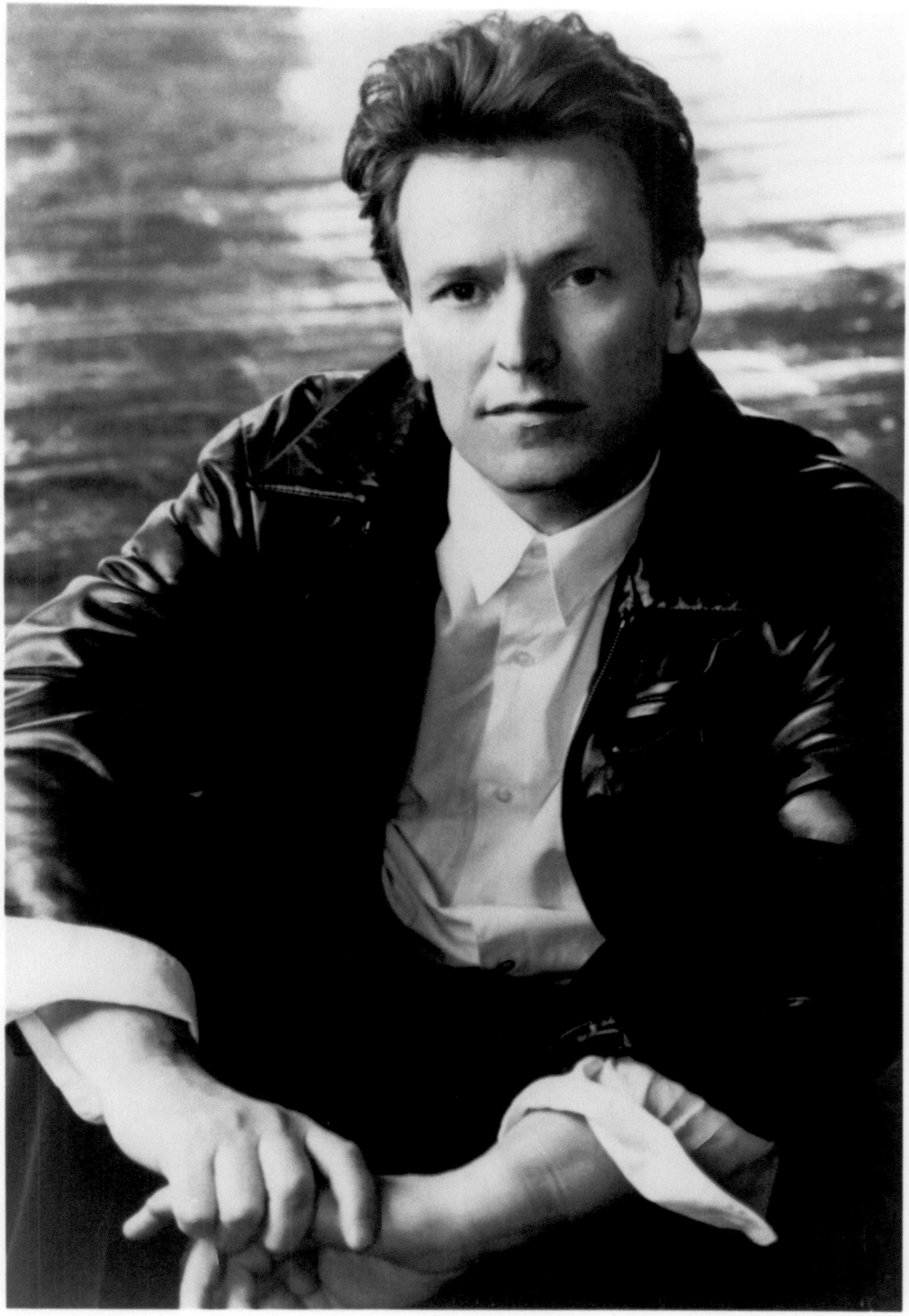

PHOTO CREDIT: **HERB RITTS**

MANAGEMENT:
RON WEISNER
ENTERTAINMENT
(213) 550-8200

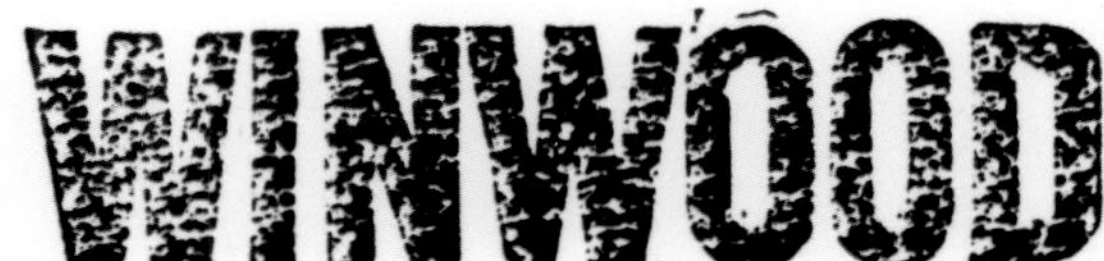

Virgin

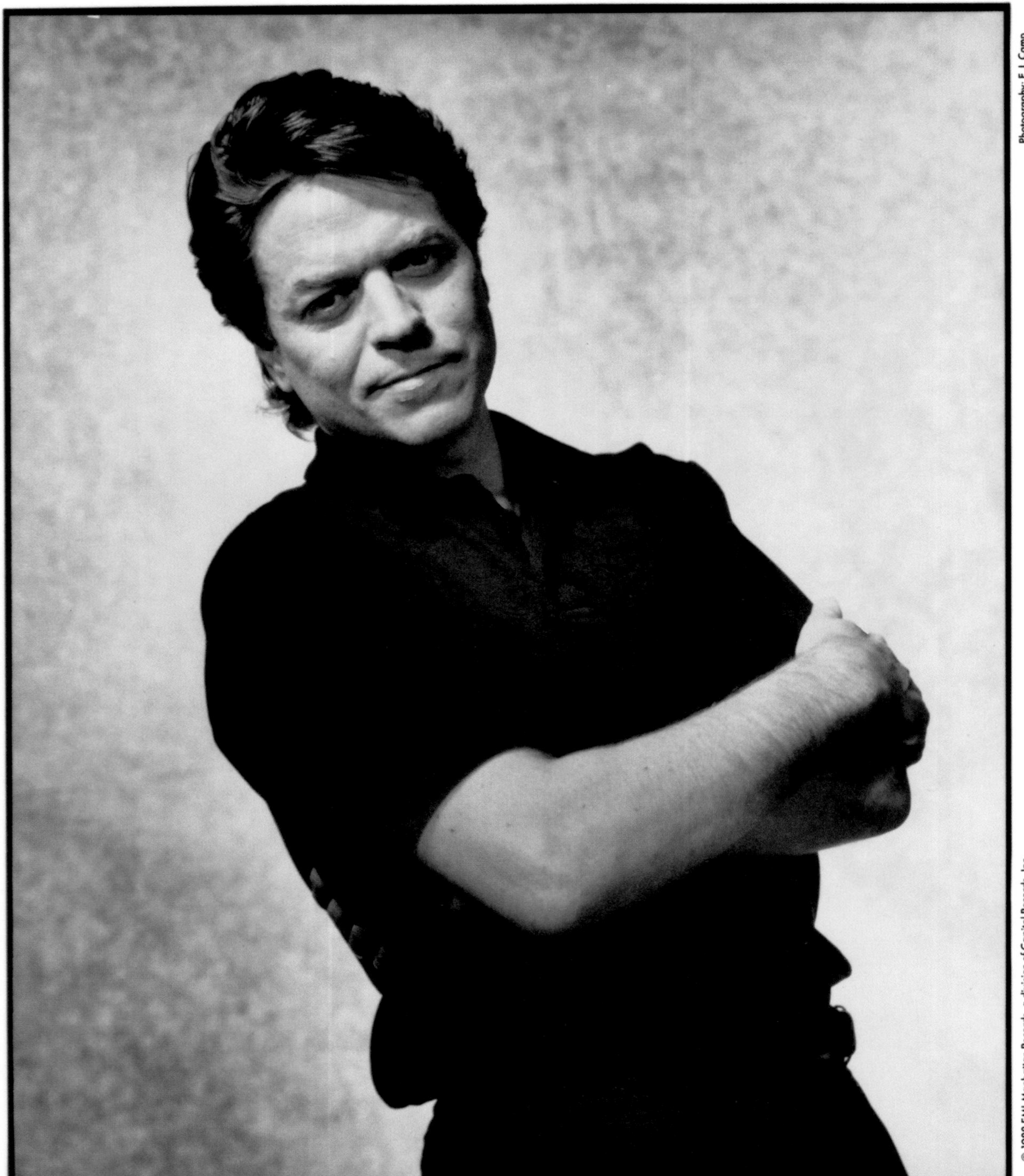

Photography: E.J. Camp

ROBERT PALMER

EMI MANHATTAN®

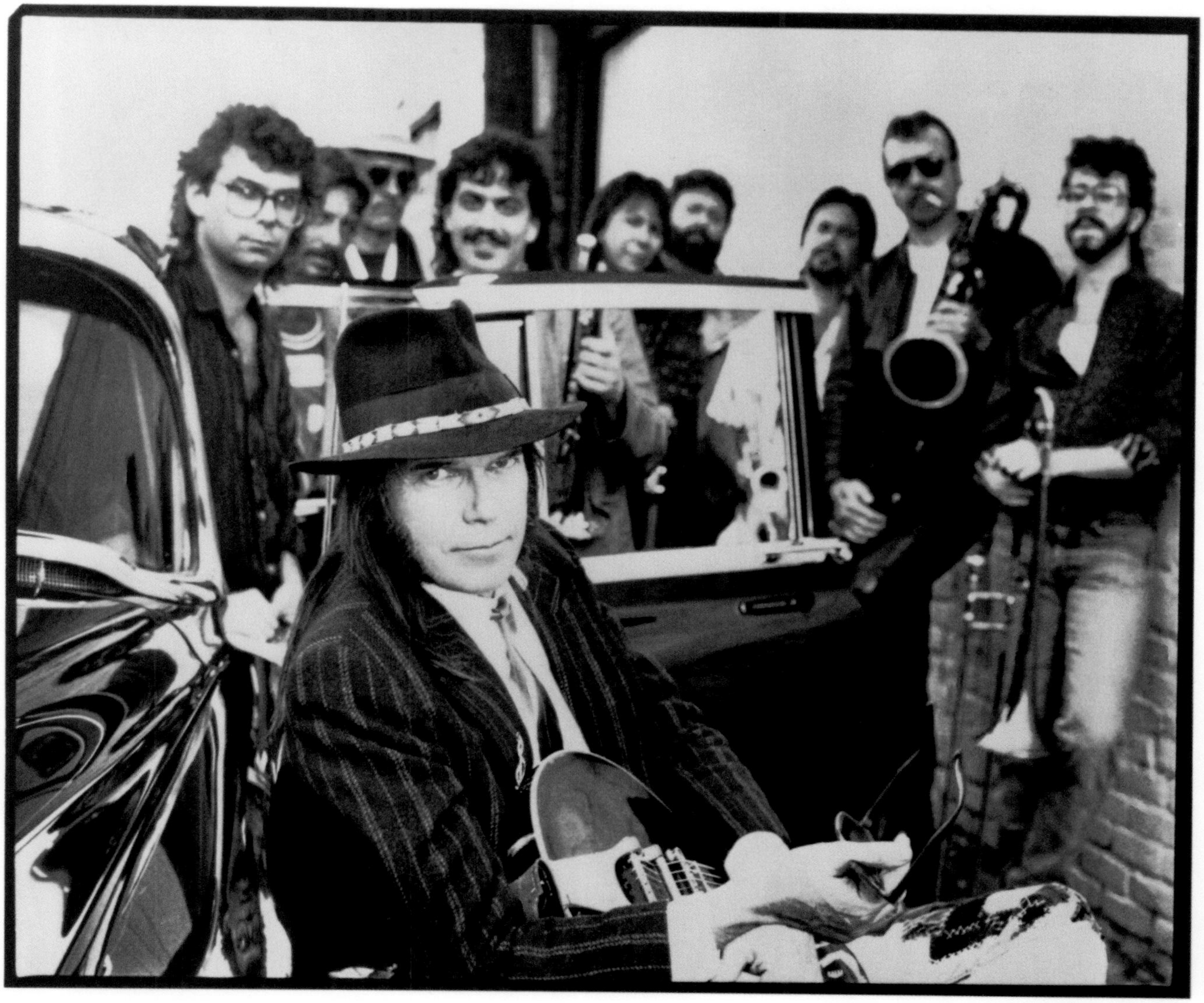

Photo Credit: Aaron Rapoport

Neil young
& the bluenotes

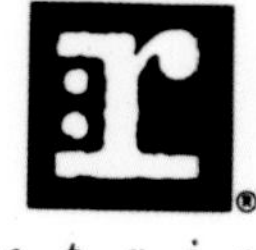

reprise

Original Chicago member **Peter Cetera** paired up with producer Patrick Leonard on "One Good Woman," earning a No. 1 adult contemporary track.

Billboard 200: *One More Story* (#58)
Billboard Hot 100: "One Good Woman" (#4); "Best of Times" (#59)

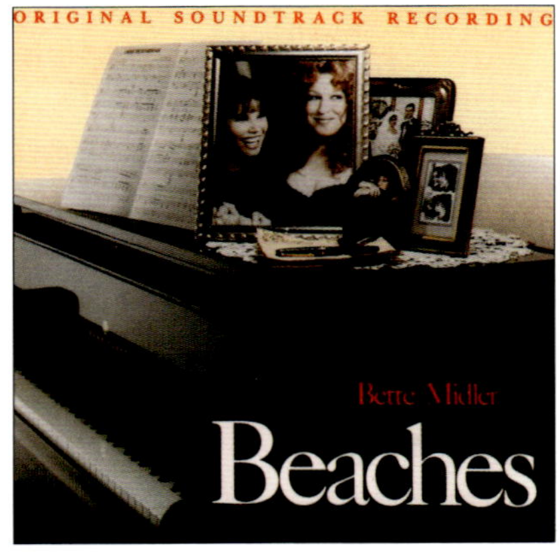

Bette Midler's heart-wrenching "Wind Beneath My Wings," from the soundtrack of her film *Beaches*, won the Grammy Award for Record of the Year.

Billboard 200: *Beaches* (#2)
Billboard Hot 100: "Wind Beneath My Wings" (No. 1)

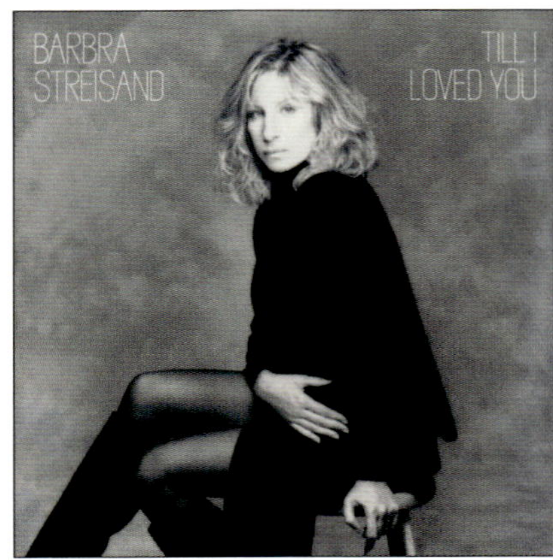

Barbra Streisand's lushly romantic *Till I Loved You* was sparked by the title track, a tender duet with her paramour, *Miami Vice* actor Don Johnson.

Billboard 200: *Till I Loved You* (#10)
Billboard Hot 100: "Till I Loved You" (#25)

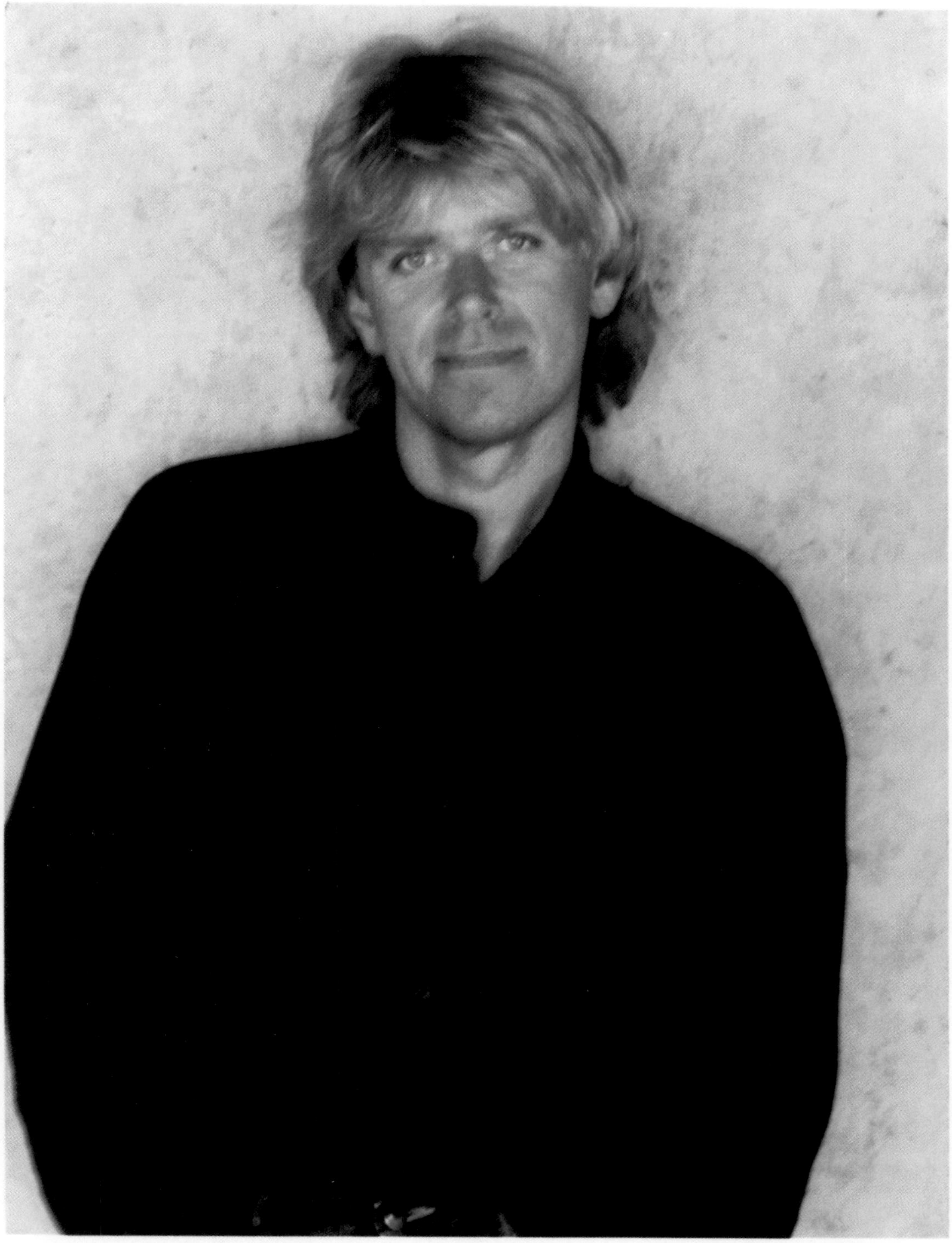

Photo Credit: Nicola Dell

PETER CETERA

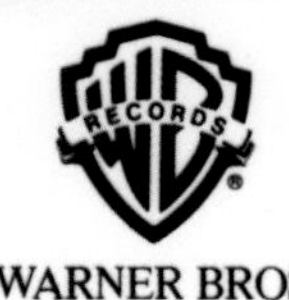

WARNER BROS.

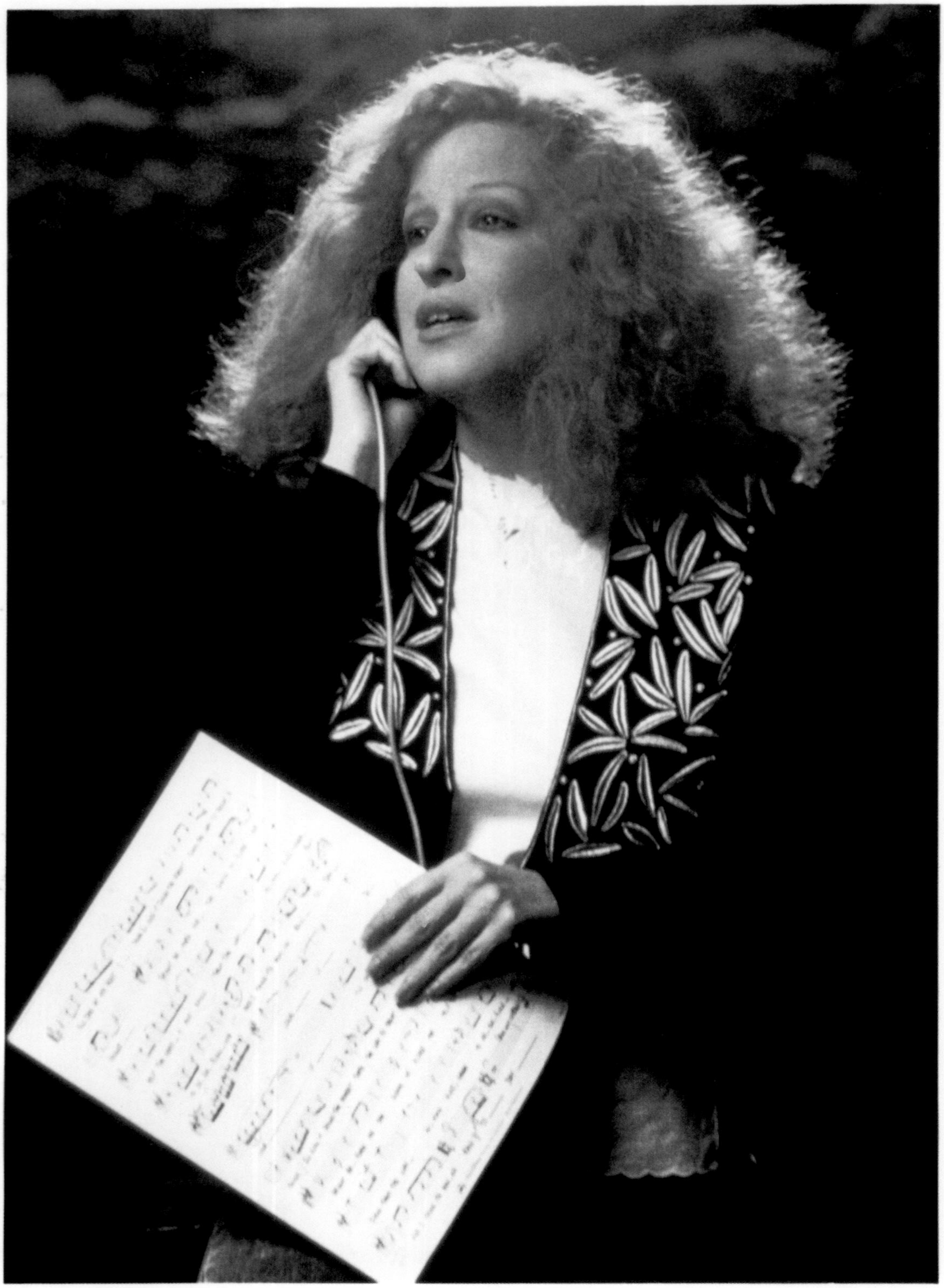

BETTE MIDLER
IN "BEACHES"

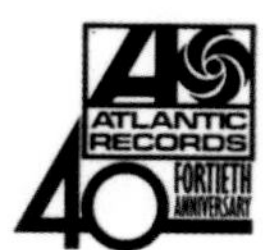

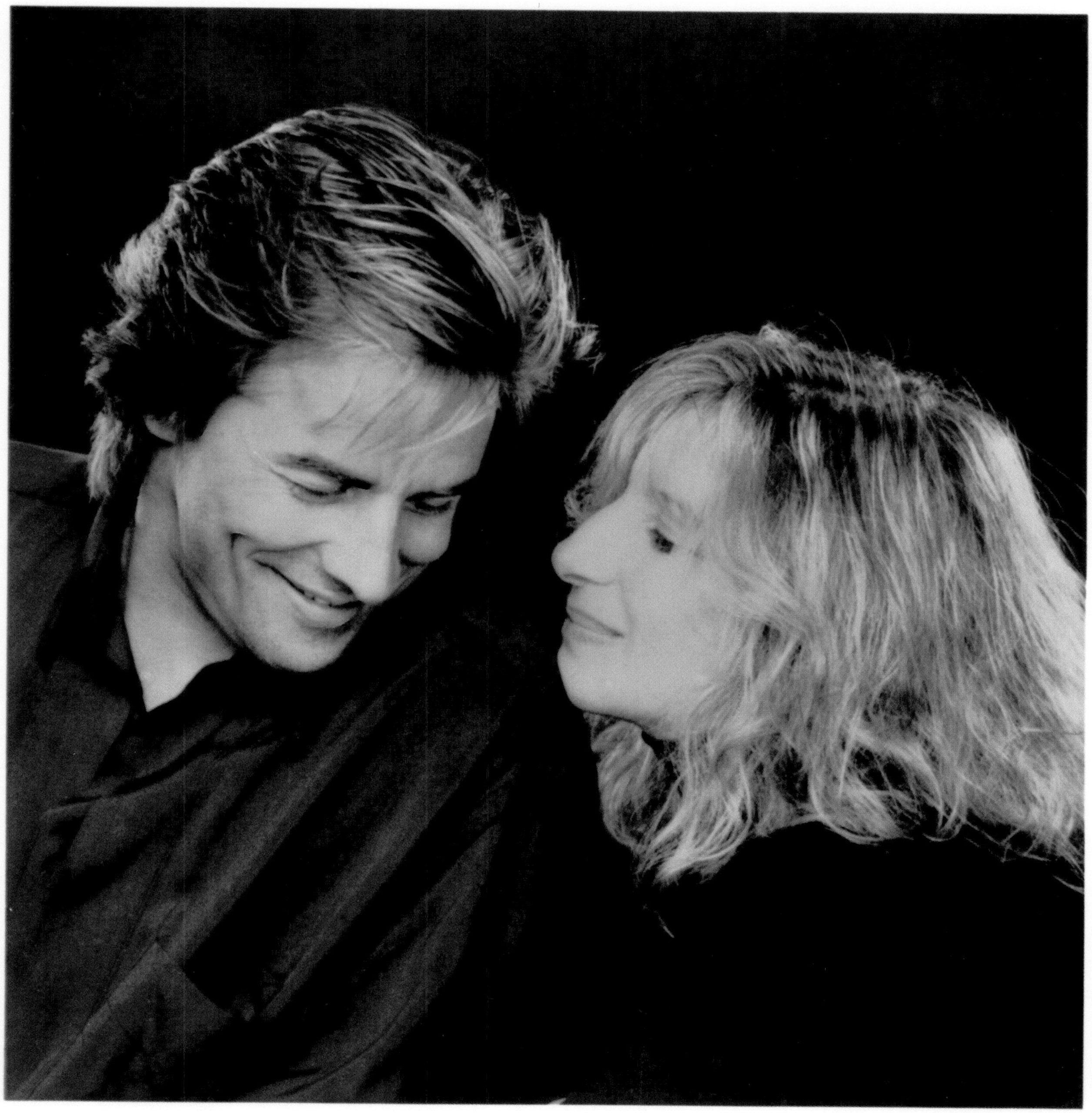

Photography Randee St. Nicholas

BARBRA STREISAND AND DON JOHNSON
TILL I LOVED YOU
(The Love Theme from *Goya*)

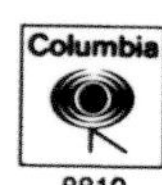

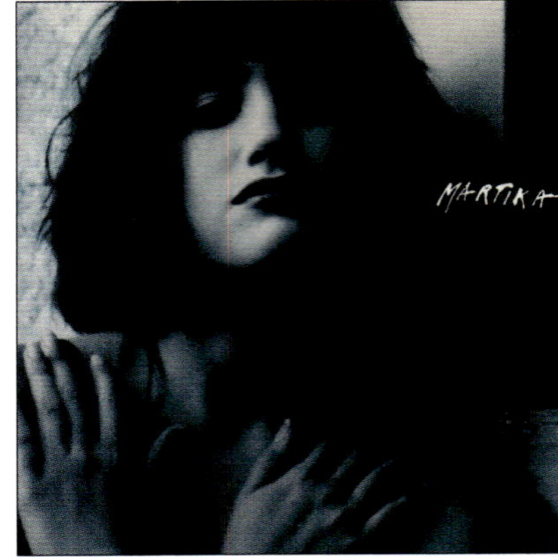

"Toy Soldiers," from pop singer **Martika**'s self-titled debut album, hit No. 1 in the US and the Top 5 in the UK, Ireland, Germany, Australia and Canada.

Billboard 200: *Martika* (#15)
Billboard Hot 100: "More Than You Know" (#18); "Toy Soldiers" (No. 1); "I Feel the Earth Move" (#25)

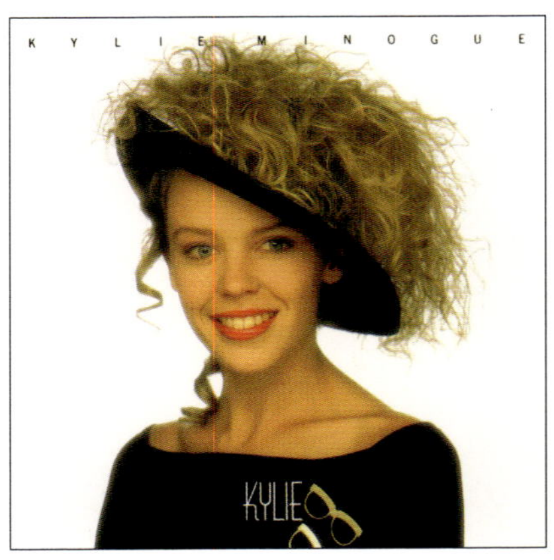

Kylie, the debut album of Australian dance-pop sensation **Kylie Minogue**, landed a cover version of "The Loco-Motion" atop the charts in many countries.

Billboard 200: *Kylie* (#53)
Billboard Hot 100: "I Should Be So Lucky" (#28); "The Loco-Motion" (#3); "It's No Secret" (#37)

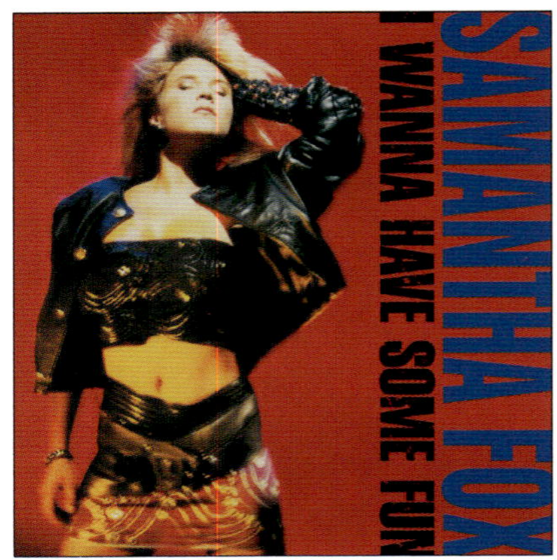

Former topless model **Samantha Fox** offered "I Wanna Have Some Fun," another come-hither dance-pop hit that got right to the crux of her popularity.

Billboard 200: *I Wanna Have Some Fun* (#37)
Billboard Hot 100: "I Wanna Have Some Fun" (#8); "I Only Wanna Be with You" (#31)

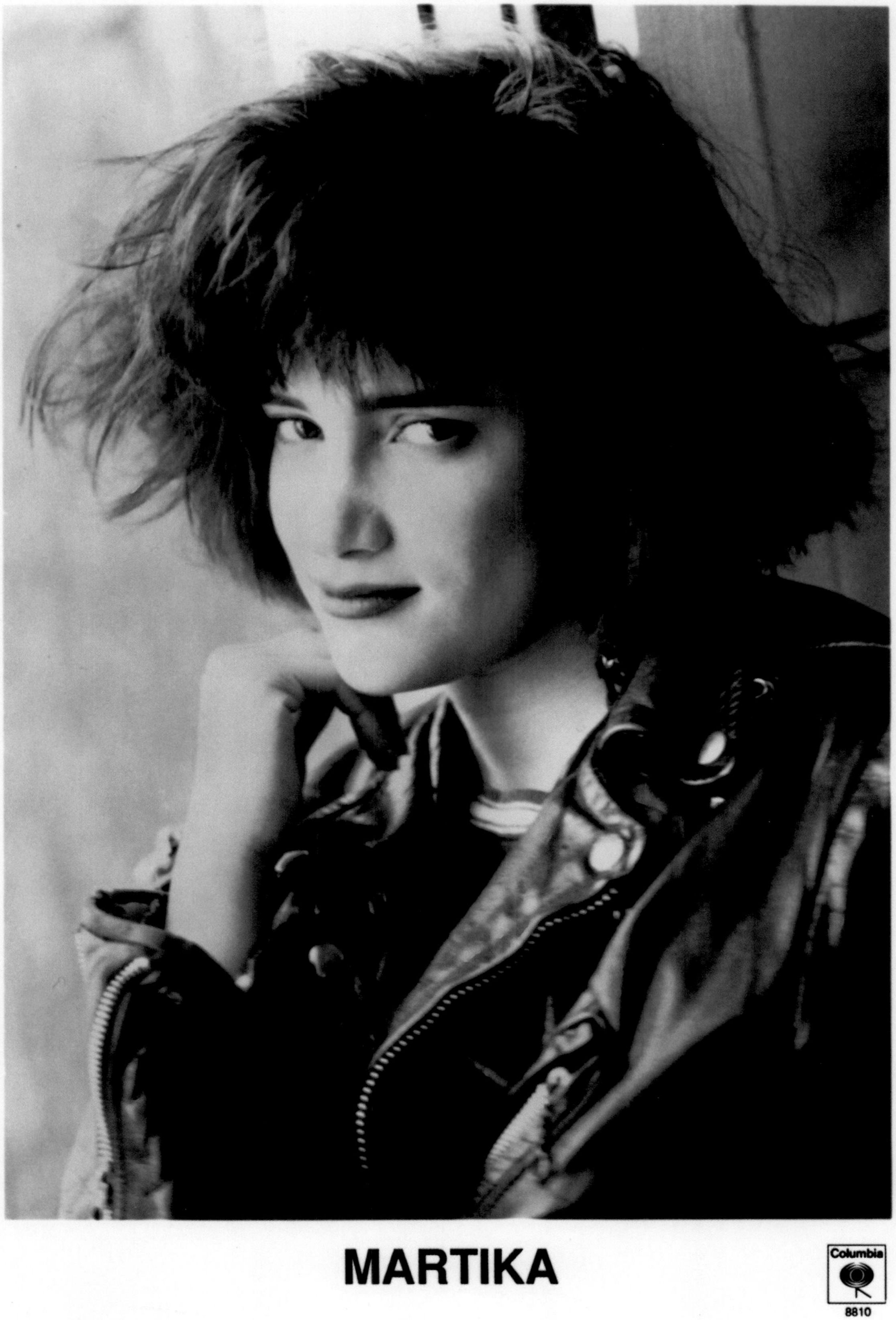

PHOTO: ALBERTO TOLOT

MARTIKA

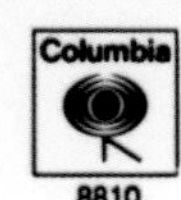

8810

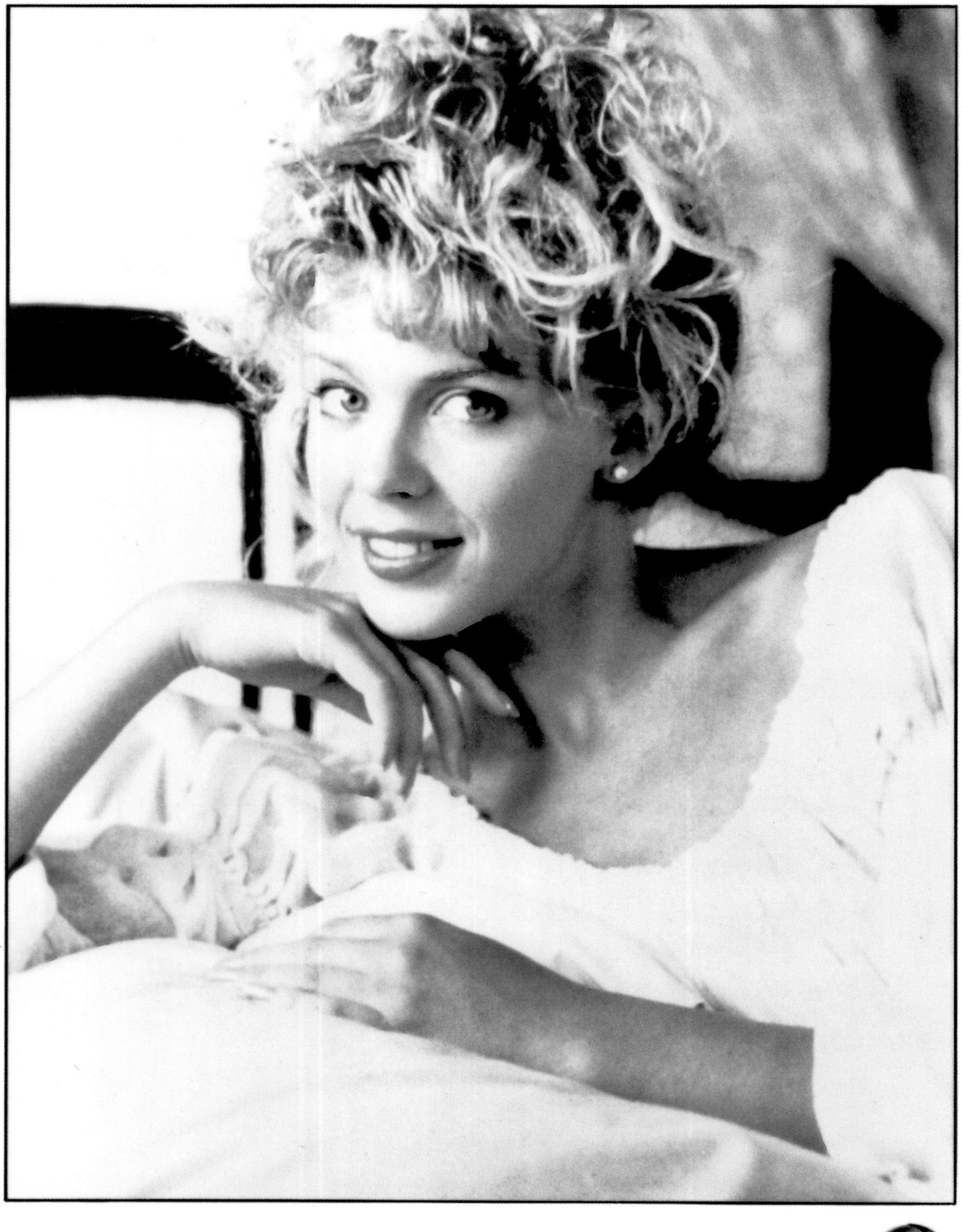

Photo Credit: Andrew Lehmann

KYLIE MINOGUE

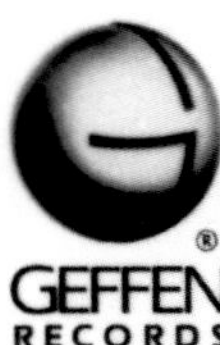

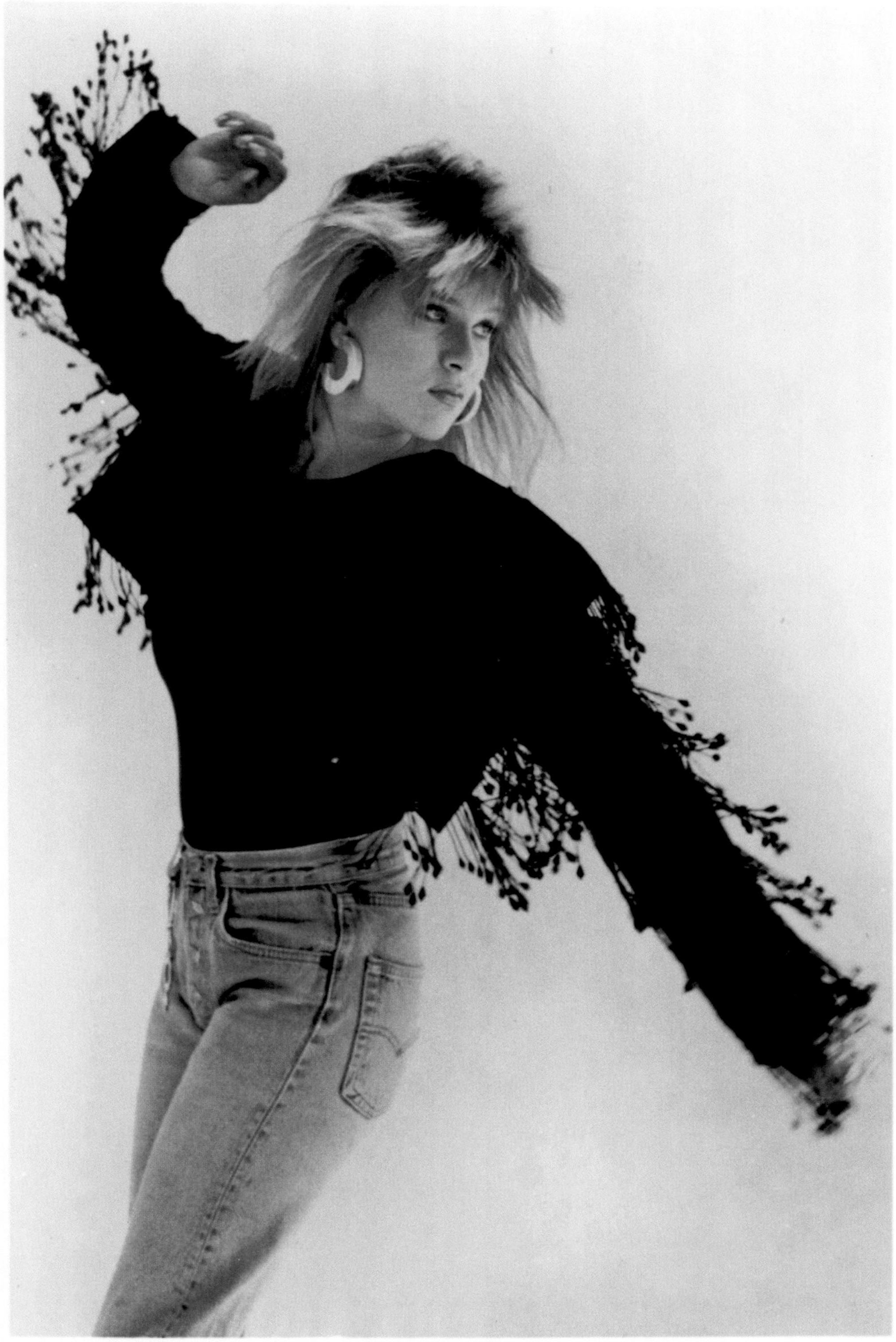

SAMANTHA FOX

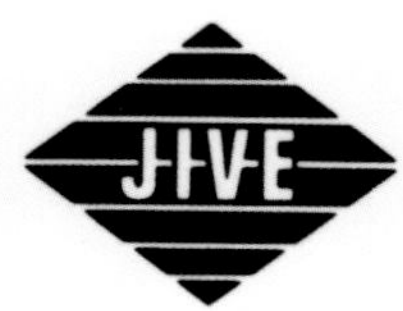

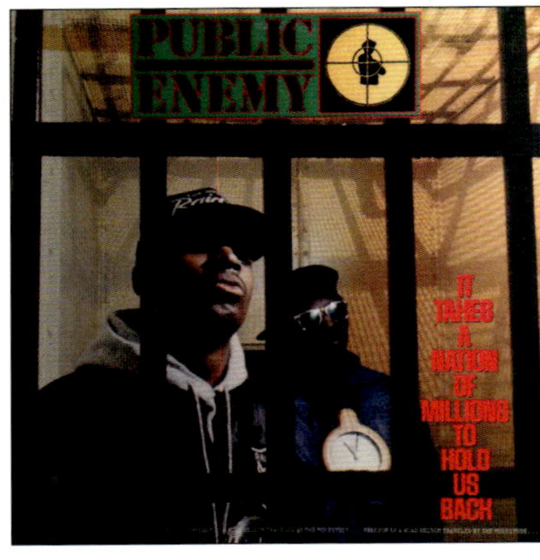

Public Enemy's militant *It Takes a Nation of Millions to Hold Us Back* included the ornery "Bring the Noise" and the advisory "Don't Believe the Hype."

Billboard 200: *It Takes a Nation of Millions to Hold Us Back* (#42)

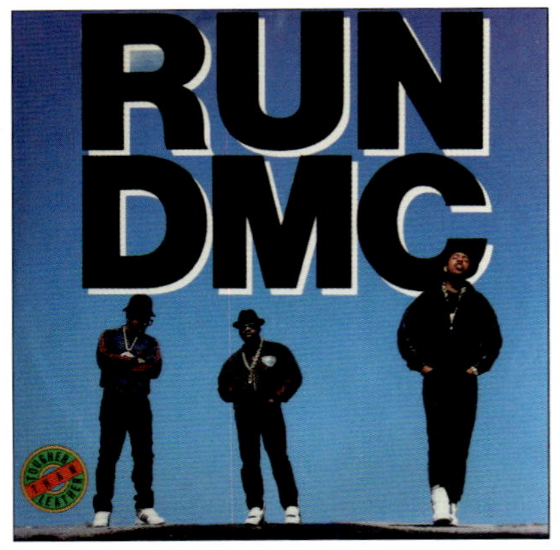

A follow-up to the hit *Raising Hell*, Run-D.M.C.'s *Tougher Than Leather* spawned "Run's House" and a rap-rock cover of the Monkees' "Mary, Mary."

Billboard 200: *Tougher Than Leather* (#9)
Billboard Hot 100: "Mary, Mary" (#75)

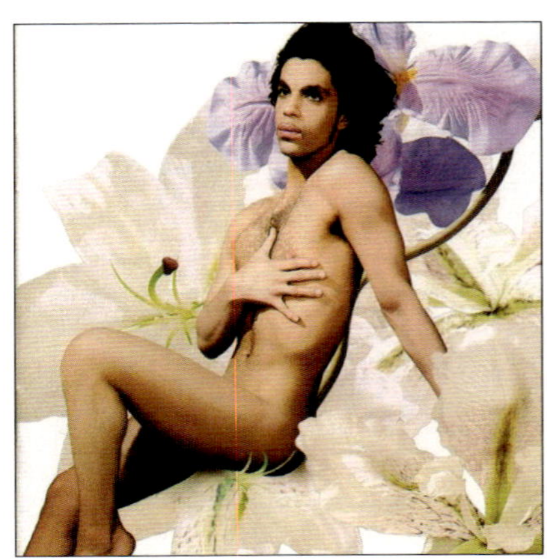

After withdrawing the release of *The Black Album*, Prince proclaimed his spiritual growth with *Lovesexy* and an international Top 10 hit, "Alphabet St."

Billboard 200: *Lovesexy* (#11)
Billboard Hot 100: "Alphabet St." (#8)

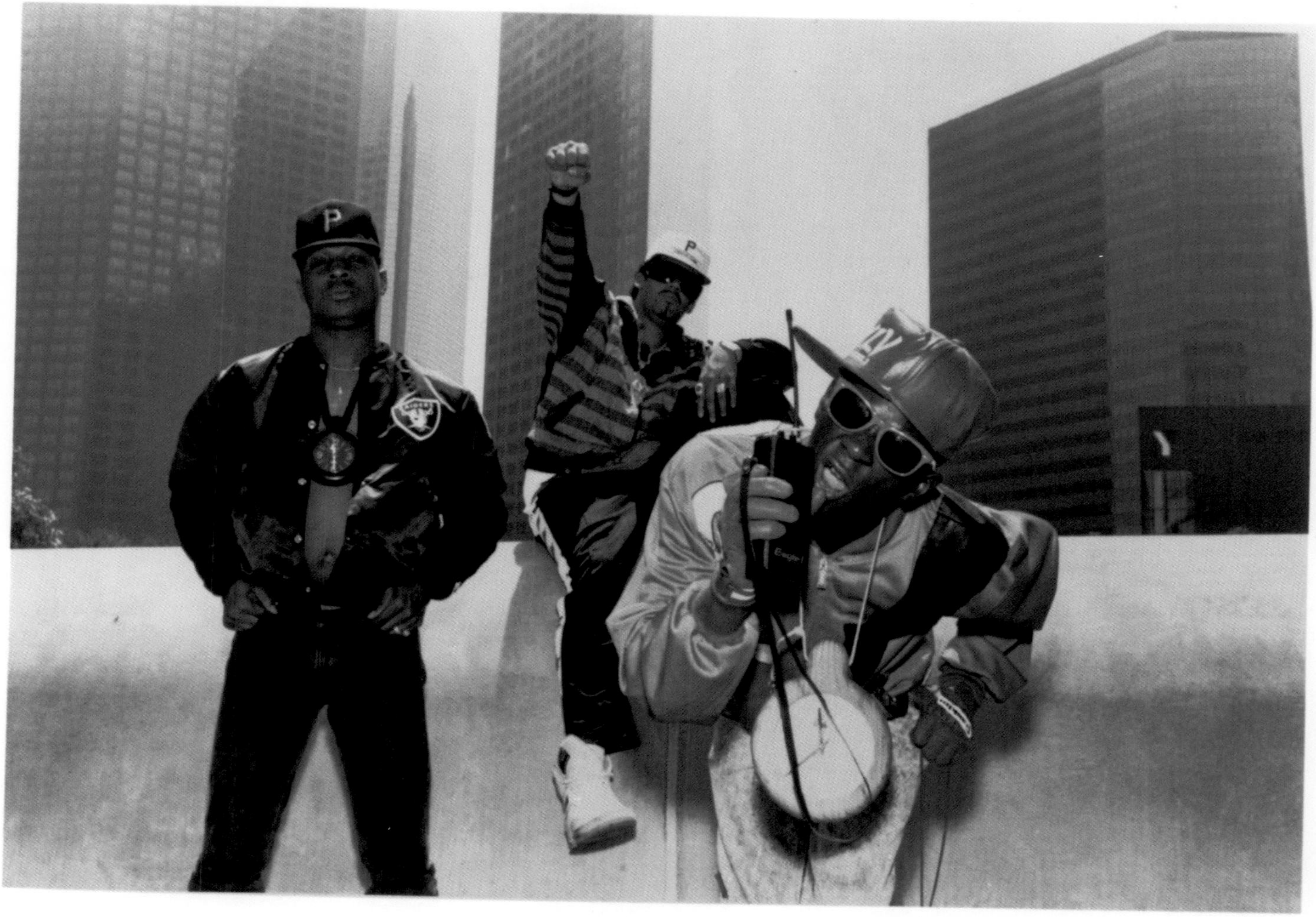

PHOTOGRAPH: c DEACON CHAPIN

From left. CHUCK D, TERMINATOR X, and FLAVOR FLAV.

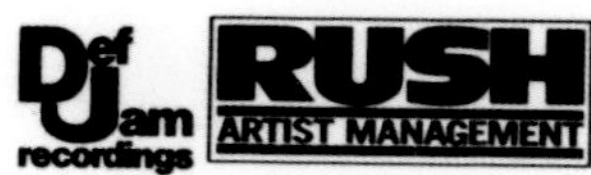

PUBLIC ENEMY

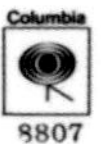

8807

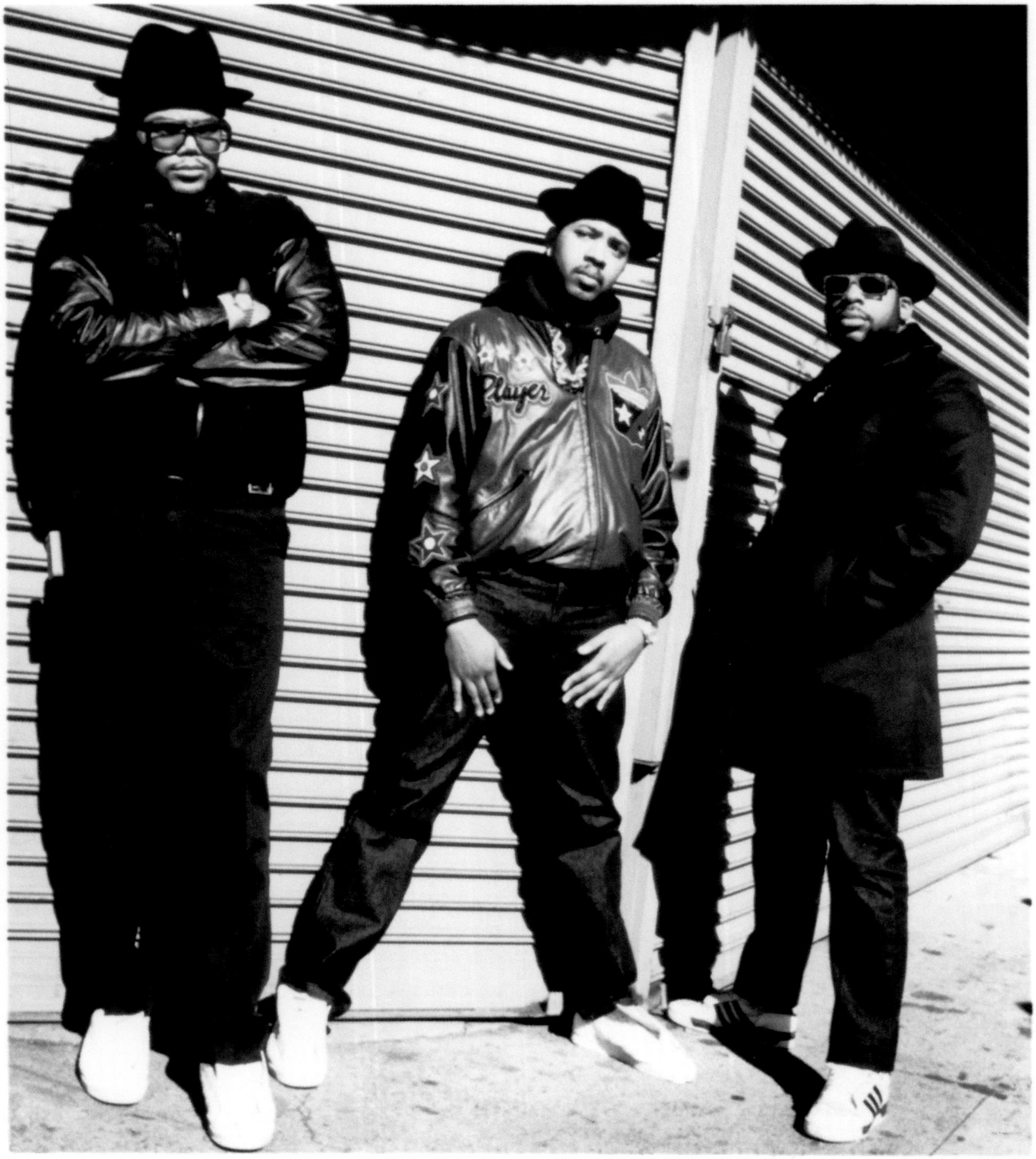

RUN-D.M.C.

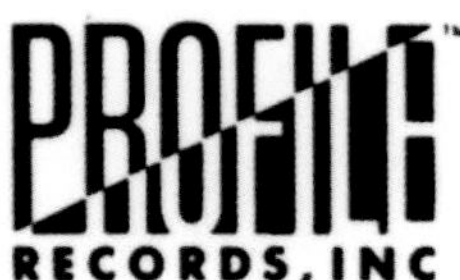

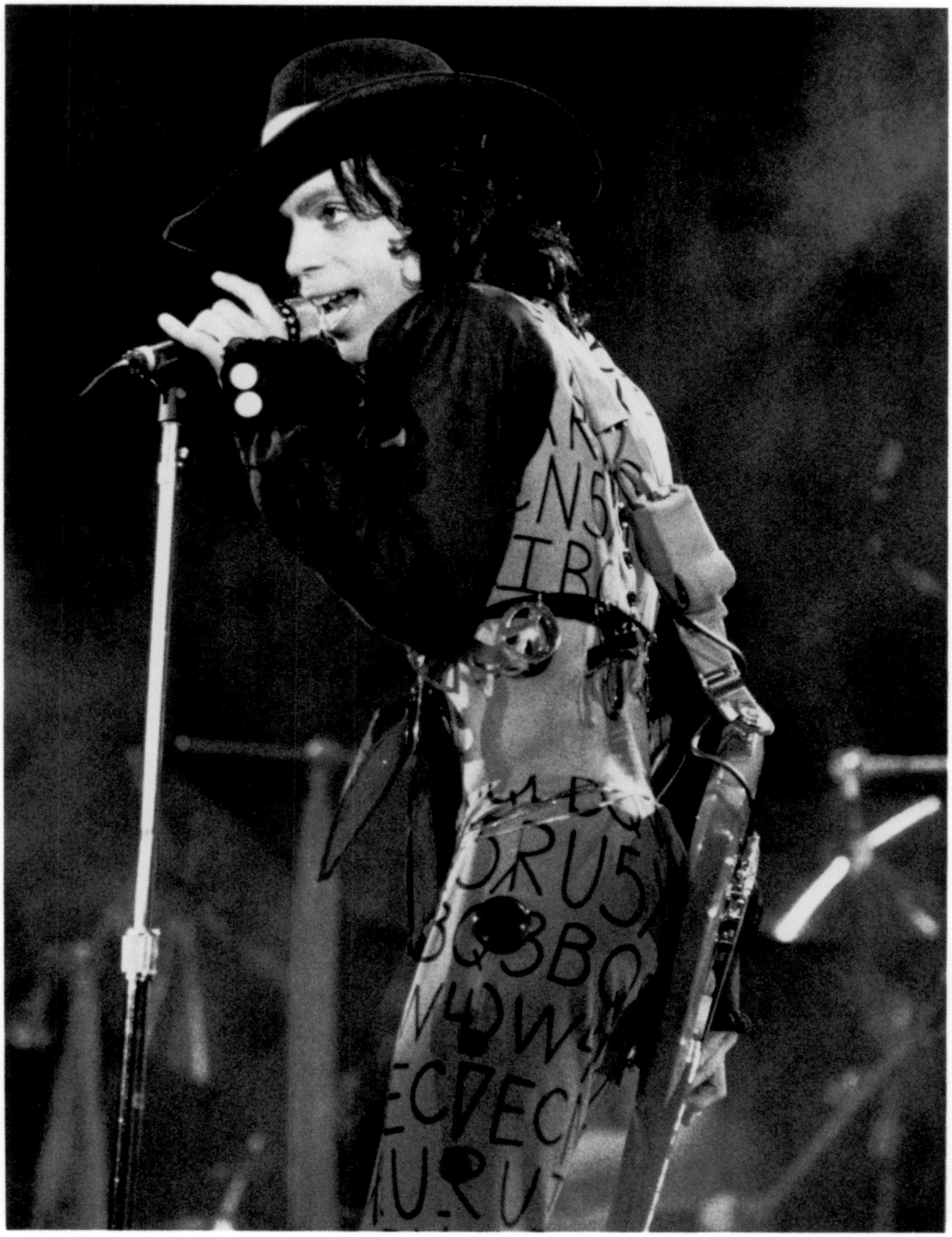

Photo Credit: Frank Griffin

PRINCE

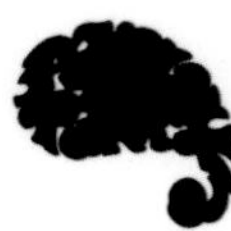

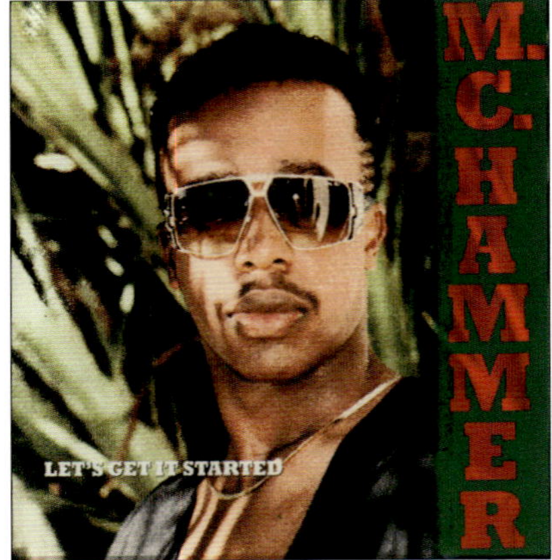

A revamping of his first independent album, **M.C. Hammer**'s *Let's Get It Started* topped the R&B charts and produced the hit "Turn This Mutha Out."

Billboard 200: *Let's Get It Started* (#30)

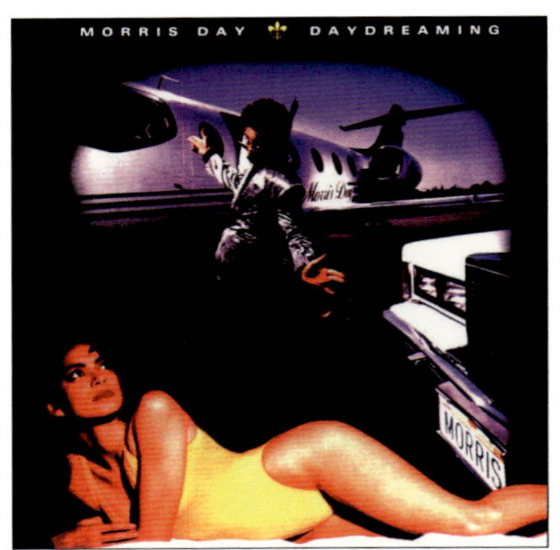

Morris Day's *Daydreaming* was highlighted by "Fishnet," a collaboration with his ex-bandmates in the Time, iconic producers Jimmy Jam & Terry Lewis.

Billboard 200: *Daydreaming* (#41)
Billboard Hot 100: "Fishnet" (#23)

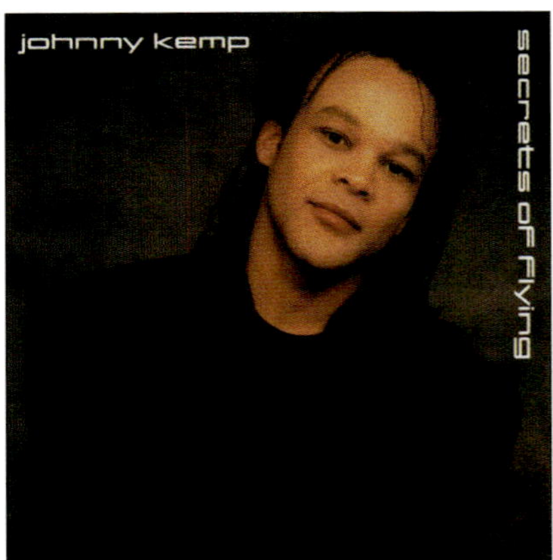

Johnny Kemp's Grammy-nominated "Just Got Paid," one of the first hits produced by Guy's Teddy Riley, reached No. 1 on the R&B and dance charts.

Billboard 200: *Secrets of Flying* (#68)
Billboard Hot 100: "Just Got Paid" (#10)

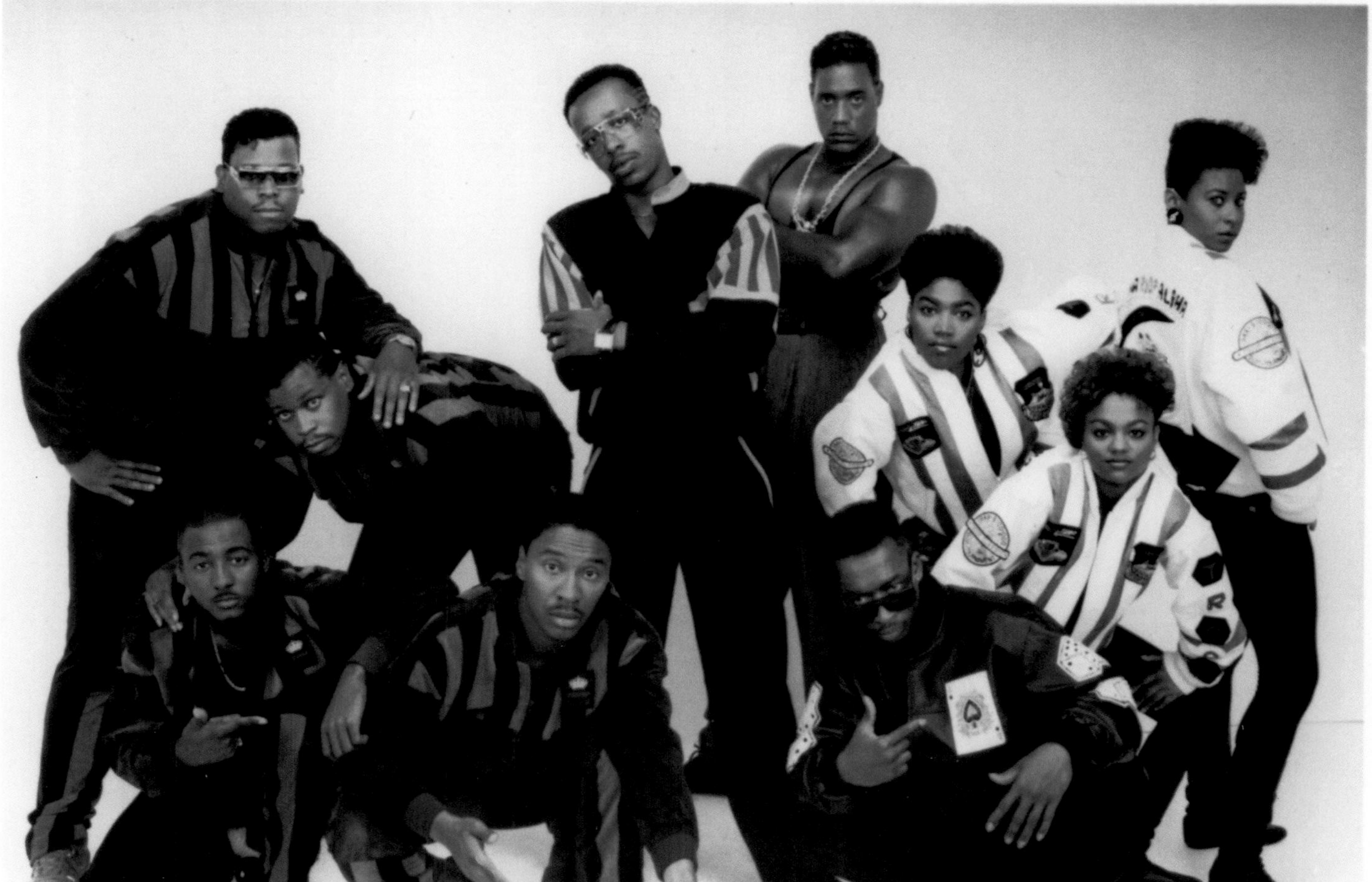

Photo: Pat Johnson / 1988

M. C. HAMMER

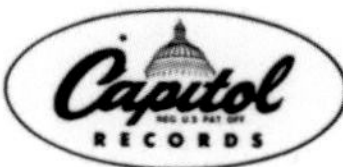

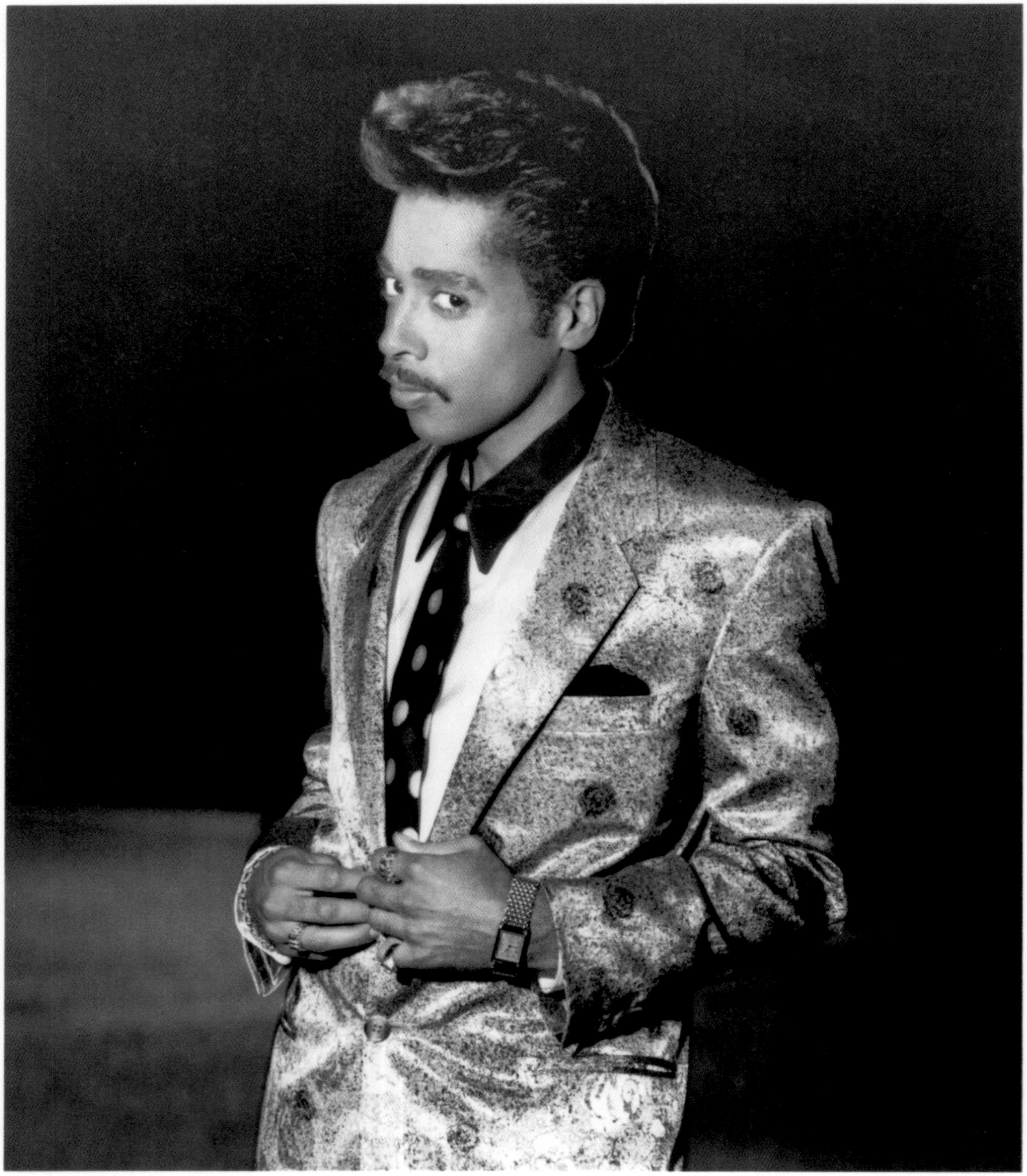

Photo Credit: Jeff Katz

MORRIS DAY

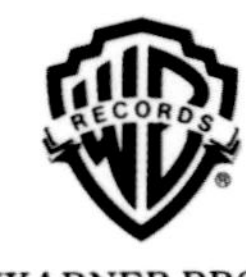

WARNER BROS.

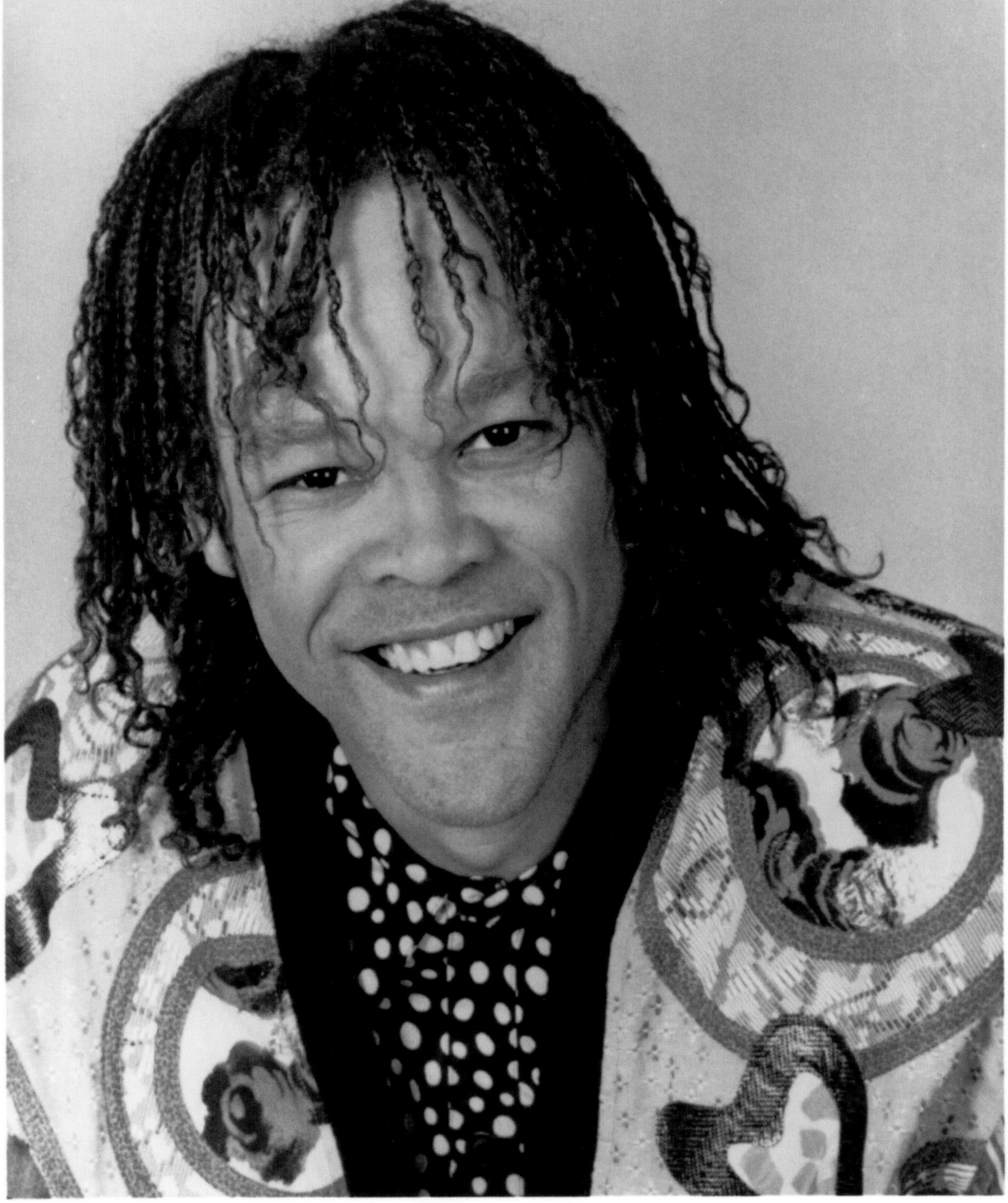

JOHNNY KEMP

Columbia

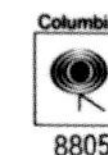

8805

PHOTOGRAPH: JOYCE TENNYSON

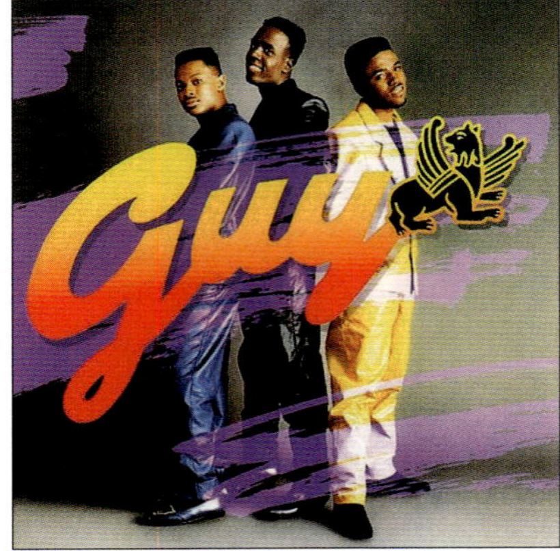

Guy's self-titled debut peaked at No. 1 on the R&B album chart, triggered by the hits "I Like," "Groove Me," "Teddy's Jam" and "Round and Round."

Billboard 200: *Guy* (#27)
Billboard Hot 100: "I Like" (#70)

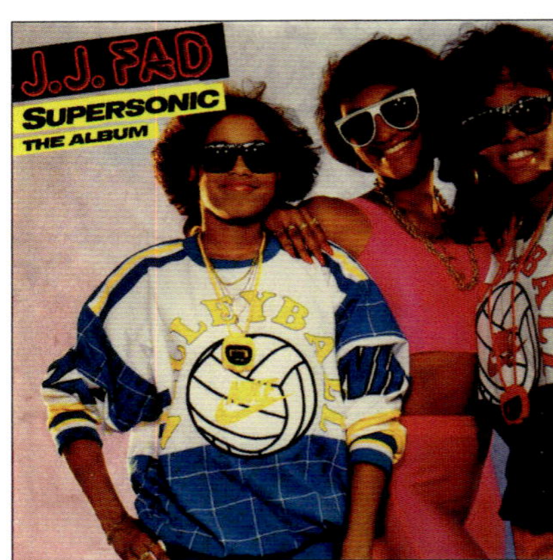

Signed to Eazy-E's Ruthless Records, a label known for gangsta rap, the hip-hop girl trio J.J. Fad offered a pop option with the catchy "Supersonic."

Billboard 200: *Supersonic* (#49)
Billboard Hot 100: "Supersonic" (#30); "Way Out" (#61); "Is It Love" (#92)

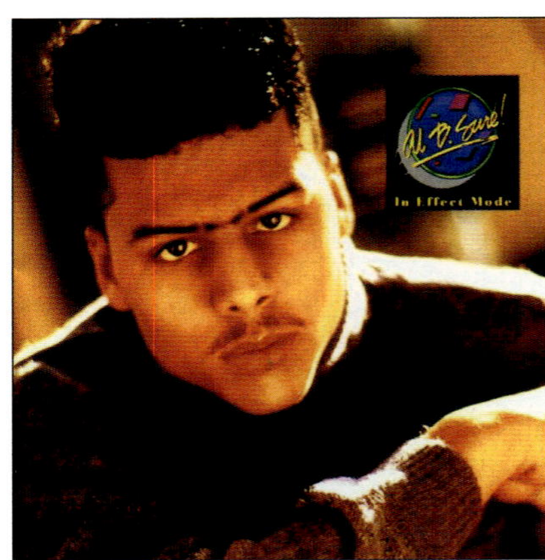

With *In Effect Mode*, his debut album of new jack swing ballads, romantic singer Al B. Sure! spent seven consecutive weeks at No. 1 on the R&B charts.

Billboard 200: *In Effect Mode* (#20)
Billboard Hot 100: "Nite and Day" (#7); "Off on Your Own (Girl)" (#45); "Killing Me Softly" (#80)

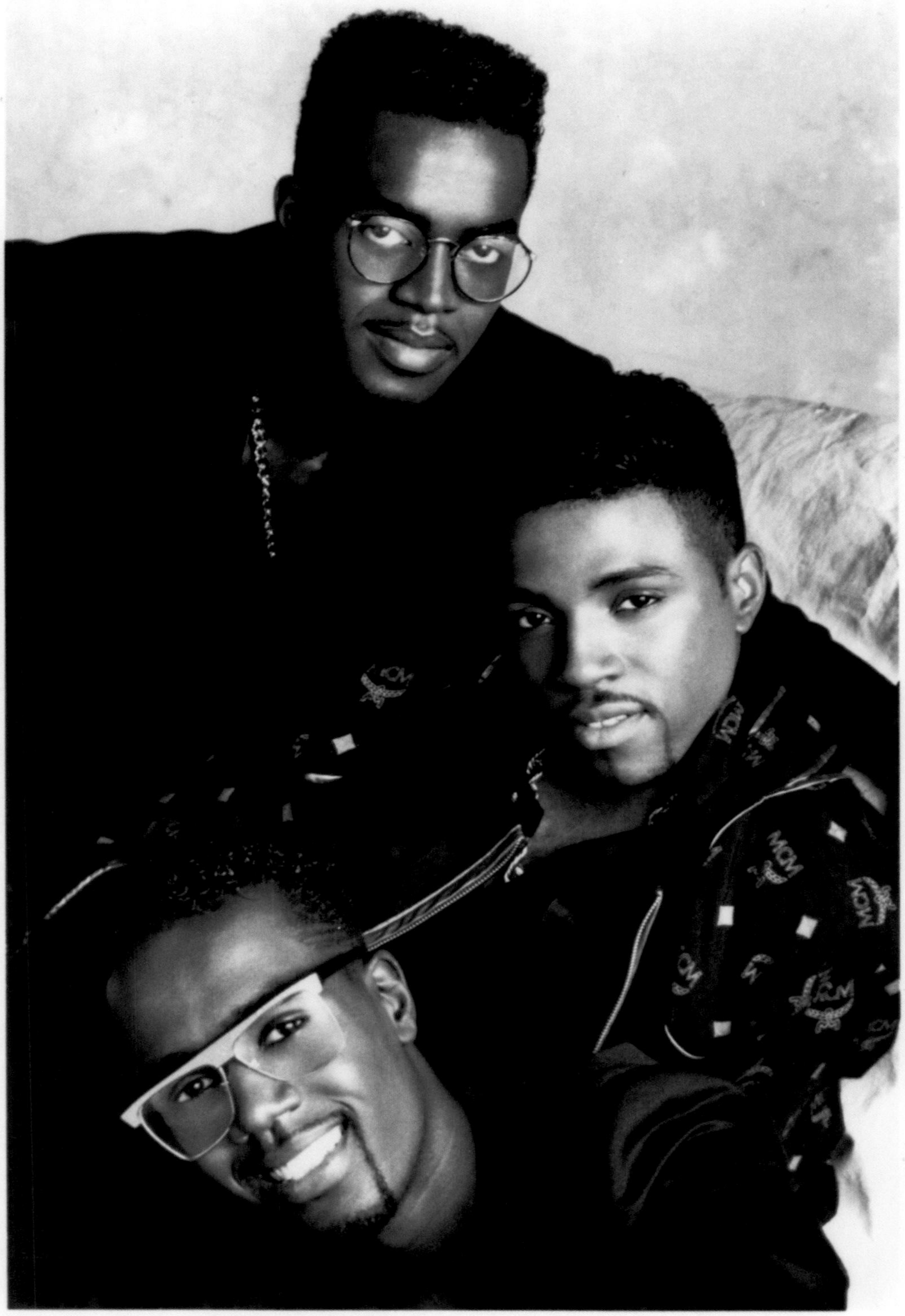

Photo Credit: Todd Gray/MCA

DAMIEN HALL
AARON HALL

TEDDY RILEY

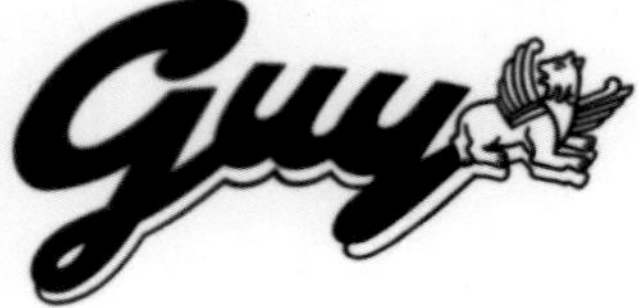

MCA RECORDS

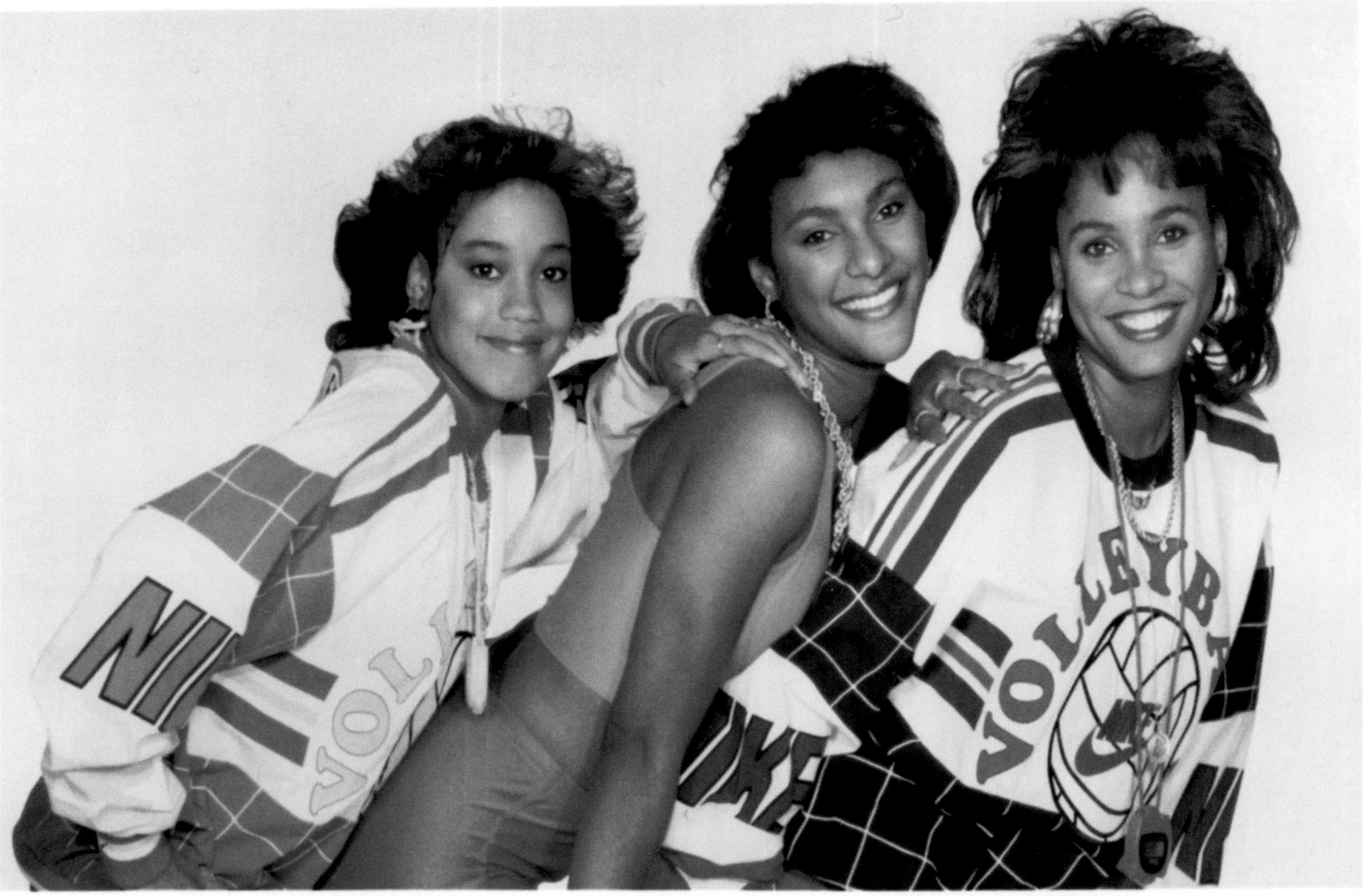

BABY D MC JB SASSY C

J. J. FAD

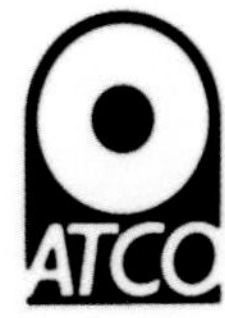

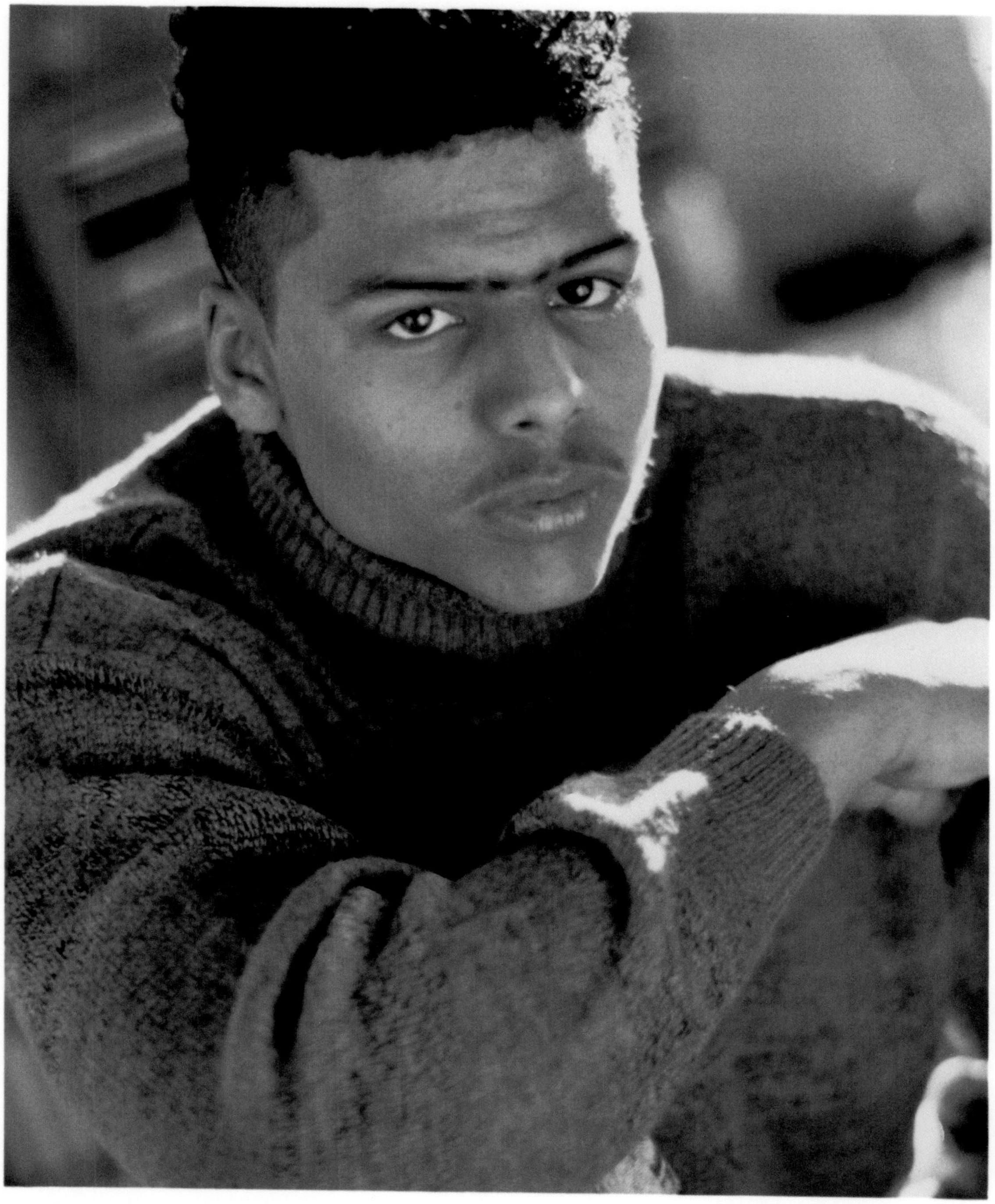

Photo Credit: Deano Mueller

AL B. SURE!

AL B. SURE! IS THE WINNER OF A

SONY INNOVATORS

AWARD

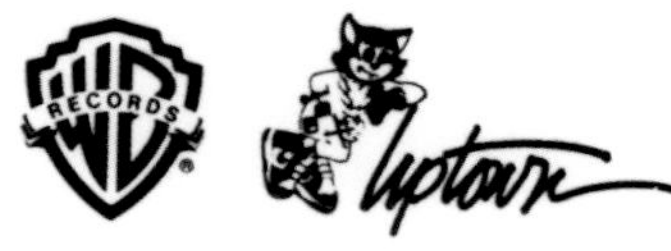

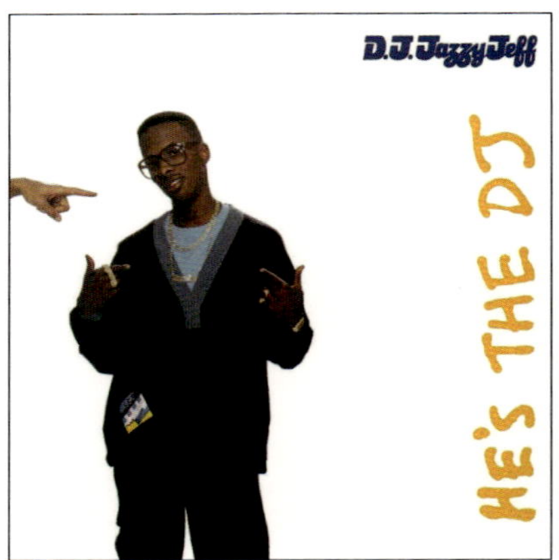

"Parents Just Don't Understand" by D.J. Jazzy Jeff & the Fresh Prince (Jeff Townes and Will Smith) won the first-ever Grammy for Best Rap Performance.

Billboard 200: *He's the DJ, I'm the Rapper* (#4)
Billboard Hot 100: "Parents Just Don't Understand" (#12); "A Nightmare on My Street" (#15)

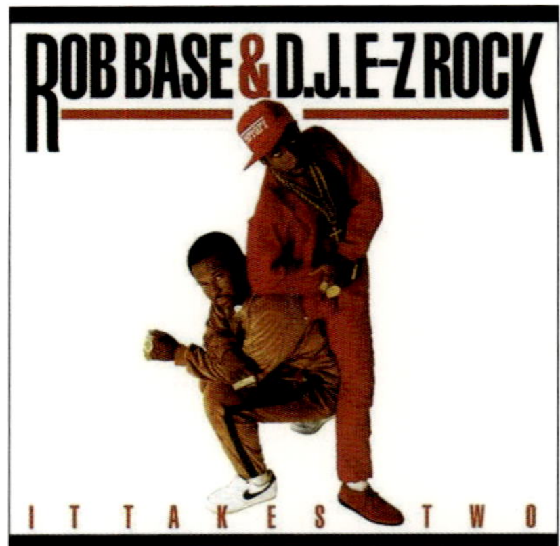

Crossing over to pop culture, the Harlem hip-hop duo Rob Base & D.J. E-Z Rock crashed the Top 40 charts with the inventive, dynamic "It Takes Two."

Billboard 200: *It Takes Two* (#31)
Billboard Hot 100: "It Takes Two" (#36); "Joy and Pain" (#58)

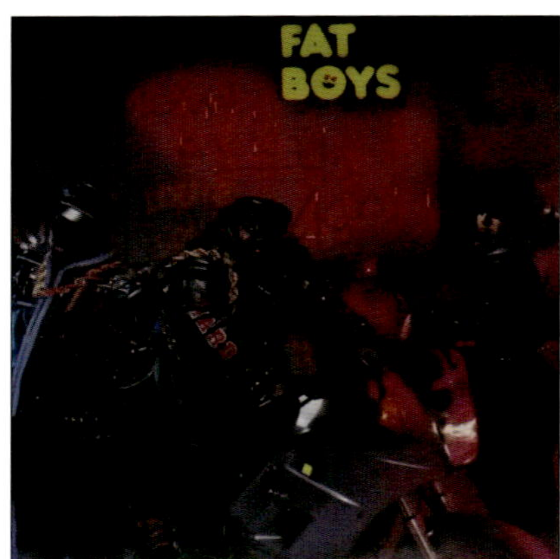

Novelty rappers Fat Boys recorded a remake of "The Twist" with backing provided by Chubby Checker, who first performed the dance-floor hit in 1960.

Billboard 200: *Coming Back Hard Again* (#33)
Billboard Hot 100: "The Twist" (#16); "Louie, Louie" (#89)

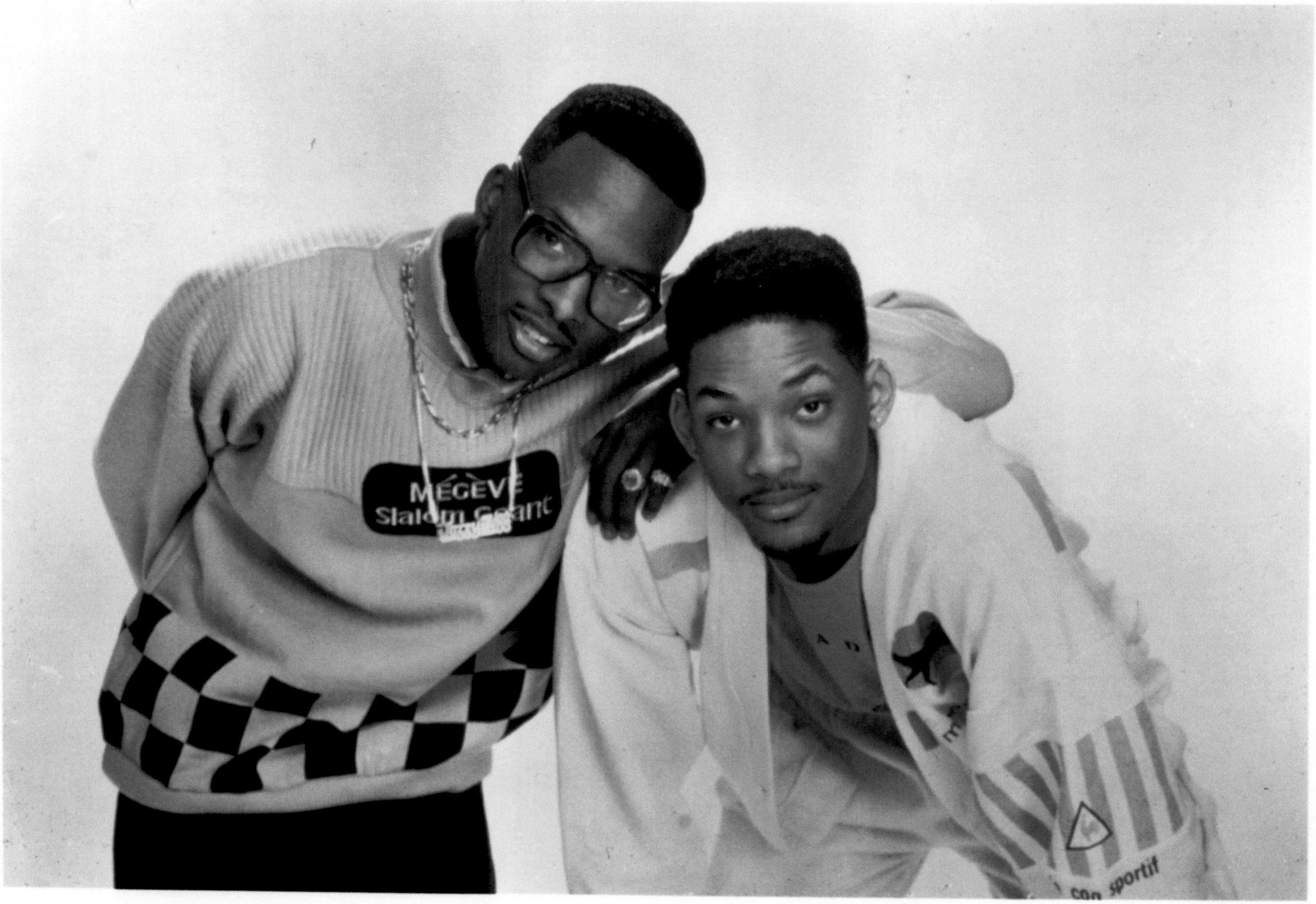

D.J. Jazzy Jeff & THE FRESH PRINCE

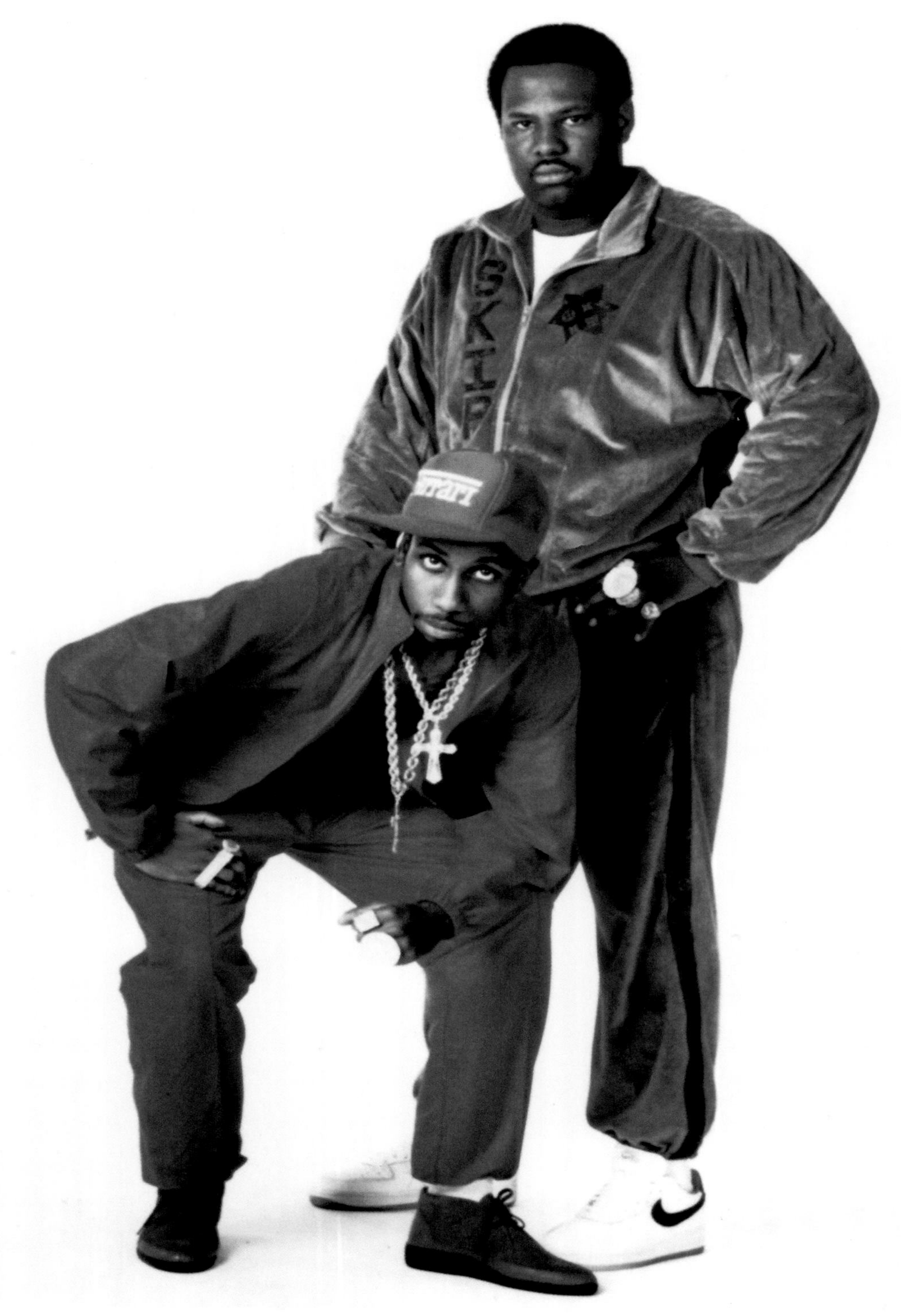

ROB BASE & D.J. E-Z ROCK

PROFILE RECORDS, INC

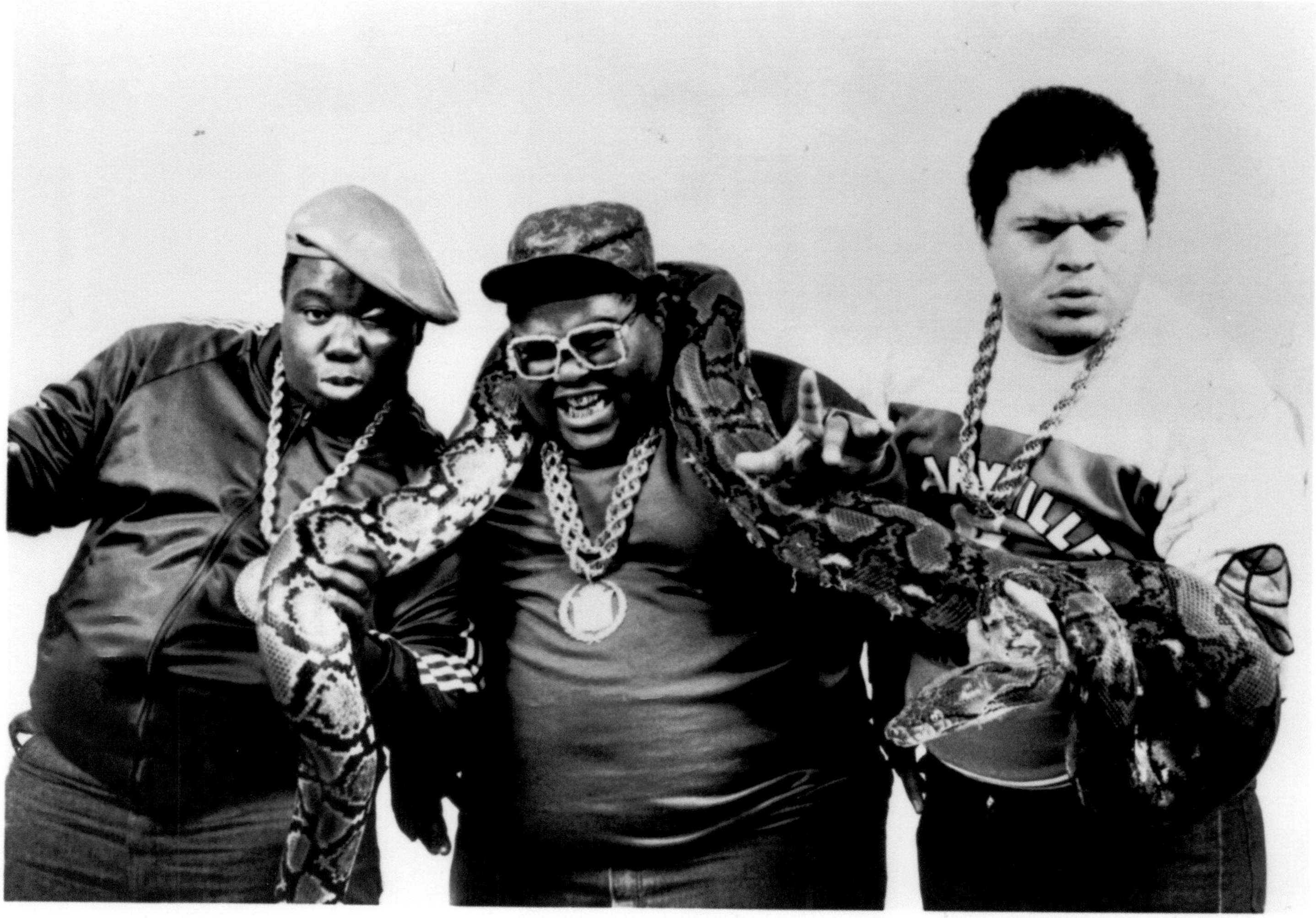

FAT BOYS

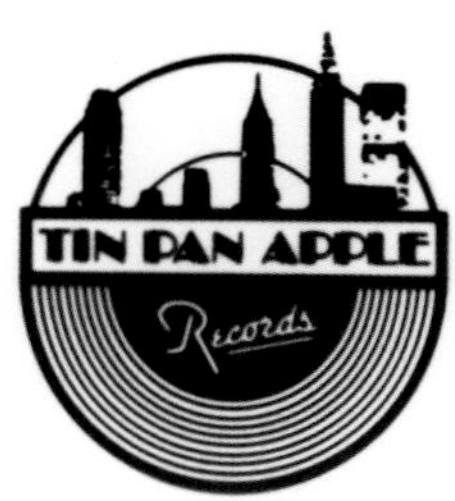

PolyGram Records

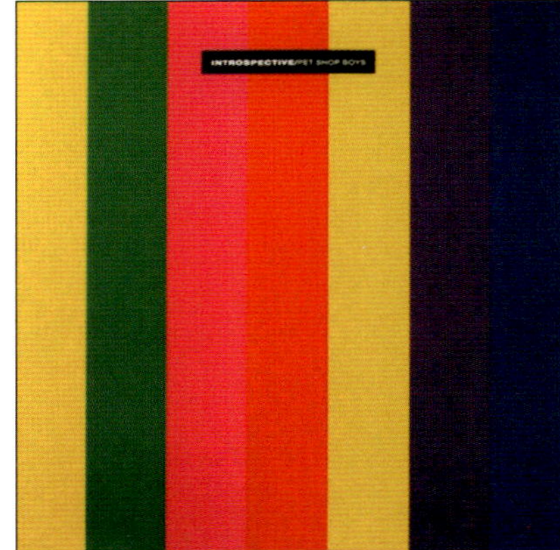

Pet Shop Boys' *Introspective* offered a synth-pop version of the timeless "Always on My Mind" and the orchestral pomp of "Left to My Own Devices."

Billboard 200: *Introspective* (#34)
Billboard Hot 100: "Always on My Mind" (#4):
"Domino Dancing" (#18); "Left to My Own Devices" (#84)

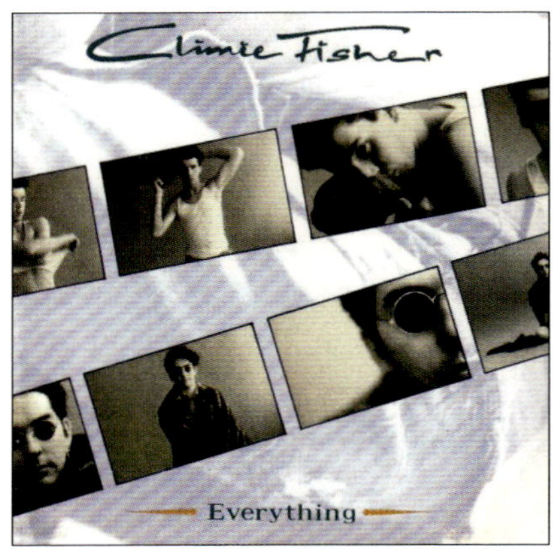

With a slight remix by Bob Clearmountain, the single "Love Changes (Everything)" brought the English pop duo Climie Fisher international chart success.

Billboard 200: *Everything* (#120)
Billboard Hot 100: "Love Changes (Everything)" (#23)

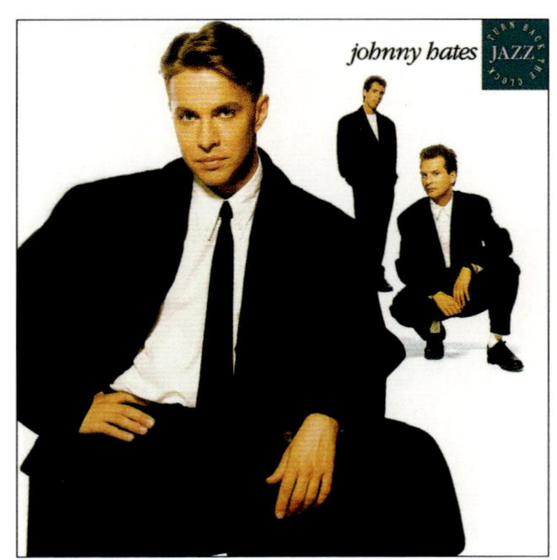

The natty British trio Johnny Hates Jazz, named after a friend who did despise jazz, burned up charts worldwide with the hit single "Shattered Dreams."

Billboard 200: *Turn Back the Clock* (#56)
Billboard Hot 100: "Shattered Dreams" (#2);
"I Don't Want to Be a Hero" (#31)

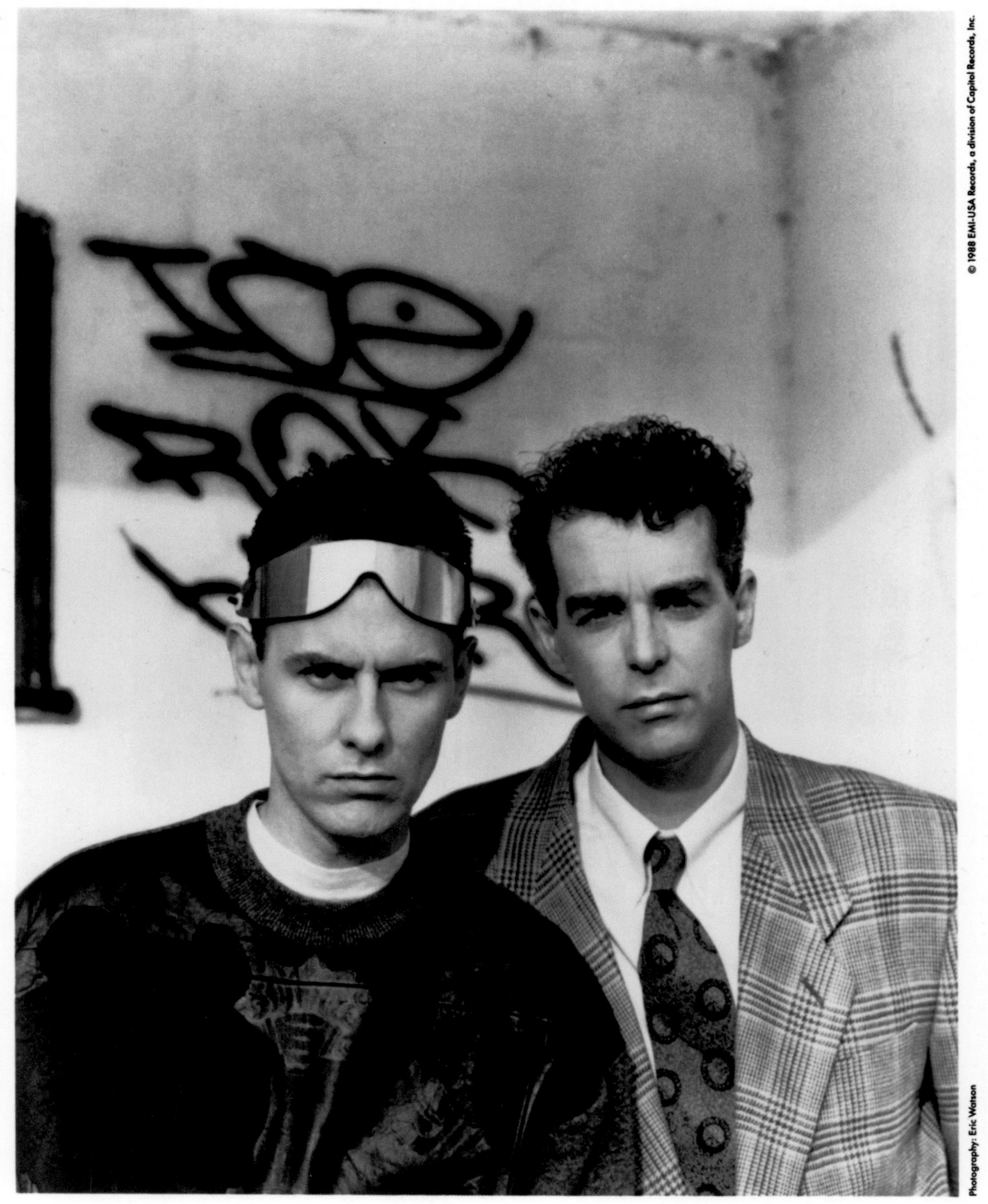

Photography: Eric Watson

PET SHOP BOYS

EMI®

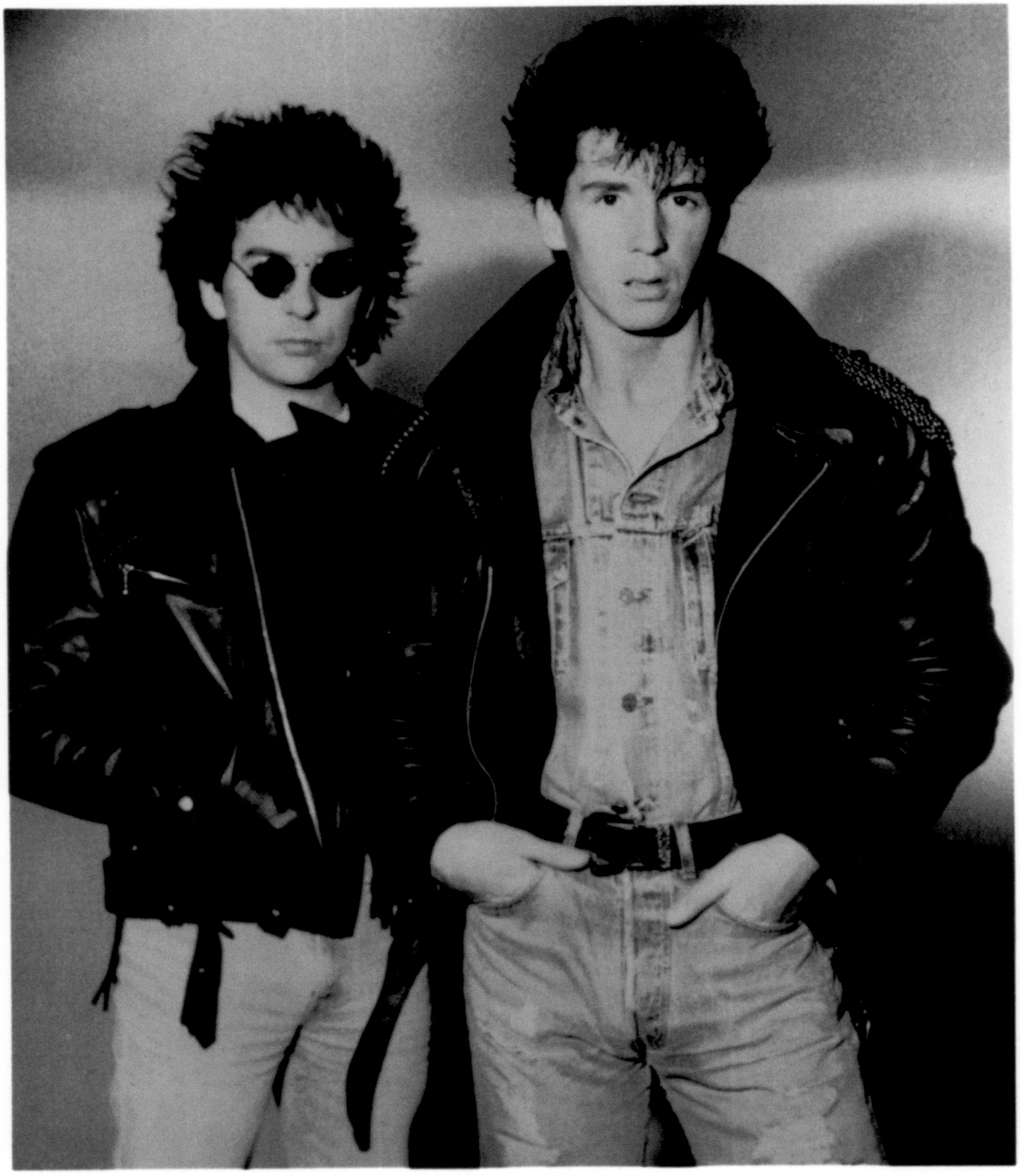

Photo: Paul Cox / 1988

Rob Fisher Simon Climie

Climie Fisher

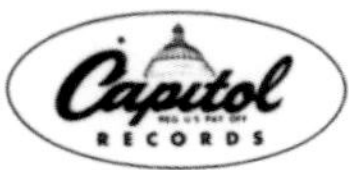

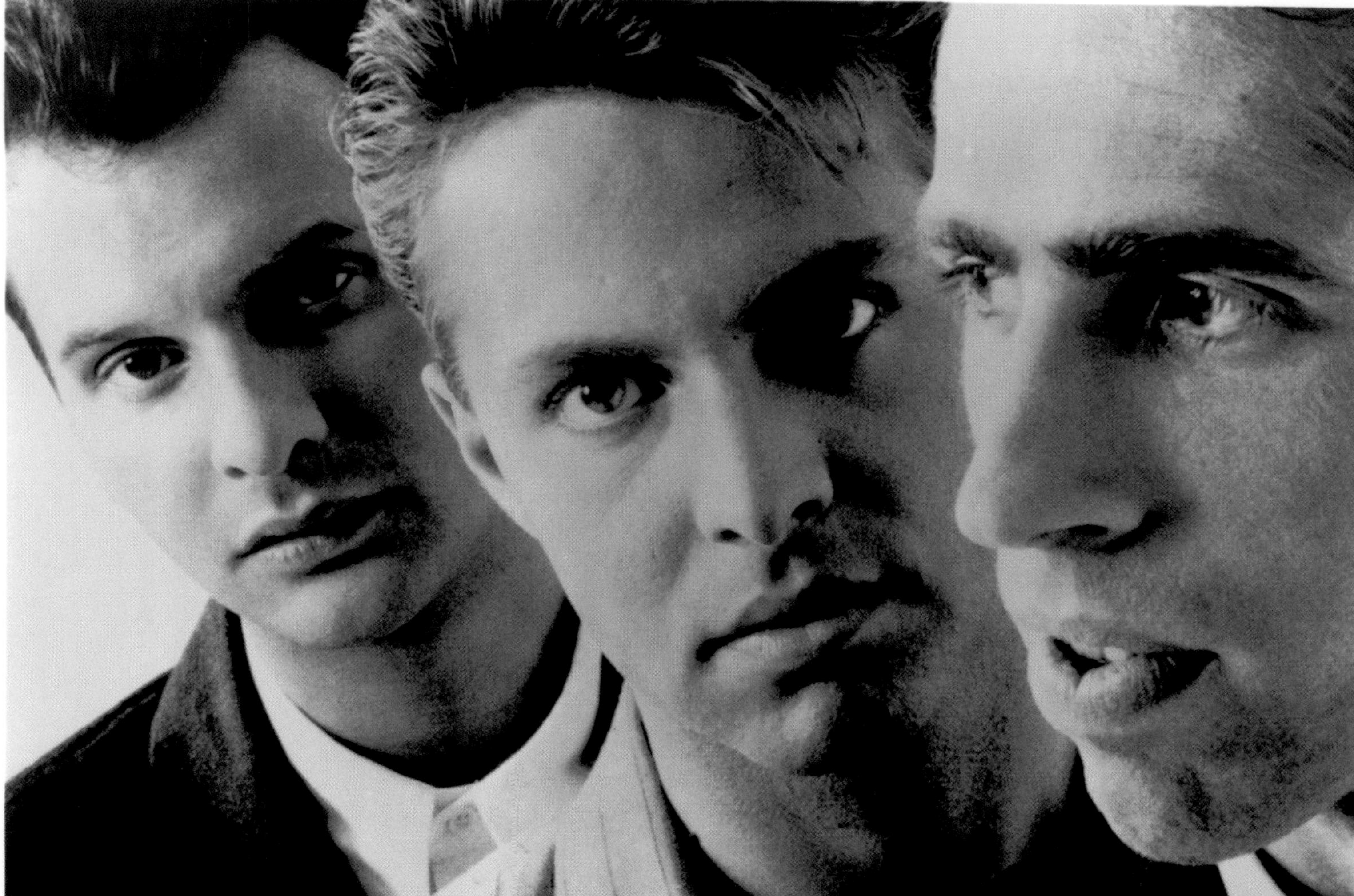

PHOTO : SIMON FOWLER

JOHNNY HATES JAZZ

Virgin

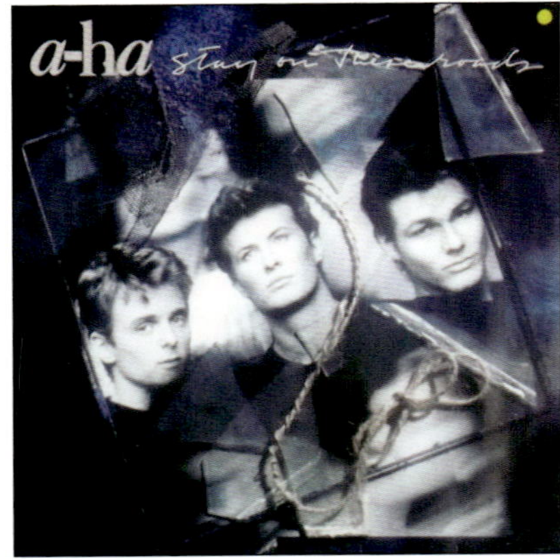

Thanks to the title song, a significant hit for Norway's **a-ha** in numerous European countries, *Stay on These Roads* sold over 4 million copies worldwide.

Billboard 200: *Stay on These Roads* (#148)

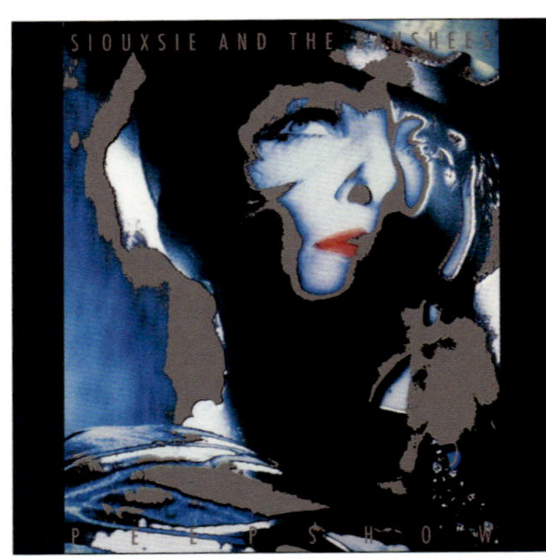

English post-punk band **Siouxsie & the Banshees** made a commercial breakthrough in the US with *Peepshow* and the modern-rock single "Peek-a-Boo."

Billboard 200: *Peepshow* (#68)
Billboard Hot 100: "Peek-a-Boo" (#53)

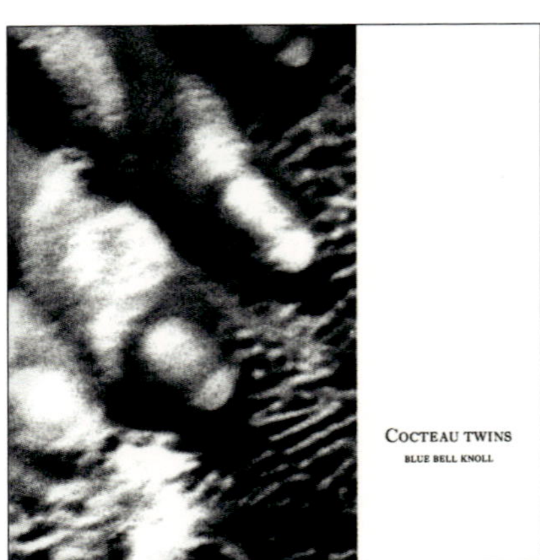

Finally signing a major label contract in the US, the UK trio **Cocteau Twins** released *Blue Bell Knoll* and a standout track, the lush "Carolyn's Fingers."

Billboard 200: *Blue Bell Knoll* (#109)

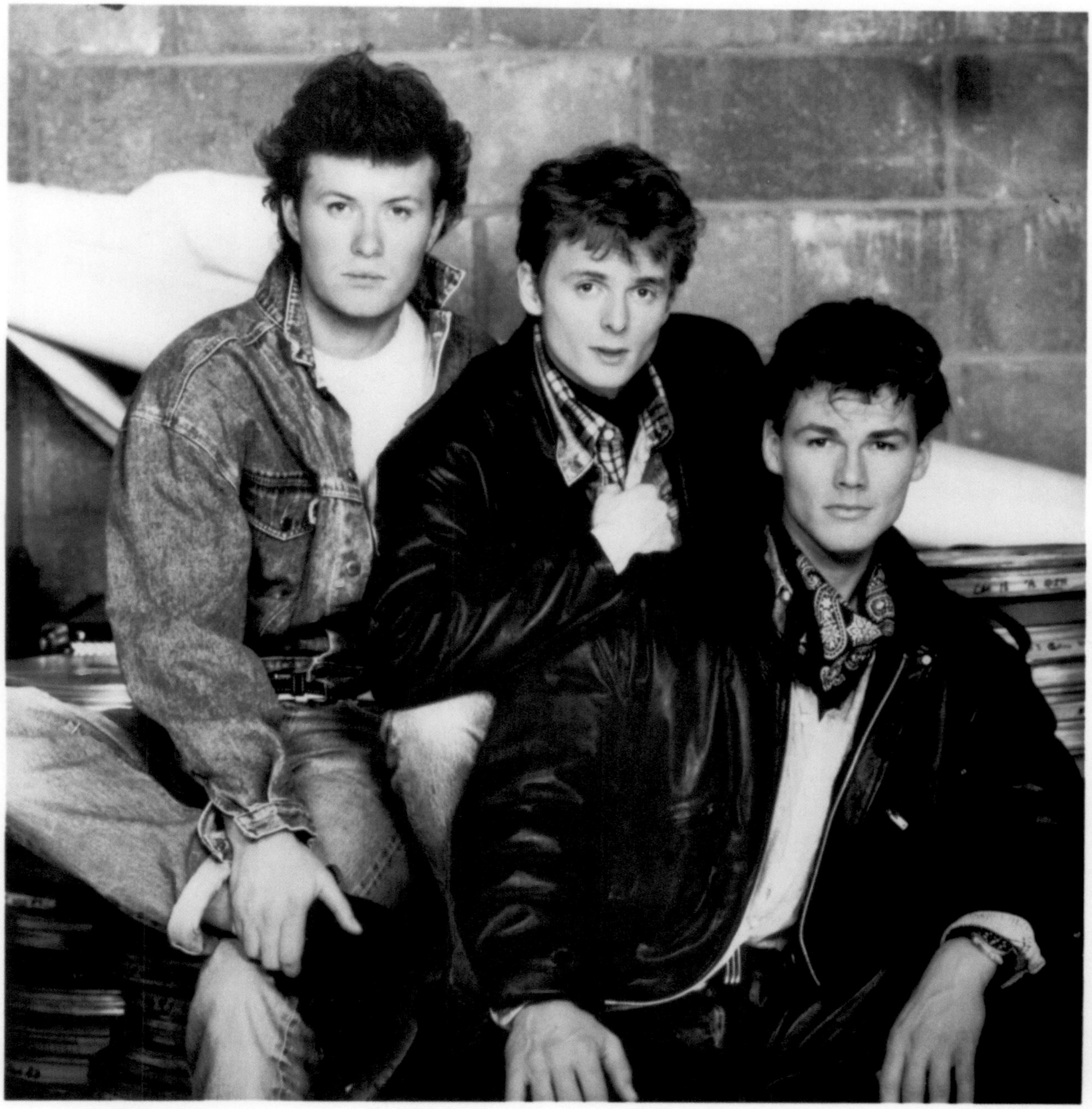

Photo Credit: John Paul

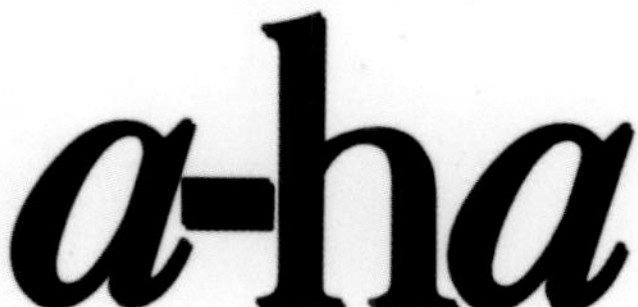

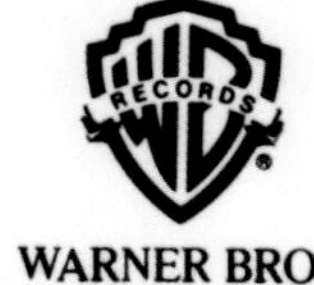

WARNER BROS.

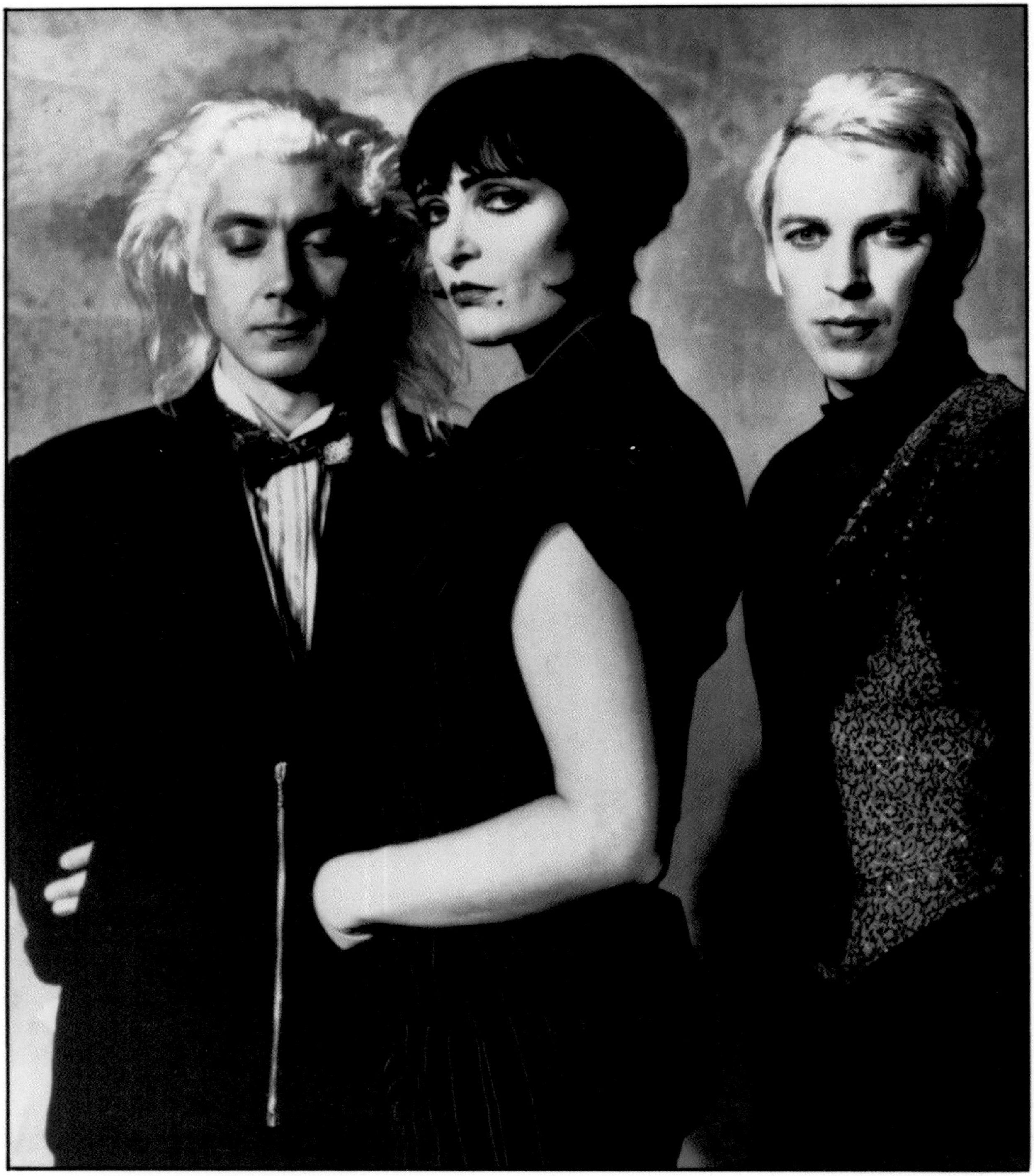

Photo Credit: John Stoddart

SIOUXSIE AND THE BANSHEES

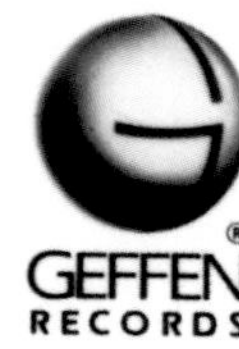

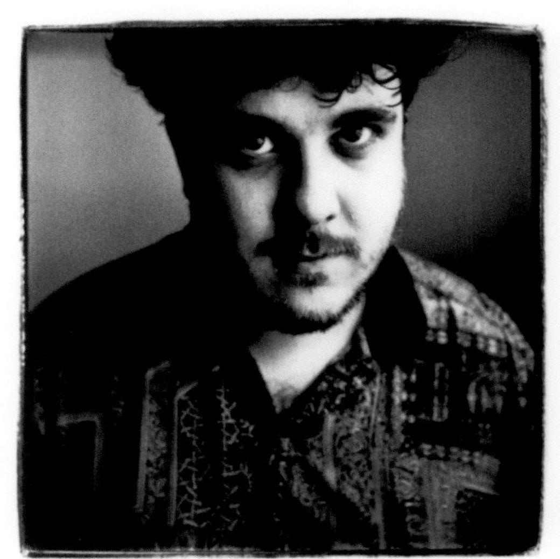

ROBIN GUTHRIE

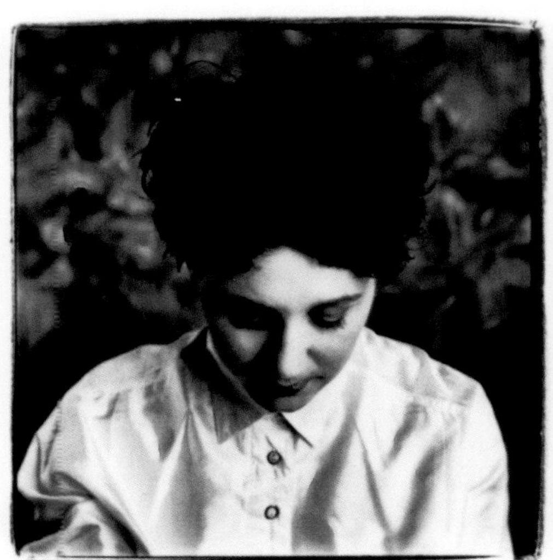

ELIZABETH FRASER

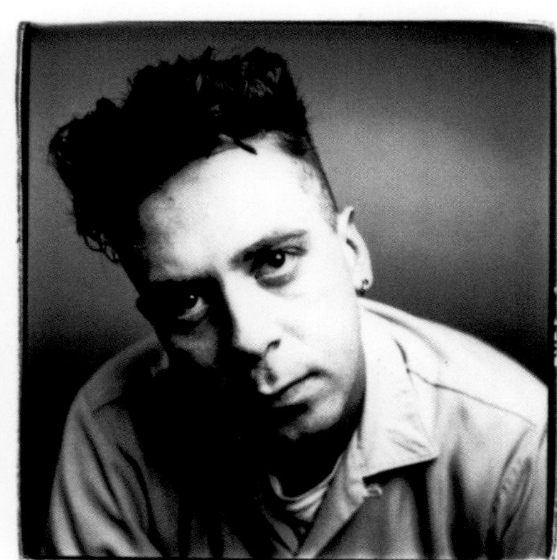

SIMON RAYMONDE

PHOTOCREDIT:STEVE PYKE

COCTEAU TWINS

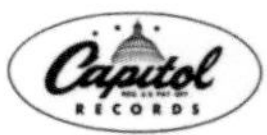

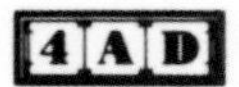

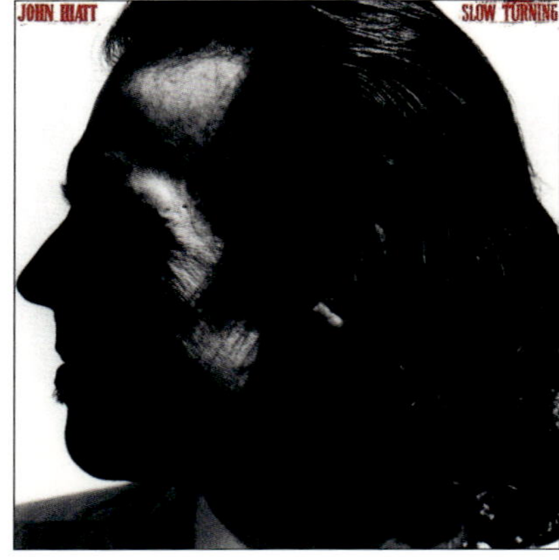

The prolific John Hiatt provided keen observations of adulthood on *Slow Turning*, a collection of impassioned paeans to shaping up and settling down.

Billboard 200: *Slow Turning* (#98)

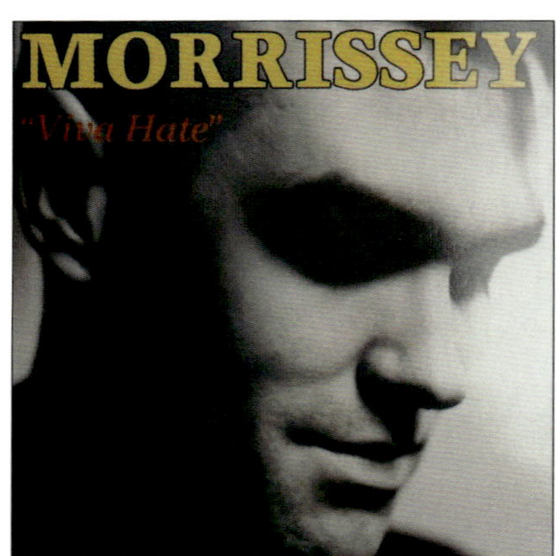

After the dissolution of the Smiths, iconoclastic singer Morrissey launched his solo career with the UK hits "Suedehead" and "Everyday Is Like Sunday."

Billboard 200: *Viva Hate* (#48)

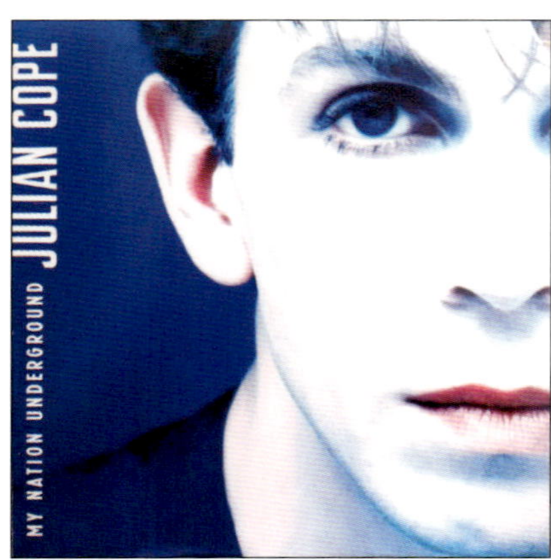

One of pop music's legendary eccentrics since his days in The Teardrop Explodes, Julian Cope emerged with "Charlotte Anne," a No. 1 modern-rock track.

Billboard 200: *My Nation Underground* (#155)

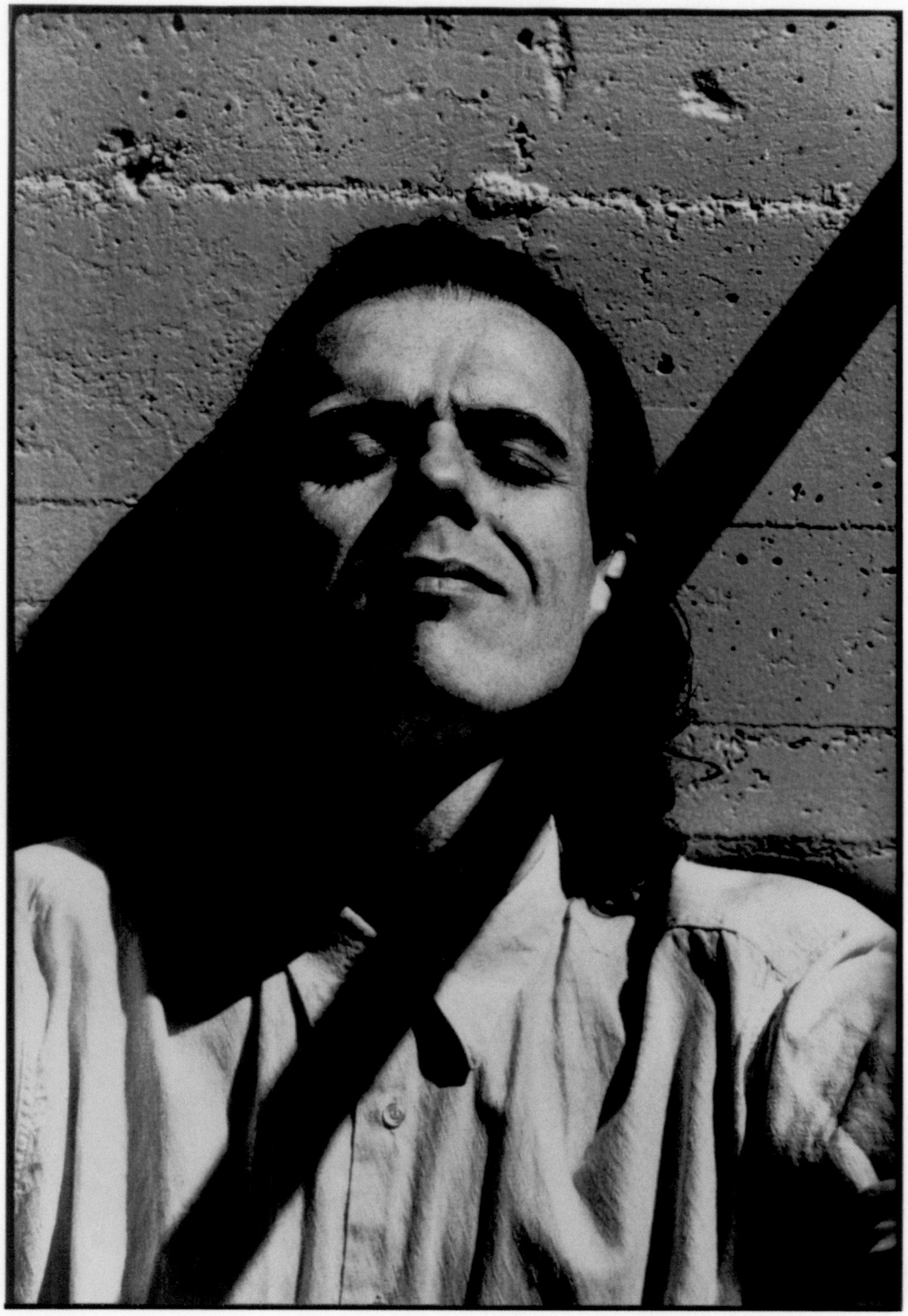

JOHN HIATT

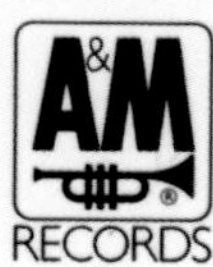

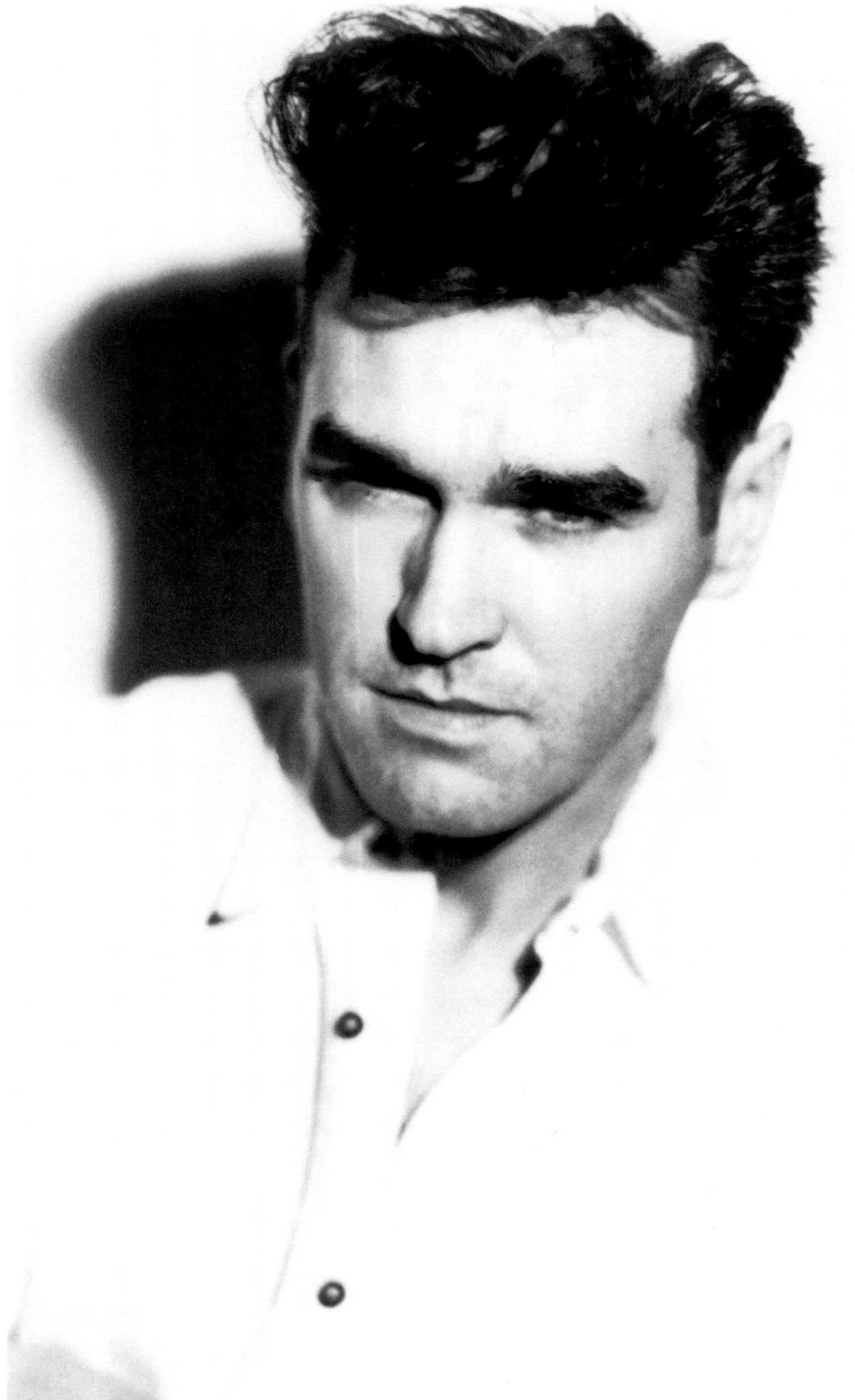

Photo Credit: Eamonn J. McCabe

MORRISSEY

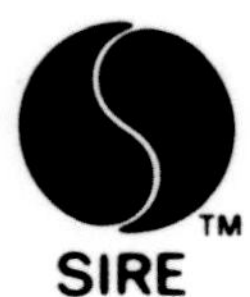

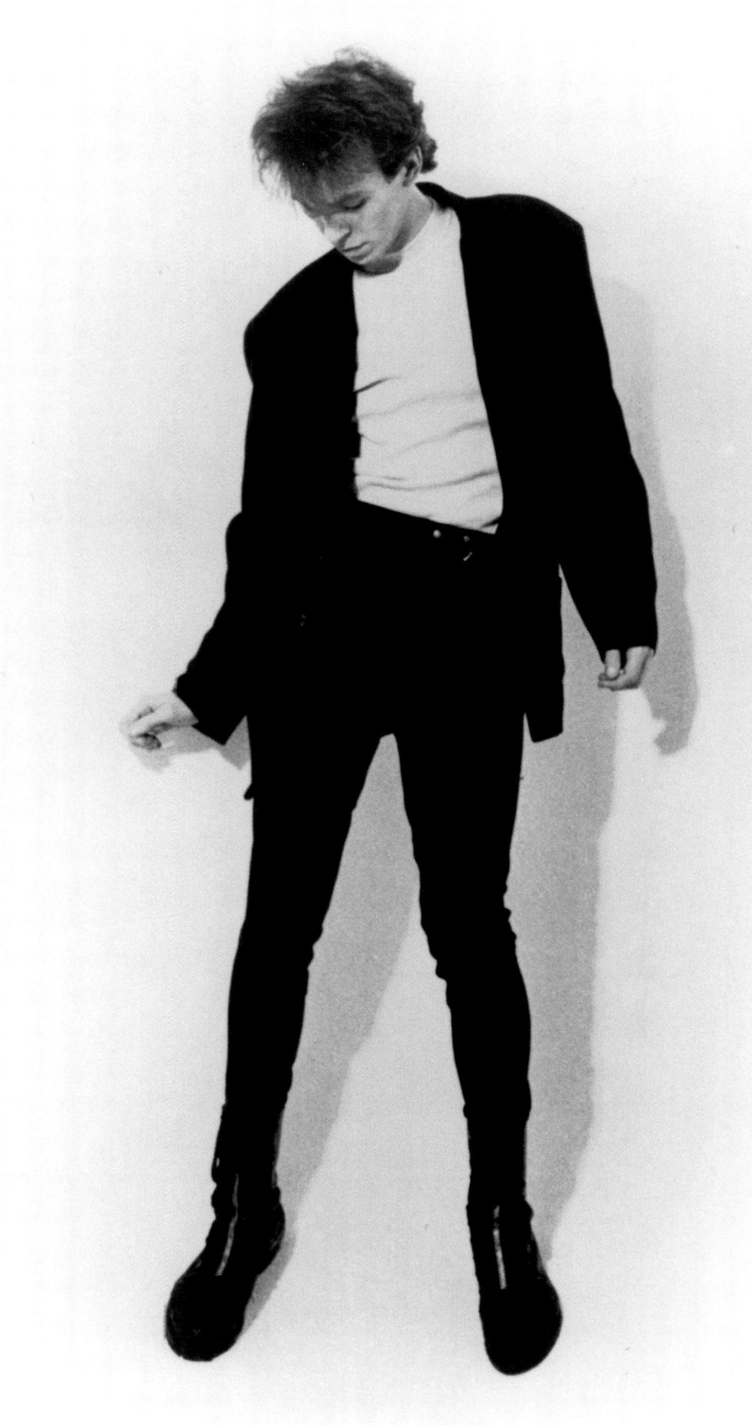

JULIAN COPE

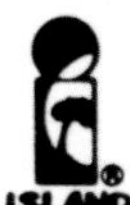

A lilting cover of Cat Stevens' "Wild World" established **Maxi Priest** as England's top reggae singer and accorded him his first charting American hit.

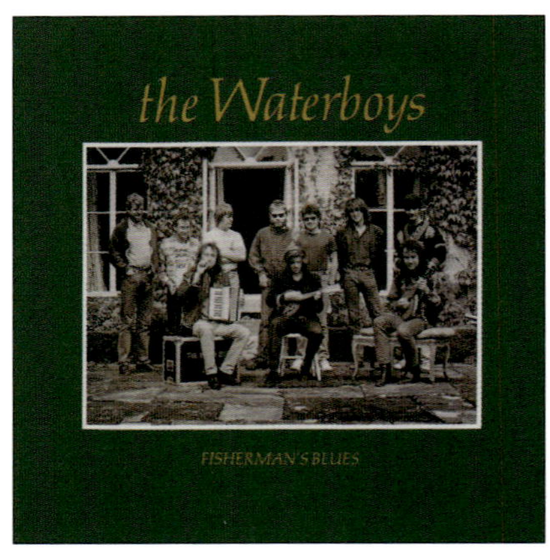

The Waterboys, fronted by Mike Scott, embraced traditional Irish music influences and reached #3 on the modern rock charts with "Fisherman's Blues."

Billboard 200: *Fisherman's Blues* (#76)

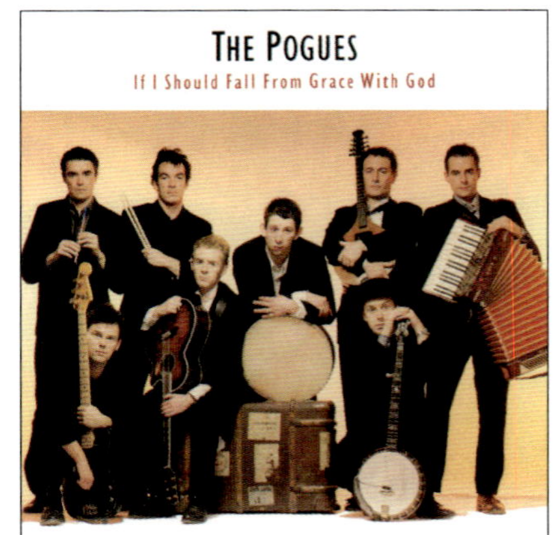

The Pogues, a politically charged Celtic folk-punk band led by Shane MacGowan, famously peaked with the Christmas-themed "Fairytale of New York."

Billboard 200: *If I Should Fall from Grace with God* (#88)

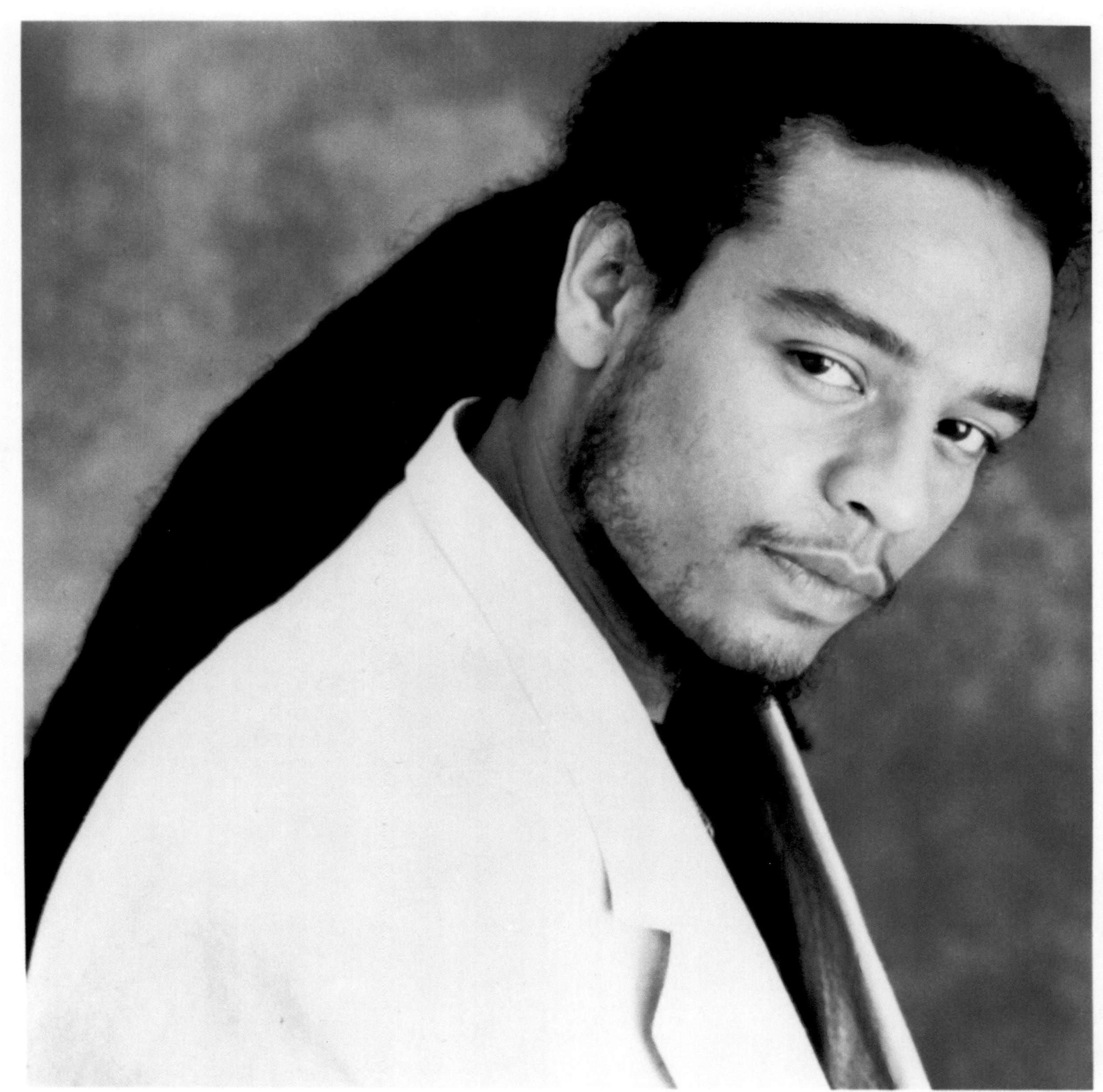

Photo Credit: Sheila Rock

MAXI PRIEST

Virgin

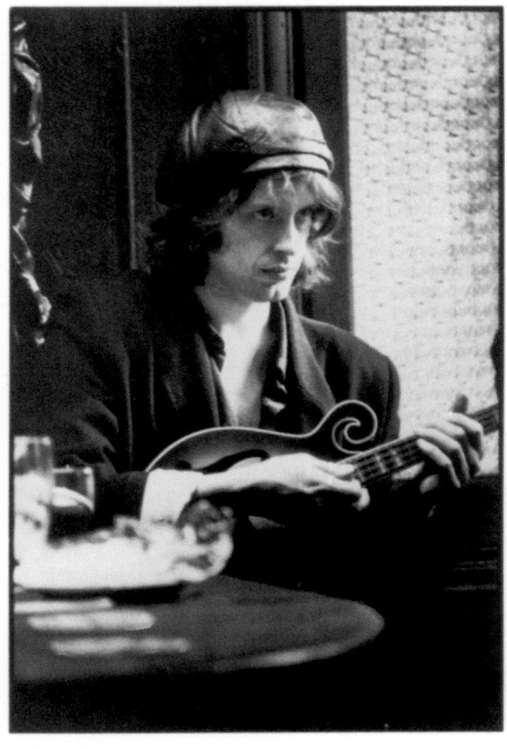

Mike Scott

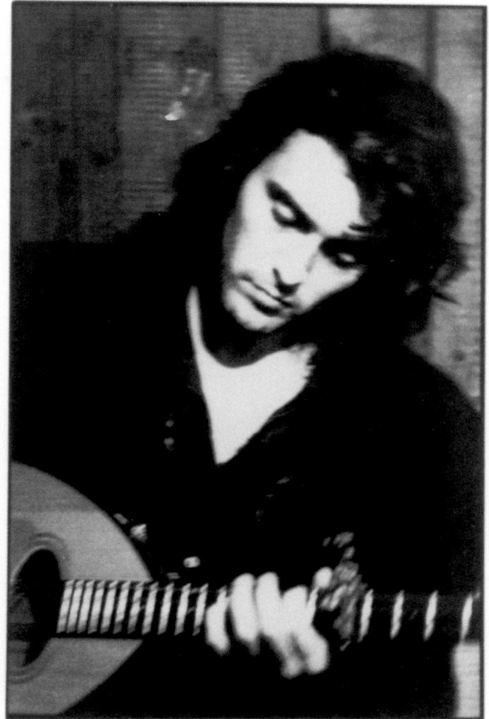

Trevor Hutchinson

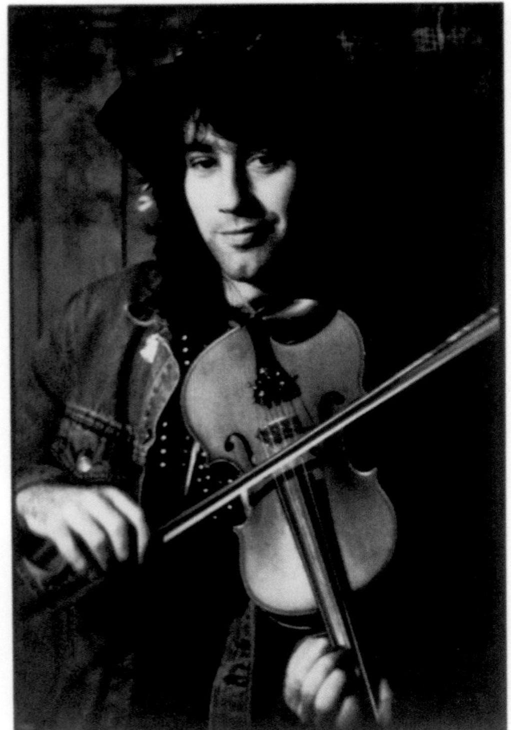

Steve Wickham

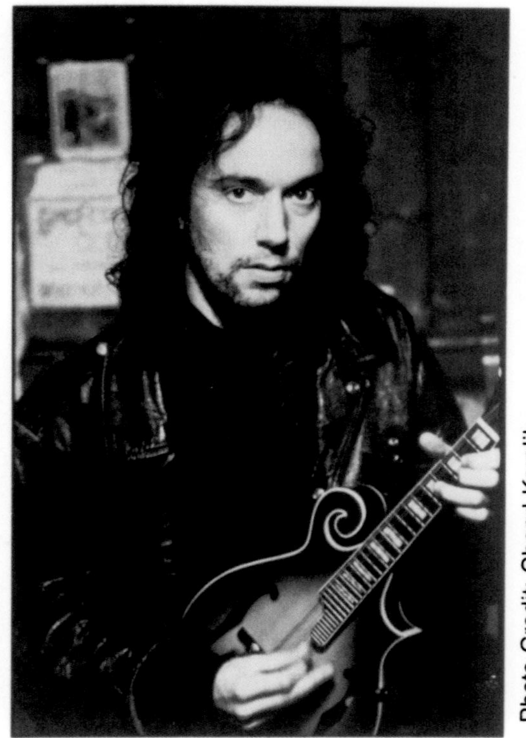

Anto Thistlethwaite

Photo Credit: Cheryl Koralik

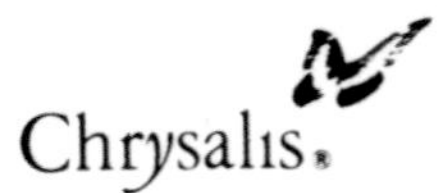

the Waterboys

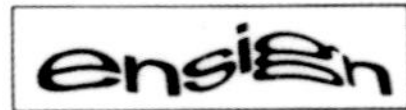

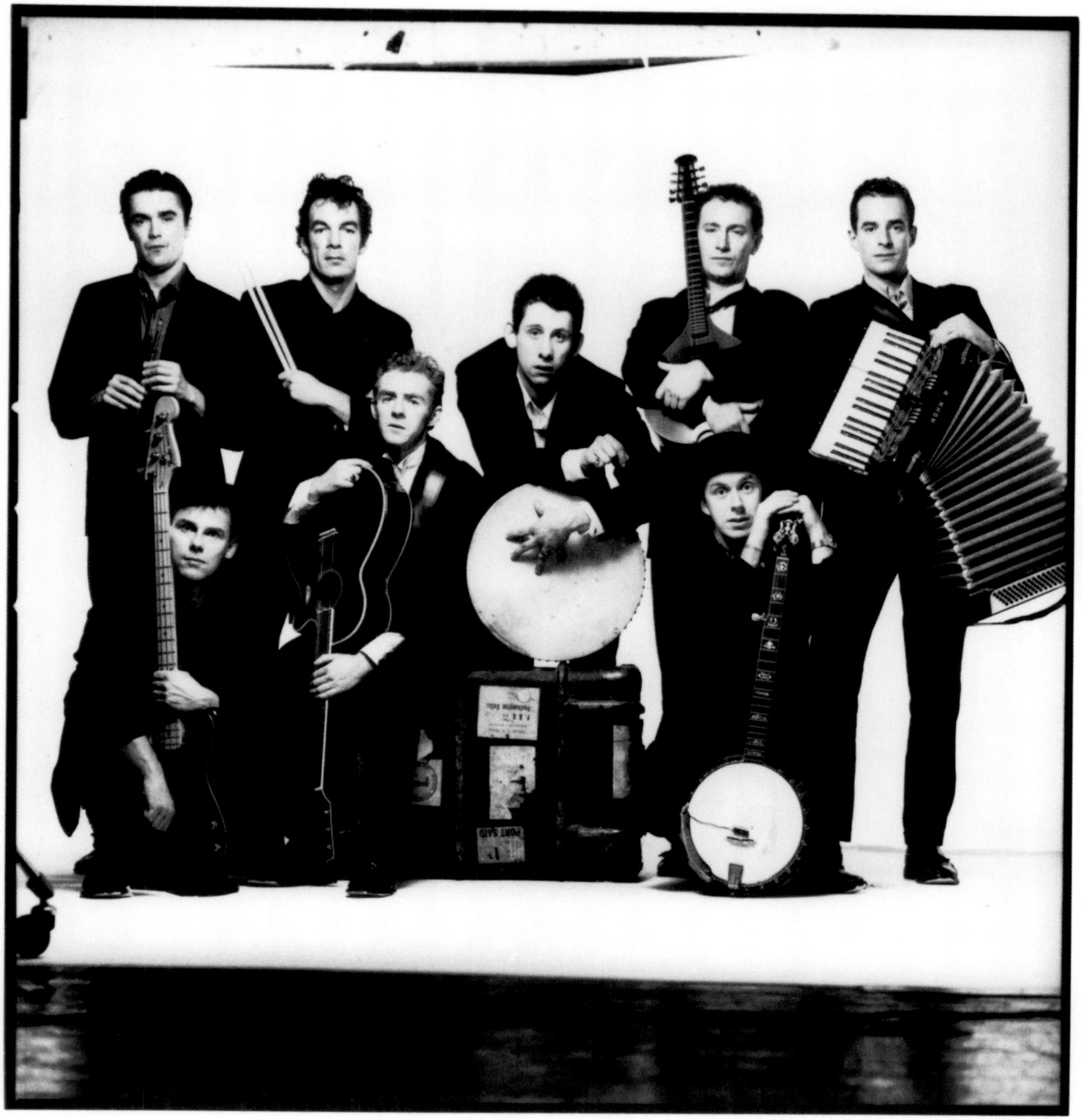

The Pogues

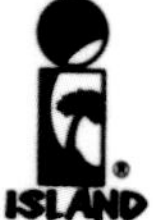

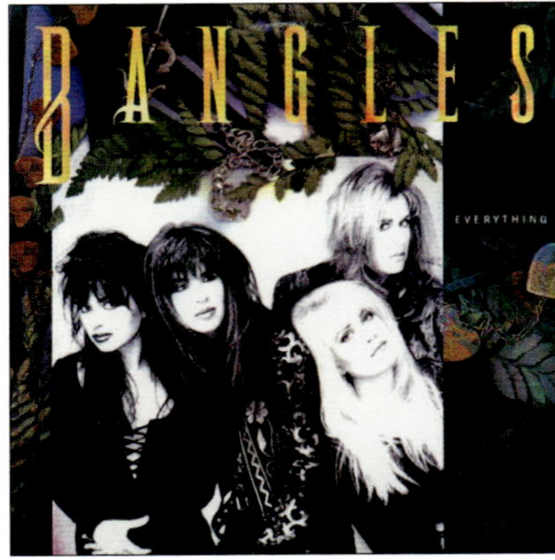

The Bangles' *Everything* included "Eternal Flame," a glossy ballad co-written by member Susanna Hoffs and the group's biggest hit around the world.

Billboard 200: *Everything* (#15)
Billboard Hot 100: "In Your Room" (#5);
"Eternal Flame" (No. 1); "Be with You" (#30)

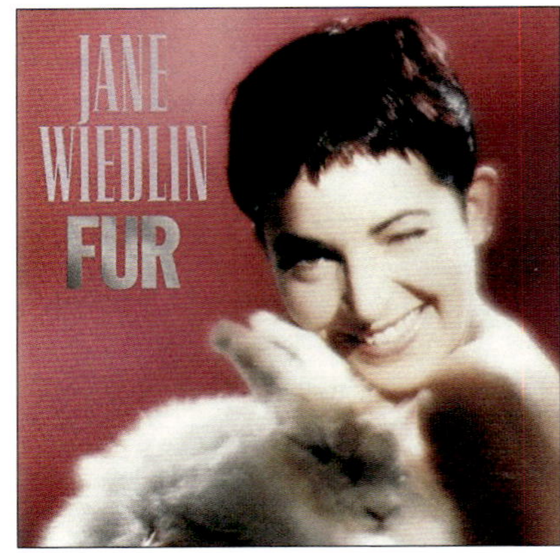

Pursuing a solo career after exiting the Go-Go's, **Jane Wiedlin** climbed the US and UK charts with "Rush Hour," a glittering synth-pop track from *Fur*.

Billboard 200: *Fur* (#105)
Billboard Hot 100: "Rush Hour" (#9); "Inside a Dream" (#57)

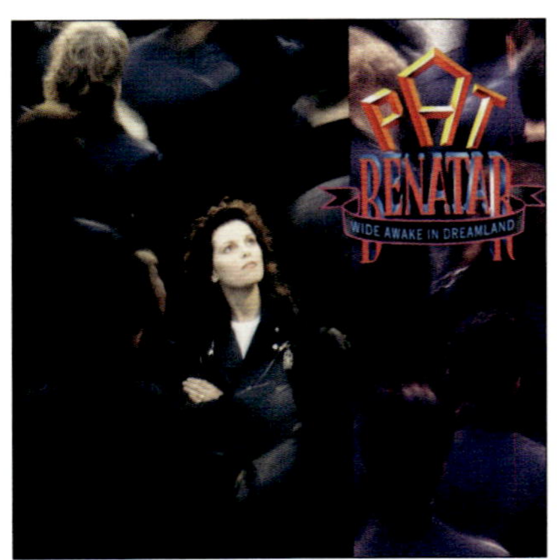

Rock singer **Pat Benatar** offered the melodic *Wide Awake in Dreamland*, her eighth album, and another Grammy-nominated Top 40 single, "All Fired Up."

Billboard 200: *Wide Awake in Dreamland* (#28)
Billboard Hot 100: "All Fired Up" (#19)

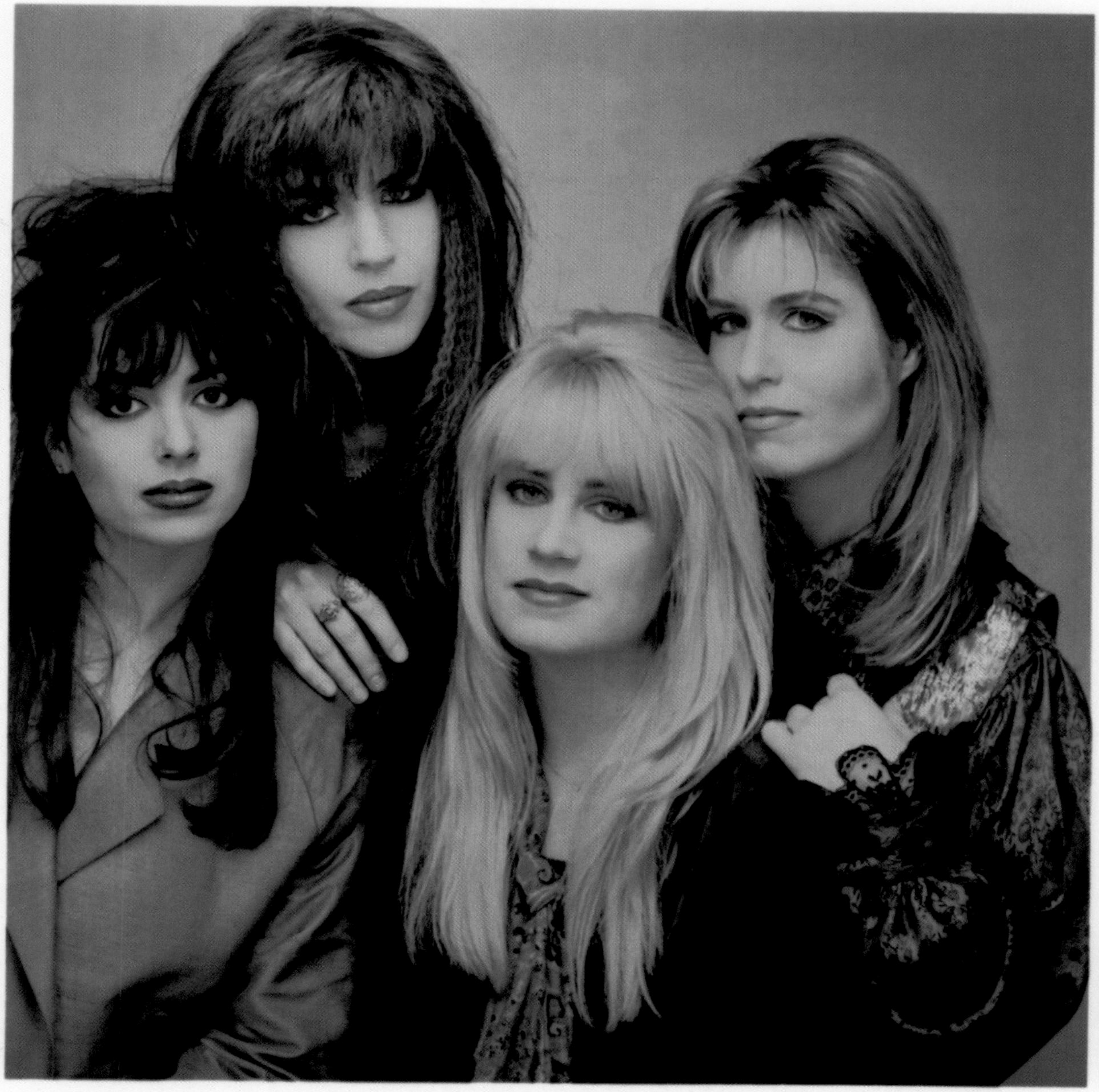

Susanna Hoffs Michael Steele Debbi Peterson Vicki Peterson

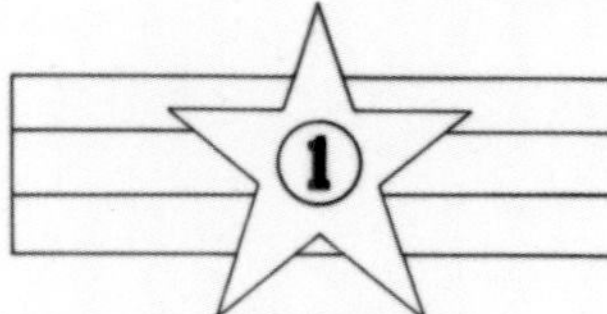

BANGLES

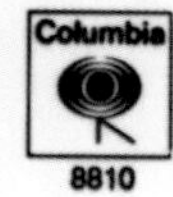

PHOTO: SHEILA ROCK

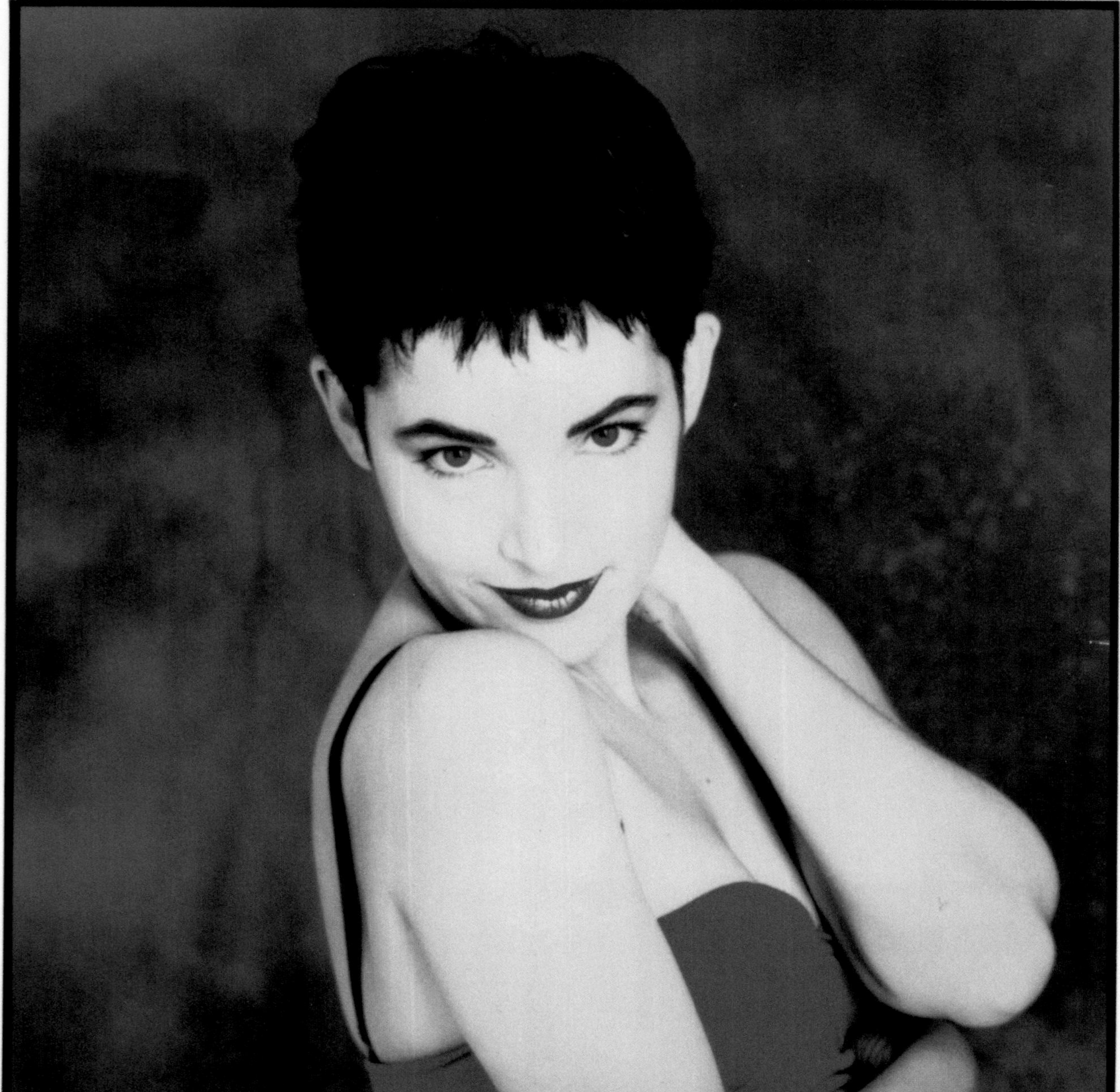

Photography: Mike Owens

JANE WIEDLIN

EMI MANHATTAN®

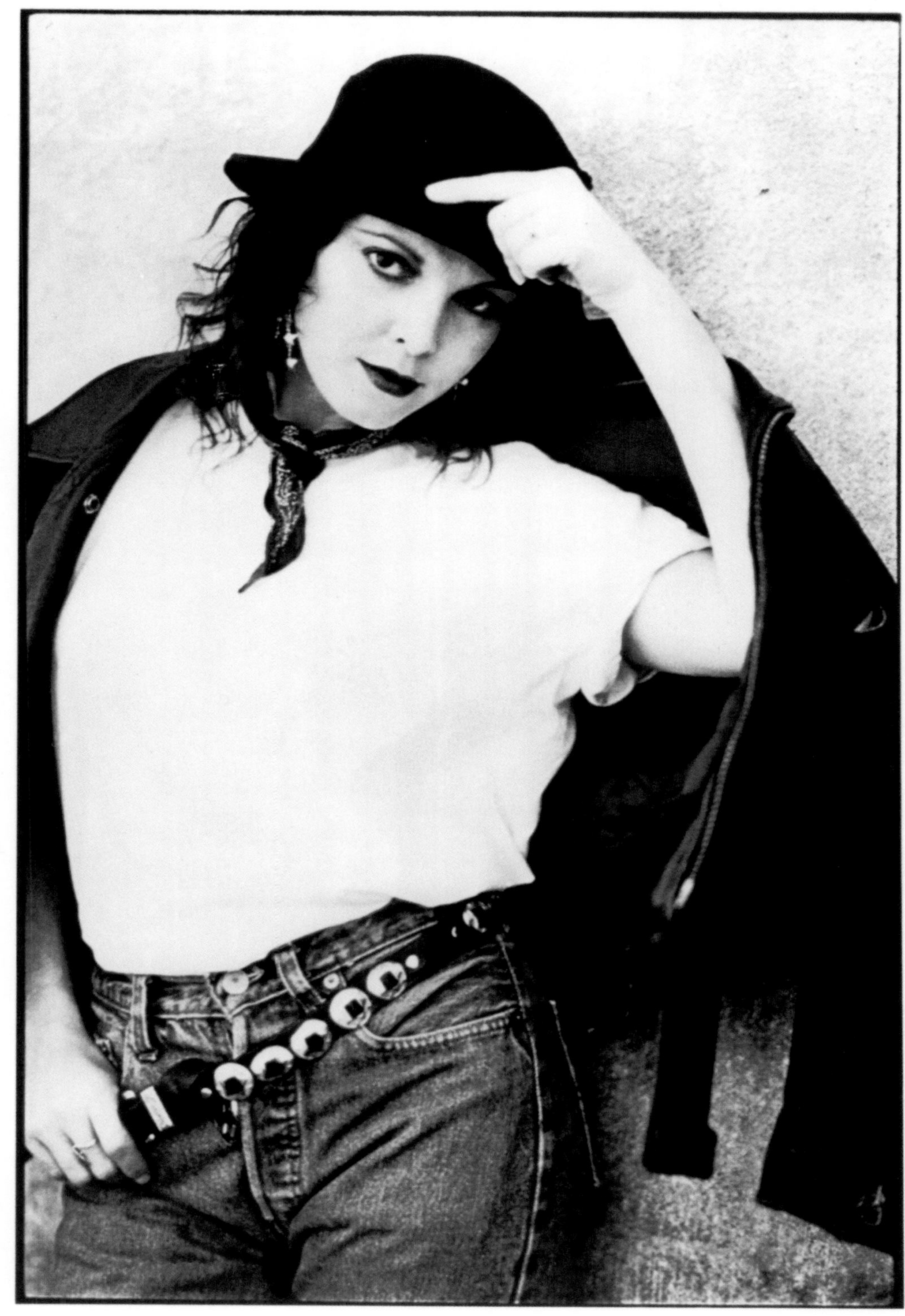

Photo Credit: Moshe Brakha

PAT BENATAR

Chrysalis®

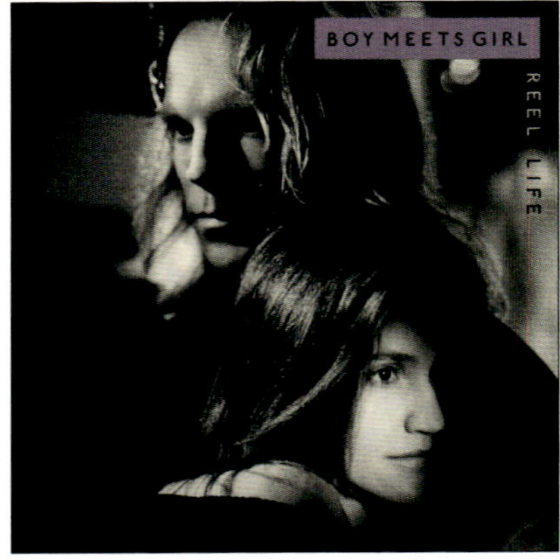

After years of writing for Whitney Houston and other acts, the duo **Boy Meets Girl** earned global success with the hit single "Waiting for a Star to Fall."

Billboard 200: *Reel Life* (#50)
Billboard Hot 100: "Waiting for a Star to Fall" (#5); "Bring Down the Moon" (#49)

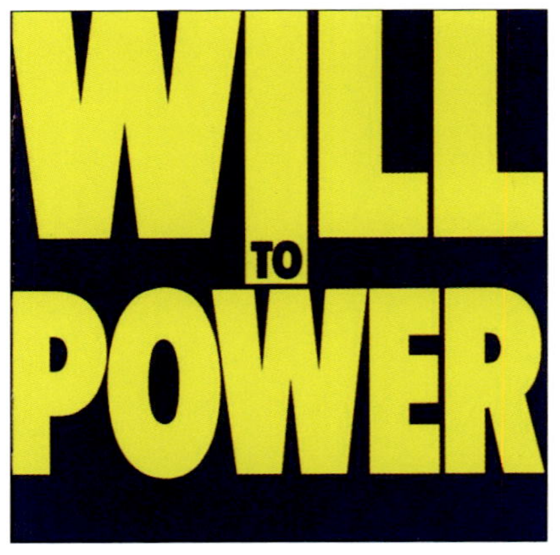

Will to Power reached No. 1 with "Baby I Love Your Way/Freebird Medley," a pop hybrid of Peter Frampton and Lynyrd Skynyrd hits from the Seventies.

Billboard 200: *Will to Power* (#68)
Billboard Hot 100: "Dreamin'" (#50); "Say It's Gonna Rain" (#49); "Baby I Love Your Way/Freebird Medley" (No. 1); "Fading Away" (#65)

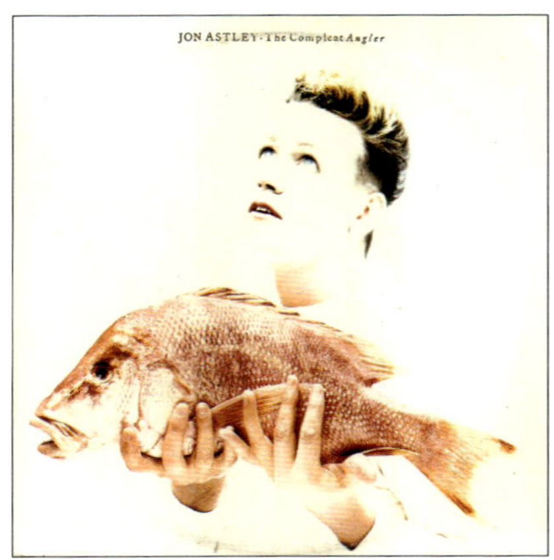

English producer **Jon Astley** delivered his second album as a singer-songwriter, and the "Put This Love to the Test" scaled the modern rock charts.

Billboard Hot 100: "Put This Love to the Test" (#74)

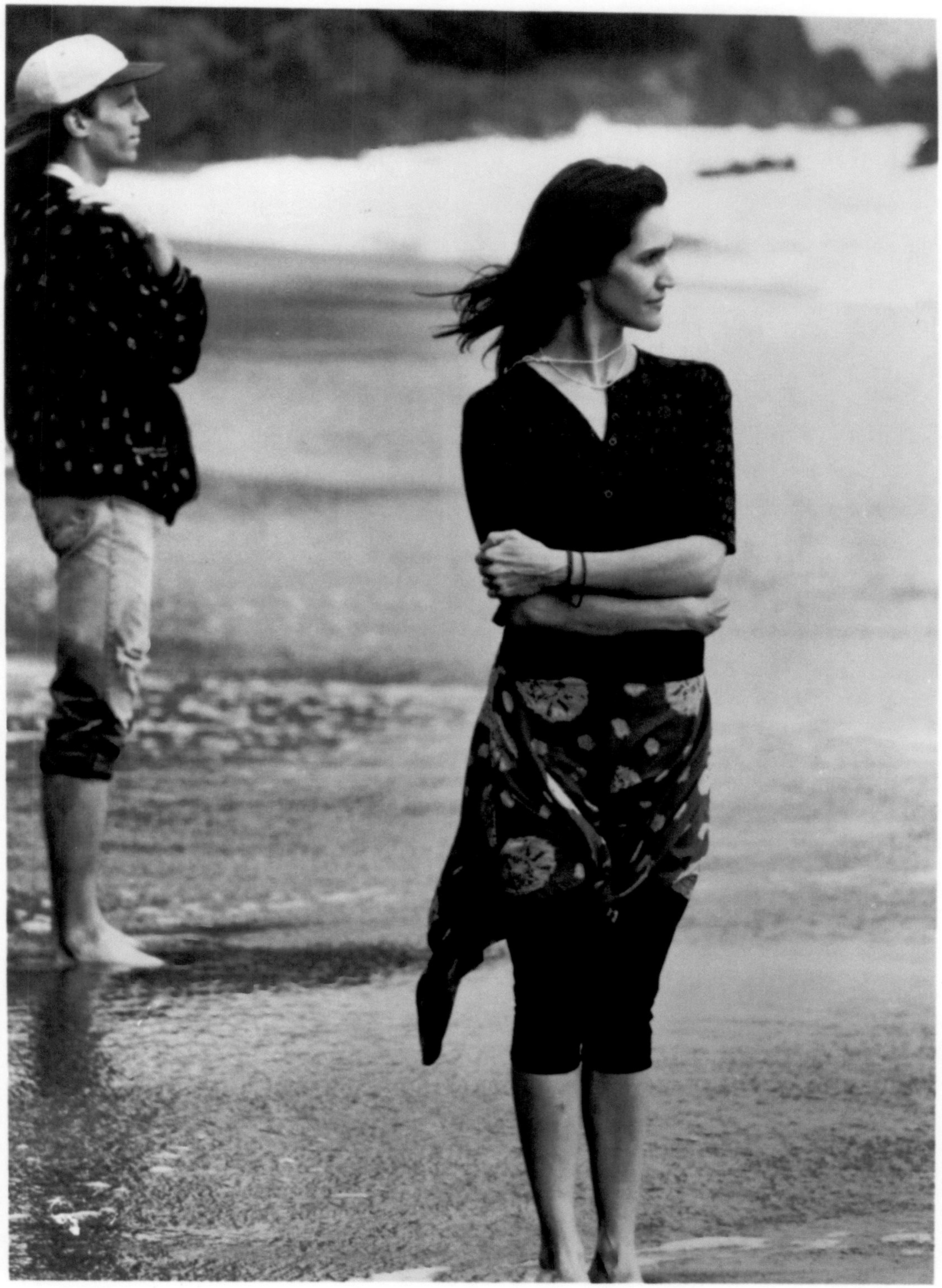

BOY MEETS GIRL

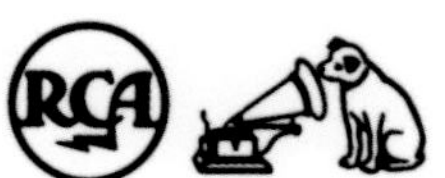

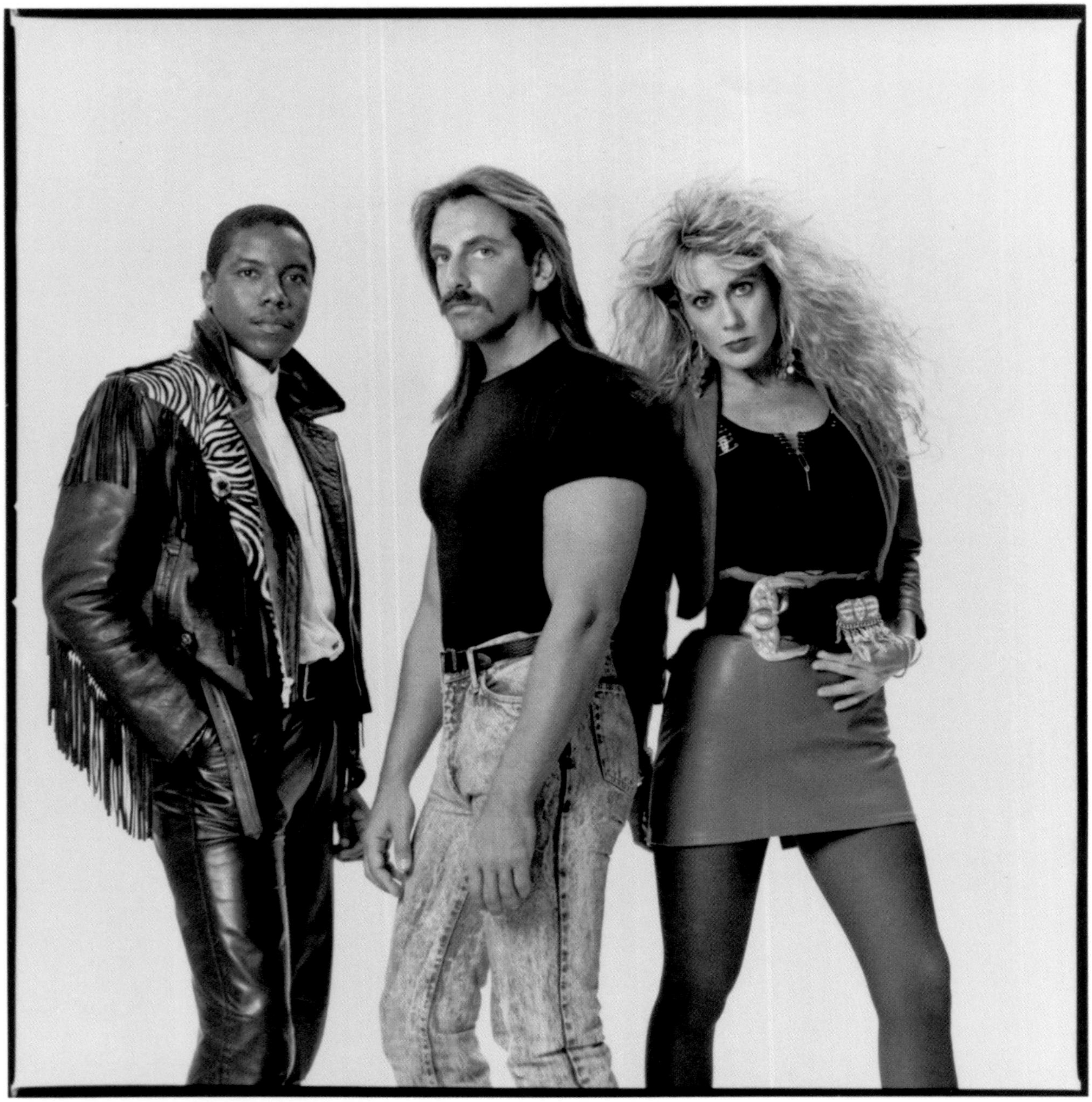

DR. J | BOB ROSENBERG | SUZI CARR

WILL TO POWER

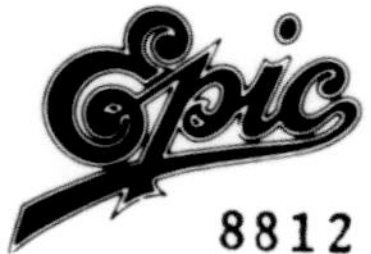

8812

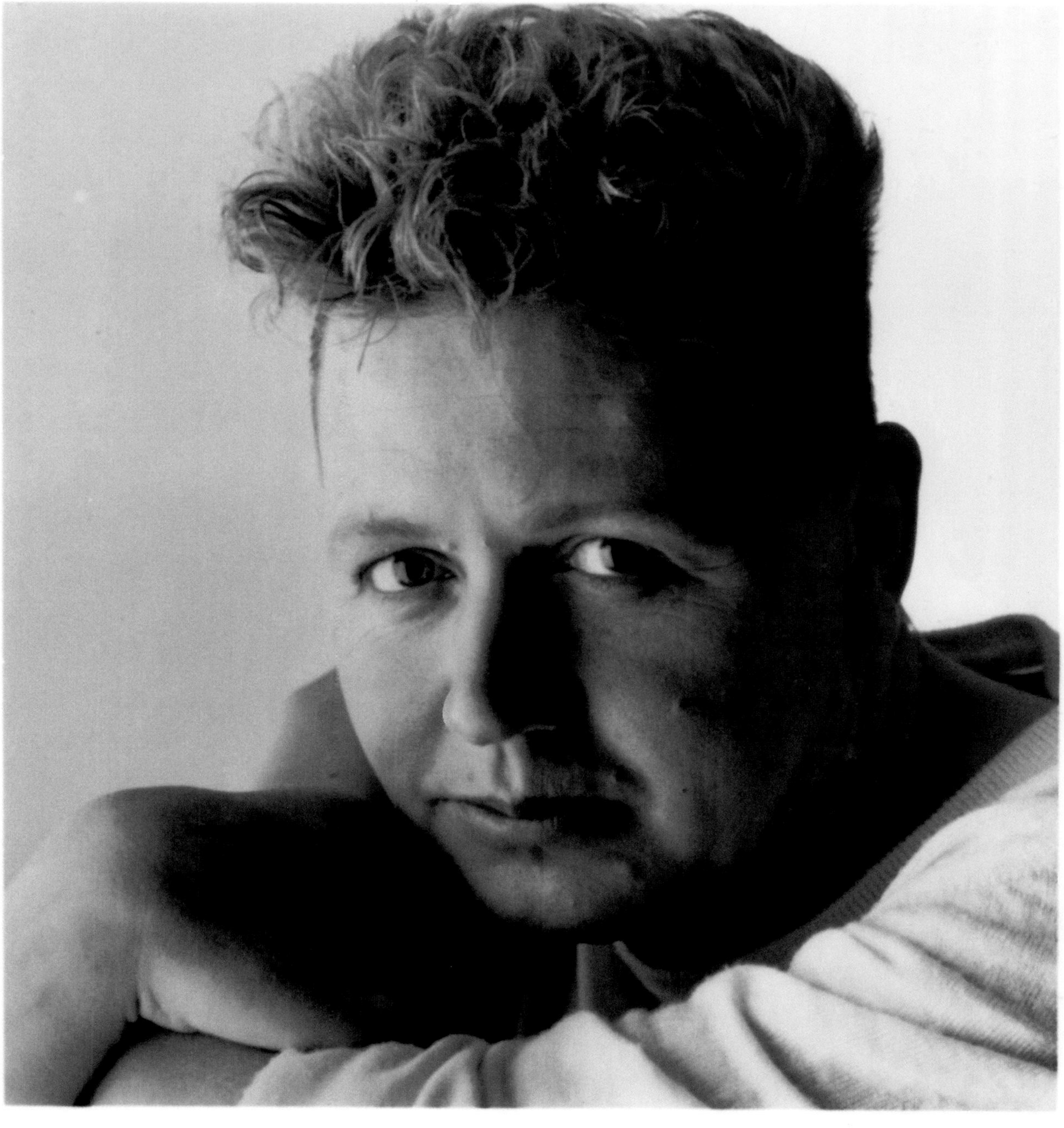

JON ASTLEY

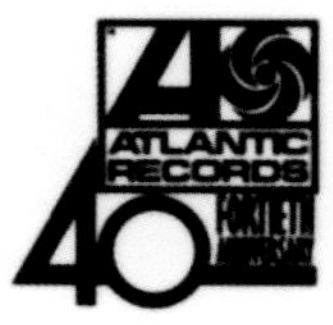

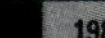

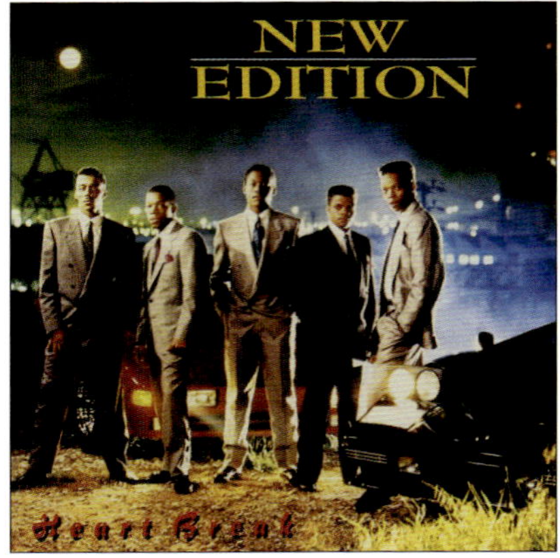

Evolving from a teen-pop group, **New Edition** introduced a more adult sound on *Heart Break* and claimed a No. 1 R&B hit, "Can You Stand the Rain."

Billboard 200: *Heart Break* (#12)
Billboard Hot 100: "If It Isn't Love" (#7); "You're Not My Kind of Girl" (#95); "Can You Stand the Rain" (#44)

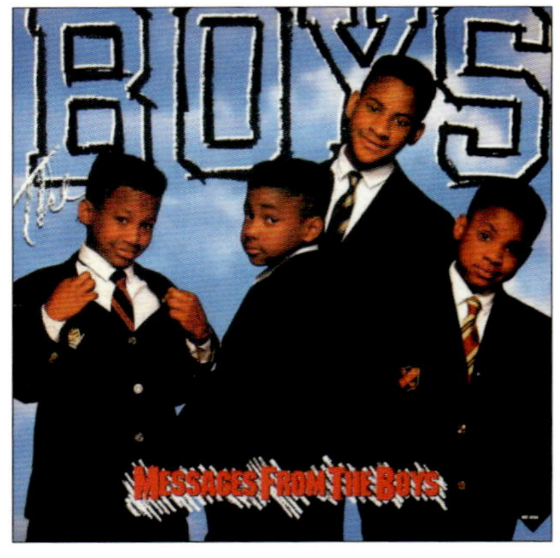

The Boys, composed of the four Abdulsamad brothers, showcased "Dial My Heart" and "Lucky Charm" on their debut album *Messages from the Boys*.

Billboard 200: *Messages from the Boys* (#32)
Billboard Hot 100: "Dial My Heart" (#5)

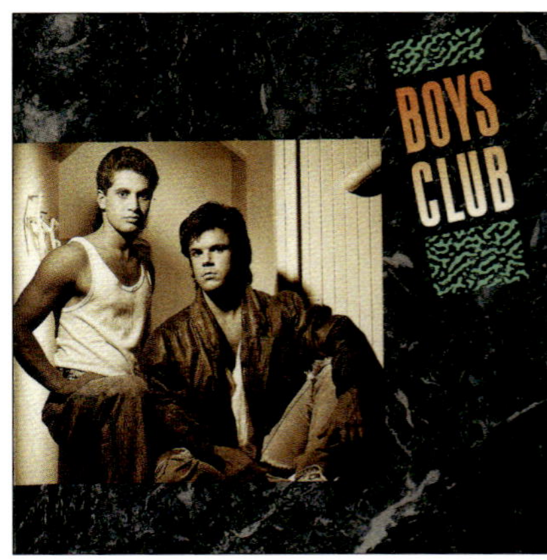

A partnership of Gene Hunt, formerly with the Jets, and Joe Pasquale, **Boys Club** secured a big pop hit with the yearning "I Remember Holding You."

Billboard 200: *Boys Club* (#93)
Billboard Hot 100: "I Remember Holding You" (#8)

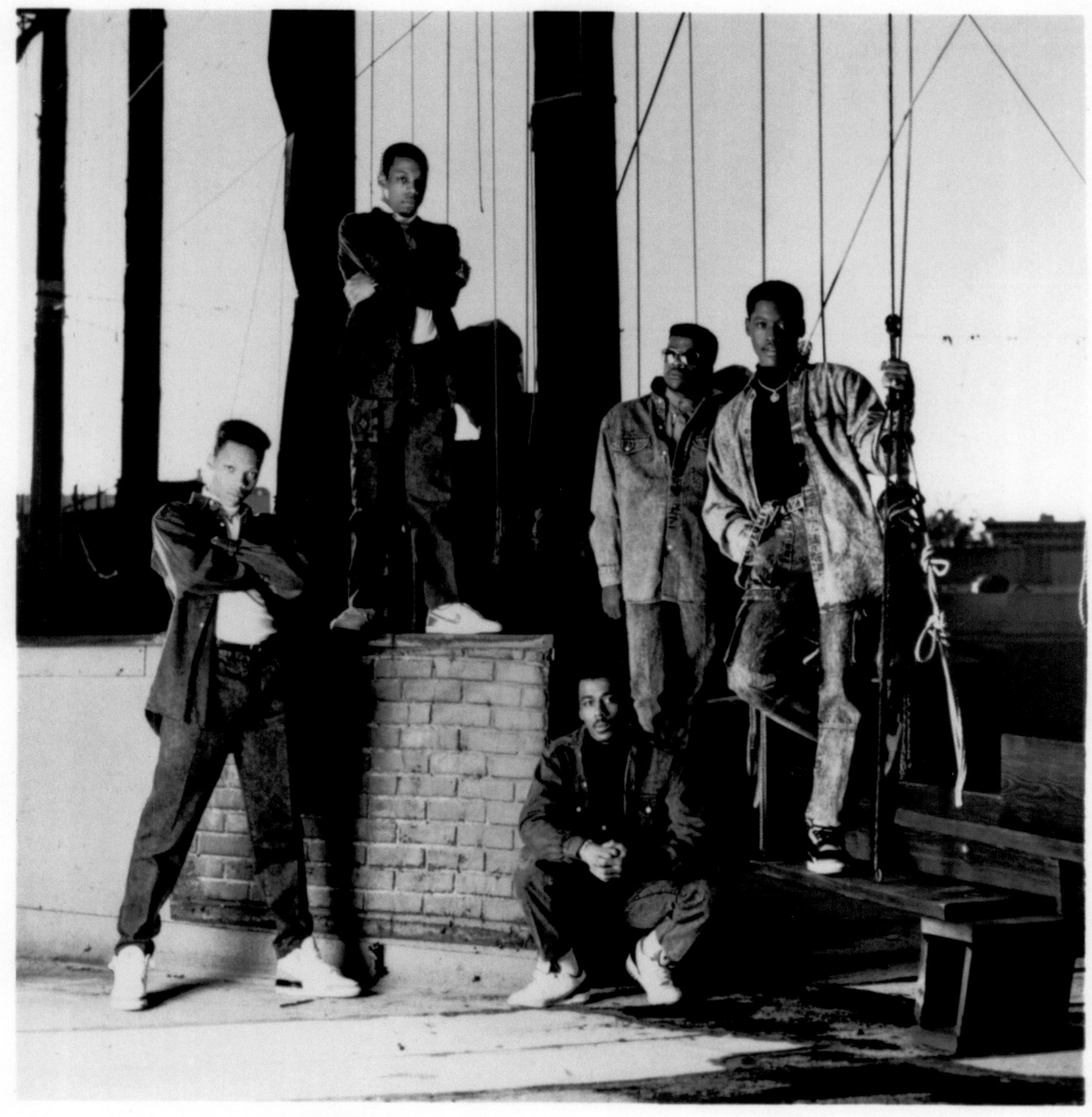

RONNIE DeVOE MICHAEL BIVINS RALPH TRESVANT RICKY BELL JOHNNY GILL

NEW EDITION

MCA RECORDS

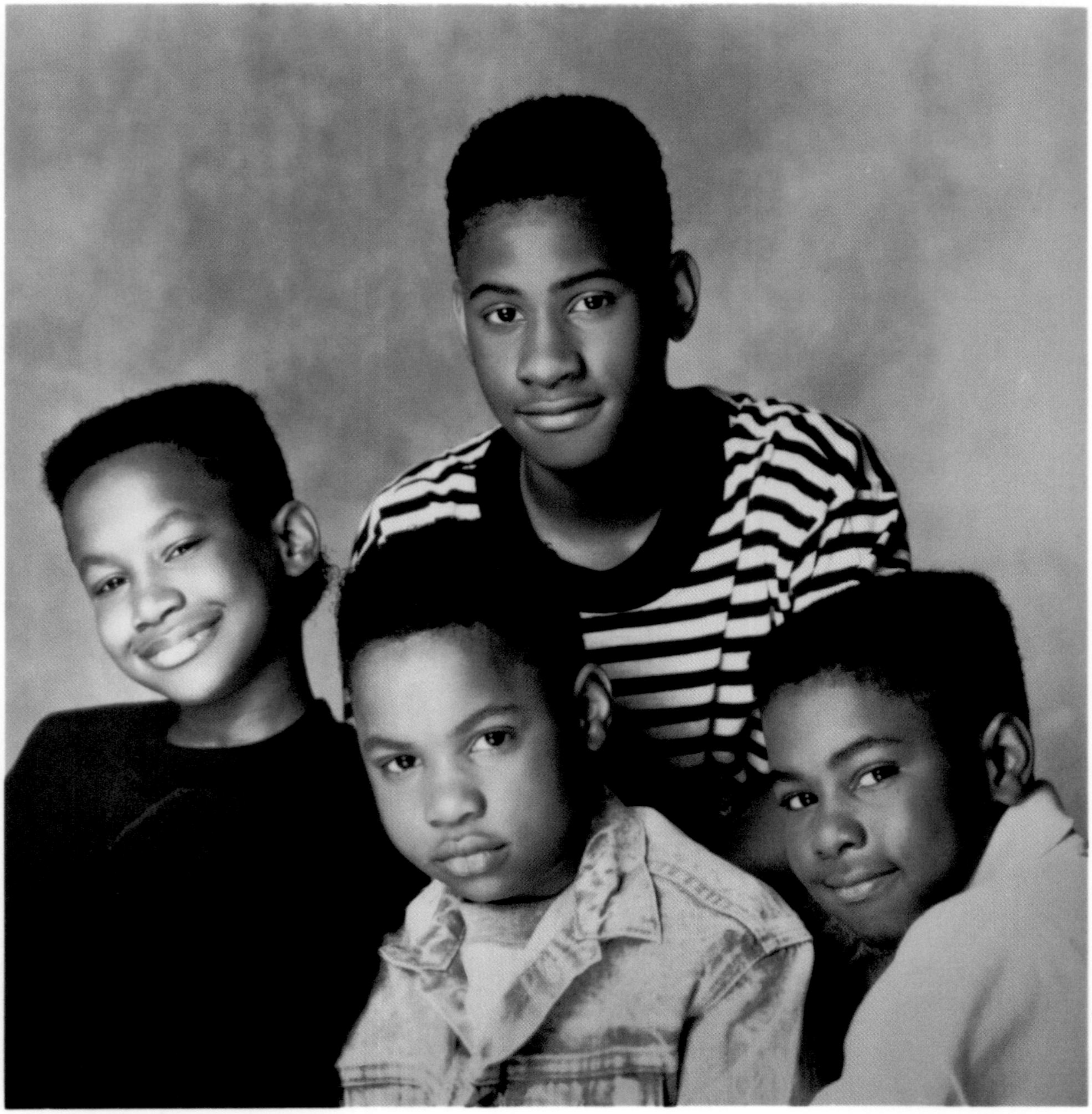

HAKEEM BILAL TAJH KHIRY (TOP)

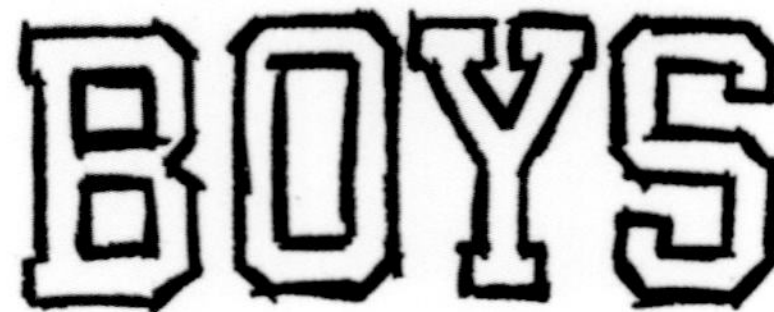

The

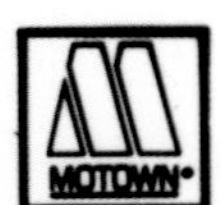

Photo Credit: Joe Stafford/MCA Records

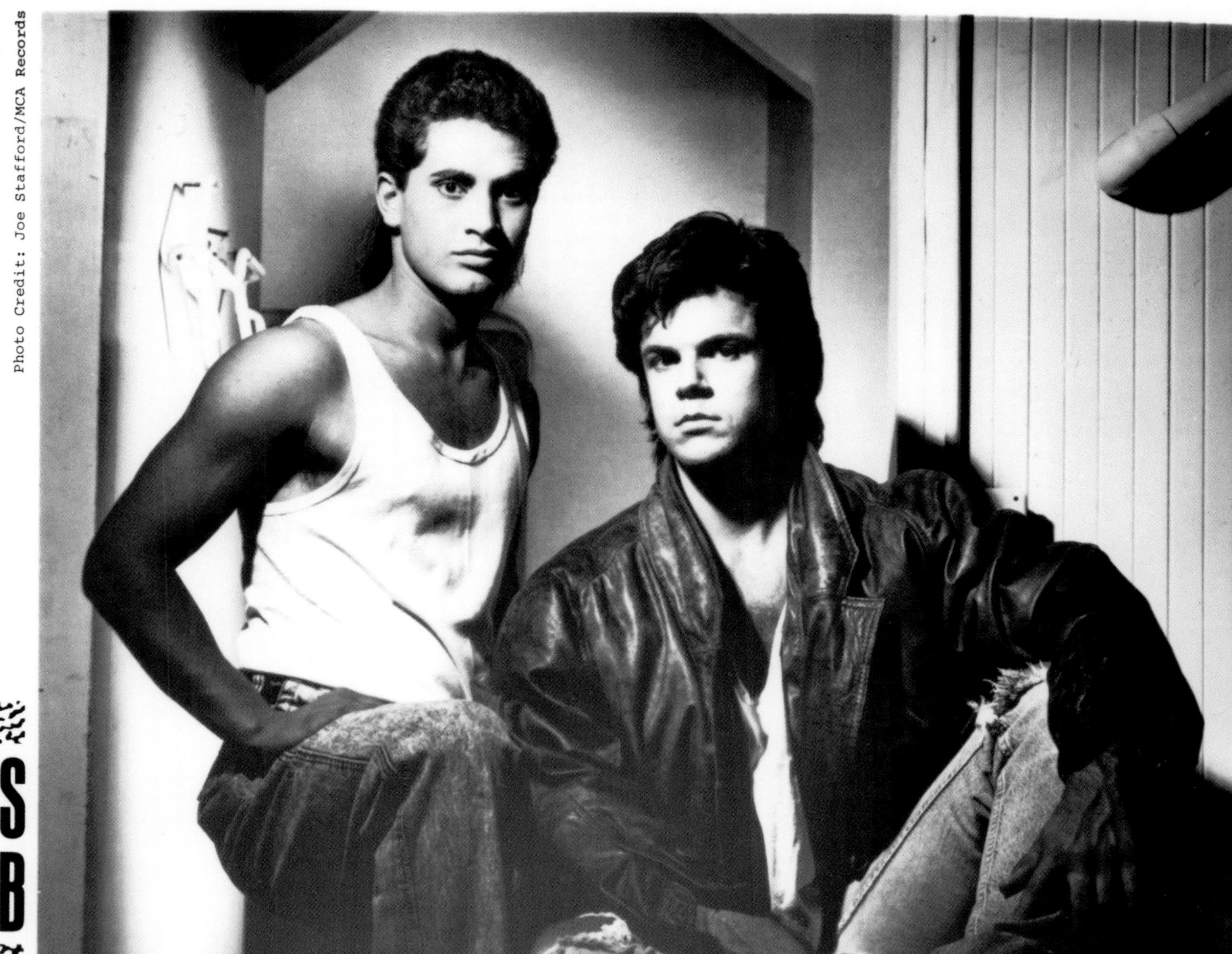

BOYS CLUB

Gene Hunt Joe Pasquale

MCA RECORDS

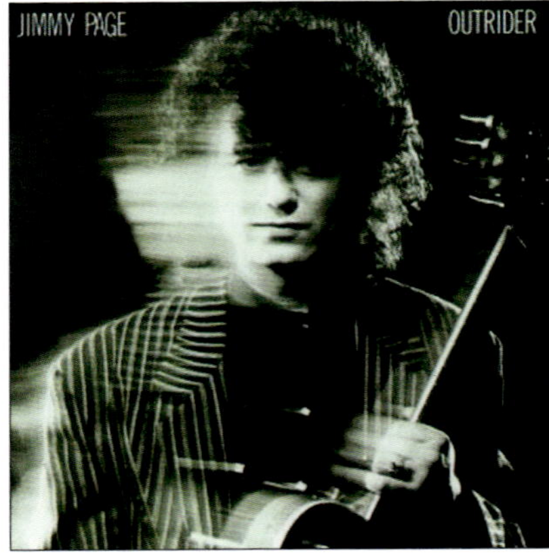

The legendary guitar hero of Led Zeppelin, **Jimmy Page** released *Outrider*, featuring a guest appearance from vocalist Robert Plant, his former bandmate.

Billboard 200: *Outrider* (#26)

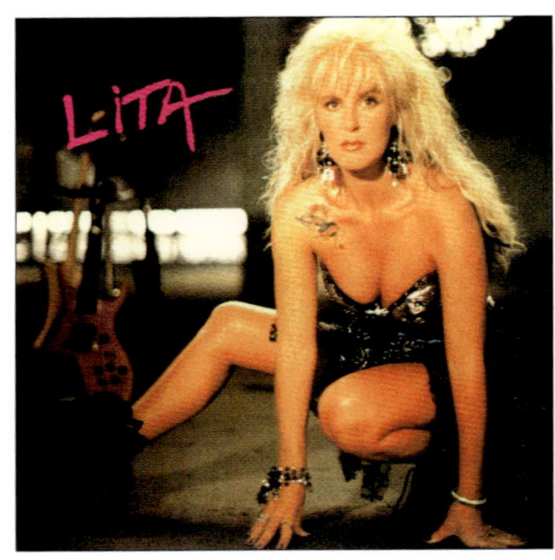

Lita Ford's *Lita* contained the hard-rock hit "Kiss Me Deadly," her signature song, and the ballad "Close My Eyes Forever," a duet with Ozzy Osbourne.

Billboard 200: *Lita* (#29)
Billboard Hot 100: "Kiss Me Deadly" (#12);
"Close My Eyes Forever" (#8)

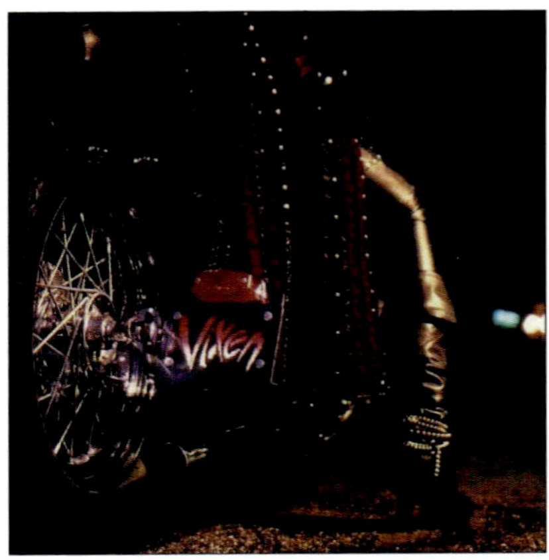

Portrayed as "the female Bon Jovi" of Los Angeles' glam-metal scene, **Vixen** rose up the charts with the songs "Edge of a Broken Heart" and "Cryin'."

Billboard 200: *Vixen* (#41)
Billboard Hot 100: "Edge of a Broken Heart" (#26); "Cryin'" (#22)

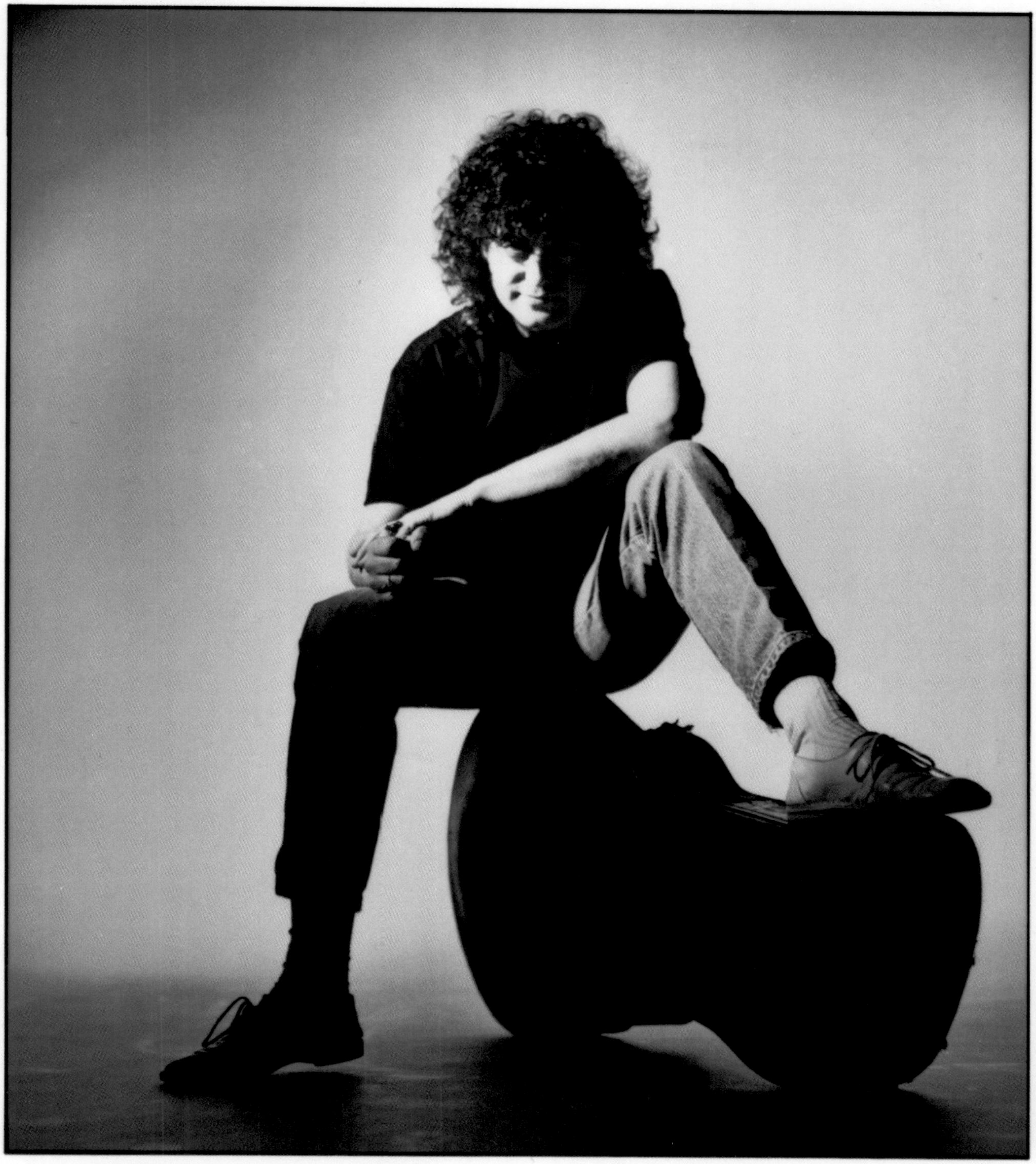

Photo Credit: Peter Ashworth

JIMMY PAGE

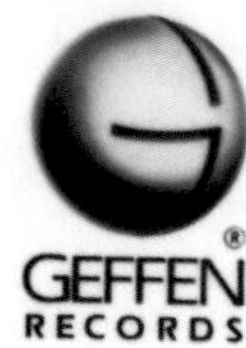

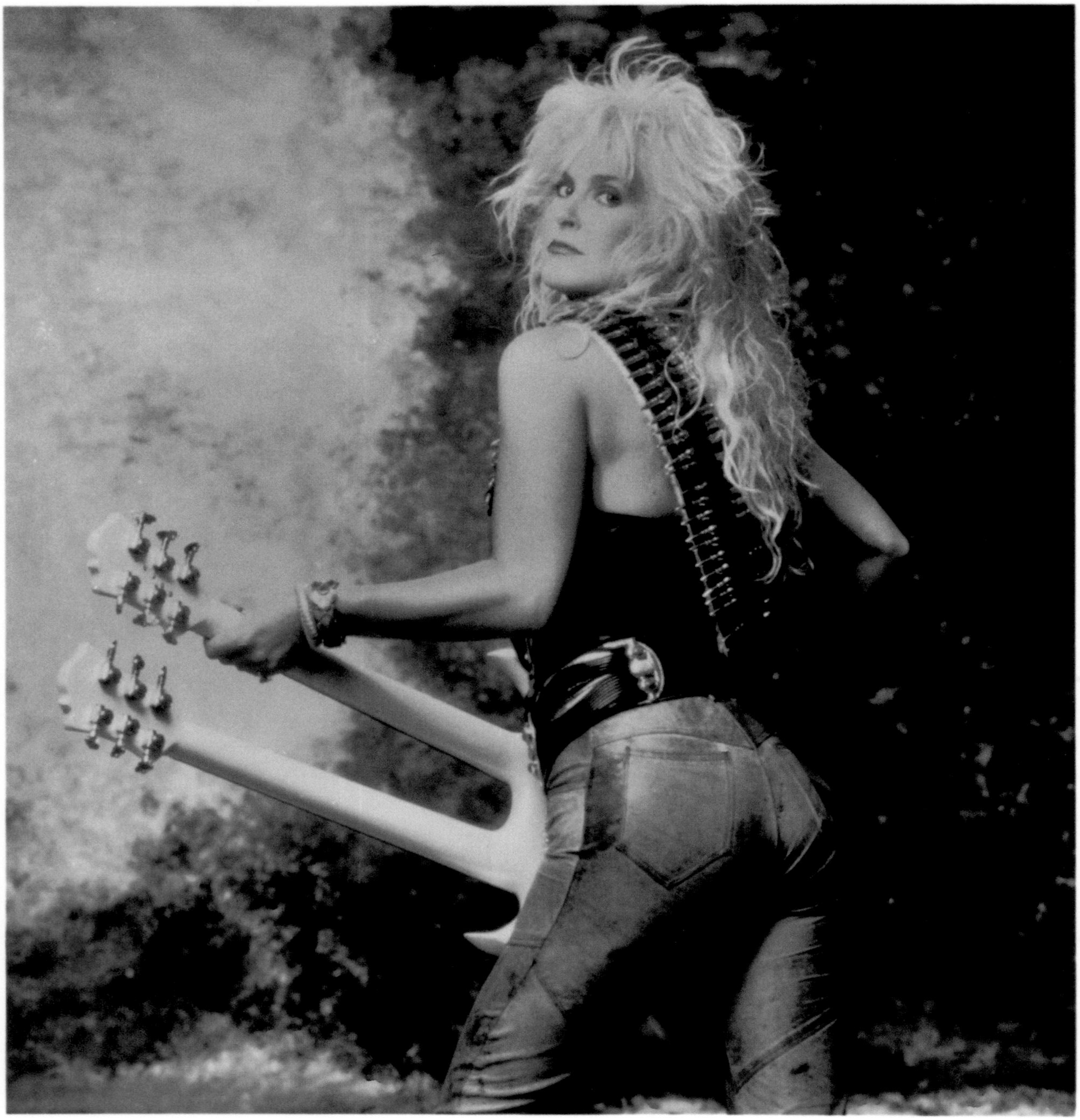

LITA FORD

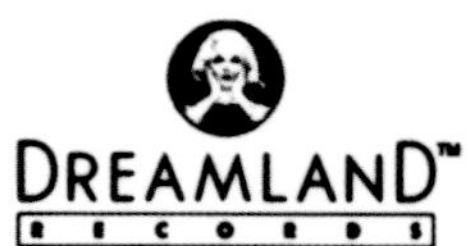

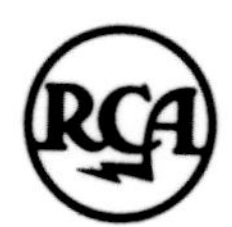

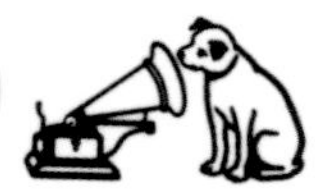

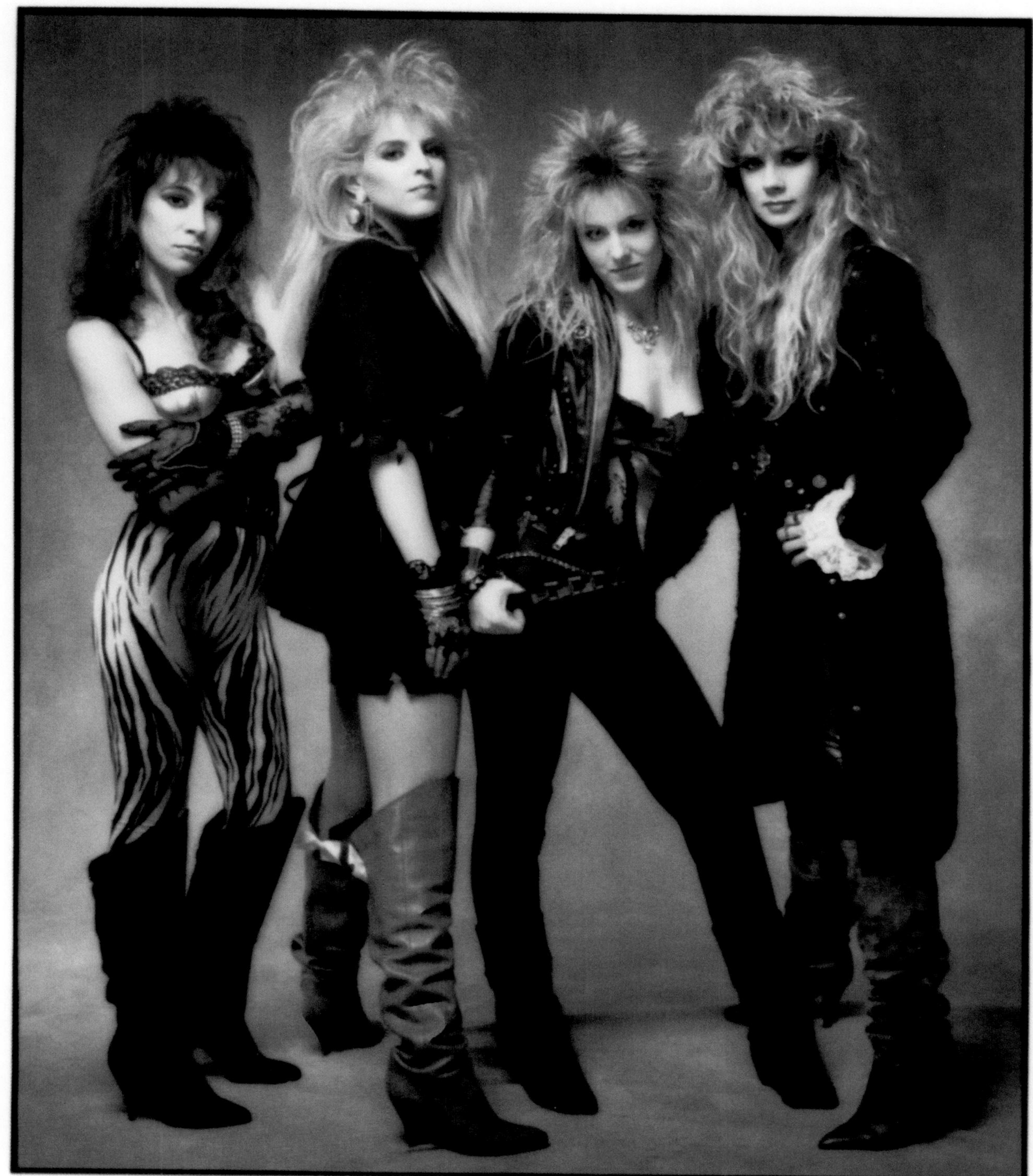

Photography: Glenn La Ferman

Vixen

EMI
MAN
HAT
TAN®

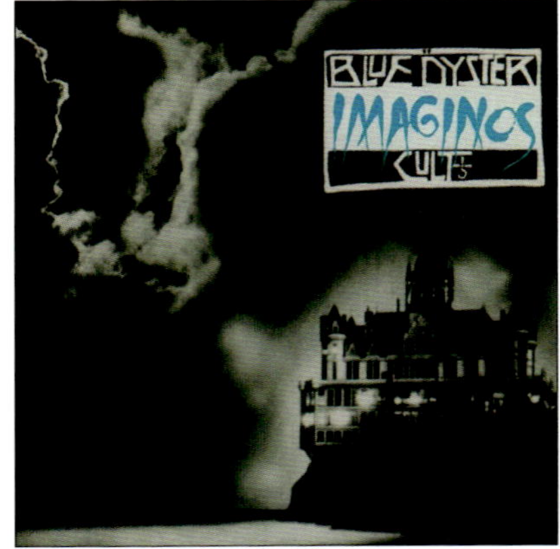

Recorded over six years, **Blue Öyster Cult** finished *Imaginos*, a song-poetry cycle composed by Sandy Pearlman, the group's producer and manager.

Billboard 200: *Imaginos* (#122)

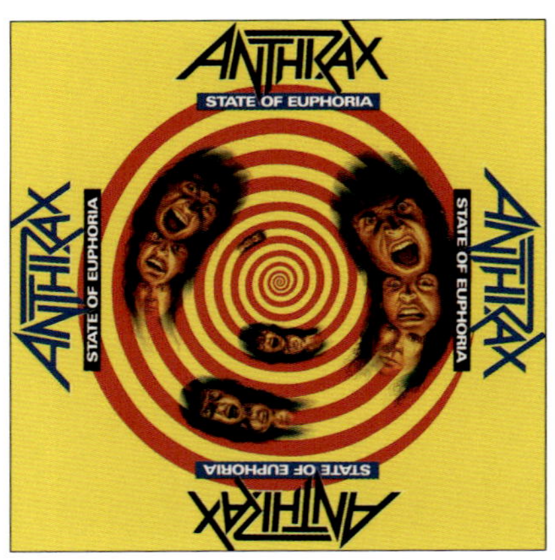

On *State of Euphoria*, thrash-metal outfit **Anthrax** covered "Antisocial," a song by the political French hard-rock band Trust, with alternate English lyrics.

Billboard 200: *State of Euphoria* (#30)

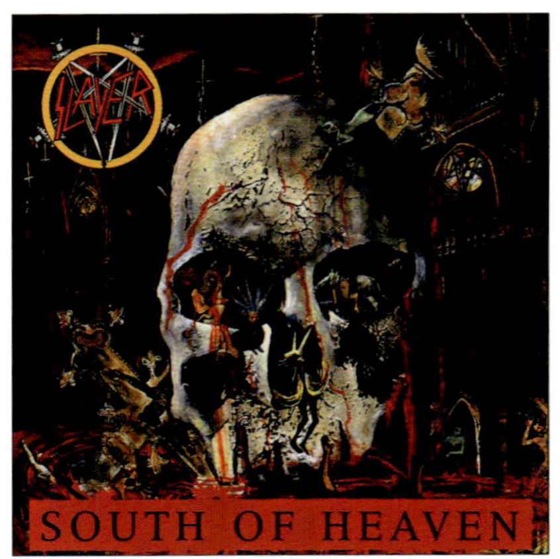

Slayer decelerated its frenzied tempos on *South of Heaven*, disconcerting the fans who had venerated the speedy metal of the previous *Reign in Blood*.

Billboard 200: *South of Heaven* (#57)

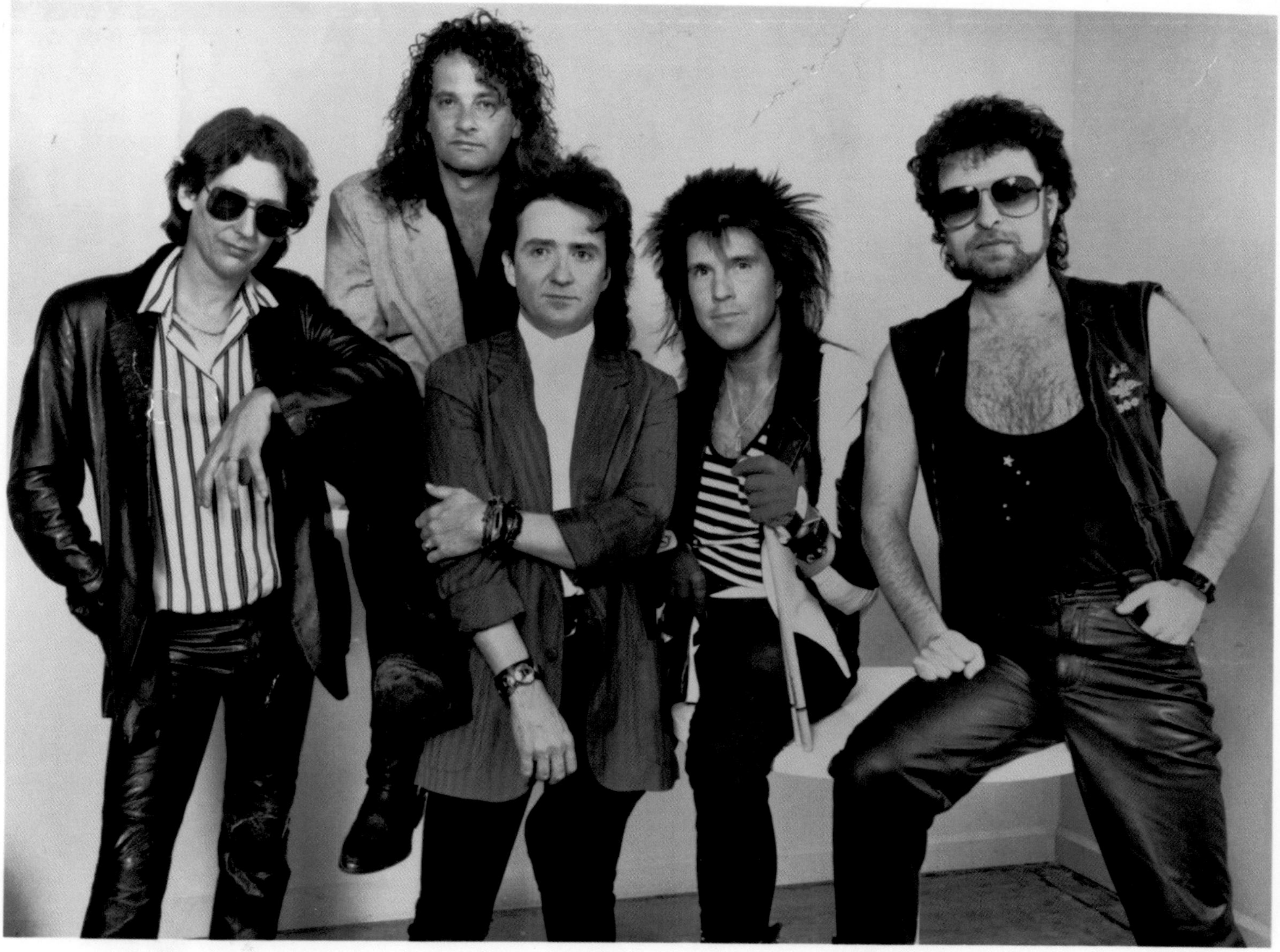

From left. ALLEN LANIER, JON ROGERS, DONALD "BUCK DHARMA" ROESER, RON RIDDLE, ERIC BLOOM.

BLUE OYSTER CULT

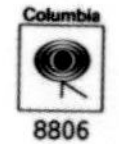

8806

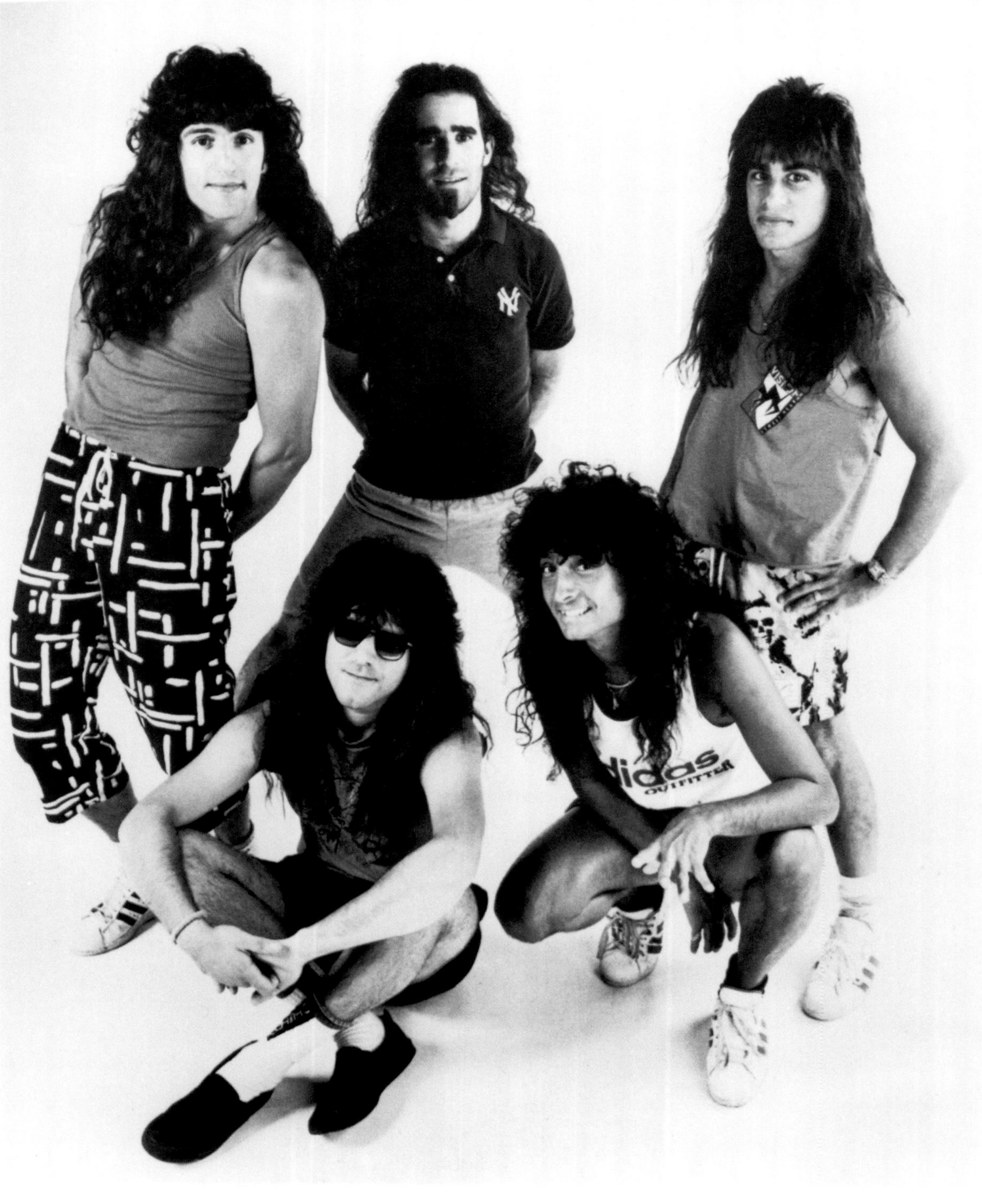

Photo Credit: Studio B

MEGAFORCE WORLDWIDE

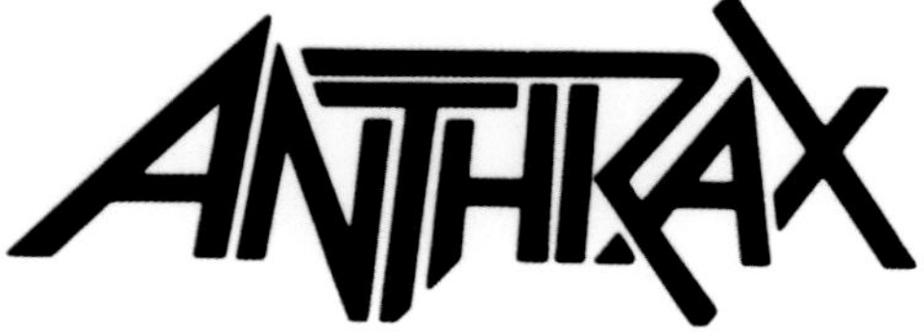

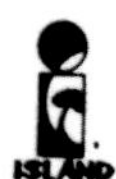

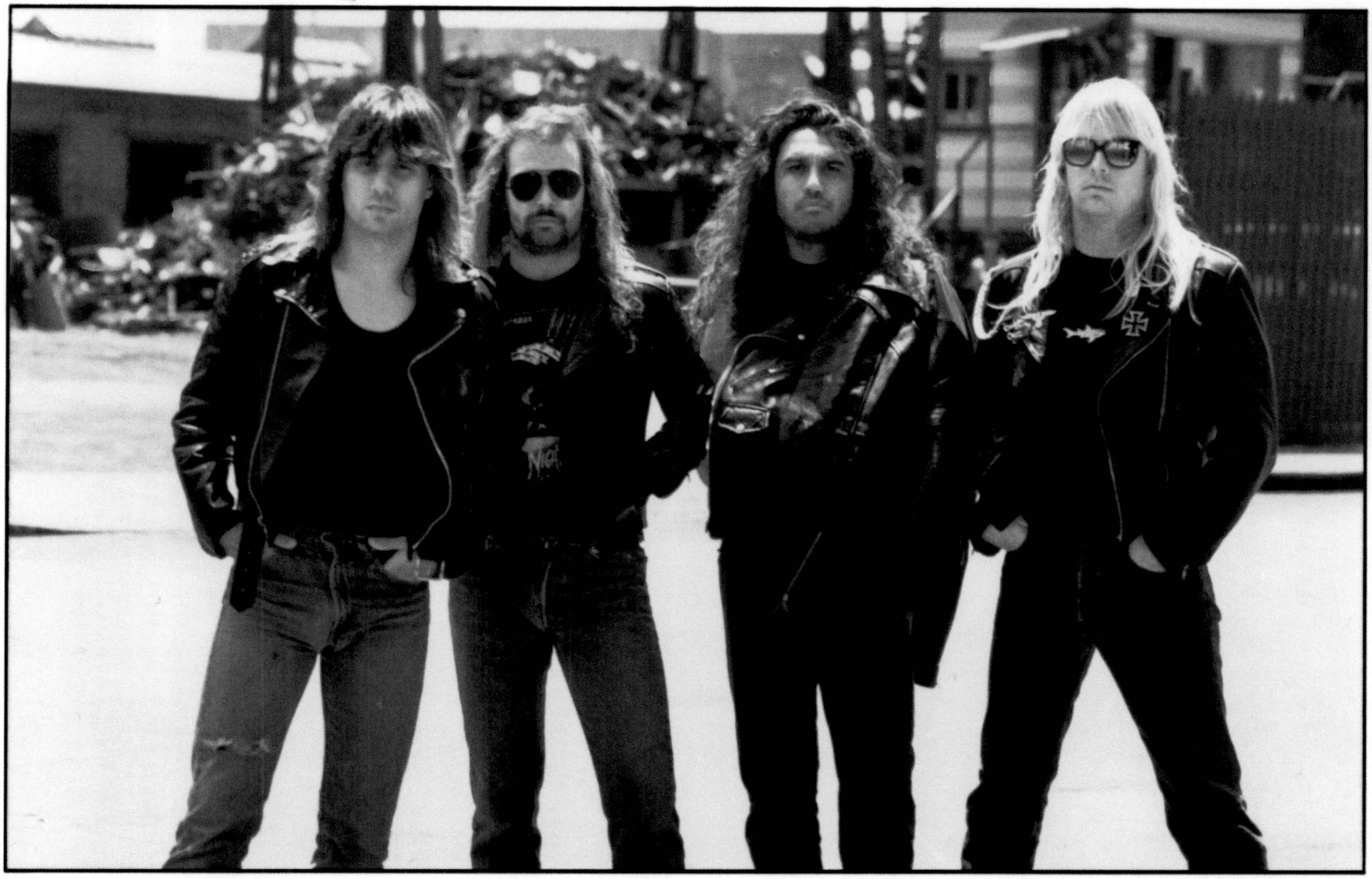

LOMBARDO KING ARAYA HANNEMAN

Photo Credit: Alex Solca

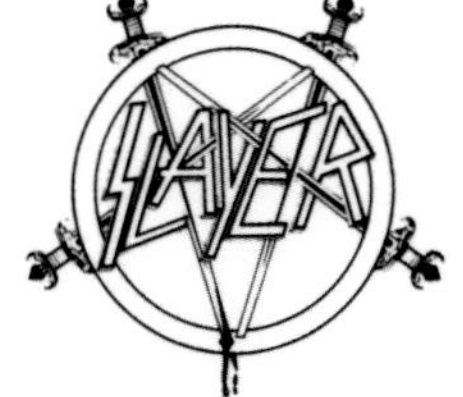

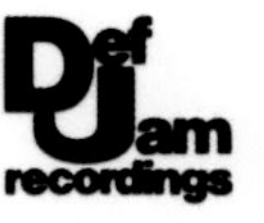

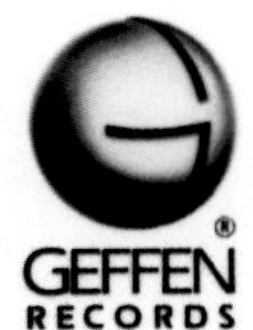

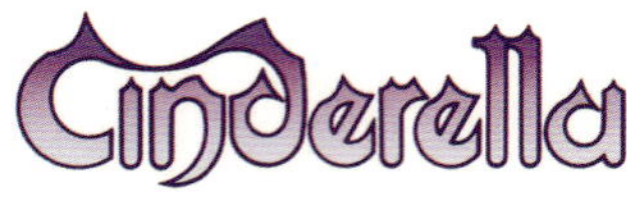

On *Long Cold Winter* and the ballad "Don't Know What You Got (Till It's Gone)," **Cinderella** changed its sound from glam metal to gritty, bluesy rock.

Billboard 200: *Long Cold Winter* (#10)
Billboard Hot 100: "Don't Know What You Got (Till It's Gone)" (#12); "The Last Mile" (#36); "Coming Home" (#20); "Gypsy Road" (#51)

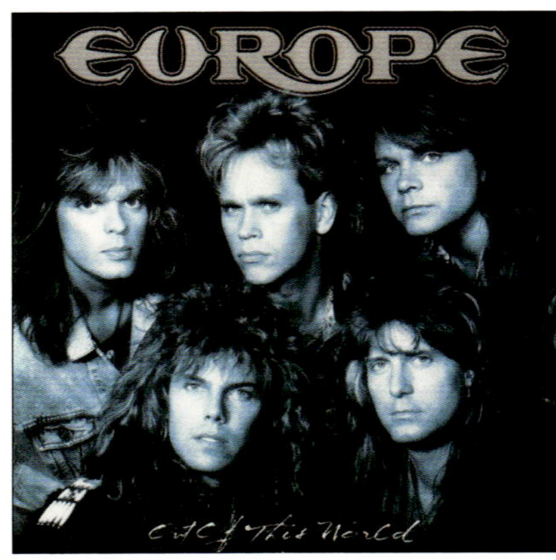

With *Out of This World*, produced by hitmaking hard-rock specialist Ron Nevison, the five Swedes known collectively as **Europe** stayed on a hot streak.

Billboard 200: *Out of This World* (#19)
Billboard Hot 100: "Superstitious" (#31)

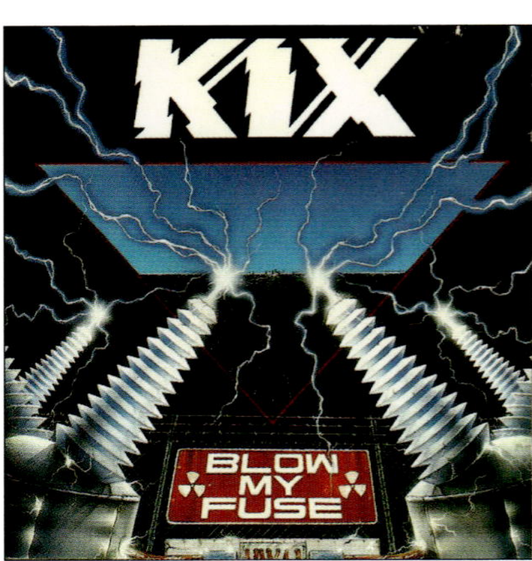

Melodic hard rockers **Kix** gained attention for *Blow My Fuse*, the hit power ballad "Don't Close Your Eyes" and a rambunctious video for "Cold Blood."

Billboard 200: *Blow My Fuse* (#46)
Billboard Hot 100: "Don't Close Your Eyes" (#11)

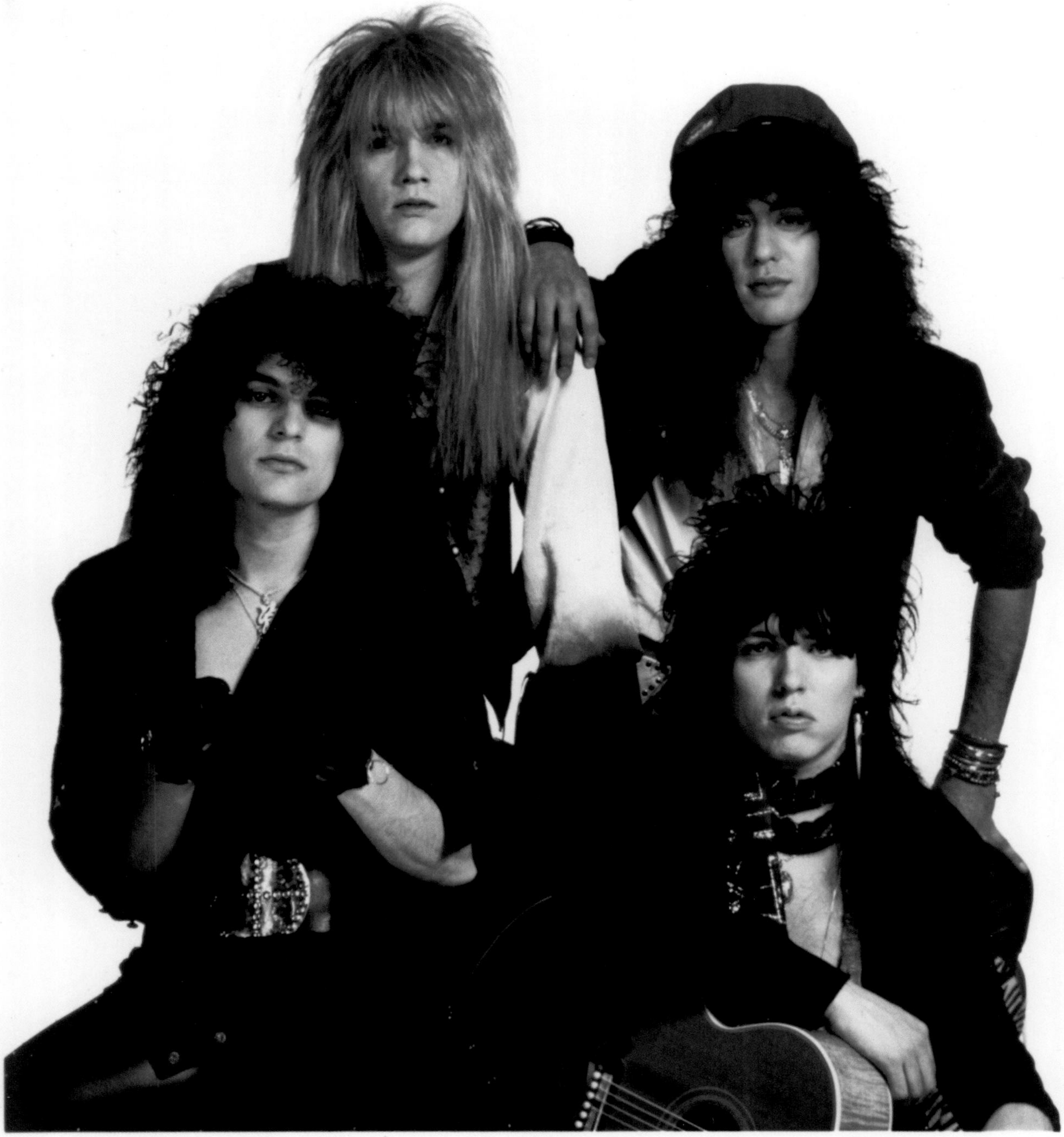

ERIC BRITTINGHAM JEFF LABAR

FRED COURY TOM KEIFER

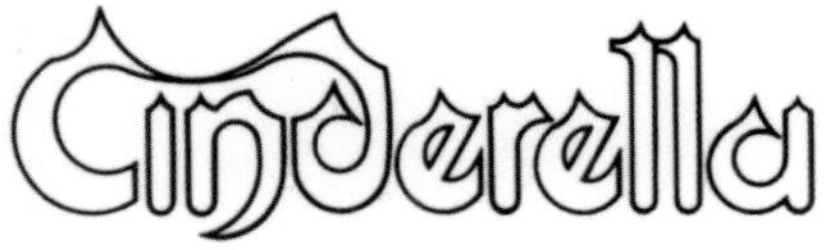

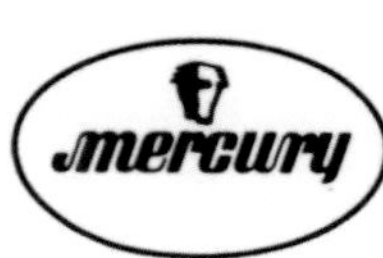

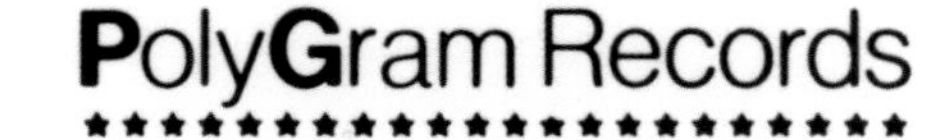

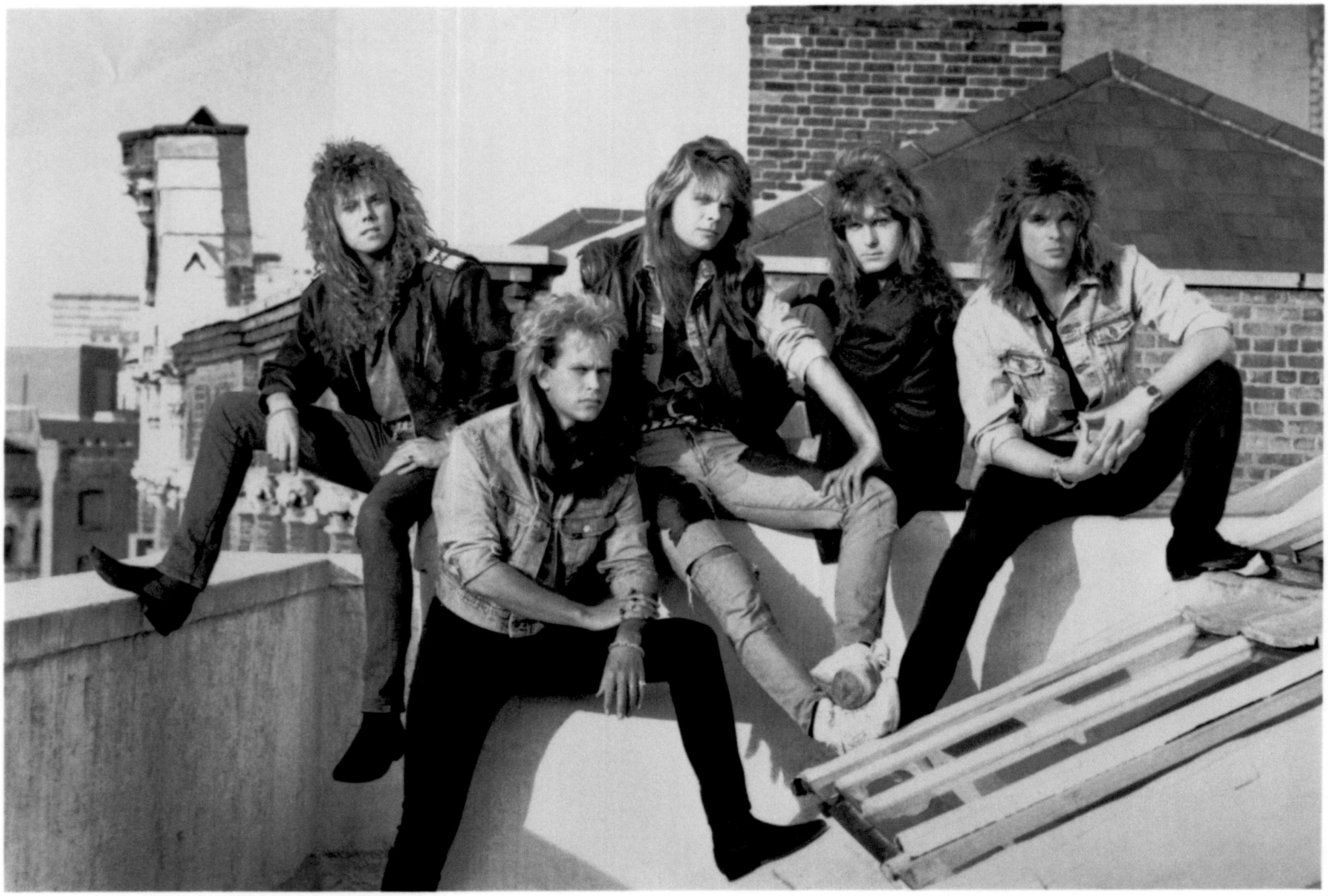

PHOTO: LYNN GOLDSMITH

L-R: JOEY TEMPEST (Vocals); IAN HAUGLAND (Drums); MIC MICHAELI (Keyboards); KEE MARCELLO (Guitar); JOHN LEVEN (Bass)

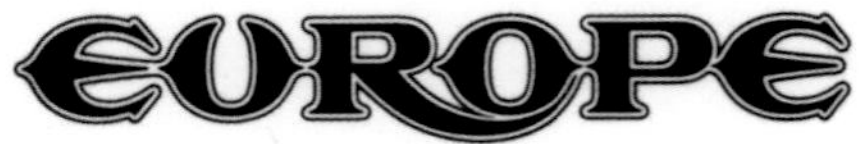

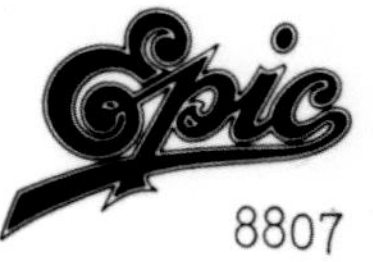

8807

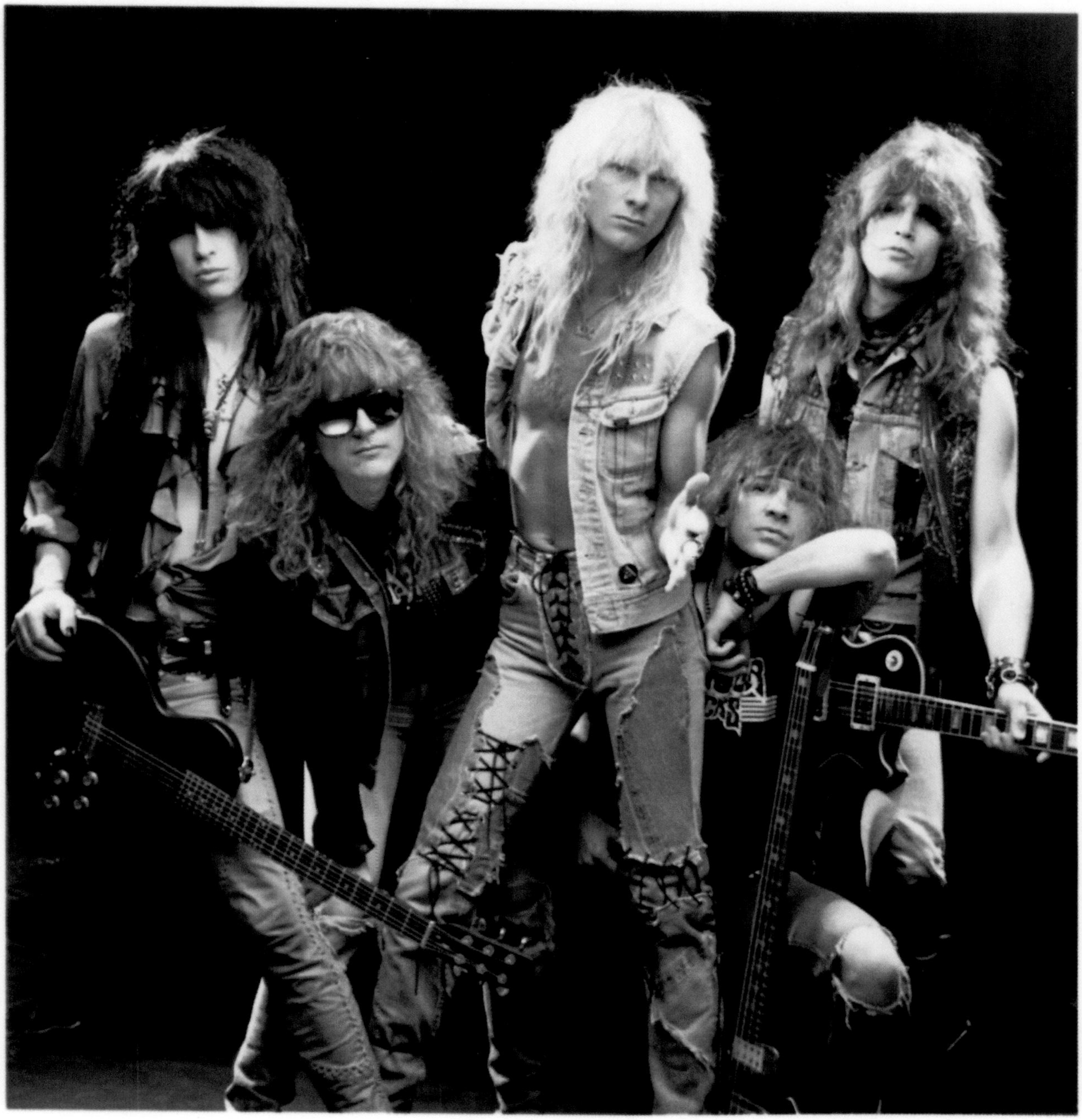

BRIAN "DAMAGE" FORSYTHE   JIMMY "CHOCOLATE" CHALFANT   STEVE WHITEMAN   DONNIE PURNELL   RONNIE "10/10" YOUNKINS

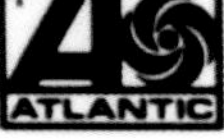

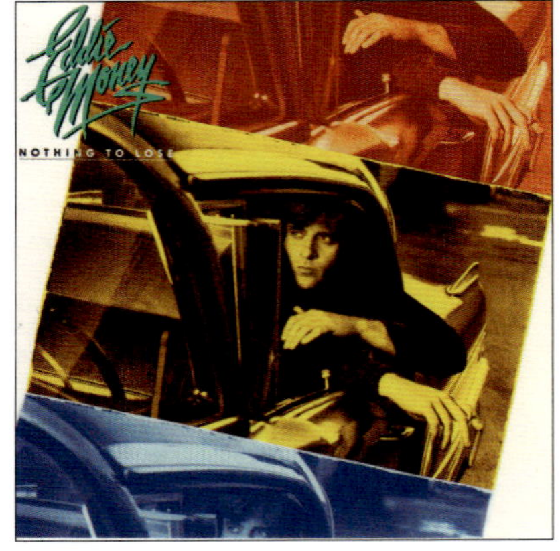

Eddie Money reunited with Jimmy Lyon, his guitarist from the "Baby Hold On" era, for the album *Nothing to Lose* and the Top 10 hit "Walk on Water."

Billboard 200: *Nothing to Lose* (#49)
Billboard Hot 100: "Walk on Water" (#9);
"The Love in Your Eyes" (#24); "Let Me In" (#60)

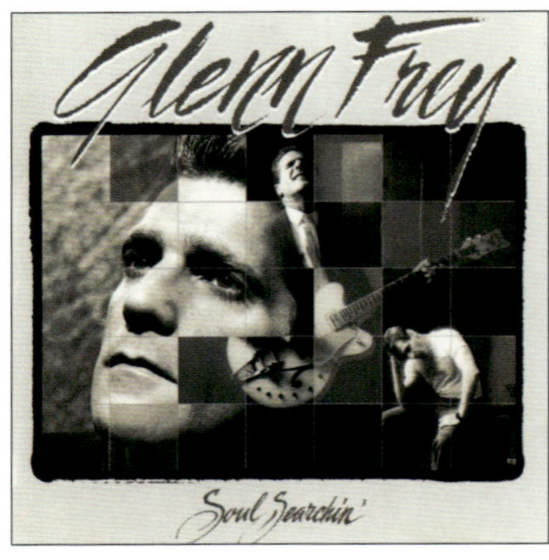

Eight years after the Eagles' demise, **Glenn Frey** notched one of his biggest adult contemporary hits, "True Love," from the solo album *Soul Searchin'*.

Billboard 200: *Soul Searchin'* (#36)
Billboard Hot 100: "True Love" (#13); "Livin' Right" (#90)

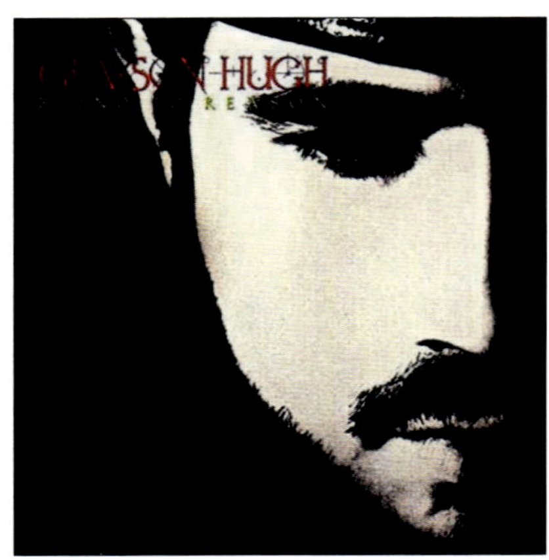

Keyboardist and singer **Grayson Hugh** reached the pop Top 20 with "Talk It Over," a blue-eyed soul delivery of his lyrics about a fractured relationship.

Billboard 200: *Blind to Reason* (#71)
Billboard Hot 100: "Talk It Over" (#19); "Bring It All Back" (#87);
"How 'Bout Us?" (#67)

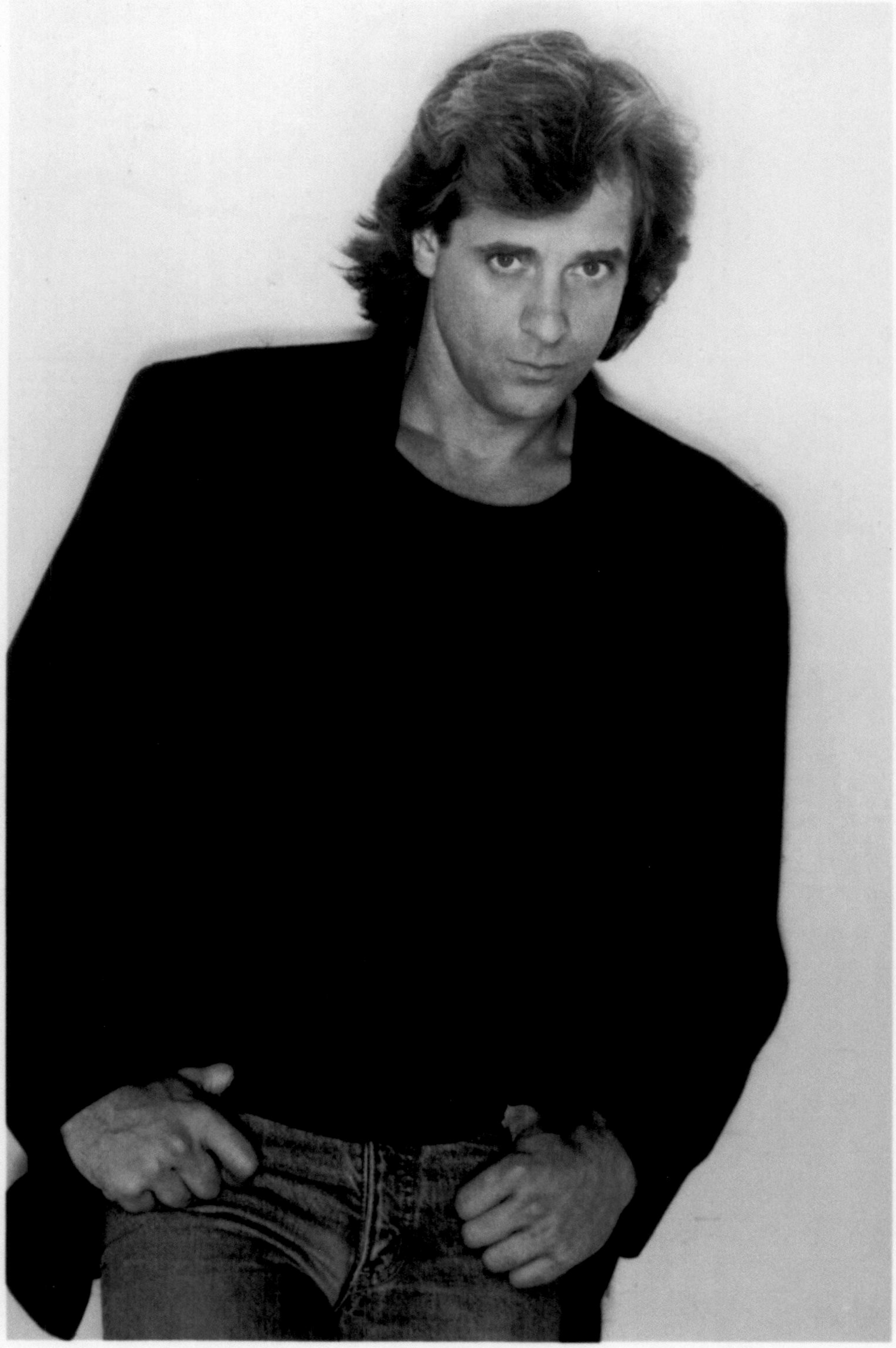

PHOTO: JEFFREY MAYER

Direction:
Bill Graham Management
(415)541-4900
Premier Talent
(212)758-4900

EDDIE MONEY

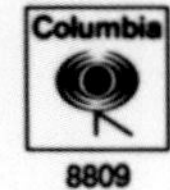

8809

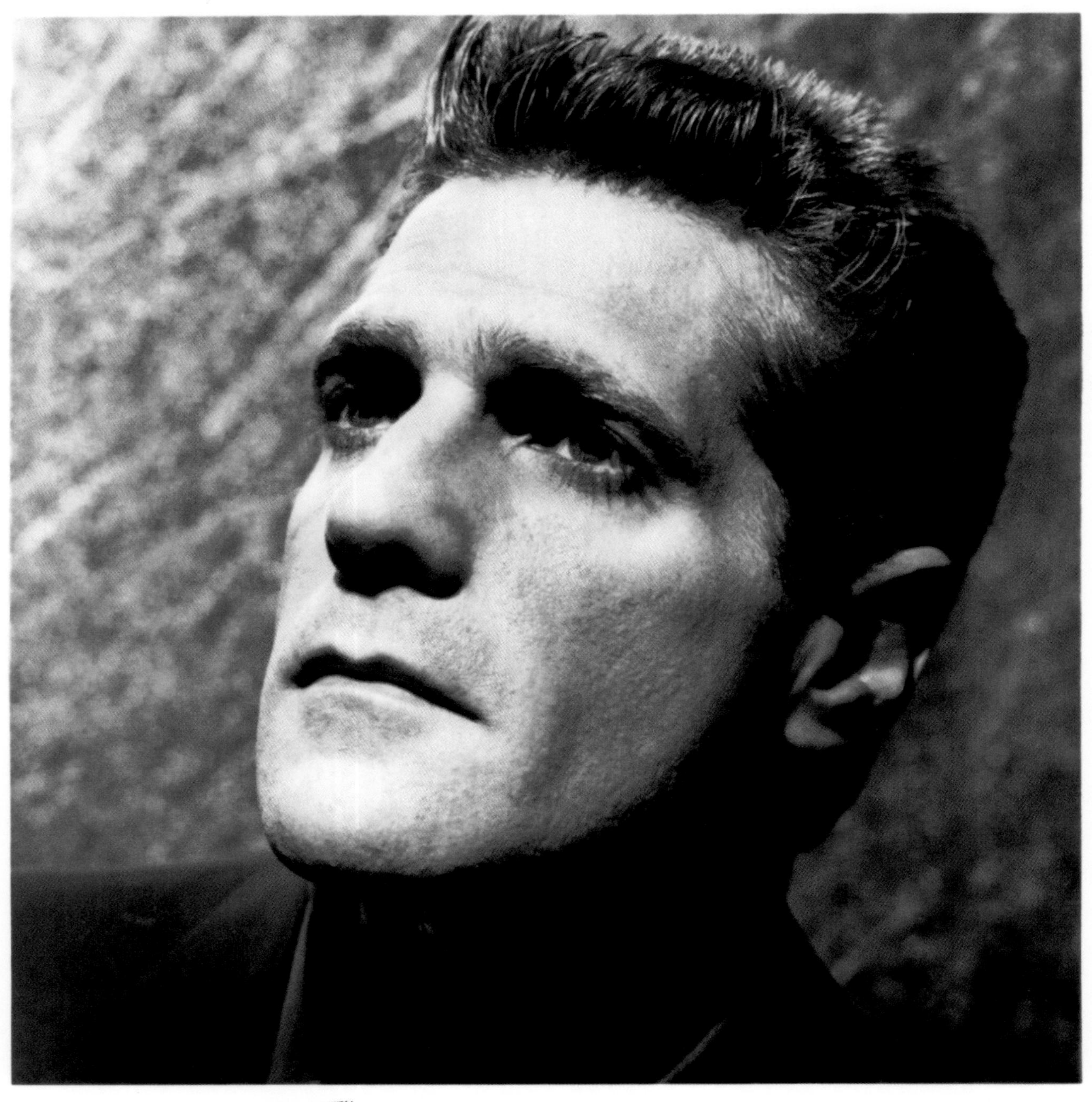

Glenn Frey

MCA RECORDS

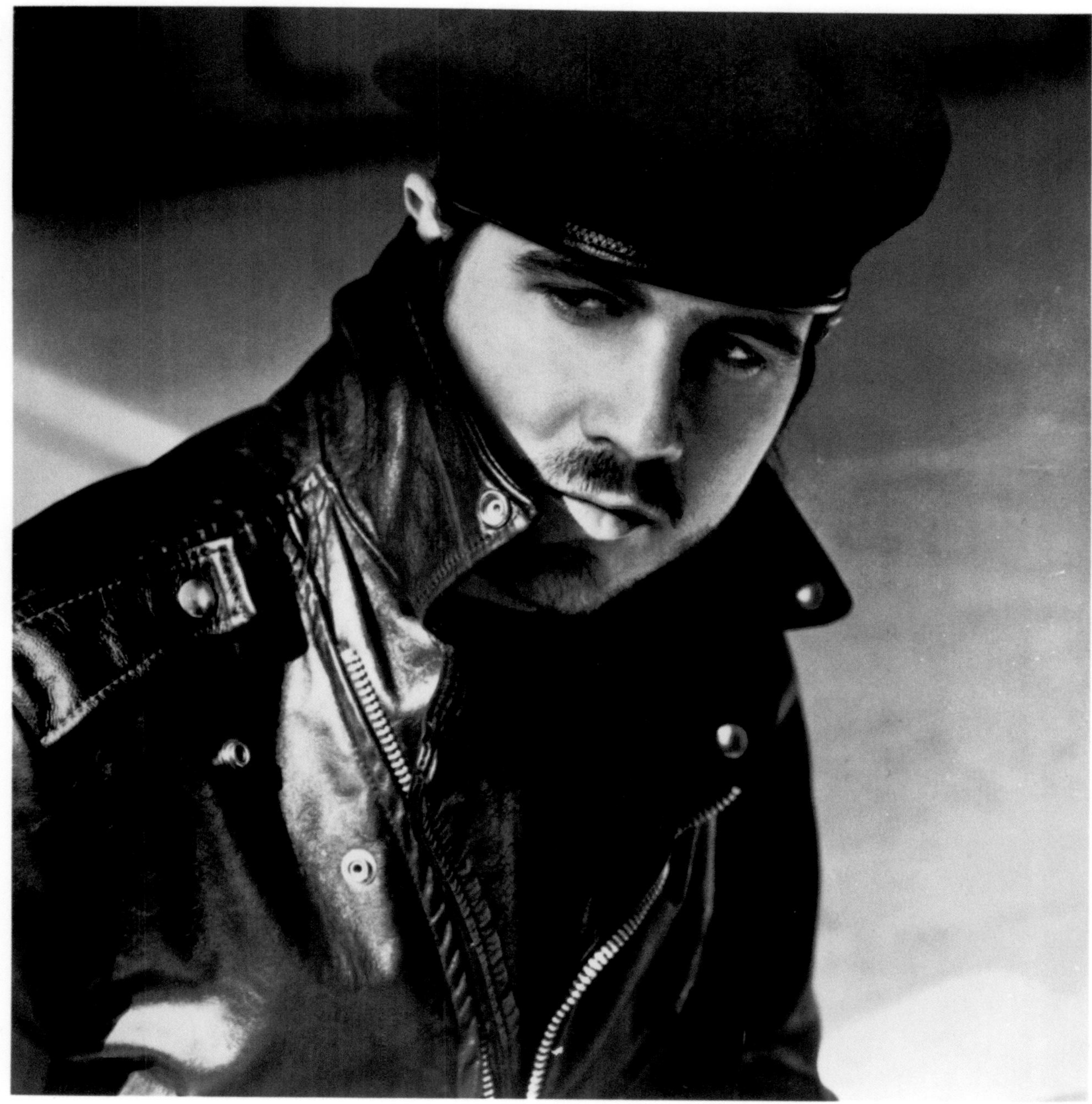

GRAYSON HUGH

McGUIRE/WEIN ARTIST MGMT.
CONTACT: MARY McGUIRE
(212) 772-6818

RCA

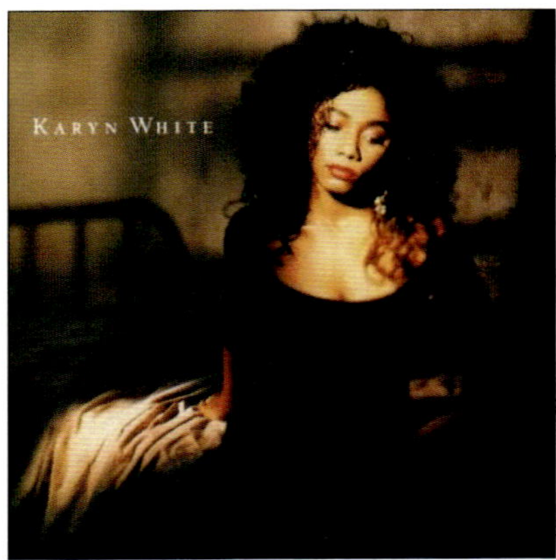

The chart-topping R&B hits "The Way You Love Me," "Superwoman" and "Secret Rendezvous" propelled Karyn White into the pop-star stratosphere.

Billboard 200: *Karyn White* (#19)
Billboard Hot 100: "The Way You Love Me" (#7); "Superwoman" (#8); "Secret Rendezvous" (#6)

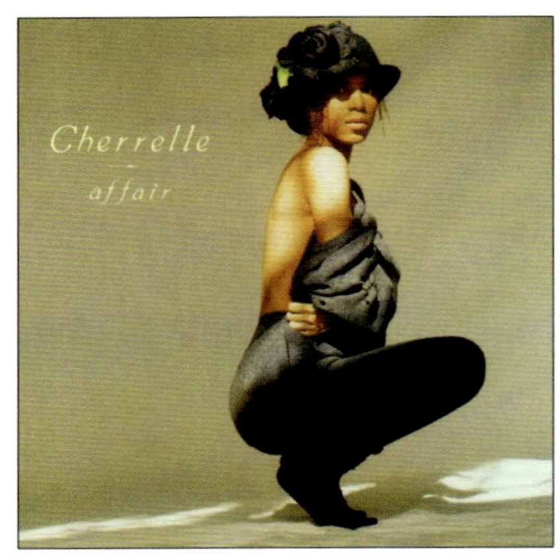

Detroit-born songstress Cherrelle's *Affair* held the No. 1 R&B single "Everything I Miss at Home," produced by the team of Jimmy Jam & Terry Lewis.

Billboard 200: *Affair* (#106)

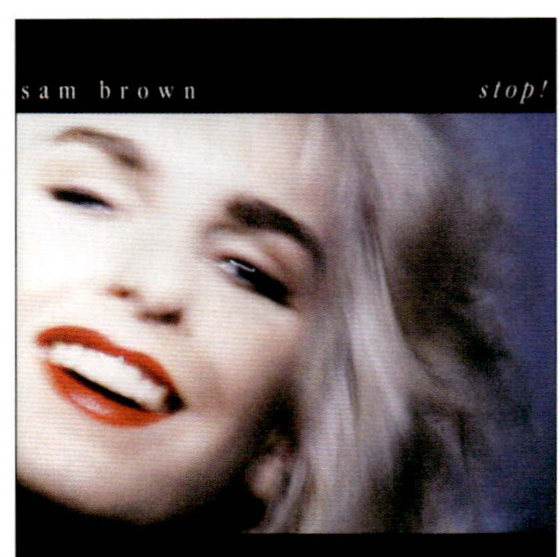

Sam Brown's debut album *Stop!* brought the British singer-songwriter to renown via the title track, a febrile soul ballad that unfolded as a global smash.

Billboard Hot 100: "Stop!" (#65)

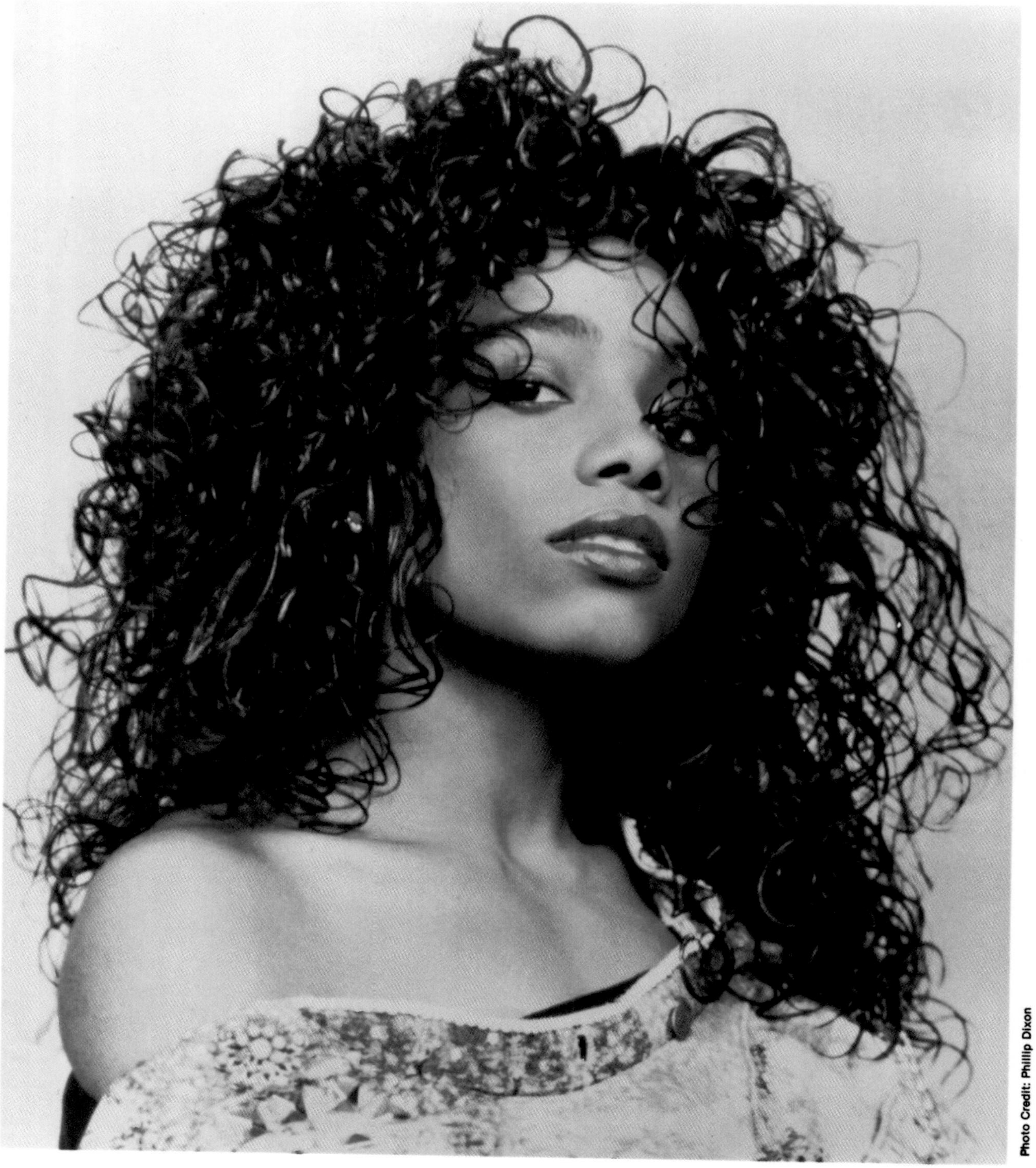

Photo Credit: Phillip Dixon

KARYN WHITE

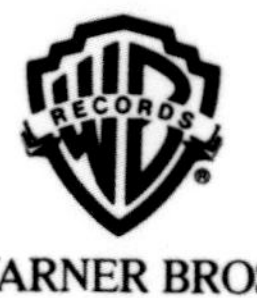

WARNER BROS.

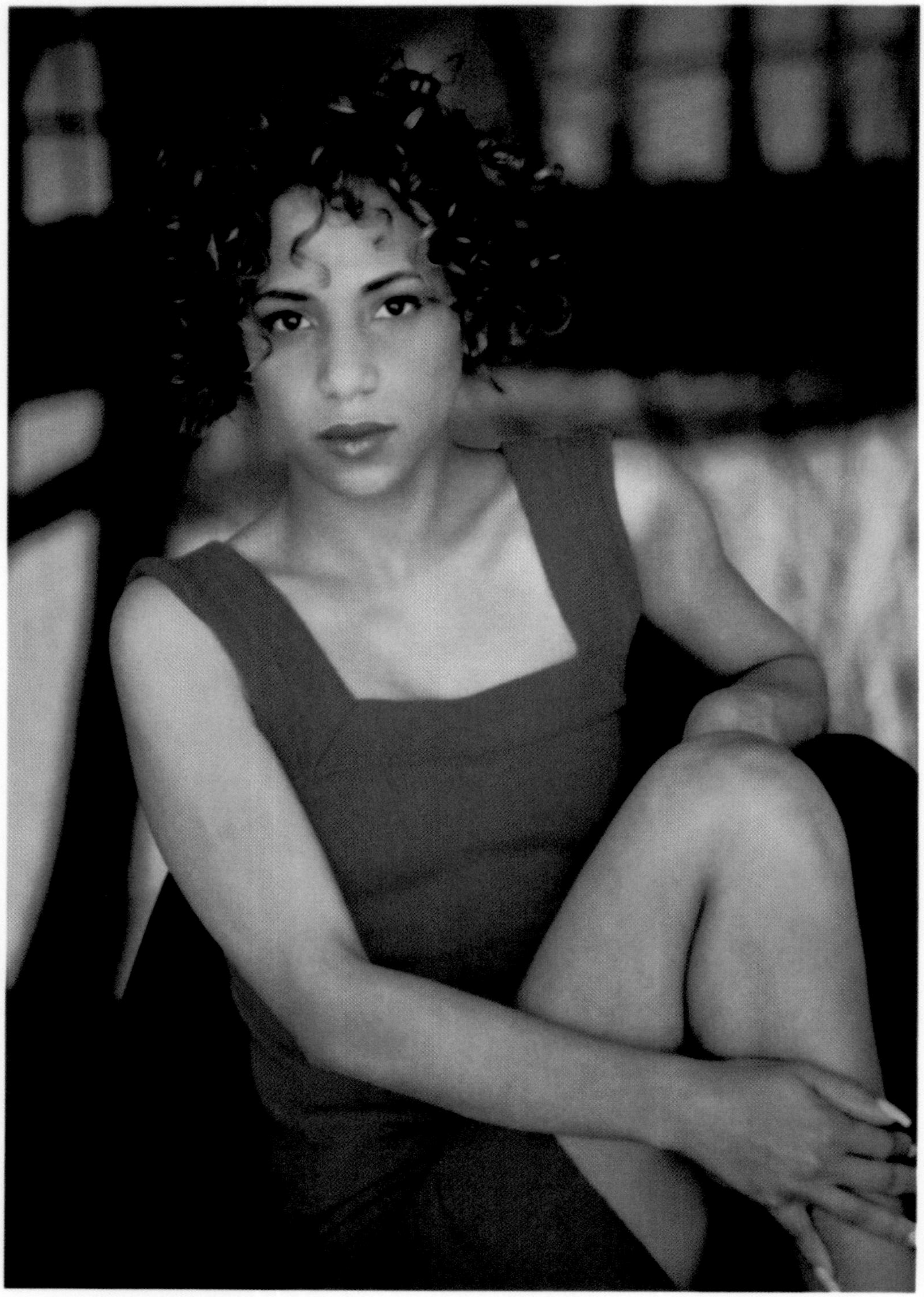

PHOTO: ALBERTO TOLOT

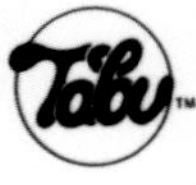

Cherrelle

EPIC PORTRAIT ASSOCIATED
8811

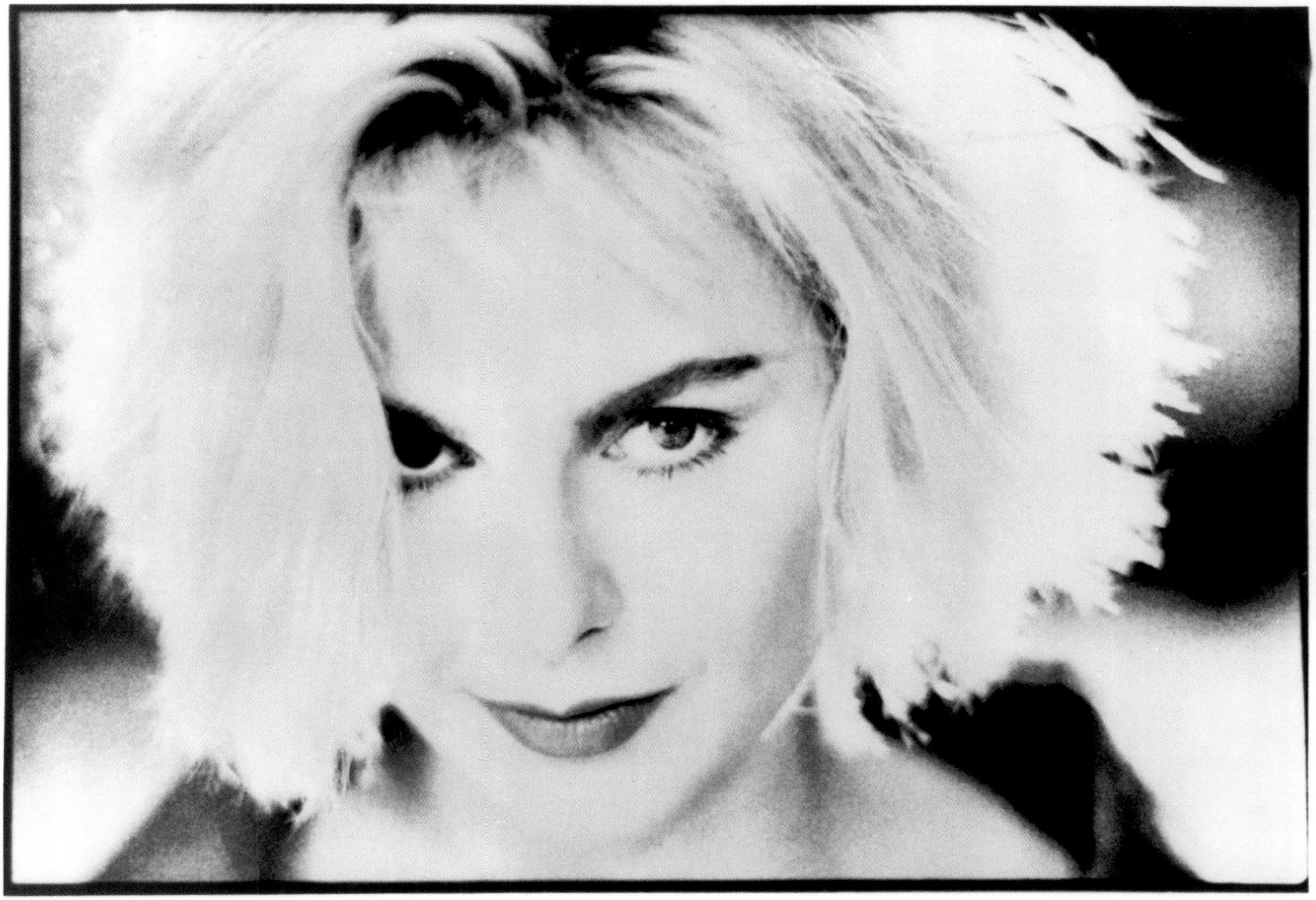

SAM BROWN

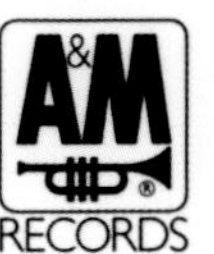

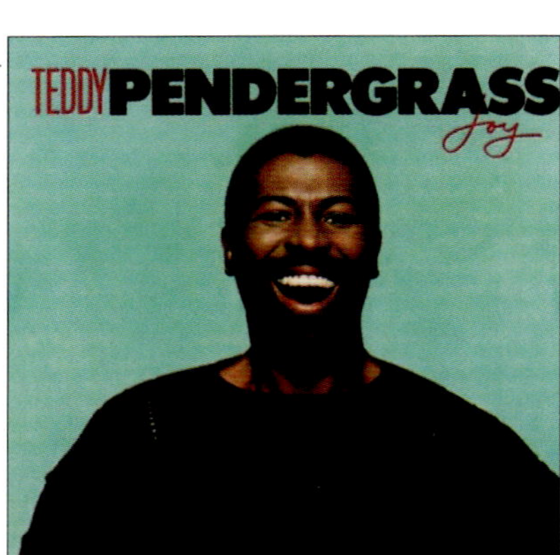

With the title track from *Joy,* **Teddy Pendergrass** secured his first No. 1 R&B hit in a decade—and his first since the 1982 car crash that left him paralyzed.

Billboard 200: *Joy* (#54)
Billboard Hot 100: "Joy" (#77)

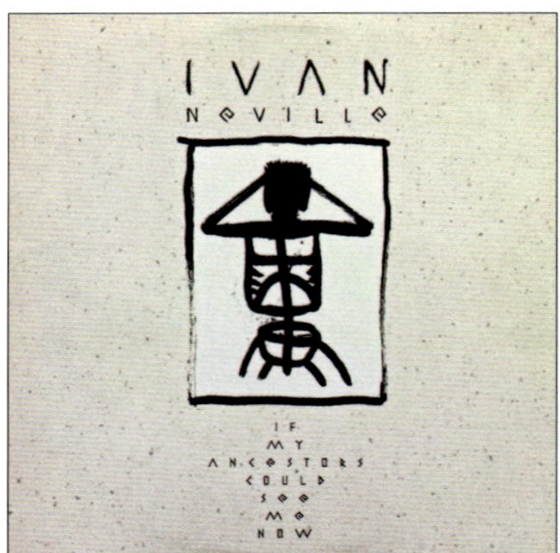

Ivan Neville, Aaron Neville's son, began his solo career with "Falling Out of Love," a duet with Bonnie Raitt, and "Not Just Another Girl," a Top 30 hit.

Billboard 200: *If My Ancestors Could See Me Now* (#107)
Billboard Hot 100: "Not Just Another Girl" (#26);
"Falling Out of Love" (#91)

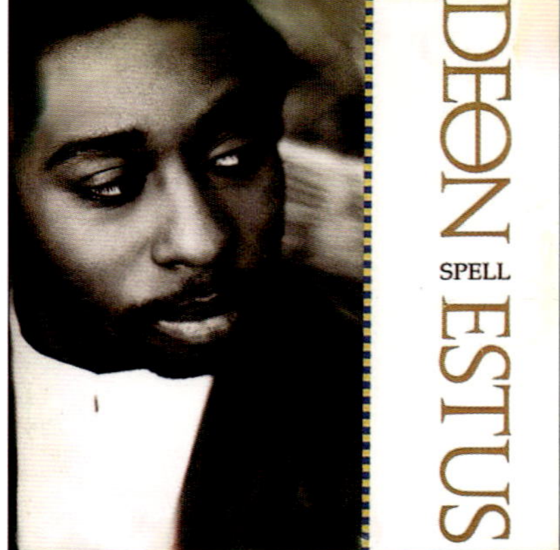

Former Wham! and George Michael bass player **Deon Estus** released *Spell,* which spawned "Heaven Help Me," featuring additional vocals by Michael.

Billboard 200: *Spell* (#89)
Billboard Hot 100: "Heaven Help Me" (#5)

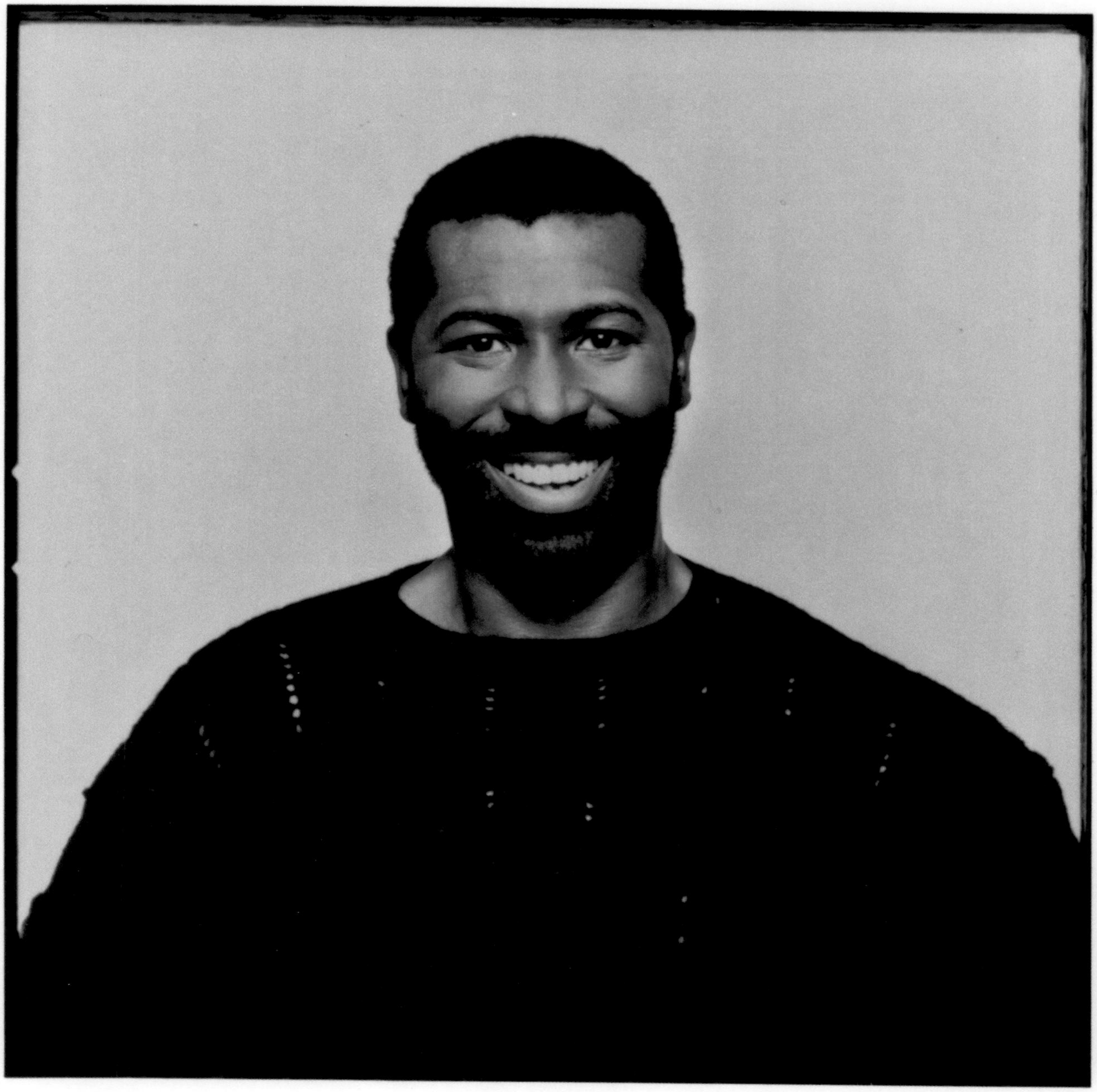

TEDDY PENDERGRASS

PHOTO CREDIT: CAROL FRIEDMAN

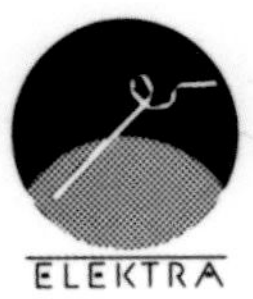

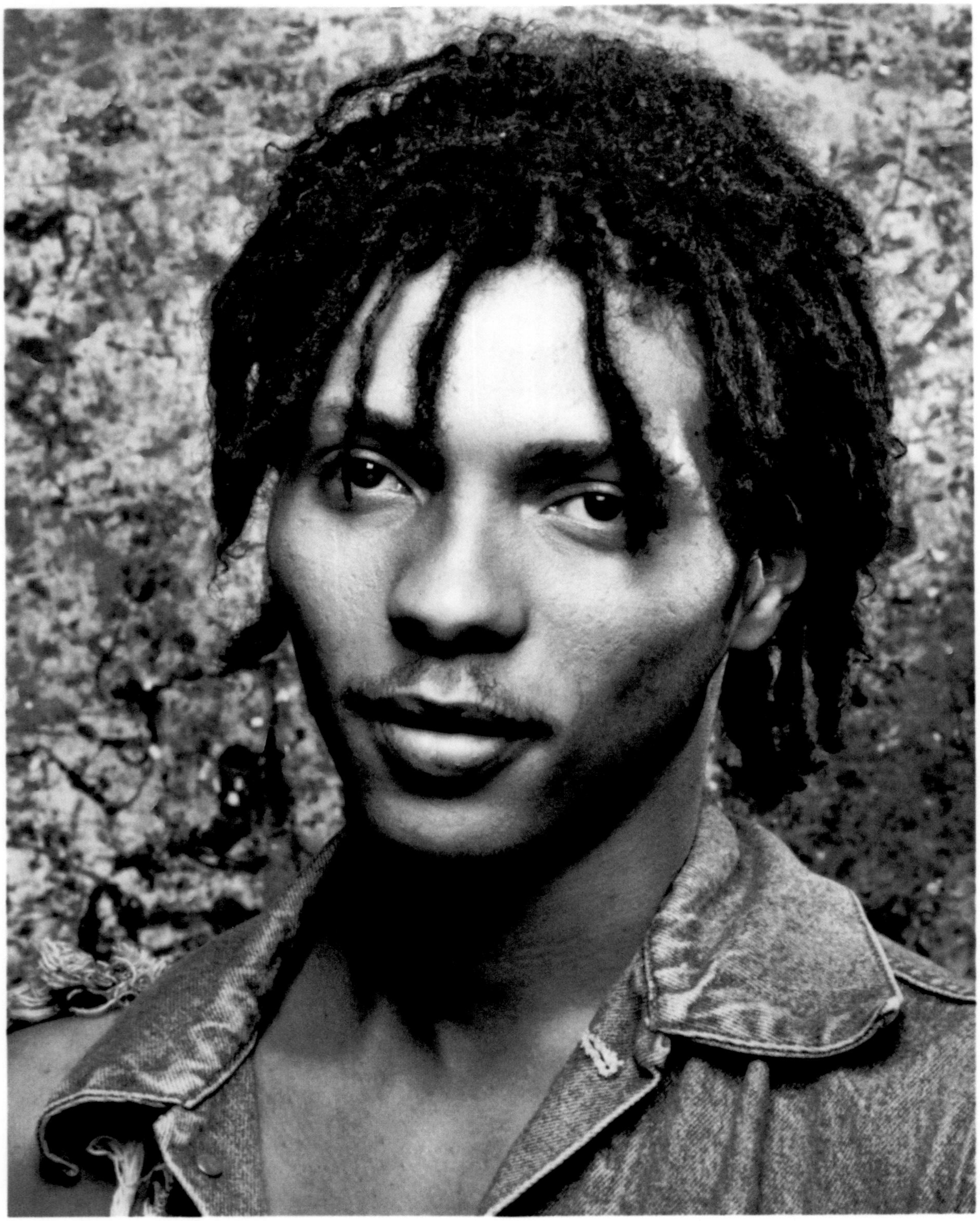

PHOTO CREDIT: LEVON PARIAN

IVAN NEVILLE

PolyGram Records

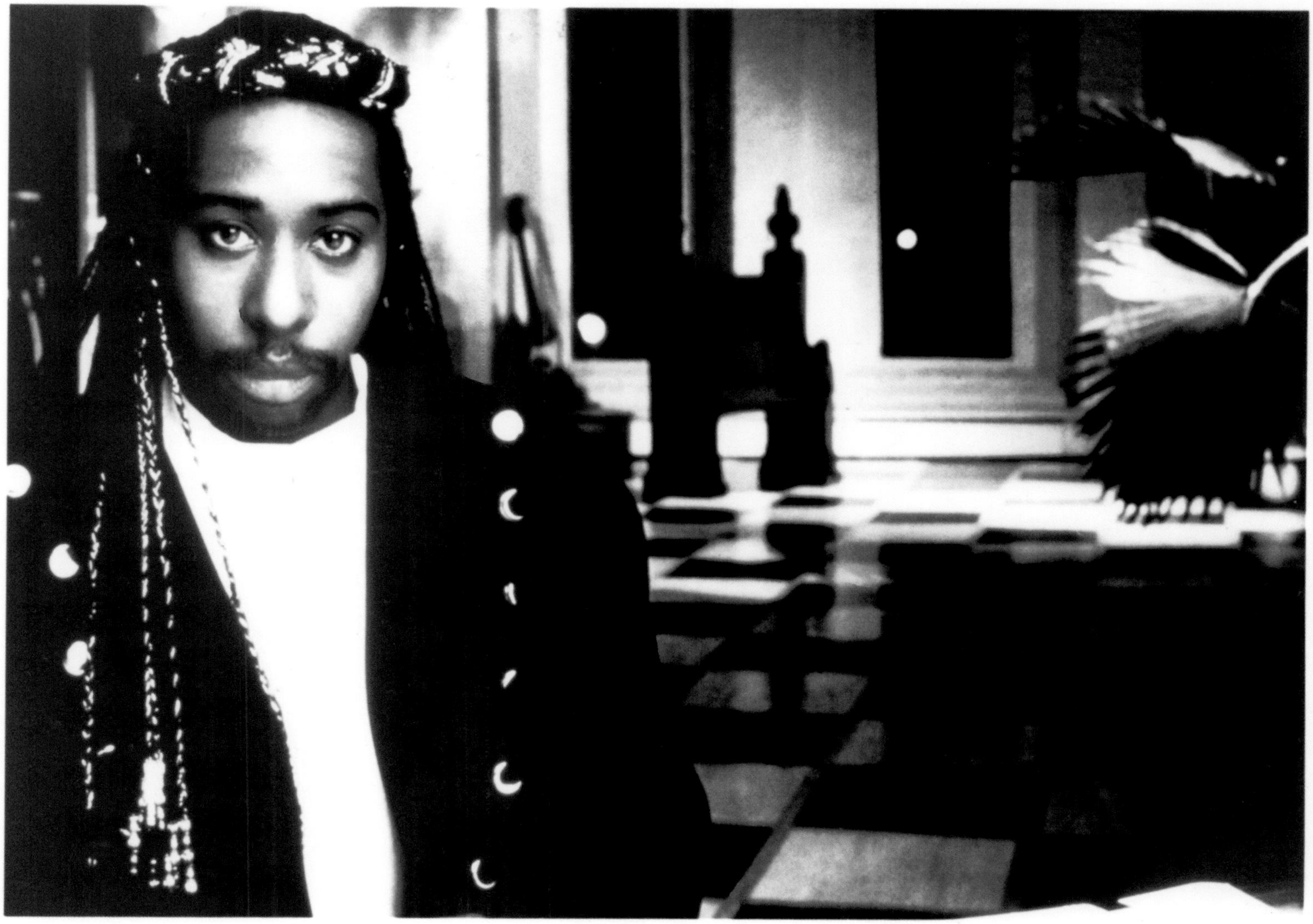

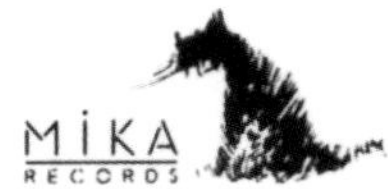

DEON SPELL ESTUS

PolyGram Records

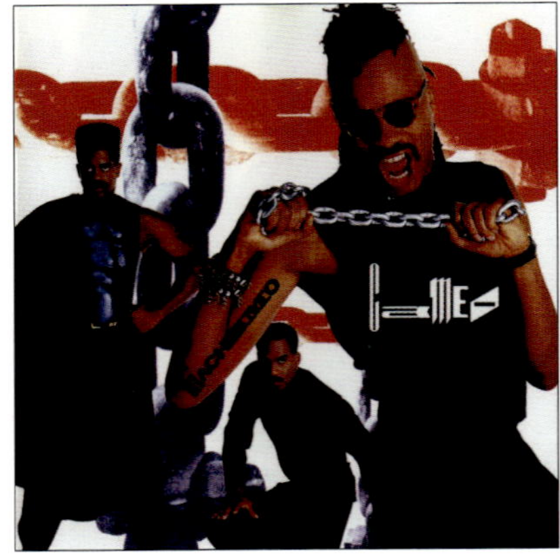

After the classic *Word Up!* album, Larry Blackmon and the funksters in **Cameo** reappeared with *Machismo* and a crisp single, "You Make Me Work."

Billboard 200: *Machismo* (#56)
Billboard Hot 100: "You Make Me Work" (#85)

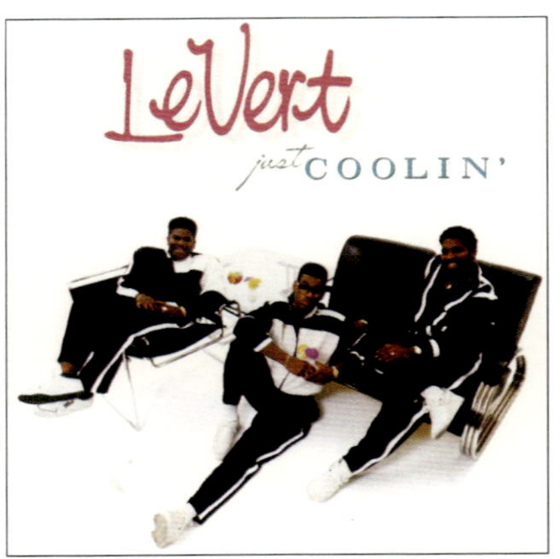

With the Top 5 R&B singles "Addicted to You," "Pull Over," "Gotta Get the Money" and the title track, *Just Coolin'* showed **LeVert**'s knack for hit-making.

Billboard 200: *Just Coolin'* (#79)

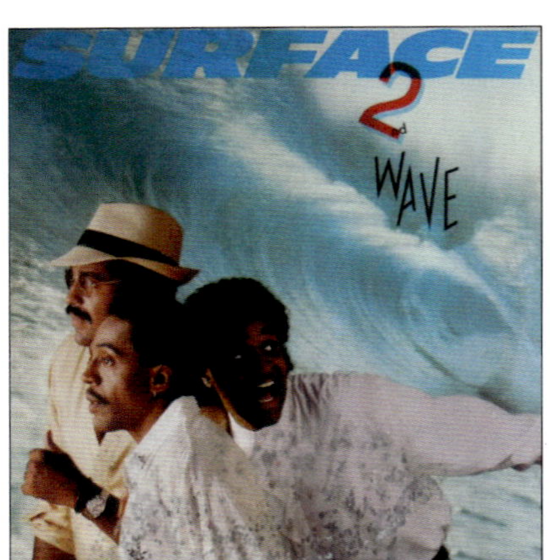

2nd Wave, soul trio **Surface**'s second album, introduced "Shower Me with Your Love," a classic wedding song that qualified for a gold certification.

Billboard 200: *2nd Wave* (#56)
Billboard Hot 100: "Closer Than Friends" (#57);
"Shower Me with Your Love" (#5); "You Are My Everything" (#84)

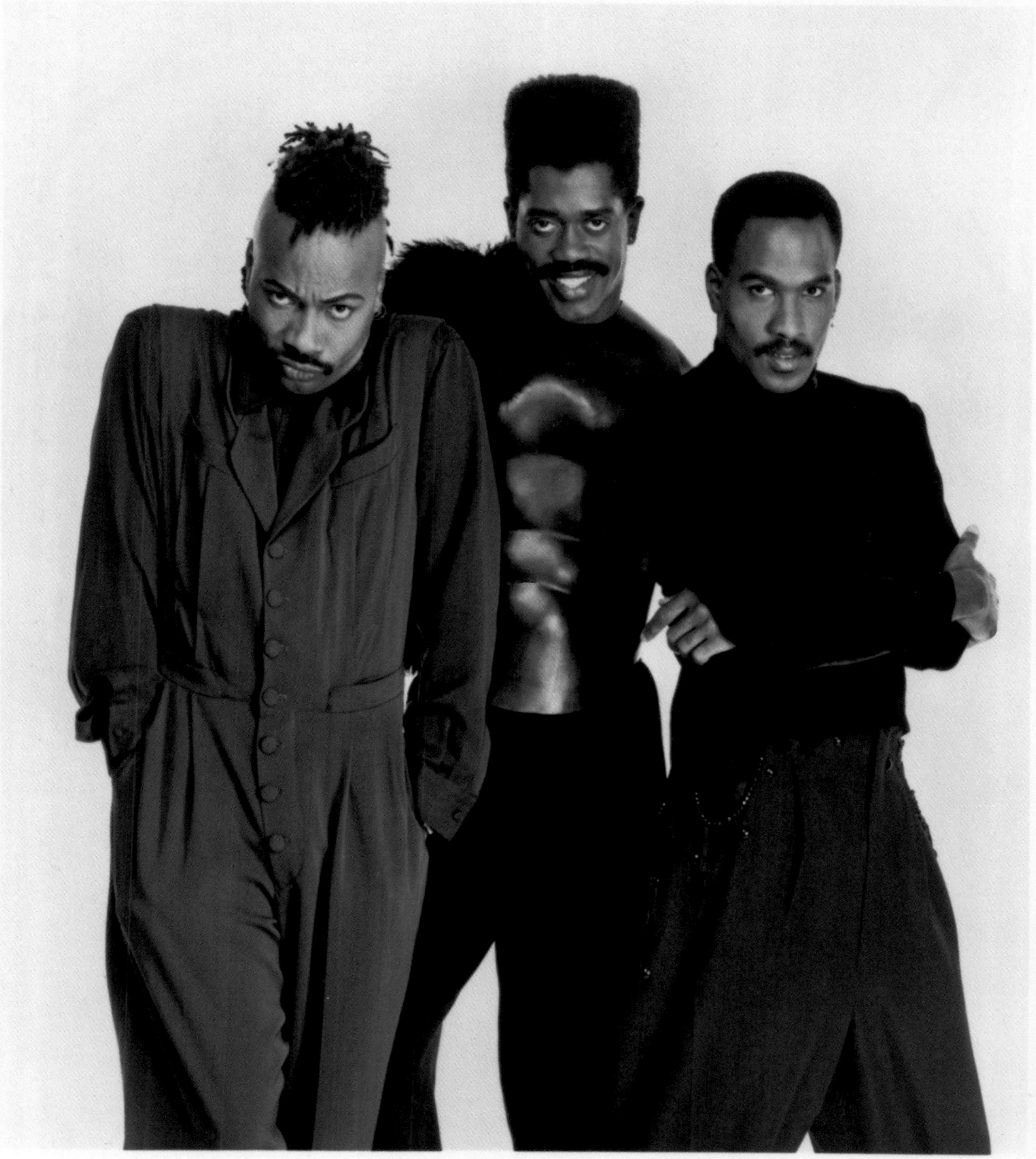

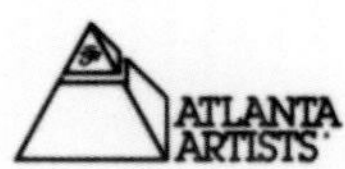

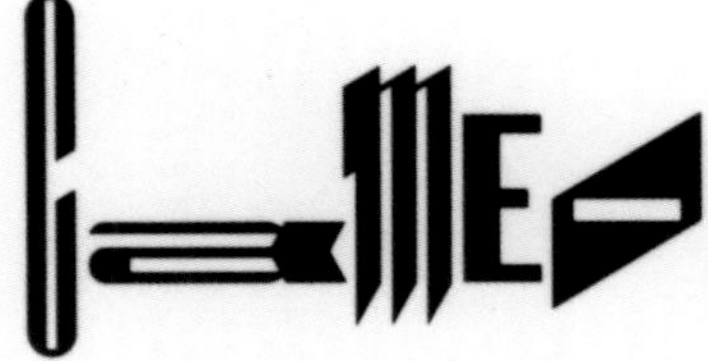

PolyGram Records

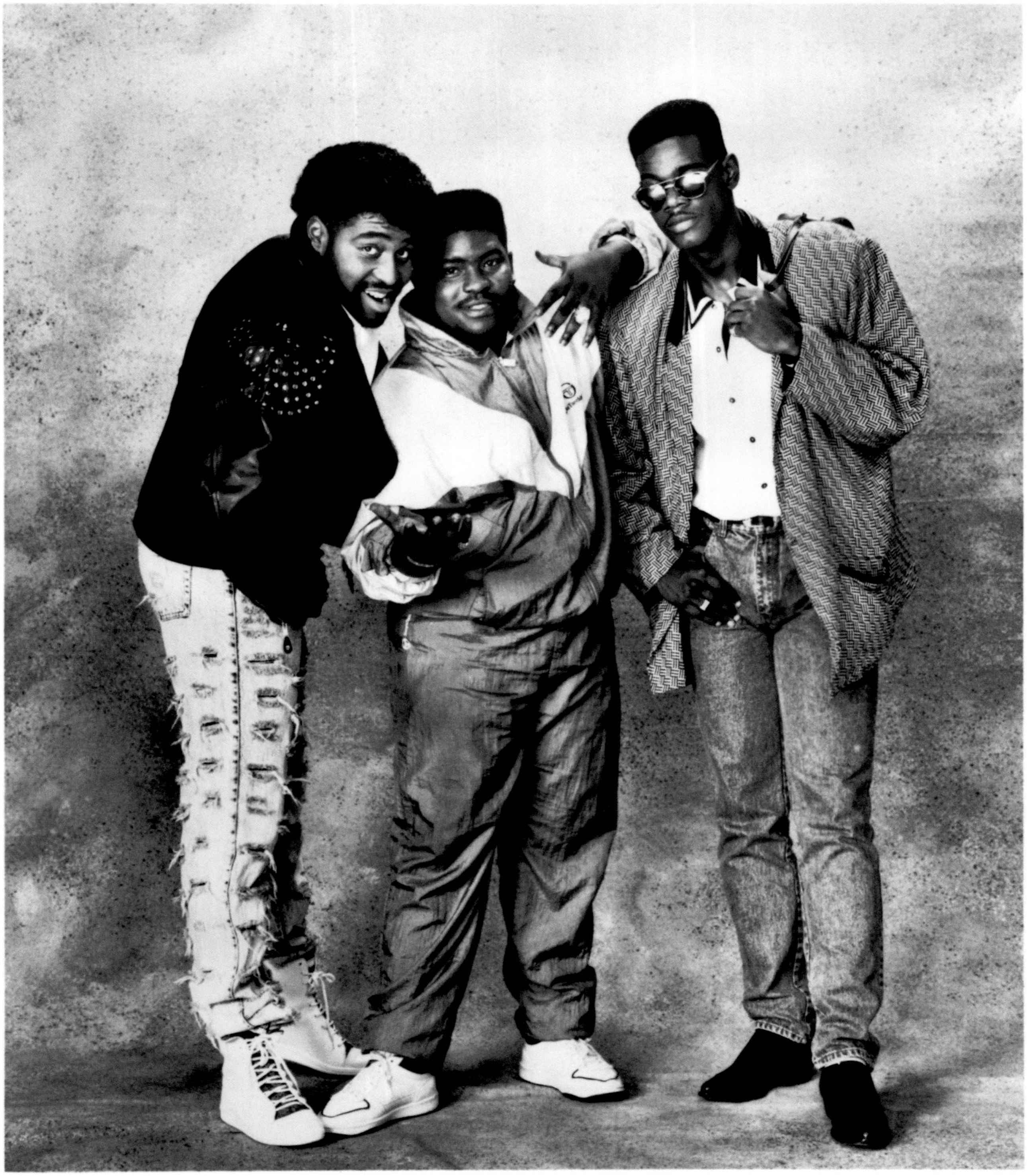

Gerald LeVert **Sean LeVert** **Marc Gordon**

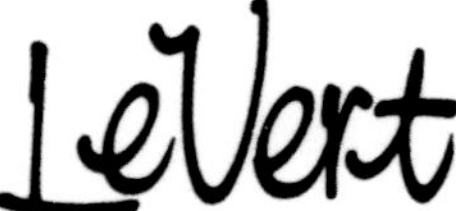

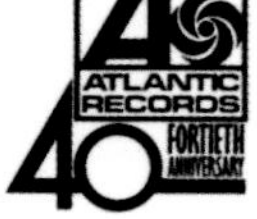

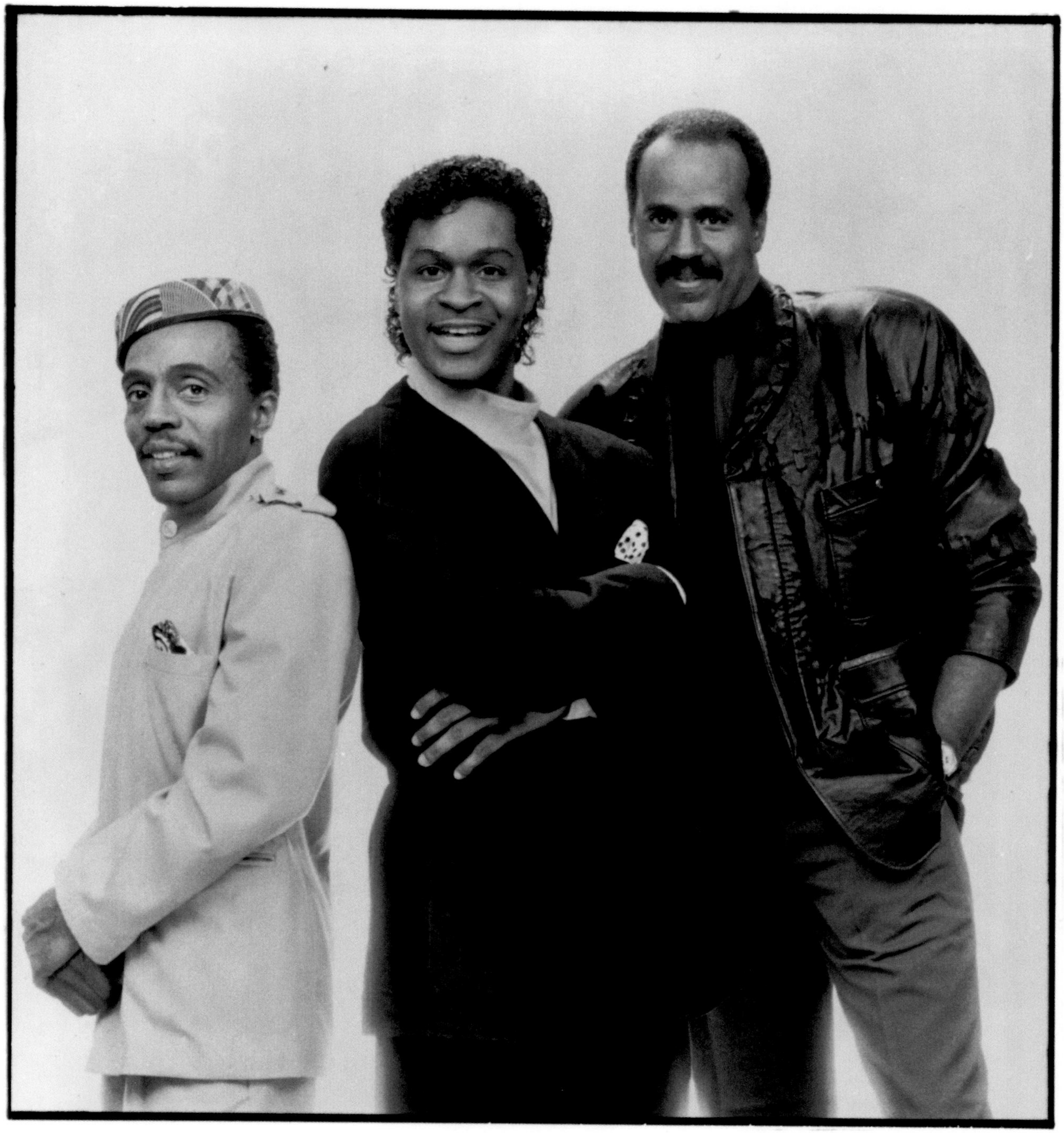

PHOTOGRAPH: GEORGE LIGON / MAKEUP & STYLING: ANGELA SLATE

From left DAVE "PICK" CONLEY, BERNARD JACKSON, DAVID TOWNSEND.

SURFACE

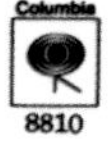

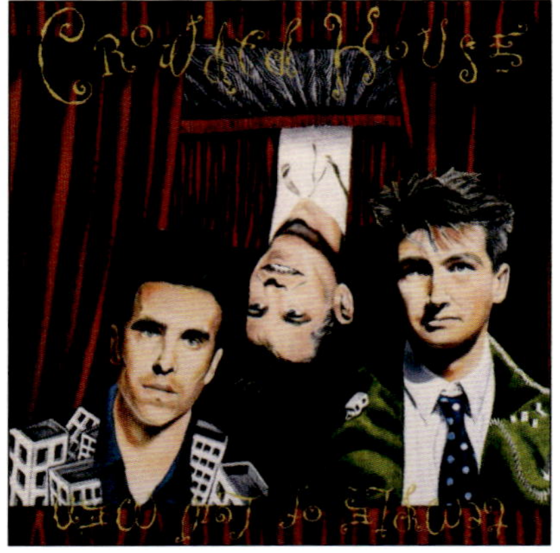

Led by Neil Finn's songcraft, Crowded House showcased the exquisite melody and pensive lyrics of "Better Be Home Soon" for its Australasia fan base.

Billboard 200: *Temple of Low Men* (#40)
Billboard Hot 100: "Better Be Home Soon" (#42)

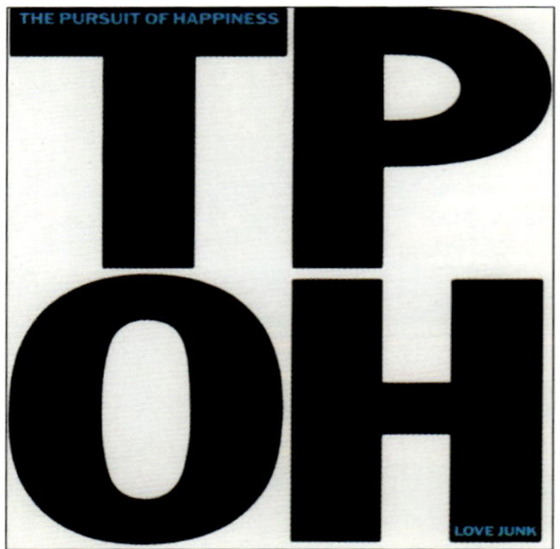

The Pursuit of Happiness, a Canadian group steered by Moe Berg, placed a caustic hit on rock radio with the Todd Rundgren-produced "I'm an Adult Now."

Billboard 200: *Love Junk* (#93)

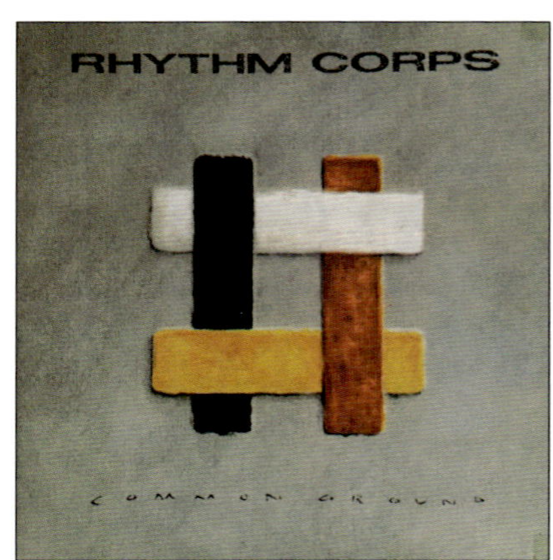

Coming out of Detroit's alternative music scene, Rhythm Corps landed a track on the mainstream rock charts with the title track from *Common Ground.*

Billboard 200: *Common Ground* (#104)

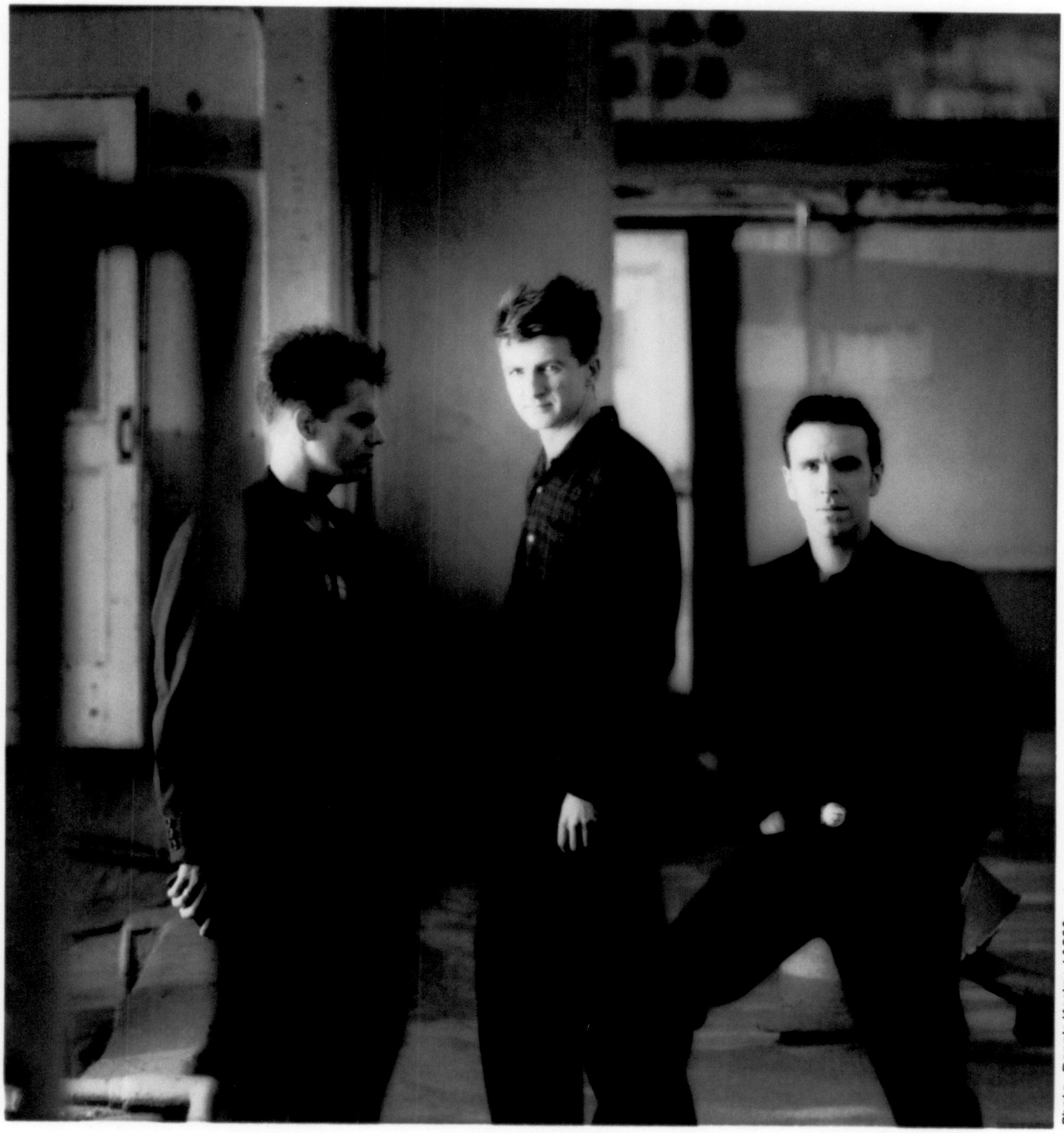

Photo: Dennis Keeley / 1988

Paul Hester Neil Finn Nick Seymour

CROWDED HOUSE

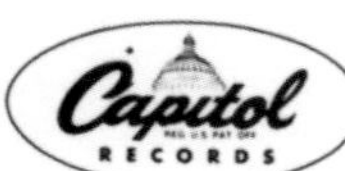

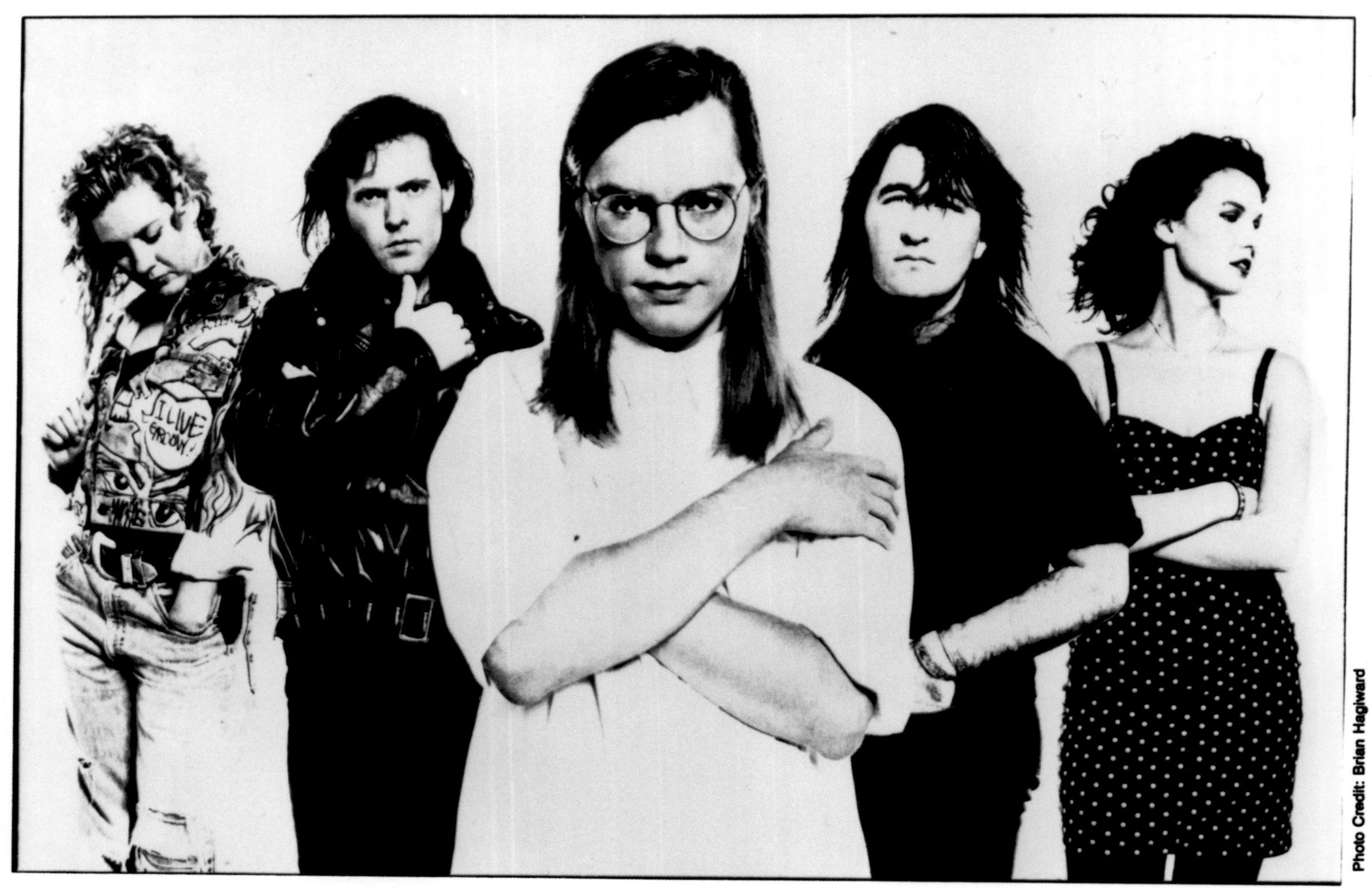

Photo Credit: Brian Hagiward

THE PURSUIT OF HAPPINESS

Chrysalis.

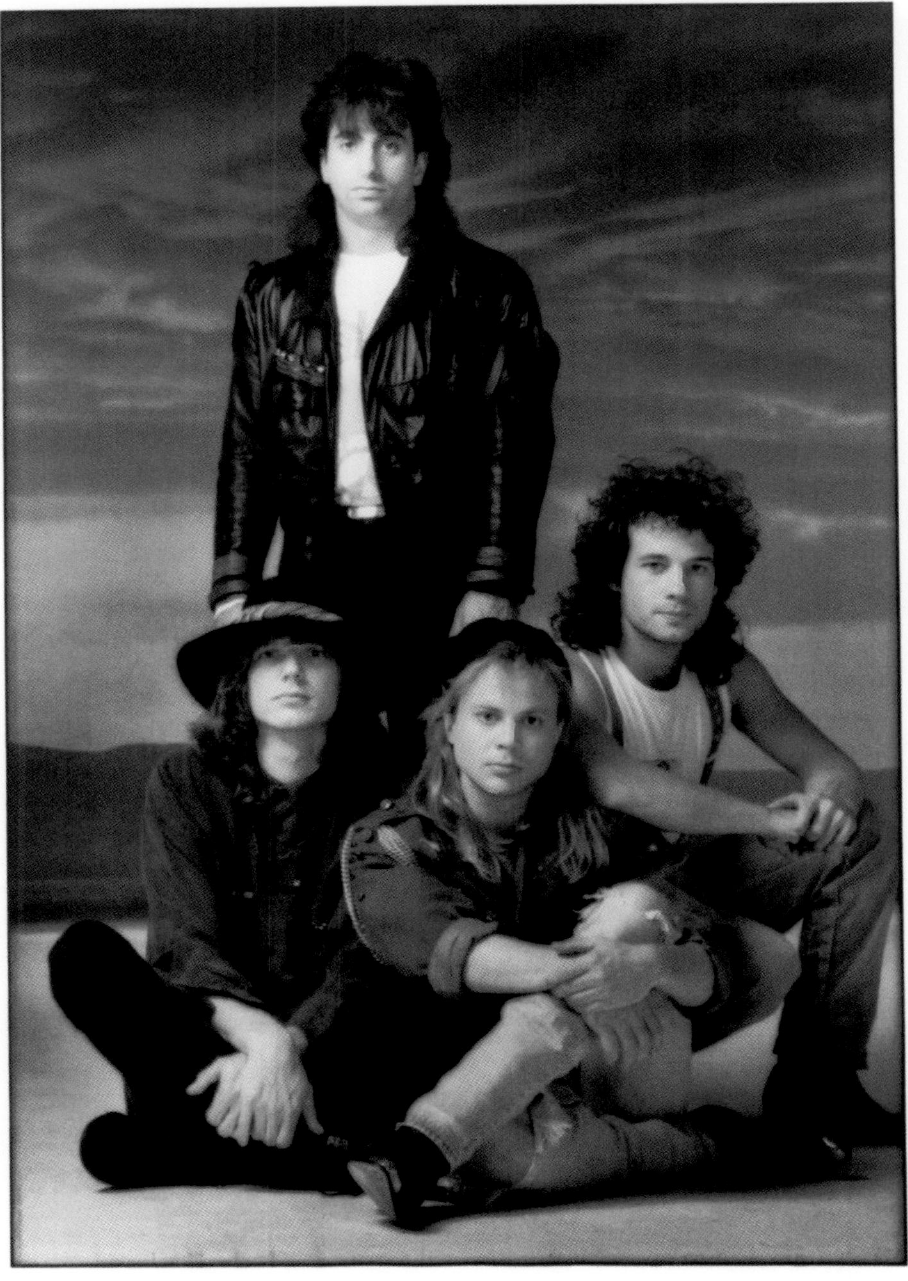

PHOTO: JAY DAVID BUCHSBAUM

L to R: DAVEY HOLMBO GREG APRO (Standing) MICHAEL PERSH RICHIE LOVSIN

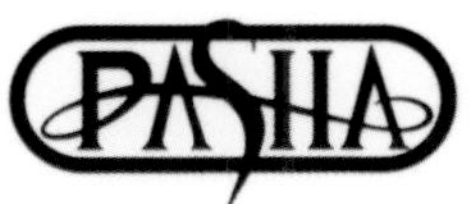

RHYTHM CORPS

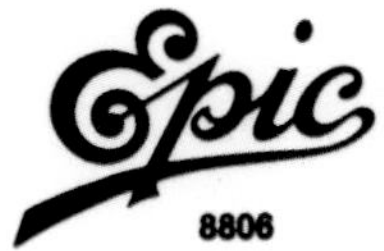

MANAGEMENT· RANDY SOSIN /LEFT BANK MANAGEMENT

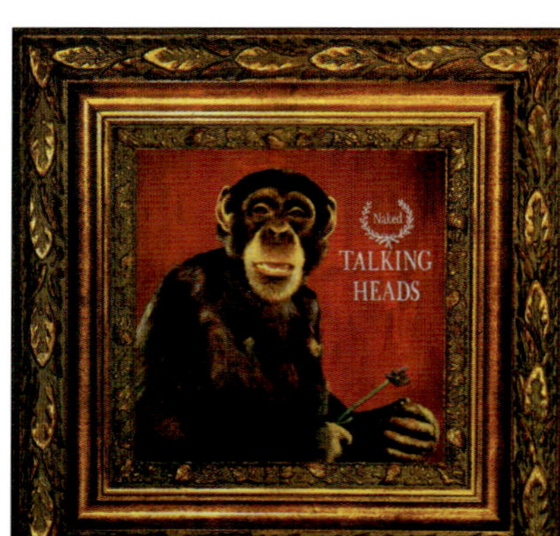

Under David Byrne's command, **Talking Heads**' *Naked* marked a return to fusing polyrhythmic styles, manifested on the song "(Nothing But) Flowers."

Billboard 200: *Naked* (#19)

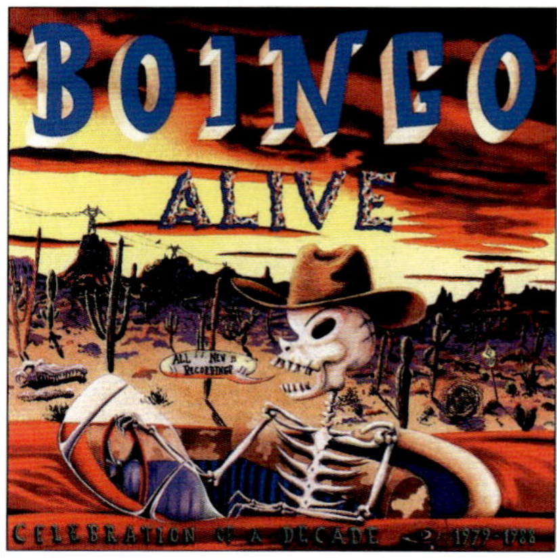

Recorded "live" on a soundstage, the double album *Boingo Alive* commemorated **Oingo Boingo**'s most popular tunes plus the recent "Winning Side."

Billboard 200: *Boingo Alive* (#90)

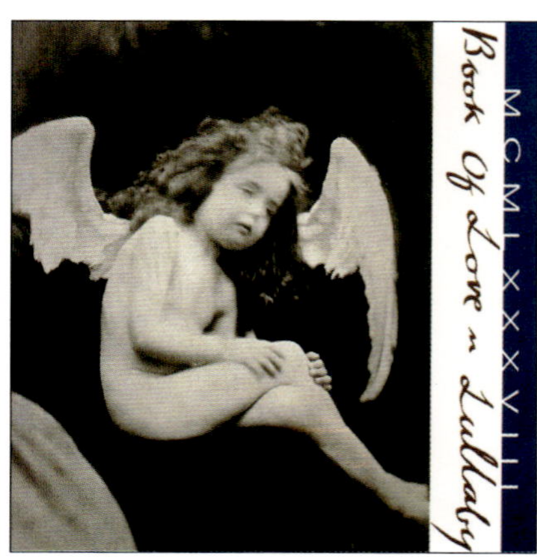

"Pretty Boys and Pretty Girls," one of the earliest songs to address the AIDS crisis, gave the synth-pop act **Book of Love** exposure on pop radio stations.

Billboard 200: *Lullaby* (#156)
Billboard Hot 100: "Pretty Boys and Pretty Girls" (#90)

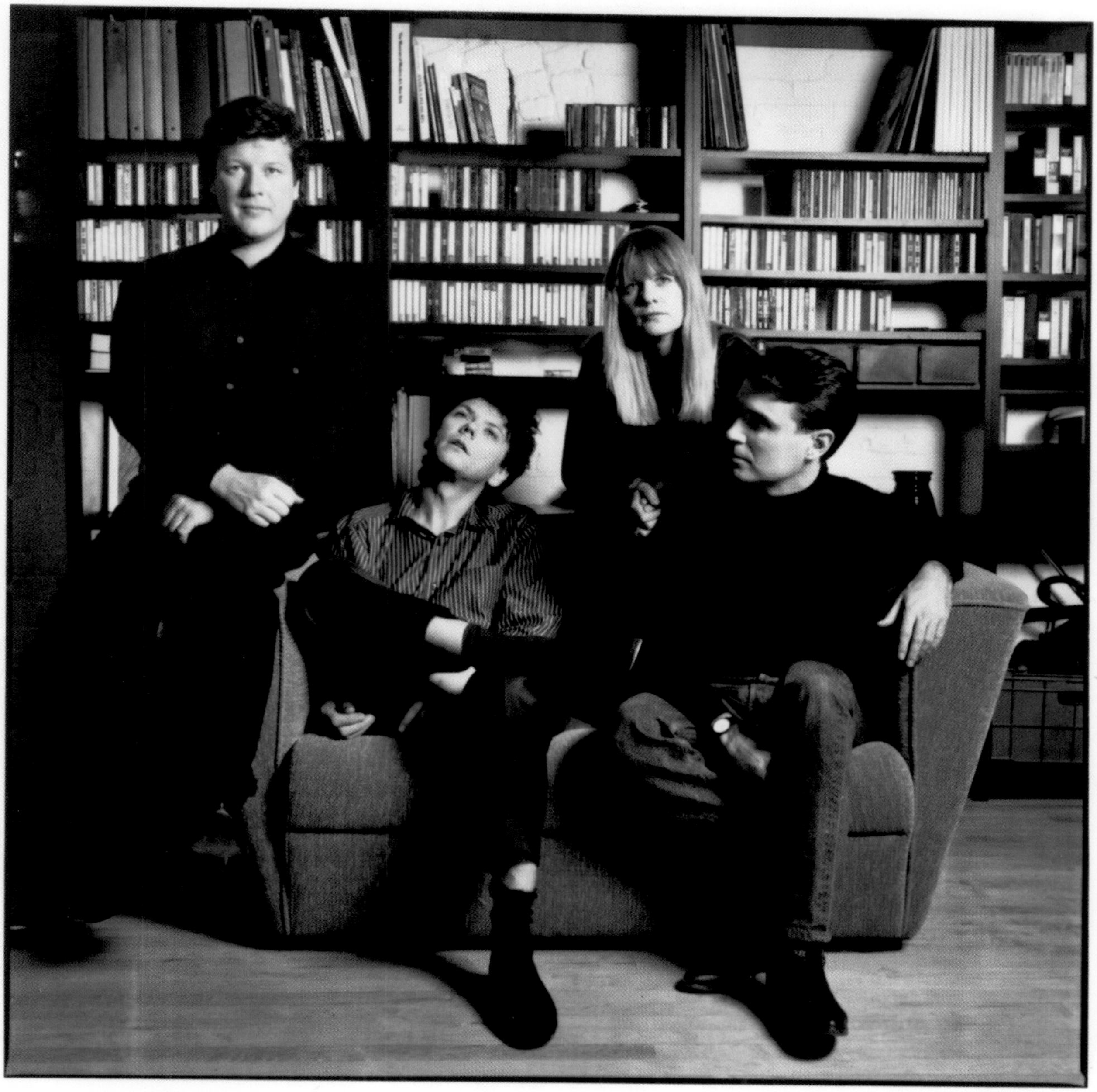

Photo Credit: Deborah Feingold

TALKING HEADS

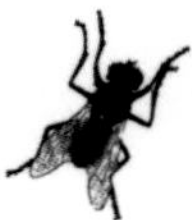

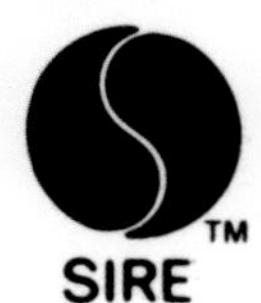

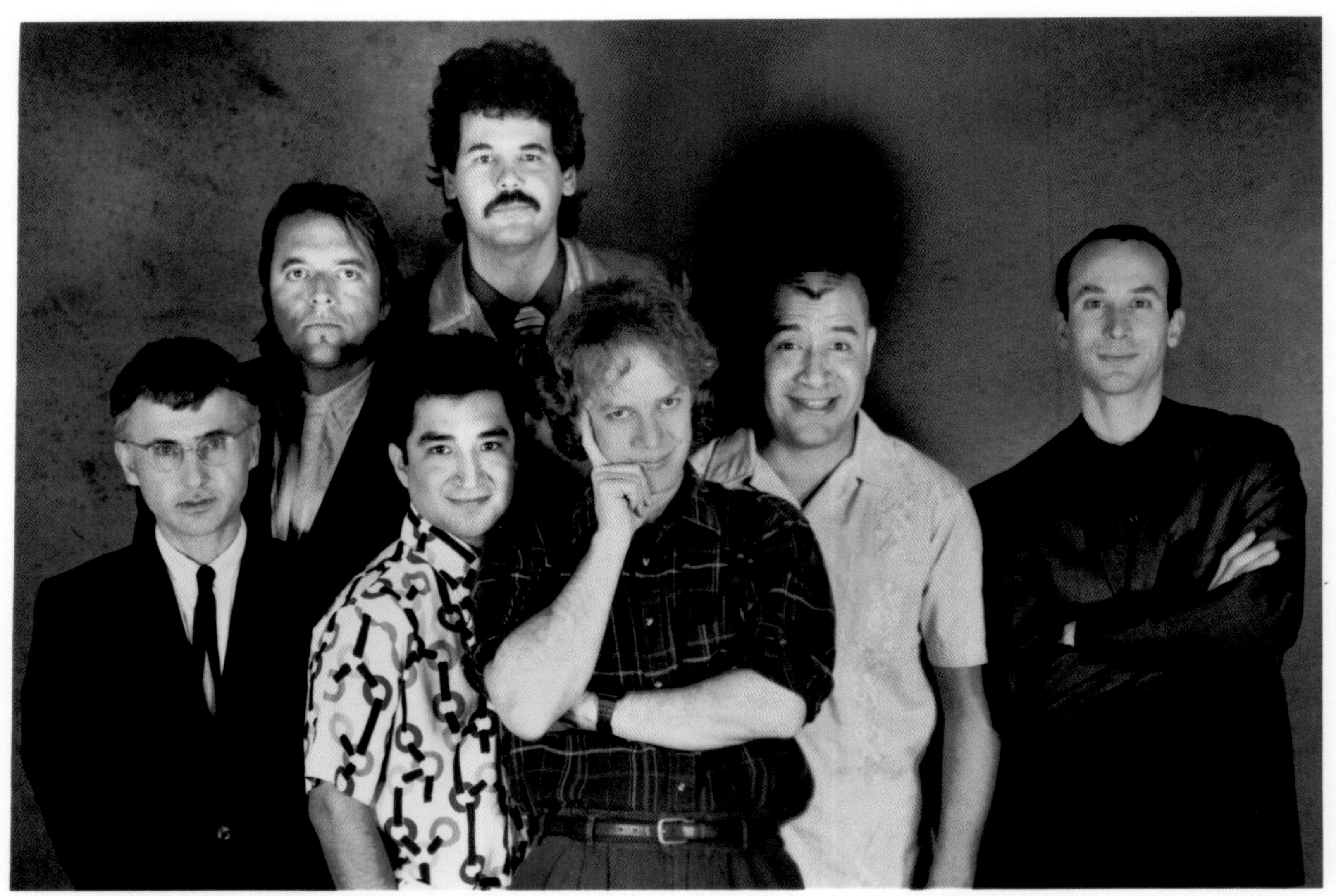

(left to right) Dale Turner, Sam Phipps, John Avila,
Steve Bartek, Danny Elfman, Johnny "Vatos" Hernandez,
Leon Schneiderman

OINGO BOINGO

MCA RECORDS

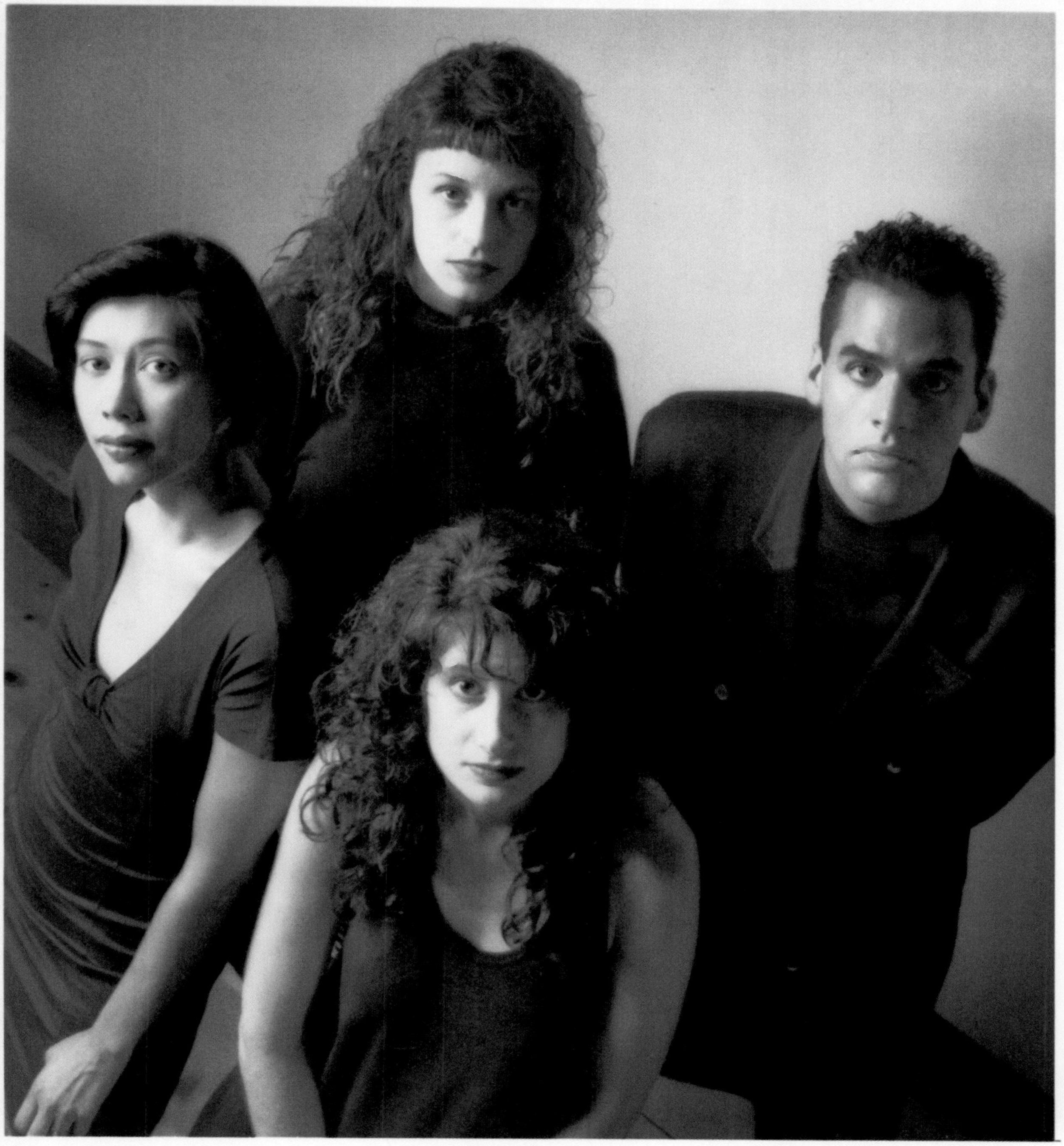

Photo Credit: Melodie Gimple

JADE LEE LAUREN ROSELLI SUSAN OTTAVIANO TED OTTAVIANO

Book Of Love

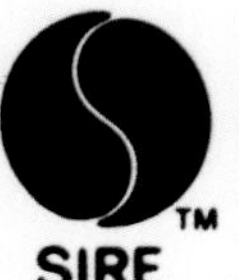

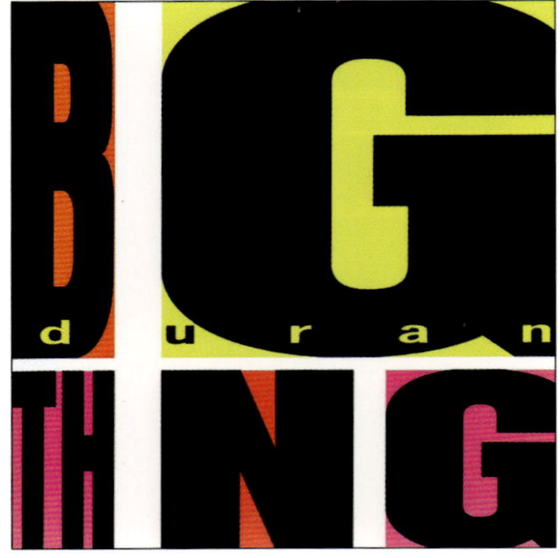

Duran Duran's single "I Don't Want Your Love" coalesced a more assertive dance direction involving former Missing Persons guitarist Warren Cuccurullo.

Billboard 200: *Big Thing* (#24)
Billboard Hot 100: "I Don't Want Your Love" (#4); "All She Wants Is" (#22); "Do You Believe in Shame?" (#72)

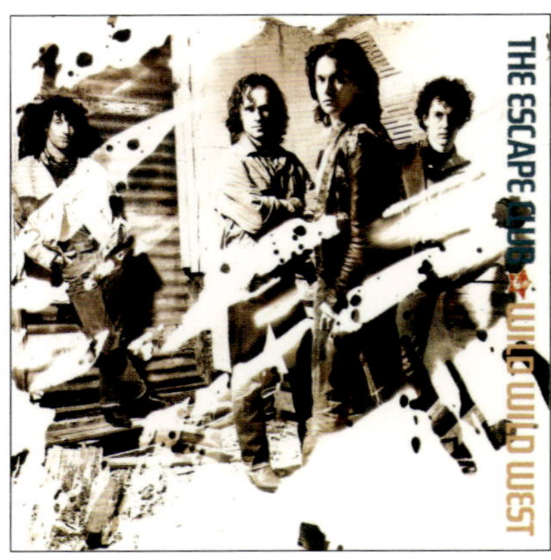

The Escape Club's "Wild, Wild West" was played in heavy rotation on MTV and hit No. 1 in the US—while never charting in the English band's homeland.

Billboard 200: *Wild Wild West* (#27)
Billboard Hot 100: "Wild, Wild West" (No. 1); "Shake for the Sheik" (#28); "Walking Through Walls" (#81)

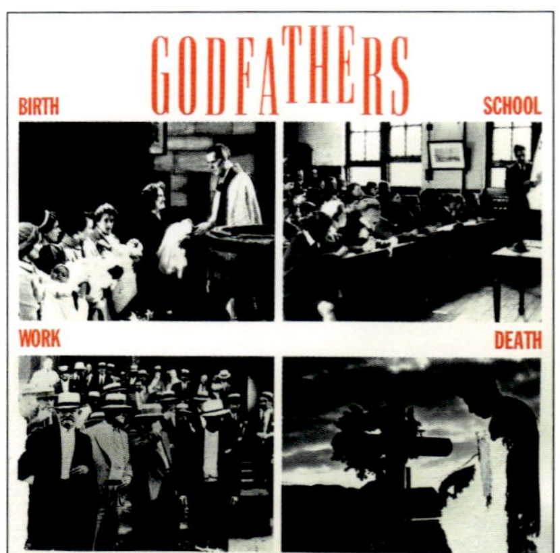

The Godfathers, a South London quintet, offered up "Birth, School, Work, Death," a working-class anthem that became a college radio smash in America.

Billboard 200: *Birth, School, Work, Death* (#91)

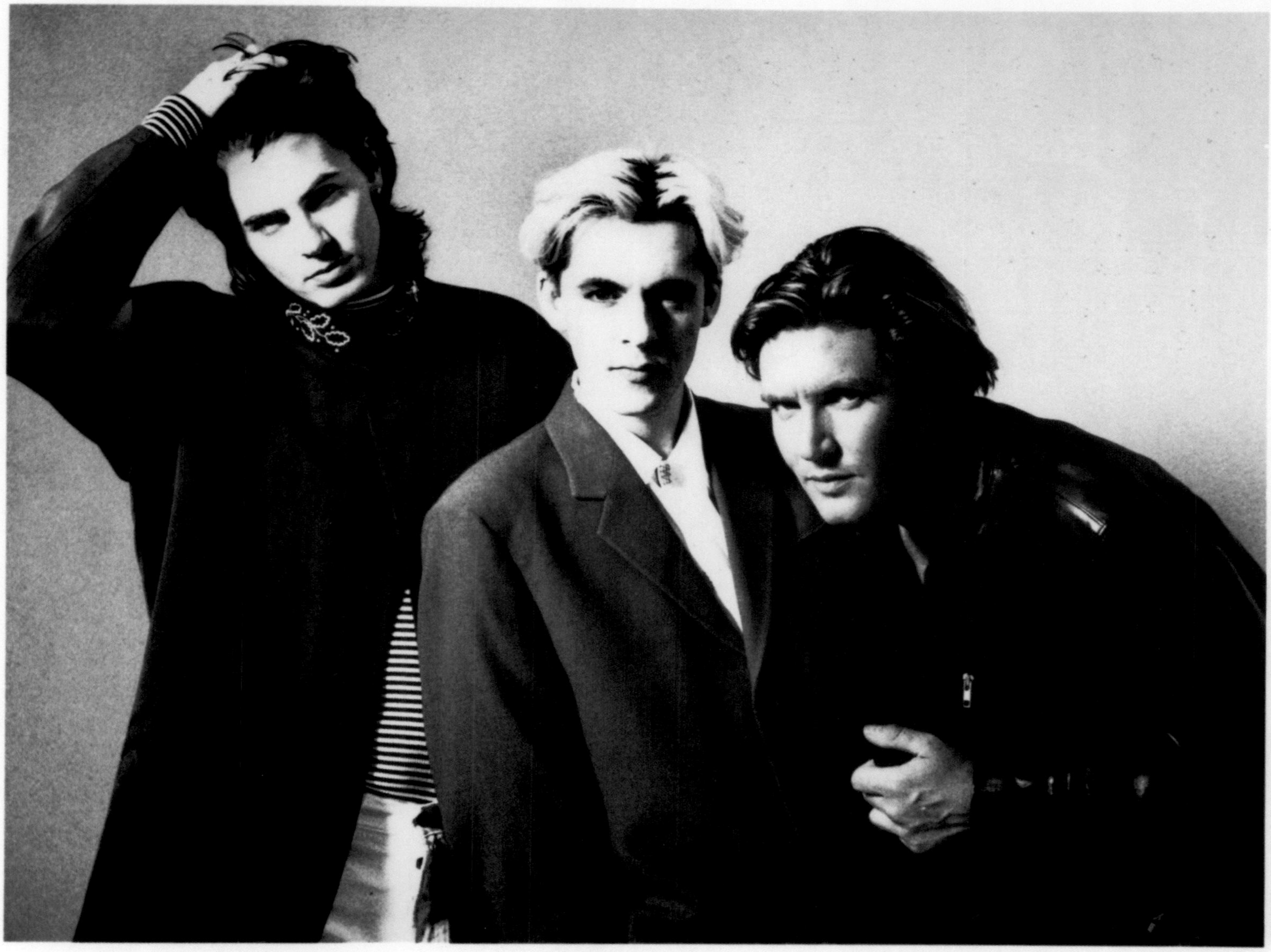

1988 Copyright DD Productions Ltd. Photographer: Mark Bayley

John Taylor

Nick Rhodes

Simon LeBon

DURAN DURAN

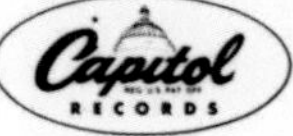

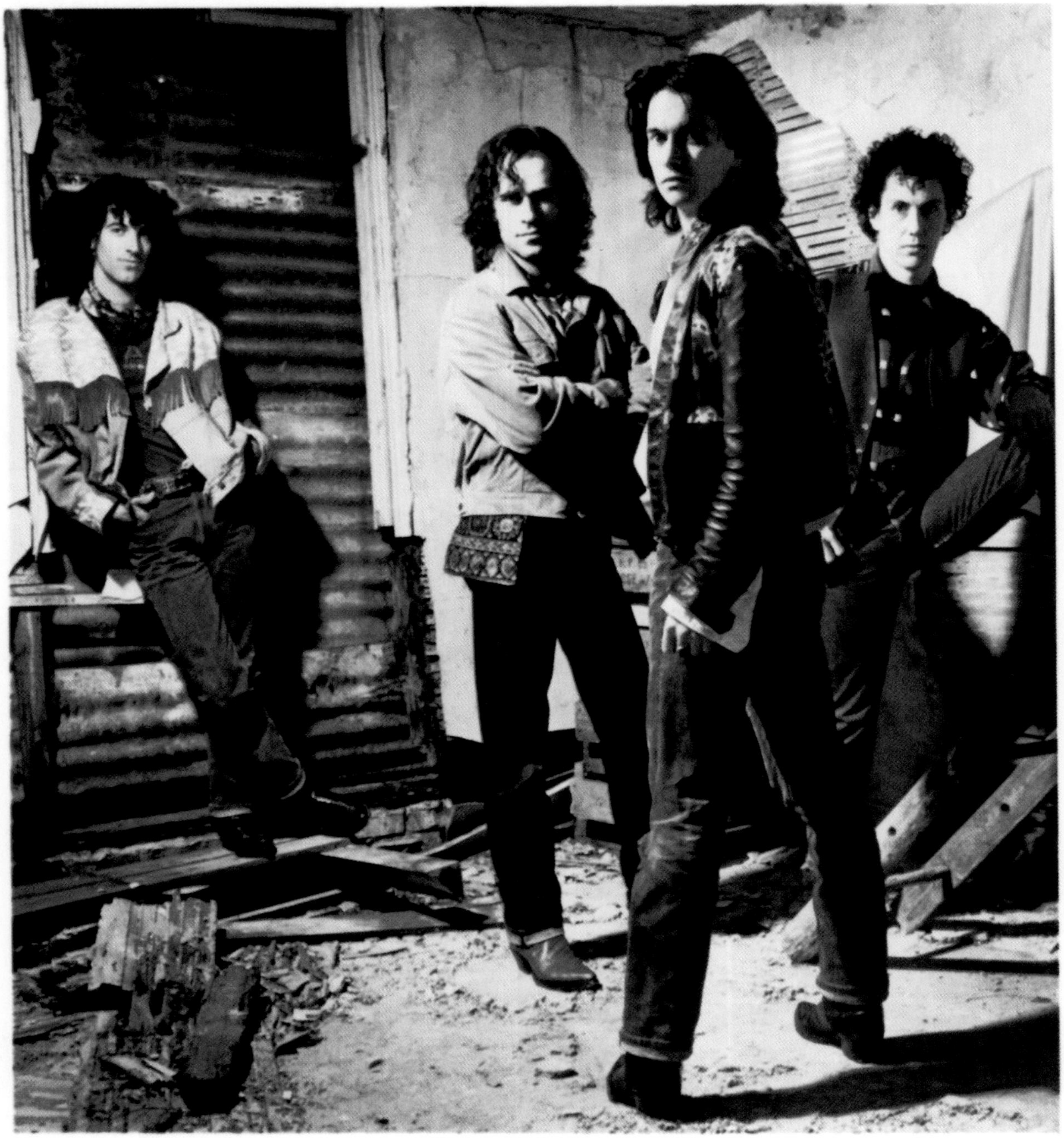

JOHNNIE CHRISTO MILAN ZEKAVICA TREVOR STEEL JOHN HOLLIDAY

THE ESCAPE CLUB

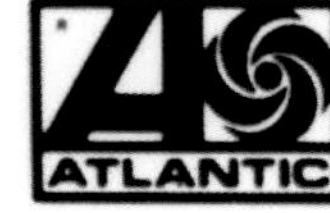

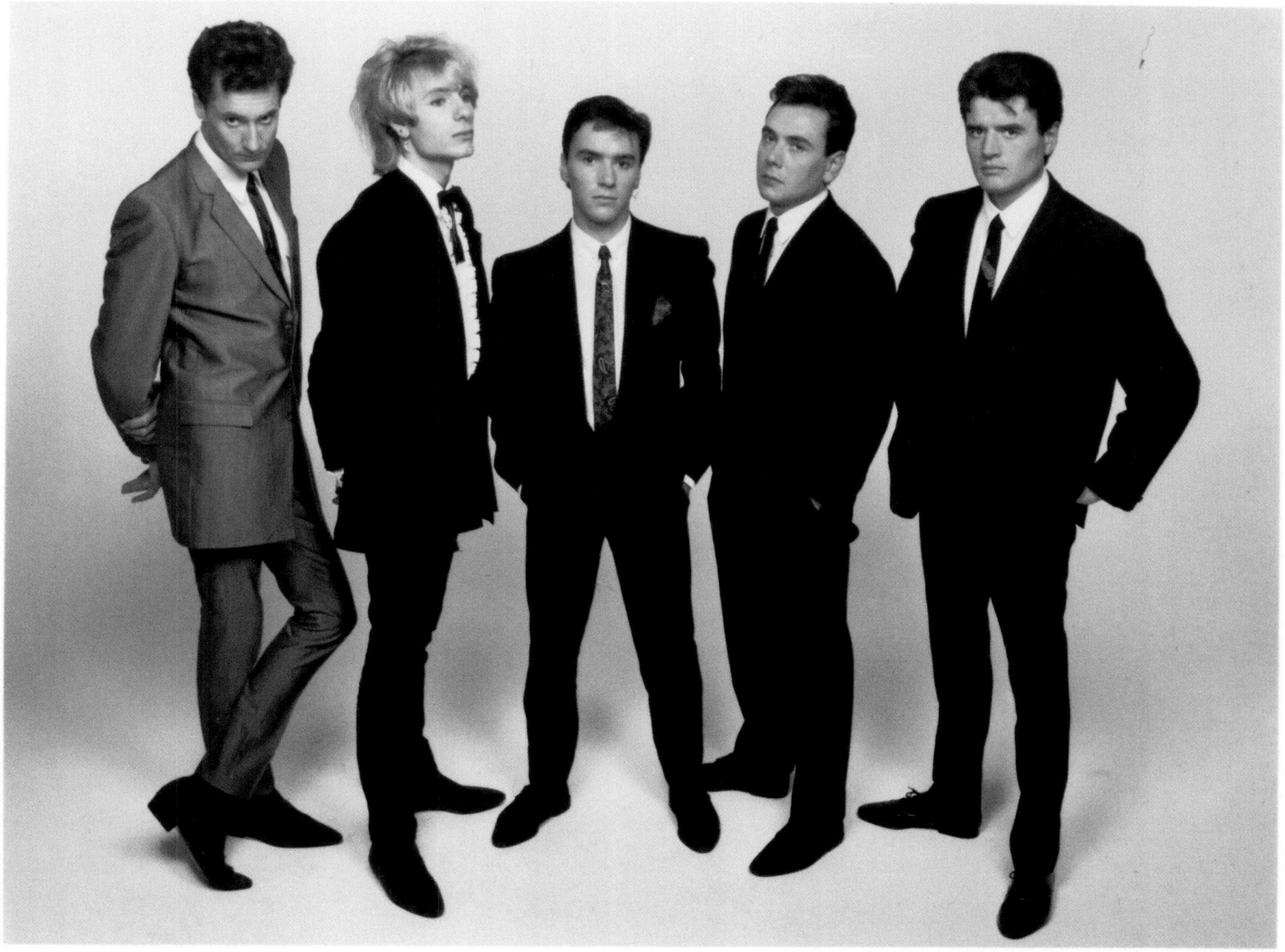

L-R: Mike Gibson Guitar ; George Mazur Drums ; Kris Dollimore Guitar ;
Pete Coyne Vocals ; Chris Coyne Bass

THE GODFATHERS

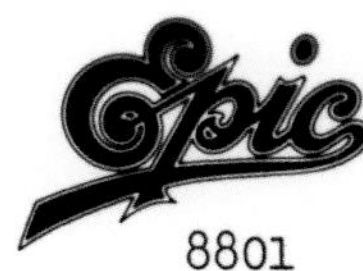

8801

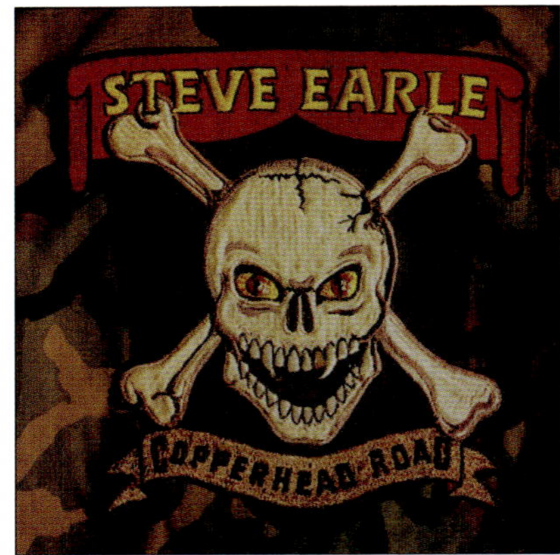

"Copperhead Road" found maverick **Steve Earle** breaking from country's stylistic constraints, but the song found acceptance from rock radio stations.

Billboard 200: *Copperhead Road* (#56)

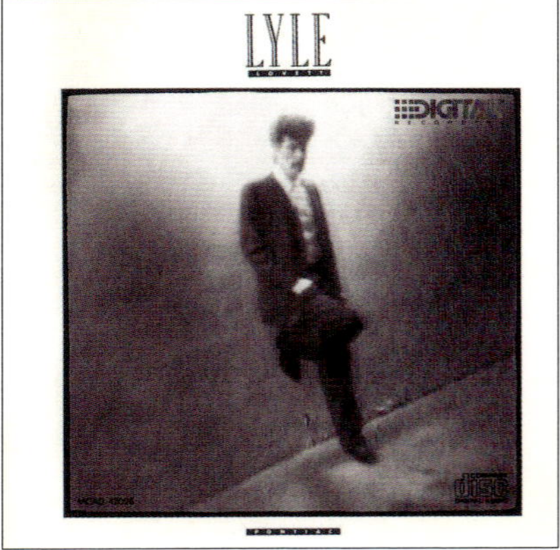

Pontiac, **Lyle Lovett**'s second album, enhanced his reputation as a rare, provocative songwriter with the cynical "She's No Lady" and "If I Had a Boat."

Billboard 200: *Pontiac* (#117)

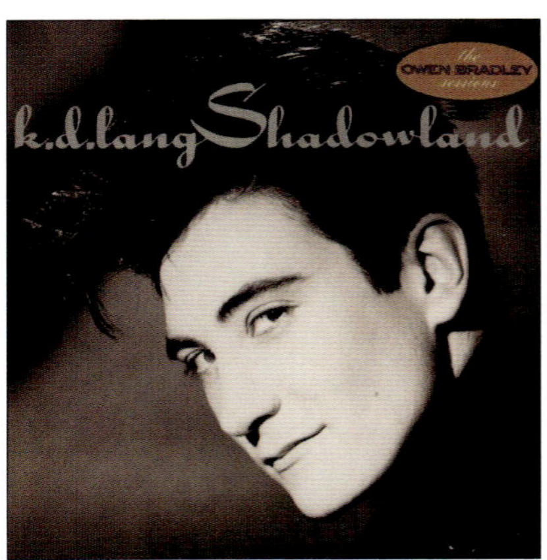

Country legends Loretta Lynn, Brenda Lee and Kitty Wells appeared on **k.d. lang**'s *Shadowland*, lending their voices to "Honky Tonk Angels' Medley."

Billboard 200: *Shadowland* (#73)

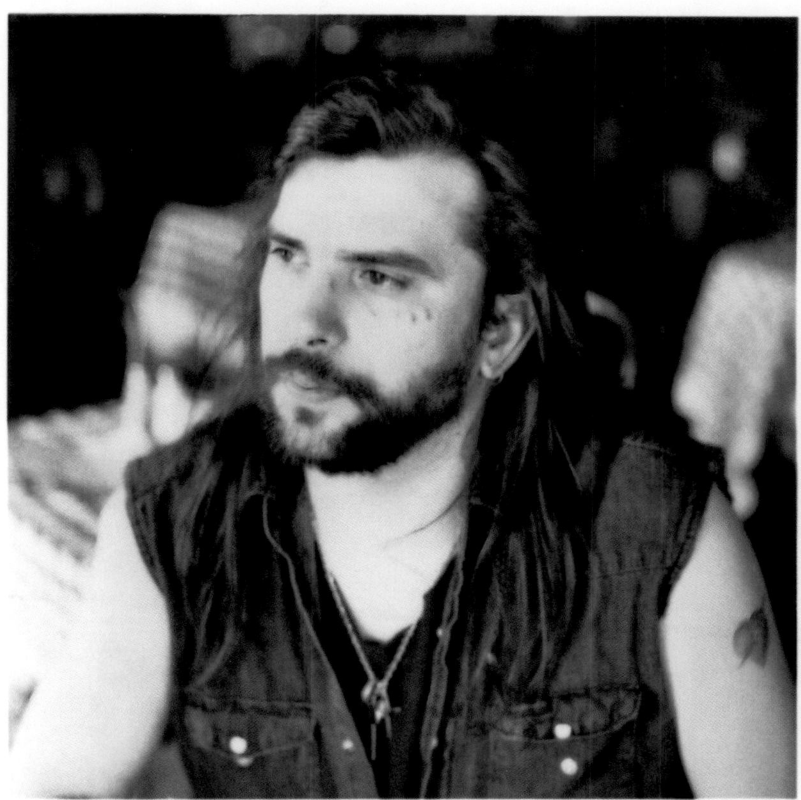

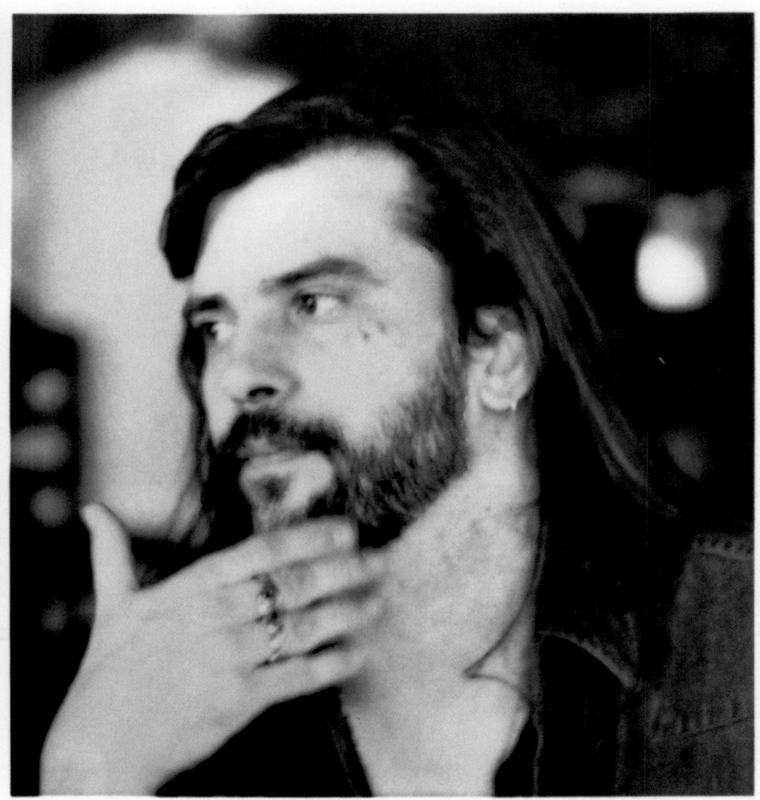

PHOTO CREDIT: EMPIRE STUDIOS

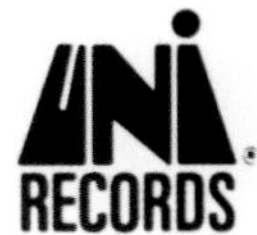

Steve Earle

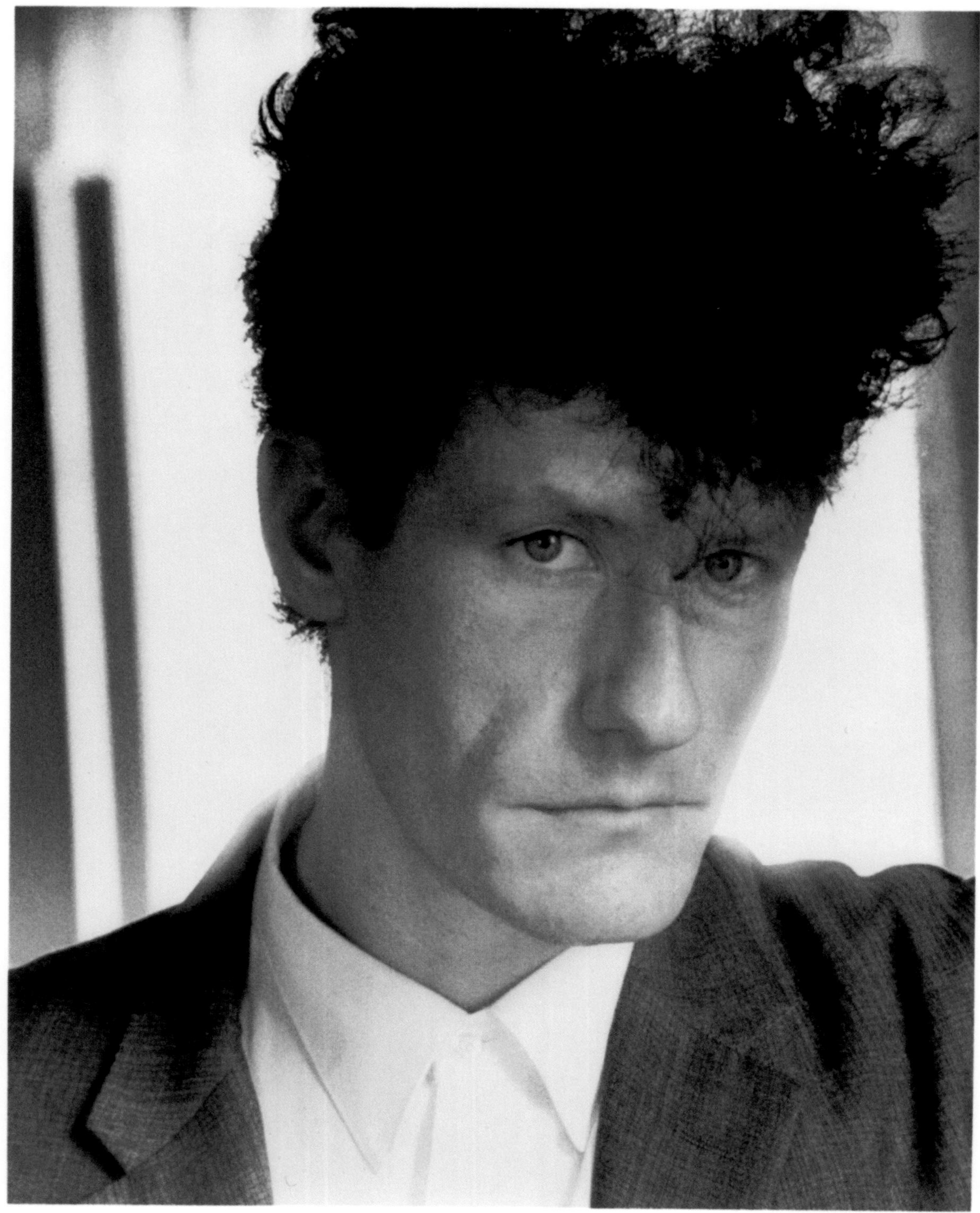

photo: Peter Nash 0887 A

LYLE LOVETT

MCA RECORDS CURB RECORDS

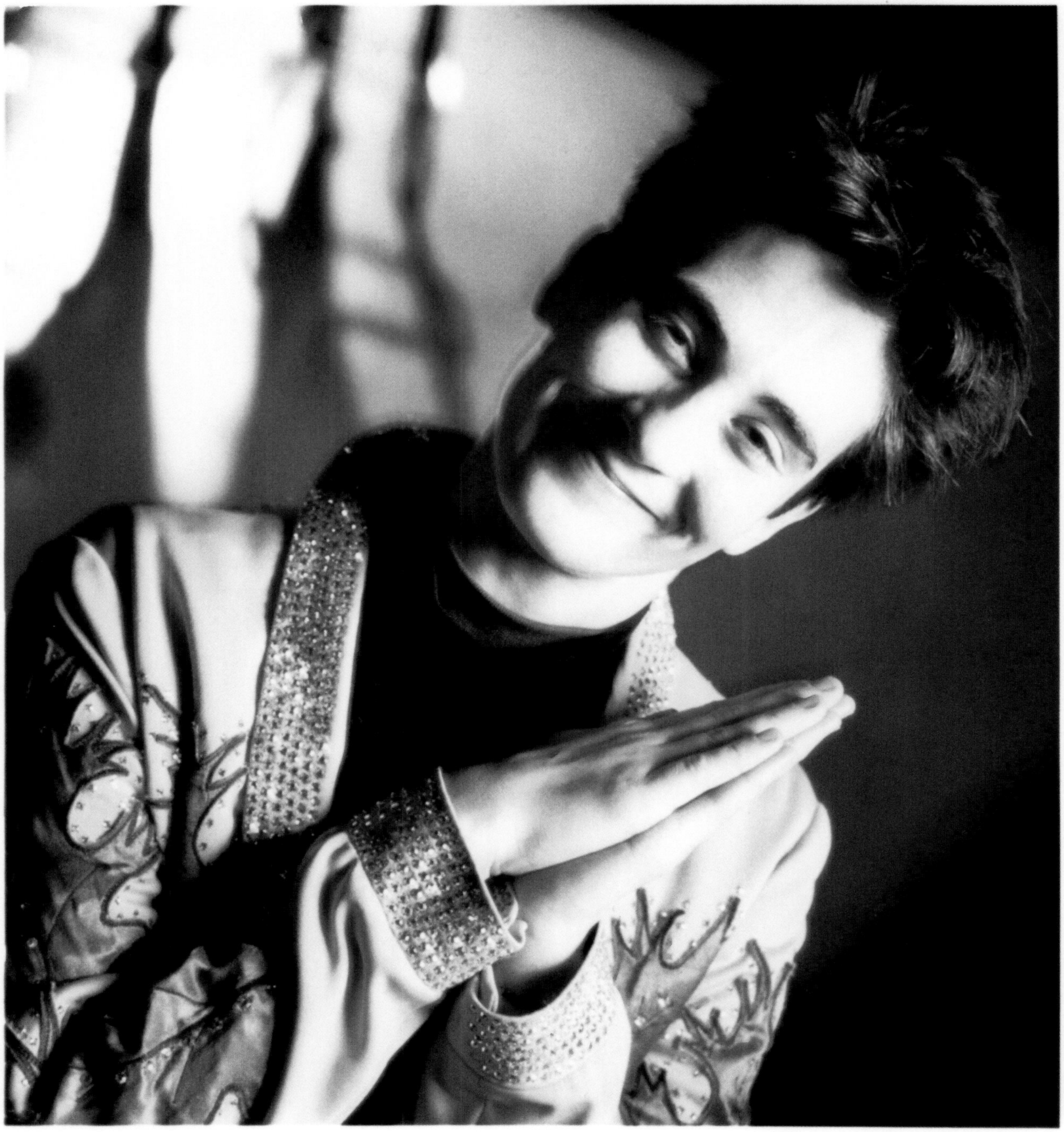

credit: Empire Studio 3/88

k.d.lang

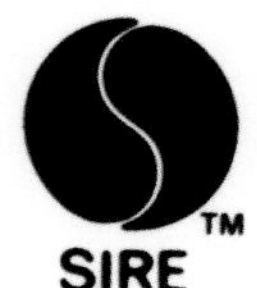

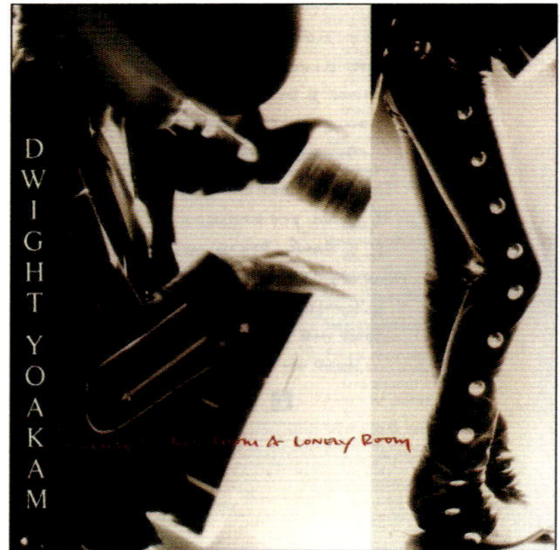

Dwight Yoakam's third album spawned his first country chart-topper, a duet with his musical hero, Buck Owens, on a cover of "Streets of Bakersfield."

Billboard 200: *Buenas Noches from a Lonely Room* (#68)

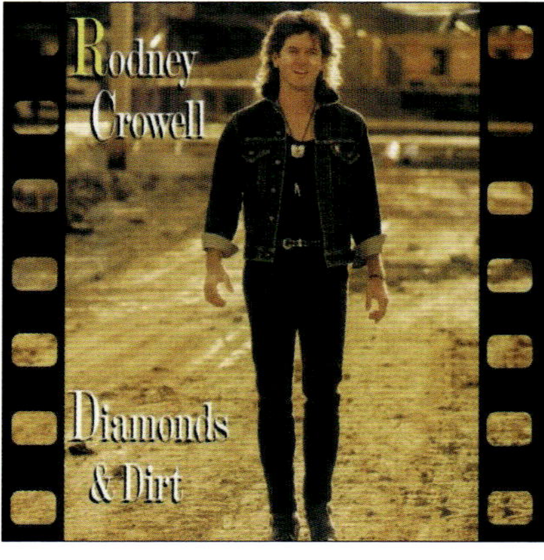

A record-setting five consecutive No. 1 singles on the country charts came from *Diamonds & Dirt,* singer-songwriter **Rodney Crowell**'s milestone album.

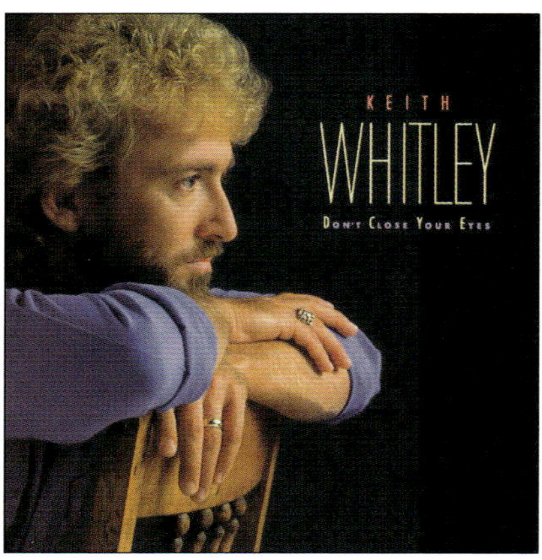

Budding country music superstar **Keith Whitley**'s *Don't Close Your Eyes* delivered three No. 1 tracks before his untimely death due to alcohol abuse.

Billboard 200: *Don't Close Your Eyes* (#121)

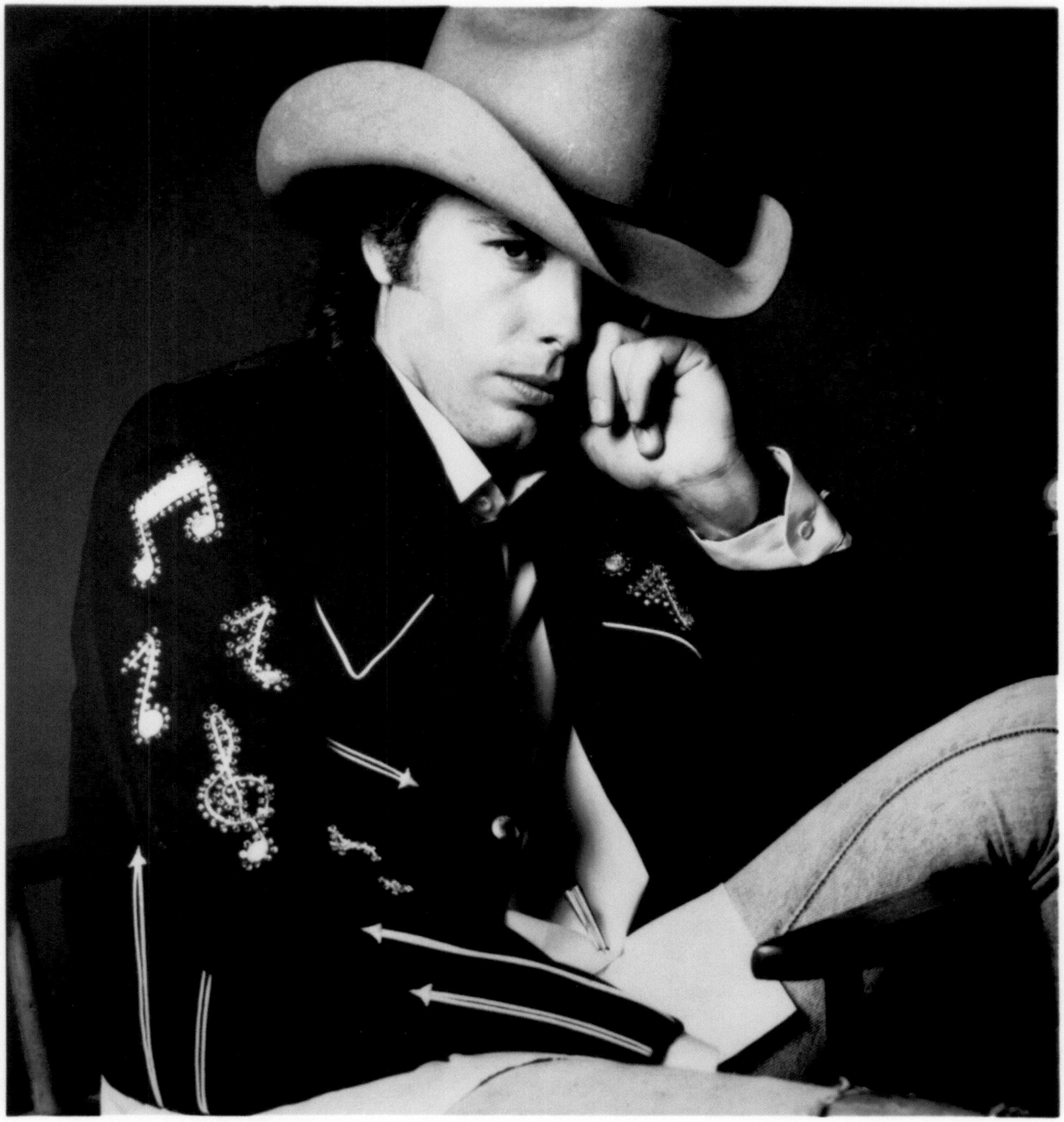

credit: Graham Hughes 0787

DWIGHT YOAKAM

Dwight Yoakam Tours
6363 Sunset Blvd., Suite 712
Hollywood, CA 90028
213/467-0669

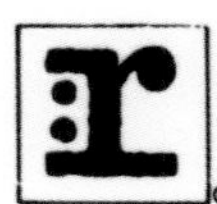

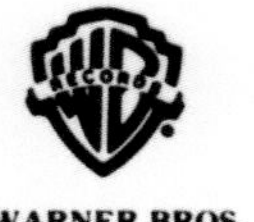

WARNER BROS.

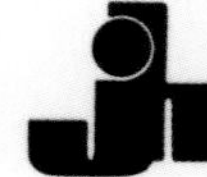

THE JIM HALSEY ©. INC
24 MUSIC SQUARE WEST
NASHVILLE, TENNESSEE 37203
615-244-7900 TELEX 49-2335

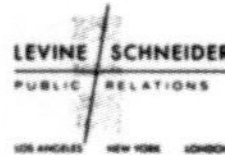

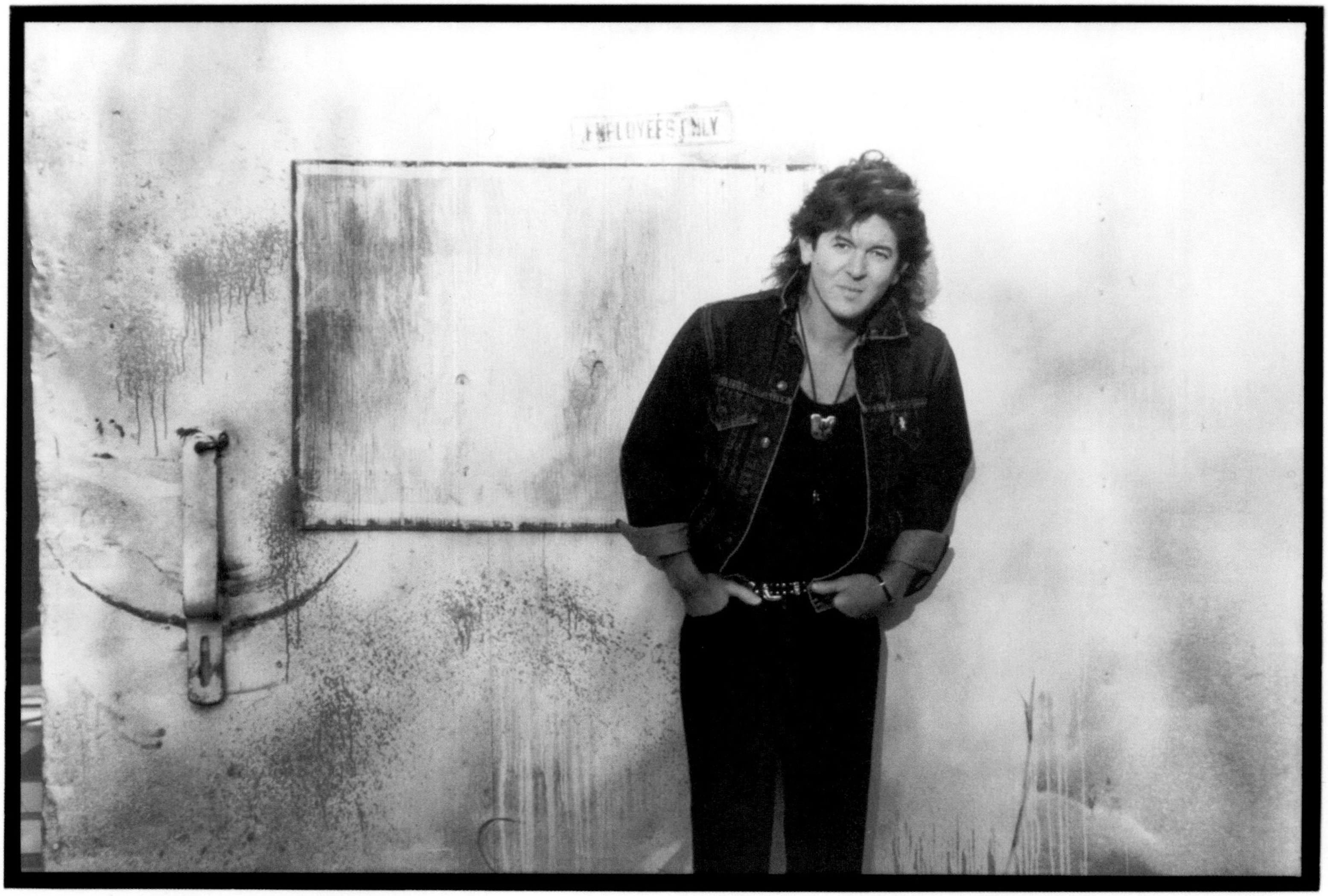

credit: McGuire

Rodney Crowell

Columbia

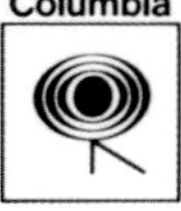

8802

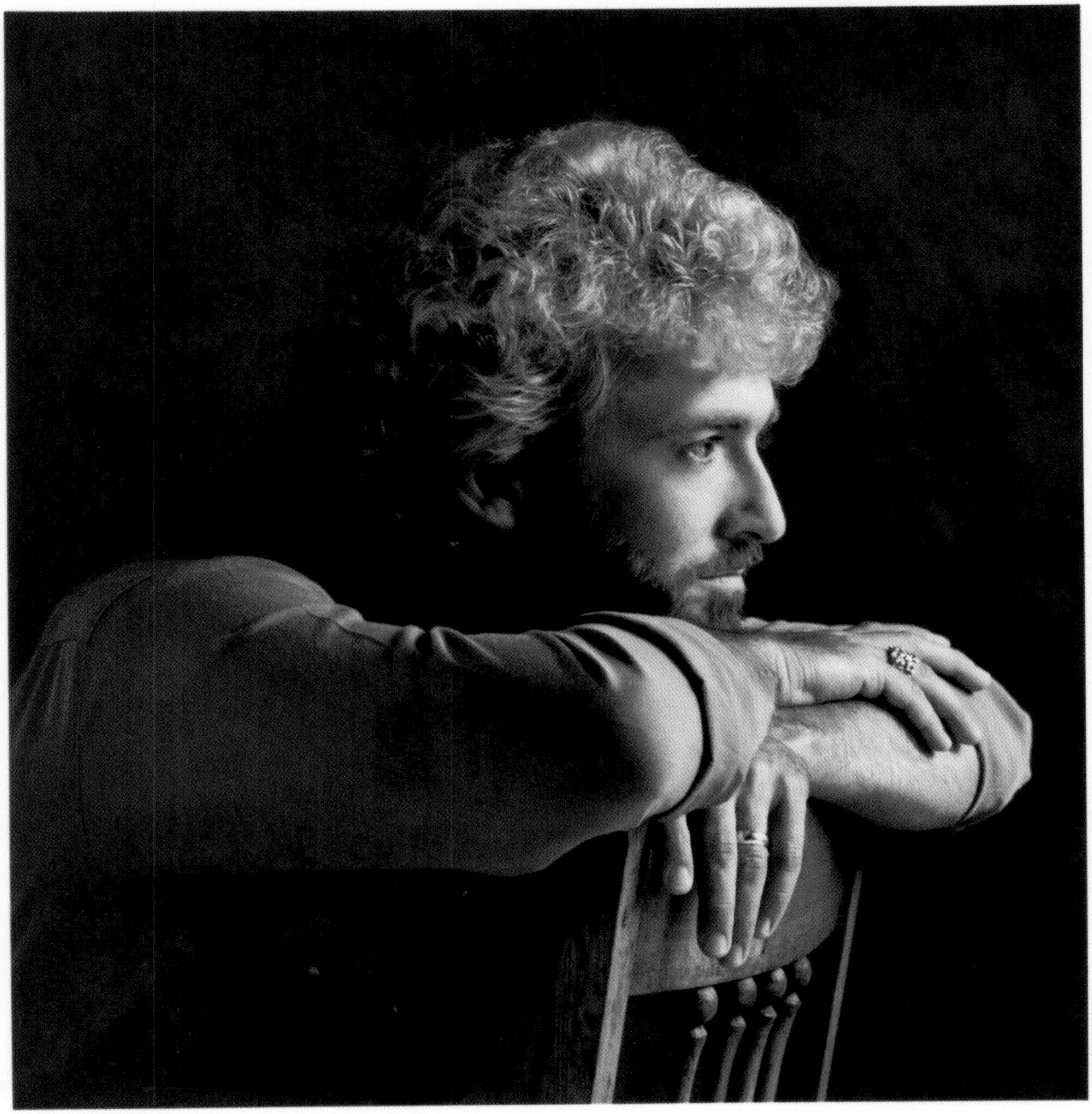

KEITH WHITLEY

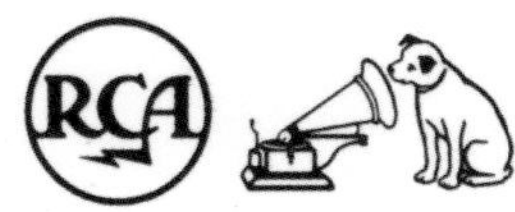

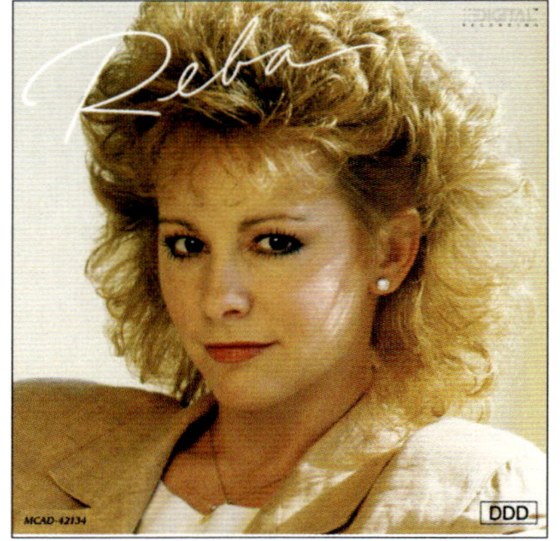

Country vocalist **Reba McEntire** moved toward a contemporary pop style on *Reba* and the No. 1s "I Know How He Feels" and "New Fool at an Old Game."

Billboard 200: *Reba* (#118)

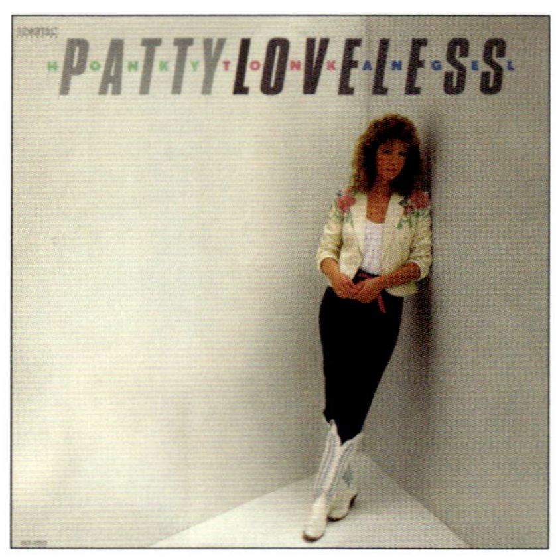

Honky Tonk Angel, the album that made **Patty Loveless** a star, included two of her biggest country singles, "Chains" and "Timber, I'm Falling in Love."

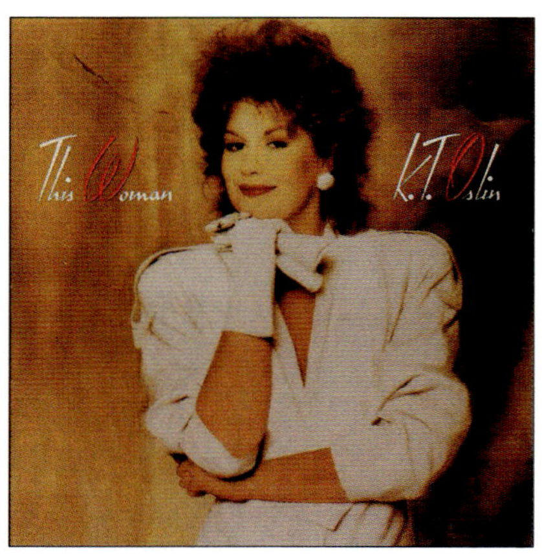

K.T. Oslin was 45 when she recorded her second album, *This Woman*, and "Hold Me," her third country No. 1 and the winner of two Grammy Awards.

Billboard 200: *This Woman* (#75)

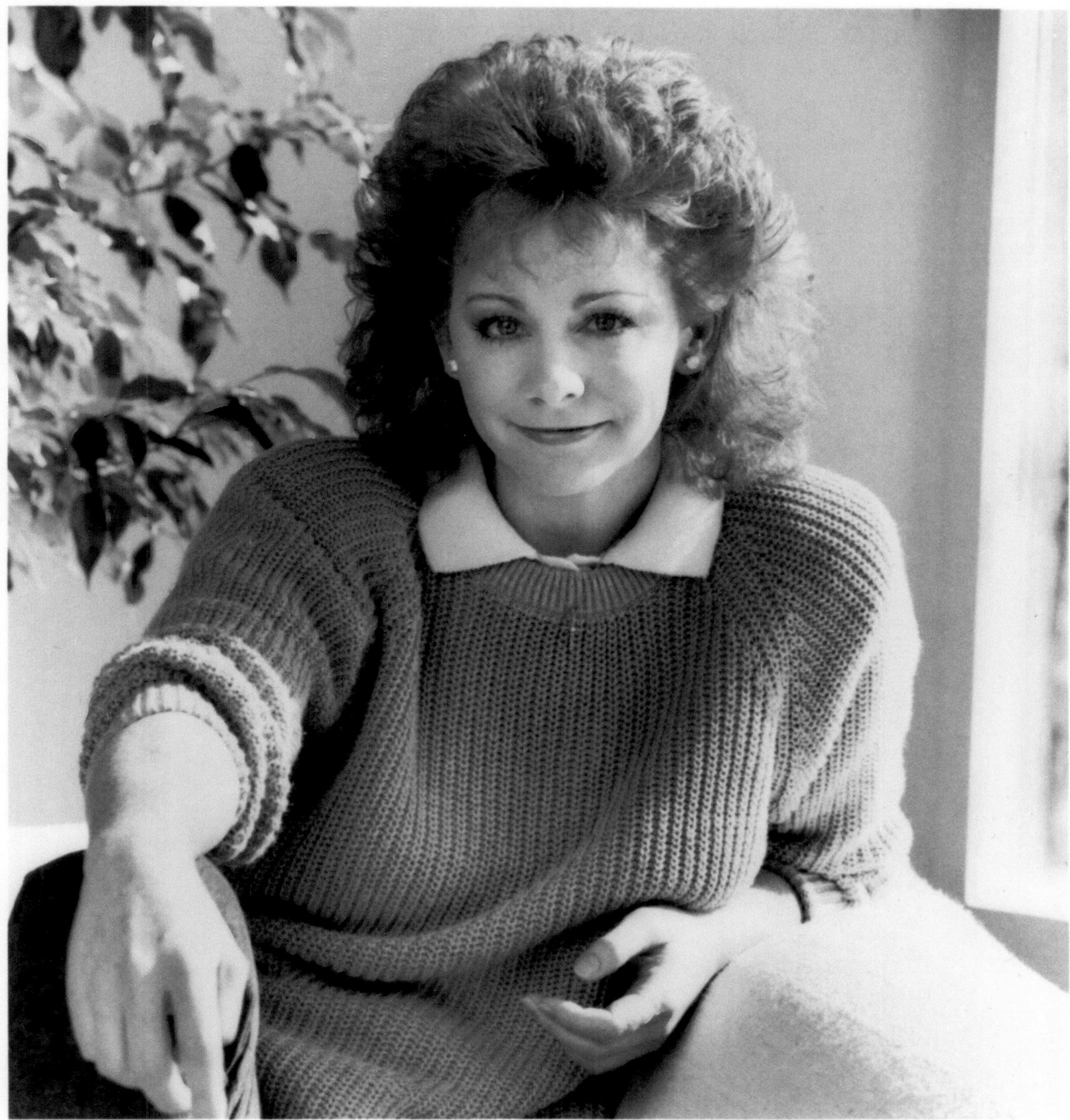

photo: McGuire 0388A

REBA McENTIRE

MCA RECORDS
NASHVILLE

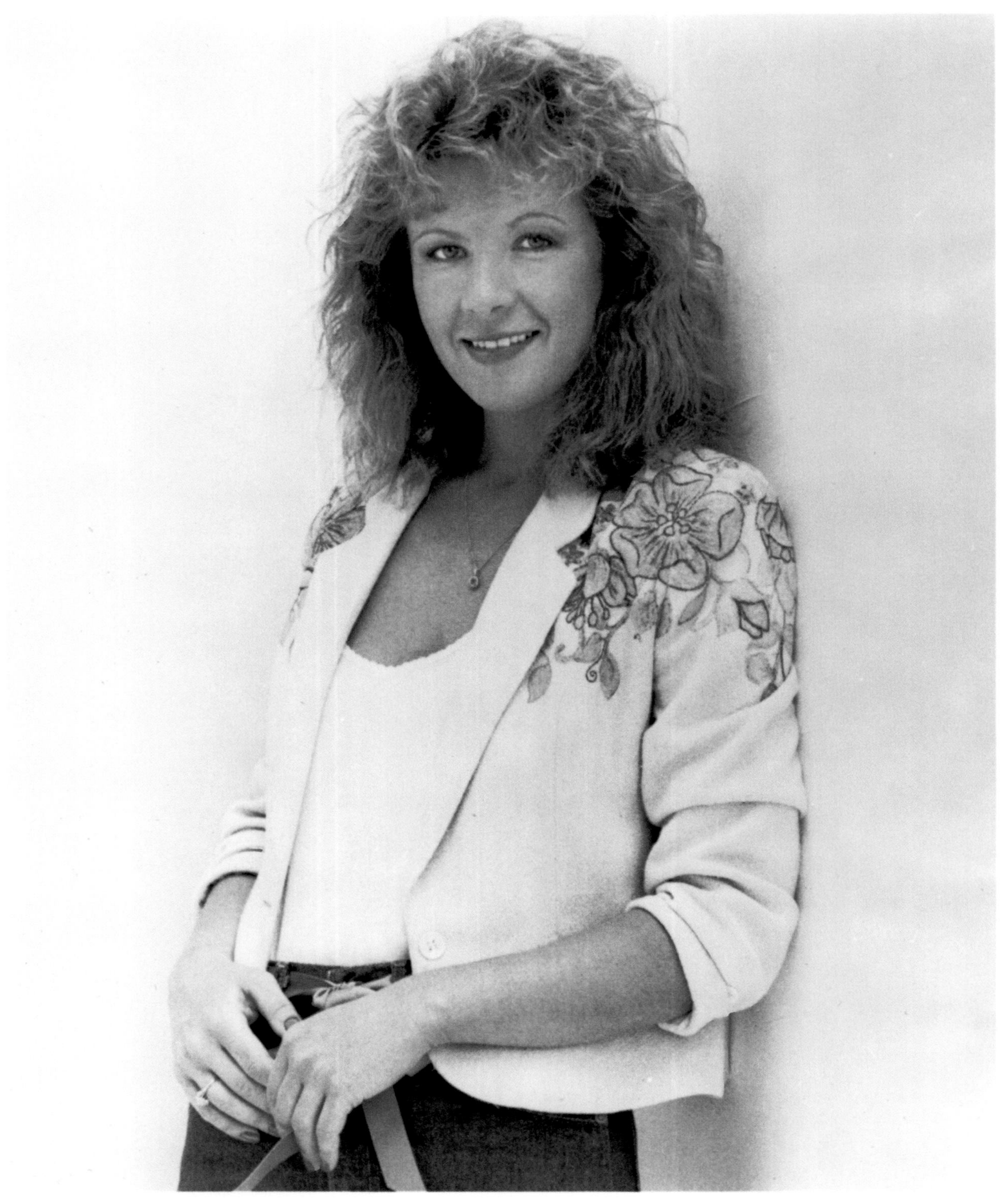

photo: McGuire 0988

PATTY LOVELESS

MCA RECORDS
NASHVILLE

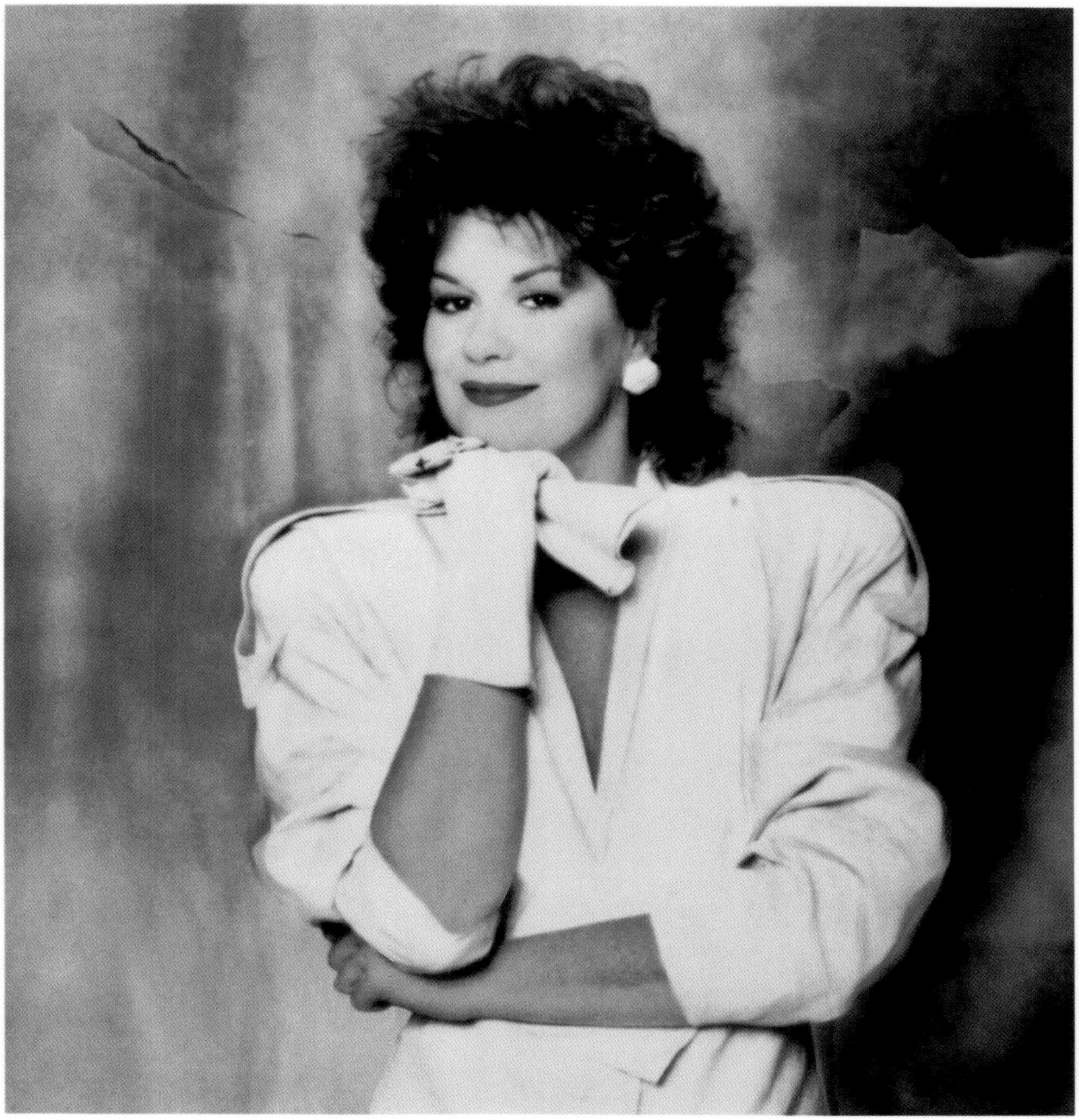

K.T. OSLIN

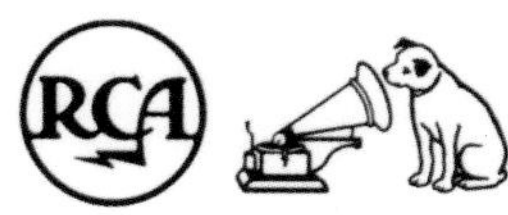

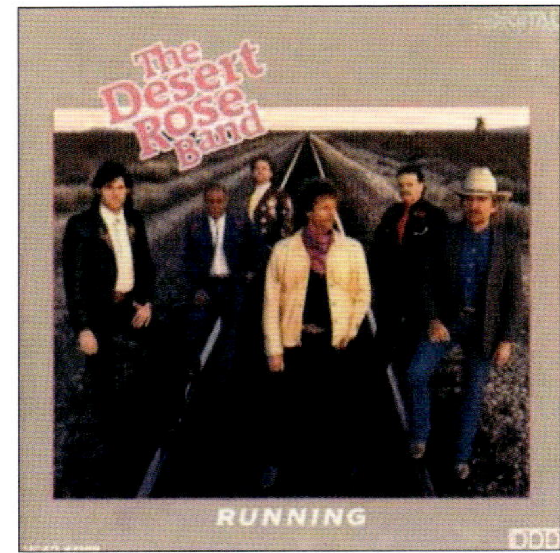

The Desert Rose Band, led by Chris Hillman, served up the major country singles "I Still Believe in You," "Summer Wind" and "She Don't Love Nobody."

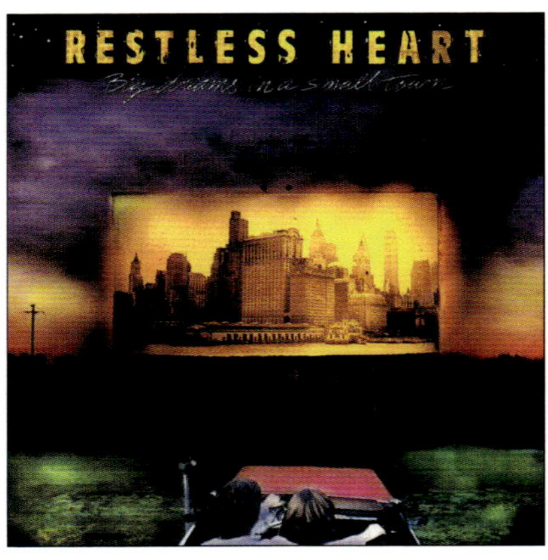

Big Dreams in a Small Town, Restless Heart's third album, continued the country band's hot streak with "The Bluest Eyes in Texas" and "A Tender Lie."

Billboard 200: *Big Dreams in a Small Town* (#114)

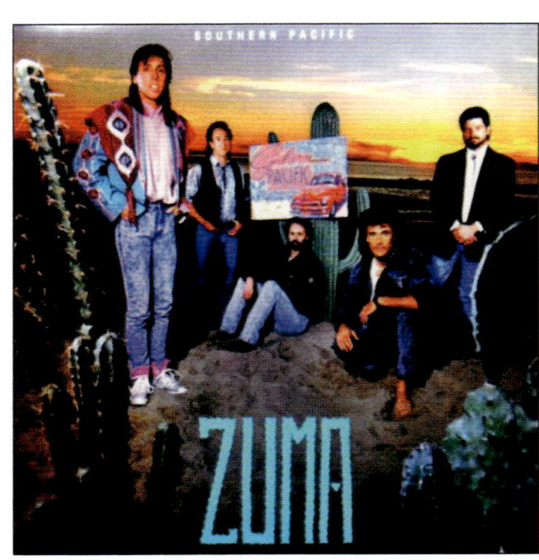

Adding vocalist and guitarist David Jenkins, formerly of Pablo Cruise, engendered Southern Pacific's highest charting country hit, "New Shade of Blue."

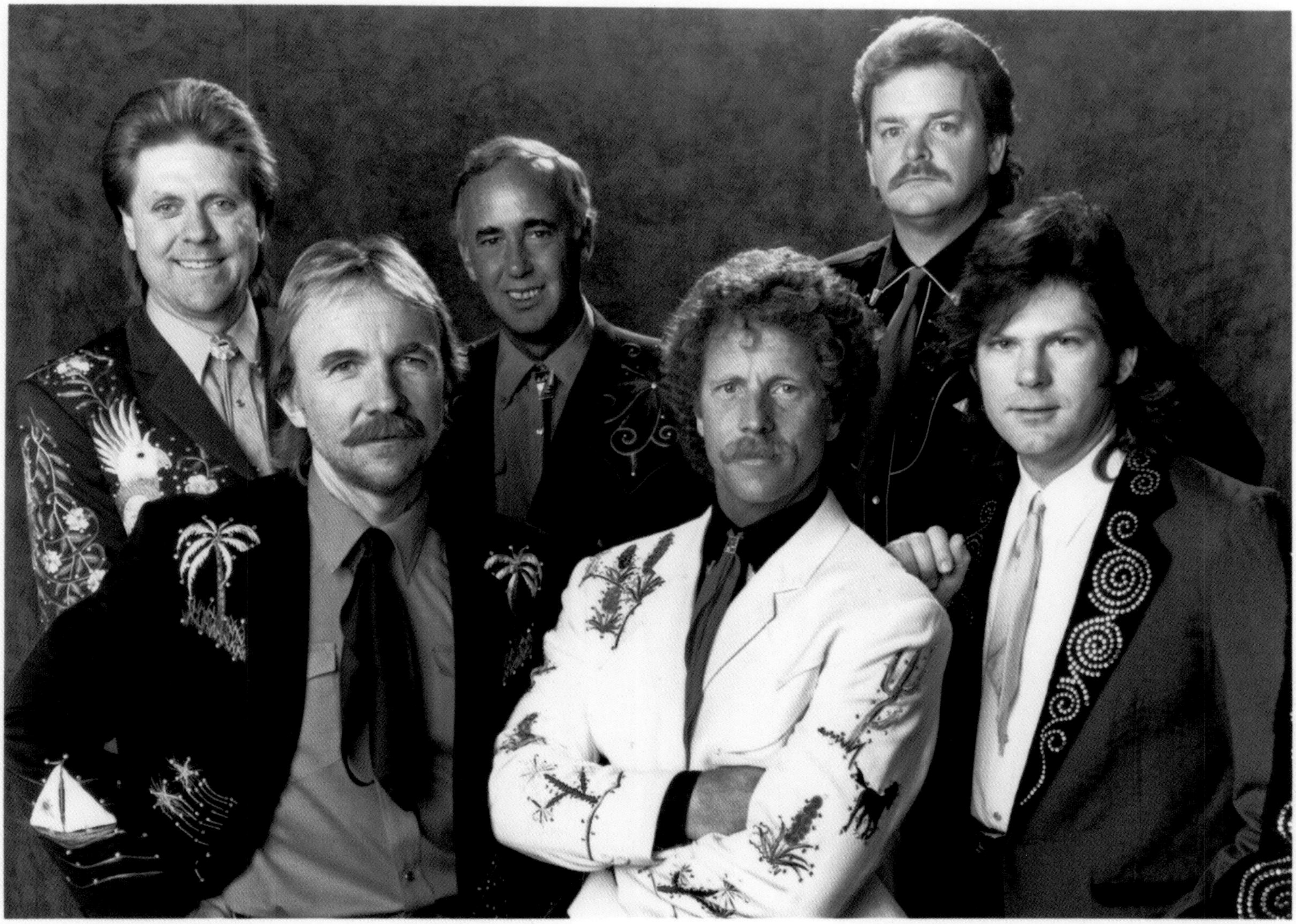

photo: Peter Figen 0588 A

THE DESERT ROSE BAND

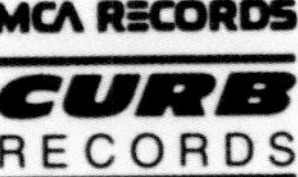

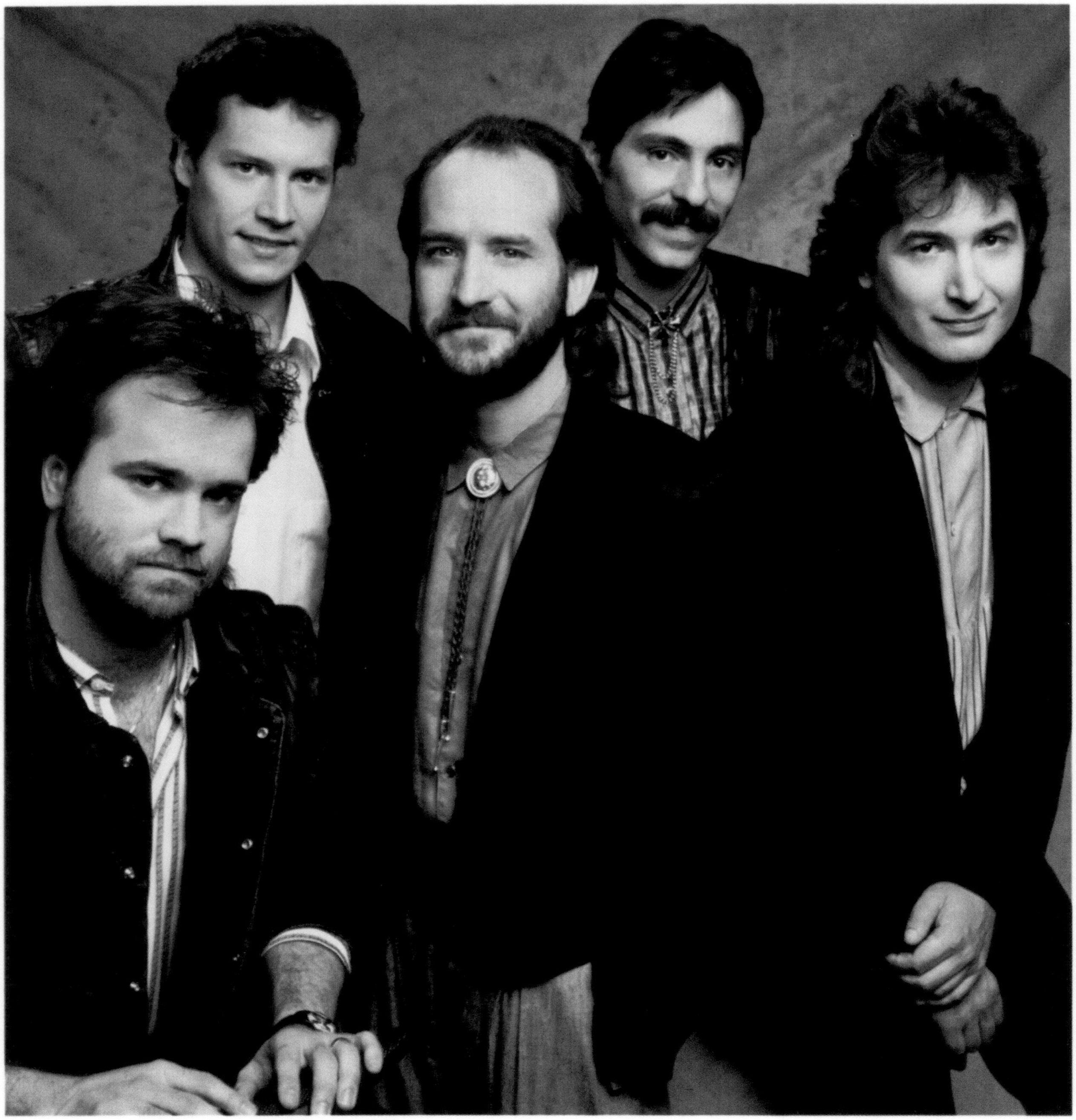

RESTLESS HEART

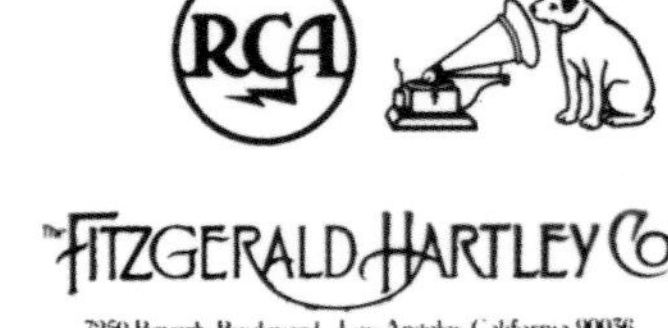

TRIAD ARTISTS, INC.
TALENT AND LITERARY AGENCY

7250 Beverly Boulevard Los Angeles California 90036
(213) 934-8002

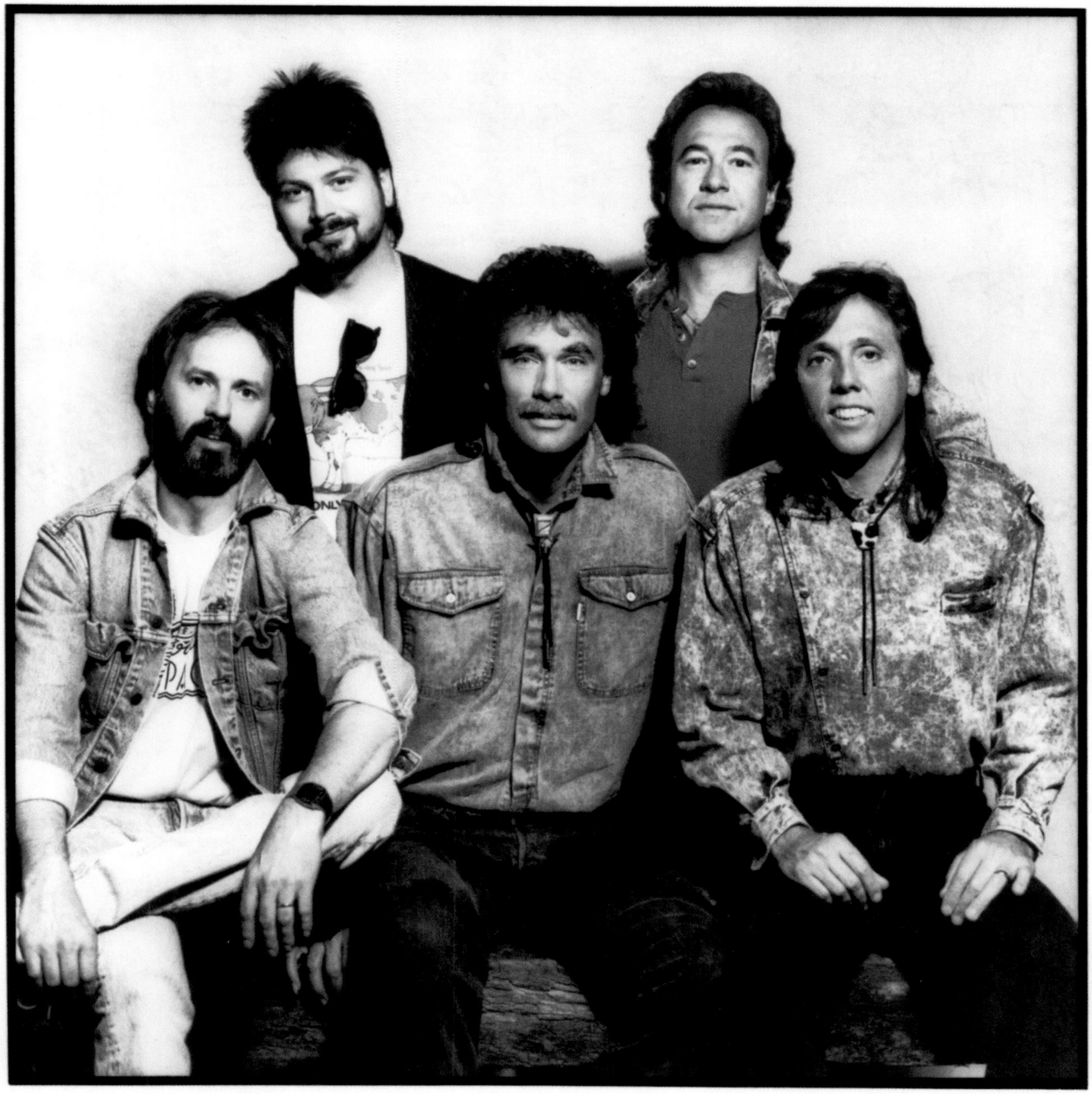

Keith Knudsen Kurt Howell David Jenkins Stu Cook John McFee

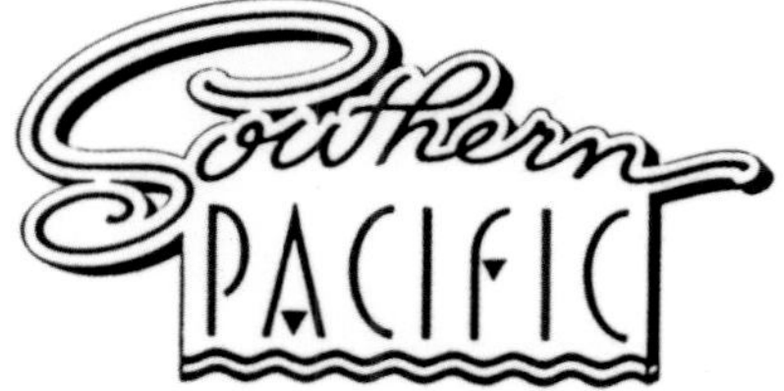

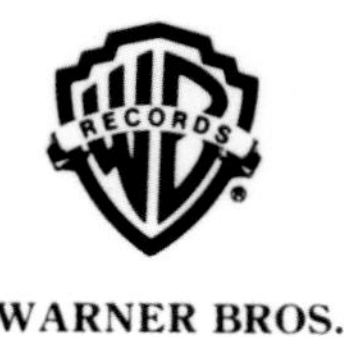

WARNER BROS.

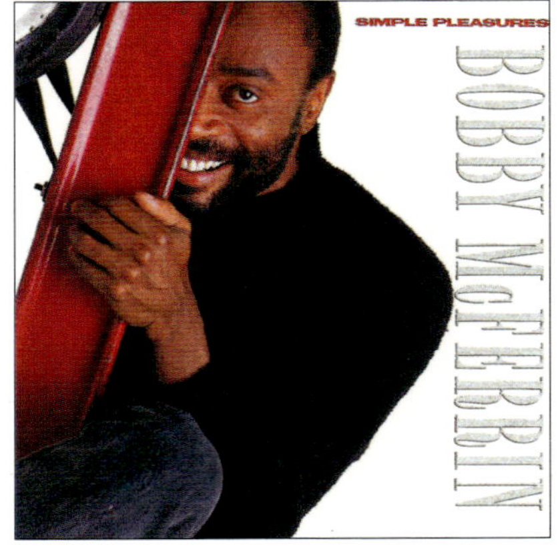

Vocal virtuoso **Bobby McFerrin** won Grammy Awards for Record of the Year and Song of the Year for "Don't Worry, Be Happy," his a cappella pop hit.

Billboard 200: *Simple Pleasures* (#5)
Billboard Hot 100: "Don't Worry, Be Happy" (No. 1)

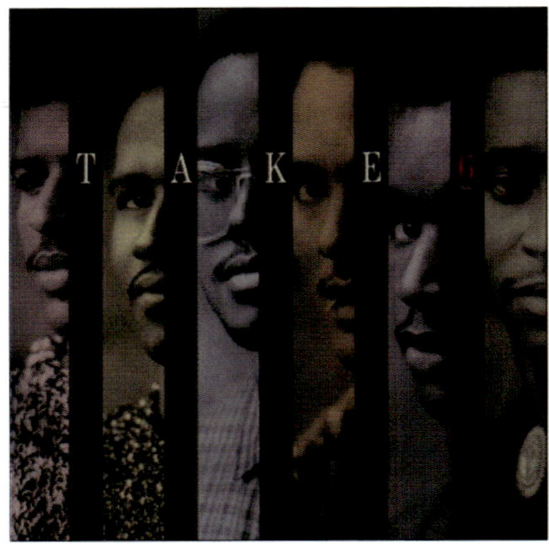

Take 6's self-titled debut album collected Grammy Awards in both gospel and jazz categories, captured three Dove Awards and was certified platinum.

Billboard 200: *Take 6* (#71)

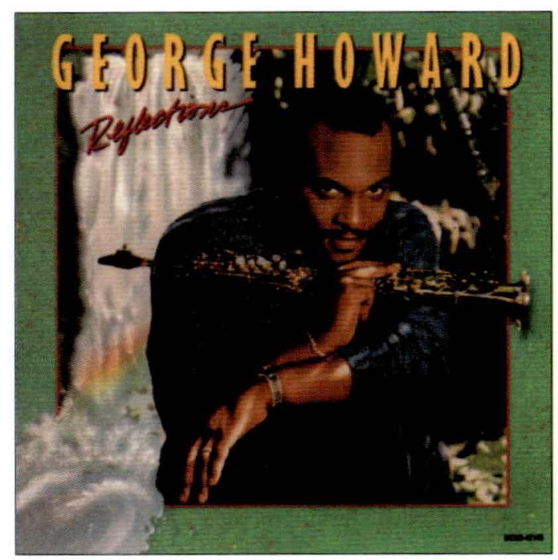

Reflections by **George Howard** was the Philadelphia-born soprano saxophonist's fourth consecutive recording to top the contemporary jazz charts.

Billboard 200: *Reflections* (#109)

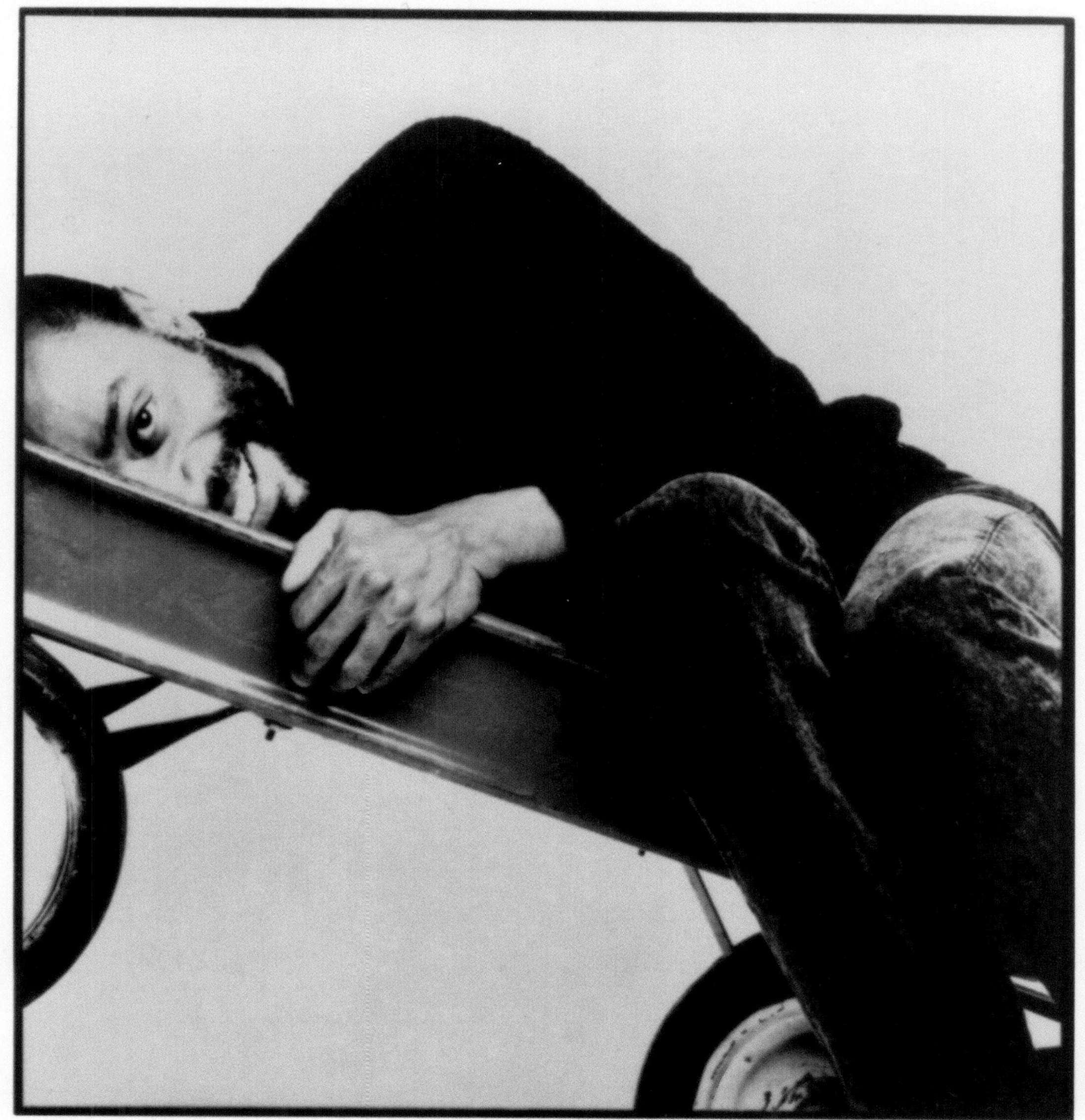

Photography Carol Friedman

BOBBY McFERRIN

EMI MAN HAT TAN®

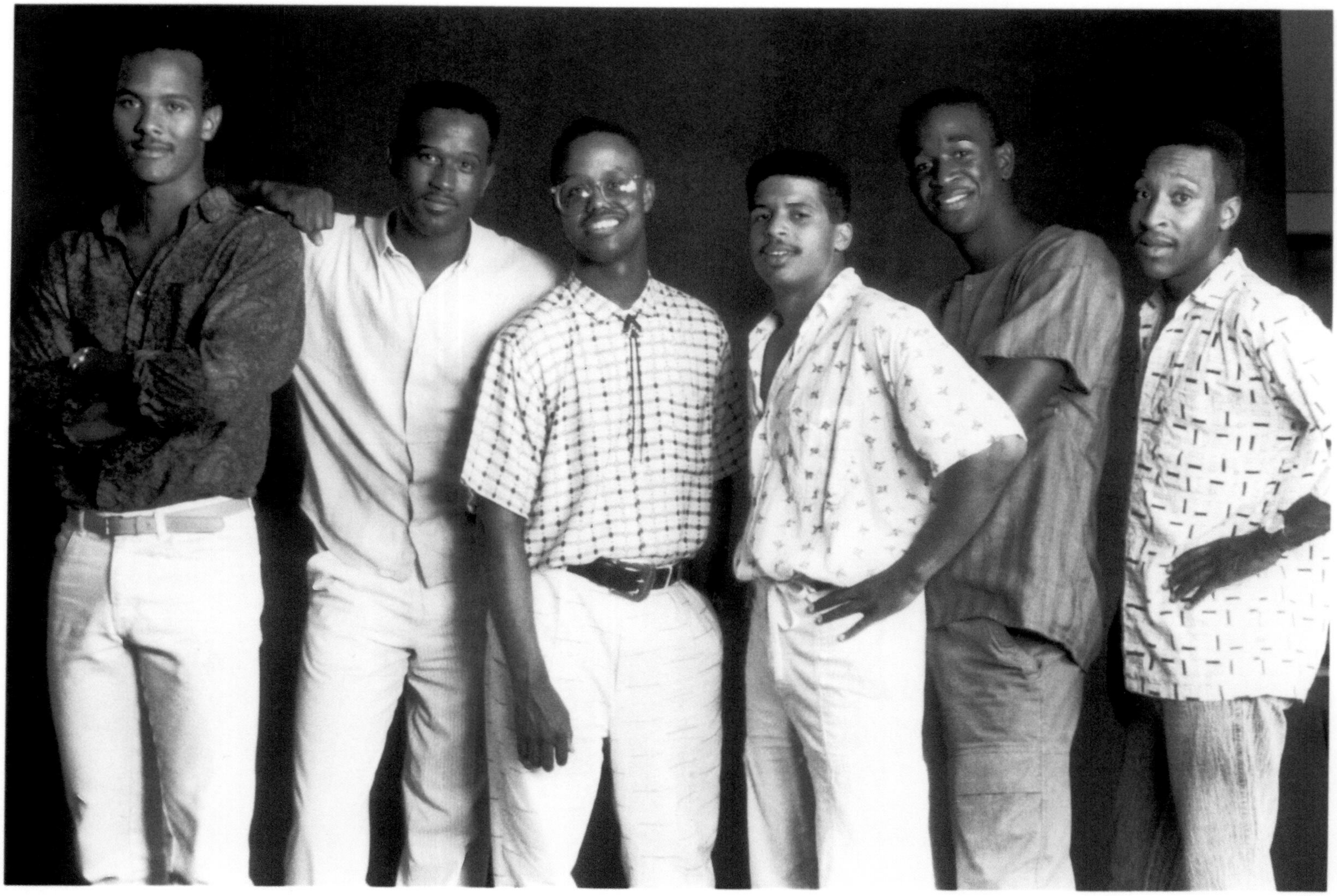

credit: Greg Miller

David Thomas | Claude V McKnight, III | Mervyn Warren | Mark Kibble | Alvin "Vinnie" Chea | Cedric Dent

TAKE 6 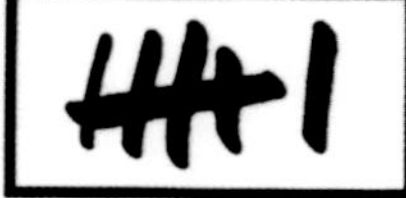

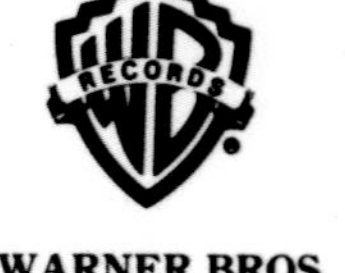

WARNER BROS.

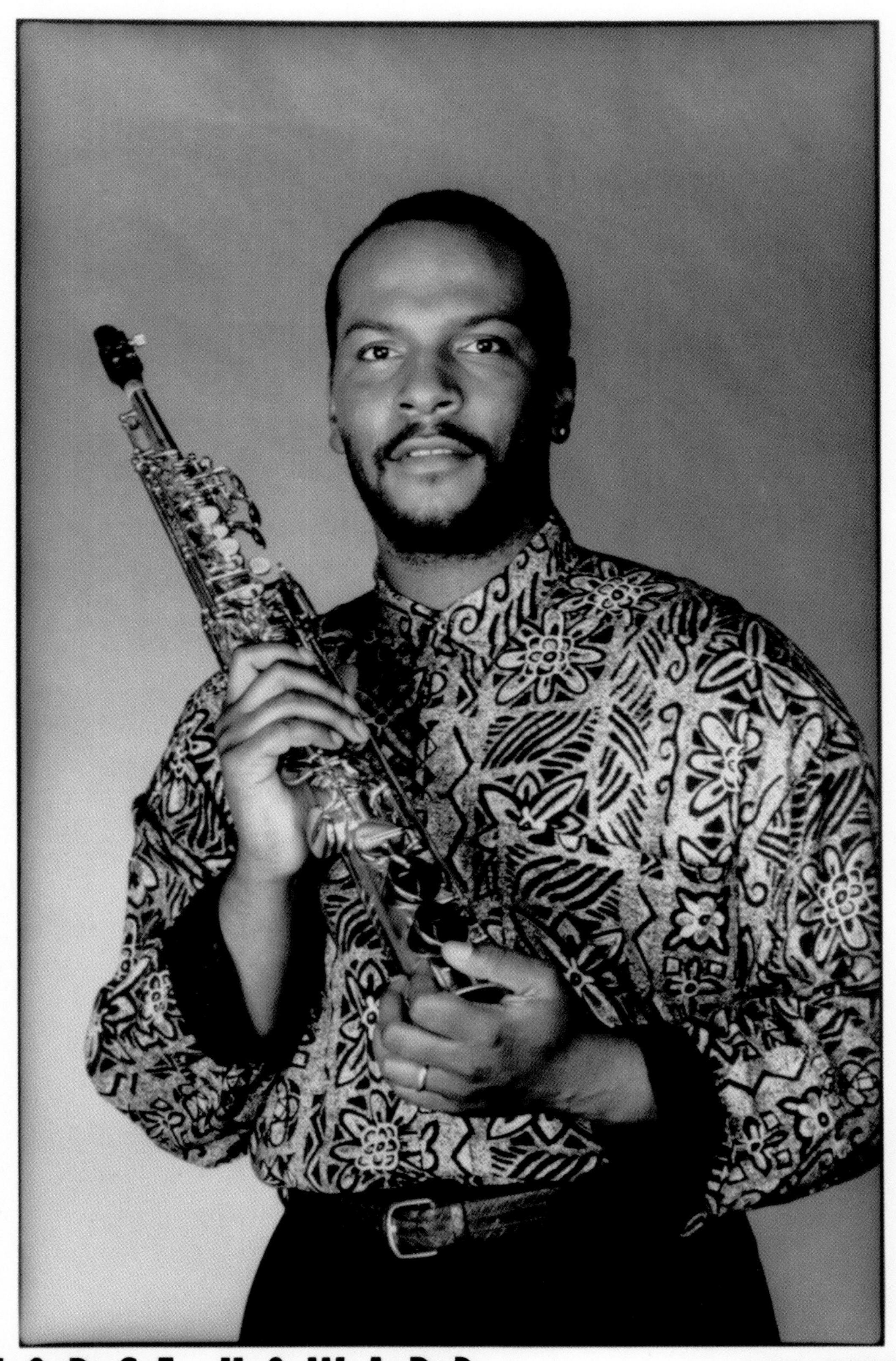

GEORGE HOWARD

.MCA RECORDS

One of south Louisiana's premier two-fisted pianists, **Katie Webster** cut *The Swamp Boogie Queen* with guests Bonnie Raitt, Robert Cray and Kim Wilson.

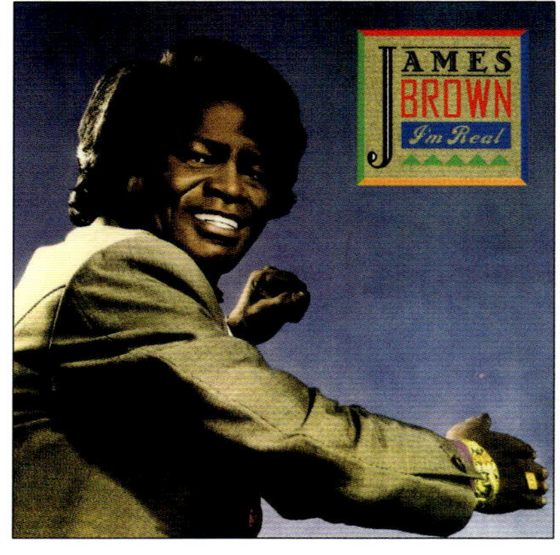

With his prime work being sampled by a new generation of funksters, **James Brown** was back on the good foot with *I'm Real*, guided by the Full Force crew.

Billboard 200: *I'm Real* (#96)

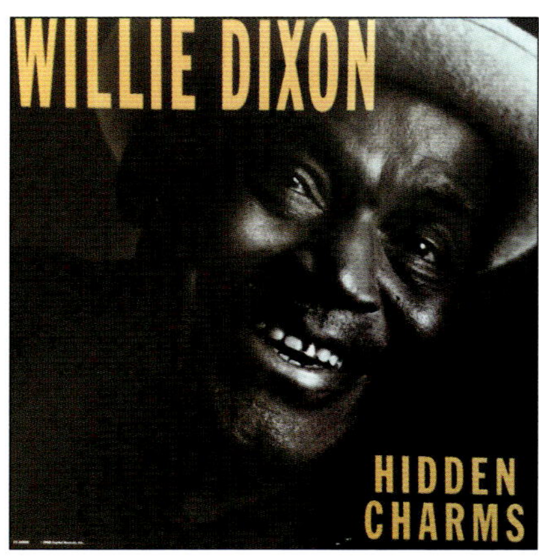

Willie Dixon, the most celebrated songwriter in fashioning the Chicago blues sound of the Forties and Fifties, won a Grammy for the new *Hidden Charms*.

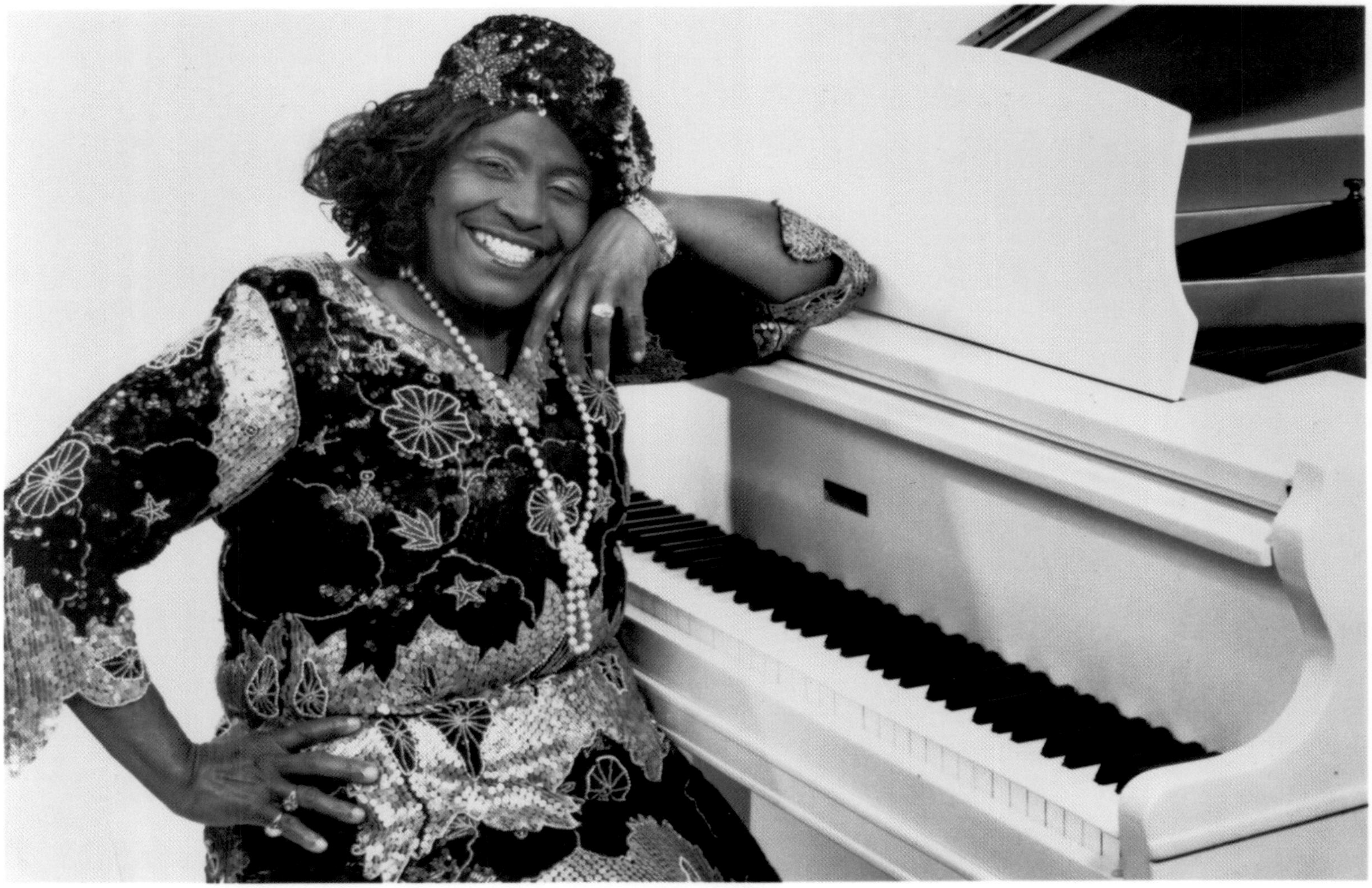

Photo: Peter Amft

KATIE WEBSTER

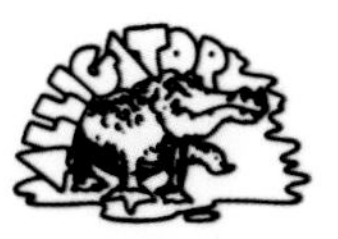

ALLIGATOR RECORDS
Box 60234
Chicago, IL 60660
(312) 973-7736

Artist representation:

BON TON WEST
P.O. Box 8406
Santa Cruz, CA 95061
(408) 425-5885
Fax: (408) 438-7367
Tlx: 171142 BONTON WEST UD

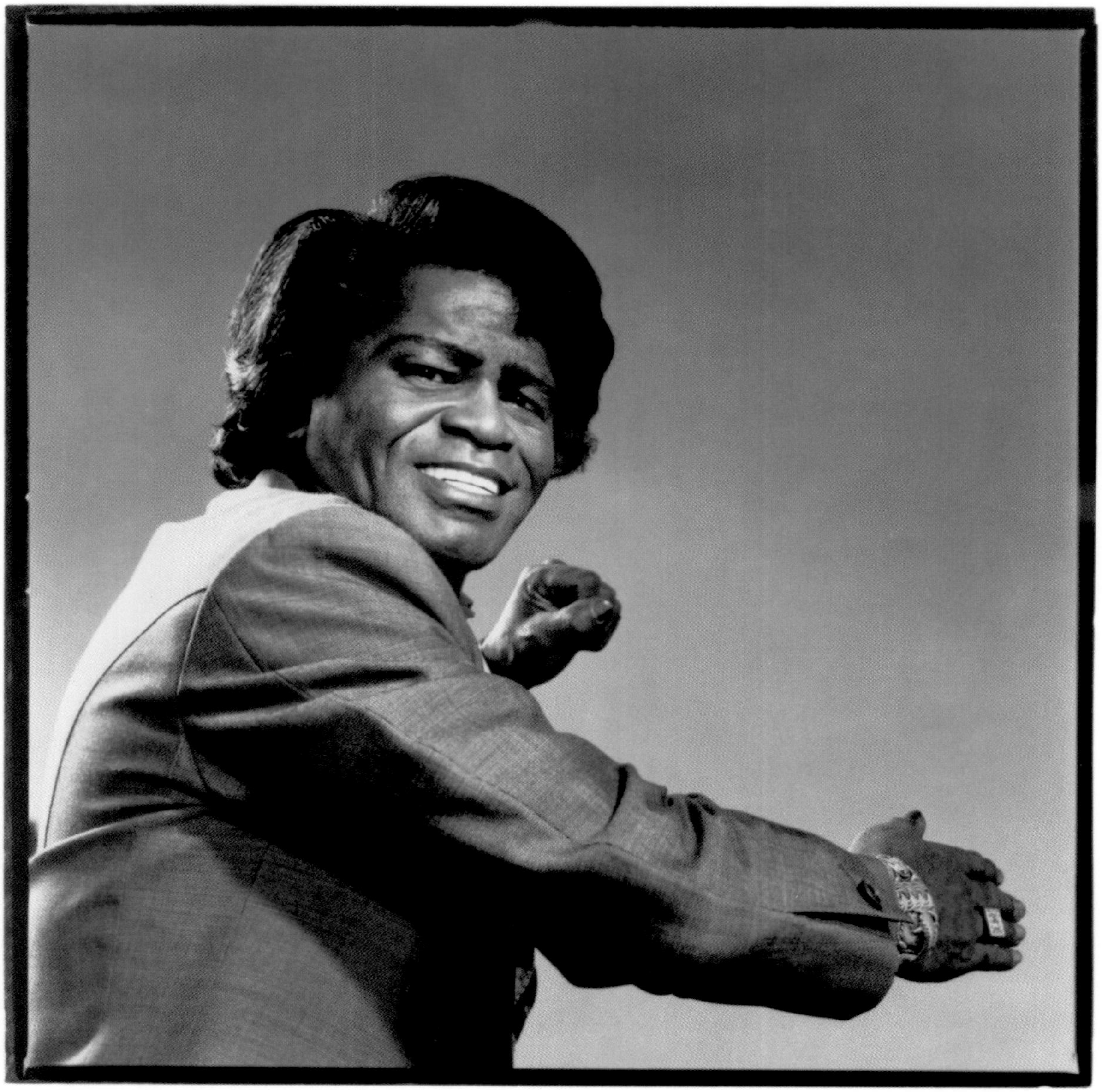

PHOTO: NELS ISRAELSON

JAMES BROWN

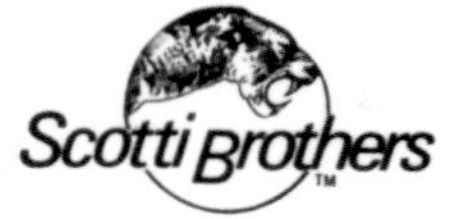

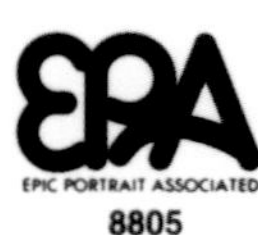

8805

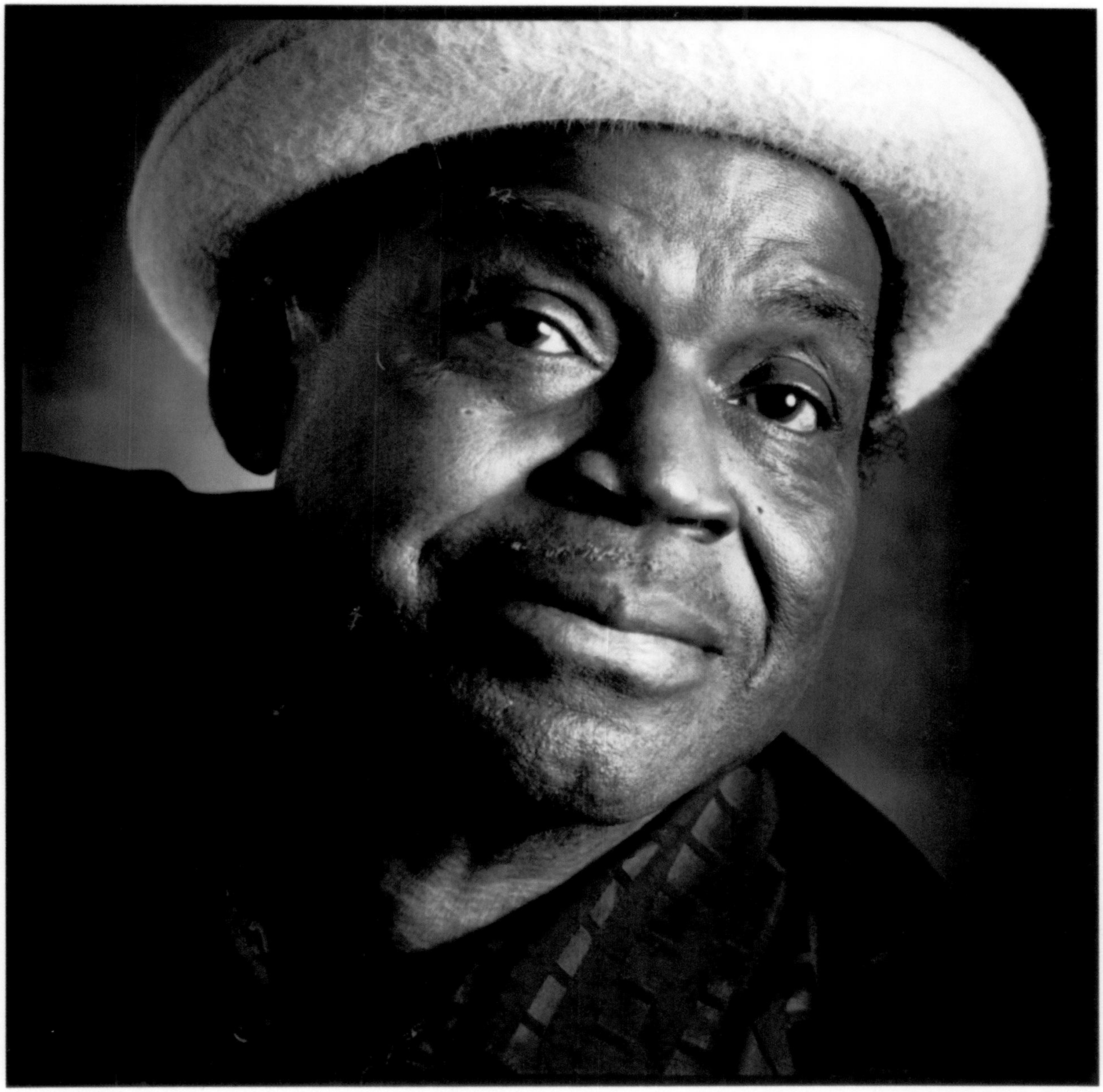

Photo: Marc Norberg / 1988

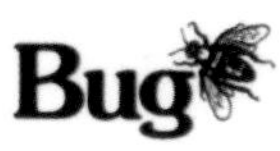

WILLIE DIXON

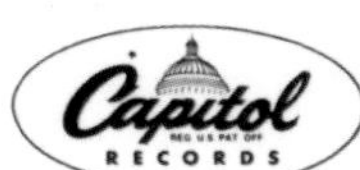

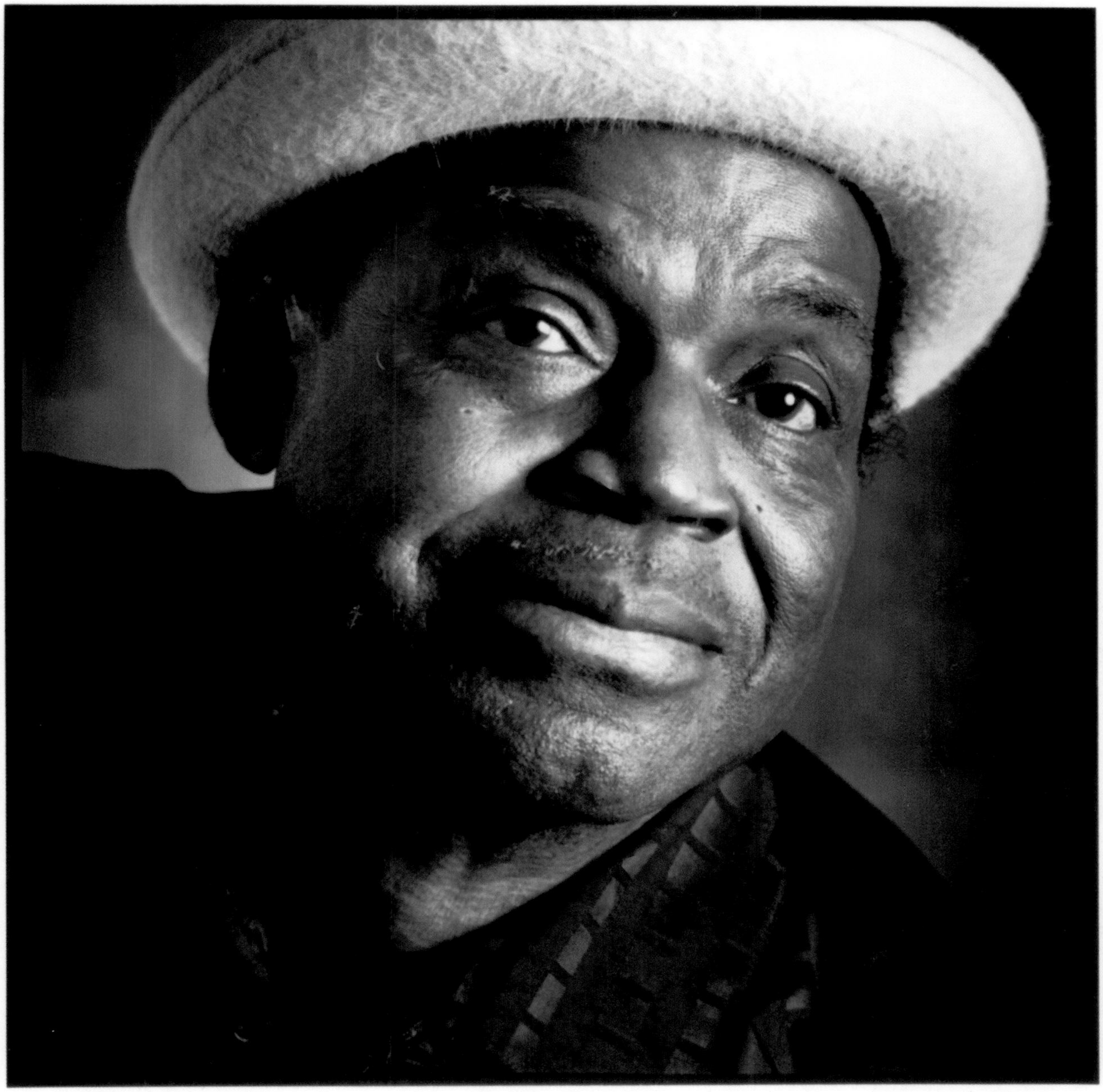

Photo: Marc Norberg / 1988

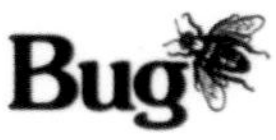

WILLIE DIXON

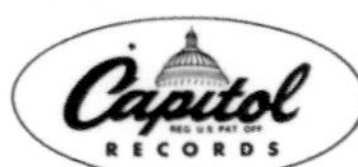

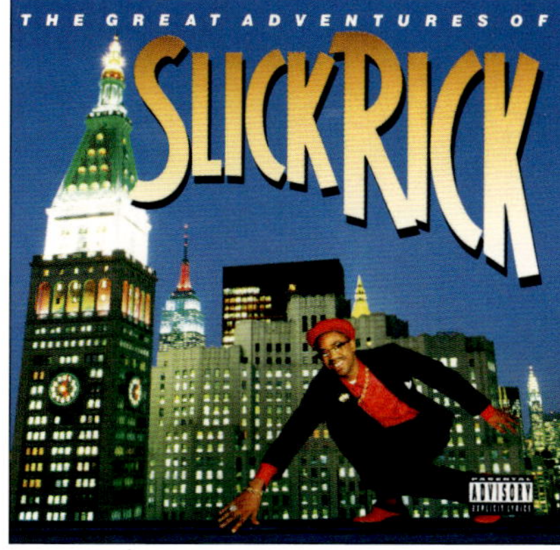

Raconteur rapper **Slick Rick** produced his debut, *The Great Adventures of Slick Rick*, a No.1 hip-hop album known for its message song, "Children's Story."

Billboard 200: *The Great Adventures of Slick Rick* (#31)

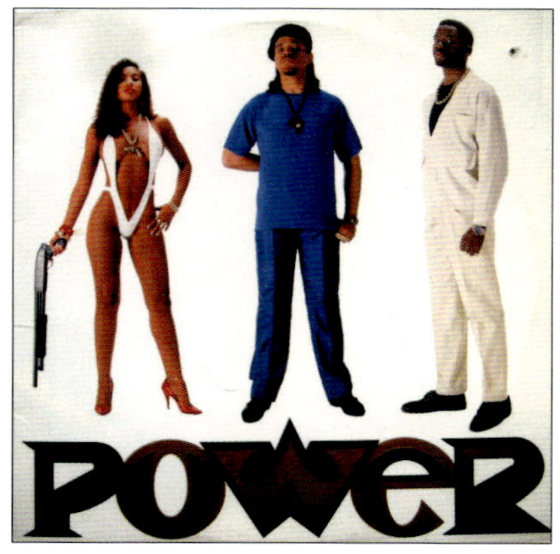

Founding his own Rhyme Syndicate label, West Coast hip-hop artist **Ice-T** proved himself with "I'm Your Pusher," a sociopolitical gangsta-rap gem.

Billboard 200: *Power* (#35)

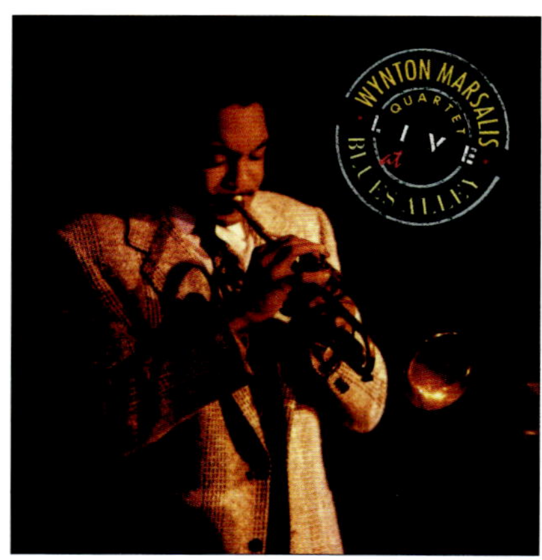

Live at Blues Alley, recorded in Washington, D.C., was a jazz hit for trumpeter **Wynton Marsalis** and his quartet featuring pianist Marcus Roberts.

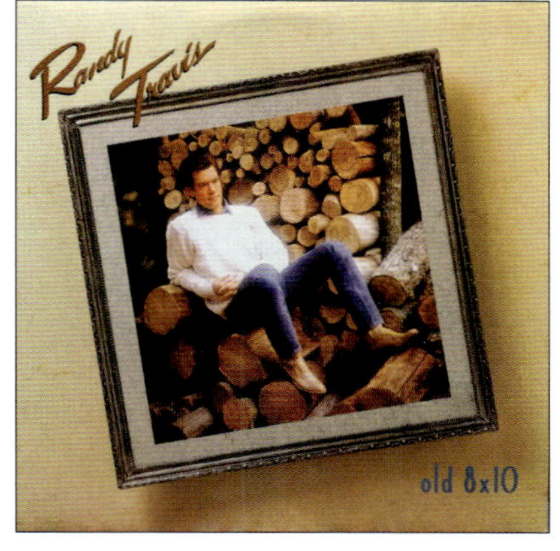

Country star **Randy Travis** got to No. 1 with the first three singles from *Old 8x10*, "Honky Tonk Moon," "Deeper Than the Holler" and "Is It Still Over?"

Billboard 200: *Old 8x10* (#35)

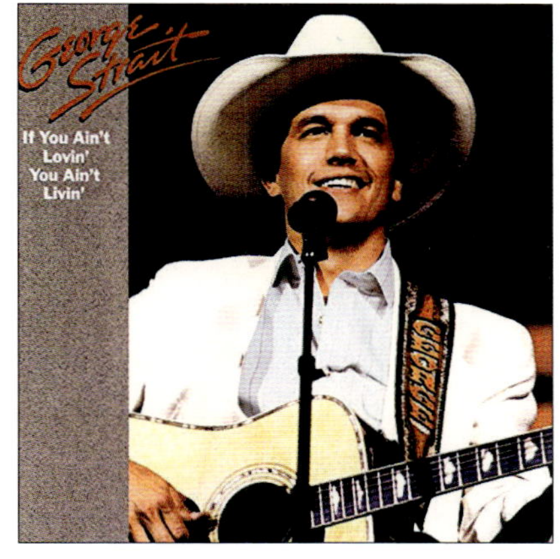

George Strait's *If You Ain't Lovin' You Ain't Livin'* offered a triad of No. 1 country hits, "Baby Blue," "Famous Last Words of a Fool" and the title track.

Billboard 200: *If You Ain't Lovin' You Ain't Livin'* (#87)

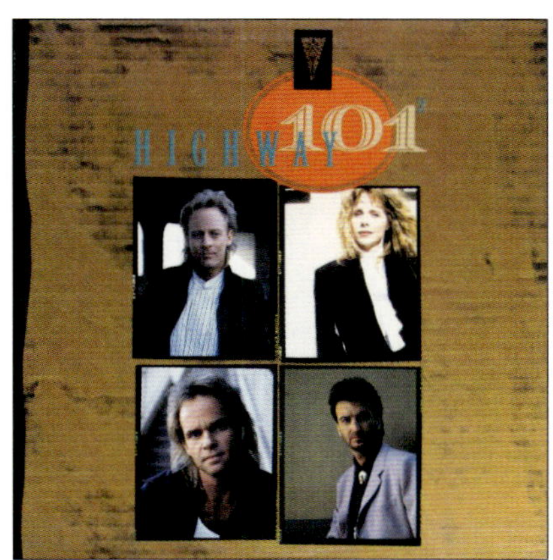

Highway 101's second album accounted for four Top 10 country singles, notably "(Do You Love Me) Just Say Yes," the band's third consecutive No. 1.

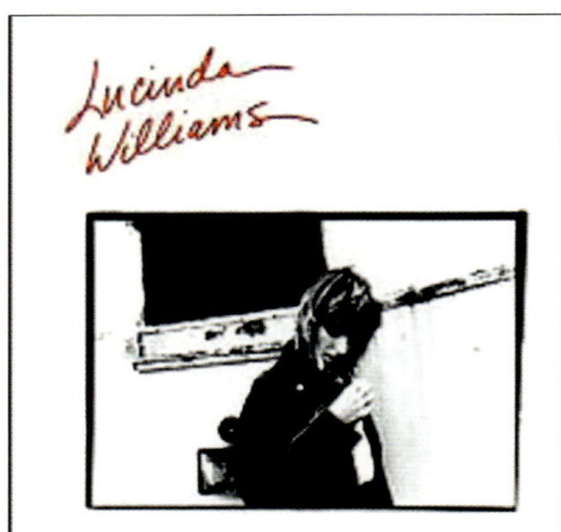

Lucinda Williams' self-titled album offered "Changed the Locks" and "Passionate Kisses," which later garnered her a Grammy for Best Country Song.

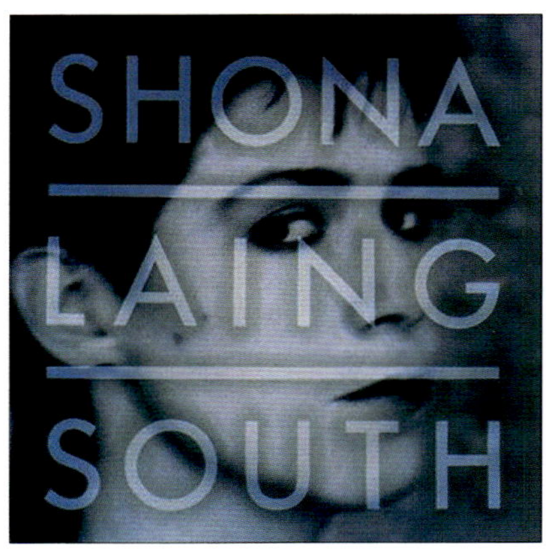

Retooling her acoustic sound to a synth-pop style, New Zealand singer-songwriter Shona Laing landed a worldwide hit with "(Glad I'm) Not a Kennedy."

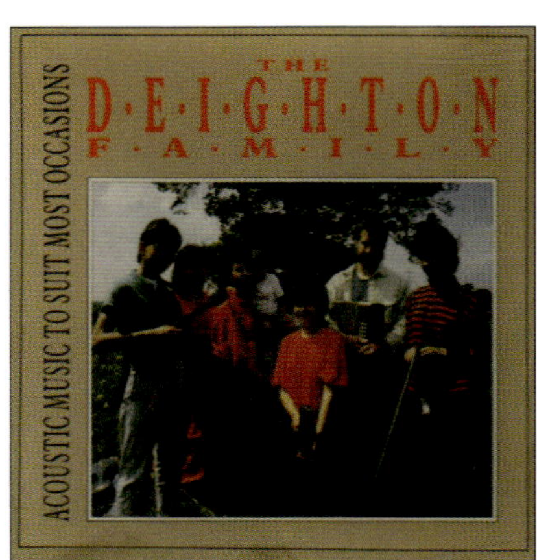

The Deighton Family, a musical menage from Yorkshire, England, picked up NPR's Record of the Year honor for *Acoustic Music to Suit Most Occasions*.

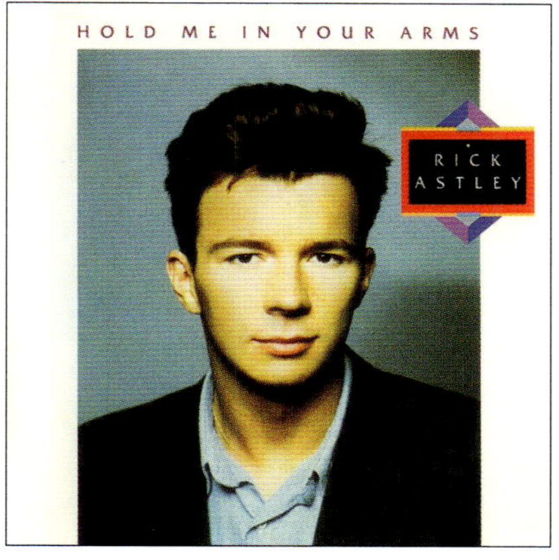

Singer **Rick Astley** followed his best-selling first album with *Hold Me in Your Arms* and "She Wants to Dance with Me," a self-penned international hit.

Billboard 200: *Hold Me in Your Arms* (#19)
Billboard Hot 100: "She Wants to Dance with Me" (#6); "Giving Up on Love" (#38); "Ain't Too Proud to Beg" (#89)

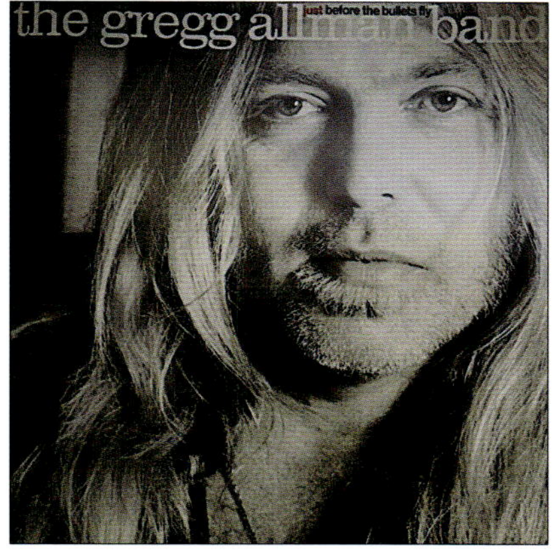

The Gregg Allman Band, the Southern rock legend's road-seasoned quintet, issued another album before the Allman Brothers Band's second reformation.

Billboard 200: *Just Before the Bullets Fly* (#117)

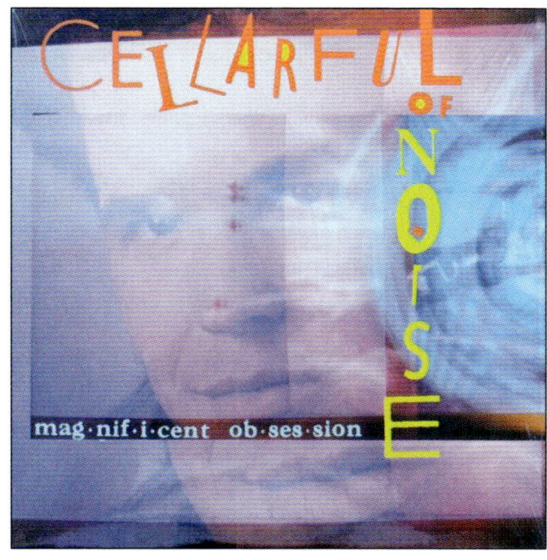

Cellarful of Noise, a recording project created by Mark Avsec of Donnie Iris & the Cruisers, scored a fab chart hit, "Samantha (What You Gonna Do?)."

Billboard Hot 100: "Samantha (What You Gonna Do?)" (#69)

{ IN MEMORY OF **SPENCER CHARLES WEDUM** }

ACKNOWLEDGMENTS

Many people were essential to the creation of this book. My first thanks go to my amazing publishing team—Jon Rizzi for bringing his special brand of wit and intelligence, and Kate Glassner Brainerd for her design artistry and unflagging pursuit of excellence. Special appreciation goes to Eric Pirritt's The Love We Bring Foundation and the Michael & Patricia Matthews Fund, whose facilitation was indispensable, as well as John Cerullo and Kevin Votel.

Mike Dickson, Chip Garofalo, Jennifer Soulé, Mark Zaremba, Peter Marcus, Matt Rue, Jay Elowsky, Dave Zobl and Mark Lewis contributed expertise and resources. I am especially indebted to my dear friend Michael Jensen, as well as Sue Satriano, Janice Azrak, Bryn Bridenthal, Byron Hontas, Kathy Acquaviva, Shelly Selover, Sue Sawyer, Glen Brunman, Rick Ambrose, Bob Merlis, Bill Bentley, Heidi Ellen Robinson, Les Schwartz, Rick Gershon, Jim Merlis, Judi Kerr and Susan Blond—all of whom supported my efforts.

I specifically treasure the beneficence of Dave Rothstein, Greg Phifer, John Tope, Kevin Knee, Dick Merkle, Jeff Cook, Michael Brannen, Zak Phillips, Rich Garcia, Jason Minkler, Burt Baumgartner, Mitch Kampf, Don Zucker, Carl Walters, Charlie Reardon, Robin Wren, Jimmy Smith, Sharona White, John Ryland, Geina Horton, Michael Linehan, Mike Prince and Jeffrey Naumann, who all graciously furnished information and assistance.

I gratefully acknowledge the editing and reviewing skills of Dick Kreck, Tom Walker, Diane Carman, Mike Rudeen, Ed Smith, Jay Whearley, Mark Sims, Jeff Bradley and Peggy McKay.

I also salute David Gans, Leland Rucker, Steve Knopper, David Menconi, Jon Iverson, Gil Asakawa, Mark Bliesener, Butch Hause, Ricardo Baca, John Moore, Justin Mitchell, Michael Mehle and Harvey Kubernik, whose writings formed a vital index for the music-obsessed.

Finally, I would like to acknowledge with gratitude my beloved wife, Bridget, for her constant devotion and kindness. I cherish her—the love of my life.

EDITOR | **JON RIZZI**
ART DIRECTOR | **KATE GLASSNER BRAINERD**

ISBN 978-0-9915668-8-4 | PRINTED IN CHINA | Asia Pacific Offset

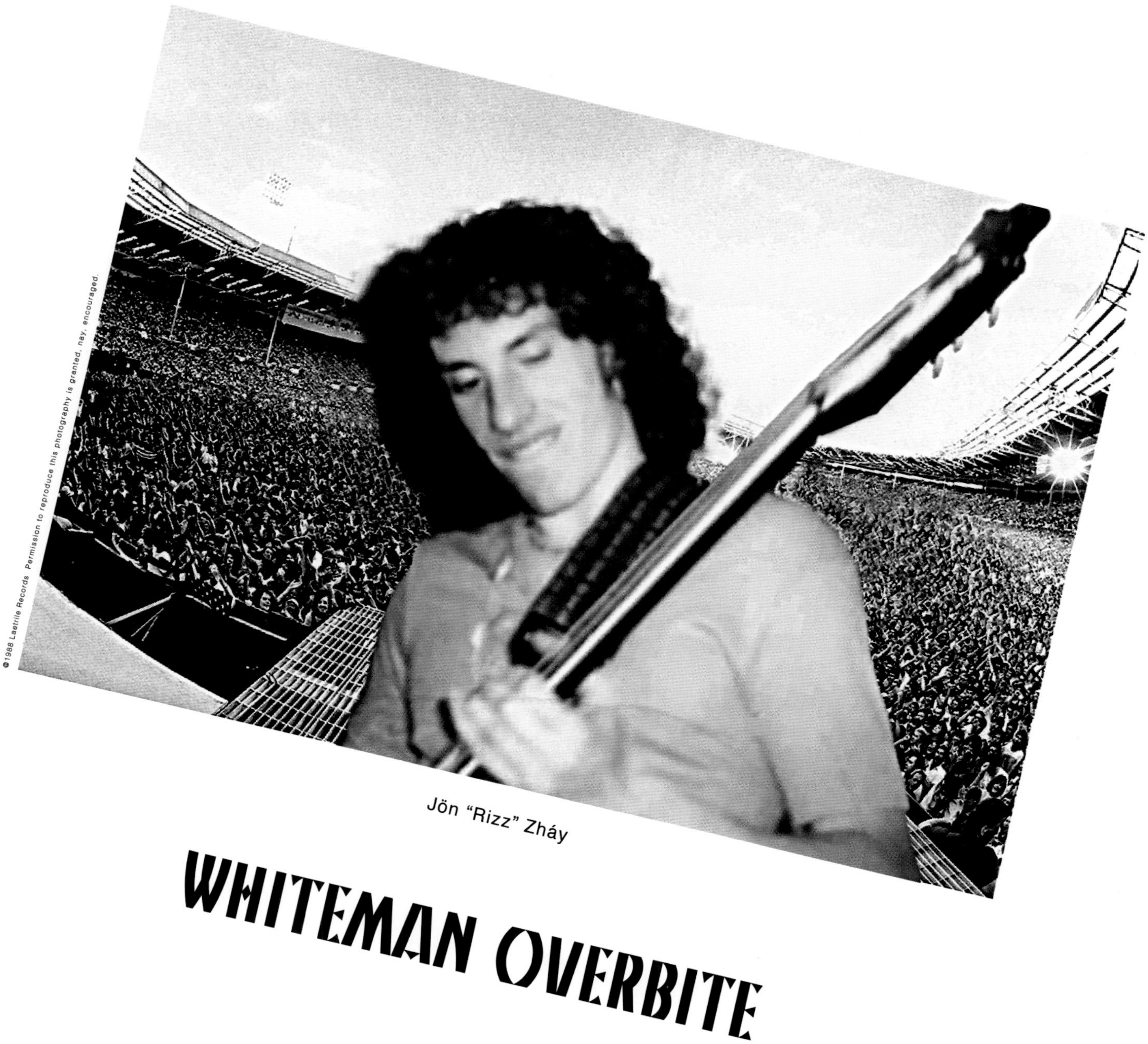

Jön “Rizz” Zháy

WHITEMAN OVERBITE

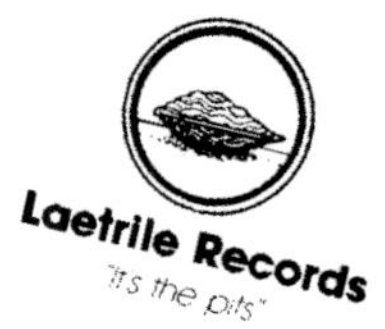

Next in the *ON RECORD* book series

Vol. 6 1995

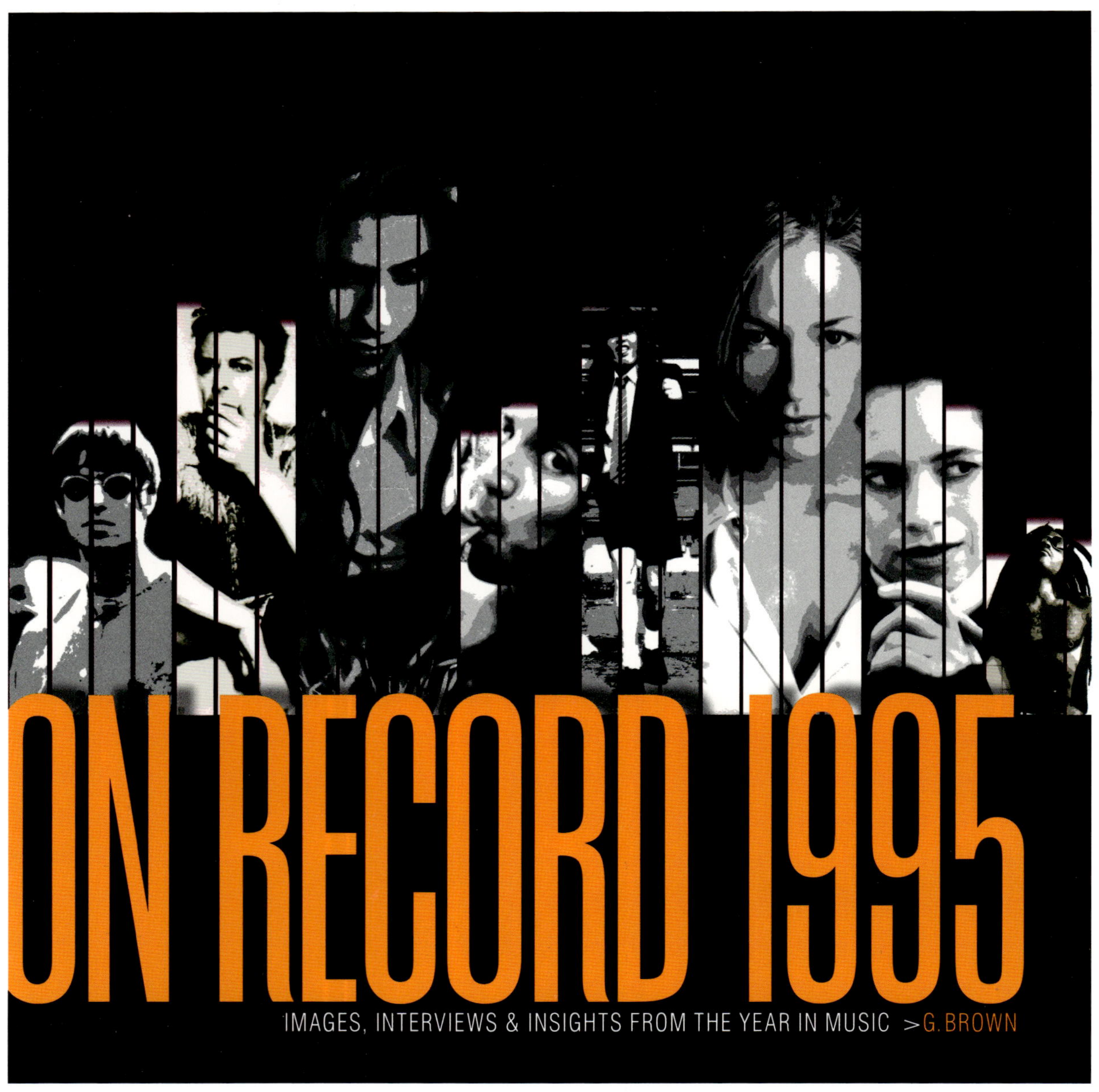